The Sound of Virtue

THE SOUND OF VIRTUE
Philip Sidney's Arcadia *and Elizabethan Politics*

Blair Worden

Yale University Press
New Haven & London

Set in Bembo by Best-set Typesetter Ltd, Hong Kong
Printed in Great Britain by St Edmundsbury Press

Library of Congress Cataloging-in-Publication Data

Worden, Blair.
    The sound of virtue: Philip Sidney's Arcadia and Elizabethan politics/Blair Worden.
    Includes bibliographical references and index.
    ISBN 0–300–06693–7
    1. Sidney, Philip, Sir, 1554–1586. Arcadia. 2. Sidney, Philip, Sir, 1554–1586 – Political and social views. 3. Politics and literature – Great Britain – History – 16th century. 4. Didactic literature, English – History and criticism. 5. Pastoral literature, English – History and criticism. 6. Great Britain – Politics and government – 1558–1603. 7. Arcadia in literature. 8. Virtue in literature. I. Title.
PR2342.A6W67 1996
823'.3 – dc20
                                              96–18713
                                               CIP

A catalogue record for this book is available from the British Library.

10 9 8 7 6 5 4 3 2 1

The author and publishers would like to thank Oxford University Press for kind permission to quote from the following: *The Prose Works of Fulke Greville, Lord Brooke* (1986), edited by John Gouws; *Miscellaneous Prose of Sir Philip Sidney* (1973), edited by Katherine Duncan-Jones and Jan van Dorsten; Sir Philip Sidney, *The Countess of Pembroke's Arcadia (The New Arcadia)* (1987), edited by Victor Skretkowicz; Sir Philip Sidney, *The Countess of Pembroke's Arcadia (The Old Arcadia)* (1973), edited by Jean Robertson; and Fulke Greville, Lord Brooke, *The Remains* (1965), edited by G. A. Wilkes.

Synopsis illustration by Philippa Stockley.

Endpapers: woodcut of a royal hunting picnic, 1575, from *The Noble Arte of Venerie*. Bodleian Library, Oxford.

To the memory of Angus Macintyre

For conclusion, I say . . . the poet is indeed
the right popular philosopher, whereof
Aesop's tales give good proof: whose pretty
allegories, stealing under the formal tales
of beasts, make many, more beastly than
beasts, begin to hear the sound of virtue
from these dumb speakers.

(Sidney, *A Defence of Poetry*)

Contents

PART FOUR: POLITICAL THOUGHT

PART FIVE: LOVE AND POLITICS

Illustrations

Abbreviations

Included in the list below are the books which are identified in the footnotes only by their author or editor. The titles of other publications are normally cited, after the first citation, in shortened forms: the full forms can be found in the Bibliography.

BL	British Library
Bodl.	Bodleian Library
Bullough	Geoffrey Bullough, ed., *Poems and Dramas of Fulke Greville*, 2 vols (Edinburgh and London, 1939)
CSPD	*Calendar of State Papers Domestic*
CSPF	*Calendar of State Papers Foreign*
CSPS	*Calendar of State Papers Spanish*
CSPV	*Calendar of State Papers Venetian*
Feuillerat	Albert Feuillerat, ed., *The Prose Works of Sir Philip Sidney*, 4 vols (Cambridge, 1912–26)
Garnett	George Garnett, ed., *Vindiciae, Contra Tyrannos* (Cambridge, 1994)
GP	John Gouws, ed., *The Prose Works of Fulke Greville, Lord Brooke* (Oxford, 1986)
Hatf.	Hatfield House, Cecil Papers
HMC	*Historical Manuscripts Commission*
K. de L.	Baron J. Kervyn de Lettenhove, ed., *Relations Politiques des Pays-Bas et de l'Angleterre*, 11 vols (Brussels, 1882–1900)
KAO	Kent Archives Office
MP	Katherine Duncan-Jones and Jan van Dorsten, eds, *Miscellaneous Prose of Sir Philip Sidney* (Oxford, 1973)
NA	Sir Philip Sidney, *The Countess of Pembroke's Arcadia (The New Arcadia)*, ed. Victor Skretkowicz (Oxford, 1987)
NRO	Northamptonshire Record Office
OA	Sir Philip Sidney, *The Countess of Pembroke's Arcadia (The Old Arcadia)*, ed. Jean Robertson (Oxford, 1973)
Oram	William Oram, ed., *The Yale Edition of the Shorter Poems of Edmund Spenser* (New Haven, 1989)

Pears Steuart Pears, ed., *The Correspondence of Sir Philip Sidney and Hubert Languet* (London, 1845)

PRO Public Record Office

Ringler William Ringler jr, ed., *The Poems of Sir Philip Sidney* (Oxford, 1962)

Stubbs Lloyd Berry, ed., *John Stubbs's Gaping Gulph* (Charlottesville, Va, 1968)

Wilkes Fulke Greville, Lord Brooke, *The Remains*, ed. G. A. Wilkes (Oxford, 1965)

The Principal Characters
(The *Old Arcadia*)

BASILIUS   Duke of Arcadia
GYNECIA   the Duchess

PAMELA   their elder daughter
PHILOCLEA   her sister

MUSIDORUS   Duke (or King) of Thessalia (alias Dorus, alias Palladius)
PYROCLES   Prince of Macedon, his younger cousin (alias Cleophila, alias Timopyrus)

PHILANAX   Basilius' faithful counsellor
DAMETAS   Basilius' foolish favourite

KERXENUS   a hospitable nobleman
TIMAUTUS   an ambitious nobleman

MISO   wife to Dametas
MOPSA   their daughter

EUARCHUS   King of Macedon, father to Pyrocles and uncle to Musidorus

SHEPHERDS: Dicus; Geron; Histor; Lalus and his betrothed, Kala; Mastix; Nico and Pas; Philisides

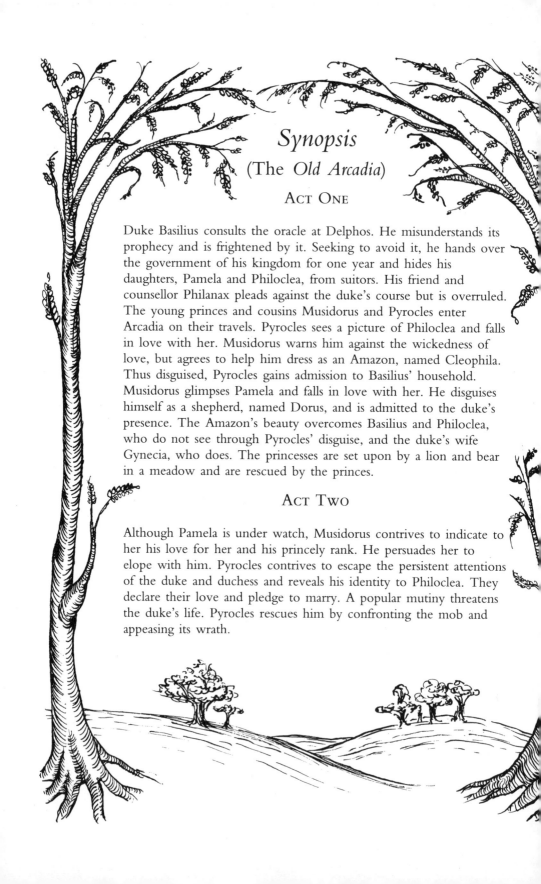

Synopsis
(The *Old Arcadia*)
ACT ONE

Duke Basilius consults the oracle at Delphos. He misunderstands its prophecy and is frightened by it. Seeking to avoid it, he hands over the government of his kingdom for one year and hides his daughters, Pamela and Philoclea, from suitors. His friend and counsellor Philanax pleads against the duke's course but is overruled. The young princes and cousins Musidorus and Pyrocles enter Arcadia on their travels. Pyrocles sees a picture of Philoclea and falls in love with her. Musidorus warns him against the wickedness of love, but agrees to help him dress as an Amazon, named Cleophila. Thus disguised, Pyrocles gains admission to Basilius' household. Musidorus glimpses Pamela and falls in love with her. He disguises himself as a shepherd, named Dorus, and is admitted to the duke's presence. The Amazon's beauty overcomes Basilius and Philoclea, who do not see through Pyrocles' disguise, and the duke's wife Gynecia, who does. The princesses are set upon by a lion and bear in a meadow and are rescued by the princes.

ACT TWO

Although Pamela is under watch, Musidorus contrives to indicate to her his love for her and his princely rank. He persuades her to elope with him. Pyrocles contrives to escape the persistent attentions of the duke and duchess and reveals his identity to Philoclea. They declare their love and pledge to marry. A popular mutiny threatens the duke's life. Pyrocles rescues him by confronting the mob and appeasing its wrath.

ACT THREE

Musidorus tells Pyrocles of his plan to take Pamela to his native Thessalia. He asks him to raise an army that will enable the two princes to force Basilius to grant them his daughters. Musidorus and Pamela get away. As they rest on their journey, Pamela falls asleep. Musidorus, who has promised to respect her virginity until their marriage, breaks his vow. He is thwarted by the arrival of a remnant of the mob of Act Two. Meanwhile Pyrocles lures the duke and duchess out of the way by promising both him and her a meeting in a dark cave. There, as he has planned, they mistake each other for him. He makes love to Philoclea.

ACT FOUR

In the cave the duke and duchess realise their error and resolve to end their foolishness. Basilius is thirsty and takes a potion which Gynecia has intended for Cleophila. The liquor gives those who drink it the appearance of death. Meanwhile the mutineers have seized Musidorus and Pamela, only for horsemen of Philanax to rescue them. Philanax, told that the duke is dead, has Musidorus and Pyrocles imprisoned and the princesses placed under guard. The succession to the throne is unclear. The Arcadians panic and turn against each other and the survival of the state is in jeopardy.

ACT FIVE

Pyrocles' father, Euarchus King of Macedon, enters Arcadia. His purpose is to persuade Basilius, on whose assistance all Greece depends for survival against its enemies, to resume his duties. Learning of Arcadia's crisis, he agrees to act as its temporary protector and to judge the princes, who have taken new disguises, Musidorus as Prince Palladius, Pyrocles as Prince Timopyrus. They are charged by Philanax with responsibility for the duke's death and with the rape of his daughters. The princes plead that the court has no proper jurisdiction over them. Euarchus overrules them and condemns them to death. He then discovers that the prisoners are his own son and nephew, but adheres to his sentence. Basilius comes to life and the sentence is not carried out.

1 Sir Philip Sidney.

Preface

Sidney's *Arcadia* is the unread classic of English literature. Few books so widely known about have been so narrowly known. Of course, it has always had its devotees. Yet even in our time, when universities and publishers bring the literature of the English Renaissance to the largest audience it has had, I have been surprised to find how many well-read people will own to not having read it.

For its neglect there have, I think, been two reasons. The first has been the difficulty of telling what 'the *Arcadia*' means and where to find a copy of it. The second, even when that obstacle has been surmounted, has been to know how to read it.

Around 1580, when he was in his mid-twenties, Sidney wrote a complete version of the *Arcadia*. A little later he wrote a revised and incomplete one. In modern times the earlier version has come to be called the *Old Arcadia*, the revised version the *New Arcadia*. The *New Arcadia* was first published, under the direction of Sidney's friend Fulke Greville, in 1590, four years after Sidney's death. The *Old Arcadia* survived, as an independent text, only in manuscript. Forgotten in the seventeenth century, it was not reclaimed until the early twentieth. There is also a third version, at once the most familiar and, for all its attractions, the least satisfactory. It was published in 1593 under the direction of Sidney's sister Mary Countess of Pembroke. Only with the recovery of the *Old Arcadia* in 1907 did it become clear what the countess had done. Printing the uncompleted *New Arcadia*, she had completed it by stitching the later part of the *Old* to it; the rest of the *Old* she jettisoned.

Twentieth-century readers can find it hard to grasp which of the three texts is which. Until recently they have been unable to read any of them in a readily accessible and intelligible form. Over the past two decades or so that impediment has been removed, mainly by publications of Oxford University Press, which has produced definitive editions in hardback of the *Old Arcadia* and the *New Arcadia* and an excellent paperback version of the *Old Arcadia*. It has also published scholarly versions of works invaluable to an appreciation of Sidney's fiction: his miscellaneous prose works and the account of his career and art by his friend Fulke Greville. Penguin Books has played its part too, by publishing a paperback text based on the countess's composite version of the *Arcadia*.[1]

So Sidney's story is now accessible in its various forms. Yet its spirit remains elusive. He wrote it not for publication but for circulation in manuscript. His early readers, or at least his close friends among them, would have recognised private allusions of which, even when we sense them, we can only guess the significance.[2] There are also allusions to public events and public problems, allusions which may or may not have been self-evident to his early readers but which cannot be self-evident to us. To be unaware of them is to confront puzzles of structure and content and tone.

The public allusions are less resistant to recovery than the private ones. They are also, as far as can be judged, of larger consequence. My aim is to recover them. I seek to relate the *Arcadia* to the political concerns of Sidney and his friends and to the language in which they expressed them. There are limitations to any single approach to a great work of literature. Many features of the *Arcadia*, among them some for which it has been most dearly loved and will remain so, lie beyond my scope and intention. Yet without a knowledge of Sidney's political preoccupations, I believe, we lose the guiding thread of his fiction, a thread of which politics are an essential component. In dwelling on the political content of his narrative I am very far from wishing to belittle its other themes. On the contrary, those themes take on fresh life when, seeing their relationship to the political argument, we realise how many things Sidney is doing at once. The readier we are to recognise the multiplicity of his purpose, the likelier we may be to perceive the vitality and cunning of his prose. Some critics and readers have wearied of Sidney's prose, finding in its calculated artifice only a nerveless artificiality, not a controlling instrument of analysis and irony. Yet the artifice, as Richard Lanham has suggested, is the choice, not the limitation, of a writer who knew how to write differently.[3] A study of Sidney's politics confirms Lanham's perception.

My book has five parts. The focus of Part One is Sidney's beliefs: beliefs about the purpose of poetry that point us towards the political concerns of the *Arcadia*; and beliefs about the purpose of living that inform both his writing and his political career. I examine the philosophy of virtue that links the themes of his fiction with each other and connects his fiction with his

---

1   The paperbacks are: Katherine Duncan-Jones, ed., *The Old Arcadia* (Oxford, 1985); Maurice Evans, ed., *The Countess of Pembroke's Arcadia* (Harmondsworth, 1977). There is also a modern facsimile reproduction, likewise published in paperback, of the *New Arcadia* of 1590: Carl Dennis, ed., *The Countess of Pembroke's Arcadia* (Kent State University Press, Ohio, 1970).

2   By the middle of the seventeenth century an editor of Sidney was conscious of the same difficulty: *The Countess of Pembroke's Arcadia* (London, 1655), sig. b3.

3   Richard Lanham, 'The Old Arcadia', in Walter Davis and Richard Lanham, *Sidney's Arcadia* (London and New Haven, 1965), pp. 332–7, 403–4. Cf. *Dictionary of National Biography*, xviii. 231 ('Sidney, Sir Philip'); Neil Rudenstine, *Sidney's Poetic Development* (Cambridge, Mass., 1967), p. 53.

life. Part Two explores the context, biographical and political, in which that philosophy developed. Central to its evolution was the dismay of Sidney and his friends about the character and policies of the Elizabethan regime and about the condition of the Protestant cause in Europe and England. The *Arcadia* addresses those deficiencies. If Sidney's aim is to be grasped we need to re-create the political events that are the background to the work. We cannot say whether, had those events taken a different course, he would still have written the *Arcadia*. What will be evident is that had he done so it would have been a different book.

If the political events of Elizabeth's reign can help us to understand Sidney's writing, his writing can help us understand the events. That is why, or one reason why, the *Arcadia* deserves to be known by readers not only of literature but of history. The approaches of literary critics to the Elizabethan political scene, especially when indebted to literary theory and its related abstractions, sometimes strike historians as fanciful or anachronistic. The approaches of historians to the same subject, especially those which anatomise parliamentary procedures or patterns of political allegiance, sometimes strike literary critics as narrow or antiquarian. There is, I believe, a middle way.

The presence of political events in the *Arcadia* is the subject of Part Three, which explores analogies between the Arcadian setting and the public world of Sidney's time. Part Four moves, as his mind did, from events to the institutional defects that he took them to reflect. It traces his thinking about problems of monarchy and tyranny which he held to be present in all ages and which he found dominant in his own. Exploring, in fictional writing, subjects that his English contemporaries were exploring less interestingly in factual writing, he made innovative contributions to the political and historical thought of his time.

In Part Five the perspective broadens beyond politics. The *Arcadia* is a romance, a love story, which can seem far removed from the concerns of public life. I want to show that the themes of love and politics cannot be properly understood if viewed as separate exercises. They are the private and public dimensions of a single argument.

It is uncertain quite when Sidney wrote his two versions of the *Arcadia*. I adopt the standard view that the *Old Arcadia*, though it may have been planned and even in some form begun as early as 1577, was mostly and perhaps entirely written between the autumn of 1579 and the spring of 1581. We are on firmest ground in taking the most intense period of its composition to have been between March and August 1580, when he was at Wilton and Ivychurch in Wiltshire. I likewise adopt the standard view that the *New Arcadia*, though it grew out of the earlier version by a complex and protracted process, was essentially written between 1582 and 1584.[4] Some readers may prefer slightly different dates for either text, but I know of no

---

4   *OA* xv–xvii; Katherine Duncan-Jones, *Sir Philip Sidney. Courtier Poet* (London, 1991), p. 168; *NA* xiii–xvii.

alternatives in circulation that would affect, unless on its periphery, the argument of my book.

My focus is the *Old Arcadia*. So 'the *Arcadia*' will mean 'the Old *Arcadia*'. I draw extensively on the *New Arcadia* with the aim of illuminating the *Old*, sometimes by observing the expansion or illustration, in the later version, of material in the earlier one, sometimes by pointing to contrasts between the two. To read the *Old* and the *New Arcadia* is to wonder that two books can be at once so alike and so unlike. Sometimes in this book (especially in Chapter 2 and in Part Five) it will make sense to treat writing that is new in the second version as continuous with and complementary to the first: at other times the two versions will need to be kept apart. A book which centred on the political content of the *New Arcadia* would have to be a different enterprise from mine. It would also be a harder one, for political events are closer to the front of Sidney's mind in the first version than in the second.

Three choices of presentation should be explained at the outset. First, I refer with intentional looseness to the political 'party' to which Sidney belonged. No party in Tudor England was anything more than a provisional grouping of people of varying experiences and outlooks who, while they agreed about some things, might disagree about others. Nevertheless the politicians to whom my term 'party' refers were united in their diagnosis of the ills of Elizabethan policy. They worked together in vain attempts to remedy them. Using a term contemporaries would have understood, I call them forward Protestants. They sought the vigorous advancement of Protestantism at home and abroad. In 1577–8, when our story begins, Protestantism seemed to them in retreat. In 1578–9 the conviction grew that the queen intended to marry a Roman Catholic, the Duke of Anjou, the heir apparent to the Valois throne of France. That episode was the most convulsive and divisive to have beset Elizabeth's reign. Not everyone who opposed the marriage was a forward Protestant; not every forward Protestant opposed the marriage; but to spare the reader wearisome qualification I sometimes treat those two groups, which so extensively overlapped, as if they were the same. My account of mid-Elizabethan politics is not rounded. I look at them mainly through the eyes of Sidney and his allies. Seen mainly through the eyes of their opponents, the politics would look different.

The second choice of presentation is minor in itself but raises a less minor issue. I part with tradition in calling our author Philip Sidney, not Sir Philip. His knighthood was bestowed only in February 1583, after the *Old Arcadia* was written. If that seems a pedantic reason, there is a larger one which the smaller one sanctions. Two processes of posthumous mythology, both of them aided by his knighthood, have obscured the historical Sidney. In the seventeenth century he was claimed for (though never monopolised by) the tradition and decorum of Cavalier culture. In the nineteenth century 'the shepherd knight' became an image of courtierly chivalry and ardent loyalty.[5] Both myths had bases in facts, but both of them seriously distorted them, in two complementary respects. First, his afterlives, while preserving the Sidney who felt, forgot the Sidney who thought. Secondly, in commemorating the Sidney who approved, they neglected the Sidney who questioned and opposed. His knighthood was granted not as a mark of favour or reward but to qualify him to stand proxy for his friend John Casimir, the militantly Protestant Count Palatine, whom Elizabeth had made a Knight of the Garter in 1579 and who was now formally installed in the Order. She had bestowed the honour rather than give Casimir the money and men, and the open endorsement, which he sought for his campaign on behalf of the Protestant cause in the Low Countries, and which Sidney and his allies sought on his behalf. The knighthood symbolises not an affinity between Elizabeth and Sidney but the gap between them.[6] The queen did recognise merits in Sidney, but ardent loyalty was not among them. Modern literary criticism has outgrown the Victorian legend. Yet the character and extent of his political dissent, and its place in the *Arcadia*, have yet to be realised.

Thirdly, in advancing my argument I make extensive use of quotation, both from Sidney and from his contemporaries. I do so in two beliefs: the first, that thought is best understood through an acquaintance with the language which expresses it; the second, that language is the register and proof of continuities within Sidney's fiction, and of correspondences between it and the public realm, which have gone unnoticed and which reveal central concerns of the *Arcadia*. Quotation can be an uneasy practice. The term 'quoting out of context' is tautologous. We know what we mean by it and what to seek to avoid: the distortion of an author's meaning by the suppression of surrounding matter which balances or complicates the passage quoted. I trust there is a distinction between those derelictions and the methods of compression which I sometimes use in striving to uphold the reader's patience. Yet any quotation will supply a new context and thus a new meaning. Sidney might sometimes have been surprised by the uses to which I put his words. If I have been true to my aim, however, he would not have dissented from them.[7]

There are technical points of presentation to explain too. Using as I do the Oxford University Press editions of my main literary sources, where spelling and punctuation are normally modernised, I modernise the writing of all but one of the authors whom I quote from unmodernised texts, except in a

---

5 John Gouws, 'The Nineteenth-Century Development of the Sidney Legend', in M. J. B. Allen *et al.*, eds, *Sir Philip Sidney's Achievements* (New York, 1990), pp. 251–60; and see Pears, Introduction.

6 Duncan-Jones, *Sir Philip Sidney*, pp. 158, 249.

7 Some complexities are bypassed by my decision to quote a number of works and letters, written in ancient or foreign languages, as if they were written in the English of the translations that have been made of them.

handful of instances when changes of punctuation would confuse the sense, or destroy the flavour, of the original. (I have preserved the original spelling of the titles of books, except in modernising 'j' to 'i' and 'u' to 'v'.) The excepted author is Edmund Spenser, where modernisation, which is always translation, would over-translate. I silently change capital letters to lower case and lower case to capitals, and silently eliminate tiny inconsistencies in the punctuation of Sidney's texts. In quotations from verse I justify the text at the left-hand margin. When quoting manuscripts in the Public Record Office, and at Hatfield House, which have been calendared in print, I cite only the calendars (which are where the reader would look first) except where the wording of the manuscripts differs from them. A word is perhaps needed about the terms 'counsellor' and 'councillor'. The first means adviser, the second a member of the council; naturally the two categories overlap.

Scholars with heavy duties of teaching and administration long for time to write their books. I wonder if I would have written this book but for three institutions which gave me that time. The first, the Radcliffe Trust, awarded me a fellowship which was intended for, and mostly given to, a larger and longer-term project, but during which the seeds of the present venture were sown. At the second, the Huntington Library in California, I was first an Andrew W. Mellon Visiting Fellow and then, for a longer period, Fletcher Jones Foundation Visiting Professor. It was in the library that the greater part of the book was written, and in the gardens, where the *Arcadia* demands to be filmed, that much of it was meditated. I owe more than I know how to say to the staff of that marvellous place and to my colleagues there: above all Barbara Donagan, Roy Ritchie and Mary Robertson. The third institution is my Oxford college from 1974 to 1995, St Edmund Hall, whose Principal and Fellows were generous in permitting my absences. I have especially appreciated the forbearance of my fellow tutors in history, John Cowdrey and David Priestland.

There are many kindnesses to acknowledge. Viscount De L'Isle, MBE, permitted me to make use of the De L'Isle and Dudley Papers. George Garnett made available to me the proofs of his edition of the *Vindiciae, Contra Tyrannos*. I profited from invitations to test portions of my argument before constructive audiences chaired by David Armitage at Columbia University, Paulina Kewes at Oxford University, Fritz Levy at the University of Washington in Seattle, and Steven Pincus at the University of Chicago. During the approach to publication I have had invaluable aid and guidance from Nicola Bennett, Paulina Kewes and, at Yale University Press, Robert Baldock, Candida Brazil and their colleagues. Another debt is broader. Behind the book, as behind other recent writings of mine, there lies an undergraduate course in the literature and politics of early modern England in the Oxford History Faculty. I owe the warmest of thanks both to my colleagues in the teaching of that subject, with whom it has been such a pleasure to collaborate, and to my pupils in it, who have given me some of my most rewarding experiences as a teacher.

A draft of this work, even longer than the final version, was read by Patrick Collinson, Katherine Duncan-Jones, Nicholas von Maltzahn, Penry Williams, Susan Wormell and Henry Woudhuysen. The seriousness with which they have taken the book has been ample reward for the writing of it. I am profoundly grateful for their suggestions and criticisms, even on those matters where my obstinacy has prevailed. All but one of those readers can, I hope, be safely cleared of implication in the outcome. There is more difficulty in exonerating the reader on whose time and friendship I have drawn most fully, Susan Wormell, so generous, so steadfast and so sustaining has been her counsel.

PART ONE: POETRY AND PRECEPT

CHAPTER I

Teaching and Delight

that delightful teaching which is the end of poesy . . ..

(Sidney, *A Defence of Poetry*)

The place of politics in Sidney's *Arcadia* is not a new subject, though it has never been a large one. His friend Fulke Greville, the only one of his contemporaries to refer more than fleetingly to Sidney's purpose, gave priority to the political component of the work. The subject is then lost to sight for three hundred years. I know of no discussion of it between the early seventeenth century, when Greville wrote, and the early twentieth, when it was rediscovered by the critic Edwin Greenlaw.

In 1913 Greenlaw published an article entitled 'Sidney's *Arcadia* as an Example of Elizabethan Allegory'. His principal insight was to discern Sidney's interest in the misrule of Arcadia's ruler, Duke (or King) Basilius. In Basilius' retreat from his regal duties, which exposes his realm to what Sidney calls 'the pangs of uttermost peril',[1] Greenlaw saw a parallel to the inactive response of Queen Elizabeth, in the years around 1580 when the *Arcadia* was written, to the international threat of Counter-Reformation Catholicism. The *Arcadia* 'was intended by Sidney to apply to political conditions in his own time and to the crisis that he saw was coming upon England'. Sidney 'does not hold up the pastoral life of Basilius as a model; he does not find in it an admirable withdrawal from the cares of life; it is no idyllic existence in the forest of Arden, but a criminal evading of responsibility that will bring ruin to any state'.

Greenlaw was right. But his argument was thinly stated and still more thinly supported. He planned but failed to expound it 'more fully in another place'.[2] An article of 1931 by W. D. Briggs offered a general endorsement of

1   *OA* [page] 351/[lines] 3–4.
2   Edwin Greenlaw, 'Sidney's *Arcadia* ...', *Anniversary Papers by Colleagues and Pupils of George Lyman Kittredge* (Boston and London, 1913), pp. 327–37, at p. 337. Greenlaw's short essay 'The Captivity

Greenlaw's approach and advanced fresh claims about Sidney's political intention.[3] The most influential passage of Briggs's essay pointed to the presence in the *Arcadia* of the sixteenth-century debate about the legitimacy of armed resistance to tyrants. In subsequent writing on politics in the *Arcadia*, that theme has attracted more attention than any other. It certainly merits exploration. In Chapter 16 we shall explore it. Yet of all the political issues raised in Sidney's story it is the most perplexing and may be the least central. The theme that interested Greenlaw, the irresponsibility of Basilius, is a more fertile and substantial one.

Some critics have been more sympathetic to Greenlaw's case than others. Yet in the eighty years and more since he wrote, few of them have significantly developed it. Their difficulty has been to know what politics are doing in a romance. Unless we can relate the politics to the other themes of the work, we are left to think of the passages that seem political as asides, where Sidney has contrived to work concerns about current events into a story which is really about something else.[4] If that were all they were, the study of them, though it might be of value to historians of Elizabethan politics, would not do much for our literary understanding.

Perhaps it will be thought that we should not expect it to. For did not Sidney himself, in his *A Defence of Poetry*, explain that history belongs to the territory of mere fact, poetry (by which he meant fiction) to the higher ground of fancy? How then can the 'historian in his bare *Was*', as the *Defence* labels him,[5] hope to illuminate the workings of Sidney's imagination? A writer of imaginative literature, after all, may take his raw materials – political or non-political – from the world around him, but what he does with them, how he transmutes them into art, how he discovers or surprises himself in the process, is his incommunicable secret. What purpose, then, can be served by returning to those materials?

Yet once we recognise the scale of the political engagement of Sidney's fiction, a scale much larger than Greenlaw or his successors perceived, it becomes impossible to think of politics either as peripheral to the meaning of the *Arcadia* or as separable from its author's artistic impulse or achievement. He wrote at a grave political moment, when he believed the survival of Protestantism and liberty to be at stake. The crisis of 1577–81, during which the *Arcadia* was conceived and composed, drew him into a searching examination of what he took to be the ethical inadequacy of English and European public life. His imagination was the servant of that enterprise. We cannot

---

Episode in Sidney's *Arcadia*', *The Manly Anniversary Studies in Language and Literature* (Chicago, 1923), pp. 54–63, proved not to be a significant advance.

3 'Political Ideas in Sidney's *Arcadia*', *Studies in Philology* 28 (1931), pp. 137–61. Briggs too returned to the subject: 'Sidney's Political Ideas', *Studies in Philology* 29 (1932), pp. 534–42. The following year produced an acute but slender essay by Gordon Zeeveld, 'The Uprising of the Commons in Sidney's *Arcadia*', *Modern Language Notes* 48 (1933), pp. 209–17.

4 A like objection is raised by Robert Stillman, 'The Politics of Sidney's Pastoral: Mystification and Mythology in the *Old Arcadia*', *English Literary History* 52 (1985), pp. 795–814, at pp. 799–800.

5 *MP* 89/4–5.

separate it from the ideas it explores. Here I part company with that excellent modern editor of Sidney, Jean Robertson, to whose labours this book is profoundly indebted. Emphasising the 'light-hearted' aspects of his fiction, she offers us a warning: 'it must never be forgotten that he set out to produce a story rather than a treatise'.[6] Sidney, I think, would have been troubled by the postulation of those alternatives.

For the 'delight' of poetry, as the *Defence* explains, serves to 'teach'. 'Moving', which is poetry's prerogative, 'is well nigh both the cause and effect of teaching'. It was, as Fulke Greville tells us, the 'intent and scope' of the *Arcadia* 'to turn the barren philosophy precepts into pregnant images of life'. Greville's phrase 'philosophy precepts' recalls the *Defence*, where Sidney, having declared that poetry does what philosophy does but does it better, endorses the view of Joseph Scaliger that 'no philosopher's precepts can sooner make you an honest man than the reading of Virgil'.[7] By philosophy Sidney meant 'moral philosophy'. Elsewhere he represented moral philosophy as the partner of poetry in the discernment of men's 'virtu[es]' and 'vices': the *Defence* commends poetry as the superior means to the same end.[8]

Virtues and vices, in Sidney's mind, are at once public and private. Greville's account of Sidney's fiction leaves out its private or romantic plot. The omission is misleading. Yet treatments of the *Arcadia* which leave the politics out are no less so. The challenge, which I shall try to meet, is to recover the philosophical unity of the *Arcadia*, which holds the themes of love and politics together.

Politics, it is true, can sharply interrupt the love story, surprising the characters by their intervention and surprising us too. In Book (or Act) Two the lovers are in antic pursuit of their desires 'when suddenly the confused rumour of a mutinous multitude' announces the popular rebellion that threatens the duke's life. In the Third Eclogues, where the shepherds, free for once of the presence of princes, celebrate a wedding among themselves, the mood is abruptly changed by Philisides, Sidney's fictional representative, who perplexes the company by singing the song he learned from Sidney's mentor Hubert Languet about the origins and rise of tyranny. He is rebuked for choosing so gloomy a subject 'when rather some song of love, or matter for joyful melody, was to be brought forth'. No less sudden and unexpected is the information which in Book Four follows the decision of Philanax to keep the princesses under guard. 'But high time it was for Philanax so to do, for already was the whole multitude fallen into confused and dangerous divisions. There was a notable example how great dissipations monarchal governments are subject unto.'[9] Arcadia is plunged into a public crisis from which it will be rescued only at the very end of the work. Politics seem an interruption of

6 *OA* xxix, xxv.
7 *MP* 91/8–9, 121/8–9; *GP* 10/24–5.
8 Feuillerat, iii. 126: *MP* 81/37, 86/28.
9 *OA* 123/26–7, 259/31–2, 320/3–6.

the romance because the lovers, who are absorbed in themselves, have forgotten the public world, and perhaps also because we, having been absorbed in their misadventures, have forgotten it too. Private lives – especially the private lives of princes, both in the *Arcadia* and in Sidney's own world – have public consequences. If we set aside the private business of loving from the responsibilities of politics, politics will have their revenge. *Et in Arcadia Civis.*

There is a side to Sidney that forgets politics, or would like to. Some critics have discerned in the composition of the *Arcadia* his retreat from the stern demands of public life. They have detected his discovery of, and his self-discovery within, a private world beyond the reach of the Polonius-figures who had trained him for unremitting public commitment.[10] I share that view, as will appear. Yet Sidney's private instincts had to contend with his philosophy of public action. It is in that contention, I suggest, that the creative tension of the *Arcadia* lies.

The *Arcadia* is, among other things, a political allegory. As a subject of literary criticism, political allegory has a record of awkwardness, even of embarrassment. The search for analogies, once it is separated from the study of the artistic character and design of a work, can become mere tail-chasing. Greenlaw and Briggs were conscious, perhaps over-conscious, of that hazard. Greenlaw explained that 'of course' Duke Basilius 'is not Elizabeth'.[11] Briggs agreed. Identifications of Sidney's characters with real people, he wrote, are 'of course' to be avoided, at least 'in most cases'. 'Basilius, quite obviously, cannot stand for Queen Elizabeth.' Briggs did allow that there is a correspondence between Basilius' wicked sister-in-law in the *New Arcadia*, Cecropia, and Elizabeth's cousin Mary Queen of Scots. But he thought that 'the parallel, if Sidney intended it, is only remote'.[12]

Sidney, we shall see, plainly did intend the parallel, which, far from being remote, is close and pressing. Analogies between the real and the fictional world – analogies sometimes of situation, sometimes of character, sometimes of situation and character alike – are in the lifeblood of the *Arcadia*. Part Three of this book is about them. Difficulties arise only if we suppose the analogies to be ends in themselves, or if we expect Sidney's characters to be confined within them or conform consistently to them. His imagination moves, as an artist's will, from fact to invention. Yet it also moves back again. The *Arcadia* holds up contemporary politics to a revolving mirror, where our glimpses of them can be fleeting. But sometimes the mirror slows. Sometimes it halts.[13]

10 Rudenstine, *Sidney's Poetic Development*, chs 1, 2; Richard McCoy, *Sir Philip Sidney. Rebellion in Arcadia* (New Brunswick, N.J., 1979), ch. 2. Cf. John Buxton, *Sir Philip Sidney and the English Renaissance* (London, 1966), pp. 51–2; Duncan-Jones, *Sir Philip Sidney*, pp. 24, 62, 71–4.
11 Greenlaw, 'Captivity Episode', p. 57.
12 Briggs, 'Political Ideas', p. 139 & n.
13 Greenlaw, breaking (or half breaking) his own rule, thought (or half thought) that Cecropia 'is' (or 'equals') the Queen Mother of France, Catherine de Medici ('The Captivity Episode', pp.

If political analogies are prominent in Sidney's fiction, what political effect did he want them to have, and on whom? The question points us into unknowable territory. That is partly because there is so little evidence to tell us how and by whom the *Arcadia* was read in its early life. More fundamentally it is because of the difficulty that always attends the recovery of literary impulse. Sidney writes, as a writer of substance will, because he has to, in dialogue with the prompter within him. He also wants his fiction, as his *Defence* indicates, to improve the world. The interaction of those two incentives is unlikely to be a straightforward or constant process or to be tangible by his readers.

Even so, common sense can venture some suggestions about his political purpose and his intended audience. The poet, says the *Defence*, 'can . . . readily direct a prince'.[14] In the *Arcadia*, failed politician that he had become, Sidney took the only path to political influence that remained open to him. Writing in the literary tradition of advice to princes, he complained of misgovernment and called for good government. Yet if a poet can readily direct a prince, he rarely has that chance. Sidney cannot have expected – any more than most providers of literary advice to princes – that his prince would read his advice. If the interpretation of the *Arcadia* offered in this book is correct, he might have had reason to be alarmed by the thought of Elizabeth reading it.

Even if the queen – or, let us suppose, her close advisers – had read the *Arcadia*, she would have been unlikely to amend, in consequence, those policies and practices which dismayed Sidney. In any case the crisis of Elizabethan mismanagement required, he believed, swift redress. It might have been realistic for him to hope that a political paper, such as the letter he wrote to the queen in 1579 advising her not to marry the Duke of Anjou, would have that effect. No writer of Sidney's intelligence would have expected a long love story to do so. It seems likely that he began to write the *Arcadia* in the autumn of 1579, when the danger that the queen would marry Anjou, and the alarm and opposition provoked by that prospect, were at their height. Sidney's opinion of the match is unmistakably reflected (we shall find) in the opening pages of the *Arcadia*. Yet by the months of 1580 in which he evidently gave most time to that work, the danger was reduced.

It had by no means passed, however, and it would not easily be forgotten. The politics of 1580 were characterised, as one student of them has suggested, by the 'after-effects of these tremors' and by the 'prevailing mood of fear' generated by the international Catholic menace,[15] the menace from which Elizabeth had seen the match as a refuge. There persisted too the weaknesses

57, 58n.). There is something in Greenlaw's case (which perhaps gains strength from *OA* 387/ 17). For Cecropia, as a type, can stand for more than one figure of Sidney's time. So (we shall see) can Basilius. But, just as Basilius more often stands for Elizabeth than for anyone else, so the parallel with Cecropia which Sidney sustains is with Mary Queen of Scots.

14 *MP* 86/32.

15 M. M. Leimon, 'Sir Francis Walsingham and the Anjou Marriage Plans 1574–1581' (Cambridge Univ. Ph.D. thesis, 1989), pp. 153, 158–60, 185.

of government and society that Sidney believed to have made England vulnerable to that danger and to leave it vulnerable still. He is likeliest to have hoped, in writing the *Arcadia*, that his images of virtue and vice, and his account of the consequences of misrule, would imprint themselves on the minds of the Elizabethan ruling class and help guide its judgement and conduct in the face of present and future perils. The failings he saw in that class are shared by the ruling class of Arcadia.[16]

More than that we cannot say. Yet if the relationship of Sidney's artistic impulse to the political events amid which the *Arcadia* was written is inevitably elusive, we mistake him if we suppose that, in his mind, his fiction rose above those events. Nothing could have seemed more urgent to him, nothing more vividly illustrative of the ethical failings which the *Arcadia* describes and explores, than the developments which threatened, in the late 1570s, to surrender his country to popery and tyranny. We cannot properly understand the *Arcadia* without exploring those circumstances.

Equally we cannot properly understand it without familiarising ourselves with the language in which he and his patrons and friends and allies addressed them. People who share a political outlook will develop (not always consciously) a common political language in which to express it. The language used in politics by the party to which Sidney belonged has a large presence in the *Arcadia*. Perhaps our post-Romantic sensibilities expect the vocabulary of imaginative literature to be freshly minted, and are disappointed if it proves to have reproduced the phraseology of ephemeral political debate and polemic, if the language of poetry proves also to be the language of state papers. Yet the interchange of literary and political vocabulary is a recurrent phenomenon of the early modern period. Elsewhere I have tried to illustrate its operation in the writing of Ben Jonson, of Andrew Marvell, of John Milton.[17] This book will observe its operation in the *Arcadia*.

Did Sidney and those later writers plant the phraseology of current political debate in their work and invite their readers to notice its presence there? Or did they reach without deliberation for the language of the moment? We cannot often be sure, though there are occasions in the *Arcadia* when the presence of that language is manifestly calculated. Either way, the contemporary resonance of Sidney's language is a key to his art, not a debasement of it. It has no warrant to trouble us. If it does so, it may be because we think of politics as more pragmatic, and literature as more transcendent, than they always are. The language of Elizabethan politics could find a home in the

---

16   Below, Chapter 11.

17   Blair Worden, 'Ben Jonson among the Historians', in Kevin Sharpe and Peter Lake, eds, *Culture and Politics in Early Stuart England* (London, 1994), pp. 67–89; 'Andrew Marvell, Oliver Cromwell, and the Horatian Ode', in Kevin Sharpe and Steven Zwicker, eds, *Politics of Discourse* (Berkeley and Los Angeles, 1987), pp. 147–80; 'Milton, *Samson Agonistes* and the Restoration', in Gerald MacLean, ed., *Culture and Politics in the Stuart Restoration* (Cambridge, 1995), pp. 111–36.

Arcadia because, like the language of politics in most times, it was largely ethical. In incorporating it, Sidney was following, in a form which surprises us, a practice of literature which in another form we take for granted. We acknowledge, without complaint, that writers of the early modern period took words from other writers. They made a virtue of their borrowings from or allusions to classical or more recent literature, and we happily find virtue in the borrowings. Of course, the communion of spirit between a writer and a predecessor is a relationship of a different order to a debt to the political language of the present. But it may not be a larger one. To foreclose interpretation when literature carries echoes, not from other literature, but from public experience, is to deny the place of that experience in it. No literature is fuller of public experience than Sidney's.

To locate its presence we need to do what neither Greenlaw nor his successors attempted: to recover the context of political events within which, and the political pressures under which, Sidney wrote. By doing so we shall be able to watch not only politics illuminating literature but literature illuminating politics. The imaginative literature of the early modern period was often able to say things that could not be said in parliaments or pamphlets or pulpits.[18] Some recent studies of Elizabethan politics have allowed little importance to conflicts or to the voices of dissent. The evidence of literature challenges that perspective.

The prospects that shaped Elizabethan political conflicts were precarious. England had moved from Protestantism under Edward VI to Catholicism under Mary to Protestantism under Elizabeth, whose presumptive heir was the Catholic Mary Queen of Scots. We, who know that Protestantism would survive her death and become the nation's enduring religion, know what Elizabethans did not. No one in the middle of Elizabeth's reign could have expected that she would live so long or in continued domestic peace, or that when invasion came in 1588 it would be thwarted, or that on her demise England would be spared the domestic strife and foreign incursion against which the *Arcadia* warns. 'If the queen had died at any time before 1587,' observes Wallace MacCaffrey, 'there would almost certainly have been civil war.'[19] A similar anxiety, I have suggested elsewhere, provides the political context for an understanding of Ben Jonson's play *Sejanus his Fall*, written at the end of the reign.[20] For Sidney and Jonson alike, the feebleness of the realm before the dangers confronting it was an illustration not merely of dynastic misfortune or religious strife, those inherited afflictions of the Elizabethan regime, but of the misgovernment, and of the consequent corruption, of the commonwealth.

---

18 Blair Worden, 'Literature and Political Censorship in Early Modern England', in Alistair Duke and C. A. Taamse, eds, *Too Mighty to be Free* (*Britain and the Netherlands* 9, 1988), pp. 45–69; Worden, 'Tolerant Repression', *London Review of Books* 10 May 1990, pp. 14–17.

19 Wallace MacCaffrey, *Queen Elizabeth and the Making of Policy, 1572–1588* (Princeton, 1981), p. 445.

20 Worden, 'Ben Jonson among the Historians'.

There are two sources of evidence, external to the *Arcadia*, for Sidney's possession of a political purpose in writing it. Neither of them gives us detailed directions, but both of them supply signposts. The first is Sidney's *Defence of Poetry*, which, though it cannot be dated with confidence, seems likeliest to have been written at the time he was composing the *Old Arcadia*.[21] The second is Fulke Greville's 'A Dedication to Sir Philip Sidney' (a work which has traditionally but, as its modern editor insists, misleadingly been called a *Life* of Sidney).

Sidney's *Defence of Poetry* is a rhetorical work. It pleads a case which its author half believes. Proclaiming the superiority of poetry to other forms of instruction, particularly philosophy and history, it mocks them in terms which are at odds with what he writes in other places. But what it says about the purpose of poetry has never been said better. What it says explicitly about poetry it says implicitly about the *Arcadia*.

For though the greater part of the *Arcadia* is prose, we know from the *Defence* that 'verse' is 'but an ornament and no cause to poetry'; that 'one may be a poet without versing, and a versifier without poetry'. Rather, in those famous words, 'it is that feigning notable images of virtues, vices, or what else, with that delightful teaching, which must be the right describing note to know a poet by'. The poet:

> cometh to you with words set in delightful proportion . . . and with a tale forsooth he cometh unto you, with a tale which holdeth children from play, and old men from the chimney corner. And, pretending no more, doth intend the winning of the mind from wickedness to virtue – even as the child is often brought to take most wholesome things by hiding them in such other as have a pleasant taste . . . .[22]

So the poet has guile. He says more than he seems to say. Sometimes he says it obscurely or disturbingly. Since Hesiod and Homer, explains the *Defence*, 'many mysteries' of knowledge and philosophy have been 'contained in poetry, which of purpose were written darkly', 'under the veil of fables'. There are Virgil's *Eclogues*, which 'can show the misery of people under hard lords or ravening soldiers, and . . . what blessedness is derived to them that lie lowest from the goodness of them that sit highest; sometimes, under the pretty tales of wolves and sheep, can include the whole considerations of wrong-doing and patience'.[23] It was 'under the names and veils of shepherds and lovers', noted Sidney's contemporary Sir Thomas Wilson in a work dedicated to Fulke Greville, that 'many noble actions and affections of the [English] nation' were 'covertly discoursed' in the *Arcadia*.[24] 'Under the plain

21 *MP* 59–63.
22 *MP* 81/24–5, 100/23–4, 81/36–82/1, 92/7–15.
23 *MP* 121/11–14, 94/36–95/5; cf. C⁾ 43/29–30.
24 Quoted by Richard Helgerson, *The Elizabethan Prodigals* (Berkeley and Los Angeles, 1976), p. 134; cf. *NA* lviii. (Sir Thomas Wilson is not to be confused with the Thomas Wilson who figures elsewhere in this book.)

and easy emblems of lovers', remarked Sidney's editor of 1655, the *Arcadia* 'shadow[s] moral and politic results'.[25]

Sidney invokes the example of Virgil so as to commend pastoral, the genre – or a genre – to which the *Arcadia* belongs. The passages about pastoral in the *Defence*, and passages of the *Arcadia*, wink at each other. In the *Defence*, the use of pastoral to 'show the misery of people' is the province of the 'poor pipe': in the *Arcadia* the 'silly shepherd's poor pipe . . . testifies our woes'.[26] The information given by the *Defence* that poetry can proceed 'under' a 'veil', or 'under the pretty tales of wolves and sheep', is confirmed in the *Arcadia*, where the shepherds, as we learn when we are introduced to their eclogues, 'sometimes . . . under hidden forms utter such matters as otherwise were not fit for their delivery' – or, as the statement appears in the *New Arcadia*, 'such matters as otherwise they durst not deal with'.[27] The 'pretty allegories' of Aesop are described by the *Defence* as 'stealing under the formal tales of beasts': Sidney labours to tell us that the song about tyranny sung by Philisides in the Third Eclogues of the *Arcadia*, which adapts a fable of Aesop, is 'a tale of . . . beasts'.[28] Its 'words', some of its auditors notice, are 'fit to frame a pastoral style'. The concluding couplet of the fable, which almost all critics allow to be politically charged, addresses the 'considerations' of 'wrong-doing' and 'patience' to which the *Defence* alerts us: it exhorts the 'beasts' to respond to their oppression with 'patience' or by the opposite of wrong-doing, 'do[ing] well'. The term 'doing well' or 'doing good' – or, more commonly, 'well-doing', a more precise reverse of 'wrong-doing' – carries, we shall find, an emphatic function in Sidney's writings.[29]

Though Sidney's political commentary can be at its sharpest in the eclogues, it is at its fullest in the action which precedes them and on which they comment. There too the pastoral guise gives ample scope for political signals. It also gives scope for amatory signals. Musidorus, who in circumventing Basilius' decision to lock up his daughters has learned to speak of his love 'in a secret manner', gains access to Pamela 'under the baseness of' a shepherd's 'form'. Wanting her to grasp that 'under that veil there may be hidden things to be esteemed', he wonders 'if I be understood'. He is, for she sees that 'he did under that covert manner make her know the great nobleness of his birth'.[30]

An ageless tradition of literary usage and biblical exposition sanctioned the deployment of pastoral forms for political allegory. Literary critics among Sidney's contemporaries were as alive as he to the political scope of pastoral. William Webbe's *A Discourse of English Poetrie* (1586) noticed that in Spenser's

25 *The Countess of Pembroke's Arcadia* (London, 1655), sig. b3. The editor did not elaborate.
26 *MP* 94/35–95/1: *OA* 84/4–5.
27 *OA* 56/8–9; *NA* 24/33–4; Annabel Patterson, *Censorship and Interpretation. The Conditions of Writing and Reading in Early Modern England* (Madison, Wis., 1984), pp. 29–30.
28 *MP* 87/27–8 (cf. *MP* 103/3–4): *OA* 259/30–1.
29 *OA* 259/25–6, 259/15–16; below, Chapter 2.
30 *OA* 82/18, 105/34–106/25; Daniel Javitch, *Poetry and Courtliness in Renaissance England* (Princeton, 1978), p. 80 n. 5.

The Shepheardes Calender 'there is . . . much matter uttered somewhat covertly, especially the abuses of some whom he would not be too plain withal'.[31] George Puttenham's *The Arte of English Poesie* (1589) observed the capacity of the pastoral eclogue:

> under the veil of homely persons and in rude speeches to insinuate and glance at greater matters, and such as perchance had not been safe to have been disclosed in any other sort; which may be perceived by the *Eclogues* of Virgil, in which are treated by figure matters of greater importance than the loves of Titirus and Corydon.[32]

The *Arcadia* treats by figure matters of greater importance than the loves of its princes and shepherds.

The pastoral form of Sidney's romance is complemented by, or merges with, the genre of the beast-fable. Here too the conventions were understood. As the *Defence* indicates, beast-fables enabled the poet to provide, under the protective cover of allegory, 'food for the tenderest stomachs'.[33] In 1570 Thomas North, who is best known as the translator of Plutarch, dedicated to his patron, Sidney's uncle the Earl of Leicester, his translation of the collection of beast-fables published as *The Morall Philosophy of Doni*. 'As concerning the morality and sense of the philosophy' of the work, North explained to Leicester,

> it is shadowed by the manner and speech of brute and dumb beasts, and by the examples and gests of their lives . . . wherein you may my lord see into the court, look into the commonwealth, behold the most part of all estates and degrees: and the inferior and common sort may also learn, discern, and judge what way is to be taken in the trade of their life: but courtiers above all others attending on the prince's presence. A glass it is for them to look into, and also a meet school to reform such scholars as by any manner of device, practice, or subtlety, unjustly seek to abuse their prince.

In a preface North explains that the reader 'shalt most lively behold', in the same 'looking glass', 'the daily and present dangers and deceits of a man's most miserable life'. But 'to read such a book (worthy reader) thou must keep thy wits together'; 'the discreet reader must give attentive care . . . diligently marking the secret lessons'.[34]

Fulke Greville's 'Dedication' to Sidney, or rather to Sidney's memory, is our second external guide to the political purpose of the *Arcadia*. It appears to

---

31 Quoted in Javitch, *Poetry and Courtliness*, p. 79.
32 George Puttenham, *The Arte of English Poesie*, ed. Gladys Willcock and Alice Walker (Cambridge, 1936), p. 38; Patterson, *Censorship and Interpretation*, p. 29.
33 *MP* 87/24–7.
34 *The Morall Philosophy of Doni* (London, 1570), sigs A4ᵛ, bii, biiiᵛ; Eleanor Rosenberg, *Leicester Patron of Letters* (New York, 1955), pp. 160–3.

have been written, or at least largely written, between 1610 and 1612, a quarter of a century after Sidney's death and around thirty years after the composition of the *Arcadia*.[35]

No two lives belonging to different families can ever have been more closely intertwined than those of Greville and Sidney. The two men were born in the same year, 1554. They entered Shrewsbury School together ten years later. In 1575 they began their lives at court together. Two years later Greville joined Sidney, and their common friend Edward Dyer, on the diplomatic mission to Germany that formed Sidney's political apprenticeship. In 1585 Greville would have sailed with Sidney to the New World had not the queen forbidden their departure. Greville and Sidney formed, with Dyer, a 'happy blessed trinity' of poets. With those friends Sidney led England into its literary Renaissance, 'Striving with my mates in song, / Mixing mirth our songs among'. The friends, wrote Sidney, 'make but one mind in bodies three'.[36]

Sidney's death in 1586 was a blow from which Greville would never recover. The memory of his friend remained 'ever in my eyes'[37] as a yardstick both of his own loss of direction and of his country's. Time and again the plays and poems of the later part of Greville's life revert to Sidney's preoccupations and repeat his ideas, even his words. There are times when Greville seems concerned less to find his own voice than to project Sidney's beyond the grave.[38]

Greville poured his affection into the 'Dedication'. Despite – and largely because of – the proximity between the two men, the 'Dedication' is a difficult source and sometimes a treacherous one. We struggle to untie the knots and penetrate the vapours of a prose which testifies to the 'restless working and banding of his own thoughts' that afflicted Greville around the time he wrote the work.[39] Though he would never have wished to misrepresent his friend, his memory inevitably slips into confusions and conflations. Other problems arise from his laudatory purpose. The 'Dedication' is an exercise in idealisation, conducted according to the conventions of Renaissance biography, of which the prime requirement is ethical instruction, the task that Sidney set himself in poetry.

---

35 *GP* xxi–xxiv; cf. Ronald Rebholz, *The Life of Fulke Greville, First Lord Brooke* (Oxford, 1971), appendix 1.
36 Ringler, pp. 260–1, 263.
37 *GP* 88/18.
38 A fuller discussion of the problems which the 'Dedication' raises is offered in my review–essay 'Friend to Sir Philip Sidney', *London Review of Books* 3 July 1986, pp. 19–22, and 24 July 1986, p. 4. Greville's other surviving works are his *Remains*, consisting of 'A Treatise of Monarchy' and 'A Treatise of Religion' (edited by Wilkes); the verse treatises, and the sequence of poems 'Caelica', that are printed in Bullough, i; his plays, *Alaham* and *Mustapha* (Bullough, ii); and 'A Letter to an Honourable Lady' (*GP*). All but the last are in verse. The dating of Greville's writings is often problematical: see F. J. Levy, 'Fulke Greville: the Courtier as Philosophic Poet', *Modern Language Quarterly* 3 (1972), pp. 433–48. I have tried to avoid the more contentious issues (of which the most contentious relate to Greville's theological positions).
39 Rebholz, *Greville*, p. 196.

2 Philip Sidney's funeral in 1586, a demonstration of the strength of the forward Protestant part
Fulke Greville is in the foreground, as is his and Sidney's close friend Edward Dyer.

The work has a political purpose too. It holds up Sidney's life and opinions
in order to shame the corruption and policies of the regime of King James I
and to plead for its reform. James's critics could not attack the king openly.
Instead they praised his predecessor and prodded their readers into observing
the contrast. Greville's difficulty, as he pursues that strategy, is to square his
retrospective glorification of the queen's reign with her refusal to acknowledge his hero's worth or adopt his programme. What Greville thinks about
Elizabeth in retrospect is very different from what he and Sidney thought
about her at the time.

The difficulties in using Greville as a source for Sidney's political career
and opinions are set out more fully in Appendix A. He is unlikely to have
hallucinated and he would not have invented. But he did distort and exag-
gerate. We need to be alive to those tendencies. We need too to listen for
Greville's silences, for the anger and distress which the queen's conduct
induced in Sidney and his friends and which the 'Dedication' hushes.

At least Greville's account of Elizabethan politics, and of Sidney's place in
them, can often be tested against other, less subjective documents, written at
the time to which Greville looks back. His account of his friend's purpose in
writing the *Arcadia* cannot be independently measured. Yet he claims for it
the special authority to which his intimacy with Sidney entitles him. 'I
know', he twice tells us, what his friend had wanted to do:

his intent and scope was to turn the barren philosophy precepts into pregnant images of life, and in them, first on the monarch's part, lively to represent the growth, state and declination of princes, change of government and laws, vicissitudes of sedition, faction, succession, confederacies, plantations, with all other errors or alterations in public affairs; then again, in the subject's case, the state of favour, disfavour, prosperity, adversity, emulation, quarrel, undertaking, retiring, hospitality, travel and all other moods of private fortunes or misfortunes. In which traverses . . . his purpose was to limn out such exact pictures of every posture in the mind that any man, being forced in the strains of this life to pass through any straits or latitudes of good or ill fortune, might (as in a glass) see how to set a good countenance upon all the discountenances of adversity, and a stay upon the exorbitant smilings of chance.[40]

We might wish for a more concrete description. For the present we need notice only the prominence Greville gives to politics. He represents the work as a guidebook for monarchs and subjects. He also gives 'instance[s]' of the lessons of the *Arcadia*. All of them are political. All relate to the misgovernment of the monarch Basilius and to the 'map of desolation' to which it reduces his country. All have to do with the loss or diminution of regal majesty or authority and with its consequences. The *Arcadia*, he explains, shows that 'when sovereign princes . . . will put off public action' they risk bringing 'ruin' on themselves and their country.[41] The pertinence of that warning to the political situation of the years around 1580 will appear.

Yet Greville, for all his emphasis on Sidney's political purpose, gives few indications of its sharpness. That is partly because, though most of what he says is pertinent to the *Old Arcadia*, he says it with the *New Arcadia* principally in mind. For the *Old Arcadia* has a political edge which Greville, concentrating on the *New*, misses.[42] It would be misleading to call the *New Arcadia* a less political work than the *Old*. In two respects indeed it is more political, or at least has more politics in it. First, its commentary on politics, like its commentary on most things, is more explicit. Secondly, there is some new political subject-matter. Book Two of the *New Arcadia* introduces us to politics outside Arcadia: to the conflict between monarchy and oligarchy in Euarchus' kingdom of Macedon, and to the wars and tyrannies of countries visited by the princes on their travels. Yet if in those senses the political content expands in the *New Arcadia*, its contemporary application becomes in general less pointed. That adjustment is produced partly by the emblematic method of representation that characterises the *New Arcadia* and perhaps also by the striving for timelessness that the method seems to reflect. It is also produced by a change of political situation. The *Old Arcadia* was written at

40 GP 11/2, 11/9, 10/24–11/8.
41 *GP* 8/17ff., 9/27; cf. *GP* 9/14–10/5.
42 That and other statements in this and the following paragraphs are amplified in Appendix A.

a time of deep divisions within the Elizabethan regime, which were intensified by the marriage negotiations between the queen and Anjou. The anxiety
roused in Sidney by those negotiations, which were held from 1578 to 1581,
did not die with them. The influence of them, and of the meditations they
induced in him, persisted into the *New Arcadia*. But the years in which the
New Arcadia was written, 1582–4, while they by no means ended the
antagonisms of court politics, did something to moderate them. At least there
was now a common willingness to focus on that threat from Catholic Spain
which Sidney's party had long urged the queen to confront.

The *New Arcadia* has contemporary political points of its own to make,
particularly about the menace to the Elizabethan regime posed by Mary
Queen of Scots and about the dangers of conspiracy and rebellion.[43] Basilius'
misrule, which in the *Old Arcadia* proves disastrous only after his (apparent)
death, leads, in the *New Arcadia*, to civil war in his lifetime. But Sidney's
account of that war concentrates more on chivalric deeds than on the
political failings that caused it. There is nothing so politically biting in
the *New Arcadia* as the description, in the *Old Arcadia*, of the dissolution of
the Arcadian state when Basilius dies. Another shift occurs too. In the *Old
Arcadia* political criticism is characteristically barbed and interlinear. The
criticism added in the *New Arcadia* sometimes has those qualities too. But it
coexists with, and is sometimes muted by, a gentler method. Sidney's fiction
was now readier to follow the deferential conventions which permitted, amid
idealised praise of a monarch, mild indications of a gap – a small one of
course – between ideal and reality. That technique is at its most conspicuous
in the description in the *New Arcadia* of the government of Helen of Corinth,
the resemblances of whose person and rule to those of Queen Elizabeth are
unmistakable.[44]

Greville would not have mentioned those resemblances. Though the
'Dedication' supplies signposts to the Elizabethan application of Sidney's
fiction, Greville himself reads that fiction as a criticism, not of Elizabeth, who
is now his heroine, but of her successor.

Greville's omission of the romantic plot leads him to do what modern seekers
of contemporary political references in Sidney's writing have sometimes
done. He separates Sidney's political from his imaginative purpose. Amid the
protracted gloom that besieged Greville after his friend's death he developed
a profound mistrust of the literary imagination and of its claims to improve
its audience. That distrust places question-marks against his account of his
friend's literary intentions. For is not his claim that Sidney wanted 'to turn
the barren philosophy precepts into pregnant images of life' too prosaic? Is
not poetry something more, and something more complicated, than the

---

43   Below, Chapters 9, 10.
44   *NA* 253/19–254/6.

projection of philosophy precepts? Critics, noticing Sidney's delight in paradox and uncertainty, take the 'artist' in him to have been at war with any unified or coherent account of the moral universe.[45] The ending of the *Arcadia* tells us how 'uncertain are mortal judgements, the same person most infamous and most famous, and neither justly'.[46] In Greville's mind, at least by the time he writes the 'Dedication', the uncertainty of mortal judgements derives from the corruption of reason in fallen man. Sidney shares that perception, but adds to it a charitable delight, foreign to Greville in his later years, in the folly of our certainties.

The *Arcadia* is full of unexpected shifts of perspective, of experiments in the relationship of author to reader, of movement between didacticism and what Joel Altman calls 'the Tudor play of mind', which rejoices in the juxtaposition of opposing insights.[47] Does Sidney adroitly guide our responses through those variations? Or can we be sure that a writer so young and inexperienced, whose work betrays such frequent evidence of haste, knows what he is doing? He wants us to grasp that he has adopted the style and spirit of *sprezzatura*, the art that does most to conceal art.[48] Does his art triumph through its concealment, or is *sprezzatura* his excuse for untidiness and inconsistent characterisation? The conclusion of his narrative seems casual and evasive, even wilfully so. Is it a sophisticated reproach to the falsity of neat or happy endings, or merely an acknowledgement of literary defeat? Sidney saw the 'dulling' of intellectual or ethical alertness as an insidious threat to virtue. Yet the bedraggled final sentence of the *Arcadia* ends with the statement that its author's 'pen . . . is already dulled'.[49]

Greville makes the relationship of philosophy to art sound too tidy. What then of the relationship of philosophy to experience? Musidorus greets the lovesickness of Pyrocles, which opens the romantic plot, with 'philosophy precepts'. They explode in his face. He has to learn that 'all is but lip-wisdom which wants experience'. We might be among the student princes of *Love's Labours Lost*, where love is the beginning of growing up. Yet there is a difference. In Shakespeare's play Berowne and his friends withdraw from life into learning, from action into contemplation. At least Musidorus, who spurns 'contemplation', knows that learning must be a guide to 'action', from which it must never retreat.[50] Greville himself explained what he believed to be the deficiencies of his friend's literary legacy by referring to the demands made on Sidney by his philosophy of action: 'the truth is, his end was not

45   See the statements quoted by McCoy, *Rebellion in Arcadia*, p. 29, from Stephen Greenblatt's essay 'Sidney's *Arcadia* and the Mixed Mode', *Studies in Philology* 70 (1973), pp. 269–78, and Richard Lanham's 'The Old *Arcadia*'.
46   *OA* 416/34–5.
47   Joel Altman, *The Tudor Play of Mind* (Berkeley and Los Angeles, 1978); cf. McCoy, *Rebellion in Arcadia*, p. 45.
48   Javitch, *Poetry and Courtliness*, pp. 55–6.
49   *OA* 417/24–5; cf. *OA* 350/19.
50   *NA* 106/4–5; *OA* 16/14–21.

writing even while he wrote, nor his knowledge moulded for tables or schools, but both his wit and understanding bent upon his heart to make himself and others, not in words or opinion, but in life and action, good and great'.[51]

'Philosophy precepts' prove more resourceful in the 'life and action' of the *Arcadia* than the shock administered to Musidorus' philosophical system leads us to expect. Musidorus' mistake is not to turn to philosophy but to get his philosophy wrong. Or rather, half wrong: for he has got it (we shall find) half right.[52] Amid the puzzles and paradoxes that Sidney's narrative can spring upon us, there runs, through both versions of the *Arcadia*, a continuous philosophical and ethical thread. Didacticism may be softened and complicated by debate. 'Philosophy precepts' may be questioned, contradicted, jested with. Readers have repeatedly to make their own judgements about Sidney's stance or tone and about the conclusions, if any, which he wishes us to draw; and perhaps no two readers will judge identically. Yet through the diversions and complications his guidance follows a clear general direction. His plot illustrates convictions about love and politics which this book will explore.

Those convictions are serious. The *Arcadia* is witty and funny (the *Old Arcadia* more so than the *New*). But seriousness is not synonymous with solemnity. In 1574, at a grim moment for the international Protestant cause, Sidney wondered what he and Hubert Languet were doing in their correspondence, 'jesting in times like these'. He found the answer in the tradition of *joco-serio*, which, 'in the midst of most grave affairs', allows a 'seemly play of humour . . . so natural, and so ingrafted, so to speak, in the characters of some of the wisest men, that neither Socrates nor our own More could lose their jest even in the hour of death'.[53] Languet in turn explained that he had jested to Sidney because 'the present state of affairs' left him 'benumbed by hopelessness'.[54] Sidney, a prey to melancholy,[55] swings rapidly to its opposite. He finds it easier to make a straight face than keep it.

Laughter is not a natural friend to intellectual systems. The wit of the *Arcadia* can run ahead of the philosophy which the work commends. Sidney's mind is restless. He is among the pioneers of his time in philosophy, history, literature, science, geographical exploration.[56] Nothing will pin him down. He commits himself to literary conventions, only to mock them when they rein him in. 'Ordinary it is that two princes fall in love,' he explains when lamenting, in the *Defence*, the predictable absurdities of English drama. He means, by 'two young princes', not two male princes, such as those who fall

51   *GP* 12/5–9.
52   Below, Chapter 18.
53   Pears, p. 65.
54   Charles Samuel Levy, ed., 'The Correspondence of Sir Philip Sidney and Hubert Languet' (Cornell Univ. Ph.D. thesis, 1962), no. 40.
55   Pears, pp. 25, 29, 108–9.
56   Cf. Sir Philip Sidney, *An Apology for Poetry*, ed. Geoffrey Shepherd (Manchester, 1973), p. 11.

in love with two princesses in Arcadia, but a prince and princess who fall in love with each other.[57] Even so his plot hints at its own predictability, with which he likes to play.

Yet the high spirits of the *Arcadia*, if they can divert us from Sidney's 'delightful teaching', are more often its means. The teaching is cleverest when it is funniest, when the comedy points us to the ironies of the action. The test which he would, I think, have applied to his wit is whether it sharpens the critical alertness of his readers. A theme both of the public and of the private story of the *Arcadia* is the loss of wakefulness, of ethical vigilance.[58] Sidney's readers, like his characters, must keep awake. To him poetry, like love, is a charm or enchantment, with power for both good and ill. The poet's 'well enchanting skill' can win 'the mind from wickedness to virtue': yet, 'contrariwise', the 'sweet charming force' of poetry can 'infect the fancy with unworthy objects' and so 'do more hurt than any other army of words'.[59] Poetry instructs through 'delight': yet Basilius, 'daily delighted' with the shepherds' eclogues,[60] is fortified by them in his irresponsibility. Healthy enchantment is 'that delightful teaching which is the end of poesy': unhealthy enchantment is that which dulls, instead of fortifying, our vigilance.[61]

Vigilance is enjoined from the start of the *Arcadia*, in its opening sentences. There, for the attentive reader, the picture of Arcadia's political and social contentment is darkened (we shall find) by troubling maxims of political theory.[62] There too we are invited to discern the dual character of Arcadia, that never-never land, that place of pristine simplicity and beauty, which yet also mirrors the world around us and reproduces its pressures and miseries. The duality is subtly afforced, in those same sentences, by Sidney's account of the 'reputation' of Arcadia's 'seem[ingly]' prosperous happiness, which is celebrated in the poetical 'fancies' and 'conceits' of the shepherds.[63] Between appearance and reality a gap soon emerges.

If the *Arcadia* is funny, not all of it is. It becomes less funny as it goes on. The gorgeous comedy of Book One, so tightly sprung and superficially so innocuous, sets Arcadia and its princely lovers on the path to destruction. Thereafter the emotional landscape is crossed, and covered, by cloud. At the start of Book Two 'the cup of poison' is 'deeply tasted of all this noble company',[64] and the racked Gynecia issues a soliloquy of despair. The comedy

57 Compare too his use of the word 'traverses' at *MP* 113/28 with *OA* 10/37.
58 Below, pp. 63–5, 300–1, 345–6.
59 *MP* 92/9–13, 104/17–27; cf. the observation in Cicero's *De Oratore* II. viii. 34 cited by Quentin Skinner, 'Scientia Civilis in Classical Rhetoric and the Early Hobbes', in Nicholas Phillipson and Quentin Skinner, eds, *Political Discourse in Early-Modern Britain* (Cambridge, 1993), pp. 67–93, at p. 74.
60 *OA* 9/28–9.
61 *MP* 116/4–5.
62 Below, pp. 168, 262–3.
63 *OA* 4/4, 4/14, 4/17; cf. *OA* 4/31, 12/16, 15/20.
64 *OA* 91/3–4.

returns, but in the Third Eclogues Philisides' fable about tyranny signals its approaching end. The opening of Book Four, by announcing the sombre themes of providence and sinfulness, brings that end closer still.

Sidney's dedicatory epistle to his young sister Mary describes the *Arcadia* as 'but a trifle, and that triflingly handled'. The work, he tells her, is to be read only by her and her well-disposed friends, for 'indeed, for severer eyes it is not'. Those statements, which conform to the conventions of *sprezzatura*, need not over-impress us.[65] In narrating his tale Sidney toys with the picture of a cosy audience of 'fair ladies', whose interest in the story can be expected to extend only to the amatory adventures. Perhaps those ladies existed; perhaps they gathered at Wilton to listen to his drafts. Yet their presence in the narrative is in one respect a decoy. It tempts us to indulge flawed preoccupations or values. When the moral going gets tough the ladies are silently forgotten.[66] Sidney's sister – the only female among the people whom we can name as having certainly or probably read the *Arcadia* in his lifetime[67] – was no dewy-eyed 'fair lady'. Mary's own writings, particularly her translation of Robert Garnier's play about Mark Antony, are not those of a reader who, even in youth, would have been likely to miss the public theme of the *Arcadia*.

Though Sidney's dedication honours his affection for his sister, its picture of a private family audience may be intended less to convey his purpose than to protect it. We saw that the Arcadian shepherds sing of 'such matters as otherwise they durst not deal with'; and that pastoral, in Puttenham's words, can 'glance at greater matters, and such as perchance had not been safe to have been disclosed in any other sort'. The 'chief safety' of the *Arcadia*, Sidney tells his sister, 'shall be the not walking abroad'; 'the bearing the livery of your name' will be its 'chief protection', for his sister's name is 'worthy to be a sanctuary for a greater offender'.[68] Sidney, at the time he composed the *Arcadia*, would have had good reason to worry about his 'safety' and to look for literary devices with which to guard it. At that same time he was also circulating his letter of advice to the queen against the Anjou match, a document with a potent presence in the *Arcadia*. The circulation, thought his mentor Hubert Languet, was 'by no means a safe proceeding'.[69] Fulke Greville indicated that the writing of the letter was 'dangerous'.[70]

Greville knew the need to worry about such things. In writing his own poem 'The Declination of Monarchy', he recalls, he 'well weighed the tenderness of that great subject' and remembered 'the fate of many [writers]

65   *OA* 3/10–15; Kenneth Myrick, *Sir Philip Sidney as a Literary Craftsman* (Lincoln, Nebr., repr. 1965), pp. 42–3; Ringler, p. lx.
66   Below, p. 311.
67   For the male names see *OA* xvi–xvii; Buxton, *Sir Philip Sidney*, p. 136; Jan van Dorsten, *Poets, Patrons and Professors* (Leiden and London, 1962), p. 101; cf. Dennis Kay, ed., *Sir Philip Sidney. An Anthology of Modern Criticism* (Oxford, 1987), introduction, p. 10.
68   *OA* 3/22–5.
69   Pears, p. 187.
70   *GP* 37/2–3.

before me who had lost themselves in teaching kings and princes how to govern their people'. He burned his play 'Antony and Cleopatra', he acknowledges, because it was 'apt enough to be construed or strained to a personating of vices in the present governors and government'.[71] The *Arcadia* was likewise 'apt enough' to be so construed.

We can learn or guess much about how Sidney's fiction was meant to be read. Unfortunately we can learn very little about how it was read by his generation (a generation that outlived him). But three of his early readers did leave records of their responses which disclose an alertness to the political dimension of the work. To the first of them, the historian Sir John Hayward, who around 1611 borrowed from the *Arcadia* to describe the political problems of Tudor England, we shall come later.[72] We do not know the name of the second reader, who was probably a friend or relation of Sidney's brother Robert, and who took notes, towards the end of Elizabeth's reign, on the composite *Arcadia* of 1593. The notes, which are among the Sidney family papers, reveal their author's interest in Philip's treatment of tyranny, oligarchy and the corrupting properties of peace. They mingle with other notes by the same reader. There he justifies the execution of Mary Queen of Scots by arguments close to those directed at her – we shall find – in the *Arcadia* (and in notes by Robert Sidney on the same subject); he reproduces material from Sidney's letter to the queen against the Anjou match; and he makes extracts from leading texts of the new 'civil' or 'politic' history in which Philip Sidney took a pioneering interest, and which leaves its mark on the *Arcadia* (as on the writing of Sir John Hayward): the works of Sallust, Tacitus, Machiavelli, Lipsius, Bodin.[73]

The third record consists of the annotations of one W. Blount – we know only the initial of his first name – in a copy of the composite *Arcadia* of 1593 which is in the Folger Library in Washington. Blount was likewise aware, if less sharply or subtly so than the two other readers, of the political dimension of the work. He too was abreast of the new 'civil' history and saw its pertinence to Sidney's work. We cannot assume that he believed the passages from classical and Renaissance texts which came to his mind as he read Sidney's text, and which he cited in its margins, to have been in Sidney's mind too. What is evident is that, like the other two readers, he recognised Sidney's fiction as an exercise not only in imagination but in ideas.

The next chapter will address two sets of ideas which inform Sidney's life

---

71 *GP* 90/26–7, 91/12–19, 93/10–12.
72 Below, pp. 205–6 and Appendix B.
73 KAO, U1475 (De L'Isle and Dudley Papers): Z1/11; below, Chapter 14. The manuscript belongs largely or wholly to the years between 1593, when the composite *Arcadia* was published, and the death of Elizabeth (fo. 203ᵛ). The passage taken from Sidney's letter is on fo. 63 (cf. *MP* 48/24ff.). Parts of the manuscript are unfoliated, of which some are also unbound. Passages of Sidney's fiction which will be discussed in this book and which are quoted in the manuscript are: *OA* 362/29–363/1, 363/15–16; *NA* 34/7, 160/14–15.

and writing and on which the political argument of the *Arcadia* is built. One of them concerns virtue, the other faith. Those ideas, at least in some aspects, were far from unconventional, even though on other fronts Sidney was a daring and avant-garde thinker. Historians do not always attend much to conventional ideas. Perhaps regarding them as too elementary to need or repay exploration, they can neglect to explore them. Perhaps regarding them as platitudes, they can fail to grasp their importance to those who held them. To think of Sidney's ideas about virtue and religion as elementary or platitudinous would be to miss their central and nourishing place in his thinking.

CHAPTER 2

Virtue and Religion

Virtue had a larger meaning for the Elizabethans than it has for us. It meant not only conformity to moral principles but the possession of divinely endowed gifts and powers. Those properties, if cultivated by education, would carry the authority of example and could change the world. There are people in the *Arcadia* who 'count' virtue 'but a vain name' or 'but a school name'.[1] They could not be more wrong. Through virtue we honour the divinity of our souls, and through it we serve the public community to which we belong.

Virtue was hardly a novel ideal. But the Humanism of the Renaissance brought a new phase in its development. Behind virtue, in the Renaissance conception of it, there stands an ethical system which trains us for, and tests us in, both our public and private lives. Though virtue is God-given, and though Sidney's God is Christian, the ideal of virtue expressed in Sidney's writings is essentially classical. It derives from Plato and Aristotle and Cicero. The God who enjoins it in the Renaissance differs from his medieval predecessor in the demands he makes on individual action and decision-making and on something we can loosely call citizenship.[2] He differs from his Puritan successor in the scope he gives to, and the demands he makes of, freedom of will. Scattered through Sidney's fiction and his other writings is a vocabulary which, when drawn together, reveals a coherent and insistent philosophy of virtue and religion. This chapter will outline the morphology of that scheme.

Sidney, who was set by his mentors on what the chief of them, Hubert Languet, described to him as 'that toilsome path which leads to virtue', himself commends poetry as the readiest 'path . . . to lead a man to virtue'.[3]

1 *OA* 91/31, 322/10; cf. *MP* 93/7.
2 Arthur Ferguson's book *The Articulate Citizen in the English Renaissance* (Durham, N.C., 1965) seems to me undervalued.
3 Pears, p. 183 (cf. p. 166); *MP* 83/21.

The poet's purpose is to 'teac[h] what virtue is', to inspire 'virtuous action', to accomplish, through 'virtue-breeding delightfulness', 'the winning of the mind from wickedness to virtue'.[4] That is why the *Arcadia* makes use of Aesop, 'whose pretty allegories . . . make many, more beastly than beasts, begin to hear the sound of virtue from these dumb speakers'.[5] The principal characters of the *Arcadia*, the young princes Musidorus and Pyrocles, are seekers of virtue and in some respects exemplars of it. The first thing we learn about them is that they have entered Arcadia 'following the train their virtues led them'. 'Born to the exercise of virtue', they are said to be 'worthy . . . for their excellent virtue to be monarchs of the world'. They have 'a youthful longing to have some trial of their virtue' and are 'desirous more and more to exercise their virtues'. That ambition is their homage to 'the divine part of man', which, they know, 'was not enclosed in this body for nothing'.[6] Sidney knew it too. Writing to Languet in 1578 he described the human mind as a 'particle of the divine mind': Languet, for whom the fulfilment of Sidney's 'virtue' was a tireless concern, replied by encouraging him to 'make use then of that particle of the divine mind (as you beautifully express it) which you possess', and to 'exercise' his God-given gifts.[7]

Though the virtue of Musidorus and Pyrocles is in their blood, they owe the development of it to their education, which King Euarchus of Macedon, Pyrocles' father and Musidorus' uncle, has arranged for them. Pyrocles is 'framed by education to the true exercise of virtue'; he and Musidorus 'were so brought up that all the sparks of virtue which nature had kindled in them were . . . blown to give forth their uttermost heat'. The young princes, occupying a time so remote from Sidney's own, are also, in effect, being trained for membership of the ruling class to which he belongs and at which his philosophy of virtue is directed. In Arcadia as in Renaissance England, virtue and learning are held to be inseparable allies. 'No learning', explains Sidney's *Defence*, 'is so good as that which teacheth and moveth to virtue.' The education of the princes, as the *New Arcadia* describes it, is informed by the thinking of the *Defence*,

> excellent devices being used to make even their sports profitable, images of battles and fortifications being then delivered to their memory, which, after, their stronger judgements might dispense; the delight of tales being converted to the knowledge of all the stories of worthy princes, both to move them to do nobly, and teach them how to do nobly, the beauty of virtue being still set before their eyes . . . their bodies exercised in all abilities . . . and their minds

---

4   *MP* 83/22, 83/7, 120/30–1, 92/12–13. Cf. *MP* 84/3, 85/3–4, 90/2–6.
5   *MP* 87/26–9.
6   *OA* 9/36, 10/25, 325/34–326/1; *NA* 186/30–1; *OA* 10/28–9.
7   Pears, pp. 143, 147–8. The *Vindiciae, Contra Tyrannos* of 1579, written by Languet and by his and Sidney's friend Philippe Duplessis-Mornay, observes that 'the mind is a particle of the divine breath': Garnett, p. 98.

acquainted by degrees with dangers; and in sum, all bent to the making up of princely minds . . ..[8]

The loved ones of the young princes, Pamela and Philoclea, the daughters of Duke Basilius, have had an 'education . . . such as hath been most fit to restrain all evil, giving their minds virtuous delights'. Unfortunately the duke himself – the opposite of Pyrocles, who has 'a mind well trained . . . in virtue' – was 'not trained in the way of virtue', a deficiency for which Arcadia pays a heavy price.[9]

Cicero taught that virtue consists in action. Musidorus, an orthodox Ciceronian, sees that we live for 'honourable action', not for 'contemplation', which can be a 'glorious title to idleness'.[10] So, as the *Defence* tells us, 'the ending end of all earthly learning' must be 'virtuous action', 'all [good] government of action' being 'gotten by knowledge.'[11] That knowledge begins with knowledge of the self. During the composition of the *Arcadia*, when he and his friend Edward Denny were being denied 'fit employments' by the government, Sidney advised Denny 'to keep yourself awake with the delight of knowledge', of two kinds: 'the one as concerning ourselves, the other an outward application of ourselves'.[12] The *Defence* confirms the point: 'the highest end of the mistress-knowledge . . . stands . . . in the knowledge of a man's self, in the ethic and politic consideration, with the end of well-doing'.[13]

'Well-doing' (or 'doing good') – the goal to which Euarchus, the prime moral exemplar of the *Arcadia*, devotes his declining years[14] – is synonymous with virtuous action. The term runs through Sidney's writing. The *Defence* explains that poetry, the intimate ally of learning, should 'mov[e]' us to 'well-doing and not . . . well-knowing only'.[15] It is with the same end that 'knowledge' is imparted to Musidorus and Pyrocles, who in their upbringing 'gave themselves wholly over to those knowledges which might in the course of their life be ministers to well-doing'.[16]

Though well-doing originates in knowledge of ourselves, its focus is the betterment of the world outside us. Greville, we saw, says that Sidney sought the improvement not only of 'himself' but of 'others'.[17] Musidorus acknowledges the same rule of virtue: 'in action', he believes, 'a man d[oes] not only

---

8   *NA* 163/22–164/2; *OA* 18/33–4 (cf. *OA* 21/6–8); *MP* 102/7–8; cf. Nancy Lindheim, 'Sidney's "Arcadia", Book II: Retrospective Narrative', *Studies in Philology* 64 (1967), pp. 159–86, at p. 184.

9   *OA* 8/5–7, 13/9, 45/16; cf. *NA* 61/29–32.

10 *OA* 16/14–16.

11 *MP* 83/7, 105/28–9.

12 James Osborn, *Young Philip Sidney 1572–1577* (New Haven and London, 1972), pp. 537–8.

13 *MP* 82/35–83/2.

14 *OA* 357/8–9, 357n., 362/3.

15 *MP* 90/36, 83/2–7; cf. Wilkes, p. 157 (st[anza] 488).

16 *NA* 163/32–3; *OA* 10/29–30; cf. *OA* 13/30–3.

17 Above, pp. 17–18.

better himself but benefit others'. Virtue, being for social use, requires sociability. Musidorus rebukes his cousin for 'subjecting [him]self to solitariness, the sly enemy that doth most separate a man from well-doing'.[18] The 'solitary' Basilius, deaf as usual to the commentary supplied by his precepts on his conduct, seeks to lure the 'solitary' Pyrocles out of his 'loneliness' by reminding him that 'virtue seeks to satisfy others'.[19]

Since the end of learning is virtuous action, 'those skills that most serve to bring forth' that quality, says the *Defence*, 'have a most just title to be princes over all the rest'.[20] 'The beauty of virtue' is therefore 'taught' to the young princes 'with far more diligent care than grammatical rules'.[21] What is taught by precept in the schoolroom is illustrated and improved by 'practice' outside it. Again, Sidney's phrasing is insistent. The princes are brought up to 'put' their 'learn[ing]' and 'knowledge' 'in practice'; 'the mind', they learn, 'should best know his own good or evil by practice', 'which knowledge was the only way to increase the one and correct the other'; they seek, in battle, 'the practice of those virtues which they before learned'; in the experience of seamanship they had 'leisure to see the practice of that which before they had learned by books . . . delighting their conceits with confirming their knowledge'.[22] Again, too, Sidney's fiction projects the philosophy of his circle. Languet, says Greville, was 'wise by the conjunction of practice in the world with that well-grounded theory of books'.[23] Sidney himself complained to Languet that the failure of his own public career was denying him the opportunity of 'putting' his 'knowledge . . . into practice'.[24]

'Practice' is also, we are told, a feature of the education of Philisides,[25] the character who moves most often and easily between mythical Greece and the Renaissance. He learns things 'which carried in themselves some serviceable use'.[26] Sidney was educated for service too, to be 'a good servant to [his] prince and country'.[27] For the ruling classes of Renaissance Europe, that was the practical goal of education.[28] The aim of learning, maintained Sidney's friend and patron Sir Francis Walsingham, was 'to serve [one's] country', 'to serve the commonwealth', 'to serve all public service'.[29] In the hope that his brother Robert would be 'serviceable to his country', Philip Sidney urged him to 'furnish yourself' with 'knowledge'. Philip himself 'much more

---

18   *OA* 16/15–16 (cf. *NA* 179/6–7); *OA* 14/4–6.
19   *OA* 35/7–19.
20   *MP* 83/6–8.
21   *NA* 163/33–5; cf. Ringler, p. 196 (sonnet 63).
22   *OA* 13/30–2; *NA* 164/32–3, 165/20–33.
23   *GP* 6/2–3.
24   Pears, p. 143.
25   *OA* 334/26–7.
26   *OA* 334/27.
27   Osborn, *Young Philip Sidney*, p. 13.
28   J. H. Hexter, 'The Education of the Aristocracy in the Renaissance', in Hexter's *Reappraisals in History* (Evanston, Ill., 1962), pp. 45–70.
29   Conyers Read, *Sir Francis Walsingham*, 3 vols (Oxford, 1925), i. 18–19; cf. Hexter, *Reappraisals*, p. 65.

desire[d] the being busied in a thing of some serviceable [public] experience, than . . . any other commodity'.[30]

He hoped in vain. His 'noble soul', judged Languet, was 'compounded' of 'exceptional virtue'.[31] Languet delighted, he told his young friend, in the 'sweet fruit' which 'in early manhood your virtue bears'.[32] If he held to the path of virtue, 'your country' could expect to 'find no small assistance in dangers from your virtue'.[33] Yet Sidney's country, instead of employing his virtue, rejected it. The result was the *Arcadia*, where his virtue projects itself by other means.

The imperative of virtue is uncompromising. Good ends cannot justify bad means – or, as Euarchus has it, 'what is evil in itself no respect can make good'.[34] That principle was dear to Sidney's friends and patrons, even if the pressures of politics could undermine their practice of it. It had been voiced in the early 1570s by those leading figures of Sidney's party Sir Francis Walsingham and Walsingham's brother-in-law Sir Henry Mildmay, in reply to the argument that the marriage of Elizabeth into the Catholic house of Valois, albeit an evil, would be a necessary one. God, Mildmay then explained, 'hath set us a rule that we should not do evil that good may come of it'.[35] Walsingham declared himself 'not persuaded that an evil may be done whereof good may come'. No man, he affirmed on another occasion, could honour himself or serve his country without following what Cicero 'calls the rule of honesty', which 'account[s] no act as good that proceedeth not from that fountain'.[36] Philoclea, in the *Arcadia*, follows Cicero too: thinking of Pyrocles as 'the fountain of virtue', she is confident that from that 'fountain . . . nothing but virtue could ever proceed'.[37]

In Sidney's thinking good and evil have opposite 'ground[s]' and 'foundation[s]' and move on 'straight' and opposite 'line[s]'. Both have a natural tendency to grow. His fiction tells us more about the growth of evil than of good. 'Mischief' is 'of such nature that it cannot stand but with strengthening one evil by another'. So men 'with use of evil' become 'more and more evil'.[38] Wickedness expands in life as in fiction. Sidney's letter to the queen concerning the Anjou match remarks that, 'according to the nature of evil', 'abuse grow[s] upon abuse'.[39] That belief may help to explain why, when Sidney's fictional characters renounce evil, their repentance can carry so little conviction. Musidorus and Pyrocles stray 'from the right line of

30 Feuillerat, iii. 125, 142–3.
31 Levy, 'Correspondence', no. 56; cf. van Dorsten, *Poets*, p. 31.
32 Osborn, *Young Philip Sidney*, p. 149.
33 Pears, p. 183.
34 *OA* 358/14.
35 S. E. Lehmberg, *Sir Walter Mildmay and Tudor Government* (Austin, Tex., 1964), p. 109.
36 Read, *Walsingham*, i. 133, 18.
37 *OA* 305/30–1; cf. *OA* 209/26–7.
38 *OA* 128/22–4, 265/8–9, 357/13–358/2; *NA* 178/17–18; cf. *OA* 19/28–30.
39 *MP* 53/31–2.

virtue', but no one deviates on to it. Sidney is less happy in describing repentance than in relating the dissimulation of such a man as Plexirtus in the *New Arcadia*, 'who, seeming a quite altered man, had nothing but repentance in his eyes'.[40]

Sidney has much to say about the dissimulation of evil persons. By contrast, virtue, in the *Old* and *New Arcadia*, is characteristically candid. The countenances and tongues of the virtuous speak their minds and hearts. The relationship of inner thought or feeling to the outward expression of it is a constant subject of his fiction, where disordered ethics and emotions are invariably reflected in disordered countenances, and where a 'countenance troubled . . . comes not out of virtue; for virtue, like the clear heaven, is without clouds'.[41] When Philoclea, in the *New Arcadia*, refuses to let her 'tongue' be 'traitor to [her] heart', she touches a chord in the life of Sidney, whom Languet advised 'to have the same thing on your face as in your heart', and of whom Greville says that 'his heart and tongue went both one way'.[42] On his German embassy of 1577, Sidney reported to Sir Francis Walsingham that John Casimir had given a 'very good' answer to Sidney's message from Queen Elizabeth, 'with a countenance well witnessing it came from his heart'.[43] Later Sidney would ask the queen 'to read my heart in the course of my life'.[44]

Yet truth of feeling and expression, though evidence of virtue, is not a sufficient condition of its effectiveness. Virtue needs an ally: wisdom. Euarchus rules Macedon 'virtuously and wisely'; in preparing his people for war he promotes 'the progress of wisdom and virtue'; he is moved to journey to Arcadia by 'rightly wise and virtuous considerations'. Philanax urges Basilius, in vain, to understand that 'wisdom and virtue' would be the proper foundation of his rule; later he selects men of 'wisdom and virtue' to preserve order in the realm.[45] Virtue and wisdom are intimately connected with each other in Renaissance thinking, but not synonymous. In the sixteenth century, wisdom, though it has more than one branch, has ever less to do with the contemplation of divine mystery and ever more with the pursuit of virtue

---

40 *NA* 109/29, 272/20–1. Sidney's view (as so often) is close to that of his fellow advocate of militant Protestantism Thomas Wilson, who analyses 'dissimulation' while warning against the benign 'outward appearance' of Don John of Austria in 1577 (K. de L., ix. 292). Wilson gives Nero and Caracalla as 'especial examples' of the vice: the *New Arcadia*, putting – in accordance with the principles of Sidney's *Defence of Poetry* – fiction before history, gives fictional examples. Wilson's understanding of the relationship of virtue to action likewise conforms to Sidney's: see his *The Three Orations of Demosthenes* (London, 1570), p. 103.

41 *OA* 13/35–6.

42 *NA* 429/38–9; Osborn, *Young Philip Sidney*, p. 209; GP 22/11–12. For Sidney's interest in the relationship of words, faces and demeanours to inner feeling, see too: *OA* 5/27–8, 8/33–4, 13/13–17, 14/9, 15/8–11, 16/4–10, 33/25–7, 46/33–47/4, 58/18–20, 103/9–10, 117/18–19, 120/18–19, 131/31–2, 281/33–5, 305/6–7; *NA* 10/14–16, 13/1–2, 15/33–4, 26/2–4, 28/10–11, 58/26–7, 60/24–7, 73/30–1, 146/12–13, 154/39–155/1, 287/18–20, 288/16–17.

43 Feuillerat, iii. 105.

44 Ibid., 147.

45 *NA* 161/14; *OA* 356, 357n., 7/3–4, 286/10; cf. *OA* 281/28, 393/33.

through human agencies.[46] In the life of virtuous action urged by Sidney, wisdom must include political prudence. To possess virtue without wisdom is the misfortune of 'the virtuous Leonatus', Prince of Galatia in the *New Arcadia*, whose 'goodness' is 'apt to be deceived' by 'craft'.[47] Euarchus by contrast is a tough and skilful statesman. Otherwise he would never have been in a position to establish good government in Macedon or to rescue Arcadia from itself or to save Greece from the Latin and Asiatic threats.[48]

Sidney recognises no tension between the claims of virtue and those of wisdom. For as Greville observes in his 'Dedication' to Sidney, 'nothing can be wise that is not really honest'.[49] Yet political skill involves the manipulation of men. To practise it we must direct, to our advantage, the thoughts and impressions of those with whom we deal. Will our tongues and hearts 'go one way' if we need to seem something different from, or something more or something less than, what we are? 'Wisdom' has to concern itself with appearances as well as realities. Euarchus, in making the arrangements for the trial of the princes, 'did wisely consider the people to be naturally taken with exterior shows far more than with inward consideration of the material points; and therefore . . . he would leave nothing which might be either an armour or an ornament unto him; and in these pompous ceremonies he well knew a secret of government much to consist'. Kerxenus, the virtuous ally of the accused princes, proceeds on the same principle, 'wisely considering' that the judges will be influenced by the clothes in which the princes appear before them. In Book Two, Pyrocles, struggling to quieten the mutinous multitude, likewise takes advantage of 'exterior shows': he finds that 'outward graces are not without their efficacies'.[50]

Those 'shows' and 'graces' are friends, not enemies, to virtue. The 'wisdom' that makes use of them is the fortification of virtue, not a dilution or perversion of it.[51] Yet the same techniques are available to the enemies of virtue too. For the skills of man-management are morally neutral. In the *New Arcadia* we watch Pyrocles virtuously suppressing a rebellion and Amphialus wickedly inciting one. Pyrocles finds it to be 'no evil way' to manipulate the naivety of the rebels: Amphialus exploits the inability of his prospective followers to see the difference 'between truth and truthlikeness, between shows and substance'.[52]

With Niccolò Machiavelli, who influenced him in other respects[53] and

46 Eugene Rice, *The Renaissance Idea of Wisdom* (Cambridge, Mass., 1958).
47 *NA* 271/6, 272/28, 262/33–4.
48 *OA* 355–7; *NA* 159–61.
49 *GP* 37/22–3.
50 *OA* 375/1–6, 374/19–21, 129/13–14.
51 We may be less convinced by the virtue of Musidorus, who 'did wisely consider' how to deceive the family of Dametas so as to make his own escape (*OA* 186/16). Here the word 'wisely' may be an ironic criticism of his self-deception. Though wisdom should be allied to virtue, it is not always so: *OA* 320/30 (cf. *OA* 319/21).
52 *NA* 287/34–288/1 (cf. *OA* 131/28–30; *NA* 325/10–11).
53 Below, Chapter 14.

perhaps in this one, Sidney sees that the political battlefield has its own laws, which apply to the virtuous and the vicious alike. If the virtuous are to prevail they must be wise as serpents. Otherwise, he and his allies understood, they will play into their enemies' hands. The case for evil means, or at least for means at odds with Sidney's conception of virtue, can be pressing. Sir Francis Walsingham, who commended Ciceronian 'honesty' as the means to living well, established a ruthless espionage network which thrived on duplicity. Apparently he once told Philip Sidney's brother Robert 'that if, after a promise made, [a] prince found that it were against the good of his estate he was not bound to observe it'.[54] We do not know whether Philip would have agreed. What do emerge consistently from his writings, fictional and non-fictional, are a recognition of, and an interest in, the facts of power.

Where Sidney departs from Machiavelli is in holding the goodness of virtue to be a significant determinant of those facts. In Sidney's fiction the virtuous have an inner and thus an outer strength denied to the wicked. The inner strength of 'virtue', particularly when it serves the cause of 'justice', gives men the 'confidence' to 'prevail'.[55] Euarchus is sustained in adversity by 'the secret assurance of his own worthiness (which, although it be never so well clothed in modesty, yet always lives in the worthiest minds)'.[56] The outer strength of 'virtue' derives from its 'wonderful effects' on others, from what Euarchus knows to be 'the mighty force of example', from the 'natural imperiousness' which, as the impression he makes on the Arcadians shows, 'rests in a well formed spirit'.[57] 'Magnanimity', the classical quality of great- ness of soul, of which 'the confidence in oneself is the chief nurse', gives power, through the awe and respect which it carries, to Euarchus and to the young princes.[58] 'The very shining force of excellent virtue' in Musidorus and Pyrocles extracts 'a kind of reverence' from their Phagonian captors. At their trial the princes hope 'to conquer the expectation of the onlookers with an extraordinary virtue. And such effect, indeed, it wrought in the whole assembly.'[59]

In the wars of the *New Arcadia*, 'virtue' is a military gift,[60] and the 'authority' bestowed by it is a source of military prowess. The performance of the princes in battle derives a decisive advantage from the 'sparks of virtue' which 'inflamed the affections of all that knew them'. That impact explains why Pyrocles holds such 'authority' in commanding the Laconian forces, and why, when Musidorus appears on the battlefield in the anonymous guise of the Black Knight, 'followed by none, and adorned by nothing', 'virtue quickly made him known, and admiration bred him such authority

---

54 KAO, U1475: Z1/10, p. 513.
55 *NA* 243/10–11, 246/38–247/1, 265/28–9.
56 *OA* 362/5–7.
57 *NA* 377/18–22; *OA* 364/15–16.
58 *OA* 289/21–2, 129/14–16, 377/20–2; *NA* 161/26.
59 *OA* 314/27–9, 377/213; cf. *OA* 302/33–303/1.
60 *NA* 463/17–18, 463/30, 463/37–8.

that . . . all knew it was fit to obey him'.[61] (It was because of the sway exerted by Sidney's virtue, says Greville, that 'wheresoever he went he was beloved and obeyed'.)[62] Characters of the *New Arcadia* are moved by their 'liking' for the princes to draw swords on their behalf; a nobleman who fights under Euarchus is 'so mind-stricken by the beauty of virtue in that noble king that, though not born his subject, he even professed himself his servant'; Prince Plangus is able, in the cause of the princess Evona, to enlist a 'good number of friends (whom his virtue, though a stranger, had tied unto him)'; by contrast Antiphilus is the object of such 'contempt' and 'hatred' that Plangus can 'get nobody to join with him' on his behalf.[63] Perhaps the example of Plangus would be lost on Antiphilus, for, as Greville indicates, it takes a 'free spirit' to respond to 'superior worth'.[64] In the *Old Arcadia* the example of Basilius' faithful friend Philanax is lost on the corrupt nobleman Timautus, who is blind to 'the lovely beauty of his virtue, whose image he had so quite defaced in his own soul that he had left himself no eyes to behold it'.[65]

The authority of virtue explained to Sidney's father why Philip had become the 'very formula that all well-disposed young gentlemen of our court do form . . . their manners and life by'.[66] It explained to Greville why, as his 'Dedication' recalls, 'many gentlemen', moved by 'this one man's example and personal respect', paid their 'natural tribute' to Sidney's 'superior worth' and 'affected to row and steer their course in his wake'; 'by which only commendable monopoly of alluring and improving men, look how the sun draws all winds after it in fair weather – so did the influence of this spirit draw men's affections and understandings to depend upon him'.[67] The hopes which were held by Sidney's party of their hero William of Orange, the leader of the Dutch revolt, were inspired by the authority of his virtue, for 'surely such a man . . . cannot but prosper, that loveth virtue'.[68] Like Sidney's Euarchus, whom he much resembles,[69] the Orange described by his English admirers and their continental friends has not only 'virtue' but 'wisdom'. Languet links Orange's 'virtues' with the 'wisdom' of that leader, whom he 'cannot enough admire', there being no 'wiser man' among 'the great men in Christendom'.[70] In the eyes of Sidney, who admires his virtue no less than Languet, Orange has 'the greatest sagacity'.[71]

61 *NA* 163/23–6, 38/20, 39/23, 344/13–17. Cf. *NA* 184/8–10, 263/17–20; *OA* 193/16–17.
62 *GP* 12/11–12.
63 *NA* 274/19–20, 171/18–20, 304/4–5, 303/28–33.
64 *GP* 70/2–3.
65 *OA* 322/35–323/1.
66 Arthur Collins, ed., *Letters and Memorials of State*, 2 vols (London, 1746), i. 246.
67 *GP* 12/11–12, 21/33–22/3, 70/2–3, 12/16–20.
68 K. de L., ix. 230.
69 Below, Chapter 13.
70 Pears, pp. 159–60, 166.
71 Quoted by Charles Samuel Levy, 'The Sidney–Hanau Correspondence', in Arthur Kinney *et al.*, eds, *Sidney in Retrospect* (Amherst, Mass., 1988), pp. 15–24, at p. 19.

Greville says that Sidney 'made the religion he professed the firm basis of his life'.[72] The emphasis of the 'religion he professed' was ethical (and, we shall see in Chapter 4, political) rather than theological. Greville expressed the same priority on his own account. In his judgement, wise princes enjoin:

> that people from the pulpit hear
> Nothing, but that which seems man's life to mend . . .
> Not idle theoric, to tickle wit,
> Empty of goodness, much more nice than fit.[73]

When Sidney writes the *Arcadia*, English lay Protestantism has yet to enter its dogmatic phase, though it soon will. Sidney, who is sometimes called a Calvinist, cannot properly be given that description (unless we call everyone a Calvinist who found points of agreement with Calvin or lamented the fall of Adam). His Protestantism, as far as we can see, carries light credal baggage. It is a Platonist Protestantism, or, as it has been called, a 'postlapsarian' Platonism.[74] It dwells on essence rather than form. Though its inmost truths can be understood best by the beneficiaries of Christian revelation, they are not (it seems) exclusive to them. In the pagan setting of the *Arcadia*, where men pray to Apollo or Jupiter or the stars, Sidney addresses, with no apparent sense of incongruity, the issues of faith and devotion that concern him as a Christian in his own time. His characters recognise a supreme source of divinity and virtue and beauty and truth and spiritual light. They are content to describe God as 'the Eternal'. Sidney, in his letters, does the same.[75]

The harmony of paganism and Christianity in Sidney's mind was manifest, in Greville's account, on his deathbed. Surrounded by ministers, he 'entreated this choir of divine philosophers about him to deliver the opinion of the ancient heathen touching the immortality of the soul, first, to see what true knowledge she retains of her own essence out of the light of herself; then, to parallel with it the most pregnant authorities of the Old and New Testament'.[76] Christianity has enlarged heathen wisdom, not contradicted it. The subscription of the ancients to the idea of the immortal soul was one of the tenets in which Christians sympathetic to classical antiquity found evidence that divine illumination had preceded the revelation of the gospel. Another was the belief in providence.[77] Sidney, when thinking about

---

72 *GP* 22/15–16.
73 Wilkes, p. 91 (st. 225).
74 *MP* 64.
75 Feuillerat, iii. 78, 99–100, 101–2, 114, 119; Osborn, *Young Philip Sidney*, 459. (That habit was not unique to Sidney.) A more theological Protestantism is discerned in Sidney's writings by Andrew Weiner, *Sir Philip Sidney and the Poetics of Protestantism* (Minneapolis, Minn., 1978), and 'Sidney, Protestantism, and Literary Critics', in Allen, *Sir Philip Sidney's Achievements*, pp. 117–26.
76 *GP* 81/27–82/2.
77 Cf. Thomas More, *Utopia*, ed. Edward Surtz and J. H. Hexter (New Haven and London, 1965: vol. iv of *The Yale Edition of The Complete Prose Works of St. Thomas More*), pp. 221, 523–4; W. R. Elton, *King Lear and the Gods* (San Marino, Calif., 1966), pp. 38, 41.

providence in his own time, conceived of it in Christian terms. Yet it is a theme of the pagan story of the *Arcadia*.[78]

If pagan and Christian religion are on friendly terms, so are pagan and Christian virtue. In the *Arcadia* virtue is effectively synonymous with the God who is its source. Sidney pits the supremacy of virtue, and thus of God in our souls, against a potent enemy: fortune. That theme is developed in the later part of the *Arcadia*, where virtue, which Sidney has until now portrayed as a creed of action, becomes a creed of endurance against evil fortune. Books Four and Five, where the princes are placed under guard and await the terrors of punishment, begin to expound what the *New Arcadia* will explore more fully: the Stoic – or, as in its Renaissance form it is sometimes called, neo-Stoic – doctrine of fortitude. The Stoicism of the Renaissance found its chief exponent in the Low Countries, in Sidney's friend Justus Lipsius, whose work *De Constantia* was its most influential expression. The doctrine scorns the vagaries of evil fortune, scorns those external afflictions to which virtue, whose strength is internal, is properly indifferent.[79] As Musidorus 'well know[s]', 'there is nothing evil but within us; the rest is either natural or accidental'. So in the later part of the *Arcadia* he and Pyrocles, who have hitherto demonstrated their virtue in action, in 'well-doing', resolve to 'triumph over adversity' by 'well suffering all accidents'. Virtue, urges Sidney, is to sustain itself through constancy and through what the *Arcadia* calls the 'patience' which 'is, as it were, the material cause of making a man happy or unhappy'.[80]

If virtue must be superior to external affliction, it must be no less superior to external prosperity. For goodness is not to be measured by its successes. 'Virtue', as Sidney observed to Languet, is 'its own reward'.[81] Euarchus and Philanax perceive the same truth: the 'reward' or 'prosperity' of 'virtue' lies 'in itself'. Philanax explains to Basilius that 'although the wickedness of the world should oppress' virtue, 'yet could it not be said that evil happened to him who should fall accompanied with virtue; so that, either standing or falling with virtue, a man is never in evil case'.[82] Sidney applied that point to himself at a low ebb in his life and career: 'I think a wise and constant man', he wrote to Walsingham, 'ought never to grieve while he doth play as a man may say his own part truly.'[83] In the *Arcadia* the elderly shepherd Geron declares the same conviction: we should follow the dictates of virtue and

78 Below, Appendix A.
79 Blair Worden, 'Constancy', *London Review of Books* 3 February 1983, pp. 13–14. Machiavelli too demanded the subordination of fortune to virtue, but in a different spirit. Fortune, in his account, is a whore which we must master if it is not to master us. But though Fulke Greville absorbed Machiavelli's teaching on that point (Bullough, ii. 268, ll. 63–6), there is no evidence that Sidney did so, indebted as he was to Machiavelli in other ways.
80 *OA* 318/13–20, 413/10–11, 318/1–2 (cf. *OA* 9/33–4, 319/9–14); below, Appendix A; cf. Wilson, *Demosthenes*, sig .*iii*ᵛ.
81 Osborn, *Young Philip Sidney*, p. 223.
82 *OA* 357/9–10, 7/7–10.
83 Feuillerat, iii. 166.

nature, 'and for th'event we never ought be sad'. The governing 'wisdom' of the world, Musidorus reminds Pamela, 'hath not his judgement fixed upon the event'.[84]

To measure virtue by its outward rewards, knows Euarchus, is to confuse it with the gifts of fortune.[85] It is a similar mistake to measure God's approval by the distribution of those gifts. Like Philisides, who asks 'what essence dest'ny hath; if fortune be or no',[86] Sidney explores the relationship between providence and fortune. Fortune (or chance), which is for him normally the enemy of providence, is sometimes its servant, for providence may make use of the 'traverses . . . of good and evil fortune' to train us in virtue;[87] but it allows no independence to their operation. Fortune is likewise normally the enemy but sometimes the servant of virtue.[88]

Sidney associates providence with permanence. The 'everlasting', 'everliving', 'eternal gods' are 'the eternal truth', or 'the immortal truth' or 'immortal goodness' or 'immortal beauty', or 'the eternal' or 'everlasting' justice.[89] Virtue is associated with permanence too. The gods are 'the eternal givers of virtue' or 'the eternal spring of virtue'.[90] Fortune, by contrast, is 'changeable'. It is thus, again, the contrary of both providence and virtue. 'Eternity and chance', Pamela explains to Cecropia in the New Arcadia, 'are things unsufferable together, for that is chanceable which happeneth . . . but we see [God's] work is steady and permanent.'[91] Sidney's own principle, as recorded by Greville, is at one with Pamela's: 'being once resolved' on a virtuous path 'he never brought any question of change to afflict himself with, or perplex the business, but left the success to His will that governs the blind prosperities and unprosperities of chance, and so works out His own ends by the erring frailties of human reason and affection'.[92]

With his friends – perhaps with Sir Francis Walsingham and Hubert Languet above all – Sidney shared an alertness to the providence that was at work in European politics and to its tendency to confound human calculations. In the last months of his life, when he acknowledged his own dependence on 'the higher power that must uphold me or else I shall fall', the grasp of providentialism on his political thinking seems to have strengthened. He meditated on the 'means' which 'God useth', on God's 'great work indeed in

84 OA 262/1–5, 311/8–9; cf. OA 312/29–30.
85 OA 357/4–10.
86 OA 336/24.
87 OA 10/37–8.
88 Below, Chapter 18.
89 OA 17/22, 173/10–11, 234/23, 265/2, 296/9, 298/17, 307/10, 371/18; NA 178/29; MP 116/ 30–1; cf. OA 407/9–10.
90 NA 79/15; OA 197/5–6.
91 OA 43/15; NA 360/4–5, 360/22.
92 GP 18/4–9; cf. GP 11/4–8. Cf. the view, quoted in OA xxviii, of Sidney's friend Philippe Duplessis-Mornay, expressed in the work of his, De la vérité de la religion chrétienne, that Sidney began to translate.

hand, against the abusers of the world'.[93] Yet God, though he demands
an alertness to that 'great work', permits his followers only a limited understanding of it. 'It is a strange event', writes Sidney to Languet on the death
of Charles IX of France in 1574. 'I am at a loss what to think of it, whether
his death is a wound to our cause, or, as I hope, a healing salve. The Almighty
is ordering Christendom with a wonderful providence in these our days.'[94]

Those words reflect a conception of providence which, though Sidney
does not acknowledge the fact, draws the Christian world, to which he
belongs, apart from the pagan one, in which he sets his fiction. Christians saw
providence, as pagans did not, as a pattern which gives shape to history: as a
spinal chord of which events are the vertebrae.[95] Pagans lacked too a counterpart to Adam's fall. The shadow of Adam's transgression is cast across the
Arcadia. Sidney gives no historical or theological definition to it. For all we
can tell it might be not an event but a metaphor. That is why it can be
inserted, with no sense of strain, into a pagan narrative. Yet its effect there,
our separation from God, is a Christian one and, in its emphases, a Protestant
one. 'So are we from our high creation slided' that we live in 'inward
darkness' or 'foggy mist' or 'dusty way'.[96] Our 'corrupted reason', being
'darkened with error', 'deface[s]' 'heav'nly rules', while our 'passions', which
'deceive' us and impair our sight, 'kill' them.[97] God is too 'high', too far
'beyond the heav'n, far more beyond our wits',[98] for us 'worms'[99] to understand him. Our souls are 'wrapped in flesh', in 'fleshly bondage'.[100] In relation
to God our 'eyes' are not 'clear'; they are 'owly' or 'dimmed'; or, being
'dazzled', they 'their way do miss'.[101] God's ways are 'unsearchable' or
'unreachable' and 'not [to be] searched into'.[102] Basilius searches into them,
with disastrous results for himself and his country. He shows himself to be
among the 'many who, making a perpetual mansion of this poor baiting-
place of man's life, are desirous to know the certainty of things to come,
wherein there is nothing so certain as our own continued uncertainty'.[103]

---

93 Feuillerat, iii. 166–7; cf. John Bossy, *Giordano Bruno and the Embassy Affair* (London and New
    Haven, 1991), pp. 150–1.
94 Pears, pp. 75–6.
95 C. A. Patrides, *Milton and the Christian Tradition* (Oxford, 1966), ch. 8.
96 *OA* 152/9, 182/28, 148/31, 374/2; cf. Osborn, *Young Philip Sidney*, p. 538 ('this fleshly darkness
    of ours').
97 *OA* 389/26–7, 365/14–15, 136/29–30, 148/32.
98 *OA* 148/34, 255/21; cf. *NA* 362/22.
99 *OA* 79/25, 91/26, 148/34, 385/31–2 (echoed in the penultimate sentence of Bosola's dying
    speech at the end of Webster's *The Duchess of Malfi*); cf. *MP* 168/6–7.
100 *OA* 147/12, 336/11. Cf. *OA* 371/22–3; Elton, *King Lear and the Gods*, pp. 61–2.
101 *OA* 373/33–374/2, 149/3.
102 *OA* 292/12, 371/17–18, 413/19, 7/11–12.
103 *OA* 5/5–8; cf. *OA* 150/27–9. Sidney's early biographer Thomas Moffet says that, 'as a young
    man . . . inspired with true religion', Sidney 'feared lest, too receptive to the fables of sooth-
    sayers, he might in rashness diminish the divine majesty (everywhere and always the disposer of
    all things) to particular modes and means'. Thomas Moffet, *Nobilis or the Life and Death of a
    Sidney*, ed. Virgil Heltzel and Hoyt Hudson (San Marino, Calif., 1940), p. 75. But Moffet, not
    for the only time, may have been wise after the writing of Sidney's fiction.

Yet our uncertainty before God's inscrutable purpose is no reason for faintheartedness or resignation. If our faculties are impaired they have not been destroyed. 'Our erected wit', explains Sidney's *Defence*, 'maketh us know what perfection is.' It is true that, since 'that first accursed fall of Adam', we have been prevented from 'reaching unto it' by 'our infected will'.[104] But the exercise of our faith and of our virtue demands that we try. We must aspire, however imperfectly, to the ideal with which Sidney credits Languet: to that

> concord between our wit and will,
> Where highest notes to godliness are raised,
> And lowest sink not down to jot of ill.[105]

If we embark on that task we shall find that God has left us the resources with which to strive towards him. Above all he has given us learning. For though 'books be but supplies of defects'[106] – the defects we inherit from the Fall – they are aids towards the 'purifying of wit'. The 'final end' of 'learning' is 'to lead and draw us to as high a perfection as our degenerate souls, made worse by their clayey lodgings, can be capable of': 'to lift up the mind from the dungeon of the body to the enjoying his own divine essence'. There is the same purpose to poetry, which God inspires with 'the force of a divine breath'.[107]

He inspires our reason with it too. Reason is flawed, and we must be careful to pay only 'tribute', not 'oblation', to 'human wisdom'.[108] But we must respect it and exercise it. Sidney's and Languet's intimate friend the Huguenot grandee Philippe Duplessis-Mornay denies, as Sidney does, the power of reason to measure God's purposes.[109] Yet when Mornay observes the fatalism with which Europe succumbs to the slaughters of religious war, his emphasis changes. 'We are men, and capable of reason', he declares. 'We should do what reason can do.'[110] Even when Sidney, in the last months of his life, faced disaster and disgrace in the Netherlands, he thought it 'no greater fault to have confidence in man's power, than it is too hastily to despair of God's work'.[111] With Mornay, and with the young Greville, Sidney believes that God allows and requires us to make our own free choices and thus to contribute to the bettering of ourselves and the world.[112]

---

104 *MP* 79/24–6.
105 *OA* 255/23–5; cf. *OA* 150/30–2.
106 *NA* 362/13.
107 *MP* 82/11–27, 79/22.
108 *NA* 457/37–8; cf. Rice, *Renaissance Idea of Wisdom*, p. 87.
109 Weiner, *Poetics of Protestantism*, p. 45.
110 *Mémoires et correspondance de Duplessis-Mornay*, 12 vols (Paris, 1824), ii. 47. Cf. ibid., iii. 532. Mornay shared Sidney's Platonism: Sidney, *Apology for Poetry*, ed. Shepherd, p. 158.
111 Feuillerat, iii. 166. Cf. Hatf. 148, fo. 49ᵛ; [Thomas Norton], *Orations, of Arsanes against Philip the Trecherous King of Macedon* (London, n.d.), sig. *iiii (the pertinence of Norton's work to the *Arcadia* will become evident below, Chapters 9, 11).
112 For Mornay and Greville, see Rebholz, *Greville*, pp. 24–5; cf. A. C. Hamilton, 'Sidney's Humanism', in Allen, *Sir Philip Sidney's Achievements*, pp. 109–16, at p. 110.

In that endeavour we have a solid base on which to place our trust and build our virtue. That base is the permanence of providence. Providence's enemy, fortune, being mutable, can provide no such base. Sidney's characters mistake the operation of providence for that of fortune or conflate the two. The 'despairing conceit' which Gynecia 'took of the judgement of God in her husband's death and her own fortune' is one of a series of such misapprehensions on her part.[113] The characters rage or 'blasphem[e]' against providence,[114] calling it 'blind' (even though blindness is properly the characteristic of fortune) or 'unjust' (even though 'justice' is, in the *Arcadia*, the essence of providence).[115] Musidorus, in his wiser vein, recognises that pitfall. As he tells Pyrocles during their adversity, 'we should [not] be . . . diligent auditors of the chances we like not. We have lived, and have lived to be good to ourselves and others. Our souls . . . have achieved the causes of their hither coming.'[116]

An understanding of providence, as of virtue, gives us courage, resolution, independence. Sidney's characters stand alone before God and before each *Self-* other. So do the English of his time. For men, in Sidney's philosophy, are *reliance* not links in a Great Chain of Being. They are not members of an elect or reprobate class. They are free agents, facing, in Renaissance politics as in Arcadian fiction, free tests of their virtue. They may voluntarily surrender their freedom from within, by servitude of the spirit. They may lose it to political tyranny, imposed from without. But God will not remove it from them. 'If God have made us masters of anything', declares Pyrocles, 'it is of our own lives.' Philoclea dissents. 'That we should be masters of ourselves we can show . . . no other right but [God's] gift.'[117] Yet the two positions complement each other. God's gift (we shall see) is the gift of self-reliance. In the political circumstances in which Sidney wrote the *Arcadia*, self-reliance would seem to him and his party the key to the survival, political and ethical, of their country.

The next section of this book will explore the context, biographical and political, in which that conviction was formed and from which the *Arcadia* emerged. For to follow the argument of Sidney's fiction, and to recognise the sound of virtue that it makes, we need first to know more about his life and times.

---

113 *OA* 384/18–20, 287/27–9, 366/33–4, 367/6–12.
114 *OA* 148/30, 367/8–9.
115 *NA* 431/22–3, 435/20; below, Appendix A.
116 *OA* 371/19–24. Earlier, in his less wise vein, Musidorus has contrived to muddle providence (even while explaining it correctly) with fortune: *OA* 311/1–16.
117 *OA* 297/17–18, 297/34–298/2.

Part Two: The Context

CHAPTER 3

Sidney's Loyalties

In 1579 Sidney composed and addressed to Queen Elizabeth his 'Letter ... touching her marriage'. By alienating England's Protestant leadership, he warned her, her marriage to Anjou would destroy the foundations, political and religious, of her reign. It would sacrifice her own and her country's independence to a ruthless and self-seeking foreign prince, who would plot to take over her government and to restore Catholicism. Anjou would pursue those goals through his influence within the regime and perhaps by conniving at rebellion against it. The queen was looking to end, through the marriage, her diplomatic isolation. Instead, argued Sidney, she could and should stand alone.

The 'Letter' is a delicate achievement. Criticism of Elizabeth's errors, and notice of the calamities to which they are leading, are circumscribed – at least on the surface – by deference and good manners. Yet Sidney risked the grave displeasure of the queen. As Greville says, a 'judicious reader' might 'ask whether it were not an error – and a dangerous one – for Sir Philip, being neither magistrate nor counsellor, to oppose himself against his sovereign's pleasure'.[1] Sidney was a junior politician in his mid-twenties. He was, it is true, in regular attendance upon the queen at court and was often present when she spoke of the match.[2] She evidently had a certain fondness for him. But she mistrusted him and prevented his advancement. In June 1577, at the age of twenty-two, he had returned, to general congratulation, from a diplomatic mission to Germany. 'There hath not been any gentleman ... these many years', wrote Elizabeth's Secretary of State Sir Francis Walsingham to Sidney's father, 'that hath gone through so honourable a charge with as great commendations as he.'[3] Yet that triumph, which looked

reception of mission

---

1   GP 37/1–4.
2   MP 51/3–4, 51/21, 53/7–9; GP 17/25; Pears, p. 120 (cf. p. 117); van Dorsten, Poets, pp. 65–6.
3   Osborn, Young Philip Sidney, p. 494.

to be an early foothill of the career in statesmanship for which he had been prepared, proved to be its summit.

The hazard Sidney ran in writing the 'Letter' can be measured by the queen's treatment of opponents of the match who, as privy councillors, were entitled to offer their advice. They were sharply rebuked by her, and some of them were banished from her presence.[4] It can be measured too by her response to the sensational pamphlet that attacked the marriage proposal in September 1579, John Stubbs's *The Discovery of a Gaping Gulph*. For writing what the queen's proclamation against it called his 'lewd, seditious book'[5] Stubbs had his right hand struck off before a public audience. The *Discovery* was an incendiary publication, intended to reach a large readership: Sidney's letter was an exercise in courtly persuasion, circulated only in manuscript. Yet, as the Oxford editors of the 'Letter' observe, there are 'parallels in argument and phrasing' between the two texts.[6] Sidney probably did not risk the punishment inflicted on Stubbs, but he certainly risked his career and possibly destroyed it.

The 'Letter' is as impolite about Elizabeth's prospective husband as it is polite about the queen. Its circulation provoked or intensified the dislike of Sidney felt by Anjou, who if ever he became Elizabeth's husband, Hubert Languet feared, would drive Sidney into exile. Writing to Sidney from Antwerp, Languet admired his former pupil's 'courage' in 'resisting the queen's will' but questioned his prudence.[7] Yet Languet came to realise that the 'Letter', though it expressed its author's own views, had not been written on his initiative. On other occasions, it is true, Sidney seems to have been capable of independent political action and of mobilising pressure on the queen to implement policies he favoured.[8] But in this case, as Languet wrote to Sidney, 'you were ordered to write as you did by those whom you were bound to obey'. Sidney's instructors, Languet suspected, 'either did not know into what peril they were thrusting you, or did not care for your danger, provided they effected their own object', the defeat of the match.[9]

There were two men above all whom Sidney was 'bound to obey': his father Sir Henry Sidney; and the figure whom Languet is likely to have had principally in mind, Sir Henry's brother-in-law and Philip's uncle, Robert Dudley, Earl of Leicester. Neither man would have underestimated the risk Philip ran. Neither would have wanted to sacrifice Philip's future. But the survival of a country, of a religion and of a political affinity was in the balance, or was thought to be. Leicester was the leading opponent of the match, Sir Henry Sidney his lieutenant. The royal disfavour which fell on

---

4   Below, Chapter 9.
5   Stubbs, p. 148.
6   *MP* 33–4; cf. Leonard Tennenhouse, 'Arcadian Rhetoric: Sidney and the Politics of Courtship', in Allen, *Sir Philip Sidney's Achievements*, pp. 201–13, at p. 205.
7   Pears, pp. 170, 177, 187–8.
8   *GP* 56/36–7, 75n.
9   Pears, p. 187.

Philip in the late 1570s was an extension of the queen's attitude towards his father and uncle.

In 1551, when Leicester's father, the Duke of Northumberland, held sway over the boy king Edward VI, Sir Henry had married Northumberland's sister Mary. The marriage marked and furthered the spectacular rise of the Sidneys in Edward's reign, when they gained their country seat at Penshurst in Kent from the crown. Sir Henry, it was said, 'acquired so great an influence next to the king that he was able to make all his motions conform to those of the duke'.[10] When Edward died, in Sir Henry's arms, Sir Henry committed himself to Northumberland's attempt to enthrone Lady Jane Grey. After the failure of the coup Northumberland was executed. His sons, Ambrose (Earl of Warwick) and Robert, were placed under a suspended sentence of death, which was lifted only after they had distinguished themselves on the crown's behalf at the Battle of St Quentin in 1557. Sir Henry by contrast was soon in Queen Mary's favour. In 1554 Philip was born, his first child. The baptism was a moment of historical irony, for the son was named after Mary's husband, Philip II of Spain, who stood at the font as godfather and to whose defeat Philip Sidney would devote and sacrifice his life.

Yet the Sidneys, like the Dudleys, would never regain their Edwardian standing. Sir Henry served Elizabeth ably and indefatigably, both as Lord President of Wales and as Lord Deputy (or Viceroy) of Ireland. But her ingratitude, and her reluctance to support his efforts to reduce Ireland to order and civility, brought him to despair. They also brought him close to insolvency, so that he was obliged to decline a peerage, 'in consideration', his wife said, of the family's 'inability to maintain a higher title than they now possess'.[11] Philip, who loved to spend what he did not have, lived in a state of debt-ridden 'necessity'.[12] It was poverty that kept him from court (even though his absence may not have been unwelcome to him) in 1580, when he retreated to Wilton House and wrote the *Arcadia*.

The retreat was the culmination of a long process of political disappointment and frustration. His fortunes were tied to those of Leicester, which sank low in the late 1570s. The earl had long hoped to lead, and Philip Sidney to belong to, a military expedition to the Netherlands in support of William of Orange, the leader of the armed resistance to Spanish hegemony in the Netherlands. Orange in turn was eager to cultivate Leicester and his affinity. Philip, on his return journey from Germany in 1577, had an opportunity to wait upon Orange, who said afterwards that he had 'conceived a great

10   Dale Hoak, 'Rehabilitating the Duke of Northumberland', in Jennifer Loach and Robert Tittler, eds, *The Mid-Tudor Polity* (London, 1980), pp. 29–51, at p. 44.
11   Osborn, *Young Philip Sidney*, p. 5; cf. Simon Adams, 'The Patronage of the Crown in Elizabethan Politics', in John Guy, ed., *The Reign of Elizabeth I. Court and Culture in the Last Decade* (Cambridge, 1995), pp. 20–45, at p. 29 & n. 41.
12   Feuillerat, iii. 129, 138, 139.

opinion' of him.[13] At that meeting the two men must have discussed the wish recently formed by Orange that Philip should marry his eldest daughter Mary. As a dowry Philip was offered what loose report (which is all we have) described as the lordship of Holland and Zeeland.[14] The marriage would have given him a prominent role in the revolt of the Netherlands. It would have struck a powerful blow, in symbolic and perhaps in practical terms too, for the cause of militant international Protestantism. We cannot tell whether it was that marriage, or the betrothal to a Protestant German princess which Philip also contemplated, that Languet was trying to arrange in the summer of 1577.[15] Philip's wish for a marriage that would assist international Protestantism illustrates his priorities. Only the diminution of his own standing and the deterioration of his finances would lead him, in 1583, to settle for an English bride.[16] Even then he gained as his father-in-law England's most prominent champion of the European Protestant cause, his friend and guide Sir Francis Walsingham.

Elizabeth had 'well liked' Philip's report on his German embassy.[17] But when, soon afterwards, she learned of his proposed marriage to Orange's daughter, approval yielded to indignation. The match would have made Philip the ally of a foreign power. It would have drawn him into a rebellion against her fellow monarch, Philip II. If there was a cardinal principle in the queen's political and religious policies, it was that her subjects owed their allegiance to her and her country, not to those imaginary international obligations which religious zeal, whether Catholic or Protestant, too often suggested to them. Greville, who attended on Orange in 1579, records that Orange then asked him to pass on a request to the queen that she give advancement to Sidney, who '(as he heard) lived unemployed under her'. Greville adds that Sidney dissuaded his friend from conveying that message, partly on the prudent ground that 'princes love not that foreign powers should have extraordinary interest in their subjects, much less to be taught by them how they should place their own'.[18]

In 1577 the queen made plain her view of Philip's proposed marriage in words that she must have expected to get back to his family. To Daniel Rogers, an intimate of the Sidneys, she wrote that she could not approve of any initiative in the Low Countries that would assist 'the withdrawing the subject from the sovereign' there. 'For *we* could not like that any foreign prince should enter into any such secret combination with *our* President of Wales or Deputy of Ireland or any other governor under us, which might any way estrange him from the obedience he oweth us.'[19] Where Sidney's

---

13   K. de L., ix. 411.
14   Osborn, *Young Philip Sidney*, pp. 491, 496–7.
15   Pears, pp. 109–10, 120.
16   Duncan-Jones, *Sir Philip Sidney*, p. 225.
17   Osborn, *Young Philip Sidney*, p. 494.
18   GP 17/3, 17/29–32.
19   Osborn, *Young Philip Sidney*, p. 496. The italics are mine.

plan to marry Orange's daughter was a pledge of commitment to international Protestantism, Elizabeth's negotiations with Anjou signalled her repudiation of it. Leicester's hopes of heading an army in Orange's cause were now ended. Only after Orange's assassination in 1584 would the earl be allowed to lead, the following year, his expedition to the Netherlands, on which Philip would meet his death in 1586.

Elizabeth's discovery of Philip's marriage plan was a sharp setback to his father. In Ireland a year earlier, fresh from the suppression of a rebellion there, Sir Henry had been at the height of his reputation. Walsingham, expressing the pleasure of Sir Henry's 'private friends' at the general recognition of his achievements, assured him that 'your very enemies cannot but commend you'.[20] Yet in September 1577, when the story of the proposal had broken, we find Walsingham trying to assure Sir Henry that the 'bitterness' of the queen's recent letters to him had merely 'proceeded of some passion for the time'.[21] The tide had turned against Sir Henry in Ireland. By vigorously challenging oligarchical interests there, he had aroused opposition at the English court and alarmed even his supporters around the queen.[22] By 1578 father and son both knew how deeply they had offended. In the spring, Philip came to despair of achieving political or military service under Elizabeth. He was contemplating, he told Languet, a voyage of exploration ('some Indian project').[23] Yet even now, when he knew the queen's views on the subject, there was 'much talk' of his continuing intention to marry Orange's daughter.[24] In September Sir Henry left Ireland for the last time. It was said that he went on board reciting the 114th Psalm, 'alluding thereby to the troublesome state of Moses in the land of Egypt'.[25]

The Sidney family was not new to independent negotiations with foreign powers. In the past, Sir Henry's dealings had been with Spanish agents. For, like Leicester, he had been a slow convert to the cause of international Protestantism. Though the two brothers-in-law had built support for themselves among England's radical Protestants, they had maintained communications with Catholics too. In 1574 Antonio de Guaras, a Spanish agent in England, reported to Philip II a conversation with Sir Henry. According to the record of it made by the Spanish king, Sir Henry:

> had asked to see Guaras and spoken in great secrecy to him, and offered that he had a way to serve his majesty with 6000 chosen English soldiers; and since Guaras expressed two or three times his belief as to the difficulty of doing so with the queen's will, *and even more without it*, he replied . . . that as security for

20   Collins, *Letters and Memorials of State*, i. 124.
21   Ibid., 226.
22   Leimon, 'Walsingham', pp. 18–21; Ciaran Brady, *The Chief Governors. The Rise and Fall of Reform Government in Tudor Ireland, 1536–1588* (Cambridge, 1994), ch. 4, esp. p. 149.
23   Pears, p. 146.
24   *CSPS 1568–79*, pp. 575–6; Osborn, *Young Philip Sidney*, p. 491n.
25   *MP* 5.

the fulfilment of it he pledged his only heir . . . whose name is Philip whom his majesty lifted from the font.[26]

At the time of that conversation Philip Sidney was abroad, on his extended grand tour. If he learned of the proposal he would have been unlikely to welcome it, for though he was eager for military experience his anti-Spanish views were already firmly set. What he did share with his father was a readiness to form international attachments that might conflict with his monarch's understanding of his national loyalties. A few months before his death he wrote from the Netherlands a letter to Walsingham, now his father-in-law, which confronts the disastrous predicament of Leicester's expedition and the consequences of the queen's failure to give it adequate backing. His words place a higher value on his God than on his queen.

> If her majesty were the fountain I would fear considering what I daily find that we should wax dry, but she is but a means whom God useth and I know not whether I am deceived but I am faithfully persuaded that if she should withdraw herself other springs would rise to help this action. For methinks I see the great work indeed in hand, against the abusers of the world . . ..[27]

Philip knew from an early age the truth he would express late in his life: that 'my chiefest honour is to be a Dudley'.[28] Until the birth of Leicester's son in 1581 he was heir to the titles and estates of Leicester and his brother Warwick. The Sidneys, Philip knew, were a 'youngly . . . fortuned family'.[29] The fortunes of the Dudley family were not much older; indeed their youth was bitterly remarked by Leicester's opponents among the ancient nobility; but the Dudleys were grandees as the Sidneys were not. In his schooldays Philip had been urged by his father to remember 'the noble blood you are descended of by your mother's side', and to strive to 'be an ornament to that illustrious family'.[30] Sir Henry, tied to Leicester, may not have liked the earl, for he is said to have also told his children 'that if they meant to live in order, they should ever behold whose sons, and seldom whose nephews they were'.[31] Nevertheless Philip understood the primacy of his obligations to Leicester, who was consistently his patron and protector. Always he had to obey Leicester's wishes. Always he had to look to his uncle's influence as his chief hope of securing a career in the state's service.[32] It is likely to have been

---

26 Duncan-Jones, *Sir Philip Sidney*, p. 88 (my italics); cf. ibid., p. 89.
27 Feuillerat, iii. 166.
28 *MP* 134/17–18.
29 Feuillerat, iii. 139.
30 Osborn, *Young Philip Sidney*, p. 13.
31 *MP* 124.
32 For his dependence on and deference to Leicester, see e.g. Pears, pp. 59, 89–91; Sir Harry Nicolas, ed., *Memoirs of the Life and Times of Sir Christopher Hatton* (London, 1847), p. 69; Feuillerat, iii. 78–9 (cf. 132); K. de L., x. 679, 744; van Dorsten, *Poets*, p. 66; Moffet, *Nobilis*, p. 79; cf. *CSPF 1583–4*, p. 579.

as Leicester's man that Philip was appointed, at so young an age, to lead an embassy to Germany in 1577. Throughout that mission a tablet was hung outside his lodgings proclaiming his relationship to his uncles, as well as to the '*pro-rex* of Ireland'.[33] Following the birth of Leicester's son, Philip is said to have appeared at a tournament at court bearing the motto 'Speravi' ('I have hoped'), with the word 'dashed through, to show his own hope therein was dashed'.[34] The hope was restored in 1584, when Leicester's son died.

If Philip Sidney ever needed reminders of his dependence on Leicester, his friends at home and abroad were ready to provide them. The hopes they held of his future derived not merely from his abilities, impressive as they were, but, as Languet put it, from 'the expectation of great wealth, the authority and influence of your relations ... and all those other things which are commonly called gifts of fortune'.[35] Sidney was seen not only as the prospective inheritor of his uncles' titles and estates but as the heir to their political influence. It would be his task to help England assume, in the generations to come, the leadership of international Protestantism.

Philip's relationship with Leicester, like Sir Henry's, may not have been comfortable. The 'Defence' of Leicester which he wrote in answer to that notorious libel of 1584, *Leicester's Commonwealth*, is the least assured of his writings. Its portrait of the earl has neither life nor warmth. Sidney's letters reveal no fondness for him and may sometimes hint at a lack of it. When, in December 1581, a stressful time for Philip,[36] Leicester's patronage procured for him the offer of only an unattractive and unremunerative post, Sidney wrote to him with breathless petulance: 'Well my lord your lordship made me a courtier do you think of it as seems best unto you.'[37] In the month before his death Sidney described to Walsingham the wretched state of the expedition to the Netherlands. 'To complain of my Lord of Leicester you know I may not,' he wrote;[38] plainly he would have liked to. Sidney's imaginative writings, too, contain what may be indications of trouble in his feelings about Leicester and the Dudleys.[39] Dissatisfaction, if he felt it, is

---

33 Duncan-Jones, *Sir Philip Sidney*, p. 123; cf. van Dorsten, *Poets*, p. 49.
34 Duncan-Jones, *Sir Philip Sidney*, pp. 194, 218 (cf. *NA* 61/20–3).
35 Pears, pp. 183–4; cf. Osborn, *Young Philip Sidney*, p. 297.
36 Duncan-Jones, *Sir Philip Sidney*, p. 220.
37 Feuillerat, iii. 140.
38 Ibid., 180.
39 (i) In the *New Arcadia* the description of the oligarchy which ruled Macedon during the nonage of King Euarchus answers to the description by its critics of the regime of Leicester's father Northumberland during the nonage of Edward VI (*NA* 159/25–160/23); those critics included Marian exiles whose works we shall find echoed in the *Old Arcadia*. (ii) There is a sharp aside in the *New Arcadia* where Sidney tells how 'great men' 'shak[e] off ... their friends' (*NA* 189/ 8). The words recall a letter written by Leicester in October 1579, at a low ebb in his own career and (probably) shortly after Sidney had been directed to write against the Anjou match. Pleading for understanding, almost for mercy, from his rival Lord Burghley, Leicester reminds him 'what friends ... I have shaked from [me], chiefly in respect of your lordship'. (Quoted by Conyers Read, *Lord Burghley and Queen Elizabeth* (London, 1960), p. 204.) (iii) Sidney's masque *The Lady of May*, written in 1578 or 1579 for the queen's visit to Leicester's house at Wanstead, describes the earl as 'foully commaculated with the papistical enormity'. The description is a jest (*MP* 13),

understandable. What must Sidney have thought of Leicester's wavering tactics (as we shall find them to have been) during the Anjou crisis of 1579, when Sidney was required to risk political suicide on his uncle's behalf? Leicester had learned to speak, even to feel, the language of forward Protestantism. He had given indispensable support to its programme, and to its agents, at home and abroad. Yet forward Protestants continued to mistrust him. Sidney must have been well informed about the publication in 1579, and the republication in 1580 and again in 1581, of an English translation of a work by his beloved friend Philippe Duplessis-Mornay under the title *A Treatise of the Church*. Leicester, to whom the translation is dedicated, is sharply warned by the dedication, in which the zealous Puritan John Field urges him to 'stop your ears against the enchanting and fawning whisperings of hollow-hearted papists and dissolute oppressors: for there can be no greater trespass against the Lord than to lean upon Assyria'.[40]

Sidney's want of warmth towards Leicester may have been reciprocated. Fulke Greville, whose 'Dedication' to Sidney indicates so few shortcomings in its hero, relates on Leicester's authority that the earl appointed Sidney to a place in the Netherlands expedition only 'as one among the rest, not only despising his youth for a counsellor, but withal bearing a hand upon him as a forward young man'.[41] Leicester is a shadowy figure in the 'Dedication', even though the Grevilles and Dudleys were close.[42] The 'Dedication' calls him 'this grandee', not an approving noun in the vocabulary of Greville, who refers to the self-interested conduct, which he contrasts with Sidney's purity of motive, of the 'grandees at court' – Leicester among them? – at the time of the Anjou crisis.[43]

There was a happier and more intimate relationship in Sidney's public life: his friendship with Sir Francis Walsingham. Walsingham and Leicester were allies but not friends.[44] Though Walsingham, too, was a much older man than Sidney, the bond of political and religious sympathy between them crossed the gap of generations. It was probably formed in 1572, when Walsingham was ambassador in Paris and when Sidney took refuge in his house from the Massacre of St Bartholomew. In that traumatic episode many of their friends

---

but a strange one. Strange too is the failure of *The Lady of May* to distance Leicester from that 'servile flattery' of 'courtiers' on which the masque is so severe (*MP* 28/17–18).

40   Rosenberg, *Leicester*, pp. 245–50. Cf. *Le Reveille-Matin* ('Edinburgh', 1574), dialogue ii, pp. 62–3; K. de L., ix. 303. Leicester's religious beliefs and his relationship with his Puritan clients are luminously treated by Patrick Collinson, *Godly People* (London, 1983), ch. 3.

41   *GP* 18/19–21.

42   Rebholz, *Greville*, p. 5.

43   *GP* 88/12, 37/25. Greville showed no wish to rescue Leicester's reputation from its posthumous disfavour. One literary partner of Greville sought to intensify that disfavour. Greville's 'Dedication', observes its modern editor, has a 'very close relationship' to the *Annals* of Elizabeth's reign written under James I by Greville's close friend William Camden, who recorded Greville's 'exceeding great deserts toward me' (*GP* xx). Camden's *Annals*, which laud Sidney, breathe hatred of Leicester: Hugh Trevor-Roper, *Renaissance Essays* (London, 1985), pp. 142–3.

44   Leimon, 'Walsingham', p. 37.

3 Robert Dudley, Earl of Leicester.

4 Sir Francis Walsingham.

were killed or had to flee for their lives; Walsingham himself was lucky to escape.[45] Three years later, when Sidney entered court politics, he found that he had 'friends which . . . were Sir Philip's for [Walsingham's] sake'.[46]

In a letter to Sir Francis a few months before his own death, Sidney disclosed his feelings about the miserable condition of God's 'cause'. He reflected too on the 'danger, want and disgrace' likely to be soon visited on himself. His gloom was countered by a declaration of the faith which he knew his father-in-law to share, and which opened Sidney's heart to the man 'to whom for my particular I am more bound than to all men besides'.[47] Walsingham, deprived by Sidney's death of 'my chief worldly comfort',[48] was left with the younger man's debts, a burden that would cripple his estate. It was Walsingham who made the arrangements for Sidney's funeral, that massive show of strength by the forward Protestant party which is commemorated in Thomas Lant's roll. On his own death Walsingham would be quietly buried beside Sidney in St Paul's Cathedral.[49]

As a friend of Walsingham, Sidney belonged to a circle which included his own closest friends. Edward Dyer, who was a client of Leicester but grew away from him, developed a strong allegiance to Walsingham.[50] Fulke Greville came to think of Walsingham as a second 'father' to him and was described in 1580 as a 'link' in the 'chain' of Walsingham's associates.[51] Two years earlier he had risked the queen's anger by accompanying Walsingham, 'that wise and active Secretary' as the 'Dedication' calls him, on a diplomatic mission to the Netherlands without her knowledge. On his return he was 'forbidden her presence for many months'.[52] In the summer of 1580, when Sidney was writing the *Arcadia*, Greville was leading a naval expedition off the Irish coast and sending reports to Walsingham which confirm his dependence on him.[53] Other friends of Sidney who were close to Walsingham were Robert Beale, who was Sir Francis's brother-in-law and who acted as his secretary and often as his deputy, and Beale's friend the scholar and poet Daniel Rogers, that key figure in the diplomatic relations of England and the Netherlands. Rogers thought of Walsingham as his 'especial friend and patron'.[54]

Sidney, Greville, Beale and Rogers were all, like Walsingham, urgently

45   Read, *Walsingham*, i. 221–2, 229, 233.
46   *GP* 19/2–3. Walsingham's relations with Sidney's father were not easy: Leimon, 'Walsingham', pp. 18–21.
47   Feuillerat, iii. 166–7.
48   John Bruce, ed., *Correspondence of Robert Dudley, Earl of Leycester* (London, Camden Society, 1844), p. 454.
49   *CSPD 1580–90*, p. 670.
50   Ralph Sargent, *The Life and Lyrics of Sir Edward Dyer* (Oxford, 1968), pp. 21, 91.
51   PRO, SP 63/74/30; Rebholz, *Greville*, p. 20.
52   *GP* 18/29, 88/7, 110/9–10.
53   Leimon, 'Walsingham', p. 195; PRO, SP 63/74/3, 32; Rebholz, *Greville*, pp. 41–3.
54   Van Dorsten, *Poets*, pp. 19, 31n. Rogers was a close friend of the printer of John Stubbs's attack on the Anjou match, *The Discovery of a Gaping Gulph*: Stubbs, p. li.

committed to the continental Protestant cause. All, like him, were on close terms with continental Protestants. One continental Protestant in particular was a large presence in their lives and a dominant one in Sidney's. Hubert Languet was born in 1518. He was eleven years older than Sidney's father and about fifteen years older than Walsingham and Leicester. A Frenchman, he spent the greater part of his career as a roving diplomat in the Protestant cause. On learning of Languet's death in September 1581 Walsingham was overwhelmed by distress.[55] To Walsingham's secretary Robert Beale, with whom, as with Sidney, he would conduct a correspondence over many years, Languet wrote as early as 1569 about the perils confronting England's and Europe's Protestants.[56] Beale visited Languet on his continental missions. So did Daniel Rogers. Languet delighted in his conversations with both men, which were warmed by affectionate discussions of Sidney's virtues. Languet worked to bring Beale closer to Sidney, Sidney to bring Rogers closer to Languet.[57] In 1581, the last year of his life, Languet told his and Rogers's friend George Buchanan that he had 'cultivated a particular intimacy' with Rogers 'for many years'.[58] Greville, who escorted Languet back to the continent after the older man's visit to England in the winter of 1578-9, was on affectionate terms with him; so was Edward Dyer.[59]

The friendship of Walsingham and Languet was built on a common perception of the international peril facing Protestantism and of the need for international cooperation to withstand it. The two men made each other's acquaintance while both were ambassadors in Paris in 1571-2, Walsingham as the representative of Queen Elizabeth, Languet of the Lutheran prince Augustus of Saxony. It may have been Walsingham who arranged for Languet to monitor Sidney's travels from 1573 to 1575. We do not know whether Sidney and Languet met when both of them were in Paris in 1572. Both of them fled from the city in that year at the time of the Massacre of St Bartholomew. Greville tells us that they got to know each other soon afterwards in Frankfurt, where, he says, they were fellow lodgers in the house of that doyen of international Protestant publishing, the printer Andreas Wechel.[60] The friendship deepened in 1573 when Sidney spent time in Vienna, whither Languet had removed to become Augustus' representative at the Imperial court.[61]

55 *CSPF 1581-2*, p. 338. For Walsingham and Languet see also ibid., *1577-8*, pp. 277, 303, *1578-9*, p. 503; *CSPD 1547-80*, p. 497; Osborn, *Young Philip Sidney*, pp. 149-50; Pears, p. 36.
56 BL, Egerton MS. 1693, fos 3ff.
57 Pears, pp. 129-36, 143, 146-9, 189-90; van Dorsten, *Poets*, pp. 31, 67, 70; Charles Wilson, *Queen Elizabeth I and the Revolt of the Netherlands* (London, 1970), p. 32; cf. *CSPF 1577-8*, pp. 97, 185, 277.
58 David Irving, *Memoirs of the Life and Writing of George Buchanan* (Edinburgh, 1817), p. 217.
59 Rebholz, *Greville*, p. 29; Pears, pp. 145, 158, 159, 191.
60 *GP* 6/9-16. For Wechel see R. J. W. Evans, *The Wechel Presses: Humanism and Calvinism in Central Europe 1572-1627* (*Past and Present* supplement 2, 1975).
61 In his invaluable study *Poets, Patrons and Professors*, pp. 30, 64-5, van Dorsten overrules Greville's evidence about the meeting at Frankfurt, and claims, on the basis of a poem about Sidney by

By 1575, as Sidney learned from a common friend, Languet was 'in ill favour' with Augustus and 'in great peril'.[62] Languet's eagerness for Protestant militancy had come up against the peaceable inclinations of German Lutheranism and had exposed him to what he described to Sidney as 'unbelievable discourtesy, and even treachery', from his ostensible friends.[63] The Peace of Augsburg in 1555 had given the Lutheran princes of the Holy Roman Empire the right to establish their faith in their principalities. Their reluctance to jeopardise that gain helps to explain their passive response, which exasperated Sidney and his English patrons and allies, to the international Catholic threat. 'The princes of Germany', complained the queen's agent at Antwerp, the forward Protestant William Davison, in 1578, were 'hirelings and coldly affected'.[64] The Peace of Augsburg had granted no such toleration to Calvinist princes, from whom there might thus be more hope of militancy.

Languet (who had learned his Protestant faith from Philip Melanchthon) was not a Calvinist in doctrine. But in 1577 he entered the service of the younger brother of the Elector Palatine, the Calvinist John Casimir, Count Palatine, who had committed himself and his troops to the international Protestant cause. Languet came to England with Casimir in the winter of 1578–9. Casimir's sister may have been the German princess with whom he had earlier tried to arrange a marriage for Sidney.[65] Certainly Casimir, who held Sidney 'greatly . . . in admiration' for his 'noble towardness and virtue', was eager to enlist him as a fellow commander in his army.[66] Sidney was no less eager to fight beside him.[67] Languet's relations with Casimir, however, turned sour. For Casimir's military ambitions proved inconvenient to William of Orange, to whom Languet and Sidney alike looked as the leading hope of international Protestantism. In the late 1570s Languet acquired a prominent place in Orange's counsels.

There he was joined by another intimate friend of Sidney, another Frenchman who, like Languet, had spent much of the 1570s outside France. This was Philippe Duplessis-Mornay, who was five years Sidney's senior. Mornay too had been in Paris in 1572, when he had helped the Protestant leader Gaspard de Coligny to push King Charles IX into agreeing to invade the Low Countries and fight the Spaniards there. Elizabeth had been as reluctant

Daniel Rogers, that Sidney and Languet met for the first time in Vienna. Greville's evidence seems to me to be worth more, and Rogers's poem to say less, than van Dorsten thinks (though I agree with Duncan-Jones – Sir Philip Sidney, p. 71 – in doubting whether, as Greville suggests, Languet and Sidney lodged together in Frankfurt by 'chanc[e]').

62   Osborn, Young Philip Sidney, p. 380.
63   Ibid., p. 446.
64   Nicolas, Hatton, p. 45.
65   Osborn, Young Philip Sidney, pp. 478–9; Duncan-Jones, Sir Philip Sidney, pp. 133–4; and see H. R. Woudhuysen, 'Leicester's Literary Patronage: A Study of the English Court, 1578–1582' (Oxford Univ. D.Phil. thesis, 1982), p. 236n.
66   CSPF 1577–8, pp. 638, 731; Pears, pp. 131, 166 (cf. p. 160); van Dorsten, Poets, p. 65.
67   Pears, pp. 153–4; Nicolas, Hatton, p. 69.

to endorse the plan as her ambassador in Paris, Walsingham, had been eager.[68] The assassination of Coligny and the Massacre of St Bartholomew put an end to that initiative. Mornay's narrow (and dramatic) escape from Paris was secured by Languet. First Mornay went to England, where Walsingham arranged for his favourable reception.[69] Mornay and Walsingham would remain close.[70] Mornay returned to England in 1576, now in a vain bid to extract money from Queen Elizabeth for the French Protestant cause. He received a disappointingly 'meagre' answer from her.[71] But he was back in 1577, in the hope of winning support for the Huguenots' ally Henry of Navarre.

This time he stayed for eighteen months. During that visit Walsingham and Sidney were (as Mornay's widow would recall) 'ses plus confidens amis'.[72] Their assistance could not win the queen to his cause. Walsingham reported that Mornay had told him 'with tears' of her 'hard speeches' to him.[73] By March 1578 Sidney had recognised the failure of the mission.[74] Mornay was distressed too by Elizabeth's failure to aid the forces fighting Spain in the Netherlands, by her abandonment of them in their hour of need.[75] So was Languet.[76] It was during Mornay's stay in England that the Anjou marriage was proposed. Mornay knew Anjou's character, having acted as agent for him at a time when Anjou had found it convenient to cultivate the Huguenots. Mornay's widow would remember that her husband had 'heartily disapproved of this marriage both on account of religion and no less for reasons of state, and this notwithstanding that the queen did him the honour to discuss it with him confidentially'. She would recall too that the marriage negotiations had been 'the chief reason' why he had 'left England in such a hurry'.[77] He was back, again as an agent for Navarre, in 1580, while Sidney was writing the *Arcadia*. After his return to France he and Sidney would sustain a regular and frequent correspondence.[78]

Languet was hostile to the Anjou match too.[79] Like Sidney, Mornay owed

---

68 Read, *Walsingham*, i. 217–18, 295.

69 Lucy Crump, ed., *A Huguenot Family in the XVI Century* (London and New York, n.d., ?1926), pp. 131–2.

70 Read, *Walsingham*, i. 263, 302; *Mémoires et correspondance de Duplessis-Mornay*, ii. 102, 235–41, iii. 327; Raoul Patry, *Philippe Du Plessis-Mornay* (Paris, 1933), pp. 71–3, 109n., 118n., 135n.; *CSPF 1577–8*, p. 81, *1578–9*, p. 349, *1579–80*, p. 138.

71 Read, *Walsingham*, i. 294 & n.; Mack Holt, *The Duke of Anjou and the Politique Struggle during the Wars of Religion* (Cambridge, 1986), p. 73; *CSPF 1575–7*, p. 322 (cf. pp. 325–6).

72 *Mémoires et correspondance de Duplessis-Mornay*, i. 117.

73 Read, *Walsingham*, i. 302.

74 Pears, p. 146.

75 *Mémoires et correspondance de Duplessis-Mornay*, ii. 240–1.

76 Osborn, *Young Philip Sidney*, p. 364; Pears, p. 151.

77 Crump, *Huguenot Family*, pp. 132, 170–1 (cf. p. 133).

78 *Mémoires et correspondance de Duplessis-Mornay*, ii. 304. See too Margaret Hannay, '"This Moses and This Miriam": the Countess of Pembroke in the Legend of Sir Philip Sidney', in Allen, *Sir Philip Sidney's Achievements*, pp. 217–26, at p. 220.

79 Pears, pp. 170, 188. (The import of Languet's remarks is evident from the correspondence which surrounds them.)

much of his political education to Languet. Languet taught him, as he did
Sidney, to study the political lessons of history and to apply them to current
events.[80] Those lessons were put to sensational effect in a book which has
been attributed sometimes to Languet, sometimes to Mornay, and which
appears to have been written by both of them: the *Vindiciae, Contra Tyrannos*,
the most influential of the sixteenth-century treatises which justified armed
resistance to tyranny.[81] It is a work, we shall find, with a strong presence in
the *Arcadia*. Languet was godfather to a son of Mornay and was 'just like a
father' to Mornay and his wife.[82] On his deathbed, wishing that his young
friend, to whom he had 'left his heart', could be present, Languet asked that
he commemorate their friendship in print. Mornay duly did so, paying
homage to Languet's memory and affirming his own wish to preserve it. In
the *Arcadia* too Languet is 'mentioned for honour's sake'.[83] Eight years after
Languet's death Mornay would remark that his love for Languet made him
love all those who had loved him.[84]

Sidney's death, no less than Languet's, was a landmark in Mornay's life. Of
all the responses to Sidney's demise, which devastated his friends and dismayed even some of his critics, none seems more heartfelt than the tears shed
by Mornay. Even amid the miseries of that war-torn age, he wrote, nothing
had touched him more deeply than the loss of Sidney to England and to
Christendom.[85] Though Sidney and Mornay had met in Paris in 1572,[86] the
bond between them was formed while Mornay was in England in 1577–8.
Soon after Mornay's arrival Languet wrote to Sidney asking 'if the similarity
of your characters has made you friends'.[87] If it had not, it soon did. It was
during Mornay's stay that Sidney stood as godfather to his daughter.[88] The
two men had much to discuss. Both of them had an interest in new ideas
about poetry.[89] Jacopo Sannazaro, whose *Arcadia* was a principal source for
Sidney's *Arcadia*, was esteemed by Mornay 'an excellent poet'.[90] Mornay and
Sidney shared their literary interests with the Scottish poet George Buchanan,
whom Sidney's *Defence of Poetry* commends as a 'piercing wit'.[91] They also

---

80 *Mémoires et correspondance de Duplessis-Mornay*, ii. 80–3; Henri Chevreul, *Hubert Languet* (Paris,
    1852), pp. 90–1. (Both writers studied the English chronicler Matthew Paris, about whom
    Languet corresponded with Sidney, and of whose *History* – published in 1571 – Sidney's father
    owned a manuscript copy. Osborn, *Young Philip Sidney*, p. 157; Philippe Duplessis-Mornay, *The
    Mysterie of Iniquitie* (London, 1612), p. 392; May McKisack, *Medieval History in the Tudor Age*
    (Oxford, 1971), pp. 40–1.)
81 Shared authorship is the conclusion reached in the recent, and only scholarly, edition of the
    work: George Garnett, ed., *Vindiciae, Contra Tyrannos* (Cambridge, 1994).
82 Crump, *Huguenot Family*, p. 181.
83 David de Liques, *Histoire de la vie de Messire Philippe de Mornay* (Leiden, 1647), pp. 56–7; below,
    p. 267.
84 *Mémoires et correspondance de Duplessis-Mornay*, iv. 318.
85 Ibid., iii. 488.
86 Osborn, *Young Philip Sidney*, p. 268.
87 Pears, pp. 111–12.
88 Crump, *Huguenot Family*, p. 170.
89 Van Dorsten, *Poets*, p. 41.
90 Duplessis-Mornay, *Mysterie of Iniquitie*, p. 615.
91 Van Dorsten, *Poets*, p. 41; *MP* 110/19–20.

shared their political concerns with him, among them their dismay at the Anjou suit, about which Sidney's friends kept closely in touch with Buchanan.[92] Sidney and Mornay had religious convictions and tastes in common too. Sidney (like Buchanan) made translations from the Psalms: Mornay wrote meditations on the Psalms.[93] Like Sidney, Mornay was eager to combat the advances not only of popery but of atheism and epicureanism.

The French wars of religion cast a long and profound shadow over Mornay's career and thinking. So did they over Languet's. The destructiveness of that conflict in their native land shook both men to their foundations. At least Mornay, like Languet, led a life of public action, as Sidney did not. Yet no more than Sidney did Mornay feel fulfilled. Like Sidney he contemplated, in dark moments, emigration to the New World. He also thought of going to Ireland, 'to fight the savages there'.[94] Had he done so he would probably have fought under Philip Sidney's father, under whom Philip himself briefly served against the Irish rebels in 1576.

Sidney's own interest in emigration would produce the 'very hard resolution'[95] which he made to accompany, with Greville, Drake's expedition to the Caribbean in 1585. His intention, like his plan to marry Orange's daughter in 1577, was kept 'secret' from the queen.[96] It was thwarted only as he was preparing to sail, when she discovered and forbade his departure. Having gained advance notice of her command, Greville tells us, Sidney employed 'two resolute soldiers in mariners' apparel' to 'intercept' her messenger, seize his letters and bring them to him.[97] It is a story which might belong to Sidney's fiction, but which Greville, who likes to present Sidney in a loyal and obedient light, would not have invented. Elizabeth's refusal did not discourage Sidney for long. What Greville calls his 'heroical design of invading and possessing America' was soon revived. Revealing once more the internationalism of his outlook, Sidney 'contrived' a plan for a 'plantation' that would be 'as an emporium for the confluence of all nations that love or profess any kind of virtue or commerce'.[98] There can have been no one he would have welcomed more warmly to that emporium than Mornay, and perhaps no one who would have been more at home in it.

Sidney's perception of the events of his time was shared with his closest friends. It rested on the memories common to his and Mornay's generation and on those passed on to him by Walsingham's and Languet's. Walsingham's outlook had been shaped by the overthrow of English Protestantism in 1553

---

92 James Phillips, 'George Buchanan and the Sidney Circle', *Huntington Library Quarterly* 12 (1948–9), pp. 23–55, at pp. 32–4.
93 Crump, *Huguenot Family*, p. 218.
94 Ibid., p. 132.
95 Marjon Poort, '"The Desired and Destined Successor": a Chronology of Sir Philip Sidney's Activities 1585–1586', in Jan van Dorsten *et al.*, eds, *Sir Philip Sidney. 1586 and the Creation of a Legend* (Leiden, 1986), pp. 25–37, at p. 26.
96 *GP* 42/14, 43/11, 43/29.
97 *GP* 44/27–31.
98 *GP* 45/27–8, 70/9–13.

and by the Marian persecution that followed it. It had been coloured too by reports of the discussions at Bayonne in 1565 between Catherine de Medici (the Queen Mother of France) and Philip II's representative the Duke of Alva, whose reign of terror in the Low Countries would begin soon afterwards. In that meeting Walsingham saw proof of the readiness of 'the two great monarchs of Europe together with the rest of the papists' to join forces so as to 'root out . . . the professors of the gospel' everywhere.[99] In the face of that conspiracy, he believed, 'the common cause of religion'[100] was at once the only conscionable and only practicable basis of English foreign policy. His conviction was reinforced by the Massacre of St Bartholomew and by the subsequent international developments of the 1570s. Languet shared Walsingham's perspective. In educating Sidney he explained to him the pope's responsibility for the gravest disasters of recent years: the execution of leading noblemen in the Netherlands by Alva's regime in 1568, the Massacre of St Bartholomew, the election of the King of France to the throne of Poland in 1574.

With Languet, Sidney shuddered at the 'cruelty' of the pope and the Catholic princes.[101] He watched with distress the grim progress of the continental wars of religion, 'the wounds', as he called them, 'from which the Church of God is now suffering'. He thought of the Protestant struggle as 'the cause', 'our cause', 'the good cause', 'the true cause'.[102] Greville tells us that Sidney discussed with his friends how best to thwart 'this fatal conjunction of Rome's undermining superstitions with the commanding forces of Spain', 'this masked triplicity between Spain, Rome and the sovereign Jesuits of France'; that he longed for his country to break the union of 'popish and Spanish . . . arts' and the 'servile yoke' imposed by 'Spanish Rome'; that he grasped that the threat posed to his 'native country' by 'this immense power of Spain . . . was not like to be prevented . . . by any other antidote than a general league among free princes'.[103]

What Sidney called the pope's 'wicked and detestable counsels to the Christian princes'[104] alarmed Mornay too. The counsels of most Catholic rulers, he reminded Walsingham in 1583 after the discovery of Catholic plotting in England, are 'refined' in the 'furnace' of Rome, to serve the pope's ends.[105] Sidney and Languet used equivalent imagery: Italy, they

99   Read, *Walsingham*, i. 239; cf. ibid., 69; BL, Harleian MS. 6265, fo. 109ᵛ.
100 Read, *Walsingham*, i. 214; cf. ibid., 199.
101 Languet: Pears, pp. 14, 44; Osborn, *Young Philip Sidney*, p. 156. Sidney: Osborn, *Young Philip Sidney*, p. 477. Cf. (e.g.) *CSPF 1577–8*, p. 301, *1578–9*, p. 182; Osborn, *Young Philip Sidney*, p. 367.
102 Pears, pp. 47, 75, 91, 146; Feuillerat, iii. 166.
103 GP 14/25–6, 25/34–26/2, 59/32–3, 16/8, 49/14–16, 57/23–4, 102/15–17, 52/1–5. Cf. GP 49/14–16, 102/15–17, and Sidney's remark to the Landgrave of Hesse in 1577: Osborn, *Young Philip Sidney*, p. 477.
104 Pears, pp. 90–1.
105 *Mémoires et correspondance de Duplessis-Mornay*, ii. 236–7.

agreed, was 'the forge in which the causes of all these ills are wrought'.[106] If Rome was the forge, the arsenal was Madrid. Mornay shared the fear of Sidney and Languet that Spain, in alliance with the papacy, would gobble all Christendom. Greville, in recalling Sidney's thoughts about the best means of meeting that threat, ascribed to him a global perspective which we likewise find in the thinking of Mornay, who, like Sidney, wanted to see Spain's weak points in the Mediterranean and the New World identified and attacked.[107]

Upon the international cooperation of Protestantism there depended, its advocates maintained, the survival of England. It was the guiding premise of forward Protestantism that 'those abroad who are . . . of the same religion that we profess must be united to us, and we to them'; that the 'surety' of queen and country 'cannot be otherwise than by alliance made' with Protestants and Protestant rulers 'everywhere'.[108] The queen was immune to that conviction. Sidney's mood and conduct in the late 1570s were the product of her immunity.

---

106 Pears, pp. 45, 48.
107 Ibid., p. 175; GP 47–51; *Mémoires et correspondance de Duplessis-Mornay*, ii. 27–8, 238; Patry, *Philippe Du Plessis-Mornay*, pp. 73–4. There were also points of difference between Sidney's (English) and Mornay's (French) strategic perspectives.
108 PRO, SP 12/123/17 (fo. 54ᵛ); K. de L., ix. 301; cf. Lehmberg, *Mildmay*, p. 162.

CHAPTER 4

An Unelected Vocation

> myself, who (I know not by what mischance) in these my not old years and
> idlest times having slipped into the title of a poet, am provoked to say
> something unto you in the defence of that my unelected vocation . . ..
>
> (Sidney, *A Defence of Poetry*)

Sidney and his friends maintained that Protestantism, having the will of God
and the conviction of truth behind it, would always be a more dependable
basis of foreign policy than worldly calculation. So in calling for 'a general
league in religion', says Greville, Sidney 'affirm[ed] that to associate by an
uniform bond of conscience for the protection . . . of religion and liberty
would prove a more solid union, and symbolise far better against [the
Catholic] tyrannies, than any factious combination in policy [or] league of
state'. 'To temporise with the enemies of our faith' would be 'false-
heartedness to God and man', which 'would in the end find itself forsaken of
both'.[1] The Chancellor of the Exchequer Sir Walter Mildmay, Walsingham's
brother-in-law and close ally, agreed: 'God will not endure any . . . temporising . . . for any respect, derogatory to his honour,' he argued in 1579.
'There is no counsel or wisdom either against or besides him.'[2]

Policy, then, is to be no more than the servant of religion. Yet its service
is indispensable. In recording that Sidney 'made the religion he professed the
firm basis of his life', Greville offers a revealing explanation of that commitment. Sidney judged, 'as he often told me', that 'true-heartedness to the
reformed religion . . . brought peace, safety and freedom' to England, and
that 'the wisest and best way' was that of William of Orange, 'who never
divided the consideration of estate from the cause of religion'. Because the
Catholic powers 'mix[ed] the temporal and spiritual swords', Protestant
powers must do the same. Sidney's party took that 'mixture' to be a fact of

---

1 GP 26/28–27/3, 22/23–7.
2 BL, Harleian MS. 6265, fo. 108. Cf. NRO, F(P)M, fos 5, 9; NRO, F(P)M 68.

life. Walsingham argued that the cooperation between the pope and Catholic princes against Orange's cause 'showeth that the quarrel is mixed and consisteth as well of religion as of state'.[3] Greville commends Walsingham for having 'upheld both religion and state by using a policy wisely mixed with reflections of either'.[4]

In Greville's account, Sidney saw the Protestant 'religion' as the ally of political 'liberty', and associated Catholic 'superstition' with political 'tyran[ny]'.[5] Languet thought in the same terms. The 'despotism' of Spain in the Netherlands, he wrote in 1578, depended on the maintenance of Catholic 'idolatry' there.[6] At the same time Sidney and his allies knew that the survival of Protestant regimes correspondingly depended on the inculcation of Protestant beliefs. Sidney's father wanted to have a 'spiritual pastor' appointed to the see of Armagh so that the Irish people 'might be drawn' 'by good teaching and doctrine . . . first to know their duties to God, and next their obedience to their prince and civil order'.[7] 'Strong princes', Greville thought, 'plac[e] the first foundation of their reigns' on 'religion', which 'reverence breeds / In . . . subjects'.[8] The forward Protestant Thomas Wilson, Walsingham's fellow Secretary of State, urged upon the English the example of the ancient Athenians, who bore 'such love to their country, that all their sacrifices and church religion tended only to the long preservation and good welfare of their state'.[9]

If Catholicism were to be defeated, Protestantism must be united. Unfortunately, as Leicester observed in 1572, there was 'no more hate or displeasure almost between papist and Protestant than is now in many places between many of our own religion'.[10] Protestant churches were divided against each other and within themselves. Sidney's party was distressed by the disputes fought over issues of ecclesiology and doctrine, by what that vigorous polemicist against popery Thomas Norton called 'civil wars of the church of God'.[11] One argument in Sidney's mind for an offensive war against European Catholicism, says Greville, was that it might end the 'petty dividing schisms' among Protestants, which sprang not 'from any difference of religious faith' but from 'misty opinion . . . moulded first upon the desks of busy idle lecturers' and then 'blown abroad to our disadvantage' by papists.[12] Languet too believed that Catholics were fomenting theological disputes among Protestants.[13]

3   GP 22/15–21, 49/18–19; Read, *Walsingham*, i. 215–16.
4   GP 18/30–1.
5   GP 25/28–9, 26/31–27/1, 65/16–20; cf. Osborn, *Young Philip Sidney*, p. 477.
6   Pears, p. 151.
7   Collins, *Letters and Memorials*, i. 142. Cf. Walsingham's point in Thomas Wright, ed., *Queen Elizabeth and her Times*, 2 vols (London, 1838), ii. 80; NRO, F(P)M 68.
8   Wilkes, p. 85 (sts 201–2).
9   Wilson, *Demosthenes*, sig. A2ᵛ; cf. below, Chapter 9.
10 Collinson, *Godly People*, p. 71.
11 Ibid., p. 73.
12 GP 27/15–20.
13 Pears, p. 107.

The dispute most damaging to international Protestantism was that in Germany over the Lord's Supper. The quarrel, which cost Languet his job at the Saxon court, turned orthodox Lutherans against unorthodox Lutherans and against orthodox Calvinists. In wanting the Germans to sink their differences, at least, Elizabeth was at one with England's forward Protestants, even if her motives were different from theirs. They wanted the Germans to unite with each other and with England in fighting the Catholic threat: she wanted them to unite in fighting against Spain and so spare her from having to fight. In 1577 she sent first Sidney, then Daniel Rogers, then Robert Beale, to Germany to try to resolve the controversy. Sidney, on his mission, tried, together with friends of Languet, to establish a broad-based confession of faith and so outflank the diehard Lutherans.[14] The squabble reminded Beale of earlier 'contentions and useless questions' which, to satisfy the ambition of divines, had been 'raised . . . concerning *adiaphora*, free will, predestination, justification, good works, original sin'.[15] Milton's fallen angels, lost in the wandering mazes of soteriology, were in a Protestant tradition.

Beale himself had taken a divisive stand against the order of episcopacy in England five years earlier. He had thus irritated Leicester, whose aim was the 'reconcilement' of the contending Protestant factions in England and the presentation of a united front against Catholicism.[16] By 1577 Beale had learned his lesson. He saw now that 'the authority of princes' was needed to keep religious disputes under control.[17] His master Walsingham knew that truth. He too knew the need for a common Protestant front. He understood that only princely authority could secure it, and that Protestants therefore needed to please their princes. In 1578 he feared lest radical English noncon-formists, by alienating the queen, should strengthen the conservative reaction that was gathering around her. He was likewise worried lest too precipitate an advance of Protestantism in the Netherlands should stiffen Elizabeth's reluctance to aid Orange's cause. It might also, as Walsingham and Orange himself recognised, divide the revolt, that tenuous alliance of Protestant and Catholic against an external foe. So this, Walsingham thought, was a time when doctrinal 'zeal', in England and Europe, should make way for 'policy'.[18]

For Sidney, too, the doctrinal codes of Protestantism mattered less than the thwarting of Catholicism. The superstition and external observances of Catholicism, he believed, crush and chain the spirit. They make men servile and rob them of that ethical and political independence which the *Arcadia* enjoins on them. An acquaintance with the language in which Sidney's party voiced that concern will aid our study of his fiction.

14 Jan van Dorsten, 'Sidney and Languet', *Huntington Library Quarterly* 29 (1965), pp. 215–22, at pp. 220–2; cf. Levy, 'Correspondence', no. 65.
15 PRO, SP 81/1/23 (*CSPF 1577–8*, pp. 216–17).
16 Collinson, *Godly People*, pp. 71, 74.
17 PRO, SP 81/1/23 (*CSPF 1577–8*, p. 216).
18 *CSPF 1577–8*, p. 670, 1578–9, p. 50; cf. Greville's Erastianism: Wilkes, p. 91 (sts 224–5).

It is the language of sleep, dreams, enchantment, idleness. Sidney complained that Europe's princes were 'spellbound' by the papacy, Languet that they were 'beguile[d]' by its 'sorceries'.[19] Sidney, says Greville, saw that the 'superstitious princes' of Europe were lost in 'enchanted dreams', and that the papists, by 'filling people's minds with apparitions of holiness, specious rites, saints, miracles', had 'lulled inferior powers asleep'.[20] Sidney's friends thought in the same way. Mornay contrasted the spiritual 'sleep' of Catholicism with the 'wake[fulness]' of Protestantism.[21] Greville himself compared 'active spirits' with 'dull spirits' sunk in 'the idle sleeps of ignorance'.[22]

If there was idleness of the spirit, there was political idleness too. Above all there was the 'idleness' of the English response to the Catholic threat. In 1573 Languet complained to Sidney that the English 'look on idly' while the godly cause succumbed to persecution in France and the Netherlands.[23] Sidney echoed his mentor's phrasing in October 1580, when England was offering no resistance to the Spanish annexation of Portugal: 'how idly we look on our neighbours' fires', he remarked to his brother Robert.[24] A few weeks earlier, in a letter to Philip which explained the plight of the Netherlanders, Languet criticised 'those who are idle spectators of [their] dangers, and offer them no help in their need'.[25] Sidney, who (says Greville) thought the English 'apt . . . to corrupt with peace',[26] rebukes in the *Defence of Poetry* the 'overfaint quietness' of 'idle England', and hints at the shame of nations which, shunning 'the honourable enterprise' of war, are 'lulled' into 'shady idleness' or 'the sleep of idleness'.[27] With its 'honour', idle England has lost its 'virtue'. In the Fourth Eclogues of the *Arcadia* Philisides, Sidney's fictional surrogate, imagines himself in Samothea, the mythical name of pristine England,[28]

> a land which whilom stood
> An honour to the world, while honour was their end,
> And while their line of years they did in virtue spend.[29]

Yet England was not alone in its idleness. That vice, believed Sidney and his party, was shared by other countries, both Protestant and Catholic:

---

19 Osborn, *Young Philip Sidney*, p. 477; Pears, p. 111; cf. Stubbs, pp. 25, 30, 92.
20 *GP* 59/2–3, 26/12–19.
21 Weiner, *Poetics of Protestantism*, p. 45.
22 *GP* 156/33–157/1.
23 Pears, p. 14.
24 Feuillerat, iii. 133.
25 Pears, p. 186.
26 *GP* 47/8.
27 *MP* 110/31, 111/2, 97/32–3, 101/36–102/1; cf. I. D. Macfarlane, *Buchanan* (London, 1981), p. 433.
28 Katherine Duncan-Jones, 'Sidney and Samothea: a Forgotten National Myth', *Review of English Studies* n.s. 25 (1974), pp. 174–7.
29 *OA* 336/15–17.

Protestant ones which failed to assist their afflicted co-religionists, Catholic ones which failed to grasp that the advances of Rome and Madrid were threats to the independence not only of Protestant powers but of themselves. 'Germany', complained Languet to Sidney in 1578, 'looks on idly at the tragedies which are being acted in the neighbouring countries.'[30] It was the view of Sidney and his friends that the 'idleness' of Europe's princes, or what Sidney (says Greville) thought of as their 'fatal passiveness',[31] had sent Europe's rulers to 'sleep'. Languet told Sidney in 1574 that 'the princes of Christendom', who were 'so slothful', were sunk in a 'deep sleep' from which they would be 'forced to wake up';[32] 'this at least is certain', concurred Sidney, 'that our princes are enjoying too deep a slumber';[33] Greville tells us that Sidney, 'this wakeful patriot', longed for the princes of Germany to 'awake' and that on his embassy of 1577 he sought to 'awake' them.[34] In Greville's writings the follies of political 'sleep' and 'dreams' and 'idleness', and the need for princes to 'awake', are a recurrent theme. He associates 'sleep' and 'idleness' with 'superstition', which produces 'unactive apparitions of no use'.[35] We should put our trust, he believes, in 'active' men like Sidney, not in 'idle' men.[36]

Sidney's party used 'sleep' as a metaphor for the fatal sense of 'security' which, they held, was blinding princes to dangers at home and abroad. For Greville a sense of political 'security' always spelled danger. 'Security', like 'sleep', was to him the friend of 'idleness' and the enemy to 'discipline'.[37] He attributed the rise of Spanish power to 'the fatal security of all Christendom'.[38] 'Security', than which Walsingham thought 'nothing more dangerous', was to his secretary Robert Beale 'the bane of all kingdoms and estates'.[39] In the late 1570s its perils produced a chorus of alarm. Daniel Rogers, William of Orange, Hubert Languet, despairing of the inaction of the German Protestant princes before the Catholic threat, all blamed it on 'security', in which, said Orange, they were 'lulled asleep'.[40]

30 Pears, p. 152.
31 GP 48/10. To Sidney's friends, an exasperating symptom of the idleness of Europe's princes was their tendency to indulge in what Sidney called 'absurd hunting parties', or in other frivolous pursuits, when they should have been attending to the international peril (Pears, p. 59; Read, Walsingham, i. 181; CSPF 1577–8, pp. 151, 242; cf. CSPF 1578–9, p. 373). Sidney disliked bloodsports (below, Chapter 18, n. 65). In the Arcadia, it is while hunting that Basilius befriends Dametas, that act of disastrous frivolity: OA 31/5–6.
32 Levy, 'Correspondence', no. 40; Pears, p. 48.
33 Pears, p. 59. Cf. K. de L., x. 401; Harold Laski, ed., A Defence of Liberty against Tyrants (London, 1924), p. 184.
34 GP 51/32, 16/15, 26/2, 59/2. Cf. the title of the Huguenot tract Le Reveille-Matin, a work of 1574 whose author or authors had links with Sidney's party; on it, see Robert Kingdon, Myths about the St. Bartholomew's Day Massacres 1572–1576 (Cambridge, Mass., 1988), esp. ch. 4.
35 GP 16/15–20, 48/24–6, 58/29–30, 156/33–157/1; Wilkes, pp. 47 (st. 47), 85 (st. 201), 88 (st. 211), 154 (st. 477), 157 (st. 487); Bullough, i. 130, 151 (sonnet lxxx, cviii).
36 GP 46/6–9.
37 GP 51/10–12, 66/8–11, 127/2–6; Wilkes, pp. 168, 169 (sts 530, 535).
38 GP 127/5–6.
39 Read, Walsingham, i. 58, 432.
40 CSPF 1577–8, p. 238; K. de L., ix. 418; Pears, p. 134.

The same charge was levelled by forward Protestants against England and its queen. In 1577 William Davison thought 'our whole state in peril by our secure manner of proceeding'. In that and the following year the queen's ambassador in Paris, the forward Protestant Sir Amias Paulet, repeatedly issued the same warning: 'our security' will 'throw us into danger'; England, 'lulled' in sleep, must 'wake out of this dangerous slumber of security'; 'nothing is more dangerous than security in these bad times'.[41] Thomas Wilson, on whom much of Paulet's anxiety was unburdened, shared it. In the face of the Catholic threat, he told Walsingham in June 1578, 'security and contempt of harm are the right means to lull us to ruin'.[42]

In Arcadia, the first time we encounter Basilius after his abdication he is asleep in daytime. (The first time we meet Dametas, the duke's favourite, he too is asleep in daytime.) Of course, Arcadia is a hot country; but the duke is neglecting his business and is oblivious to the dangers facing his realm.[43] The sleep of princes, an image with a long literary history, is a theme (we shall find) of the *Arcadia*.[44] It is a theme too of a poem which can profitably be read alongside it, and which we shall meet now and return to later: Edmund Spenser's *Mother Hubberds Tale*. Spenser, like Sidney, was a client of the Earl of Leicester. By the summer of 1579, when the Anjou crisis was reaching its peak, he had secured a base at Leicester's London house and had attained 'some use of familiarity' with Sidney.[45] *Mother Hubberds Tale* was not published until 1591. But it was, as he then said, 'long sithens composed in the raw conceipt of . . . youth'.[46] Though large passages were subsequent additions, the obvious context of the original composition of the work, as a number of critics have perceived, is the crisis created for England by the queen's prospective marriage to Anjou, which threatened, as its opponents argued, to surrender the independence of crown and country to a foreigner.[47] The implications of that perception have generally not been pursued.[48]

Spenser's beast-fable is, he tells us, 'a pleasant tal[e]', 'fit for that idle stound [= idle time]'.[49] Like the beast-fables of the *Arcadia* it has political judgements to pass and political warnings to issue. Its concluding line wonders if the warnings have been given too 'bluntly'.[50] They are certainly transparent.

---

41 Bodl., Rawlinson MS. A331 (letter-book of Sir Amias Paulet), fos 9ᵛ, 51ᵛ, 89ᵛ, 119 (cf. fo. 82ᵛ); *CSPF 1578–9*, p. 184. Paulet 'account[ed]' Sidney's intimate friend Edward Dyer 'one of my best assured friends': Bodl., Rawlinson MS. A331, fos 102, 123ᵛ.

42 *CSPF 1578–9*, p. 23. Cf. K. de L., x. 544; Wilson, *Demosthenes*, pp. 6, 63, 83, 88, 96–7.

43 *OA* 33/23–4, 29/23–4, 358/2–359/7.

44 Below, Chapters 17, 19.

45 S. K. Heninger, *Sidney and Spenser* (Pa, 1989), p. 3; Stubbs, p. li.

46 Oram, p. 327. My line numbers follow that edition.

47 Ibid., pp. 327–9; Edward Greenlaw *et al.*, eds, *The Works of Edmund Spenser. A Variorum Edition: The Minor Poems*, 2 vols (Baltimore, 1943–7), ii. 568ff. (cf. i. 603–4). Spenser may, for all we know, have revised the earlier material before it was published; but if so, the pertinence of his poem to the circumstances of the late 1570s survived the revision.

48 See however Stubbs, pp. liii–liv.

49 Line 26; cf. Oram, pp. 398 (l. 313)–399 (l. 322).

50 Line 1388.

Spenser's leading characters are an 'ape' (Anjou, to whose agent Jean Simier
the queen had punningly given that nickname, 'simièsque' being the French
for 'ape-like') and a 'fox' (whom critics have equated, surely correctly, with
Lord Burghley, the leading advocate of the match and Leicester's hated
rival).[51] The ape and fox establish control of a kingdom by seizing the crown
from the lion who is its monarch.[52] William Webbe might have written of
Mother Hubberds Tale what he wrote of Spenser's pastoral work *The
Shepheardes Calender*: 'there is . . . much matter uttered somewhat covertly,
especially the abuses of some whom he would not be too plain withal'.[53]
Sidney's *Defence of Poetry* explains that both the pastoral genre and beast-
fables can supply undercover political comment. To that end the *Arcadia*,
which makes principal use of the pastoral genre, also deploys beast-fables: to
the same end *Mother Hubberds Tale*, which makes principal use of a beast-
fable, also deploys pastoral. Thus the ape and fox spotted a flock of sheep
and

> when all shrowded were
> In careles sleep, they without care or feare,
> Cruelly fell upon their flock in folde,
> And of them slew at pleasure what they wolde . . ..

Advancing into the realm, they found their chance to steal the sovereignty of
the realm:

> they spide, how in a gloomy glade,
> The lyon sleeping lay in secret shade,
> His crowne and scepter lying him beside. . . .[54]

A century later John Dryden, in *The Hind and the Panther*, recognised
Spenser's target:

> And Mother Hubbard in her homely dress
> Hath sharply blamed the British Lioness,

---

51   See e.g. Stubbs, p. liv.
52   Cf. ibid.; Heninger, *Sidney and Spenser*, p. 357. Stubbs (p. 75), quoting one argument that has
      been made in defence of the proposed match, describes it as 'but Reynard [the fox]'s flattering
      of our kingly bird and well-natured Chanticleer in his goodly sweet voice and fair feathers'.
      Stubbs's quotation (though he does not say so) is from a memorandum drawn up by that leading
      advocate of the Anjou match, the Earl of Sussex, a document which Burghley either contributed
      to or (more probably) borrowed from: Nicolas, *Hatton*, p. 87; below, Chapter 6, n. 34. Animal
      nicknames were common in the politics of the Anjou match and in the protests against it: Jan
      van Dorsten, *The Anglo-Dutch Renaissance* (Leiden, 1988), p. 76; Susan Doran, *Monarchy and
      Matrimony. The Courtships of Elizabeth I* (London and New York, 1996), p. 168. For another hit
      at Burghley in Stubbs's tract see Doran, *Monarchy and Matrimony*, p. 166.
53   Above, pp. 11–12.
54   Lines 333–6, 951–3; cf. *MP* 101/36–102/1.

That queen . . .
Exposed obscurely naked and asleep.[55]

'Idleness', the partner of sleep in the minds of Sidney and his party, threatened to beleaguer Sidney himself. In September 1580, while he was writing
the *Arcadia*, Languet told him that his friends feared lest the 'vigour' and
'edge' of his mind 'would be dulled by' the 'idleness' into which his retreat
from politics had led him. Languet, who thought the German princes too
'fon[d] of ease', worried also lest Sidney should succumb to 'love of ease', a
quality, he reminded him, which the younger man 'once despised'.[56] Two
years earlier Sidney had confessed to Languet that 'indolent ease' was causing
his mind, 'if it was ever active in anything', 'imperceptibly to lose its strength,
and to relax without any reluctance'.[57] Languet laments to Sidney 'the sloth
of our princes': Sidney admits to Languet his own 'slothfulness'.[58] Spenser's
lion is 'in a traunce' (l. 1325): Languet says that Sidney, at least in the period
leading up to the Anjou crisis, was in a 'trance'.[59] Languet had long been
anxious that Sidney should 'shun that sordid siren, Idleness': the *Arcadia*, as
Sidney tells his sister in dedicating it to her, is 'this idle work of mine'.[60]
(Spenser, dedicating *Mother Hubberds Tale* to Lady Compton, calls it 'these my
idle labours'.)[61]

Poetry might be the fruit of idleness. Yet it might also be an antidote or
alternative to it. Sidney wrote his fiction, his father's secretary testifies,
because 'he could endure at no time to be idle and void of action'.[62] By
writing poems, explained Geoffrey Whitney on Sidney's death, Sidney 'used
to banish idle fits'.[63] The idleness from which he sought relief was enforced,
the product of royal disfavour. It is, he tells us, because he has, in his 'not old
years and idlest times', 'slipped into the title of a poet' that he writes the
Defence of Poetry, which vindicates 'my unelected vocation'.[64] The vocation
was unelected indeed. The *Arcadia*, in large measure a meditation on politics,
is also a substitute for them.

55 Quoted in Greenlaw, *Works of . . . Spenser . . . The Minor Poems*, ii. 569. Dryden was not the only
    friend to the royal prerogative in the reign of Charles II to observe the deployment of the genre
    of the beast-fable to criticise English monarchs. Remarks in John Nalson's *The King's Prerogative*
    (London, 1684 edn), pp. 3, 24–5, 70–1, might almost have been directed at the beast-fable in
    Book Three of Sidney's *Arcadia*; note too the title of Nalson's attack on Philip Sidney's great-
    nephew the republican Algernon Sidney, who had recently been executed for treason: *Reflections
    upon Coll. Sidney's Arcadia* (London, 1684).
56 Pears, pp. 134, 183.
57 Ibid., p. 143.
58 Ibid., pp. 120, 143.
59 Ibid., p. 168.
60 Osborn, *Young Philip Sidney*, p. 363 (cf. p. 389; Levy, 'Correspondence', nos 58, 65); *OA* 3/4.
61 Oram, p. 334.
62 *OA* xv.
63 Quoted from Whitney's *A Choice of Emblems* (London, 1586) in A. C. Hamilton, *Sir Philip
    Sidney* (Cambridge, 1977), p. 181.
64 *MP* 73/28–31.

To Languet, Sidney's political failure was a profound disappointment. The time and energy he had devoted to his young friend's education were directed, as he so often told him, to help him 'serve' and 'benefit' his 'country' and to answer the 'hope' which it had a 'right' to have of him.[65] Sidney, feared Languet, might fail not only his country but himself. Let him, he urged him, be 'true to yourself' and 'remain what you are'.[66] Two prospects particularly troubled Languet. First, he knew the side to Sidney's character that longed to be free of court life and its pressures and would sooner withdraw to the countryside than engage in political action. Secondly, there was the streak in Sidney which was eager for military action. 'A man who falls at a young age', he warned him with dreadful prophecy, 'cannot have done much for his country.'[67] Languet looked ahead, beyond his own lifetime, to the 'high station' and 'great authority' which, 'if it shall please God to grant you life', Sidney could hope to attain 'after twenty or thirty years', and which would enable 'your country' to find 'no small assistance . . . from your virtue'.[68] Yet when Languet visited England in the winter of 1578–9 he 'found', as he told him afterwards, 'a sort of cloud over your fortunes'.[69] The cloud would never pass. After Sidney's death a poem by George Whetstone gave him words which lament the waste of his education and his 'inability to do my country good': 'I studied have to benefit the state, / To execute I am forbid by fate.'[70] 'He never was magistrate,' regrets Greville, 'nor possessed of any fit stage for eminence to act upon.' The 'sparks of extraordinary greatness in him . . . for want of clear vent, lay concealed and in a manner smothered up'.[71]

In 1580, while he was writing the *Arcadia*, Sidney lamented to Edward Denny that 'the unnoble constitution of our time doth keep us from fit employments'.[72] Two years earlier, in a letter to Languet, he attributed the softening of his own mental powers to his exclusion from public service. 'For to what purpose should our thoughts be directed to various kinds of knowledge, unless room be afforded for putting it into practice, so that public advantage may be the result, which in a corrupt age we cannot hope for?'[73] In 1577–8 Sidney's 'present inactivity' became 'irksome' to him. He complained of 'too much leisure'.[74] In June 1578 there was a moment of hope, when it seemed that 'his service is to be used'. He was to be put in charge of a royal fleet, though it is not clear to what purpose.[75] But the plan fell

---

65 Pears, pp. 42, 56, 170, 184.
66 Ibid., pp. 6, 26.
67 Ibid., p. 137.
68 Ibid., pp. 42, 62, 183; Osborn, *Young Philip Sidney*, pp. 149, 297.
69 Pears, p. 185.
70 George Whetstone, *Sir Phillip Sidney* (London, 1587), sig. C1ᵛ.
71 GP 24/1–2, 7/27–9.
72 Osborn, *Young Philip Sidney*, p. 537.
73 Pears, p. 143.
74 Ibid., pp. 127, 147.
75 *Acts of the Privy Council 1577–1578*, p. 240; *CSPS 1568–79*, p. 595.

through. 'I am especially sorry to hear you say', wrote Languet to him four months later, 'that you are weary of the life to which I have no doubt God has called you.'[76]

In some moods Sidney contemplated rural retreat. In others he restlessly considered emigration to the New World or military action in Europe's wars of religion. For 'he had no delight', as Greville tells us, 'to rest idly at home'.[77] Robert Sidney, travelling on the continent in the autumn of 1580, was advised by his brother, 'if there [are] any good wars', to 'go to them'.[78] For most of the last decade of his life Philip was, as Katherine Duncan-Jones says, 'a carpet knight'.[79] He was condemned to wait upon a queen on whose favour his chances of political fulfilment and financial survival depended. Like his father before him he held the ceremonial post of cup-bearer to the queen,[80] a position symbolic of effete and subservient inactivity. When we encounter him in public life it is usually in the fulfilment of some minor and uncongenial task for the queen or as an assistant to Leicester or Walsingham.[81]

Elizabeth did toss him the occasional political or financial bone. In 1583 he was given a post in the Ordnance Office. The post became arduous in 1584,[82] which could explain why he failed to complete the New Arcadia. In July 1585 he became, with Warwick his uncle, joint Master of the Ordnance. In the autumn he left for the Netherlands campaign. Yet, if Greville is right, Sidney by that time saw little point in attacking the Spaniard in the Low Countries, 'the strongest seat of his war'. He thought England should 'strike at the root, and assail him where he is weakest': in the New World.[83] Sidney's conduct in the Netherlands did nothing to improve his relations with the queen, who was outraged by his support for Leicester's unauthorised assumption of the governorship of Holland and Zeeland, the position which – or one akin to that which – Orange would have given Sidney eight years earlier had Sidney married his daughter. Sidney noticed during the last year of his life 'how apt the queen is to interpret everything to my disadvantage'.[84] Walsingham echoed that lament: the queen, he told Leicester, was 'very apt upon every light occasion to find fault with him'.[85]

When Sidney died, an unidentified diarist lamented the passing of 'so rare a gentleman, and so accomplished with all kind of virtue and true nobility, as

76 Pears, p. 155.
77 GP 46/11–12.
78 Collins, Letters and Memorials, i. 286.
79 Katherine Duncan-Jones, 'Philip Sidney's Toys', Proceedings of the British Academy 66 (1980), pp. 161–78, at p. 165.
80 H. R. Woudhuysen, 'A "Lost" Sidney Document', Bodleian Library Record 13 (1990), pp. 353–9.
81 For the latter role, see e.g. CSPF 1583, pp. 177, 249, 1583–4, p. 314.
82 Duncan-Jones, Sir Philip Sidney, p. 270.
83 GP 52/12–25, 64/3–4.
84 Feuillerat, iii. 167.
85 Bruce, Leycester Correspondence, p. 345.

few ages have brought forth his equal, and the very hope of our age seemeth to be utterly extinguished in him'.[86] His death was received much as the (apparently) imminent death of Pyrocles is viewed in the *New Arcadia*: as 'the cutting away of the greatest hope in the world, and destroying virtue in his sweetest growth'.[87] Upon the grief which greeted Sidney's death there would be built the hagiography that served the political purposes of forward Protestantism in the decades ahead. He quickly became 'a paragon of our time'.[88] He came to seem something more than he was. Quirks and faults of character – the tendencies to violence and impetuousness and intolerance, the nervous and often tense disposition[89] – were ironed from the record.

Yet the magnetism of his personality is no posthumous invention. On his grand tour his gifts of character impressed those who met him, charmed them, sometimes astonished them.[90] On his return, as Languet would remind him in 1580, he 'carried away the admiration of all men; and all of your nobility who had a name for generosity of sentiment began eagerly to compete for your friendship'.[91] His reputation for 'eminent wit and virtue' persisted.[92] Sir Henry Sidney, a proud father but a hard-headed man, gave advice to Philip's brother Robert in March 1578, a time when, as it happened, Philip's assessment of his own and his country's prospects was particularly bleak. 'Imitate his virtues, exercises, studies, and actions,' Sir Henry urged Robert. 'He is a rare ornament of this age . . . . In truth I speak it without flattery of him or of myself, he hath the most rare virtues that ever I found in any man.'[93]

So there is plausibility in Fulke Greville's claims for the influence of Sidney's virtue,[94] and in his statement that, as 'will be confessed by all', his 'example and personal respect did not only encourage learning and honour in the schools, but brought the affection and true use thereof both into the court and camp'. Yet, striking as Greville took Sidney's influence on his contemporaries to have been, he knew that his friend's lack of favour had severely restricted it. The 'honour' of 'princes', Greville believed, should impel them to select 'one man' to be, as 'a reformed standard', 'a nourisher of virtue in their courts or service'. In Elizabeth's service, he was sure, Sidney would have been the perfect 'standard'. Yet Greville acknowledged that his friend had been 'no received standard' there.[95]

Greville remembered that he himself had been made by the queen to 'live

86 Duncan-Jones, *Sir Philip Sidney*, p. 303.
87 *NA* 171/7–8.
88 Whetstone, *Sir Phillip Sidney*, sig. A4.
89 Duncan-Jones, *Sir Philip Sidney*, pp. 21–3, 41, 153, 197–8, 269, 272, 274. Cf. Pears, pp. 25, 26, 87–8, 101, 108, 137, 147, 154; Osborn, *Young Philip Sidney*, p. 420.
90 Van Dorsten, *Poets*, p. 31.
91 Pears, p. 184.
92 *CSPF 1579–80*, p. 130 ('praestanti ingenio et virtute iuvenis': PRO, SP 83/13/3).
93 Collins, *Letters and Memorials*, i. 246; cf. *GP* 5/21–3.
94 Above, p. 31.
95 *GP* 21/26–22/1, 24/22.

in her court a spectacle of disfavour, too long as I conceived'.[96] He hoped for military service abroad, and in 1582 seems to have planned to fight in the Netherlands, together with 'a good force of gentlemen' of England.[97] But his appetite for 'foreign employments' was, he found, 'offensive' to the queen. He secured her favour, he wistfully recalls, only when he learned 'to bound my prospect within the safe limits of duty in such home devices as were acceptable to my sovereign'.[98] In Sidney's lifetime Greville, sharing his friend's frustration, was well equipped to understand it. The two men were linked, observes Greville's biographer, by the 'common failure' of their careers.[99]

For Greville, Sidney's failure in politics is the defeat of 'worth'. He sees it as the triumph of 'the idle censuring faction' which prevailed over such 'active' and 'unbounded spirit[s]' as Sidney, of 'cautious wisdoms' over 'greatness of heart', a quality which, together with 'worth', he saw being snuffed out by the corruption and servility of modern politics.[100] The regime had been 'lulled asleep' in a false sense of 'security'; and 'security', Greville knew, 'is no true nurse of worth'.[101] The government of 'kings' is, in Greville's mind, innately unfriendly to merit, for promotion is at best a lottery, in which men of 'worth' compete on unequal terms with 'the children of favour and chance'.[102] Only 'little hearts', believes Greville, thrive in the company of princes. In 'pleasing' those princes they 'do corrupt them too'.[103] Greville's views recall the observation of Languet to Sidney in 1574 that 'in monarchies virtue is more often the cause of ruin than vice for men of high rank'.[104] They also correspond to observations in the *Arcadia* about the failings of kings and courts.

96 *GP* 88/18–19.
97 *CSPF 1581–2*, pp. 633–4 ('une bonne troupe de monsieur de vôtre nation': PRO, SP 83/15/116); Rebholz, *Greville*, p. 41.
98 *GP* 87/6–10, 89/14–15.
99 Rebholz, *Greville*, pp. xxiii–xxiv, 47.
100 *GP* 46/6–8, 75n., 11/24, 24/24, 18/10–12, 79/6. Cf. *GP* 147/2–6; Wilkes, p. 162 (st. 507); Rebholz, *Greville*, p. 285; George Buchanan, *The Powers of the Crown of Scotland*, ed. Charles Arrowood (Austin, Tex., 1949), p. 87. The contrast drawn by Greville between the manly and martial virtue of men such as Sidney who wanted to fight abroad, and the effeminacy of those who sought peace abroad because they lacked 'honour', may owe something to later developments. Greville is perhaps thinking of the hostility to the martial aspirations in the 1590s of the Earl of Essex, whose side Greville took and in whose 'active worth' and 'active heart' he saw the continuation of Sidney's virtues. Or he may be thinking of the suppression of martial merit under James I. (*GP* 47/3–6, 52/9–10, 95/19, 96/3, 97/11, 127/2–6; Worden, 'Friend to Sir Philip Sidney'; below, Appendix A.) Yet, as so often, Greville, though he may distort, does not invent: as early as 1587 the dedication to the English translation of Mornay's treatise *De la vérité de la religion chrétienne* observed gladly that Sidney 'died not languishing in idleness and riot and excess, nor as overcome with nice pleasures and fond vanities, but of manly wounds' (Philippe Duplessis-Mornay, *A Woorke concerning the Trewnesse of the Christian Religion* (London, 1587), sig. ★3ᵛ; cf. Moffet, *Nobilis*, p. 87).
101 Wilkes, p. 114 (st. 318).
102 *GP* 7/29–8/3, 47/2–3. In the *Arcadia* the advancement of Dametas is 'unworthy': *OA* 269/16–17.
103 Bullough, i. 129 (sonnet lxxviii, ll. 1–6).
104 Osborn, *Young Philip Sidney*, p. 155.

To understand Sidney's representation of those failings we shall need a fuller acquaintance with the international and national context from which the *Arcadia* emerged. That will be the purpose of the next two chapters. They will equip us not only to approach the political content of the *Arcadia* but to perceive the unity of its ideas. For in response to the events of the late 1570s there emerged, in the minds of Sidney and his friends, a political and ethical philosophy which is tested and illustrated both in the public and in the private themes of his fiction.

CHAPTER 5

A Losing Cause

The Elizabethan regime was rarely free of a sense of precariousness and peril. In the late 1570s it became ever more subject to it. So far, the government had thwarted its enemies at home. The Northern Rising of 1569 had been suppressed; the Ridolfi plot of 1571 had been exposed; the pope's demand for the murder of Queen Elizabeth remained unfulfilled. Yet the threats of rebellion, conspiracy and assassination persisted. They were made to seem graver by the fresh vitality of English Catholicism in the later 1570s, when leading advisers of the queen warned of the 'contemptuous growing' and 'daily bold obstinacy' of 'the disobedient papists', who 'find the laws very weak against them'.[1] Their boldness, it was held, thrived on encouragement or at least connivance from above. There persisted the belief, voiced by an M.P. in 1572, that 'the papists' were 'placed in authority in all places, in commission of peace, in seat of judgement, in noblemen's houses, in the court, yea about the queen's own person'.[2]

The unresolved succession to the throne, that permanent anxiety of Elizabethan politics, created a national plight as hazardous as can be imagined within the European system of hereditary monarchy. Elizabeth had no husband or children and no answer to the problem of Mary Queen of Scots, her prisoner since her flight to England in 1568. That practised conspirator was not only next in line to the succession but, in her own and her supporters' eyes, the rightful occupant of the throne Elizabeth had gained. 'Many', as Sidney's 'Letter' opposing the Anjou match reminded Elizabeth, 'thin[k] you an usurper; many thin[k] the right you had, disan[n]ulled by the pope's excommunication'.[3] As the friend and relation and co-religionist of

---

1 Wright, *Queen Elizabeth*, ii. 75; Read, *Burghley*, p. 236; BL, Harleian MS. 6992, no. 26, Huntingdon to Burghley, 12 September 1576.

2 T. E. Hartley, ed., *Proceedings in the Parliaments of Elizabeth I 1558–1581* (Leicester, 1981), pp. 349–50; cf. BL, Harleian MS. 6265, fo. 104.

3 *MP* 48/19–20.

Catholic princes, Mary was the natural focus of Catholic discontent at home
and of intrigue by Elizabeth's enemies abroad. At the least, English Catholics
could expect – provided that Mary, aged thirty-six in 1578 and nine years
Elizabeth's junior, outlived her – a Catholic reign after Elizabeth's death,
when the Reformation would surely be reversed. The bolder spirits among
them had higher hopes: the overthrow of Elizabeth in her lifetime and the
enthronement of Mary in her stead.

The regime knew how frail were the roots of its support and of the
Protestantism with which it had identified its authority. Protestantism, which
had captured the establishment, could expect to fall with it. Walsingham,
who believed that 'misliking . . . reigneth generally . . . though men make
outwardly a fair show',[4] in 1579 identified three 'inward diseases' that were
endangering the realm: 'discontentment in the subjects' on account of the
queen's failure to resolve the succession; 'the disunion of the subjects' minds
in respect of the diversity of religion'; and 'the falling away in devotion of the
subjects of this realm unto the competitor [Mary]'.[5] 'For the love of God,
good madam,' he urged the queen in 1581, 'look into your own estate and
think that there can grow no peril so great as to have a war break out in your
own realm, considering what number of evil subjects you have.'[6]

The courtliness that characterises Sidney's 'Letter' becomes conspicuous
when we set the document beside opinions expressed by Walsingham. Sidney
thinks the same as Walsingham but says the opposite. Walsingham urges the
queen to 'look into your own estate' and recognise the disloyalty and
discontent that prevail there: Sidney encourages her to 'look in your own
estate' and realise how 'devoted' her subjects are to her. In Walsingham's
mind the queen's problem is to remove, or at least avoid, 'the contempt
of her people': Sidney's 'Letter' assures the queen that her 'people' do not
hold her rule in 'contempt'.[7] Walsingham habitually thinks in terms of the
'sickness' and 'disease' of the realm and of the 'medicine' needed to cure
its 'corruption':[8] Sidney, though privately sharing Walsingham's sense of
England's 'corruption',[9] tells the queen that 'so healthful a body' as her
regime needs no such 'weary medicine' as marriage to Anjou.[10]

Grave as the dangers and problems at home were, they could seem less
immediate than those from abroad. In Book Five of the *Arcadia* it looks as if

---

4   SP 83/9/3x (*CSPF 1578–9*, p. 172).
5   Read, *Walsingham*, ii. 14; cf. Hatf. 148, fos 31, 35.
6   Read, *Walsingham*, ii. 70. For comparable assessments see K. de L., x. 544; *HMC Cecil*, ii. 250–
    1; Huntington Library, Hastings MS. HA 5086 (Sir Francis Hastings to Walsingham, 4 April
    1582), HA 13065 (Walsingham to the Earl of Huntingdon, 21 March 1580); Bodl., Rawlinson
    MS. A331, fo. 82ᵛ.
7   Read, *Walsingham*, i. 292; *MP* 54/7–17; cf. K. de L., ix. 303.
8   Read, *Walsingham*, i. 70, 237, 239, 289, ii. 14, 70, 87, 92 (cf. ii. 216); Wright, *Queen Elizabeth*,
    ii. 93. Cf. K. de L., viii. 358, x. 315, 819; Huntington Library, Hastings MS. HA 5086; Wilson,
    Demosthenes, p. 28.
9   Pears, p. 143; *GP* 47/8; cf. Wilson, *Demosthenes*, pp. 52–3.
10 *MP* 47/4–5.

Basilius' dukedom will 'either run itself upon the rock of self-division or be overthrown by the stormy wind of foreign force'.[11] The same prospect confronted Elizabeth's advisers, who thought of 'division at home' and 'foreign invasions' as complementary dangers.[12] It seemed, intermittently at least, that the great Catholic powers were bent on the extinction of Protestant regimes and on the imposition of Tridentine Catholicism on Protestant lands. England's difficulty was to foresee the policies, and to estimate the power, of France, torn as that country was by civil and religious wars. As the rival of Spain, France could sometimes seem the principal obstacle to the Catholic advance. Yet in the late 1570s it increasingly appeared to be its ally. Henry III, King of France since 1574, was believed to be variously manipulated by Spain, by his mother Catherine de Medici, and by the most militant champion of Catholic resurgence, the Guise family. Catherine, to Sidney, was 'the Jezebel of our age'.[13] The fear and detestation she inspired had been whetted by her leading part in the Massacre of St Bartholomew in 1572, that defining event in the escalation of Europe's religious hatreds. The Guises worked with or against the crown as it suited them, veering between loyalty and treason, between authoritarianism and rebellion. Their power was strengthened in 1576 by the formation of the Catholic League and by the decision of the States-General to endorse the League's goal of extinguishing French Protestantism.

The Guises, an international force whose contacts drew the threads of Catholic intrigue together, were in the thick of what William Davison, Elizabeth's envoy in the Low Countries, described in 1578 as the 'holy league of . . . Catholic princes long since projected, often renewed, and now like to be put in execution' so as to secure the 'ruin' of 'the reformed religion'. Of the targets of that holy league, thought Davison, Elizabeth was 'the mark they principally shoot at', the Catholic powers 'holding it for a maxim that if she, being the chief protectrice of our religion, were once supplanted, they should the more easily prevail over the rest'.[14] For England, while its military resources could not compete with those of France or Spain, was the strongest of the Protestant powers, strong enough to impede the ambitions of the great monarchies and to aid their continental enemies. Though zealous Protestants, inside and outside England, regarded Elizabeth's response to the Catholic threat as pitifully inadequate, she had done enough to provoke her Catholic neighbours and give them pretexts for attack. She had aided the Huguenots, financed German princes, condoned the seizure of Spanish treasure-ships, countenanced attacks by her subjects on Spain's possessions in the New World.

In the late 1570s the long peace of Elizabeth's reign was widely believed

11 *OA* 360/23–4.
12 Hatf. 148, fos 37ᵛ, 48ᵛ.
13 *MP* 48/6; cf. NRO, F(P)M, fo. 1ᵛ.
14 K. de L., x. 315; cf. NRO, F(P)M, fo. 5.

by Englishmen to be doomed.[15] By 1578 English statesmen, ever more alarmed by the evidence of 'amity and intelligence' between France and Spain, believed it to be only a matter of time before those 'two mighty and potent powers' fell upon the queen's realm 'with conjunct force and fury', in 'deadly hatred', 'full of enmity and revenge', using the quarrel of religion as 'the chiefest pretext' to wreak 'the destruction and ruin of this . . . kingdom'.[16] Like the Arcadia of Sidney's fiction, Elizabethan England was 'brought . . . to feel the pangs of uttermost peril'. Like Arcadia too it needed to 'make timely provision against this peril'.[17] The queen's advisers joined in acknowledging the 'most imminent' and 'most certain' 'peril' posed by the prospect of a Franco-Spanish alliance with the full resources of international Catholicism behind it. This was 'a suspicious and dangerous time', or these were 'dangerous and perilous times'; 'never stood this crown in like peril'; 'there was never so dangerous a time as this is'.[18]

The principal source of alarm was Mary Queen of Scots, that likely abettor and inspiration both of invasion and of rebellion. Though neither France nor Spain would willingly see England in the hands of the other, there was always the prospect that, as Walsingham had put it in 1572 with Mary in mind, 'they both may consent to advance a third person, who pretendeth right to the crown (especially being provoked thereto by the pope) which is my chief fear'.[19] That prospect was brought closer in 1576 by the aspirations of Don John of Austria, a military commander of towering achievement and ambition, whom Philip II, frustrated by the resilience of the revolt of the Netherlands, had sent to crush it. Don John aspired to lead an invasion of England, depose Elizabeth, marry Mary and join her on the English throne. Intimations of his intentions grew in the spring of 1577, when Sidney relayed reports of them to Elizabeth from Germany.[20] If Mary could claim the English throne she would surely reclaim, de iure or de facto, her Scottish one, which had descended to her son, the boy king James VI. In the late 1570s the fear grew that James would be incited to make war on England.[21]

Mary's natural ally was France, of which, as the wife of Francis II, she had been queen. She was sister-in-law to the present king, Henry III, and cousin to Henry Duke of Guise. Yet by 1577 her French sympathies were vying with, perhaps yielding to, Spanish ones. The Guises had no qualms in seeking Spanish support on her behalf. The death of Don John in 1578, though a relief to the English government, did not diminish the Spanish threat. In the

15 Collinson, *Godly People*, p. 380.
16 K. de L., x. 571, 634; Nicolas, *Hatton*, pp. 40–1; PRO, SP 12/123/17 (fos 53&ᵛ). For the fear of 'revenge' see also *MP* 50/8; *HMC Cecil*, ii. 250–1; NRO, F(P)M 123, fo. iᵛ; *CSPF 1578–9*, pp. 172, 473; K. de L., x. 153; Read, *Walsingham*, i. 143, 154, 417n.
17 *OA* 351/3–4, 355n.
18 Bodl., Rawlinson MS. A331, fos 33, 63, 79, 89ᵛ, 118ᵛ, 124; Nicolas, *Hatton*, p. 40; K. de L., x. 614, 711.
19 Read, *Walsingham*, i. 238.
20 Osborn, *Young Philip Sidney*, p. 459; cf. *CSPF 1575–7*, pp. 566–7.
21 Hatf. 148, fos 49, 52, 58.

same year the outbreak of the Portuguese succession crisis made Spain more formidable still. In 1580 Philip II seized the Portuguese throne for himself while England, to the distress of Sidney and his party, stood back.

Spain's weakness remained the Netherlands. The revolt there had begun in 1566.[22] In 1576 its course was transformed by the Pacification of Ghent. Hitherto its strength had been mainly confined to the provinces of Holland and Zeeland. But in 1576 outrages committed by mutinous Spanish troops in Antwerp drove Spain's more lukewarm opponents in the southern provinces into alliance with the more committed actors and with their leader, William of Orange. The Pacification gave the revolt, through the authority of the States-General which sanctioned it, a claim to constitutional respectability. Orange himself, whose enemies had hitherto been able to portray him as a leader of desperadoes, became a figure of incontestable stature. Yet even in the Low Countries Spain was able to reassert itself in the late 1570s, thanks to a recovery in the crown's finances and to a truce with the Ottoman Turks which freed Philip's hands from the Mediterranean.[23] In 1579 the new-found unity of the revolt and of the Netherlands collapsed. The Union of Utrecht in January 1579 and the Treaty of Arras in May brought a permanent split between north and south. The division was intensified by the diplomatic and military brilliance of Don John's successor, Alexander Farnese, Duke of Parma, who wooed the southern nobility and began a campaign of reconquest.

Yet it was French, not Spanish, diplomacy that struck the heaviest blow against England in the late 1570s. The *sine qua non* of England's safety in Europe, as the forward Protestants insisted, was control of Scotland.[24] For half a decade Elizabeth had exercised a decisive influence on Scottish politics through the regency of James Morton, Earl of Douglas. (Sidney, who followed events in Scotland closely, befriended Morton's nephew and 'delighted much to impart' the *Old Arcadia* to him.)[25] By 1577–8 Morton's regime, seen by its enemies as a covetous clique ruling in a foreign interest,[26] was in jeopardy. Yet what Walsingham described as Elizabeth's 'indisposition to deal effectually in the Scottish causes' was immovable. One consequence of it, he feared, was that her aggrieved subjects in the north of England would look to Scotland for deliverance.[27] Her inactivity threatened to bid farewell to 'the quietness and good days of England'.[28]

Elizabeth's advisers had three particular fears about James VI. The first,

---

22 I shall, for convenience, occasionally use the loose adjective 'Dutch', to describe the revolt and its participants.
23 Geoffrey Parker, *The Dutch Revolt* (Ithaca, N.Y., 1977), pp. 187–9.
24 Nicolas, *Hatton*, p. 41; Bodl., Rawlinson MS. A331, fo. 70; BL, Harleian MS. 6265, fo. 106ᵛ; *CSPF 1578–9*, p. 182.
25 *OA* xvii.
26 Wright, *Queen Elizabeth*, ii. 65, 78; *CSPF 1578–9*, p. 172.
27 Huntington Library, Hastings MS. HA 13065.
28 Nicolas, *Hatton*, p. 66; cf. K. de L., x. 744.

which did not materialise, was that he would be 'convey[ed] . . . out of Scotland' by the French.[29] The second, that he would be betrothed into a Catholic royal house hostile to England,[30] did not materialise either. The third fear, that he would shake off his English monitors, did materialise.[31] In March 1578, three months before his twelfth birthday, he assumed the reins of government with the support of Morton's enemies. The following year Esmé Stuart, a Catholic cousin of James and an ally of the Guises, arrived in Scotland. Gradually he came to dominate the boy king, a process completed by the execution of Morton in December 1580. England's 'postern gate' in the north, which Elizabeth's agents had worked so hard to keep closed, was once more wide open. With the loss of Scotland, as Walsingham observed, 'a great gate' was opened 'for the loss of Ireland'.[32] For it was by intervention in Ireland, Elizabeth's advisers believed, that the Scots had the greatest chance of damaging the queen.[33] England's other enemies looked to Ireland too. The papacy sponsored a military expedition there in the summer of 1579 and another in the summer of 1580. Though those enterprises were quickly dealt with, they strengthened the belief of the queen's counsellors that Spain and the pope were conspiring towards England's downfall.[34]

Historians observe a change in the character both of international diplomacy and of English politics in the late 1570s. The language of both spheres became more urgent and more desperate. So long had the cold war of Counter-Reformation Europe lasted, so intense had its pressures become, that judgements were clouded by frayed nerves, even by hysteria. In England the heightening of tension produced a new polarisation among Elizabeth's councillors and, with it, a sharpening mood of bitterness and division.[35]

Admittedly the factional allegiances of Elizabethan England were never clear-cut. Three factors complicated them. First, the elaborate fluctuations of European diplomacy produced corresponding fluctuations of opinion among the queen's advisers. As Walsingham's secretary Robert Beale observed, 'when counsels are daily taken and varied according to the uncertainty of affairs, the wisest men have been often overtaken and put to hard shifts and have not known what counsel to give or take'.[36] A group of politicians might agree on principles but not about how to meet the choices they confronted in implementing them. Secondly, conflicts of party could be buried in moments of immediate peril, when survival demanded unity and when

29   K. de L., x. 450; cf. Nicolas, *Hatton*, pp. 41–2.
30   Hatf. 148, fo. 52; BL, Harleian MS. 6265, fo. 107.
31   Phillips, 'Buchanan', pp. 40–1.
32   Huntington Library, Hastings MS. HA 13067, Walsingham to the Earl of Huntingdon, 5 April 1581.
33   Hatf., Cecil Papers 148, fo. 81.
34   MacCaffrey, *Policy*, pp. 129–30.
35   Read, *Walsingham*, ii. 2; MacCaffrey, *Policy*, pp. 3, 162–3.
36   Read, *Walsingham*, i. 432.

convictions and postures yielded to facts and necessities. However sharply the queen's advisers might divide, they were all committed to and dependent on the survival of the regime. The plot of the *Arcadia* enacts the political nightmares of Sidney's party; and yet the worst of those nightmares, the eruption of civil discord on the queen's death – the dreadful prospect which Sidney conveys in relating the disintegration of the Arcadian commonwealth on the death of Basilius – troubled all parties within the regime. Thirdly, the rules of Elizabethan political conduct operated to conceal or deny conflict. Differences were obscured (or can be obscured from us) by obligatory courtesies, treacherous charm, silken arts of misinformation. They were obscured too by the ties of kinship and patronage and personal affection that crossed the party lines.[37]

The principal source of disagreement was the question whether England should intervene in the Low Countries. To those who favoured English involvement the arguments were clear and urgent. 'The avoiding of her majesty's danger', warned Sir Francis Knollys, 'doth consist in the preventing of the conquest of the Low Countries betimes.' If she spurned that advice, as she seemed determined to do, she would be 'utterly overthrown'.[38] Sir Nicholas Bacon, weakened by age and illness and burdened with 'great grief' by the queen's inaction, begged her 'to keep the Prince of Orange in heart and life'. To the argument, voiced so often by the queen and her Lord Treasurer, Burghley, that an assertive foreign policy would be expensive, Bacon replied that 'every thousand pounds that shall be thus bestowed will save . . . a hundred thousand' later.[39] Other forward Protestants pressed the same point.[40]

Another of Bacon's convictions was likewise widely shared. Tactfully but firmly he explained to Elizabeth that England's immunity from the recent and current continental wars had resulted not, as she liked to tell herself, from political skill but from good fortune and from those preoccupations of her enemies that were now ceasing to distract them.[41] Walsingham shared that view: her timid response to the Catholic threat, he believed, 'heretofore hath accidentally (in respect of the weakness of the princes her neighbours) continued her majesty in a peaceable kind of government', but now she 'is to look for another kind of reckoning'.[42] The forward Protestant Thomas Wilson, Walsingham's fellow Secretary of State, concurred. 'We deceive ourselves greatly', he told Leicester in 1577, if we imagine that England's

---

37 A more eirenic view of Elizabethan politics than the one I shall propose is given by Simon Adams in 'Eliza Enthroned? The Court and its Politics', in Christopher Haigh, ed., *The Reign of Elizabeth I* (London, 1984), pp. 55–77, and in 'Favourites and Factions at the Elizabethan Court', in Ronald Asch and Adolf Birke, eds, *Princes, Patronage and the Nobility* (Oxford, 1991), pp. 265–87.

38 Wright, *Queen Elizabeth*, ii. 75.

39 Collinson, *Godly People*, p. 152; Nicolas, *Hatton*, p. 42.

40 Read, *Walsingham*, i. 237, 296; *CSPF 1578–9*, p. 171; cf. Wilson, *Demosthenes*, p. 97.

41 Nicolas, *Hatton*, pp. 40–1; cf. Hatf. 148, fo. 48ᵛ.

42 Read, *Walsingham*, ii. 88.

'quietness' has derived from 'our own political wisdom'. The queen's 'policy' of intermittent, underhand and grudging assistance to continental Protestants, Wilson argued, 'is not good, because it is not perpetual but temporary and for a season'.[43] Though 'temporising hath been thought heretofore good policy', he remarked, the chances which had been lost by it would soon haunt the English memory.[44]

Forward Protestants knew that the unity achieved in the Netherlands by the Pacification of Ghent was frail and might be short-lived. The years 1576–8 seemed to them to present an 'opportunity' or 'occasion', of which Elizabeth was 'not like to have the like again', to defeat the claims of political and religious tyranny in the Low Countries and to free England from the Spanish threat. God had offered the queen 'speedy and undelayed remedies' which she must not be 'negligent to use' and which she must 'take when they are offered', before it was 'too late' and she was left to 'repent' the consequences of inaction.[45] If only England would commit itself promptly to Orange's cause and send large supplies of men and money to the Low Countries, there was a chance to change the whole course of the war. The 'union or disjunction, prosperity or peril' of the Netherlanders 'dependeth upon her resolution'.[46] Moments of Spanish military weakness, particularly those in the late summers of 1577 and 1578, seemed to forward Protestants to cry out for English intervention. In return for it, as had long been known, the Dutch were willing to grant Elizabeth the sovereignty or protection of a portion of the Netherlands.

Elizabeth feared Spanish power in the Low Countries and hoped to weaken it. But she did not mean to destroy it. Though, with the forward Protestants, she thought of the Spaniards as bent on a 'conquest' of the Netherlands that would suppress the 'ancient liberties' of that land,[47] she was also inclined to regard Spain's enemies there as rebels against a legitimate monarch. She would have liked to see the Netherlands return to the times of the Emperor Charles V, Philip II's father, when they had accepted Habsburg sovereignty but preserved their constitutional liberties. To that end, she believed, the correct means was diplomacy, not war. Armed intervention on the Netherlanders' behalf would 'irritate the King of Spain, the French king and all other princes Catholic to be revenged of the queen's majesty, which otherwise she thinketh they would not'.[48]

43 K. de L., ix. 304.
44 Ibid., x. 711; cf. the remark of Edmund Grindal described by Patrick Collinson, *Edmund Grindal 1519–1583* (London, 1979), p. 244.
45 K. de L., viii. 287, ix. 301, 529, x. 444, 711, 819; *CSPF 1575–7*, p. 323, *1577–8*, p. 592; Bodl., Rawlinson MS. A331, fos 90ᵛ, 99ᵛ, 118ᵛ, 119ᵛ (cf. fo. 88ᵛ). Cf. *MP* 11/23–6; K. de L., viii. 330, x. 333; *HMC Cecil*, ii. 427; BL, Harleian MS. 6265, fo. 107ᵛ; Wright, *Queen Elizabeth*, ii. 93; Nicolas, *Hatton*, p. 46; Bruce, *Leycester Correspondence*, pp. 304, 366; Wilson, *Demosthenes*, sigs ci, ciii, and pp. 11, 22; Peter Medine, *Thomas Wilson* (Boston, Mass., 1986), pp. 141–2; Read, *Walsingham*, i. 153.
46 Nicolas, *Hatton*, p. 50.
47 BL, Harleian MS. 6992, no. 30; cf. Hatf. 148, fo. 81.
48 K. de L., x. 153; cf. Nicolas, *Hatton*, pp. 47–8, 49.

Forward Protestants argued an opposite case. It was, they maintained, a 'conceit' to imagine that England could appease France or Spain.[49] The 'underhand' aid to England's co-religionists to which the queen wished to confine herself would provoke the Catholic powers no less than the 'open' and wholehearted commitment which forward Protestants craved.[50] Forward Protestants concurred with the observation made by Orange to Sidney in 1577 and reported by Sidney to his queen: that 'neither the King of Spain, nor yet the French king, is able to make war upon the realm of England if England, Holland, and Zeeland be linked together in amity'.[51] Sidney's 'Letter' endorsed that perspective: as long as England's co-religionists abroad 'may be kept from utter falling, your majesty is sure enough from your mightiest enemies'.[52] To Sidney's party the Dutch, with 'our [other] good friends abroad', were 'our best assured buckler to defend the blows prepared against us'. If Elizabeth allowed Philip II to defeat them she would be left without allies, and 'our own army cannot defend us against so mighty and conjured ememies'.[53] But if she would 'proceed roundly' and keep Spain's 'hands full in the Low Countries', Philip would 'be an enemy more terrible in opinion than in effect unto us'. He could be swiftly brought to a peace that would give honour and security to the Dutch and English alike.[54] Sooner or later, maintained the forward Protestants, war between Spain and England was inevitable. It was England's interest to choose the time and place of war, and the sooner she moved against Spain's gathering strength the better her chance of thwarting it.[55] In the *New Arcadia* Amphialus, who at first 'would not be persuaded by danger to offer any offence', discovers that 'who stands only upon defence stands upon no defence'.[56] The forward Protestants maintained the same principle. It is 'better', reasoned Thomas Wilson, 'to annoy by offence than to stand at defence, and to begin war than to withstand war'.[57]

Despite such counsel, Elizabeth had not yet come to think of Spain as an enemy. In forward Protestant eyes she was too vulnerable to Spanish (as indeed to French) professions of friendship.[58] For her, England's natural enemy was its traditional one, France. The queen's preoccupation was that of English foreign policy down the centuries: the prevention of French control of the Low Countries and thus of the Channel seaboard.[59] The French, she feared, would take advantage of Spain's weakness in the Netherlands and

49 Read, *Walsingham*, i. 217, 417n.
50 Nicolas, *Hatton*, pp. 47–9.
51 Osborn, *Young Philip Sidney*, p. 488; cf. NRO, F(P)M 123, fo. 4ᵛ.
52 *MP* 56/26–8.
53 Bodl., Rawlinson MS. A331, fo. 78ᵛ; cf. Wilson, *Demosthenes*, p. 89.
54 Nicolas, *Hatton*, pp. 49–50; K. de L., x. 333.
55 Read, *Walsingham*, i. 153–5; cf. Wilson, *Demosthenes*, p. 90.
56 *NA* 196/33–4, 197/7–8.
57 Wilson, *Demosthenes*, p. 9. Cf. ibid., sig. Bii and pp. 8, 48, 75; K. de L., ix. 329; Read, *Walsingham*, ii. 70.
58 Below, pp. 164–5.
59 Read, *Walsingham*, i. 202.

seize them for themselves. The moments when she was readiest to contemplate armed involvement in the Low Countries were those when she most feared 'that the Low Countries may become French'.[60] Burghley, her chief minister, was more often ready to advocate assistance to the Dutch than the queen was to favour it. Yet in him too the fear of a French annexation of the Low Countries overrode all other considerations. There were times when, for that reason, he was even willing to offer aid to the Spaniards there.[61]

It was not that either the queen or Burghley was blind to the alternative hazards: control of the seaboard by Spain and the consequent dangers to England of invasion and economic blockade.[62] Elizabeth had somehow to steer between the two perils, adjusting her course amid the constant and subtle shifts in the balance of continental power. Yet in the eyes of forward Protestants she had failed to grasp the implications of recent diplomatic history for English policy. The queen, they sensed, instinctively thought of Spain's presence in the Low Countries as a continuation of the old Burgundian counterweight to France. That perspective, believed Walsingham, had been made anachronistic: first by the loss of Calais under Mary Tudor, which had ended or at least reduced the ground of natural enmity between England and France; secondly by the weakening of France during the religious wars; and thirdly by the rise of Spain to world power.[63] On the continent, Walsingham's and Sidney's friends Languet and Mornay also argued that the old balance of European power had been broken in Spain's favour.[64] Languet insistently impressed upon Sidney the gravity of the Spanish threat to England and lamented the queen's unreadiness to acknowledge it. Once the Dutch were overcome, he advised, Spain would turn on England 'as the chief author of their misfortunes'.[65] Sidney tried to bring those warnings home to his English superiors.[66]

England's forward Protestants were no more indifferent to the French threat than the queen was to the Spanish one. Forward Protestants saw the French as the most duplicitous of statesmen.[67] French control of the Low Countries, they acknowledged, would be at least as dangerous as Spanish domination.[68] It was indeed their frequent complaint that Elizabeth's inactivity in the Low Countries had increased that very threat.[69] Yet in 1577–8

---

60 K. de L., viii. 304, x. 465, 710. Cf. ibid., xi. 82; BL, Harleian MS. 6992, no. 30; Read, *Walsingham*, i. 295; Read, *Burghley*, p. 189.

61 Read, *Burghley*, chs 11, 12; cf. Hatf. 148, fo. 81.

62 K. de L., x. 153; Read, *Walsingham*, i. 373; Hatf. 148, fo. 81.

63 Read, *Walsingham*, ii. 91–2.

64 Pears, pp. 102–3; Patry, *Philippe Du Plessis-Mornay*, p. 82.

65 Pears, pp. 56, 62–3, 102–3, 108, 131, 185 (cf. p. 78); Levy, 'Correspondence', no. 58; Osborn, *Young Philip Sidney*, pp. 363–4.

66 Pears, pp. 59, 102.

67 K. de L., x. 789; Bodl., Rawlinson MS. A331, fos 12ᵛ, 120&ᵛ; NRO, F(P)M, fo. 5ᵛ; *CSPF 1577–8*, pp. 592, 711; Read, *Walsingham*, i. 237, ii. 15, 18, 93.

68 K. de L., xi. 144.

69 Ibid., ix. 132, x. 818, xi. 130; Nicolas, *Hatton*, pp. 65–6; Wright, *Queen Elizabeth*, ii. 93. Cf. Read, *Walsingham*, ii. 38; Lehmberg, *Mildmay*, pp. 156–7.

it was to the menace of Spain that they were the more alert. Spain was the political and military head of the popish interest. It was on Spanish might that the ambitions of international Catholicism, and the intrigues of the pope, of the Jesuits, of the Guises, must depend.

The hostility to Spain among England's forward Protestants produced differences between the queen and themselves not only of perspective but of goal. Walsingham and his friends, being Elizabeth's servants, were obliged to speak her language and pursue her stated aims. Yet when they did so she was apt to question their sincerity and to suspect that their ultimate loyalties were international ones.[70] Certainly they had a thin line to tread. The forward Protestants often professed to share the queen's wish for a negotiated compromise to end the war in the Netherlands. There were in any case black periods for Orange's cause when a peace treaty seemed the best they could hope for.[71] Yet such a peace, they believed, would leave dangers for England behind it. Indeed by stabilising Spain's power it might create new ones.[72] The only satisfactory peace would be one imposed on Spain by the Dutch from a position, which Elizabeth could help bring them, of military superiority.[73] Orange, as Walsingham saw, 'is determined utterly to shake off the Spanish government'. In their hearts the forward Protestants were with him.[74]

To the argument that the overthrow of Spain would open the way to the French, Walsingham and his allies replied that England must beat France to it. The queen must take the Netherlands under her own protection. England could and must stand up to France, as she could and must stand up to Spain. As well as sending men and money to the Low Countries she should keep the French monarchy 'occupied at home'. That might 'easily' be done[75] if the queen would do two things. First, she must aid the Huguenots and their French allies, Henry of Navarre and the Prince of Condé. Secondly, she must encourage and pay German princes to impede Valois ambitions and, if France should 'grow too great', to 'change the balance' against her.[76]

The forward Protestants saw diplomacy in confessional terms. The queen did not. Where she viewed with 'dislike' the rapid advances of Dutch Protestantism, Walsingham thought that its progress – provided its leaders showed political discretion – was 'like to bring . . . the greatest strength and surety' to the Netherlands and thus to be 'no less beneficial' to England's interests 'than the change of religion in Scotland' had been. The common interest of Protestantism, he hoped, would bind the Dutch and English

---

70 Read, *Walsingham*, i. 325, 334–5 (cf. 287, 335); K. de L., x. 458.
71 K. de L., x. 581, 777, 815, 832, xi. 200; *CSPF 1578–9*, p. 174; NRO, F(P)M III, fo. 11; Read, *Burghley*, p. 199.
72 *CSPF 1578–9*, p. 182.
73 Cf. Nicolas, *Hatton*, p. 48; *CSPF 1577–8*, p. 591.
74 K. de L., x. 488; Nicolas, *Hatton*, p. 74.
75 Nicolas, *Hatton*, p. 49.
76 Read, *Walsingham*, ii. 92; cf. ibid., i. 154, 285, ii. 17.

together, 'no union carrying so great an assurance as that which is grounded upon consent of religion'.[77]

In 1578, that terrible year for forward Protestants, the differences between Elizabeth and them became acute. At the end of January the Dutch revolt suffered a heavy defeat at Gembloux. 'If her majesty should now in their need disappoint' Orange and his followers, wrote Davison from Antwerp, 'it would in the judgement of the wisest [here] bring forth some great and dangerous alteration.'[78] For once, the queen recognised the gravity of Orange's position. She undertook to send an army to the Netherlands under Leicester. Here at last, it seemed, was the act of commitment for which forward Protestants had so long hoped. Yet Elizabeth had made promises to the Dutch before, and broken them. She broke this one too. Her reversal of policy, which became clear by March, was a shattering blow to the forward Protestants and their Dutch friends. Now it was that Sidney wrote the melancholy letter to Languet which declared that 'our cause' was 'withering away' and that he was 'meditating . . . some Indian project'. Sidney and Languet, who had always to remember that their letters might fall into unfriendly hands,[79] were wary of describing in them the alignments or the intensity of the political conflicts of which they were witnesses. Yet now Sidney's curbed language came closer to candour than at any other moment of that correspondence. The queen, he reported, had found occasion 'to defend her tardiness in executing her designs, against Leicester, Walsingham, and others, who had persuaded her to a more active course; which I much regret'.[80]

In May 1578 the queen sent Walsingham and Lord Cobham on an embassy to the Low Countries, instructing them to assess the situation and help procure a peace. (This was the mission which Fulke Greville joined without the queen's consent.) Their humiliating journey, from which they returned in October, exposed them to the full blast of Dutch resentment. Meanwhile Walsingham's allies at home strove to revive the plan for a military expedition. There were moments of optimism, enough of them to enable Walsingham to 'entertain' the Dutch 'with hope of the continuance of her majesty's favour', but his protestations were greeted with mounting disbelief.[81] Then, in August, Elizabeth's mind changed again. Alarmed by the prospect of French involvement in the Netherlands, she was 'suddenly minded, without all scruples', to send Leicester over 'without delay, and the army shall follow'. 'She seemeth ready', Burghley wrote to Walsingham, 'to hazard any expense.' 'Nevertheless,' he added with long experience to support him, 'though this be for the present earnestly meant, I can assure

---

77 K. de L., x. 832; cf. ibid., x. 410, 570–1.
78 Ibid., x. 276.
79 Pears, pp. 70, 78 (cf. p. 45); Osborn, *Young Philip Sidney*, p. 157.
80 Pears, p. 146.
81 K. de L., x. 599, 814–15. Walsingham's absence also enabled the cautious Burghley to exert a larger influence on foreign policy: Read, *Burghley*, pp. 193–4, 203.

nothing.'[82] Elizabeth's abandonment of her momentary resolution was a bitter blow to Walsingham, the more so because the Dutch had just won a dramatic victory at Rijmenant, a triumph which left 'the estate of their affairs', he believed, 'upon making or marring'.[83]

Despair, a mood never alien to Walsingham's mind, plumbed new depths in it in the second half of 1578. In 'quite abandon[ing]' the Dutch 'when they stood in greatest need of her assistance', he reflected, the queen had committed 'a most dangerous . . . error'.[84] Not only had she betrayed her natural allies: she was driving them into the arms of the French. That peril was signalled by the alliance formed in August 1578 between the Low Countries and the heir to the French throne, the Duke of Anjou. Walsingham feared that Orange and the States-General, having until recently been 'altogether at her majesty's devotion', would now 'of assured friends grow most dangerous enemies'.[85]

Indeed, judged Walsingham, Elizabeth's entire diplomacy might have been calculated to leave her with 'no friends abroad', with 'all the world [her] enemies at once'.[86] The Dutch had been 'alienat[ed]';[87] Scotland had been 'aliened';[88] Ireland had been 'aliened';[89] and Navarre and Condé, whose requests for assistance the queen had long parried, 'are to learn' from her 'dealings' with Orange and the States-General 'what they are to look for in the time of their necessity'.[90] Then there was Sidney's friend John Casimir, who alone among the German princes had been willing to intervene in the Low Countries, and whose army the queen had grudgingly and covertly subsidised in 1578 as a substitute for direct intervention; earlier she had subsidised his troops in France in a similar spirit. In August 1578 Sidney was spared, by Leicester's intervention, from being the bearer of a message of 'cold comfort' from the queen to Casimir. The message carried, not the gratitude to which Walsingham thought Casimir entitled, but a rebuke for revealing her support for him.[91] Casimir, wrote Walsingham from the Low Countries in September, 'doth curse the time he ever departed out of his country, seeing her majesty deals so coldly in these causes, especially finding her now grown hateful to this people, and he himself for her sake the less esteemed'.[92]

---

82 K. de L., x. 710, 712. The habit of scepticism bred by the queen's conduct can be sensed in an echo of Burghley's statement in a letter by Sidney six years later: 'her majesty seems affected to deal in the Low Country matters, but I think nothing will come of it'. Feuillerat, iii. 145.

83 K. de L., x. 819.

84 Ibid., 814–15, 818.

85 CSPF 1578–9, p. 172.

86 Read, Walsingham, ii. 92; K. de L., x. 815; cf. K. de L., x. 777.

87 CSPF 1578–9, p. 171; K. de L., x. 815.

88 Read, Walsingham, ii. 88; cf. Wright, Queen Elizabeth, ii. 65.

89 Read, Walsingham, ii. 92.

90 K. de L., x. 815; cf. CSPD 1578–9, p. 172.

91 K. de L., x. 679, 744.

92 Ibid., 815.

Such were the circumstances from which there emerged the dominant issue of English politics in the period which produced Sidney's *Arcadia*: the proposal – a revived proposal – that Elizabeth marry Francis Duke of Alençon and Anjou, the younger brother, and heir apparent, of the childless King Henry III of France. The origins of the Anjou match, and of the passions which it aroused, were intimately related to the course of the Dutch revolt and to the divisions within the English government over the question of direct involvement in it.

The Duke of Anjou, a Roman Catholic half Elizabeth's age, a footloose adventurer in search of a kingdom, was viewed by forward Protestants with fear, hatred, profound mistrust. In France, by unscrupulous alternations between support for his royal brother and collaboration with the crown's enemies, he had built the semi-autonomous power-base to which princes of the blood customarily aspired. The Huguenots had had particularly bitter experience of his opportunism. He had been implicated in the Massacre of St Bartholomew in 1572, an episode vividly recalled in England during the marriage negotiations between Anjou and Elizabeth, as was the duke's involvement in it.[93] In 1573 he had taken part in the siege of the Huguenot stronghold of La Rochelle. In 1575, in one of his many reversals of allegiance, he left the court and joined the Huguenot forces. His aim was to put pressure on King Henry to grant him a freer and more prestigious political role. In December 1576, that goal accomplished, he returned to the royal fold. As Sidney's 'Letter' put it, he had acquired 'his liberty and principal estates chiefly by the Huguenots' means', and had then turned on them. Referring to the massacre of Huguenot families by Anjou's troops in the Loire Valley in the spring of 1577, Sidney asserted that the duke 'did sack La Charité and utterly spoil Issoire with fire and sword'.[94] Anjou had not in fact borne direct responsibility for the massacres.[95] They nonetheless fostered a belief that if given the chance he, like members of the French royal family, would sanction similar outrages in the future.[96] In February 1578, however, he was in trouble with his brother again. He was placed under guard, only to escape from court a few days later.[97] His conduct and motives in the months which followed were a source of intense speculation.

Anjou was unattractive in person, his face pock-marked, his body ill-shapen. His character was unattractive too. He was not quite the ogre imagined by forward Protestants. The same instinct which led them to demonise Mary Queen of Scots – and which so confused them when, on

93   Stubbs, pp. 7–8, 40; Nicolas, *Hatton*, p. 134; BL, Harleian MS. 6265, fo. 108; Kingdon, *Myths*, p. 21; cf. NRO, F(P)M, fos 3, 5.
94   *MP* 48/9–11. Cf. BL, Harleian MS. 6265, fo. 108; PRO, SP 15/26/*35, fos 114ᵛff.
95   Holt, *Anjou*, pp. 90, 121, 124.
96   Bodl., Rawlinson MS. A331, fos 22ᵛ, 25&ᵛ, 36; K. de L., x. 457.
97   Read, *Walsingham*, i. 373–4.

5 Francis Duke of Alençon and Anjou.

meeting her, they found her so personable[98] – made it hard for them to think rationally about Anjou. Walsingham, who for all the excesses of his pessimism could think as rationally as anyone, met the duke in August 1578 and confessed to having found him 'very wise, well spoken and not so deformed as he was'.[99] Advocates of the match claimed that Anjou was 'by all men [who knew him] commended to have a good wit, and to be of courteous condition'.[100] Even so, he was not a man to trust. The judgement of the nineteenth-century historian of the Dutch revolt, J. L. Motley, is at least half fair: the duke was 'ferocious without courage, ambitious without talent and bigoted without opinions'.[101]

Those defects did not impede his political rise. By 1578 he was a substantial figure not only in French but in European politics. For some time he had

98 Below, p. 329.
99 Read, *Walsingham*, i. 40–3; cf. PRO, SP 15/26/*35, fo. 120&ᵛ.
100 *CSPF 1578–9*, p. 473.
101 Quoted by Wilson, *Netherlands*, p. 65.

seen in the troubles of the Low Countries the chance of martial adventure and personal aggrandisement. At least since 1576, as England's forward Protestants knew, he had been putting out feelers to the leaders of the revolt in the hope of acquiring the sovereignty of their land. Elizabeth's abandonment of her pledge to send an army under Leicester played into his hands.[102] In the summer of 1578 her envoys, Walsingham and Cobham, were left to look on helplessly as plans advanced for a treaty that would bring an army under Anjou into the Low Countries.[103] Signed in August, the treaty described him as 'defender of the liberty of the Netherlands against the tyranny of the Spanish and their allies'.[104] That was the role which the forward Protestants had wanted Elizabeth to fill. They knew that Orange and his followers, nervous of French ambitions in the Netherlands, would greatly have preferred an English alliance, but also that the queen's conduct had left them no choice.[105] Besides, the Dutch dared not alienate Anjou, whose 'hatred' they 'fear[ed]'.[106] It had long been known that he intended to fight in the Netherlands: what was not clear was on which side. Many had thought he would ally himself with Spain and join forces with Don John, another figure with high martial and personal ambitions.[107] In 1578 Anjou allowed the Dutch to understand that he would fight either for them or against them, 'as whether they do accept or refuse his offers'.[108] Orange believed he was more likely to fight against them than for them.[109]

The hardest puzzle for English statesmen was Anjou's relationship not with the Dutch or Spain but with his elder brother and mother. Henry III professed to be troubled by Anjou's offer of aid to the Dutch. If so, the duke, as Walsingham remarked, might 'serve for a good counterpoise of his brother's malice'.[110] But was Henry's posture, as some suspected, a pretence? The expedition, after all, would get Anjou and his military following off French soil. If it succeeded, Spain would suffer a blow from which Henry could reap the benefit while disclaiming the responsibility. If it failed, Anjou would be weakened and his power to trouble France reduced.[111]

Elizabeth's advisers, as they peered into the mists of French politics, formed still graver suspicions. They feared that Henry and Anjou were colluding so as to annex part or all of the Low Countries to the French crown. On that reading, Anjou's flight from court in February 1578 had been a ruse. His subsequent conversations with the Duke of Guise, the Spanish ambassador in Paris, 'and such like', it was argued, showed him to be an

---

102   K. de L., x. 313, 426.
103   Ibid., x. 599, 662.
104   Holt, *Anjou*, p. 104.
105   Nicolas, *Hatton*, pp. 44–6; cf. K. de L., x. 811–12.
106   K. de L., x. 424.
107   Nicolas, *Hatton*, p. 83; K. de L., x. 465, 488; *CSPF 1578–9*, p. 185.
108   K. de L., x. 402, 448. Cf. ibid., 443–4, 624; *CSPF 1577–8*, p. 494.
109   K de L., x. 402; cf. *CSPF 1577–8*, p. 494.
110   Nicolas, *Hatton*, p. 67.
111   *CSPF 1577–8*, p. 711; Hatf. 148, fo. 49; K. de L., x. 457; Nicolas, *Hatton*, pp. 82–3.

agent not only of Henry but of the international Catholic conspiracy.[112] Walsingham was left to wonder which was 'the greater peril' to England, an alliance between Anjou and Spain or one between Anjou and the Dutch. The duke, he feared, would establish 'a further foot' in the Low Countries 'than ever the King of Spain will be able to remove or we to hinder'.[113]

Yet there were other, less alarming ways of interpreting Anjou's conduct. Was he not acting, as he had always done, in his own interests, which he would never consistently harness to anyone else's? Would it not be possible to turn his ambitions in the Low Countries to England's advantage? Might not Elizabeth, by giving him support, sow discord between him and his Catholic backers and among those backers themselves?[114] In their treaty with Anjou the Netherlanders obliged him to seek cooperation with the English government,[115] a provision which might be so used as to give the queen a hold over him. Forward Protestants, however mistrustful of the duke, could at least see the point of seeking to influence rather than offend him. Walsingham worried lest the queen, having alienated everyone else, would alienate him too by spurning requests for assistance from him.[116]

For much of 1578 Elizabeth was fearful of an alliance between Anjou and the Dutch. It was partly with the purpose of fending off that danger that she sent Walsingham and Cobham to the Low Countries in May 1578,[117] and it was in the hope of forestalling it that in August she momentarily revived her plan to dispatch Leicester's expedition. But her interpretation of the duke's motives, though it understandably fluctuated, gradually became more hopeful. She came to think – rightly, it seems – that Henry III's professions of distaste for his brother's behaviour were genuine and that Anjou was acting on his own initiative.[118] Though she shared the concern of forward Protestants lest he should seek absolute power for himself in the Netherlands, she found reassurance in the terms of his treaty with the States-General, which precluded him from holding constitutional authority there. She was more and more inclined to think of him not as an enemy but as a potential ally, whose friendship might deter the designs of both France and Spain against her.[119]

There were two ways in which she might seek to bind him to her. The first was to subsidise him. Here she thought of him as she thought of John Casimir: as someone to do her fighting for her without involving England in the expense of war or provoking either France or Spain to invade England. Unfortunately the causes of Anjou and Casimir came into conflict in the

112 K. de L., x. 443–4, xi. 146; *CSPF 1577–8*, pp. 534–5; cf. Hatf. 148, fo. 81.
113 K. de L., x. 457; *CSPF 1578–9*, p. 72.
114 *CSPF 1577–8*, p. 619 (cf. *1578–9*, p. 16); K. de L., x. 634–5.
115 Holt, *Anjou*, pp. 104, 107; *CSPF 1578–9*, pp. 131–2.
116 *CSPF 1578–9*, p. 172; cf. Read, *Walsingham*, ii. 93.
117 K. de L., x. 465, 486–7; *CSPF 1577–8*, p. 722; Read, *Walsingham*, i. 382–3, ii. 2–3.
118 Read, *Walsingham*, ii. 3; Read, *Burghley*, pp. 192, 197.
119 K. de L., x. 525–6, 581, 678, xi. 82; MacCaffrey, *Policy*, p. 240.

autumn of 1578, when both men headed armies in the Low Countries. Anjou's strength (though also some of the most intense of the hostility to him) lay in the Catholic and French-speaking south. But the havoc wrought by his undisciplined troops, and the ignominious failure of his campaign, played into the hands of a revolutionary movement in the southern towns which took Anjou for its enemy and which found a friend in Casimir. Casimir, swayed by his Calvinist adviser Dr Beuttrich, that 'very firebrand of contention',[120] encouraged a wave of iconoclasm and social disturbance that proved still more disastrous to Orange's cause than Anjou's intervention, antagonising the southern nobility and helping to drive it back into Spanish hands. Orange, watching the unity of the revolt collapse, was infuriated by Casimir's tactics. So were the forward Protestants. So was Elizabeth. Having given support, however limited, to his expedition, she now found herself blamed for its consequences, the more so as the revolutionaries of the south were making plain their wish that the Dutch would ally themselves with England rather than France. By November she was 'sorry that ever she brought him into' the Low Countries.[121]

There remained Anjou. But by December his plundering army was disintegrating and his fortunes were at an ebb as low as Casimir's. In that reduced condition he saw increasing merit in the second, and more ambitious, of the two steps by which Elizabeth was thinking of binding him to her: marriage.

120   K. de L., xi. 128, 147.
121   Ibid., 129.

CHAPTER 6

The Anjou Match

Sidney, relates Greville, believed that the queen's marriage to Anjou would produce a sea-change in English and European politics. In England it would lead – perhaps gradually, perhaps quickly – to absolutism on the French model and the restoration of Catholicism. Abroad – perhaps gradually, perhaps quickly – it would break England's links with the Protestants of France, of Germany, of the Netherlands, of the Baltic, and draw it into the international Catholic axis.[1] In 1579, when the marriage became an imminent prospect, everything that the forward Protestants held most dear was at risk. It was hard for them to choose their ground of opposition to the match. Their fears were speculative. They had to judge how Anjou would behave as Elizabeth's husband and how the English would respond to his behaviour, matters about which there could be no certainty. There were pragmatic arguments for the marriage which were difficult to counter and of which they could recognise the force. Yet in most of Sidney's party, and in Sidney himself, the match aroused the most profound and heartfelt distaste. To it they proposed an alternative programme. They called for the assertion, even amid the perils of the late 1570s, of the nation's independence. The queen and her people, they argued, must trust in God and in the political and ethical resources which God had given them. That conviction has a central place in the *Arcadia*. Here we shall meet the circumstances and debates out of which the conviction took its strength and depth.

Catherine de Medici had long thought of Queen Elizabeth as a suitable match for one of her surviving sons. In 1570–1, when Charles IX, the eldest of them, was King of France, there were negotiations for the marriage of Elizabeth to his brother Henry, who was Charles's heir and, until his own succession to the throne in 1574, Duke of Anjou; it was upon that succession

1 GP 28ff.

that the dukedom passed to Francis, the youngest of those three brothers. In 1572 Francis took Henry's place as the queen's prospective husband. The betrothal was mooted at various times between 1572 and 1576; in 1573–4 the prospect was strong enough to polarise Elizabeth's advisers. Yet the proposal faded.[2]

In the spring of 1578 it was revived.[3] Over the months that followed, English politicians learned to grasp its seriousness. At the end of August the Earl of Sussex, the pacemaker of the marriage initiative and perhaps the warmest advocate of the match among the queen's councillors,[4] drew up a memorandum to her in its favour. His premise was that Anjou was determined to aggrandise himself, either by marrying the queen or by ruling the Low Countries. Nothing less than marriage, maintained Sussex, would enable Elizabeth to 'hinder his greatness' in the Netherlands or prevent him from using it against her.[5] To Sussex's arguments Sir Walter Mildmay produced a swift and full reply, which revived and adapted objections he had raised to earlier proposals that Elizabeth marry into the Valois house. Now as then, that prospect affronted his deepest beliefs.[6]

Walsingham, away on his mission to the Low Countries in the summer of 1578, was slower than most to grasp the seriousness of the suit. Though he knew that Anjou would marry Elizabeth if he could, 'being as she is the best marriage in her parish', he did not see how the duke could have serious hopes.[7] Anjou's professions of interest in Elizabeth, he believed, were intended primarily to dupe her, 'thereby to win her the better to digest his proceedings' in the Low Countries.[8] Elizabeth too, Walsingham told himself, was bluffing. Walsingham's hostility to the idea of the match was already well enough known at court to risk the queen's displeasure.[9] When he returned to England in October he was dismayed to discover that the negotiations were persisting. 'I would to God her majesty would forbear the entertaining any longer the marriage matter,' he wrote. 'No one thing hath procured her so much hatred abroad as these wooing matters, for that it is conceived she dallieth therein.'[10]

But was she dallying? Whether she ever intended to marry Anjou only she, if anyone, has ever known. Initially secretive about her intentions,[11] she

---

2   There is now a comprehensive narrative of the successive matrimonial negotiations of Queen Elizabeth and especially of her negotiations with the House of Valois: Susan Doran, *Monarchy and Matrimony. The Courtships of Elizabeth I* (London and New York, 1996). It appeared too late for me to make more than the most peripheral use of it.

3   Read, *Walsingham*, i. 396–7; PRO, SP 12/123/17.

4   Doran, *Monarchy and Matrimony*, pp. 146–7.

5   Nicolas, *Hatton*, pp. 81–9; Read, *Burghley*, pp. 197, 201–2; cf. Thomas Rogers, *Leicester's Ghost*, ed. Franklin Williams (Chicago, 1972), p. 27.

6   NRO, F(P)M 111; Lehmberg, *Mildmay*, pp. 157ff.

7   K. de L., x. 744; cf. Doran, *Monarchy and Matrimony*, p. 21.

8   K. de L., x. 662.

9   Ibid., 679–80, 744. Cf. ibid., 631; Nicolas, *Hatton*, p. 66.

10 Nicolas, *Hatton*, p. 94.

11 K. de L., x. 680.

became more communicative with time. Her intimations were various and contradictory. Yet in 1579, the year when the issue came to a head, the general impression she gave was one of eagerness, even ardour. As the Spanish ambassador to England, Bernardino de Mendoza, reported in June, 'she gives every sign of being most anxious' for the match and 'is burning with impatience' for the arrival of her suitor.[12] Over the course of the summer the world of European diplomacy adjusted to the prospect of the marriage and thus of a French-controlled England.[13] At Elizabeth's court, observes Conyers Read, 'everybody believed that Elizabeth seriously contemplated marriage'.[14]

Posterity may view that belief with scepticism. There had always been one obvious political reason for Elizabeth to marry: the provision, by childbirth, of a clear heir to the throne. But had not that hope passed? Her forty-fifth birthday fell in September 1578. She was forty-six when, in October 1579, the debates over the marriage reached their peak. Burghley nonetheless argued in favour of the match. The queen's doctors, he claimed, had given assurance that she was 'very apt for procreation of children', 'even at this day'. Indeed, he argued, there were 'good reasons' to think that, unless she married, she would suffer the 'dolours and infirmities' which afflict single and childless women and which might lead her to an early grave. The same fatal consequence, if she declined the match, might arise from her 'grief' when she saw the unpopularity of her failure to provide for the possibility of children.[15] If Burghley's reasoning sounds far-fetched, it was no more so than the contrary plea of Walsingham, who claimed what his brother-in-law Sir Walter Mildmay had argued when Elizabeth considered marrying Anjou five years earlier: that her days would be shortened by the 'grief of mind' and 'miscontentation' that the marriage would bring her.[16]

Yet there were arguments for the match which had nothing to do with the procreation of children or the queen's state of mind and which, in the thinking of its advocates, may have been more pressing. As Anjou's wife, they reasoned, Elizabeth could expect to steer his actions in the Netherlands to England's advantage. She could use him to forestall the Spanish reconquest of the Netherlands, while at the same time preventing him from annexing them either for himself or for France. The combined strength of Elizabeth and Anjou would bring Spain and the Dutch to the negotiating table and impose a peace that would preserve but restrict Spanish sovereignty.[17]

12 *CSPS 1568–79*, p. 680.
13 Leimon, 'Walsingham', p. 122.
14 Read, *Burghley*, p. 206.
15 Ibid., pp. 210–11. The seriousness with which those arguments were formulated indicates the depth of the preoccupation of Elizabeth's councillors with the likely consequences of her death; cf. below, Chapter 11.
16 Read, *Walsingham*, ii. 15–16; Lehmberg, *Mildmay*, p. 108. On the closeness of Walsingham and Mildmay see Leimon, 'Walsingham', p. 130.
17 Nicolas, *Hatton*, pp. 83–4; Doran, *Monarchy and Matrimony*, pp. 4, 59.

Elizabeth herself, though unlikely to have thought in such ambitious terms, did see the match as a means of thwarting Spain. In February 1579 Walsingham, acknowledging that the suit 'hath taken greater foot than was at the first looked for', interpreted the queen's readiness as a consequence of the apparent disintegration of the Dutch revolt during that winter. To prevent a Spanish reconquest, he thought, 'she will in the end consent to the match though otherwise not greatly to her liking'.[18]

Yet, as the two historians best acquainted with the course of Elizabethan politics, Conyers Read and Wallace MacCaffrey, have concluded, the issue in the queen's mind was not only one of diplomacy. It was, or at least became, personal. What initially 'had seemed to be yet another conventional diplomatic exercise in matrimonial bargaining', explains MacCaffrey, became in 1579 'an intensely personal drama', of which 'the driving force . . . was the overpowering attraction which matrimony now exerted on Elizabeth'.[19]

In January 1579 Anjou's agent Jean Simier arrived in England to open the formal negotiations. In late March and early April the privy council held protracted debates about the desirability and terms of the marriage. It was then, too, that the match became a matter of wide public discussion.[20] The terms of the proposed marriage treaty were discussed by Elizabeth's council early in May.[21] In August Anjou came to England for ten days to conduct the wooing. Urgent deliberations among the queen's advisers continued into the autumn. There was a long and intense series of debates, lasting nearly a week, in early October. In November a preliminary treaty for the marriage was agreed.[22]

In January 1580 the queen suspended her negotiations with Anjou. It was believed that she had decided against the match.[23] Yet in February there was uncertainty once more. The subject was again debated at a conference of councillors, where the now well-worn arguments for and against it were lengthily rehearsed.[24] That, however, was the last of the major debates. Over the next two years the proposal would intermittently resurface. But as a political question, and perhaps too as a question in the queen's mind, it never regained the intensity it had acquired in 1579. She may still have occasionally contemplated marrying the duke, but it seems more likely that she persisted with the discussions in order to keep France sweet or to help her play France and Spain against each other.[25] There was a theatrical moment in November

18 K. de L., xi. 304–5.
19 MacCaffrey, *Policy*, pp. 249, 254–5; Read, *Burghley*, pp. 206–7; though cf. Doran, *Monarchy and Matrimony*, p. 163.
20 CSPS *1568–79*, p. 663.
21 Hatf. 148, fos 42–4, 75ᵛ; NRO, F(P)M 111, fos. 11ᵛ–12. (The foliation of that second manuscript is problematical; my solution differs from that adopted in Lehmberg, *Mildmay*.)
22 Doran, *Monarchy and Matrimony*, pp. 174–5.
23 Read, *Burghley*, pp. 221, 563. I do not share Read's certainty that the document he cites is by Burghley, though it may well be.
24 NRO, F(P)M 111, fos 14ᵛ–15ᵛ; Lehmberg, *Mildmay*, p. 163.
25 Lehmberg, *Mildmay*, p. 164; Read, *Walsingham*, ii. 95; though cf. HMC Cecil, ii. 387–8.

1581, when Anjou came to England as a wooer for the second time. The queen startled Leicester, Walsingham and the French ambassador, who were in attendance, by kissing the duke on the mouth, drawing a ring from her finger to give to him, and declaring that she would marry him.[26] That conduct, which struck and puzzled diplomats and politicians, may have had that intention.[27] At all events nothing came of her gesture. The match was dead.

The marriage negotiations overshadowed the English politics of 1579. Whether or not the suit would succeed, the forward Protestants knew what it signified. The confessional diplomacy which they had urged for so long had been finally rejected. Instead the queen was treating with a ruthless and unscrupulous Catholic, a demon of the Huguenots and their sympathisers. If the match proceeded, warned the pamphlet written by John Stubbs against it, all the Protestant states on the continent 'will at once throw away their Christian estimation' of the English.[28] Hitherto the queen had at least been willing to support and subsidise Protestant princes, however grudgingly and inadequately. Now, if she intervened on the continent, it would be in alliance with the heir of a mighty Catholic power. Forward Protestants did not imagine that the new situation pleased her. But her predicament had arisen, they thought, only because she had ignored their warnings so often and so long. By the timidity and negligence of her policy towards the Low Countries, towards France, towards Scotland, she had left herself diplomatically isolated. Time and again they had pressed upon her the gravity of the Spanish threat. Now that she had at last recognised it, she found herself looking, for her sole hope of protection, to the fickle and inept Anjou.

The forward Protestants sought, in Walsingham's words, 'the advancement of religion as well at home as abroad'.[29] Thwarted abroad, they felt thwarted at home too. For the Anjou match at once reflected and strengthened a shift in both politics and religion which characterised the middle period of Elizabeth's reign. The year 1577, that time of missed Protestant opportunities in foreign policy, also brought the suspension of the evangelical Archbishop of Canterbury, Edmund Grindal. His fall, writes Patrick Collinson, 'was recognised to be a portent of reaction against the progressive Protestantism which he symbolised, at a time when Protestant and conservative, even crypto-Catholic forces were in contention for the mastery, at court and in the direction of domestic and foreign policy'.[30] The forward Protestant Sir Francis Knollys, whose mind linked the queen's appeasement of Catholics abroad with her treatment of Grindal, remarked that 'if the Bishop of

---

26 Read, *Walsingham*, ii. 95.
27 For a different view see Doran, *Monarchy and Matrimony*, pp. 187–8.
28 Stubbs, p. 64. Cf. ibid., pp. 20–1; F(P)M 111, fos 2, 15. The Huguenots already thought
    Elizabeth too closely tied to the French monarchy, their enemy: Kingdon, *Myths*, p. 82.
29 K. de L., xi. 23.
30 Collinson, *Grindal*, p. 256.

Canterbury shall be deprived, then up starts the pride and practice of the papists, and down declineth the comfort and strength of her majesty's safety'.[31] The appointment in the same year of John Aylmer, that hammer of conventiclers, to the see of London confirmed the reactionary trend. Protestants who provoked the queen by their innovative zeal, suggested Walsingham in May 1578, would be less reckless if they knew 'with what difficulty we retain that we have'.[32]

A conservative reaction was one thing: the overthrow of Protestantism would be another. The Anjou match raised that larger prospect. 'Most men presaged', the historian William Camden would recall, that the marriage 'would be the overthrow of [the Protestant] religion'.[33] That was not a judgement of hindsight. A memorandum of March 1579, either written or sanctioned by Camden's patron Lord Burghley, sought to counter the wide-spread fear that the match would bring 'the overthrow of [the Protestant] religion', first in England and then abroad;[34] opponents of the match on the council voiced the belief that Anjou, who 'hath showed himself an enemy to the professors of the gospel in France', was 'therefore most likely to attempt the change of religion in England';[35] Sidney, according to Greville, thought it 'probable [Anjou] would . . . endeavou[r] to steal change of religion' into England.[36] In reality neither Anjou nor his family seems to have been interested in achieving the conversion of England to Catholicism. They may have hoped, half-heartedly, to secure toleration for English Catholics, as a means to steering the affection of recusants away from Spain towards France, but they apparently meant to leave England's established religion alone.[37] Yet the anxieties of forward Protestants on that subject were not viewed with scepticism by the advocates of the match. The most that advocates on the council argued, and even then in a gingerly manner, was that Anjou was a less fanatical Catholic than his relations.[38]

The hostility of the forward Protestants to the match intensified the

---

31 Wright, *Queen Elizabeth*, ii. 75.
32 PRO, SP 83/6/54 (*CSPF 1577–8*, p. 670).
33 Quoted by Holt, *Anjou*, p. 123; cf. Stubbs, p. xxxix.
34 *HMC Cecil*, ii. 242. The authorship of that memorandum, which Burghley describes as a 'memorial for the queen's majesty' (ibid., 245), is the subject of uncharacteristically confusing remarks by Read, *Burghley*, pp. 211, 562. Whoever wrote it, it reflects views which Burghley expressed in similar language elsewhere (and compare the remark about the lineage of Henry VIII – *HMC Cecil*, ii. 244 – with the queen's remark recorded in ibid., ii. 272). The document is also close, both in opinions and in wording, to parts of the memorandum to the queen drawn up in August 1578 by the Earl of Sussex, Burghley's ally, in favour of the match: Nicolas, *Hatton*, pp. 81–9.
35 Hatf. 148, fo. 24. Elizabeth's ambassador in Paris, the forward Protestant Sir Amias Paulet, reportedly maintained that the marriage would effect 'some change [*quelque mutation*] in the Protestant religion': PRO, PRO 31/3/27, fo. 358ᵛ. Cf. NRO, F(P)M 111, fo. 4.
36 *GP* 31/1–2. Cf. PRO, PRO 31/3/27, fo. 354; Stubbs, p. xxxix; BL, Lansdowne MS. 28, fos 156&ᵛ.
37 John Bossy, 'English Catholics and the French Marriage, 1577–81', *Recusant History* 5 (1960), pp. 2–18, esp. pp. 4–9.
38 Hatf. 148, fos 26ᵛ, 63; cf. Read, *Walsingham*, ii. 92.

queen's distaste for their evangelical sympathies. As Camden would recall, she now 'began to be a little more incensed against the Puritans, or innovators'.[39] That change was noticed at the time by the French ambassador in London.[40] In the autumn of 1579 the queen was said to be so angered and shaken by the opposition to the suit that she was contemplating the addition of four Roman Catholics to her privy council.[41] The fortunes were rising of a young group of peers and gentry of Catholic faith or sympathies, of whom the two most prominent were Edward de Vere, Earl of Oxford, and Lord Henry Howard, whose elder brother, the Duke of Norfolk, had been executed for treason in 1572.[42] They were warm advocates of the match. Oxford figures famously in Sidney's life because of the quarrel between the two men in 1579, which was ended by the queen after Oxford had challenged Sidney to a duel. The dispute erupted on the tennis-court, where it was watched from a window by French commissioners who were at court to negotiate the marriage. In Greville's account, which has Oxford and Sidney standing on their pride, 'like a dumb show', after the earl had twice 'scornfully call[ed] Sir Philip by the name of puppy', the episode has its comic aspect. Yet more was at stake than the honour and pride of the two men. Behind Oxford, Sidney knew, there lay 'a mighty faction'.[43] Oxford and Leicester hated each other. So did Howard and Leicester, who interpreted each other's conduct during the Anjou crisis in demonic terms. To Howard and his allies, Leicester was a would-be usurper of the throne. To Leicester and his following, Howard was a sinister and dangerous figure, who saw the match as a means to the restoration of Catholicism and to the proscription of the Protestant nobility. He was alleged to have given encouragement to Anjou's agent Simier by informing him that Elizabeth 'was not resolved of what religion to be of'. There was some satisfaction for Leicester and his friends when Howard was imprisoned for six months after the Throckmorton conspiracy of 1583.[44] In 1584 Howard was the object of a literary assault of savage brilliance by Giordano Bruno, who had close links with Sidney and Greville.[45]

Behind the emotional violence of Leicester's party towards their Catholic rivals there lay profound political anxiety. There seemed, as Collinson observes, 'the chance of a real palace revolution'.[46] In the event, Howard

39 Stubbs, p. xxxiv; cf. Alexandre Teulet, ed., *Relations politiques de la France et de l'Espagne avec l'Ecosse au XVIᵉ siècle*, 5 vols (Paris, 1862), iii. 70.
40 PRO, PRO 31/3/27, fo. 358ᵛ.
41 Read, *Walsingham*, ii. 21n.
42 Bossy, 'English Catholics'; Leimon, 'Walsingham', p. 123; D. C. Peck, ed., *Leicester's Commonwealth* (Athens, Ohio, 1985), pp. 14ff.; Read, *Walsingham*, ii. 5n.; MacCaffrey, *Policy*, pp. 261–2.
43 GP 38/21ff.
44 Bossy, *Bruno*, pp. 29–31, 100–1, 123.
45 The assault is marvellously reconstructed in ibid., pp. 117ff.
46 Patrick Collinson, *The Elizabethan Puritan Movement* (London, 1967), p. 200; Bossy, 'English Catholics', p. 7.

would have to wait until James I's reign (when he was made Earl of Northampton) to become a prominent statesman. But in the late 1570s, when he enjoyed the queen's liking, his star was rising. His chief ally during the Anjou negotiations was that prominent supporter of the match the Earl of Sussex, his second cousin, whose own standing improved in the same period thanks to the boldness of his advocacy. Under Elizabeth, Sussex had given up his earlier Catholicism, but he was no friend to forward Protestantism. If England became Catholic again, so might he. Like Howard he was an old enemy of Leicester. He was also an old enemy of Sidney's father Sir Henry, who had once challenged him to a duel, and who saw his hand in the attempts made at court to undermine his own policies in Ireland.[47]

For Leicester, as for the forward Protestant cause he espoused, the Anjou negotiations were a calamity. The conservative reaction of Elizabethan politics was a cause and symptom of his decline, a process in which the period of the Anjou match was critical.[48] Like other members of the Dudley family, Leicester is a hard man to know. His apparent combination of self-interested opportunism and strong (if erratic) commitment to public causes can take baffling forms. A similar and similarly puzzling combination of qualities had characterised his father, the Duke of Northumberland, who had ruled England during the later part of Edward VI's reign. The son, too, aimed for the summit.

At the time of the Anjou negotiations Leicester's chief enemy was his old rival Burghley. His chief ally was Walsingham. Yet Burghley and Walsingham shared a world different from Leicester's. Walsingham had risen through the patronage of Burghley, who in times of crisis was his 'only refuge'.[49] The differences between Burghley and Walsingham could be deep. The two men sometimes connived against each other's policies. Yet at other times they were able to cooperate amicably. They trusted each other's commitment to the regime they served, and sympathised with the strains endured by the other in serving their quixotic monarch. Their statesmanship is in essence that of civil servants. Leicester's is that of a would-be Renaissance prince, of a would-be Anjou or Don John. His is a world of semi-autonomous power-broking, of extravagant display, of munificent patronage of learning and the arts.[50]

In the career of Leicester, as in those of other great courtiers of the sixteenth century, there is a recurrent tension between the ideals of courtly service and those of noble independence. The crown and the courtly nobility were at once partners and rivals. The networks of allegiance built by Leicester, in state and church alike, were a potential challenge to the crown, as Burghley's following never was. Yet the earl remained critically dependent

47 Brady, *Chief Governors*, pp. 114–15, 121–2.
48 Collinson, *Godly People*, pp. 64–5.
49 Lehmberg, *Mildmay*, pp. 107–8.
50 Cf. the account of Leicester in Woudhuysen, 'Leicester's Literary Patronage', ch. 1.

on the queen's favour, 'a man', as she once reminded him, 'raised up by ourself'. 'If you think to rule here', she told him at another time, he should think again, for 'I will have here but one mistress and no master.'[51]

The favour, though bestowed unevenly over time, survived three decades of the reign. We do not know the secrets or extent of the love affair of the early years, and cannot safely estimate its emotional legacy. What seems to have remained constant, up to the Anjou negotiations of 1578–9, was Leicester's hope of marrying the queen. By the 1570s he had acquired a second ambition: to lead an expedition to the Low Countries. For the softening influences of the courts of the Renaissance did not eliminate the hunger of Europe's nobilities for military action. Though he was a late convert to the policy of forward Protestantism which Walsingham had consistently pressed, Leicester invested his prestige in its military fulfilment. As the arguments for English intervention in the Netherlands became stronger in 1576–8, so his hopes of military leadership rose, and so his political standing seemed to rise too.[52] When, early in 1578, the queen first made and then broke her promise to send an army under him, her change of heart devastated and humiliated him.[53] It belittled his stature not only in England but among the Orange party in the Netherlands, who had hoped keenly for his presence there.[54]

A second blow soon followed. Though Elizabeth had declined to marry Leicester, she had at least come to seem unlikely to marry anyone else. In her sounding of Anjou in 1578, the earl evidently came to see the end of his own hopes. He secretly married Lettice Knollys, the daughter of the privy councillor Sir Francis Knollys. The story leaked. Anjou's agent Simier, Camden tells us, took pleasure in relating it to Elizabeth during his mission of 1579.[55]

In the spring of that year, when the council first debated the marriage proposal, no clear balance of opinion emerged. By October, when the debates were resumed, most councillors were against the match.[56] This was not the first occasion when the council was more sympathetic to a forward Protestant position than the queen. It had happened at least four times within the previous four years, over the issues of involvement in the Netherlands and the advancement of religion in England.[57]

The leading advocate of the match in 1579 was Lord Burghley. Burghley's

---

51 Richard McCoy, *The Rites of Knighthood. The Literature and Politics of Elizabethan Chivalry* (Berkeley and Los Angeles, 1989), pp. 48, 45.
52 Rosenberg, *Leicester*, pp. 278–9; MacCaffrey, *Policy*, p. 447.
53 K. de L., x. 318; cf. Nicolas, *Hatton*, pp. 96–7.
54 K. de L., x. 334.
55 MacCaffrey, *Policy*, pp. 261–2.
56 Read, *Walsingham*, ii. 21.
57 For those episodes see: Wright, *Queen Elizabeth*, ii. 76–7; Wilson, *Netherlands*, pp. 35–6; Read, *Burghley*, p. 201 (cf. p. 187); Patrick Collinson, 'The Downfall of Archbishop Grindal and its Place in Elizabethan Political and Ecclesiastical History', in Peter Clark *et al.*, eds, *The English Commonwealth 1547–1580* (Leicester, 1979), pp. 39–57, at pp. 53–4.

political positions are sometimes hard to assess. His memoranda, endlessly
listing pros and cons, can leave us uncertain which side he was on, which of
the arguments he listed were his own, which of them were adopted or
adapted to win over his opponents. In his dealings with his colleagues – not
least with Walsingham over the Anjou match – he could be most circuitous
when he affected to be most straightforward.[58] Yet in pressing for the
marriage he was often blunt and vigorous in his tactics. His advocacy brought
him into close cooperation with the other eager advocate of the match on
the council, the Earl of Sussex.[59] Before the marriage negotiations, Burghley
had occupied a shifting middle ground between Elizabeth and the forward
Protestants. Though always anxious to be, or at least to seem, on the same
side as the queen, he sympathised, at least intermittently, with much of the
forward Protestant programme. He agreed with Walsingham, as the queen
did not, about the need for the more effective proscription of Catholics and
for the promotion of evangelical Protestantism in England. There were times
when, despite the worries which he shared with Elizabeth about the likely
financial costs, he concurred with Walsingham's judgement that English
intervention in the Netherlands had become essential. With Walsingham, he
would have liked England to press for the toleration of Protestantism there,
a goal with which the queen had less sympathy. But in 1579, when Burghley
came down in favour of the Anjou match, he and Walsingham were on
opposite sides.

The council's debates about the match in 1579 were hard fought. The
forward Protestants, ably led by Sir Walter Mildmay, maintained that the
marriage would be a needless surrender of England's strength and independence. They also regarded Anjou's Catholicism as an insuperable argument
against it. That was the ground on which Mildmay had opposed her
prospective marriage to Henry Duke of Anjou in 1570–1 and her suit with
Francis in 1573–4. Now he asserted that marriage to Francis, who 'from his
cradle . . . hath been bred and nourished up in papistry', 'will prove . . .
offensive to God and the world abroad, and dangerous to the realm at home'.
How, he asked, could the queen, who forbade Roman Catholicism among
her subjects, be ready to countenance it in a husband?[60] Knollys asked her the
same question and got a sharp answer.[61]

Advocates of the match believed that that difficulty could be overcome.
They expected Anjou to accept terms that would restrict the exercise and
influence of his religion in England. Thus he would be required to confine
his Catholic devotions to his own household, to attend Protestant services
with the queen from time to time, and to swear not to infringe the laws of
England 'in causes of religion'.[62] But what, asked forward Protestants, would

58 Read, *Burghley*, pp. 195–6.
59 *CSPS 1568–79*, pp. 648, 662–3, 669, 692, 693.
60 Lehmberg, *Mildmay*, pp. 107–9, 162.
61 *CSPS 1568–79*, p. 704.
62 *HMC Cecil*, ii. 242.

such pledges be worth? What was to be inferred from Anjou's treatment of the Huguenots, if not that he would be 'most likely to attempt the change of religion in England to the tyranny of Rome'?[63] Sidney's 'Letter' put the point more politely: the duke was 'of the Romish religion, and if he be a man, must needs have that man-like disposition to desire that all men be of his mind'.[64] Even before the suit began, the strength and confidence of English Catholicism had been on the increase; during the negotiations they may have grown further.[65] The marriage, its opponents feared, would create a momentum of Catholic activity and sentiment which the terms of the treaty would be powerless to withstand. The process would begin with the flocking of papists to mass in Anjou's chapel, which no one would dare to try to stop.[66] 'The papist subject that is ill affected already', predicted Mildmay, 'will take such courage' from the marriage, 'and the Protestant subject such discourage, as the like troubles [= wars of religion] are to be feared here that have been in other countries.'[67] Negotiations over the marriages to Catholic princes which Elizabeth had contemplated earlier had been plagued by the hostility of English Protestants to the prospect of mass being celebrated in a royal household.[68] In 1579 the fear that Anjou would celebrate it on English soil aroused profound resistance. During the council debates of October, Sidney's father Sir Henry was uncompromising: 'a mass may not be suffered in the court', and 'the marriage cannot be made good by all the counsels between England and Rome'.[69]

Public opinion, claimed the leading opponents of the match, would be bitterly hostile to it. The suit was 'misliked generally in the realm'.[70] Anjou himself was 'misliked', not only as a Catholic but, perhaps still more intensely, as a foreigner. In the words persistently used by the opponents of the match, he was a 'stranger' or 'foreign prince' who would take, or try to take, the throne and realm into his own 'possession'. That fear, and the language which expressed it, are frequently echoed in the *Arcadia*. To recognise the echoes we need to meet the voices they return. Sidney told the queen that she would lose the love of her people if she resolved on 'an odious marriage with a stranger'.[71] He spoke for a strong body of opinion both among her advisers and among a wider public. The queen, forward

---

63 Read, *Burghley*, p. 209.
64 *MP* 52/13–15. In a less courtly document Sidney would no doubt have put the point in words closer to those of Thomas Norton in *Orations, of Arsanes*, sig. Ci: 'the nature of tyranny is not only to oppress, to spoil, and to murder innocents, but also to hate all such as are not of the same disposition'; for Norton and Sidney see below, Chapters 9, 11.
65 *CSPS 1568–79*, p. 710 (cf. p. 711); Bossy, 'English Catholics', p. 5.
66 William Murdin, ed., *A Collection of State Papers relating to Affairs in the Reign of Queen Elizabeth from 1571 to 1596* (London, 1759), p. 332; BL, Harleian MS. 6265, fo. 108ᵛ; cf. Hatf. 148, fo. 58.
67 Lehmberg, *Mildmay*, p. 158; cf. Hatf. 148, fo. 31.
68 Doran, *Monarchy and Matrimony*, pp. 88ff., 106ff., 134.
69 Hatf. 140, fo. 7. Cf. Murdin, *Collection*, pp. 333, 336; Stubbs, pp. 11–12, 16.
70 Murdin, *Collection*, p. 332.
71 *MP* 55/5.

Protestants urged, must understand 'the mislike of the people to be governed by a foreign prince, and especially by the blood of France', 'the people of this realm generally hating that nation'.[72] There would be hostility to the taxation necessary to maintain Anjou's state and patronage, 'the rather because it is by the means of a stranger'.[73] 'And can it be', asked John Stubbs's *Gaping Gulph*, 'that a stranger and a Frenchman should possess as owner our queen . . . ?'[74] Calling it 'natural to all men', and to Englishmen as much as to any, 'to abhor foreign rule', Stubbs warned that 'a stranger king . . . will hardly be gotten out again'.[75] Bishop Aylmer, anxiously watching the mood of his London flock as the negotiations proceeded, observed the hatred voiced against Anjou as a 'foreign prince' and 'stranger'.[76] At court, a preacher 'said that marriages with foreigners would only result in ruin to the country'.[77]

French rule, argued opponents of the match, would be tyrannical rule. They feared 'the intolerable yoke of a stranger';[78] they warned that the duke, a 'foreign prince', might 'in time and by degrees bring this realm to his own possession and subjection', to 'servitude and subjection'.[79] He would subjugate both the queen and her country to his will and would thus terminate the independence which they had bravely sustained for the first two decades of her reign. Thus would England, having survived the threat of invasion and conquest for so long, voluntarily and needlessly deliver itself into foreign hands.

There is, then, a contemporary pertinence in the last of the predictions made by the oracle to Basilius at the outset of the *Arcadia*: 'And in thy throne a foreign state shall sit.' The pertinence is amply confirmed by Sidney's subsequent narrative. In Book Two, Basilius, echoing the forward Protestants, admits to Cleophila (the disguised Pyrocles) that her beauty has made 'a prince unconquered to become a slave to a stranger'. Pyrocles' sway over the duke soon provokes a popular mutiny, whose participants complain that 'a strange woman ha[s] now possessed their prince and government'. 'What need', they ask, will Arcadians have 'henceforward to fear foreign enemies, since they were conquered without stroke striking, their secrets opened, their treasures abused, themselves triumphed over, and never overthrown?' 'An

---

72   *HMC Cecil*, ii. 243; Murdin, *Collection*, p. 333 (cf. p. 331); BL, Cottonian MS. Vitellius C XVI, fo. 345; Hatf. 148, fos 24, 43ᵛ (cf. fo. 27ᵛ); NRO, F(P)M 111, fo. 10ᵛ.
73   K. de L., xi. 410; cf. Read, *Burghley*, p. 209.
74   Stubbs, p. 37.
75   Ibid., pp. 34, 49.
76   Nicolas, *Hatton*, p. 133.
77   *CSPS 1568–79*, p. 658. Cf. John Nicholls, *The Progresses and Public Processions of Queen Elizabeth*, 3 vols (London, 1823), ii. 148; John Strype, *The Life of the Learned Sir Thomas Smith* (Oxford, 1820 edn), p. 258.
78   BL, Harleian MS. 6265, fo. 109. Cf. NRO, F(P)M 111, fo. 8ᵛ; William Camden, *The History of . . . Princess Elizabeth . . . Selected Chapters*, ed. Wallace MacCaffrey (Chicago and London, 1970), p. 136; W. R. Morfill, ed., *Ballads Relating Chiefly to the Reign of Queen Elizabeth* (Ballad Society, Hertford, 1873), ii. 114.
79   K. de L., xi. 407; NRO, F(P)M 111, fos 14ᵛ, 15 (cf. F(P)M 99, fo. 2ᵛ); Lehmberg, *Mildmay*, p. 158; BL, Harleian MS. 6265, fo. 108ᵛ; *HMC Cecil*, ii. 240, 269.

unused thing it is', Cleophila concedes, that 'a stranger' should 'possess the regal throne'.[80] Later Philanax protests 'with a just anger' that 'strangers become our lords', and fears that the Arcadians 'will have strangers' as their 'princes'. Through the conduct of the 'stranger' Pyrocles, argues Philanax, the Arcadians have suffered 'a greater overthrow than our mightiest enemies have been ever able to lay upon us'.[81]

Elizabeth's predecessor, Mary Tudor, had married a 'stranger', Philip II of Spain. Opponents of the Anjou match compared it to that earlier union. Sidney was, he told Elizabeth, troubled to think 'what events time would have brought forth of that marriage' had Mary lived longer.[82] In reality the terms of Mary's marriage had been favourable to England. They had guaranteed the continuance of the country's laws and customs and had severely restricted Philip's formal powers in government. For that reason the English negotiators, in discussions with Anjou's representatives, insisted on the terms of the Marian treaty as the basis of the present one. Burghley was confident that conditions could be agreed that would prevent Anjou, even though he would have the title of king, 'from intermeddling with the government of the realm'.[83] Certainly the duke's wish for a legislative veto was firmly resisted by the English negotiators, as was his desire for a ceremony of coronation.[84] But of what use would be the restrictions to which Anjou agreed? Here too Burghley's opponents on the council, always alert for evidence of French duplicity, had no faith in the promises of the duke, whose instinct, they held, was to rule by the sword and not by law. 'No bonds, no acts of parliament,' they warned, 'will serve.'[85] Sidney agreed. It was not 'to be hoped for', he told Elizabeth, 'that he will be contained within the limits of your conditions', or that he would settle for being 'the second person' in England and 'pretend no way sovereignty'.[86] Of course, forward Protestants conceded, it might take a 'long time' for that 'foreign prince' to 'usurp the state'; but his 'ambitio[n]', and his readiness to 'abuse' the queen's trust, would in the end make him 'lor[d] of . . . [the] kingdom'.[87]

There were other, no less fundamental objections to the match. Outside the queen's hearing, councillors who opposed it remarked bluntly that she was 'not meet to marry considering her years', for 'few old maids escape' the perils of childbirth. Anjou, and the threat he posed to England, would probably outlive her, for she was 'old enough to be his mother'. (In fact he

---

80   *OA* 5/20, 96/23–4, 127/20–1, 127/22–5, 129/24–8, 133/32–3.
81   *OA* 324/36–8, 353/16, 388/25–6; cf. *OA* 354/25–6. Elizabeth makes a parallel mistake to that of Basilius, who imagines that the 'only way . . . a foreign prince might endanger his crown' is by invasion: *OA* 6/28–9.
82   *MP* 50/14–15; cf. F(P)M 111, fos 8&ᵛ, 9ᵛ.
83   Murdin, *Collection*, p. 333. Cf. ibid., pp. 334, 334–5; Hatf. 148, fos 63ᵛ–64.
84   *CSPF* 1578–9, p. 504; Hatf. 148, fos 42–45ᵛ; cf. Doran, *Monarchy and Matrimony*, p. 174.
85   Murdin, *Collection*, p. 332. Cf. BL, Harleian MS. 6265, fo. 109ᵛ; PRO, SP 15/26/*35, fo. 126&ᵛ.
86   *MP* 49/32–50/1.
87   NRO, F(P)M, fos 7ᵛ, 11; cf. Stubbs, pp. 21–2.

would die, after a series of miserable failures in the Low Countries, in 1584.)
It looked no less likely that the sickly Henry III of France, whose days
seemed numbered and who appeared certain to remain childless, would be
survived by Anjou, who would thus soon succeed to the French throne.[88] (In
fact Henry would live, albeit remaining childless, until his assassination in
1589.) Once he was King of France, Anjou would leave Elizabeth behind
him, 'as King Philip did . . . Queen Mary'.[89] England would thus become, in
international diplomacy, a pawn of France, as (argued opponents of the
match) it had been a pawn of Spain under Mary Tudor.[90]

And how would Anjou, if his marriage to Elizabeth produced no children,
behave on her death, particularly if he had by then succeeded to the kingdom
of France? 'What', asked opponents of the match, would he 'not do, to retain
the crown of England [in] his own actual possession'?[91] The chances were
that he would 'have a purpose to marry the Queen of Scots, by whom he
may enjoy both England and Scotland' and thus 'establish in his issue all the
three crowns of France, England and Scotland'.[92] Indeed, if his marriage to
Elizabeth proved childless, might he not, in her lifetime, use his new English
power-base to free himself from her and marry Mary instead? That last
argument may sound to us alarmist. Yet it was generally treated with respect
by advocates of the match.

And what if the marriage did, against the odds, produce an heir or heirs?
What would happen, it was especially asked, if the union were to produce a
single, male child, who would inherit the two crowns of England and
France? As the English negotiators conceded,[93] he would then live mainly in
France. England would thus be 'spoiled of the comfort of a king', 'the
greatest mischief that can come to the perpetual diminution of the glory of
this kingdom'.[94] Whatever the dynastic future, the chances were that, sooner
or later, England would be ruled, 'greatly to the discontentment of the
realm', through a viceroy, 'whereby great calamities may ensue'. The dread
of a 'viceroy' provided a rallying cry of opposition.[95] England, feared
Mildmay, would become 'a province to France', with 'the loss of our ancient
freedom, privileges and liberties'.[96] Stubbs warned that the country would
suffer the fate of Rome's provinces under its proconsuls or of Spain's modern
possessions under viceroys.[97] The uniting of the two crowns by the marriage

88 Murdin, *Collection*, pp. 332, 333; cf. Lehmberg, *Mildmay*, pp. 162–3.
89 *HMC Cecil*, ii. 269.
90 Murdin, *Collection*, p. 332.
91 Hatf. 148, fo. 57.
92 Ibid., fo. 23ᵛ; *CSPF 1578–9*, p. 474; Read, *Burghley*, p. 209; *HMC Cecil*, ii. 270. Cf. PRO, SP
    15/26/*35, fos 132ff.; *CSPS 1568–79*, pp. 668–9.
93 Camden, *History*, ed. MacCaffrey, p. 132.
94 *HMC Cecil*, ii. 270; Hatf. 148, fo. 24.
95 K. de L., x. 744, xi. 407; *HMC Cecil*, ii. 270; Hatf. 148, fo. 36; NRO, F(P)M 111, fos 2, 7ᵛ, 10ᵛ,
    14ᵛ; Read, *Walsingham*, ii. 16.
96 Stubbs, pp. 52–3; cf. BL, Harleian MS. 6265, fo. 109.
97 Stubbs, pp. 52–3; cf. PRO, SP 15/26/*35, fos 145ᵛ–6.

constituted the 'difficulty', explained Walsingham in August 1578, which 'above all others I do weigh'.[98]

Effective as such arguments against the match proved, and sincerely as they were propounded, there is an element of defensiveness in them, at moments even of desperation. The opponents of the marriage found themselves having to alter or adjust a number of the positions they had adopted earlier when pressing for military intervention on the continent. For the marriage negotiations, which damaged the fortunes both of forward Protestantism and of Leicester, enabled Burghley to turn their previous arguments against them. Walsingham and his friends might complain that only the queen's neglect of their advice had caused her even to have to contemplate marriage to Anjou. But now that England was experiencing the isolation against which they had warned, what remedy did they propose? Forward Protestants had consistently emphasised the size and imminence of the threat posed to England by the Catholic powers. Yet now, instead of addressing 'the present peril', they were resorting to hypothetical or 'imaginative' arguments about 'future' dangers which might arise when Elizabeth or Henry III should die. Those dangers were 'uncertain', 'conditional', 'contingent', 'accidental'.[99] Who could say who would outlive whom, or what Anjou would or would not do if his marriage to Elizabeth disappointed him or produced no heir? Who could tell how the diplomatic map of Europe might change in the years ahead or what opportunities they might produce for England's deliverance from the continental threat? The Anjou marriage, its advocates pointed out, was intended to meet not 'uncertain' future perils but 'certain' present ones.[100] Without it, England and its Protestant neighbours would remain helpless against the 'malice' and 'revenge' of 'the pope, the French king, and the King of Spain', who could be expected to join in 'sending some part of their forces to England, Scotland and Ireland, to stir up civil wars in each of those countries'. The Huguenots would confront the 'peril . . . of utter ruin', and 'the common cause of religion will be like to go to ruin'.[101]

Forward Protestants were not deaf to those arguments. Indeed the arguments could prevail over their deepest instincts. The forward Protestant Thomas Wilson seems to have advocated the match from the outset of the negotiations.[102] Such persistent support was exceptional among the politicians

---

98 K. de L., x. 744. Cf. Lehmberg, *Mildmay*, pp. 162–3; Murdin, *Collection*, p. 336.

99 *HMC Cecil*, ii. 241, 242; Murdin, *Collection*, p. 334; cf. PRO, SP 15/26/*35, fos 146, 163.

100 Murdin, *Collection*, p. 334.

101 *HMC Cecil*, ii. 250, 268, 245, 243.

102 PRO, SP 12/123/17; Murdin, *Collection*, p. 332; Read, *Walsingham*, ii. 27n. Wilson was a client both of Leicester and of Burghley, and thus of the most powerful opponent and of the most powerful advocate of the match. The arguments for the match which he apparently advanced as early as April 1578 (SP 12/123/17), when the negotiations were in their tentative infancy, anticipate Burghley's reasoning of 1579. Another forward Protestant, Sir Nicholas Bacon, had favoured an earlier proposal that Elizabeth marry into the house of Valois: NRO, F(P)M 99; J. Payne Collier, ed., *The Egerton Papers* (London, Camden Society, 1840), pp. 50–9. In 1578

who had urged vigorous English intervention in the Netherlands in the previous years. But in March 1580 the leaders of that party were temporarily won over to the Anjou suit. Leicester and Walsingham were now so alarmed by the prospect of an alliance between Henry III and the Guises and of French action against England that they 'earnestly moved her majesty to go through with the marriage as her most safety'.[103] It is possible that Walsingham, for the same reason, was again in favour of the match in September 1580.[104] Similar considerations had moved him in the same direction before. In 1571, seeing Elizabeth 'beset with foreign peril', he had concluded that marriage to Henry, the then Duke of Anjou, offered her only salvation.[105] In August 1578, observing the severity of the French threat to the Netherlands, he half accepted the logic of the Anjou match.[106] That logic had always to contend with his inmost convictions. But it could be hard to answer.

In 1579 the advocates of the match presented it as an opportunity, even an extraordinary one, to achieve by a single stroke of peaceful diplomacy the goals which forward Protestants had wanted the queen to meet by bloody and expensive means. The conjunction of Elizabeth and Anjou, they argued, would constitute a formidable power-bloc. Henry III would not dare to threaten England; there would be no more need to incite Huguenots to revolt or to subsidise them or their French and German allies; instead the queen's new influence over France would secure toleration for the Huguenots and counter the Catholic tendencies of Henry's policies. The danger from Spain would be ended too. Philip II would no longer 'dare to trouble or offend her majesty'. There would be no further necessity for England to intervene in the Low Countries, where Spain could be brought to reasonable terms.[107] Indeed the queen would become 'the author of an universal peace in Christendom'; she 'shall by her greatness keep a hand over France, the Low Countries, Spain, Scotland, and all her own dominions; shall be honoured and esteemed abroad for the avoiding of bloodshed'.[108]

Those grandiloquent claims may sound as strained as some of the protests against the match. Yet there were those who saw in the marriage still larger opportunities for England. Great as Elizabeth might become as a peace-maker, she could become greater still by joining her new husband in war. That was not a prospect to appeal to Burghley,[109] but Sussex, whose arguments were in other respects close to Burghley's, parted from him in holding

---

both Wilson and Bacon were readier than other forward Protestants to think that Anjou's involvement in the Low Countries might be turned to England's advantage: K. de L., x. 634; Doran, *Monarchy and Matrimony*, p. 146 (and see ibid., p. 79).

103 Read, *Walsingham*, ii. 31.
104 Bossy, 'English Catholics', pp. 7–8.
105 Read, *Walsingham*, i. 117, 136; cf. ibid., 109.
106 K. de L., x. 744.
107 *HMC Cecil*, ii. 242, 244, 270, 272; Nicolas, *Hatton*, p. 83; K. de L., xi. 408.
108 *HMC Cecil*, ii. 242, 244; cf. PRO, SP 15/26/*35, fo. 113.
109 Hatf. 148, fo. 81.

it before the queen. He suggested, albeit tentatively, that she might make use of her marriage to annex the Low Countries to the English crown, or at least to divide them between England and France.[110] That argument was taken seriously on the council.[111] There was support for it outside the council too. For it was not only forward Protestants who contemplated a militant foreign policy for England. Sussex's ally Lord Henry Howard, perhaps the Catholic advocate of the match whom forward Protestants most feared and hated, maintained that the marriage would equip England to return to its medieval days of martial greatness in Europe.[112]

How galling it must have been to forward Protestants to watch the case for courage and decisiveness in foreign policy being usurped by their rivals, who refused to see foreign policy in confessional terms. In one sense, it is true, the negotiations with Anjou might seem to have been a gain for forward Protestantism. Viewed in the long term, the marriage negotiations were a critical stage in England's adoption of the actively anti-Spanish diplomacy which forward Protestants had demanded, and which in the years ahead would lead England into war with Spain. Though Elizabeth's readiness to hearken to the marriage proposal seemed to Sidney's party a mark of weakness, her instinct for caution and neutrality and passivity was beginning to yield to more positive and assertive tendencies.[113] That is why the conflicts between the queen and the forward Protestants would lose some of their edge in the 1580s (though by no means all of it). But at the time of the Anjou negotiations the tide of royal policy seemed to be running against Sidney's patrons and allies. They did not leave the claims of Burghley and Sussex unanswered. Mildmay claimed that the marriage, far from protecting the Huguenots, would drive a wedge between them and Elizabeth and be 'the next way to overthrow them'; that it was 'marvellous unlikely' that the union would bring Spain to reasonable terms in the Low Countries; that the Netherlands were 'not so easy . . . to conquer' as Sussex had suggested; that an attempt to conquer them would 'bring us into endless war and troubles'.[114] But the initiative of debate had passed to Mildmay's opponents. That ascendancy did not translate itself, on the council, into a majority of votes. But forward Protestants had all too often seen their own majorities count for nothing in the queen's decisions. Councillors whose views were attuned to her wishes had a built-in advantage.

Forward Protestants, having a built-in disadvantage in 1579, were also confronted with new complexities, which were confusing to them and which for the same reason can be confusing to us. For just when the queen began to think of the Spanish threat as England's main priority, the forward

110 Nicolas, *Hatton*, p. 84; cf. Read, *Burghley*, pp. 201–2.
111 NRO, F(P)M, fo. 15
112 Stubbs, p. 166; cf. below, p. 166.
113 MacCaffrey, *Policy*, pp. 243–4, 252.
114 Lehmberg, *Mildmay*, p. 158; cf. Stubbs, p. 27.

Protestants ceased to do so. Walsingham saw that Elizabeth, in order to thwart Catholic Spain, was willing to marry a Catholic Frenchman. Amid the variations of English diplomatic calculation in the late 1570s, the Anjou match had for the queen and for its advocates one persistent and overriding attraction: it would give England a French ally against Spain.[115] The queen hoped to bring France, the Duke of Anjou and herself together in an anti-Spanish front. To Walsingham that remedy would be worse than the disease. If he saw a use for Anjou, it was as a means of restraining not Spain but France. It was with that end in mind that he momentarily acknowledged the case for the match in August 1578, that he momentarily advocated it in March 1580, and that he may have momentarily advocated it again in September 1580. Those moments apart, however, he and his fellow opponents of the match thought the marriage likely not to reduce the French threat but to increase it.[116] In 1579–80 the accustomed priorities both of Elizabeth and of the forward Protestants were thus reversed. She, who had feared France more than Spain, came to fear Spain more than France: they, who had feared Spain more than France, came to fear France more than Spain.[117] The Anjou negotiations, which reflected that change in her, were the cause of the change in them.

In other ways too, the Anjou suit placed its opponents on the defensive. Forward Protestants had called for the queen to marry and produce an heir. Yet it was the advocates of the match who were now favouring a course which, however poor the biological prospects, at least addressed that need.[118] The queen made it plain during the negotiations that, if she ever married, it would be to no one but Anjou.[119] Why then, asked advocates of the match, should her aim be resisted? Their opponents claimed to have the nation on their side, and Burghley conceded that Anjou was 'hateful to the people of the realm'.[120] Yet how deep, he asked, did the opposition go? Had not her parliaments time and again urged her to marry whom she wished?[121] Those were fair points. Walsingham himself explained in the spring of 1579 that the queen's failure to settle the succession was a principal source of the 'discontentment in the subjects'.[122] Advocates of the match indicated that it would be harder for the queen to carry the nation against the marriage than with it. If the negotiations succeeded, her subjects would interpret the marriage as evidence of her 'great . . . care' for them: if they broke down, they would

115 K. de L., x. 410; NRO, F(P)M 111, fo. 15. Cf. Hatf. 148, fo. 81; Read, *Walsingham*, i. 295.
116 Cf. NRO, F(P)M, fo. 11.
117 Cf. Stubbs, pp. 38, 50, 63–4.
118 K. de L., xi. 408.
119 *HMC Cecil*, ii. 272.
120 Ibid., 388.
121 Ibid., 243; Murdin, *Collection*, p. 334; Hatf. 148, fo. 23. Cf. PRO, SP 15/26/*35, fo. 135; Read, *Burghley*, p. 208.
122 Above, p. 72; cf. *CSPF 1578–9*, p. 473.

think her indifferent to their fate after her death, and their affections would increasingly turn towards Mary, that 'rising sun'.[123]

A further argument for the marriage was likewise difficult to answer. In 1578 the queen had recognised a pragmatic case for backing Anjou in the Netherlands: if he did not ally with England he would ally with one of England's enemies. There was an analogous argument for her marriage to him in 1579. For if Anjou were 'rejected' by Elizabeth, there was every danger that he would 'give himself wholly over to the papists, looking to make himself strong by them'.[124] In particular he might pursue the proposal recently favoured by Philip II that he marry the Infanta Isabel. Thus might he win the support not only of Spain but of Spain's Catholic friends. Thus might he be granted the sovereignty of the Low Countries, perhaps even Spanish blessing for an invasion of England and for his own enthronement there.[125] His vacillating matrimonial ambitions were represented in Sidney's 'Letter' as characteristic of his inconstancy, the duke 'sometimes seeking the King of Spain's daughter, sometimes your majesty'.[126] Yet his weakness of character only heightened the fears of him. In the Protestant imagination Anjou had replaced Don John of Austria as the prospective 'head' of the popish interest, whose ambitions would draw Rome and Madrid and Paris together.[127] In February 1580 the council discussed the 'peril' that would ensue if he turned from Elizabeth to Isabel. An alliance could be expected between Spain and France that would dominate Scotland, 'set up the Queen of Scots' in England, and 'supplant the [Protestant] religion in Europe'.[128]

By contrast the marriage of Anjou to Elizabeth, argued its advocates, would crush the hopes of Mary Queen of Scots, both during and after Elizabeth's lifetime. She would cease, at least in the eyes of France, to be the principal Catholic contender for the throne. If the marriage bore fruit she would cease to be a significant candidate for it at all. But if the negotiations broke down, the queen's discontented subjects would persist in the hope of a 'successor . . . who w[ould] restore popery and extirpate the true religion, in which there would be no lack of assistance from abroad'.[129] As so often in the debates of 1579, advocates of the match used language which had for long been favoured (though it had never been monopolised) by forward Protestants. The marriage would prevent 'dissensions after [the queen's] death' and their likely consequences: 'slaughter and destruction'; the 'desolation . . . and perhaps servitude' of the realm; the extirpation of the true faith 'by fire

123 For that phrase see below, p. 191.
124 *HMC Cecil*, ii. 242.
125 Ibid., 242–3, 251, 308; Murdin, *Collection*, p. 331; K. de L., xi. 408; Bodl., Rawlinson MS. A331, fo. 80ᵛ; Hatf. 148, fos 35&ᵛ, 49; NRO, F(P)M 111, fo. 15; Read, *Walsingham*, ii. 15; MacCaffrey, *Policy*, p. 245.
126 *MP* 49/24–5.
127 Hatf. 148, fos 48ᵛ–9; PRO, SP 12/123/17 (fo. 53ᵛ).
128 Lehmberg, *Mildmay*, p. 163.
129 *HMC Cecil*, ii. 268.

and sword'.[130] The leaders of international Catholicism would unite behind Mary, seeing in her accession 'a highway to overthrow the Protestant religion throughout all Christendom'. England would remain at the mercy of France, of Spain, of the Guises, of the pope. Those powers, which could 'easily procure stirs and rebellions in sundry parts of the realm at [an] instant', would achieve the 'avenge' upon England which forward Protestants had for many years expected them to attempt.[131]

Armed with such reasoning, Burghley questioned the sincerity of the opponents of the match. When their arguments were met, he complained, they improvised new ones.[132] They invoked 'the cause of religion to hinder her majesty's marriage and thereby the succession', but gave no thought to the fate of that cause, or to the occupancy of the throne, after her death.[133] In reality they gave those subjects anxious attention. One candidate for the succession, favoured by Sidney and perhaps by Mornay and Languet too, was James VI of Scotland.[134] To prepare the ground, England must reassert control over Scotland. James must be brought up – ideally, no doubt, by his former tutor, the ageing George Buchanan[135] – in sound principles of Protestantism and responsible kingship. An alternative candidate, though it is not clear whether his fellow forward Protestants were prepared to run him, was Leicester's brother-in-law Henry Hastings, Earl of Huntingdon, the President of the Council of the North, who was of royal blood.[136] But the obstacles in the way of either candidacy would be formidable. Neither of them offered a reassuring answer to Burghley's criticism.

A memorandum for the queen in March 1579, which Burghley either wrote or endorsed, struck at opponents of the match who, while pretending to 'be zealous in religion', used religion 'to serve for faction'.[137] The memorandum did not name the Earl of Leicester. It did not need to. Its animus against him is transparent. Amid numerous inconsistencies, indicated the document, Leicester had been loyal to one aim only: the prevention of Elizabeth's marriage to anyone but himself.[138] The document accused him of

130   Ibid., 270, 245, 249.
131   Ibid., 249, 250.
132   Ibid., 271.
133   Ibid., 243.
134   *MP* 54/13–14, 184; Levy, 'Correspondence', no. 40; Phillips, 'Buchanan', pp. 37–8; cf. Thomas Blenerhasset, *A Revelation of the True Minerva*, ed. Josephine Waters Bennett (New York, 1941), p. viii. If James succeeded shortly, there would be the problem, as under Edward VI, of a boy king. It is conceivable that Sidney's description of the corruption of Macedon in the nonage of Euarchus, which may point back to Edward's Protestant reign (above, Chapter 3, n. 39), also, or instead, warns of such a danger under the Protestant James.
135   Phillips, 'Buchanan', pp. 36–8.
136   S. L. Adams, 'The Protestant Cause: Religious Allegiance with the West European Calvinist Communities as a Political Issue in England, 1585–1630' (Oxford Univ. D.Phil. thesis, 1972), pp. 85–7; *MP* 132/14–24; *CSPF 1578–9*, p. 119. Cf. Peck, *Leicester's Commonwealth*, pp. 38–9; Rogers, *Leicester's Ghost*, pp. 43, 51; *CSPF 1579–80*, p. 119.
137   *HMC Cecil*, ii. 243.
138   The same charge is made in the same spirit in PRO, SP 15/26/*35, fos 123ᵛ–4.

duplicity on an earlier occasion, in 1567, when he had opposed her prospective marriage to another 'stranger', Archduke Charles of Austria. The charge was accurate. While outwardly professing enthusiasm for that match, the earl had secretly been its most determined enemy.[139] He behaved similarly in the spring of 1579, when – knowing better than to express overt opposition to the suit[140] – he represented himself to the French ambassador as the friend of France who would win over the Protestant nobility to it.[141]

For now, as in 1567, the insincerity of Leicester's support had become plain. After the Austrian suit had been broken off, recalled the memorandum, he had favoured a 'device' to marry Mary Queen of Scots to the Duke of Norfolk. Burghley had bitter reason to remember that initiative, which had been professedly designed to stabilise the realm but really intended, at least in part, to break his power. Its results, observed the memorandum, had been catastrophic. It had led to the Northern Rising of 1569 and had made necessary the execution of the Duke of Norfolk for treason. 'God grant', added the document, that if the Anjou match were thwarted 'there be not also another device to make the queen sure by her greatest enemies . . . and thereby a like practice to overthrow her majesty and religion'. Alluding to the conspiracy of Sir Thomas Wyatt against Mary Tudor and her foreign husband, the document intimated that Leicester's present objection to the queen's marriage to a 'stranger' 'doth . . . savour of Wyatt's humour'. That was a shrewd hit, for men who had been involved in Wyatt's rising formed a significant element of the Dudley connection under Elizabeth.[142] Leicester's present conduct, suggested the memorandum, 'showeth a disposition of the alienating of the crown from the right succession . . . which can never proceed from a true English heart'.[143]

While the councillors debated the match in 1579, there grew up an intense public hostility to it: a hostility which foreshadowed the emotions produced, exactly a century later, by the fear that Charles II would be succeeded by his Catholic brother. Philippe Duplessis-Mornay observed that the marriage proposal of 1579, 'agreeable to one side, odious to the other', had 'split' the country into 'leagues' ('ligues') and had set the court and council alight.[144] Of the two sides, the opposition was much the more voluble. Explaining to Anjou her decision, in the midwinter of 1579–80, to suspend the negotiations, the queen declared that public opinion was too adverse for the match

139 Conyers Read, *Mr. Secretary Cecil and Queen Elizabeth* (London, 1955), p. 333.
140 K. de L., x. 679–80.
141 MacCaffrey, *Policy*, pp. 250, 261. Cf. *CSPS 1568–79*, p. 659; Hatf. 140, fo. 6 (with which compare Murdin, *Collection*, pp. 333, 335).
142 Simon Adams, 'The Dudley Clientele, 1553–1563', in G. W. Bernard, ed., *The Tudor Nobility* (Manchester, 1992), pp. 241–65, at pp. 246ff.; cf. Peck, *Leicester's Commonwealth*, pp. 75–7.
143 *HMC Cecil*, ii. 243–4; cf. Stubbs, p. 175.
144 *Mémoires et Correspondance de Duplessis-Mornay*, ii. 238–9. Cf. Peck, *Leicester's Commonwealth*, p. 232; *MP* 47/19–20.

to go forward.[145] Though that claim may have been a pretext, used to justify the suspension of the negotiations,[146] contemporary accounts agree on the extent and intensity of public feeling.[147] It seems likely – though we can say no more – that in the autumn of 1579 the queen's wish to marry Anjou was thwarted by her own subjects.[148] If so, we can understand why she was usually less eager to press for the match thereafter.

Sixteenth-century evidence of public opinion is generally thin. But the animation and mobilisation of that opinion in 1579 are visible enough. The ballad which introduced Anjou to English folklore, 'The frog he would a-wooing go', was only one of the songs produced by the suit. Writings and placards and posters were spread in the London streets or fixed to the Lord Mayor's door or even, it was said, placed in the queen's chamber.[149] Puritan sermons became bolder and sharper and more inflammatory.[150] The government, fearing that the popular hostility might cause insurrection or disturbance, vainly tried to keep Anjou's visit in August secret.[151] Public feeling was heightened by the appearance of John Stubbs's *The Discovery of a Gaping Gulph*, which represented the match as 'the swallowing gulf of our bottomless destruction'. The tract had been written by 4 August, less than a fortnight before Anjou's arrival at Greenwich. By 7 August it had been carried to the printer, who produced a thousand copies.[152] It was published in September. Stubbs, the brother-in-law of the Presbyterian leader Thomas Cartwright, had strong ties to the radical Puritan community.[153] His pamphlet, wrote that enemy of Puritans Bishop Aylmer, had 'kindled' 'sparks of murmuring, misliking, and misconstruing of matters of state' among 'the busier sort' in London and had produced similar 'grudging and groaning' 'abroad in the country (and the further off the worse)'.[154] Copies of Stubbs's pamphlet were urgently sought out by the government and seized.[155]

The sentence on Stubbs – the smiting off of his writing-hand – was also passed on the M.P. William Page, gentleman-servant to the forward Protestant the Earl of Bedford. Page had sent fifty copies of the pamphlet to his fellow M.P. Sir Richard Greenville for circulation in Cornwall.[156] Lawyers

145   MacCaffrey, *Policy*, pp. 263–4; Doran, *Monarchy and Matrimony*, p. 175.
146   Cf. Murdin, *Collection*, p. 328.
147   MacCaffrey, *Policy*, p. 264.
148   Wallace MacCaffrey, *Elizabeth I* (London, 1993), p. 206.
149   Read, *Walsingham*, ii. 21n.; *CSPS 1568–79*, ii. 638, 701; PRO, SP 15/26/*35, fos 93ᵛ, 140ᵛ–1; cf. *CSPV 1558–80*, p. 623.
150   *CSPS 1568–79*, p. 667; PRO, PRO 31/3/27, fo. 358ᵛ.
151   *CSPS 1568–79*, pp. 680, 690, 692, 693, 705.
152   Stubbs, p. xxvi.
153   Ibid., p. xxv. Sidney's 'Letter' to the queen, for all its resemblances to Stubbs's pamphlet, is a conspicuously less Puritan document than Stubbs's.
154   Nicolas, *Hatton*, pp. 132–3.
155   Stubbs, pp. xxvii–xxix.
156   Kenneth Barnes, 'John Stubbe, 1579: the French Ambassador's Account', *Historical Research* 64 (1991), pp. 421–6, at p. 421; Leimon, 'Walsingham', p. 44. For Bedford see also *CSPS 1568– 79*, p. 692; Bodl., Rawlinson MS. A331, fo. 82ᵛ.

earned the queen's wrath by contesting the legality of the sentences. A Chief Justice of the Common Pleas was 'so sharply reprehended that he resigned his place'; another lawyer was sent to the Tower.[157] Even advocates of the match urged the queen to appease popular opinion by mitigating the sentence. She refused. Enraged as she was by Stubbs's conduct, her resolve to make an example of him was said to be 'inexorable'.[158]

On 3 November the sentences were carried out 'in the Market-place at Westminster'.[159] The executions made a deep impression on their public audience. Stubbs heightened the drama, as the blood passed from his veins, by suggesting to the crowd that the bleeding might be unstaunchable. Page, 'lifting up the stump' after two blows had struck off his hand, 'said to the people "I have left there a true Englishman's hand", and so went from the scaffold very stoutly and with a great courage'.[160] The punishment intensified the public opposition to the match, as did the proclamation which condemned Stubbs's tract.[161] Yet 'her majesty's high indignation' persisted, and Stubbs would remain in prison until 1581.[162]

For all her wrath, the queen knew that the sentiments aroused by the match required careful handling. Her proclamation against it, issued on 27 September, assured her subjects that any marriage treaty with Anjou would be submitted to parliament for confirmation.[163] There were those who believed that, if the negotiations persisted, the state of public feeling would make the recall of parliament (which was under prorogation) unavoidable in any case.[164]

Public opinion against the match was led from above. That leadership had to be discreetly managed. We nonetheless catch glimpses of it. During the council debates of the spring of 1579, preachers at court were 'somewhat too busy' in 'apply[ing] their sermons to tend covertly against this marriage, many of them inveighing greatly thereat', until the queen ordered that none of them should preach 'upon any such text as the like might be inferred'.[165] During one such sermon she angrily 'rose', though we are not told what she did next. Yet no action was taken against the offending preachers. That, suggested the Spanish ambassador realistically, was because 'they are inspired from high quarters'.[166] There was certainly inspiration from high quarters behind Stubbs's pamphlet, which was close in content to statements made by

---

157 MacCaffrey, *Policy*, p. 257; cf. Stubbs, p. xxxv.
158 Barnes, 'John Stubbe', p. 425.
159 Ibid., p. 424.
160 Stubbs, pp. xxv–xxvi; NRO, F(P)M 204.
161 *CSPS 1568–79*, p. 702.
162 Stubbs, pp. xxxvii, 112.
163 Ibid., pp. 151–2; cf. PRO, SP 15/26/*35, fos 126, 128.
164 *CSPS 1568–78*, pp. 689–90, 692. Cf. ibid., pp. 700, 703, 705; *CSPV 1558–80*, pp. 585, 587, 619, 623–6; Read, *Walsingham*, ii. 28n.; cf. Stubbs, p. xxvii.
165 Edmund Lodge, *Illustrations of British History*, 3 vols (London, 1838), ii. 150.
166 *CSPS 1568–79*, p. 659; cf. PRO, PRO 31/3/27, fo. 368ᵛ.

councillors who opposed the match.[167] The queen believed that Stubbs and his agents were merely 'the secretaries of men more wicked than they'.[168] On the continent it was known to friends of leading forward Protestants that their English allies had been implicated in the pamphlet.[169]

It was probably during or immediately after Anjou's visit in August that Leicester had an interview with the queen. Mendoza, the Spanish ambassador, reported that the earl was 'in great grief' and that on his emergence from the interview 'his emotion was remarked'. Mendoza added that a meeting was held the same night at the London home of the Earl of Pembroke, Philip Sidney's brother-in-law, 'there being present Lord Sidney [Philip's father] and other friends and relatives [Philip among them?]. They no doubt discussed the matter, and some of them afterwards remarked that parliament would have something to say as to whether the queen married or not.'[170]

By November, Leicester's position was wretched. Reportedly he sent a chaplain to the queen with a paper of arguments against the match, only for Elizabeth to have the chaplain imprisoned. Around that time the earl seems to have confined himself to his own house, perhaps voluntarily, perhaps on royal orders. He may have offered to go into exile.[171] Walsingham, whom the queen was said to suspect of involvement in Stubbs's pamphlet,[172] was fiercely rebuked by her for obstructing the marriage and ordered to leave court.[173] He was back by the end of the year, but not yet allowed to speak to her.[174]

Sidney's 'Letter' was a central contribution to the campaign against the match. It cannot be precisely dated. Its Oxford editors argue that it is likeliest to have been composed during the last two months of 1579. In the parallels of argument and phrasing between it and Stubbs's pamphlet they find an indication that Sidney 'had read Stubbs carefully'.[175] Perhaps; or perhaps Stubbs had read Sidney carefully. A likelier period of composition is the late summer, during the swelling of opposition to the match in and around August that also produced the *Gaping Gulph*. For would Sidney have risked writing the 'Letter' late in the year, when his principal protectors, Leicester and Walsingham, were in disgrace? Would he have written the passages hostile to Anjou later than 27 September, when the queen's proclamation

167 MacCaffrey, *Elizabeth I*, p. 203.
168 Barnes, 'John Stubbe', p. 425.
169 *CSPF 1579–80*, pp. 73, 99 (cf. p. 84); *Mémoires et correspondance de Duplessis-Mornay*, ii. 83; cf. Read, *Walsingham*, ii. 20. A long reply to Stubbs, which was evidently intended for publication or circulation, drew, as Stubbs did, on material that must have come from a source at the centre of government (whom I would guess to be Burghley): PRO, SP 15/26/*35, fo. 120&ᵛ, and the references above, notes 121, 138. Its anonymous author had sat in parliament: ibid., fos 140ᵛ–1.
170 *CSPS 1568–79*, p. 693; cf. ibid., p. 660.
171 *CSPV 1558–80*, p. 623; GP 36/9–10; BL, Harleian MS. 6992, no. 57.
172 *CSPV 1558–80*, p. 621.
173 *CSPS 1568–79*, p. 704.
174 *CSPF 1579–80*, p. 111.
175 *MP* 33–4.

against Stubbs's tract expressed her anger at the 'slanders' and 'lies' which it had directed at the duke, calumnies which Sidney's attacks on him resemble?[176] Would he indeed, once the queen's response to Stubbs's pamphlet was known, have risked including phrases which had appeared in it?

Whenever Sidney wrote the 'Letter', he pursued, as Greville intimates, a risky course, 'being neither magistrate nor counsellor'.[177] A sermon commissioned from high within the government attacked Stubbs, who, 'being a private man, durst so far presume to look into the secret bosom of princes' councils and high magistrates, and to meddle with matters . . . above his reach'.[178] Sidney, for all his formidable connections, was 'a private man' too, as Languet, troubled by his young friend's readiness to risk the queen's wrath, had recently urged him to remember.[179] Even privy councillors who wrote to Elizabeth expressing controversial views habitually felt it prudent to apologise for their presumption or to forestall the charge of it.[180] Greville, eager as always to present the relations between Sidney and Elizabeth as amicable, tells us that she took the 'Letter' well and that Sidney's standing with her was unaffected by it.[181] Perhaps so. The document nonetheless made a stir. It was apparently with the 'Letter' in mind that Languet, writing to Sidney in January 1580, referred to 'the unpopularity of your conduct'. He also feared that the queen might have been 'seriously offended'.[182]

Sidney had told Elizabeth that he hoped that she alone would read his 'Letter'.[183] Yet he put it into circulation, where it would long remain. 'I am glad you have told me', wrote Languet to him in October 1580,

> how your letter about the Duke of Anjou has come to the knowledge of so many persons; for it was supposed before, that you had made it known to show that you despised him, and cared nothing for his dislike; which appeared to me by no means a safe proceeding, and inconsistent besides with your natural modesty.[184]

---

176 Stubbs, p. 148. Greville, it is true, says that Sidney 'seemed to stand alone' in opposing the match (GP 38/11; cf. GP 75n.), but his meaning is, I suspect, as imprecise as his chronology of the Anjou crisis. There is another argument in favour of a date before October. Sidney tells the queen that the match 'can no way be comfortable' to 'your person', 'you not desiring marriage' (MP 56/17–18). Before, and for the greater part of, 1579, as for so long before it, the queen wished it to be thought, and her advisers and loyal subjects generally remembered to say, that her personal inclinations were against marriage: Read, Walsingham, ii. 15 (cf. ibid., ii. 69; K. de L., xi. 304–5); F(P)M 111, fo. 10ᵛ; Nicolas, Hatton, p. 85; Read, Burghley, p. 197; HMC Cecil, ii. 239; Murdin, Collection, p. 328. Cf. Helen Hackett, Virgin Mother, Virgin Queen. Elizabeth I and the Cult of the Virgin Mary (London, 1995), p. 74; PRO, SP 15/26/*35, fos 140ᵛ– 1. By early October she was taking a different line (below, pp. 149, 153, 173).
177 Above, Chapter 3.
178 Nicolas, Hatton, p. 132; cf. PRO, SP 15/26/*35, fo. 92&ᵛ.
179 Below, p. 283.
180 See, e.g., Nicolas, Hatton, pp. 40, 42–3, 82; Wright, Queen Elizabeth, ii. 74–5.
181 GP 37/13–21.
182 Pears, p. 170.
183 MP 46/14–15.
184 Pears, p. 187.

Languet, in whose circle the publication of Stubbs's tract was seen as an imprudent act of provocation,[185] was troubled in turn by the tone of Sidney's attacks on Anjou. The 'Letter', he reminded his young friend, had 'exaggerat[ed] some circumstances in order to convince' its readers.[186]

The 'Letter' was not the only deed of Sidney to risk Anjou's wrath. His quarrel with the Earl of Oxford, an episode which gave Languet 'great pain',[187] was another declaration of hostility, if a less calculated one. Languet feared that, if Anjou returned to England, Sidney would be in physical danger from the duke's followers.[188] Languet's words imply that Anjou had singled out Sidney for special dislike. In 1575–6, when Anjou was supporting the Huguenot cause, Sidney had been pleased to receive invitations from him to spend several months at his side, though nothing came of them.[189] The bad blood that subsequently developed between the two young men may be attributable to the 'Letter'. Perhaps it owed something to personal rivalry. In July 1578 William of Orange, who had so recently suggested that Sidney marry his daughter, was said to have offered her to Anjou, to whom the Dutch, abandoned by England, had now turned for leadership. Orange wanted Anjou, as he had earlier (it seems) wanted Sidney, to enjoy the lordship of the lands which had come under his influence.[190] At all events the hazard Sidney ran in antagonising Anjou, and the hazard run by his patrons in encouraging or instructing him to write against the duke, indicate the profundity of the crisis which, in the eyes of Sidney's party, had arisen in their country's fortunes and their own.

We can turn now to the philosophy with which they met that crisis, and then to the presence of that philosophy in the *Arcadia*.

185   *CSPF 1579–80*, p. 99; *Mémoires et correspondance de Duplessis-Mornay*, ii. 83.
186   Pears, p. 187.
187   Ibid., p. 165.
188   Ibid., pp. 165, 170.
189   Osborn, *Young Philip Sidney*, pp. 420–2.
190   K. de L., x. 622.

CHAPTER 7

Standing Alone

The forward Protestants had seen their hopes collapse and their arguments turned against them. Though their call for an anti-Spanish policy had been met, their confessional premise had been overturned. The Netherlands and the Protestant cause had been abandoned. The queen, instead of confronting the international Catholic threat, had failed to grasp its nature and gravity and was playing into its hands. To her, the match seemed to offer a diplomatic shelter. The marriage, she hoped, would at once appease and divide the leadership of international Catholicism and thus diminish or divert the peril confronting England. That thinking, argued Sidney's party, was doomed. Far from assuaging or weakening international Catholicism, the match would be a decisive moment in its advance. England, in trying to hide from Spain behind French and Catholic skirts, would discover the essential unity, and the implacable resolve, of Catholic ambition.

In that hour of crisis, and in response to the arguments with which Burghley had pushed them on to the defensive, the forward Protestants discovered fresh reserves of religious and political faith. For all their gloom about the external perils that beset their country, they had always been more sanguine than their opponents on the council about England's ability to overcome them. The perils, they believed, had derived from the queen's timidity and inertia. Had her country only been properly armed and prepared she would have had little cause to fear either France or Spain. Had she only taken the struggle against Catholicism to the continent she could have made the invasion of England impracticable.[1] Instead she had left England diplomatically isolated. Now, in the hope of ending that isolation, she was seeking security where none lay. To that policy there was now only one alternative. However unwelcome its isolation, England must make a virtue of it. It must trust in God and stand alone. Of course, as Sidney's 'Letter' intimated,[2] it

---

1 Bodl., Rawlinson MS. A331, fo. 88^v; *CSPF 1577–8*, p. 591.
2 *MP* 56/26–8.

must aid Protestants abroad as far as it could. But essentially it had been thrown back on its own resources. It must discover the extent of those resources and mobilise them.

In October 1579 the council debated whether the country was 'strong enough' to withstand, 'without [the] marriage', the 'dangers that might endanger this realm'. The forward Protestants were not alone in arguing that it was. For the balance of opinion had changed in their favour since the spring. Those councillors who held out for the marriage, Burghley at their head, argued that the 'perils' confronting England were 'so great, and so many' as to make it necessary; that the successes of Parma in Flanders, and the attempted incursion into Ireland, had made the perils still 'more imminent' than they had been earlier in the year. But the balance now lay with the opponents of the match, who 'do not think the perils by marrying so great as they are supposed to be if her majesty marry not'.[3]

Led on the council by Sir Walter Mildmay, the forward Protestants sounded a new note of patriotic confidence. France and Spain, they argued, had weak and effeminate rulers who lived under the curse of God's displeasure. France, plagued by internal division, was in no position to assist the cause of Mary Stuart. Spain, preoccupied by the war in Flanders and by the Turkish threat in the Mediterranean, was 'not . . . so dreadful to us as it may be pretended'.[4] Walsingham had put similar arguments to the queen in the spring of 1579. He had made light of the suggestion that, if she did not marry Anjou, the duke would seize the Low Countries or marry the Infanta. Anjou's military performance in the Netherlands, Walsingham maintained, had shown how little there was to be feared from him in war. Even if he did marry the Infanta, England would confront no greater threat now than it had known in 1559, when Philip II had married Elizabeth of Valois; and England was much stronger in ships and treasure now than then.[5] Burghley by contrast maintained that, if the queen broke off the match, England would confront perils greater than 'in these twenty years' reign past, as now by no argument can be justly denied'.[6]

Confident the forward Protestants might be. Complacent they were not. They knew that, if the queen decided not to marry Anjou, every nerve of national and Protestant resilience would need to be strained in England's struggle for survival. The administration of the navy must be reformed; the subsidy system must be overhauled and its yield maximised; insufficiently zealous or insufficiently Protestant magistrates must be purged. Above all 'papists' must be 'ke[pt]' under'. The penalties for recusancy must be stepped up, as must their enforcement. There was much in those arguments with which advocates of the match agreed. But there was a difference. The

---

3 Murdin, *Collection*, pp. 334–5, 335; BL, Harleian MS. 6265, fo. 105ᵛ; Hatf. 148, fo. 61.
4 Lehmberg, *Mildmay*, p. 162; K. de L., xi. 410, 411.
5 Read, *Walsingham*, ii. 17; cf. *MP* 51/28–31.
6 *HMC Cecil*, ii. 250.

advocates argued that reform would be necessary in the crisis that would follow if the negotiations broke down. Their opponents urged that reform be undertaken instead of the negotiations.[7]

When forward Protestants measured the queen's government by the political and religious standards to which they were committed, they knew it to be sadly wanting. But when they compared it to its continental counterparts they found cause for comfort and encouragement. The queen was 'in comparison of other princes an angel'.[8] Her 'state . . . differs from' those of her Catholic neighbours because her 'subjects take her preservation to be their own safety. She is queen of a noble nation valiant and faithful to her', 'no people in the world' being 'more ready [o]r willing' to fight for their prince.[9] 'I dare with my blood answer it', Sidney's 'Letter' told Elizabeth, 'that there was never monarch held in more precious reckoning of her people.'[10]

To Sidney and his allies, 'her people' meant her Protestant people. The foundation of the regime, which her marriage to Anjou would destroy, lay in its identification with Protestantism and anti-Catholicism. Sidney reminded Elizabeth that her subjects were:

> divided into two mighty factions . . . bound upon the never ending knot of religion. The one is of them to whom your happy government hath granted the free exercise of the eternal truth. With these, by the continuance of time, by the multitude of them, by the principal offices and strengths they hold, and lastly, by your dealings both at home and abroad against the adverse party, your state is so enwrapped, as it were impossible for you, without excessive trouble, to pull yourself out of the party so long maintained . . .. These, therefore, as their souls live by your happy government, so they are your chief, if not your sole, strength.[11]

The way for the queen to maintain the love and goodwill of the people, argued Sidney's party, was 'by zealously upholding the laws established for the Protestant religion, by which the numbers of her devout subjects will continue and daily increase, and those of a contrary religion will diminish'.[12]

Protestantism, in the eyes of its ardent proponents, was the ally of those other qualities on which the strength of the Elizabethan regime rested: liberty, virtue, justice. As Englishmen had long and often done, Mildmay compared the freedom of his country with the tyranny of France, which, he feared, Anjou would seek to extend to England. Whereas 'tyranny . . . ever

---

7   Ibid., 252, 309–10; Murdin, *Collection*, pp. 328, 339–41; K. de L., xi. 407; Hatf. 148, fos 37&ᵛ, 41, 49–51ᵛ, 58, 80; cf. below, pp. 251–2.
8   K. de L., xi. 411.
9   BL, Harleian MS. 6265, fo. 106.
10 *MP* 55/28–9.
11 *MP* 47/19–33.
12 *HMC Cecil*, ii. 268.

governeth by fear', 'monarchies be or ought to be ruled with love and fear together; neither without that commixture can that government hold, as for example our state of England', where the queen inspires both 'love' and 'reverend fear'. Thus where Henry III of France, in forward Protestant eyes, 'wanteth the loving hearts of his subjects, the only true blessing of all kings and princes',[13] and where the 'evil and unjust government' of the King of Spain made him hated by his subjects, Elizabeth 'hath as much love as any prince can have'.[14] Forward Protestants declared that the queen, by leading a 'virtuous' life and maintaining 'the true religion of God' and 'justice among her people', had made herself 'beloved, feared, and trusted'.[15] Those merits, alas, had been mixed with grave failings. Yet if she would now fearlessly adhere to them, they could be her and her nation's salvation.

That view, voiced in council when the queen was not present, was pressed on her by Sidney. His 'Letter', addressed to his 'most feared and beloved' sovereign, explains that 'love and fear' are the sources of respect for a monarchy. Elizabeth, who inspires those feelings, 'hath a people more than ever devoted to you'. In 'so rare a government . . . nothing wants that true administration of justice brings forth'. So 'let your excellent virtues of piety, justice and liberality daily, if it be possible, more and more shine'. There will then be no need to think of marriage. While the queen's subjects would of course not grudge her the 'bliss' of children, 'religion and equity' are 'sufficient stays' without them. For 'virtue and justice' are 'the only bands of the people's love'.[16]

'Virtue' and 'justice' are the sovereign qualities of the model sovereign of the *Arcadia*, that antitype to Basilius, King Euarchus of Macedon. His 'justice', and the 'awful love' it inspires, are the first things we learn about him. His commitment to the 'holy name' of justice and to its 'sacred' exercise is the lodestar of his conduct.[17] In the *New Arcadia* his justice inspires the same mixture of 'love' and 'fear' that Mildmay and Sidney describe in Elizabeth's subjects: the 'love' of his people for him has been made 'most lovely' by 'the awful fear engendered by justice'.[18] Alas, closer inspection shows Elizabeth's true counterpart to be not Euarchus but Basilius. Even so, during the Anjou crisis forward Protestants, who were so conscious of her weaknesses, also remembered her strengths.

Euarchus has other qualities which Sidney and his party urged upon Elizabeth: resolution; knowledge of, and trust in, the ethical base of his authority; superiority to worldly strength, to worldly fortune, to worldly calculation. In

13 PRO, SP 78/2/68 (*CSPF 1578–9*, p. 182); cf. BL, Harleian MS. 6265, fo. 104ᵛ.
14 Lehmberg, *Mildmay*, p. 159; BL, Harleian MS. 6265, fo. 105ᵛ.
15 K. de L., xi. 411. Cf. BL, Harleian MS. 6265, fo. 106ᵛ; NRO, F(P)M 111, fo. 5.
16 *MP* 46/5, 56/6, 54/11–12, 53/33–54/2, 56/34–5, 54/30–2, 54/27; cf. Nicholls, *Progresses*, ii. 148.
17 *OA* 10/5–7, 411/19–25; cf. *OA* 379/28–9.
18 *NA* 160/36–7, 161/21, 161/26.

commending those virtues and delineating them, forward Protestants made repeated use of a set of words which will prove to be key terms in the moral economy of Sidney's fiction.

The nouns are 'foundation' and 'ground'. The verbs are 'stand', 'depend', 'build'. (There is also the noun 'building', while 'ground' sometimes figures as a verb.) There was nothing necessarily self-conscious about the use of those words. They belong, after all, to the ordinary discourse of politics. In the Anjou crisis they were not monopolised by forward Protestants. Yet we can learn from the frequency with which, before and during that crisis, those men selected that language to define the heart of their position. They deployed it, first, to urge that Elizabeth commit her policy and her trust to God, however bleak her own and her country's predicament might seem. Dependence on God is dependence on 'truth', the quality 'whereon', explains the *New Arcadia*, 'all the other goods' are 'builded' and have their 'ground'.[19] Its opposite is dependence on man. Forward Protestants time and again explained the failures of the queen's diplomacy by her readiness to 'depend' upon 'the arm of man', to 'build upon' worldly 'policies'. Such 'policy will not stand, but God will overthrow it'. She must learn to 'depend altogether upon the advancement of God's glory', seeking her 'ground' and 'foundation' in 'so precious a work' and 'shaking off all other policy that is not grounded upon God', upon whom 'all our buildings and actions' must rest.[20] In the spring of 1579, Walsingham, advising the queen against the marriage, wrote that God would 'so long . . . extend his protection as we shall depend of his providence'. The humbling 'in these late years' of 'mighty potentates that have bent themselves against God', he claimed, showed how firm a support England would find in God's power and goodness 'if we could soundly, without wavering and distrust, depend on Him'.[21]

That philosophy, in the new mood of patriotic defiance that emerged in 1579, gave forward Protestants fresh heart. Language registers the lifting of their despair. In 1571 Walsingham had accepted the need for Elizabeth to marry Henry Duke of Anjou because otherwise 'I do not see how she can stand.'[22] In 1577 Leicester feared that if the queen failed to aid French Protestantism it would not be 'possible for her majesty long to stand' without 'God's miraculous assistance'.[23] 'Miracle', or else 'prayer', seemed to Sidney's party the only hope of deliverance in the black year 1578, when human agencies had evidently failed.[24] Yet in 1579 the forward Protestants argued that the queen could indeed 'stand' without marrying Anjou. The designs of

19 *NA* 164/6–7, 325/20–1.
20 Bodl., Rawlinson MS. A331, fo. 9ᵛ; K. de L., ix. 301, xi. 161, 169; NRO, F(P)M 111, fo. 9; PRO, SP 12/123/17 (fos 53, 54ᵛ).
21 Read, *Walsingham*, ii. 16.
22 Ibid., i. 136.
23 *CSPF 1577–8*, p. 63.
24 K. de L., x. 318, 614; *CSPF 1578–9*, pp. 172, 174, 177.

France and Spain against England, argued opponents of the match on the council, could not prosper 'if we stand fast to our God'.[25]

Sidney's 'Letter' endorsed that view. In advising the queen against the match, he urged her, as the means of safety, to 'make that religion upon which you stand to carry the only strength'. To submit to the 'hazards' of the marriage would be to rest upon the whims of fortune. For 'outward accidents do [not] much prevail against a true inward strength'.[26] Walsingham concurred. Believing that the queen's policies had preserved England in peace 'accidentally', he would later summarise the failings of her diplomacy thus: 'she greatly presumeth on fortune, which is but a very weak foundation for virtue to build upon. I would she did build and depend upon God.'[27] Councillors who urged her to effect a reconciliation with her Catholic enemies, he thought, wanted her to 'build' upon a false base.[28] The Dutch, Walsingham believed, had made a similar mistake in having 'depended' or 'built' on the 'uncertainty' of support from Elizabeth; his friend Daniel Rogers made the same point in the same language.[29] By contrast the forward Protestant William Davison thought that Elizabeth might safely 'build upon' that rock of virtue and integrity, William of Orange.[30]

It was the argument of the forward Protestants that the queen, without marrying Anjou, 'may be in safety grounded'.[31] The love of her subjects, claimed Mildmay, provided her with 'the strongest foundation of surety that can be to any prince'.[32] All she needed was resolution. Yet resolution was the very quality she lacked. The fate of the Netherlands in the late 1570s, believed forward Protestants, 'dependeth upon her resolution':[33] yet time and again they noticed how 'irresolute' was her policy there, how frail her 'resolution', how 'uncertain' were the 'resolutions' of her policy and 'how subject they are to changes'.[34] The same failing of 'irresolution', in Walsingham's judgement, characterised her proceedings towards Mary Queen of Scots.[35] He located the same defect in Elizabeth's leading minister. Always troubled by the damage that 'fearful and irresolute' men could do in public life,[36] Walsingham lamented that Burghley 'hath always liked to entertain bye-courses', a weakness 'which groweth of a lack of resolution in

25   K. de L., xi. 410.
26   *MP* 56/25–6, 47/14–15.
27   Read, *Walsingham*, ii. 88; Bruce, *Leycester Correspondence*, p. 276. Cf. K. de L., x. 832; Oram, p. 241 (ll. 197–8).
28   Read, *Walsingham*, i. 417n.
29   K. de L., x. 349, 361, 813; Wright, *Queen Elizabeth*, ii. 93.
30   K. de L., x. 101.
31   BL, Harleian MS. 1582, fo. 46ᵛ.
32   BL, Harleian MS. 6265, fo. 106ᵛ.
33   Nicolas, *Hatton*, p. 50.
34   K. de L., x. 304, 314, 342, 458, 819; Bruce, *Leycester Correspondence*, p. 239.
35   Read, *Walsingham*, i. 184; below, Chapter 10.
36   Read, *Walsingham*, i. 217.

him'.[37] Again, William of Orange offered an exemplary contrast. To forward Protestants he seemed a man of 'wonderful . . . resolution', 'resolute in all things and . . . not dismayed with any loss or adversity'.[38]

'Resolution', too, is a key word in the moral economy of Sidney's fiction, where 'a resolute constancy' is 'so goodly a virtue'; where 'resolution' is the 'chief force' of 'the mind'; where 'true fortitude' has 'a persisting resolution'; where Musidorus and Pyrocles reach a 'resolution of well suffering all accidents'.[39] Basilius' 'mind', alas, is 'in doubt for want of resolution'; weakened by superstition, he 'took the common course of men, to fly only then to devotion when they want resolution'.[40] Sidney's appreciation of the quality of resolution emerged elsewhere too. Gabriel Harvey noted that he admired Julius Caesar for his 'sound[ness] in resolution'.[41] At the crisis of his own life in the spring of 1586, when his cause and his career were apparently collapsing in the Netherlands, Sidney assured Walsingham that, 'with God's grace', adversity 'shall never make me weary of my resolution'.[42]

In the circumstances of 1579, forward Protestants knew, resolution would need courage. Unfortunately, they thought, the queen was prone to 'needless fear', ready to yield to 'fear' with 'little cause' when resolution would remove its source.[43] Advocates of the Anjou match were ready with the claim that it would deliver her from 'fear'.[44] Her councillors, reported Mendoza at that time, were alive to her 'fear in any adversity'.[45] Just as 'fear' prompts Basilius to abandon the government of his kingdom,[46] so it tempts Elizabeth to yield, by marrying Anjou, the sway of hers. Yet, forward Protestants maintained, she had nothing to fear but fear itself. For fear, though an apt and healthy quality when it promotes reverence for virtue (as it does in the account of the queen's reign offered by Sidney's 'Letter'), can also be the undoing of virtue.[47] If Elizabeth's motive in forwarding the match was to escape from her perils, warned Mildmay, then 'fear', 'the worst groundwork', 'is the foundation thereof'.[48] Sidney's 'Letter' answers 'the objections of those fears which might procure so violent a refuge' as the match, an expedient for which 'fear' is no 'reasonable cause'.

---

37 Ibid., ii. 231 (MS. facsimile reproduction); Leimon, 'Walsingham', p. 177; cf. Kingdon, *Myths*, p. 82.

38 K. de L., x. 271; K. W. Swart, *William the Silent and the Revolt of the Netherlands* (London, Historical Association pamphlet, 1978), p. 29.

39 *OA* 384/11–12; *NA* 456/7–8; *OA* 296/19–20, 413/10–11.

40 *OA* 220/12; *NA* 457/19–20. He is however capable of pig-headed 'resolut[ion]' in pursuit of folly: below, p. 144.

41 Lisa Jardine and Anthony Grafton, '"Studied for Action": How Gabriel Harvey Read his Livy', *Past and Present* 129 (1990), pp. 30–78, at p. 55.

42 Feuillerat, iii. 166.

43 Bodl., Rawlinson MS. A331, fo. 88ᵛ; *CSPF 1577–8*, p. 591.

44 *HMC Cecil*, ii. 242; cf. Murdin, *Collection*, p. 333.

45 *CSPS 1568–79*, p. 703.

46 Below, p. 135.

47 Cf. below, pp. 335–7.

48 Lehmberg, *Mildmay*, p. 160.

That assurance is necessary, he tells her, because, 'as I have often heard you in sweet words deliver', a principal motive of her courtship is 'fear of standing alone in respect of foreign dealings'. She is in error. 'Standing alone with good foresight both of peace-government, and war-defence, is the honourablest thing that can be to a well established monarchy, those buildings being ever most strongly durable which, leaning to no other, remain firm upon their own foundations.' 'For your standing alone,' Sidney adds, 'you must take it as a singular honour God hath done unto you, to be indeed the only protector of his church.'[49] Greville tells us that Sidney himself, in courageously urging the queen not to marry Anjou, 'stood upright' even though he 'seemed to stand alone'.[50]

The question of England's potential for self-sufficiency exposed fundamental differences of perspective between the forward Protestants and Burghley. Burghley, using the phrase which Sidney heard Elizabeth using and which the 'Letter' turns against her, warned that if the match were broken off England would be unable to 'stand alone' against the might of Spain, France and the papacy.[51] The Lord Treasurer does not seem to have shared the profundity of dismay felt by forward Protestants at the prospect of French control of England. Though he would not have welcomed that prospect, he may have thought of it as a price worth paying for England's deliverance from the danger of Spanish conquest. He may even have seen himself as the man best equipped to ensure that, under French control, England's faith and interests would be protected.[52] Fear of invasion was a main component of Burghley's attitude to the match, as of the queen's. The forward Protestants, for the most part, overcame that fear. A student of the Anjou crisis has observed that the memoranda written by opponents of the match carry a calm and composure of mind that are absent from those produced by Burghley.[53]

The vocabulary which expressed the forward Protestant philosophy, and which is present in Sidney's 'Letter', pervades his other writings too. His premise was shared by Hubert Languet, who in October 1578 warned him to 'stand firm', as he trod the 'slippery ground' of court life, 'on your principle and strength of mind'.[54] Sidney, reveals the *Defence of Poetry*, revered the French statesman Michel de l'Hôpital, whose 'judgement' was so 'firmly builded upon virtue'.[55] In 1580, with 'moral virtue' in his thoughts, Sidney urged Edward Denny to make Cicero 'your foundation, next to the founda-

---

49   *MP* 46/23–4, 52/26, 51/21–7, 56/21–3.
50   *GP* 38/11–12; cf. Feuillerat, iii. 166.
51   Hatf. 148, fos 30, 36; cf. Peck, *Leicester's Commonwealth*, p. 79.
52   Leimon, 'Walsingham', pp. 119, 130, 138; Hatf. 148, fos 37ᵛ–38 (with which cf. PRO, SP 15/ 26/*35, fos 145ᵛff.).
53   Leimon, 'Walsingham', pp. 127, 139, 177.
54   Pears, p. 155.
55   *MP* 110/21–3.

tion of foundations', Holy Scripture.[56] The *Old Arcadia* teaches us 'that nothing remains strongly but that which hath the good foundation of goodness', an observation echoed by Philoclea, who is wary of an argument which 'hath not his ground in an assured virtue'; it is echoed again in the *New Arcadia*, where the princes are advised 'to take heed how [they] plac[e their] goodwill upon any other ground than proof of virtue'.[57] Basilius' daughters remember, in adversity, to 'stand upon' or 'depend confidently upon' the source of virtue, God; Philanax, in his country's hour of crisis, 'stand[s] only upon a constant desire of justice and a clear conscience'. The advice of the elderly shepherd Geron to Philisides echoes Sidney's to his queen: 'upon thyself to stand'.[58] Sidney's romantic plot, no less than the European diplomacy of 1579, teaches us to 'stand alone' and rest on our 'inward strength'.[59]

In urging the queen, during the Anjou crisis, to stand on the foundations of her reign – on God, on justice, on the love of her subjects – the forward Protestants made themselves advocates of continuity. Earlier, in urging her to abandon her temporising policy and go to war in the Low Countries, they had been advocates of change. Of course, they had never been advocates of mutability. That was the fault on which they blamed so many 'changes' or 'alterations' of policy, among them her disastrous 'change of resolution' when she broke her promise to send an army under Leicester in 1578. But that same disaster, and the Anjou crisis which followed it, led them to speak of the preceding two decades as a continuum which she was now bringing to an end. In her abandonment of the Netherlands, Walsingham saw 'so dangerous a storm drawing on as is likely utterly to blemish the blessedness' of the queen's former 'course of government'.[60] In Sidney's 'Letter' a similar nautical analogy makes the same point from an opposite angle: the 'course' which Elizabeth had followed until the Anjou suit was like 'a ship in a tempest, which how dangerously soever it be beaten with waves, yet there is no safety nor succour without it'. In 1579 the peril has diminished. So 'what makes you in such a calm to change course?' Citing the 'sweet words' he has heard her speak, he attributes 'this sudden change' to her 'fear of standing alone'. No 'sudden change . . . in this body politic', he warns her, can be 'without peril'.[61]

In the opening dialogue of the *Arcadia* another monarch is warned by another public-spirited counsellor against a 'sudden' 'change' of 'course', and

---

56 Osborn, *Young Philip Sidney*, p. 539.
57 *OA* 265/8–9, 298/21–2; *NA* 264/28–30; cf. *NA* 161/8–10.
58 *OA* 298/1–2; *NA* 336/11; *OA* 321/26–7, 73/20.
59 Below, pp. 334–5.
60 Read, *Walsingham*, i. 417n.
61 *MP* 47/28–31, 47/3–4, 51/20–2, 47/8–9. The emergence of the forward Protestant philosophy of self-sufficiency is surely behind the cultivation in the late 1570s of the image of Elizabeth as a perpetual virgin. See Susan Doran, 'Juno versus Diana: the Treatment of Elizabeth I's Marriage in Plays and Entertainments, 1561–1581', *Historical Journal* 38 (1995), pp. 257–74; Hackett, *Virgin Mother, Virgin Queen*, ch. 4; cf. PRO, SP 19/26/*35, fo. 163.

is urged to 'stand' on his 'virtue'. It is time for us to read Sidney's letter to the queen, and Philanax's advice to Basilius, beside each other. The comparison will indicate the prominence in Sidney's fiction of analogies between Arcadia and England.

PART THREE: ANALOGIES

CHAPTER 8

Three Crises of Counsel

The fate of England in 1579–80 rests upon the queen's decision whether to marry Anjou. The fate of Arcadia rests upon an equally critical decision of Basilius. Both monarchs, in Sidney's eyes, confront predicaments which they have brought on themselves. Elizabeth's timid and short-sighted policy has driven her into a corner from which, misguidedly and vainly, she seeks escape through marriage. Basilius seeks escape too, albeit of another kind. Moved by the 'passion' of 'curiosity', which proceeds from the 'weakness' of desiring 'to know that which in vain thou shalt be sorry after thou hast known it', he has consulted the oracle at Delphos. When the oracle foretells – on the duke's interpretation of it – 'the loss of his crown and children' during the 'fatal year' ahead, he makes a decision that will bring his country to the edge of destruction. He resolves 'for this fatal year to retire himself with his wife and daughters into a solitary place'. He will 'leave' the 'government of the country' to 'certain selected persons' under his friend and adviser Philanax and, for his 'pleasure', devote himself to the enjoyment of pastoral sports and eclogues.[1]

There are obvious differences between Elizabeth and Basilius. Elizabeth has not consulted an oracle; she has no family to protect; she does not intend to abdicate for a year. The story launched by Basilius' retreat takes Sidney's readers into imaginative territory beyond his political preoccupations. Yet it also leads us back to them. Among the differences, of both situation and character, between the two monarchs, Sidney invites us to observe a wealth of resemblances.

The most immediate of them lie in the counsel which the two rulers are given by their loyal advisers and in their responses to it. This chapter will look closely at those parallels, for it is through them that the political purpose of the *Arcadia* is declared. Whether the writing of Sidney's 'Letter' to the queen was a decisive episode in the imagining of the *Arcadia* we cannot be

1 *OA* 5/21–6/31.

sure, but there must have been some relationship of creativity between the two works. There is certainly a close relationship of content.

The 'Letter' was probably written in the late summer of 1579. It is likely that Sidney began to write the *Arcadia*, or at least embarked on the main period of its composition, soon after that, perhaps very soon. The 'Letter' was in circulation in 1580, when the bulk of the *Arcadia* was written. Its arguments are applied to the situation of Basilius by Philanax in the opening dialogue of the *Arcadia*. The two advisers, Sidney and Philanax, confront the problems of counsel that the servants of monarchy in Sidney's time knew too well.[2] The advice of both men fails. Basilius persists in his retreat. Elizabeth in the end, it is true, does not marry Anjou, but no one would have claimed that her decision was influenced by Sidney's plea. In neither case can failure be blamed on a want of endeavour or judgement or tact on the part of the adviser. Both advisers are impelled by love and duty to speak out, Sidney 'from the deep wellspring of most loyal affection', Philanax as 'a friend . . . in affection' who 'loved' Basilius 'with incomparable loyalty'. Both men know how to behave. Sidney presents his case with 'boldness' but also 'with most humble heart': Philanax argues 'with humble boldness'.[3]

Philanax can afford to be more direct than Sidney. Living in 'that thrifty world', 'that world, not so far gone into painted vanities',[4] he has no need for the flowers of praise which Sidney, in obedience to the conventions of a Renaissance court, hands to 'the excellentest prince in the world'. 'Laying . . . myself at your feet', Sidney speaks for subjects whose 'minds' are 'joyed with the experience of your inward virtues, and our eyes delighted with the sight of you'. His 'Letter' ends by describing Elizabeth as 'the example of princes, the ornament of this age, the comfort of the afflicted, the delight of your people, the most excellent fruit of all your progenitors, and the perfect mirror to your posterity'.[5] Philanax's speech ends plainly, with the kernel of his advice.[6] Though he briefly praises Basilius' rule, he sees no need to praise his character.

There are limits to Philanax's candour. We saw that the attitude of the councillors who opposed the Anjou match was double-edged. Their praise of the love rooted in her people by the justice of Elizabeth's rule, and the contrast they drew between her benign reign and the malign reigns of kings on the continent, were at odds with their dismay at the 'diseased state' of the realm and at the failings of royal policy at home and abroad. Sidney's advice to her is equally double-edged. So is that of Philanax to Basilius. His words tell his monarch what Sidney has told his: 'you have so governed this realm',

2 Cf. below, Chapter 9; Dorothy Connell, *Sir Philip Sidney. The Maker's Mind* (Oxford, 1977), pp. 104–11.
3 *OA* 5/31, 286/7, 7/19 (cf. *OA* 304/6–7, 500); *MP* 46/18–19, 46/6, 56/20.
4 *OA* 56/13, 6/14–15.
5 *MP* 55/2–3, 46/12, 53/16–18, 57/5–8.
6 *OA* 8/30–2.

says Philanax, 'that neither your subjects have wanted justice in you, nor you obedience in them'.[7] That picture proves to be as incomplete as Sidney's.

The monarchs whom the two men advise have had long and peaceful reigns. Basilius' has lasted for three decades, Elizabeth's for two. A memorandum submitted to the queen by Walsingham in 1581, which implores her not to squander that achievement, requests her, as Sidney's 'Letter' does at its outset, to indulge the 'boldness' of the advice that is to follow. Walsingham invites her to attribute that boldness, 'without offence', to 'a care I have of your highness's preservation in that happy estate you have lived in these three and twenty years, which I pray God to continue your majesty in double those years': Philanax deploys his own 'boldness' to explain how Basilius must act if he is to preserve the justice and obedience that have prevailed 'these thirty years past'.[8]

The length and peace of Elizabeth's reign figured prominently both in her propaganda and in her self-perception. Perhaps the vigour of her assertions owed something to insecurity, for Sidney's 'Letter' reveals that she believed her 'length of government' to be a source of 'contempt' among her subjects.[9] At all events her advisers had constantly to allude to the 'long peace' of her reign, to the 'experience of twenty sweet peaceable years', to the 'justice' and 'prosperity' and 'felicity' which had flourished during them.[10] Forward Protestants, who joined in those tributes, cannot always have enjoyed delivering them, for 'long peace' had been bought, they believed, to the disadvantage of Europe's Protestantism and liberty. The queen was readiest with reminders of the length and blessings of her rule when rejecting the advice of forward Protestants or when rebuking their conduct: when explaining why she would not go to Orange's aid in the Low Countries,[11] for example, or when proclaiming the villainy of John Stubbs's *The Discovery of a Gaping Gulph*. There is, intentionally or not, an ironic parallel to her proclamation against Stubbs in Philanax's speech. The proclamation commends the queen's success in maintaining 'a long and universal peace' which has kept her realm 'free always from outward hostility and war made or denounced by any foreign prince, being oftener sued unto by the greater sort for friendship and alliance than ever irritated by any unkind messages of war or unkindness':[12] Philanax's corresponding statement to Basilius reminds him that for 'these thirty years past . . . your neighbours have found you so hurtlessly strong that they thought it better to rest in your friendship than make new trial of your enmity'.[13]

---

7   *OA* 7/21–3.
8   Read, *Walsingham*, ii. 70; *OA* 7/19–23.
9   *MP* 53/7–8, 53/22–3.
10 Nicolas, *Hatton*, p. 132; *CSPF 1577–8*, p. 186; Stubbs, pp. 115, 197, 198; PRO, SP 15/96/*35, fo. 93.
11 K. de L., x. 203.
12 Stubbs, p. 147.
13 *OA* 7/21–5.

6   Queen Elizabeth accompanied by the figures of Peace and Plenty. From an allegorical painting on the Tudor succession, commissioned by the queen in the earlier 1570s and given by her to Sir Francis Walsingham as a 'mark of her people's and her own content'.

The irony derives from the misguided diplomacy pursued by both rulers and from the frailty of the peace they have established. It is true that the peace enjoyed by Elizabethan England, and the contrast between it and the wars on the continent, gave much to be grateful for: that, as Sidney's 'Letter' says of the continental wars of religion, 'neighbours' fire gives us light to see our own quietness'.[14] 'The greatest princes and potentates of Europe', acknowledged the forward Protestant Sir Amias Paulet, 'do envy the quietness and tranquillity of the estates of England.'[15] Hubert Languet, after

14   *MP* 53/33–54/1.
15   Bodl., Rawlinson MS. A331, fo. 117ᵛ.

returning to the war-stricken Low Countries from his visit to Elizabeth's court early in 1579, wrote to Sidney of 'happy England, the abode of peace'.[16] The contrast is paralleled in the *New Arcadia*, where Musidorus, 'wearied with the wasted soil' of war-torn Laconia, moves on to neighbouring Arcadia, a 'country' of 'delightful prospects', 'decked with peace and, the child of peace, good husbandry'.[17]

Peace, however, has its price. 'Neighbours' fire' may 'giv[e] us light to see our own quietness'. Yet Sidney's *Defence of Poetry* reveals that England's 'quietness' is 'overfaint'.[18] He and his allies, in acknowledging the 'quietness', the 'rare quietness', of her reign, knew not only the cost of it to their co-religionists on the continent but its precariousness. Forward Protestants – Sir Amias Paulet, Thomas Wilson, Walsingham – argued that what they termed England's 'quietness' had bred its fatal 'security'. The luck that had brought it would soon run out.[19] Arcadia's long 'quiet' and 'tranquillity' run out too, on the (apparent) death of Basilius.[20] There has been little if anything to admire in Basilius' preservation of those conditions, and much to question. Being 'by nature quiet' and anxious to preserve 'his quiet course', the duke is 'loath to take any matter of arms in hand', even though 'vehemently urged . . . thereunto' by Philanax.[21] The 'quiet' in which Philanax protects the duke from 'disturbance' shelters him from the performance of his duties.[22] Our first information about Basilius' rule is that he is 'a prince of sufficient skill to govern so quiet a country'. The compliment (we shall see) is barbed.[23]

Sidney, as Greville says, thought the English 'apt . . . to corrupt with peace'.[24] The Anjou crisis, Sidney tells the queen, has found England 'as well by long peace and fruits of peace . . . made fit to receive hurt . . . [Anjou] being every way apt to use the occasion to hurt'.[25] Where Sidney takes England to be 'fit to receive hurt', Philanax tells Basilius that Arcadia is 'hurtlessly strong'. Here, for once, it is Philanax who prefers compliment to truth. Arcadia, it emerges later, would be an easy 'prey' to its ambitious

---

16 Pears, p. lxix.
17 *NA* 10/36–7, 11/19–29.
18 *MP* 110/31.
19 Bodl., Rawlinson MS. A331, fo. 51 (cf. fo. 122); K. de L., x. 819; *CSPF 1578–9*, p. 177; Read, *Walsingham*, ii. 88; above, pp. 77–8.
20 *OA* 361/9, 361/16, 327/16.
21 *NA* 457/12–16, 456/32.
22 *OA* 286/6–7.
23 *OA* 4/20–1; below, Chapter 14. The point that 'quietness' ought not to be the goal of kings is confirmed in the *New Arcadia*, where Pyrocles, who might 'quietly have enjoyed' the crown of Phrygia, declines the offer: *NA* 177/16–21.
24 *GP* 47/8; cf. *GP* 47/12–13.
25 *MP* 50/18–22; cf. *MP* 56/14–15. Greville shares Sidney's outlook, taking 'peace' to be 'a quiet nurse of idleness' and believing that 'war' will 'Purge the imposthum'd humours of a peace; / Which oft else makes good government decrease'. Of 'greatness of heart', the quality he reveres in Sidney and sees dying among others, Greville writes that 'war is both a fitter mould to fashion it, and stage to act it on, than peace can be'. Bullough, i. 151 (sonnet cviii); Wilkes, p. 178 (st. 573); *GP* 79/6–8.

neighbours,[26] as England, so long as it remained asleep, would be to the Catholic powers.

Twice in the *Arcadia*, at times when popular disorder provides domestic challenges to the long peace which Basilius' reign has sustained, his defenders recall that achievement. Their praises of it are unconvincing. Thus in Book Two, Pyrocles, striving to tame the mutinous rabble, charges it with being 'so ungrateful as to forget the fruit of so many years' peaceable government'. Why then is it, as Pyrocles also tells the mob, that 'your own duke after thirty years' government dare[s] not show his face to his . . . people'?[27] The mutiny, we shall find, is an indictment of the duke's misrule.[28] So, we shall also find, is the occasion of the second tribute to his peaceable record, offered after his death, an event to which his subjects respond like headless chickens. The devastated shepherds praise, among other questionable achievements, 'his peaceable government, the thing which most pleaseth men resolved to live of their own': that is (in this context), men resolved to look to their own interests. Their lamentations confirm an observation of Fulke Greville about 'princes': 'we praise them for the good they never had'.[29] The stricken howls of Basilius' subjects reflect no credit on him: they merely show 'how easy a thing it is for a prince by succession deeply to sink into the souls of his subjects'.[30] That observation echoes Sidney's 'Letter' to the queen, which applies to her the rule it observes 'of all good princes', that 'the longer they reigned, the deeper still they sank into their subjects' hearts'. The echo discloses the irony both of that compliment to Elizabeth and of another, where Sidney explains that, as a ruler 'to whom our fortunes are tied by so long descent of your royal ancestors', she owes her popularity to the habits of acceptance bred by 'length of time'.[31]

Peace, desirable as it is, must be earned, abroad as well as at home. 'Peace-government', Sidney indicates to Elizabeth, depends on the readiness of 'war-defence'.[32] As King of Macedon, Euarchus is 'prepared' against 'sudden and dangerous invasions'; he has 'kept in peace time a continual discipline of war'; 'his first care was to put his people in a readiness for war, and by his experienced soldiers to train the unskilful to martial exercises', equipping them 'for resisting the invading enemy'.[33] Forward Protestants were anxious for Elizabeth to do the same. Thomas Wilson urged that England's musters be kept up and that queen and country 'be always in a readiness for war'; Sir Nicholas Bacon beseeched Elizabeth to have her 'musters kept and

26   *OA* 358/8–13, 358/35–6. Arcadia thus exemplifies Greville's belief that 'neglect' and 'security' in the government of kingdoms make them 'preys to their ambition that be strong': Wilkes, p. 168 (st. 530).
27   *OA* 130/16–17, 129/33–4.
28   Below, p. 158.
29   Bullough, i. 102 (sonnet xlix, ll. 9–10); cf. below, Chapter 11.
30   *OA* 283/18–284/1, 320/3ff.
31   *MP* 53/15–16, 54/2–6; below, p. 262.
32   *MP* 51/23–5.
33   *OA* 10/15–17, 358/20–1, 356.

continued . . . so as your captains, men, munition and armour may be in readiness against all suddens'.[34] Elizabeth, alas, here resembles not Euarchus but Basilius, his opposite in this as in so much else, whose 'armour' has been 'long before untried'. The English, Sidney warns the queen, have become 'generally unexpert in warlike defence'.[35] Languet, sharing Sidney's anxiety, recalled in January 1580 that the English had been 'much more practised in war' in the time of Queen Mary than they were now.[36] In the *New Arcadia* Helen of Corinth, standing for Elizabeth as Elizabeth ought to be, 'made her people (by peace) warlike . . . for, by continual martial exercises without blood, she made them perfect in that bloody art'.[37] Yet when Kalander, Basilius' brother-in-law, raises an Arcadian force, his soldiers are 'like men disused with a long peace, more determinate to do than skilful how to do', not lacking 'courage' but having 'neither cunning use of their weapons, nor art showed in their marching or encamping'.[38] They sound like the potential recruits of Elizabethan England.

Among the blessings bestowed on the Arcadians by 'the peace wherein they did so notably flourish' is their gift for songs and eclogues, 'long peace having begun it'; for 'they have ease, the nurse of poetry'.[39] Yet they may have paid heavily for that benefit. Sidney's *Defence*, it is true, overrules – or ostensibly overrules – the charge that poetry is a weakening force: that 'both in other nations and in ours, before poets did soften us, we were full of courage, given to martial exercises, the pillars of manlike liberty, and not lulled asleep in shady idleness with poets' pastimes'. Yet the Arcadians, like the English, are indeed lulled asleep in shady idleness by the peace they have enjoyed. Sidney's *Defence* commends poetry as 'the companion of camps',[40] but it is no such thing in Arcadia. Philisides' lament for the lost 'virtue' and 'honour' of Samothea, and thus of England, follows Holinshed, where the Samotheans 'had given over the practice of all warlike and other painful exercises, and through use of effeminate pleasures, whereunto they had given

---

34 K. de L., ix. 230; Nicolas, *Hatton*, p. 42. Cf. Nicolas, *Hatton*, p. 48; *HMC Cecil*, ii. 269; below, pp. 251–2. The achievement of a secure peace may depend not merely on a readiness to fight, but on fighting. The forward Protestant Thomas Randolph, though sure that 'an honourable peace' is always preferable to 'the most just war', knows that war may be the only means to it. Euarchus knows it too. In the Thessalia of the *New Arcadia* he and his allies 'begat, of a just war, the best child – peace'. Hastings MS. HA 10397, Randolph to Lord Hunsdon, 7 March 1581; *NA* 162/30. Cf. Murdin, *Collection*, p. 327; *CSPF 1577–8*, p. 591; Wilson, *Demosthenes*, pp. 36, 64.
35 *OA* 124/13; *MP* 47/18–19.
36 Pears, p. 170.
37 *NA* 253/31–4; cf. Edmund Spenser, *The Faerie Queene*, ed. A. C. Hamilton (London, repr. 1984), V. ix. 30.
38 *NA* 34/7–12; cf. KRO, U1475: Z1/11, fo. 11. Martial 'discipline', the achievement of Euarchus, is the repeatedly stated ideal of Fulke Greville, who wants to see 'that discipline in peace, by which wars stand'. In 'securest times', he argues, 'strong kings must arm, and exercise / Troops of their people' and employ 'active spirits' to 'train up leaders'. *GP* 47/30; Wilkes, pp. 169 (sts 535–6), 179 (st. 574).
39 *OA* 56/19–20; *NA* 24/21–6.
40 *MP* 101/34–102/1, 105/34; cf. Duncan-Jones, 'Philip Sidney's Toys', pp. 163–4.

themselves over,' 'were become now unapt to withstand the force of their enemies'.[41]

Sidney and Philanax have tactical reasons for referring to the length and success of the reigns they describe. Like the privy councillors who opposed the Anjou match, they see in the impending mistakes of their rulers a 'change' of 'course'. Like those councillors, too, they heighten the virtue of their rulers' past courses in order to encourage the continuance of them. In other moods, we saw, the queen's advisers, instead of finding consistency in her previous record, bemoaned the mutability that had produced so many 'changes' and 'alterations' of resolution.[42] Mutability was evidently a charge to which she was vulnerable, for during the Anjou crisis the privy council had to reassure the public of the queen's 'constant' and 'firm determination to maintain the state of religion without any alteration or change, in such sort as hitherto she hath done'.[43] Sidney likes to place 'constancy', which is virtuous, in opposition to what is 'most changeable', which is not.[44] His 'Letter' praises his monarch's 'constancy', but represents the prospective marriage as 'the loss of so honourable a constancy'. Philanax in turn commends to Basilius 'a constant virtue, well settled, little subject' to 'change'.[45]

Sidney's question to the queen, 'What makes you in such a calm to change course?', is echoed by Philanax: 'Why should you', he asks Basilius, 'now seek new courses?'[46] Sidney describes the queen's 'change' as 'sudden': the duke's abandonment of his duties has been 'sudden' too.[47] Sidney wants the queen not to change but to 'be as you be'.[48] His indication that her marriage would break that rule was a sensitive point to make to a ruler who took 'semper eadem' for her motto. In September 1579 Bishop Aylmer and the councillor Sir Christopher Hatton felt the need to commission a sermon in London which, in 'sharply reprov[ing]' John Stubbs, regretted that 'he or any man should think or mistrust her that she will not continue ever herself'.[49] Yet Philanax (or Sidney through him) risks the same point, imploring Basilius not to follow new courses, 'since your own example comforts you to continue on'.[50]

In reminding the two rulers of their existing strengths, the two advisers move closer still to each other. Sidney urges Elizabeth to 'let your excellent

41 Ralph Holinshed, *The First and Second Volumes of Chronicles* (London, 1587), 'The History of England', bk i, p. 4.
42 Above, Chapter 7.
43 Stubbs, pp. xxx–xxxi.
44 *OA* 384/11–12; *NA* 239/37–9; cf. *OA* 8/25.
45 *MP* 50/25; *OA* 9/5–7; cf. *OA* 9/2, 9/8–9. Sidney calls Anjou 'inconstant': *MP* 49/23.
46 *MP* 47/3–4; *OA* 7/28.
47 *MP* 51/20–1; *OA* 8/8, 358/4.
48 *MP* 57/5.
49 Nicolas, *Hatton*, p. 132.
50 *OA* 7/28–9; cf. Nicholls, *Progresses*, ii. 147.

virtues of piety, justice and liberality daily, if it be possible, more and more shine': Philanax beseeches the duke to 'let your subjects have you in their eyes, let them see the benefits of your justice daily more and more'. Elizabeth's subjects, Sidney tells her, would prefer the 'certain good' they had known during her reign to the 'uncertain good' which she sought in the match: Basilius' subjects, Philanax tells him, 'must . . . needs rather like of present sureties than uncertain changes'.[51]

The choice confronting both queen and duke is ethical as well as political. Sidney and his seniors (we saw) argued that Elizabeth could survive without the marriage if she would only 'stand' on the sources of her strength: on God, on virtue, on the love of her subjects.[52] Philanax concludes his advice to the duke with the injunction which summarises it: 'stand wholly upon your own virtue as the surest way to maintain you in that you are, and to avoid any evil which may be imagined'. Sidney warns Elizabeth against marrying from the motive of 'fear', from 'fear of standing alone'. The 'humour' of Basilius in overruling Philanax, as Greville indicates, 'make[s] fear a counsellor'. 'Arm up your courage,' Philanax exhorts the duke. 'Why should you deprive yourself of governing your dukedom for fear of losing your dukedom, like one that should kill himself for fear of death?'[53]

As so often, Basilius stands in contrast to Euarchus. Arcadia is 'a fair field to prove whether . . . fear can make' Euarchus unequal to his public duty. We soon learn the answer: he 'had his heart no whit commanded with fear'.[54] Basilius' fear does his enemies' work for them, as Elizabeth's does hers. The forward Protestant case against the queen is swollen by further charges against Basilius. The duke, says Philanax, has resolved 'to give place' to 'blows' 'before they come' and 'in the sight of an enemy to arm himself the lighter'. Elizabeth likewise resembles Basilius as he is described later: the duke 'without either good show of reasonable cause, or good provision for likely accidents, in the sight of the world put himself from the world, as a man that not only unarmed himself but would make his nakedness manifest'.[55] The opponents of the match on the council argued that the queen should call the bluff of France and Spain, whose menaces were less potent than they looked. They dissented, in vain, from the queen's view that the match was a 'necessity' if England were to be freed from the 'dangers' which 'threaten' the country.[56] Philanax urges a corresponding case upon Basilius, likewise in vain. In the *Old Arcadia* the duke needlessly yields to the 'threatenings' of the oracle. In the *New Arcadia*, where he is as cowardly and neglectful of public duty as in the earlier version, he succumbs to the blackmail of his enemies and lifts his siege of them. Philanax, pleading against that decision, presses

51 *MP* 56/34–5, 54/16–17: *OA* 7/35–8/2.
52 Above, Chapter 7.
53 *OA* 8/30–2, 7/31–4; *GP* 9/5–7.
54 *OA* 361/12–26.
55 *OA* 9/8–13, 358/5–8.
56 Hatf. 148, fo. 128.

him not to be 'terrified' of their 'threatenings', for 'a prince of judgement ought not to consider what his enemies promise or threaten, but what the promisers or threateners in reason will do'.[57] Helen of Corinth, the idealised Queen Elizabeth, succeeds where Basilius fails: she faces down the 'threateners' of war among her neighbouring monarchs. Euarchus, in the conduct of his foreign policy, defies any 'danger' that 'would offer to make any wrongful threatening upon him'.[58]

It is the 'rule of virtue', explains Sidney, 'not to abandon oneself'. Yet Basilius, as Philanax says, 'abandons himself'.[59] He abandons his subjects too. Euarchus, learning of Basilius' retreat, perceives 'the pitiful case of the Arcadian people, who were in worse case than if death had taken away their prince', for they have 'a prince being, and not doing like a prince, keeping and not exercising the place'. Elizabeth, fears Sidney, will cease to exercise her place too. The duke has 'given over all care of government'.[60] Sidney in turn replies, bravely and firmly, to the argument that marriage to Anjou would bring 'the easing your majesty of your cares'. 'That is as much to say,' he explains, 'as the easing you of being a queen and sovereign.' If she marries Anjou she 'must deliver him the keys of [her] kingdom, and live at his discretion'. Sidney's 'Letter' implicitly asks her to do what Philanax explicitly asks of Basilius: to act 'like a prince'.[61] In the New Arcadia Helen of Corinth, at one stage an idealised Queen Elizabeth, is at another an unidealised one. Like Basilius, whose 'absented manner of living' provokes the rebellion that almost costs him his life, she 'put[s] in hazard', by her 'absence', 'how my people will in time deal by me'.[62] Elizabeth's absence would be metaphorical, not literal, but would create the same 'hazard'.

Basilius' deference to the oracle has its counterpart in Elizabeth's conduct too. It constitutes in him what Sidney's party take the Anjou match to constitute in her: an abandonment of the ethical sources of self-reliance. Those sources are internal. The 'true inward strength' on which Sidney presses the queen to take her stand is matched by the 'inward comfort' of 'wisdom and virtue' on which Philanax, assuring Basilius 'that the heavens have left us in ourselves sufficient guides', urges him to rest.[63] Basilius' error, it is true, goes beyond the queen's. She does not pry into the secrets of providence. She does not share the self-delusion of Basilius, who, 'because his mind ran wholly upon Cleophila [the disguised Pyrocles]', 'thought the gods in their oracles did mind nothing but her'.[64] Philanax's insistence that 'the

57   OA 5/23; NA 417/7–11; cf. NA 417/37–8.
58   NA 253/30, 159/15.
59   NA 167/31–2; OA 7/35.
60   OA 358/30–4; NA 325/37.
61   MP 51/16–18, 50/35–6; OA 8/3; cf. NA 23/5–12.
62   NA 65/23–4, 43/26, 60/6; OA 127/1–2.
63   MP 47/14–15; OA 7/3–6, 7/14.
64   OA 133/35–134/1.

heavenly powers' are 'to be reverenced and not searched into'[65] is not aimed at her, though it does reflect the philosophy of her forward Protestant critics. That philosophy demands maximum exertion on God's behalf and minimum inquiry into his intentions. 'Wisdom above the truth', observes Greville, 'was Adam's sin.'[66] Basilius sins, or at least errs, likewise. Elizabeth does not.

Yet she does presume, as Basilius does, upon providence. Like him she does what, in the Second Eclogues of the *Arcadia*, 'Reason' does: by trusting to earthly calculation she 'deface[s]' 'heav'nly rules'.[67] We saw Greville recalling Sidney's conviction that 'to temporise with the enemies of our faith' would be 'false-heartedness to God and man', which 'would in the end find itself forsaken of both'.[68] During the negotiations for the queen to marry Anjou, Greville tells us, Sidney believed 'that the very first breach of God's ordinance in matching herself with a [Catholic] prince . . . would infallibly carry with it some piece of the rending destiny which Solomon and . . . other princes justly felt for having ventured to weigh the immortal wisdom in even scales with mortal conveniency or inconveniency'.[69] The muddling of heavenly purpose with earthly calculation is inducing, in the queen as in the duke, the abandonment of ethical foundations.

Again we learn to recognise the queen's failings by examining the duke's. Basilius should not have consulted the oracle, Philanax tells him, because 'wisdom and virtue be the only destinies appointed to man to follow . . . since they be such guides as cannot fail'; it 'is most certain' that 'no destiny nor influence whatsoever can bring man's wit to a higher point than wisdom and goodness'. If we are true to God, God will be true to us and to the virtue with which he has entrusted us. Even if, in worldly terms, we fail, our failure will have its purpose in God's inscrutable scheme. What Philanax says to Basilius is no less applicable, in Sidney's mind, to Elizabeth's diplomacy: 'although the wickedness of the world should oppress' virtue, 'yet could it not be said that evil happened to him who should fall accompanied with virtue; so that, either standing or falling with virtue, a man is never in evil case'.[70] The *Arcadia* advises us to adhere to virtue without regard to of its worldly successes and failures. It reminds us (we saw) that God 'hath not his judgement fixed upon the event' and that 'for th'event we never ought be sad'.[71] In the eyes of William of Orange, reported William Davison, it was the error of Elizabeth's policy towards the Netherlands that she 'fram[ed] her deliberations . . . according to the event and success of things'.[72]

65 *OA* 7/11–12.
66 Wilkes, p. 220 (st. 69).
67 *OA* 136/29–30.
68 Above, p. 58.
69 *GP* 33/9–14.
70 *OA* 7/3–10, 7/29–31.
71 Above, pp. 33–4.
72 K. de L., x. 101.

By his response to the oracle, explains Philanax to him, the duke is either bringing needless affliction on himself or seeking refuge from affliction which is unavoidable. For 'soothsaying sorceries', 'wherein there must either be vanity or infallibleness', are 'either not to be respected or not to be prevented'. Philanax's words again echo Sidney's 'Letter', which explains that the 'causes' that 'drive' Elizabeth towards marriage 'are either fears of that which cannot happen, or by this means cannot be prevented'.[73] We saw Sidney and Walsingham deprecating the queen's reliance on diplomatic 'accident', and Walsingham criticising her for relying not upon 'God' but upon 'fortune', which 'is but a very weak foundation for virtue to build upon'. Basilius, who rejects Philanax's advice to follow the wisdom of 'the heavens', thinks himself 'so cruelly menaced by fortune' that he retreats from his duties, 'which he thought was the surest mean to avoid her blows'. He hopes that, if he takes evasive action, 'fortune' will 'keep him unassayed'.[74] He hopes in vain. For fortune, or chance, must be the servant of activity, not of passivity. Thomas Wilson, urging 'bold dealing' by the queen in the Netherlands in 1577, remarked that 'valiant working never wanted good fortune'.[75]

It is as a response to 'change of fortune' that Basilius justifies his 'change' of 'course', 'as the ship doth her course with the wind'.[76] We have seen Sidney's 'Letter' comparing the 'course' which the queen had followed before the Anjou negotiations, and which she now proposed to 'change', to a 'ship in a tempest' which remains firm in all dangers.[77] Sidney is not inherently averse to adjustments of policy or of tactics. In the service of a 'virtuous' inner 'constancy', he believes, a man may in prudence 'sometimes alter his course' to meet 'changes' of event or circumstance.[78] Basilius offers a comparable logic to justify his own conduct.[79] But in his case the argument will not hold, for his departure from his duties, like Elizabeth's, is an embrace not of virtue but of fortune.

Walsingham, writing against the Anjou match, intimates that Elizabeth's failure to 'depend' on God derives from a 'wavering' disposition.[80] Basilius wavers too. His change 'with the wind' has many echoes in Sidney's fiction, where time and again gusts of 'wind' sway characters into following fortune instead of virtue. Wind is a recurrent symbol of inconstancy, as when 'the inconstant people' of Iberia, faced with conflicting claims to the royal succession, 'set their sails with the favourable wind' of 'fortune'.[81] The

---

73   OA 7/13–16; MP 56/18–20.
74   Above, p. 120: OA 6/23–5, 8/24.
75   K. de L., ix. 329.
76   OA 9/2–4.
77   Above, p. 123.
78   Feuillerat, iii. 122.
79   OA 9/1–15.
80   Read, Walsingham, ii. 16.
81   NA 251/32–7. Does Sidney have in mind the inconstancy of those modern Iberians, in Portugal, who yielded to Spanish rule as a result of the succession crisis in 1580, and whose 'wretched

constant man, in Sidney's moral scheme and in the neo-Stoic scheme of his time, is inwardly indifferent to good or evil fortune, to the hollow ascendancies of chance. Subordinating passion, which is fortune's friend, to reason, which is virtue's, he is not swayed by the passions of hope and fear, which would lead him from virtue's path. The Duke of Anjou, that personification of inconstancy, is, Sidney tells the queen, 'carried away with every wind of hope'; so, in pursuit of the disguised Pyrocles, is Basilius, 'whose small sails the least wind did fill'; so, in the New Arcadia, is King Antiphilus, that 'weak fool', 'neither hoping nor fearing as he should', who is 'swayed . . . as every wind of passions puffed him', 'like a bladder swelled ready to break while it was full of the wind of prosperity'.[82]

The Arcadia advises us that it is foolish, even wicked, to 'buil[d] . . . hopes on haps', to 'build . . . upon hope'.[83] We saw that Sidney, with his party, wants the queen to 'build' upon virtue, for what is firmly 'built' will 'stand'. Wind, which blows impotently round the edifices of virtue, sweeps those of fortune away. Philanax explains to Basilius, and Sidney explains to Elizabeth, the strength of those who 'stand upon' virtue: Musidorus, thralled to fortune, is reminded by Pamela of the frailty of persons who 'stand upon chance'.[84]

In consulting and responding to the oracle, Basilius succumbs not only to the claims of fear and fortune but to the superstition of which fear is the source and fortune the ally. He is forever at 'his Apollo devotions'[85] when he should be governing his country. In the New Arcadia he 'determined for three days . . . to perform certain rites to Apollo', 'knowing well enough he might lay all his care upon Philanax'. He is 'loath to take any matter of arms in hand', being 'by superstition made doubtful'. That is why he 'took the common course of men, to fly only then to devotion when they want resolution'.[86] Greville, observing a 'gathering mass / Of superstition' in his own time, thought that its 'true base' was 'fear', for 'what fear comprehends not, it inclines / To make a god'.[87]

In 1578 Walsingham described as 'rather superstitious than religious' the 'scruples of conscience' with which Elizabeth justified her refusal to act against Mary Queen of Scots and to take the bold steps by which she might 'strengthen herself with the amity of Scotland'.[88] If Sidney's friends associated superstition with timidity, they also associated it with political 'sleep': the sleep on which they blamed the inactivity of the queen and of the German

---

state', arising from the want of royal issue, seemed during the Anjou negotiations to be similar to that awaiting England (PRO, SP 15/26/*35, fos 101ᵛ, 163)?

82 MP 49/26; OA 220/31; NA 299/16–17, 303/9–14.
83 OA 148/4–5, 297/14.
84 OA 311/28–9.
85 OA 167/25.
86 NA 297/5–6, 297/25–6, 457/13–20; cf. NA 162/13–25.
87 Wilkes, pp. 173 (st. 552), 208 (st. 21). That is the argument which, in the New Arcadia, Cecropia employs to the perverted end of denying the existence of God: NA 358/37–8.
88 Nicolas, Hatton, p. 67.

princes in the face of the Catholic threat. Sidney and his allies (we saw) thought that Europe's princes were possessed by 'enchanted dreams', by the 'sorceries' and 'superstition' of popery.[89] Sleep is linked to superstition in Sidney's fiction too. In the civil war of the *New Arcadia*, the soldier Memnon, having been led – like Basilius – by 'a certain prophecy' into misidentifying the source of the danger that awaits him, was easily slain because 'he seemed to sleep in security when he went to a battle'.[90]

Greville, who thinks that 'superstition' makes men 'unactive'[91] and identifies inactivity (as he does superstition) with political 'idleness' and 'sleep', explains that Basilius governs 'unactively'.[92] To Sidney's party, Protestantism, which in its true form quells superstition and fear and keeps us 'awake', is properly an 'active' religion. Here, as so often in the minds of Sidney's circle, Protestantism came together with Humanism. Cicero's injunction, 'virtue consists in action', a principle central to the *Arcadia*, was quoted by Sir Francis Knollys to reproach Elizabeth's failure to intervene in the Low Countries.[93] Virtuous action derives from the self-reliance which God requires of us. Basilius withdraws from government to 'avoid [the] blows' of fortune: Elizabeth, remarked Sir Walter Mildmay, mistakenly saw the Anjou match as a means 'for the avoiding of dangers to herself and her realm'.[94] The false wisdom of both rulers misses the truth explained by the forward Protestant Sir Amias Paulet with England's perils in mind: that 'God will help us to avoid' the peril confronting us 'if we help ourselves'.[95]

To help ourselves we need the courage, and the calm and decisiveness of mind, to look the future in the face and to anticipate its challenges. The 'surest way' to withstand the perils facing England, Paulet repeatedly insisted, was to 'foresee' them.[96] 'Foresight', or 'prevention', is a virtue persistently commended by the *Arcadia*. It is persistently commended too by forward Protestants in the struggle for the survival of England and of Protestantism. Sir Nicholas Bacon begged the queen to recognise the perils that will await England 'if remedy be not foreseen in time'; Sir Francis Knollys, longing for Elizabeth to acquire 'a preventing heart', coupled his reminder that 'virtue consists in action' with a plea for 'vigilance, foresight, prevention'.[97] It is 'with good foresight both of peace-government, and war-defence', that the queen, if she follows Sidney's advice, will 'stan[d] alone'; Greville commends Sidney for 'foreseeing' the likely consequences of the Anjou match, and acknowledges that the queen failed to 'foresee' them.[98] In the parliament of

---

89 Above, Chapter 4.
90 *NA* 341/18–342/1; cf. *NA* 403/1, 403/8.
91 Above, Chapter 4; cf. Wilkes, p. 37 (st. 11).
92 Above, Chapter 4; *GP* 8/21.
93 Wright, *Queen Elizabeth*, ii. 74.
94 BL, Harleian MS. 6265, fo. 104.
95 Bodl., Rawlinson MS. A331, fo. 124.
96 Ibid., fos 79, 90ᵛ, 117ᵛ–18.
97 Nicolas, *Hatton*, p. 41 (cf. K. de L., xi. 100, 130); Wright, *Queen Elizabeth*, ii. 74–6; cf. Bodl., Rawlinson MS. A331, fo. 88ᵛ.
98 *MP* 51/23–4; *GP* 29/21–2, 30/24, 33/8.

1572 Elizabeth had been implicitly charged with 'great want of . . . foresight' in failing to proceed against Mary Queen of Scots, for it was a 'certain truth that evil foreseen and advisedly looked unto doth ever the less harm'.[99]

Basilius shares the queen's failing. In vain does Philanax, a man of 'fores[ight]', urge him to 'prevent' danger and to 'forethink what his enemy in reason will do'. The duke retreats from his duties 'without . . . good provision for likely accidents'.[100] By contrast Euarchus, who 'carried a heart prepared for all extremities', seeks to 'prevent' the 'peril' planned by his enemies and makes 'timely provision against' it.[101] There is a supreme irony in the hymn of gratitude ordered by Basilius, 'after sacrifice done', at the end of Book Two. His deliverance from the rebellion of which his evasion of responsibility was the cause, and from which he hid in 'miserable fear', has given him a new buoyancy. The 'fawning humour of false hope' leads him to revise his interpretation of the oracle to his advantage. Oblivious to their significance, he has the company sing to Apollo the words 'Give us foresightful minds.'[102] Foresight eludes his subjects too. 'Few' of them can think 'how to prevent' the calamity which the death of Basilius visits on them.[103]

'Foresight' is one of the qualities through which God expects us to help ourselves. Walsingham knew that, though God's providence 'many times disposeth . . . contrary to man's judgement', we must do God's work by 'foreseeing and judging of likelihoods as men may foresee and judge'.[104] Yet of the forward Protestants it is Thomas Wilson who expresses most cogently the argument about self-reliance, foresight and destiny which Philanax urges on Basilius in the opening exchange of the *Arcadia*. In June 1578 he wrote to Walsingham, in words which might equally well be Philanax's, about the queen's failure to 'prevent' the dangers before her. 'Security and contempt of harm', he observed,

> are the right means to lull us to ruin; whereas foresight and provident care preserve states in all safety. If there be a destiny, who can avoid it; and yet because things to come are unknown to man, it were good reason so to deal . . . that we should not in our judgement be condemned as the very causes of our destruction through folly.[105]

The advice of Philanax to Basilius, which corresponds to that of Sidney to Elizabeth, has another parallel. The first dialogue of the *Arcadia*, where

99 Hartley, *Proceedings*, p. 286.
100 *OA* 326/13, 7/26–8, 358/5–6 (cf. *OA* 385/31–386/1); *NA* 417/2–3.
101 *OA* 10/16–17, 355n.
102 *OA* 134/5, 132/11, 133/33, 134/17 (though cf. *OA* 128/29–31).
103 *OA* 320/12–13.
104 Read, *Walsingham*, i. 153–4.
105 PRO, SP 83/7/20 (*CSPF 1578–9*, p. 23). Cf. K. de L., xi. 662; Wilson, *Demosthenes*, pp. 44, 91; Medine, *Thomas Wilson*, pp. 138–9; *OA* 312/29–30. Wilson's words 'because things to come are unknown to man' recall too Sidney's observation that Basilius is 'desirous to know the certainty of things to come, wherein there is nothing so certain as our continual uncertainty': *OA* 5/6–8.

Philanax' advice is offered and rejected, is followed very shortly by the second, where the advice of Musidorus to Pyrocles, whom he warns against idleness and love, is offered and rejected. (The interval introduces us to the young princes and to the antitype to Basilius, Euarchus.) Philanax's advice begins the public theme of the *Arcadia*, Musidorus' the private theme. Sidney establishes the connection between the two spheres by emphasising that both Philanax and Musidorus offer 'counsel' as exemplary 'friends'.[106] The political parallel to Musidorus' advice is heightened by a moment of jest between the two young princes, when good humour has been restored between them and when Musidorus gives Pyrocles 'absolute commandments' which, according to Pyrocles, show Musidorus to be 'far fitter to be a prince than a councillor'.[107] That passage points back to the account of Basilius as a 'prince' who dismisses his friend Philanax's 'counsel' and who then, in a manner characteristic of absolute monarchy, peremptorily commands him to implement his will.[108]

The similarities between the advice of Philanax and that of Musidorus are underlined by resemblances of situation and of form. The faces of both of the advisees, Basilius and Pyrocles, betray their discomfort on hearing the truths with which the first speeches addressed to them confront them;[109] both advisers fashion their counsel to the humours of the advisees;[110] we learn what both advisers would have said had the minds of their listeners been differently set;[111] in both dialogues, long and formulaic speeches give way to contests of rapid wit.[112]

Basilius, replying to Philanax, 'deceive[s] himself': Pyrocles, replying to Musidorus, is alleged by him to 'deceive [him]self'.[113] Basilius responds to the advice of Philanax with 'choler', which is softened by 'the goodwill he bare to Philanax': Pyrocles meets the advice of Musidorus (we learn in the *New Arcadia*) with 'anger', which is muted by 'the exceeding goodwill he bare to Musidorus'.[114] Yet between the responses of the two men there is a difference. The encounter between Basilius and Philanax consists mostly of a long speech by Philanax: the debate between Musidorus and Pyrocles gives weight to both sides. For Basilius, being 'wholly wedded to his own opinion', and using 'much dukely sophistry',[115] allows only a token discussion. There is in truth nothing to discuss. Philanax is right, Basilius wrong. Musidorus and

---

106 *OA* 5/30–1, 6/32, 9/25, 10/2, 12/31–2, 18/23, 20/30, 28/19. Cf. *OA* 133/17; *NA* 55/27.
107 *OA* 25/24–5, 25/35.
108 *OA* 6/32–6, 9/19–22.
109 *OA* 8/33–5, 14/7–10.
110 *OA* 9/25–6, 16/10–12, 16/23–6. Thomas Wilson regarded the tendency of counsellors to 'frame their talk according to the humour of others' as inimical to 'free speech' (Wilson, *Demosthenes*, p. 63).
111 *OA* 6/36–7/3, 16/12–26.
112 *OA* 9/11–17, 23/6–28.
113 *OA* 9/18–19, 19/28.
114 *OA* 8/35–9, 9/1; *NA* 72/21–2.
115 *OA* 8/34, 9/18.

Pyrocles, as events will show, are both right and both wrong. Love proves to be a morally more complicated and ambiguous subject than politics. For the present we need notice only the themes which the two opening dialogues share.

Pyrocles, like Basilius, has reached a crisis in his life. He is 'upon the point of falling or rising'.[116] Like Basilius he is about to abandon his public responsibilities. Basilius is told by Philanax to 'live or die . . . like a prince': Pyrocles, to whom 'the question is . . . now whether . . . I shall live or die', is reminded by Musidorus that he is 'born so great a prince' and urged by him to 'remember what you are'.[117] The persistence of both advisees in their courses will give Sidney many opportunities to echo those injunctions: to remind us that Basilius is 'a prince being, and not doing like a prince' and that Pyrocles has not 'done anything like a prince'.[118]

Like Basilius – and like Elizabeth – Pyrocles embarks upon a 'change' of 'course' and thus hazards his 'virtue'. Love, which in Sidney's fiction is characterised by its power to effect 'change',[119] 'wrought' a 'new course' in Pyrocles, just as the oracle 'led' Basilius from his 'own course'.[120] Basilius' 'change' is 'sudden': the 'change' in Pyrocles betrays its unhealthiness by its 'sudden' manifestation (and soon love will bring an even 'more sudden' 'change' in Musidorus).[121] In love as in politics, changes of course can be fatal to virtue. Seeing a threat to his cousin's 'well chosen course in virtue', Musidorus reminds him that 'a mind well trained and long exercised in virtue . . . doth not easily change any course it once undertakes'.[122] Pyrocles, overruling that advice, duly changes course. He has entered Arcadia 'following the course' on which his 'virtue led [him]',[123] but once stricken by love he is instead 'plunged in . . . a course of misery'.[124] Other characters created by Sidney think of their lives as a 'course' which love changes. The love-stricken Gynecia is unable to 'preserve' the 'course' of 'her long-exercised virtue', 'so long embraced by her'; Philisides is educated towards a 'well guided life', only for 'love' to 'diver[t] this course of tranquillity' and to produce 'this change'.[125]

In private as in public life, change is the enemy to constancy and to the virtue it embodies. Here too the parallel between politics and love is established at the outset of the *Old Arcadia*. Philanax pleads with Basilius for 'a constant virtue, well settled', 'little subject unto' 'change': Pyrocles is

116 *OA* 24/9.
117 *OA* 8/3, 17/30–2, 19/6, 20/24.
118 *OA* 358/32–3, 391/4, 404/13–14, 412/1; *NA* 16/33, 416/31–2, 417/28, 418/3; and see the irony at *NA* 283/35–6.
119 *OA* 46/25–6; *NA* 109/30–1.
120 *NA* 68/2–3, 295/29.
121 *OA* 15/6, 14/22, 17/12, 19/28–30, 24/37, 41/3–4, 41/37.
122 *OA* 13/18, 13/9–10.
123 *OA* 9/36; *NA* 206/20–1.
124 *OA* 18/27–8.
125 *OA* 91/15–16, 91/28–9, 335/4–10; cf. *OA* 110/13, 332/14.

enjoined by Musidorus to repair his faltering 'constancy'.[126] Basilius is urged to 'continue on': Pyrocles is advised to 'remember . . . what you have been, . . . what you must be'.[127] The advisees, resolute only in misguided stubbornness, are incorrigible. Basilius 'resolutely . . . stood upon his own determination' to abandon his duties: Pyrocles adheres to his 'determination thus to change [his] estate'.[128]

Constancy requires our adherence to what Sidney's letter to the queen calls 'true inward strength'. Basilius is advised to rest on his 'inward comfort' of 'wisdom and virtue': Pyrocles is told that 'constancy' rests on 'inward good'.[129] Constancy requires courage too: Basilius is urged to 'arm up your courage'; Pyrocles, having failed to 'arm himself' against love, is instructed, in military language, to confront its challenge with 'courage'.[130] Courage fails both characters. Where Basilius' obstinate adherence to 'his own determination' is combined with 'fear', Pyrocles' countenance betrays 'some great determination mixed with fear'.[131] Instead of relying on 'inward strength', both characters succumb to 'passion' through 'weakness'.[132] They share another failing too. Basilius, to whom 'pleasure' offers 'ease of care', abandons his duty for it – a dereliction that again contrasts him with Euarchus, who is 'n[ot] beguiled with the painted gloss of pleasure'. Pyrocles succumbs to 'pleasures', those impediments to 'well-doing'.[133]

Languet feared that Sidney would succumb to them: that, as he put it in November 1579, his protégé would 'take pleasure in pursuits which only enervate the mind'.[134] It is doubtful whether Languet knew of the 'pursuit' on which Sidney had recently embarked or would soon embark: the writing of the *Arcadia*. Is poetry a form of (or a means to) 'well-doing', as Sidney's *Defence* says it should be, or is it a diversion from it, as the *Defence* acknowledges that it can be?[135] Basilius, in retreat from well-doing, turns to poetry for 'pleasure': Pyrocles, yielding to 'the conceits of the poets', discovers 'a heap of pleasures' by projecting the beauties of Philoclea on to the landscape.[136]

The 'affected' and 'excessive praises' bestowed by Pyrocles on 'this desert' echo and confirm the passage in the *Defence* where Sidney explains that 'nature never set forth the earth in so rich tapestry as divers poets have done'.[137] For the lovers of the *Arcadia*, 'poets to a man' as Richard Lanham

126   *OA* 9/5–7, 13/15, 16/9.
127   *OA* 20/24–5.
128   *OA* 9/19–20, 28/29.
129   *OA* 7/3–6, 13/13–16.
130   *OA* 7/34, 12/20, 19/15–18.
131   *OA* 9/20, 9/27, 16/4–5.
132   *OA* 5/24–5, 19/15–20/2.
133   *OA* 6/25, 274/31, 357/12, 15/31, 104/24–5. Cf. *NA* 248/32–4; *GP* 14/31, 48/14–15.
134   Pears, p. 167.
135   Above, p. 19.
136   *OA* 6/25–7, 9/28–9, 17/4–5, 15/31.
137   *OA* 16/23–4, 16/34; *MP* 78/30–4.

calls them,[138] are in thrall to their imaginations. 'Each thing he saw', we learn of Pyrocles, 'seemed to figure out some part of his passions, and . . . he heard no word spoken but that he imagined it carried the sound of Philoclea's name.'[139] Basilius, who allows himself 'a number of intermixed imaginations', surrenders to the 'fancies' that will produce his mistakes: Pyrocles is mastered by the 'fancy' or 'fancies' of love.[140] Musidorus, reproaching Pyrocles, describes 'lovers' as 'fantastical mind-infected people'.[141] Fantasy is related to superstition and inaction. On the death of Basilius, Dametas, his ignoble favourite, 'instead of doing anything as the exigent required . . . began to make circles and all those fantastical defences that he had ever heard were fortifications against devils'.[142] Public life has its disabling fantasies too. Mother Hubberd's lion is entranced, 'for fantasie is strong'.[143]

Fancy or fantasy, in Basilius and Pyrocles alike, is both a cause and an effect of 'solitariness',[144] that enemy to 'well-doing'.[145] Sidney repeatedly draws attention to what is called the 'blameworthiness' of Basilius' self-imposed 'solitary life' and 'solitary course'.[146] The common ground which his solitariness gives him with Pyrocles is emphasised too.[147] It is a general characteristic of the lovers of the *Arcadia* that they seek 'solitar[iness]' or 'lonel[iness]'.[148] Basilius' 'strange solitariness', his 'strange resolution to live so solitary', belongs to a pattern of 'strange' conduct in him:[149] Pyrocles' solitary retreat seems to Musidorus the 'strangest' effect of his love.[150]

Thus does Sidney announce, at the outset of the *Arcadia*, its public theme and its private theme and the correspondence between them. This book is more about the public than about the private theme. The private theme will surface only intermittently until Part Five, which will draw the two themes together.

138 Lanham, 'The Old *Arcadia*', p. 249.
139 *OA* 12/16–18; cf. *OA* 369/37.
140 *OA* 45/21–2, 6/5, 25/5, 27/30, 28/7–8.
141 *OA* 17/8–9.
142 *OA* 281/15–18; cf. *OA* 363/1.
143 Oram, pp. 377–8 (ll. 1325–6).
144 *OA* 6/12, 6/24, 9/28, 9/35, 15/1, 16/13, 16/28–32, 28/25–6; cf. *NA* 107/34–5.
145 Above, p. 26.
146 *OA* 123/24, 167/23, 178/6, 194/8, 224/25–6, 287/3; *NA* 25/9–10, 90/34–6, 104/11, 279/34, 415/36–7, 457/35.
147 *OA* 35/6–13, 35/34–5, 39/9, 117/15–17.
148 *OA* 49/18–20, 91/10–11, 109/11–12, 167/23. Cf. *NA* 45/5–6; Stubbs, p. 92.
149 *OA* 8/21, 11/17, 11/33, 92/6–7, 96/27, 172/29; *NA* 24/1–2.
150 *OA* 14/1–2.

CHAPTER 9

The Reign of Basilius

Basilius, then, has created, like Elizabeth, that familiar feature of the early modern political landscape, a crisis of counsel. In the late 1570s that crisis, in forward Protestant eyes, took two forms. First, the queen heard the wrong advice. Secondly, when she heard the right advice she ignored it.

Philanax, who gives the right advice, is an exceptional counsellor. Just as Euarchus, the model ruler, is unlike 'most princes',[1] so the 'true heart' from which Philanax addresses Basilius distinguishes him from 'most men' who advise monarchs.[2] The norm of kingship is represented by Basilius, the antitype to Euarchus: the norm of courtly service is represented by Dametas, the antitype to Philanax, and by the 'flatter[er]s' who raise Dametas in the duke's esteem.[3] 'True hearts' seemed to forward Protestants to be equally scarce among the counsellors of their own time. 'Princes', observed John Stubbs in *The Discovery of a Gaping Gulph* with the Anjou match in mind, 'commonly' listen to their 'chief favourites' who 'study rather for smooth, delicate words than for plain, rough truth'. Stubbs wanted the queen to spurn the 'flatterers' around her and listen to 'loyal', 'true, plain men'.[4] Greville too contrasts counsellors who 'show princes the truth' with 'self-loving creatures full of . . . servile flatteries'. He recalls that Sidney maintained a 'constant tenor of truth' in his dealings with the queen and that during the Anjou crisis he stood 'upright' and 'alone' against 'that reigning faction which in all courts allows no faith current to a sovereign that hath not passed the seal of their practising corporation'.[5]

Philanax embodies the ideal to which forward Protestants among the queen's counsellors aspired. Walsingham clung to his 'duty' to give her true advice, however unpalatable. Where Philanax is animated by 'love' and

---

1   *OA* 358/9; *NA* 161/8.
2   *OA* 6/34, 5/32–6/2.
3   Below, Chapter 12.
4   Stubbs, pp. 30–1.
5   *GP* 117/16–18, 41/19, 38/11–12, 37/30–38/2.

'affection' to give 'bold' counsel, Walsingham explains to the queen that the 'boldness' of his own counsel derives from his 'love' and 'affection' for her.[6] While in the Netherlands, Walsingham looked to his friend and fellow Secretary of State Thomas Wilson, in England, to give her candid advice.[7] Wilson himself thought 'plain', 'bold' counsel, and the 'liberty of speech' to deliver it, essential to political health. He commended Philip Sidney for the 'plain speech' which he had heard him deliver to Don John of Austria at Louvain in 1577.[8] Wilson longed for 'true-meaning counsellors' to prevail over the 'flatterers' around the queen.[9] In words that, not for the only time in his correspondence, might almost have been Philanax's, he told Walsingham in 1577 of his fear that she would dislike the 'plain writing' about the Netherlands which he had addressed to her 'after so bold a manner; but I for my part had rather be blamed now for my free speech than that her majesty should feel the smart hereafter for want of advertisements and forewarning given'.[10]

In 1579, when the wind of royal disfavour blew on the forward Protestants, the problem of evil counsel became pressing in their minds. The report in October that the queen was thinking of adding four Roman Catholics to her privy council[11] conformed to their suspicions. The conservative reaction of the later 1570s had weakened their influence on her. They felt themselves to be fighting a losing battle against 'King Richard II's men',[12] flatterers who put their own interests before those of crown and commonwealth. Walsingham, now as so often, believed that he was being outmanoeuvred by his rivals, whom he habitually suspected of being motivated either by bribery or by secret loyalty to a foreign power and of betraying their country.[13] Similar suspicions and accusations were muttered against him in return. His predicament is shared by Philanax, whose public spirit earns him the hostility of private-spirited men. Walsingham detects 'malic[e]' behind his back: 'envy' is visited on Philanax, who has to bear with false charges of 'corrupt[ion]' and is blamed for counselling the very actions of Basilius against which he has remonstrated.[14]

6 Above, p. 128: Read, *Walsingham*, ii. 70, 87, 88.
7 K. de L., x. 819.
8 Osborn, *Young Philip Sidney*, pp. 454–5. Languet had a capacity for speaking bravely and 'plainly' before princes: Pears, p. 21; [Simon Goulart, ed.,] *Mémoires de l'estat de France*, 3 vols (Geneva, 1578 edn), ii. fos 23–8.
9 Wilson, *Demosthenes*, pp. 18, 44, 62, 63, 102, 121, 77. Cf. ibid., pp. 26, 28, 58, 78, 89; Strype, *Sir Thomas Smith*, p. 209.
10 K. de L., ix. 259. Cf. Wilson's similar statement at ibid., 300–1; and the like sentiments of Sir Amias Paulet in Bodl., Rawlinson MS. A331, fos 82ᵛ, 89ᵛ, 119, 122.
11 Above, Chapter 6.
12 Wright, *Queen Elizabeth*, ii. 75.
13 Read, *Walsingham*, i. 181, 335, 415–16, ii. 84, 101 (cf. Read, *Burghley*, pp. 188, 190, 200–1); K. de L., x. 831–2, 832, xi. 65; *CSPF 1578–9*, pp. 171–2, 172; Wilson, *Demosthenes*, pp. 71, 89, 101.
14 Read, *Walsingham*, i. 335: *OA* 321/14–16, 321/25, 323/16–17, 402/8–9; *NA* 23/9–11, 325/38–9. Cf. the 'envy, spite and malice' said to have been visited on Sidney's father by his enemies for his incorruptible service in Ireland: Holinshed, *First and Second Volumes*, iii. 1549. Thomas

Yet so long as the queen's errors of policy could be attributed to evil counsel, there was at least cause for hope. For it followed that, if she could be persuaded to take different advice, her course might be redirected. It was in the periods when Walsingham accepted the integrity of his colleagues that his anxiety ran deepest. In September 1578 he acknowledged to Wilson that 'no prince could be more faithfully and earnestly dealt with' than Elizabeth by her councillors. From her refusal of their advice he concluded that God had 'closed up her majesty's heart from seeing and executing that which may be for her safety'[15] (as, in the *Arcadia*, the oracle closes up Basilius' heart from seeing and executing that which may be for his safety). At the climax of their discussions in October 1579 her councillors, whose divisions over the marriage had been so hard fought, agreed to find what common ground they could and to present the queen with a united front. The struggle among them yielded to a larger conflict between them and her. Her advisers were witnessing the emergence of a new Elizabeth, more willing to trust and impose her opinions, ready to lead where before she had followed or arbitrated.[16]

Their position could scarcely have been more difficult. The fate of the kingdom hung on the queen's decision and thus might hang on the advice they gave her for the public good. Yet in a system of personal monarchy the public good can be at the mercy of personal decisions, privately made. It was ever thus in the monarchical politics of the Renaissance, which retained their private dimension even amid the ideological intensity of the continental wars of religion. During the writing of the *Arcadia*, where wars of dreadful cruelty in Persia are fought to satisfy a monarch's love,[17] France was suffering the phase of the religious wars which was known as 'the Lovers' War'. In that conflict, Conyers Read observes, 'the love-affairs of the Queen of Navarre and her ladies-in-waiting had a good deal to do with the actions of the leaders'.[18]

Personal considerations had no less to do with the queen's conduct during the Anjou suit. Councillors hesitated to enter that delicate political territory. One reason why Sidney's decision to offer advice to the queen was a 'doubtful' step, intimates Greville, was that her inclination to marry Anjou 'may seem private'.[19] 'This matter of the marriage', acknowledged the council in October 1579, 'differeth from all other, in that her person and her own present disposition is principally to be regarded.'[20] The councillors trod as on

---

Wilson noted that 'good men [are] maliced for speaking truth'; that 'counsellors speaking for the best, do oftentimes bear the greatest blame'; that virtuous 'magistrates [are] always subject to envy': Wilson, *Demosthenes*, pp. 58, 64, 124.

15   K. de L., x. 819; cf. Huntington Library, Hastings MS. HA 13067, Walsingham to the Earl of Huntingdon, 5 April 1581.
16   MacCaffrey, *Policy*, pp. 251–2, 254.
17   *OA* 67–8.
18   Read, *Walsingham*, ii. 35.
19   *GP* 28/1–2.
20   Murdin, *Collection*, p. 336.

eggshells round the questions of biology and emotion that confronted a woman of forty-six contemplating marriage and childbirth: questions which none of them dared raise before her face and which Burghley, whose memoranda on the Anjou match are otherwise so comprehensive, judged 'meeter by physicians to be advertised to her majesty than otherwise to be set down in writing'.[21]

In October 1579 queen and council engaged in an exercise at once of brinkmanship and of buck-passing. Both sides wished to shift responsibility on to the other. It was agreed among the councillors that they would not reach a 'resolution' until they knew the queen's wishes. The queen wanted them to divine those wishes and declare in favour of them before she stated them. To help them she hinted at her 'earnest disposition for this marriage',[22] but she declined to commit herself until the council had committed itself. She had her way. Eventually the opponents of the match, Mildmay and Sidney's father among them, joined with their colleagues on the council in a common declaration. The councillors 'offered their services in furtherance of the marriage' and stated that each of them 'wisheth and liketh her majesty to marry and to have children to succeed her, and doth think it more surety than any other provision'.[23] It had earlier been the contention of councillors who were opposed to the match, as it was Sidney's in his 'Letter', that the marriage would offer no 'surety' (or 'safety') at all. Like Philanax, the councillors were overruled.

The queen's determination to assert her authority over her councillors is understandable enough. She needed to know their minds. She needed to know whether, if she married Anjou, she could carry them with her and so carry the Protestant establishment which they represented and on which, as Sidney's 'Letter' reminded her, the strength and security of her reign rested. But for her councillors the experience was humiliating.

In such humiliation there was nothing new. Elizabeth governed by tantrum. She would round on her advisers in 'extreme' rages, sending them away or becoming so 'passionate' that further discussion became impossible.[24] In July 1578, when Walsingham was in the Netherlands, Burghley mused on her volatility in a letter to him. He told him 'how sharp her majesty hath been with some of us here as counsellors', and how sharp too had been her recent remarks about 'you Mr Secretary'. 'We must all dutifully bear', Burghley concluded, 'with her majesty's offence for the time, not despairing but, howsoever she misliketh matters at one time, yet at another time she will alter her sharpness, specially when she is persuaded that we all mean truly for her and her surety, though she sometimes will not so understand.'[25]

---

21 Read, *Burghley*, p. 211.
22 *HMC Cecil*, ii. 273.
23 Ibid., 273, 274.
24 Bruce, *Leycester Correspondence*, pp. 151, 240; Read, *Walsingham*, i. 322, ii. 22–3, 101; cf. Wilson, *Netherlands*, p. 128.
25 K. de L., x. 594.

Walsingham needed the advice. In the same month he wrote to Sir Christopher Hatton that the queen's response to his own and Cobham's pleas for intervention in the Low Countries had induced:

> an intolerable grief to me to receive so hard measure at her majesty's hands, as if I were some notorious offender. Surely sir, it standeth not with her majesty's safety to deal so unkindly with those that serve her faithfully. There is a difference between serving with a cheerful and languishing mind. If there had lacked in us either care, faithfulness, or diligence, then were we worthy of blame.[26]

His distress endured.[27] In 1581, 'in heat of duty', he exploded, telling the queen that soon there would be 'no one that serveth in place of a councillor, that either weigheth his own credit, or carrieth that sound affection to your majesty as he ought to do, that would not wish himself in the farthest part of Ethiopia rather than enjoy the fairest place in England'. Sir Francis Knollys shared Walsingham's dismay. 'Who will persist in giving of safe counsel', he asked Thomas Wilson in 1578, 'if her majesty will persist in misliking of safe counsel?'[28] ('Who will ever counsel his king', asks Musidorus in the *Arcadia*, 'if his counsel' is condemned and his motives are impugned?)[29] Sidney's 'Letter' subtly invites Elizabeth to treat her councillors with more respect. She has 'a council renowned all over Christendom for their well tempered minds' and she should 'let those in whom you find trust, and to whom you have committed trust in weighty affairs, be held up in the eyes of your subjects'.[30]

So the 'choler' with which Basilius greets the plain advice of Philanax has its Elizabethan counterpart. It is muted by the duke's 'goodwill' to Philanax,[31] and doubtless the queen's rages could be assuaged by personal regard too. Yet in October 1579 she showed 'great misliking of', and was 'greatly irritated by', 'anyone who opposes the marriage', being 'very sharp in reprehending' its opponents and speaking 'very angrily' about her councillors' conduct.[32] Councillors who voiced their opposition in front of her received short shrift: Walsingham had to leave court; Hatton was excluded from her presence for a week; Knollys – who had already learned when recommending intervention in the Low Countries 'that her majesty is loath to hear me'[33] – was roundly rebuked.[34]

26 Read, *Walsingham*, i. 393.
27 Ibid., 416; K. de L., x. 730; Wilson, *Netherlands*, p. 70.
28 Wright, *Queen Elizabeth*, ii. 75.
29 *OA* 402/12–13.
30 *MP* 52/23–4, 57/2–4.
31 *OA* 8/34–9/1.
32 *HMC Cecil*, ii. 272–3; *CSPS 1568–79*, pp. 703, 704, 705.
33 Wright, *Queen Elizabeth*, ii. 74.
34 *CSPS 1568–79*, p. 704; cf. ibid., pp. 703, 705.

In the *New Arcadia*, Kalander, the duke's brother-in-law, does in a 'true-minded' spirit what the true-minded forward Protestants on the council found themselves doing in October 1579 when they endorsed the queen's inclination to marry. Knowing what Basilius wants to hear, he speaks 'to confirm what you have already determined'.[35] At the outset of the *Old Arcadia* the duke asks Philanax's 'counsel' only 'for fashion's sake'. Having heard him out, he 'resolutely . . . stood upon his own determination' and commanded him to take the necessary steps to implement it. At the height of the debates over the Anjou match, Elizabeth treated her principal council-lors in the same way: she 'told them that she had determined to marry and that they need say nothing more to her about it, but should at once discuss what was necessary for carrying it out'.[36] In 1578, when Leicester told her 'how dangerous a course' she was pursuing in the Netherlands, he 'found her', as he told Walsingham, 'earnestly resolved and bent not to change her mind'.[37] Walsingham himself thought the queen apt to decline 'to hear before she condemn[s]'.[38]

In overruling their advisers, Elizabeth and Basilius alike govern by 'will' rather than 'counsel'. Knollys, writing to Wilson, summarised the dilemma of those advising a personal monarch:

> I do know that it is fit for all men to give place to her majesty's will and pleasure, and to her affections, in all things that touch not the danger of her estate; but I do know also that if her majesty do not suppress and subject her own will and her own affections unto sound advice of open counsel, in matters touching the preventing of her danger . . . her majesty will be utterly overthrown.[39]

Basilius for his part overrules Philanax's counsel, 'making his [own] will wisdom'. For he is 'fortified with the authority of a prince whose power might easily satisfy his will'. He abdicates from his duties, and exposes his realm to hazard, 'without the advice or allowance of his subjects'.[40]

Basilius' rejection of public-spirited counsel reveals his private-spirited nature. Like Dametas, whose appointment to 'the office of principal herdman' is itself a characteristic abuse of princely power, he puts 'private' before 'public' considerations.[41] The duke's infatuation with Pyrocles (disguised as Cleophila)

---

35   *NA* 416/33, 416/7.
36   *OA* 6/32, 9/19–25: *CSPS 1568–79*, p. 704.
37   K. de L., x. 613.
38   PRO, SP 83/9/3x (*CSPF 1578–9*, p. 172). Sometimes she would not even hear. 'Our conference with her majesty about affairs', complained Leicester in 1578, 'is both seldom and slender': Penry Williams, *The Tudor Regime* (Oxford, 1979), p. 32; cf. Patrick Collinson, *Elizabethan Essays* (London, 1994), p. 42. Basilius' advisers, as far as we can see, fare no better.
39   Wright, *Queen Elizabeth*, ii. 75.
40   *OA* 9/19–20, 45/14–15, 358/4–5.
41   *OA* 8/18–22, 31/5–27, 280/33–4; *NA* 18/31–6.

blinds him to the public consequences of his actions. After the mutiny in Book Two he sees the 'dangers' brought on himself, but not those brought on the commonwealth, by his 'solitary life'. It is merely to further his amatory cause that he tells Pyrocles that he is 'now inclined to return' to his official residence. Of course he does not return. Instead his 'quiet' has to be protected from his own subjects by garrisons built under Philanax's direction in the towns and villages close to his retreat.[42]

The same pattern emerges in the *New Arcadia*. When Basilius proposes to lift the siege of Cecropia and Amphialus so as to save the lives of his daughters and Zelmane (the new name of the disguised Pyrocles), Philanax recognises that a crisis of public duty lies before him. Commanded by the duke to give counsel, he 'obey[s] not to these excellent ladies' father, but to my prince; and a prince it is to whom I give counsel'. The responsibilities of a prince, he insists, must override those of a father of a family. 'In sum, you are a prince – and a father – of people, who ought with the eye of wisdom, the hand of fortitude, and the heart of justice to set down all private conceits in comparison of what, for the public, is profitable.'[43]

Philanax's advice is doomed, for in Arcadia 'public matters had ever been privately governed'.[44] Basilius' pursuit of his own 'pleasure' conforms to an observation of Greville: that 'power' tends to 'make pleasure / The end of crowns, which God made public good'.[45] It may also conform to the conduct of Elizabeth, as the forward Protestants perceived it. 'Often have I heard you with protestation say,' Sidney's 'Letter' reminds her, ' "No private pleasure nor self affection could lead you unto" ' marriage to Anjou.[46] Why had the lady to protest so much? The 'Letter' leaves the question in the air. Was the queen ready to put public before private interest? Or would she, like Basilius, put private concerns first?

That issue was not new. In 1572 the two houses of parliament had demanded in vain that Elizabeth, whose survival had been imperilled by conspiracies on behalf of her cousin Mary Queen of Scots, proceed with Mary's trial and execution. The M.P. Thomas Digges, a client of the Earl of Leicester,[47] declared his 'sorrow to see her majesty so uncareful of her own safety'. For her survival was 'not her private case but the only pillar whereon God's church in Christendom at this day chiefly leaneth, the only shield of all faithful and true Christian English subjects'.[48] The M.P. Thomas Norton

---

42 *OA* 178/6–9, 286/6–10.

43 *NA* 416/25–32, 418/3–6. Sidney, as described by Greville, succeeds where Basilius fails: he is swayed by '[not] a private, but a public, affection: his chief ends being not friends, wife, children or himself, but, above all things, the honour of his maker and service of his prince or country' (*GP* 25/5–9).

44 *OA* 320/7–8.

45 Wilkes, p. 68 (st. 133).

46 *MP* 51/3–4.

47 Simon Adams, 'The Dudley Clientele and the House of Commons, 1559–1586', *Parliamentary History* 8 (1989), pp. 215–39, at pp. 227, 232.

48 Hartley, *Proceedings*, p. 294.

agreed: the queen's survival was 'the only pillar . . . for our politic quiet . . . and for religion the very base and pillar throughout Christendom'; princes who show excessive 'clemency', and who thus 'expos[e] their [own] persons to perils', are 'liberal of that which is not their own to give', for 'the prince is not a private but a public person'.[49]

Sidney's question hung in the air again during the council debates of October 1579. The queen's failure to provide for the succession repeatedly exposed her to the imputation of private-spiritedness: of failing to care for the fate of her subjects after her death.[50] In her attitude to the Anjou match, too, her councillors evidently detected private-spiritedness. Earlier she had intimated that in personal respects she would prefer not to marry him, and had wished it to be understood that if she did marry the duke it would be for her country's benefit, not her own. Now she wanted her councillors to appeal to her to marry him in the public interest. They would not do so. Instead the council indicated that it would support the match if the queen's personal 'liking' for her suitor should lead her to decide in favour of it. When she called on the council to acknowledge that the match offered better 'surety' than any other course, it yielded in language which hinted that the marriage would have more to do with the queen's inclinations than with the country's interests.[51] Basilius in turn, in seeking another kind of surety – or 'certainty' – from the oracle, neglects 'the care for his country'.[52]

Basilius is guided by private affections. The queen's 'affections', as Knollys recognised, were a significant element in the politics of her reign. In the Anjou suit they were on display. She flirted ostentatiously, first with Anjou's agent Simier, that 'most choice courtier', as Camden called him, 'exquisitely skilled in love toys, pleasant conceits and court dalliances'.[53] His arrival in January 1578 was greeted with a round of extravagant entertainment: dances, feasts, jousts, masques.[54] When Anjou arrived in August she flirted with him too. At a 'grand ball' she 'danced much more than usual, [Anjou] being placed behind a hanging, and she making signals to him'. She bade him a tender farewell on his departure and exchanged ardent love-letters with him thereafter.[55] Her attitude to the suit was 'largely influenced', judged the Spanish ambassador, 'by the idea that it should be known that her talents and beauty are so great'.[56] On Anjou's second visit, in 1581, her conduct attracted scandalised comment. She brought him food in bed and 'doth not attend

---

49   Ibid., p. 203; Thomas Norton, *A Warning agaynst the Dangerous Practices of Papistes*, in *All Such Treatises as have been lately published by Thomas Norton* (London, 1570), sigs Bii^v, Biii^v.
50   Above, pp. 106–7; below, p. 225.
51   *HMC Cecil*, ii. 272–3, 274; Hatf. 148, fo. 25.
52   *OA* 5/3–6.
53   Read, *Walsingham*, ii. 8.
54   MacCaffrey, *Policy*, p. 250.
55   *CSPS 1568–79*, pp. 693, 694; Read, *Walsingham*, ii. 21.
56   *CSPS 1568–9*, p. 680.

unto other matters but only to be together with the duke in one chamber from morning to noon and afterwards till two or three hours after sunset'.[57]

So at least it was said. The queen's behaviour no doubt grew, perhaps grew substantially, in the telling. It can in any case be partly explained as a public performance, intended to raise French hopes or to impress public opinion with the seriousness of the suit. In a public life permanently surrounded by men, she had learned the political advantages as well as disadvantages of womanhood. She 'was shrewd enough to see', observes Conyers Read, 'that rules framed for chivalrous love-making might very aptly be applied to diplomatic purposes'.[58] Yet, as Read himself and Wallace MacCaffrey argue, there was more to it than that. For Elizabeth the match became, as we saw MacCaffrey arguing, an intensely personal drama.[59] Her moods swung violently. Sometimes she would be in high spirits. She could suddenly seem years younger.[60] Yet she would suffer startling moods of 'melancholy'.[61] In June 1578, when the Anjou negotiations were beginning, she was reportedly 'in continual and great melancholy'. 'She dreameth', reported her councillor Sir Christopher Hatton, 'of marriages that might seem injurious to her: making myself to be either the man or a pattern of the matter'.[62] Or she would suddenly turn on her ladies-in-waiting, those frequent witnesses and targets of her rages.[63] In the period of and around the Anjou crisis, Walsingham repeatedly referred to her conduct as 'strange', the adjective that in the *Arcadia* is repeatedly used to describe Basilius' conduct too.[64]

In the negotiations of 1579 the French ambassador thought that Elizabeth was 'swayed every way like all women'.[65] Her 'passionate' conduct answered to the expectations conventionally held of women. Passion was held to be the ally of mutability and of will. Sidney – at least while still in his teens – took it for granted that 'inconstancy' is characteristic of 'a woman'.[66] Greville associated 'women' with inconstancy and 'change' and noted the dominance of 'will' in their hearts.[67] Women were supposed to be cowardly too. A Huguenot work which remarked on Elizabeth's 'inconstancy' also reproached her 'cowardice and pusillanimity', which were characteristic 'of her sex'.[68] In

---

57   Read, *Walsingham*, ii. 90 & n.
58   Ibid., 4; cf. Doran, *Monarchy and Matrimony*, pp. 156–7.
59   Above, Chapter 6.
60   MacCaffrey, *Policy*, p. 250.
61   *CSPS 1568–79*, pp. 675, 703; cf. Read, *Walsingham*, i. 316.
62   Woudhuysen, 'Leicester's Literary Patronage', p. 39.
63   Read, *Walsingham*, i. 316, 322, ii. 101; Wilson, *Netherlands*, p. 36.
64   K. de L., x. 744, 819, 832; Nicolas, *Hatton*, pp. 65, 66–7; Read, *Walsingham*, ii. 88; above, p. 145. Cf. Read, *Burghley*, pp. 195, 232; Collinson, *Grindal*, p. 259. The 'very strange humour' displayed by the queen in her anger with Leicester in the autumn of 1579 is matched by the 'strange humours' of Basilius (Wright, *Queen Elizabeth*, ii. 103; *OA* 172/29).
65   Read, *Walsingham*, ii. 32.
66   Pears, p. 4.
67   Bullough, i. 97 (sonnet xli, ll. 18–19); Rebholz, *Greville*, p. 52.
68   Kingdon, *Myths*, p. 82.

1574 Languet observed to Sidney that 'you English', instead of assisting the beleaguered European cause on the continent, 'have slunk out of it, having a woman for your leader'.[69]

The *Arcadia*, explains Greville, describes 'dark webs of effeminate princes'.[70] In Sidney's story 'feminine love', or 'effeminate love', 'doth ... womanise a man'. Pyrocles, in becoming 'an effeminate man' in his woman's clothes, proves the point.[71] The lovesick Musidorus is made effeminate too. In his previous life he would have seized upon the invitation of Basilius, offered as his reward for saving Pamela from the bear, 'to exercise his valour in soldiery'; but now his 'ambition stretched a quite other way'.[72] For as Greville says, 'hearts effeminatish' are 'adverse to war' – as Elizabeth is and as her nation, in the eyes of Sidney and his party, has become.[73] The public life of Arcadia has also been made effeminate. Under Basilius the Arcadians have 'forgotten all manly government'. That is because they are 'commanded by him that cannot command his own undecent appetites'.[74] Appetites, in Sidney's language, are passions, the feminine territory which masculine reason should govern. Basilius, taken in by Pyrocles' feminine disguise, loves him effeminately. Only when persuaded by Gynecia that 'it is high season for us both to let reason enjoy his due sovereignty' does the duke begin 'something to mark himself in his own doings' and 'with a true resolved mind' renounce his effeminate infatuation.[75]

The fate of Arcadia and of its duke has many parallels in the Europe of the late Renaissance. The 'manly virtue' of the peoples of Italy, Languet tells Sidney in 1574, has been 'soften[ed]', and their 'spirits' have thus been 'prepare[d] for servility'.[76] Women rulers, claims Languet's and Mornay's *Vindiciae, Contra Tyrannos*, tend to 'effeminate and bastardise noble spirits'.[77] Councillors who opposed the Anjou match explained that France and Spain had been weakened by the rule of their 'effeminate' kings. They regarded Henry III as 'a person effeminate passing his time in delights neither wise nor martial'. Greville relates that Sidney thought of Henry as a prince with 'effeminate vices', 'buried in his pleasures'; he also relates, with Basilius in mind, that Sidney's fiction condemns 'sovereign princes' who 'bury

---

69 Pears, p. 63.
70 GP 9/21.
71 *OA* 174/3, 20/19–20, 388/25; cf. Mark Rose, 'Sidney's Womanish Man', *Review of English Studies* 25 (1964), pp. 353–63.
72 *OA* 53/33–6.
73 Wilkes, p. 167 (st. 527); above, Chapter 4.
74 *OA* 129/30–1, 277/14–15.
75 *OA* 277/22–3, 278/17–18, 278/11.
76 Osborn, *Young Philip Sidney*, pp. 208–9.
77 Harold Laski, ed., *A Defence of Liberty against Tyrants* (London, 1924), p. 185 (cf. Garnett, p. 144). Though my quotations of the *Vindiciae* are normally taken from Garnett's recent and authoritative translation, I occasionally quote Laski's flawed edition instead (while also giving the corresponding page numbers of Garnett's text). Laski reproduces the translation of 1648, which, for all its imperfections, is closer in language to Sidney's time, and can thus be closer to his thinking.

themselves and their estates in a cloud of contempt'.[78] Late in 1577, during a breathing-space in France's wars of religion, the forward Protestant Sir Amias Paulet, Elizabeth's ambassador at the French court, wrote to Sidney's friend Edward Dyer that Henry's entourage was turning from 'martial matters' to 'pastimes and pleasures'; to another correspondent he reported that Henry's court was turning to 'sports and pastimes'. Basilius turns, 'for his pleasure', from his public duties to 'sports and eclogues'.[79]

For the contemporary parallels that appear in Sidney's fiction, though they mostly align Basilius with Elizabeth and Arcadia with England, can range beyond that ruler and that country. We cannot say whether the parallels between Arcadia and the European continent are intentional, but they do reflect Sidney's thinking about the political condition of Europe. Sidney, says Greville, believed that Henry III's 'effeminate vices' had made 'his country apt . . . either to become a prey for the strongest undertaker, or else to be cantonised by self-division'.[80] The same alternatives face Arcadia. On the one hand the Arcadians, whose land is ready to be 'overthrown by the stormy wind of foreign force', suspect that Euarchus has 'come to conquer their country'. They are proved wrong, but only because Euarchus, unlike 'most princes', is not 'dazzled with the false light of ambition' and does not take Arcadia as 'prey'.[81] On the other hand, it is 'upon the rock of self-division' that Arcadia seems likely to 'run', for if Timautus, that nobleman 'of extreme ambition', has his way, there will be 'a partition of the Arcadian state'.[82] Greville explains, on Sidney's behalf, that the France of Henry III was saved from conquest and partition by 'the providence of chance': the deliverance of Arcadia, says Greville, is 'chanceable'.[83]

Europe had another 'buried' prince too: the Emperor Rudolf II, whose court Sidney had visited in Prague, and who like Basilius had retreated from the world. Through astrology he attempted what Basilius essays through the oracle: he sought to penetrate the mysteries of providence which Sidney thinks reserved by God.[84] In 1574 Sidney observed that Rudolf's 'so long absence' had made his Bohemian subjects 'very evil content' and that they 'seemed to bend to disobedience': in the *Arcadia* the rebels rise 'emboldened with the duke's absented manner of living'.[85] Sidney's perspective was always European as well as English. He was dismayed, Greville discreetly reveals, by the qualities of 'the present princes reigning', both 'foreign and domestic'.[86] He saw, as Greville says, that it was in the interest of Catholic and Protestant

78 K. de L., xi. 409, 410; GP 48/13–19, 8/19–24; cf. *HMC Cecil*, ii. 284.
79 Bodl., Rawlinson MS. A331, fos 102, 124: *OA* 6/25–6.
80 GP 48/17–19.
81 *OA* 360/23–4, 354/15, 357/13, 358/9–11.
82 *OA* 360/23, 321/33–4, 322/18–19.
83 GP 48/22–3, 9/14.
84 R. J. W. Evans, *Rudolf II and his World* (Oxford, 1973); and see Duncan-Jones, *Sir Philip Sidney*, p. 129.
85 Feuillerat, iii. 98, 101: *OA* 127/1–2.
86 GP 48/11–12, 65/4, 85/15–18.

princes alike to stand up to the advances of Rome and Madrid, but that they lacked the spine and wakefulness to do so. The spineless and dormant Basilius (whose name means 'kingly') is a type as well as a person. He typifies the failings of monarchy in his time and all times: failings which Sidney ponders with one eye on England, one on foreign countries.[87] Yet, as the opening exchange between Basilius and Philanax leads us to expect, it is the resemblances between the duke and Elizabeth, and between Arcadia and England, that shape the public theme of the *Arcadia*.

Greville contrasts 'effeminate craft' with 'manly wisdom'; the 'discipline of doing well', he thinks, is 'manly'.[88] 'Doing well', or – in the recurrent phrase of Sidney's fiction – 'well-doing', is virtuous action. Greville scorns 'effeminate unactiveness'[89] and explains that Sidney's fiction shows what happens when 'effeminate princes' 'unactively . . . bury themselves'.[90] Writing under James I, Greville convinced himself that Sidney had lived in 'active times' which had now yielded to 'the narrow salves of this effeminate age'.[91] Yet while Sidney was alive, 'active times' would have seemed to Greville passing or past.[92] In 1579 Stubbs's *Gaping Gulph* rebuked the effeminacy he witnessed around him, reproaching those who saw in the Anjou match a chance to reassert, through diplomatic methods, England's control of France: 'in times past the noble Englishmen delighted rather to be seen in France in bright armour than in gay clothes and in masking attire; they did choose rather to win and hold by manly force than by such effeminate means'.[93]

Walsingham disliked the queen's 'wooing matters'. He believed that 'matters of love and affection be not governed by wisdom'.[94] His words reflect an ideal of austere and rational manliness which the queen's conduct during the Anjou match can only have affronted. Sidney develops a gentler view of womankind. In his fiction effeminacy is more often the failing of men than of women. But the queen's conduct during the Anjou suit, that parade of effeminacy and passion and flirtation, can only have been distasteful to him. His distaste for the amorous conduct of Basilius is underlined in a dialogue between the duke and the disguised Pyrocles, which brings home the cowardice that Basilius shares with Elizabeth: 'you are terrified', Pyrocles tells him, 'before you receive any hurt!' The duke's hollow protestation to Pyrocles, that he will return to his official residence, is delivered, Sidney relates, in 'such honey words which my pen grows almost weary to set down'.[95] Sidney, says his early biographer Thomas Moffet, abhorred 'the wantonness' of 'doting and disgusting old men' who 'violently' pursued

---

87 Below, Chapter 12.
88 GP 22/7–8; Wilkes, p. 157 (st. 488). Cf. Wilkes, p. 156 (sts 482, 484); GP 54/26.
89 Wilkes, p. 37 (st. 11).
90 GP 9/21, 8/21–3.
91 GP 7/11–12.
92 Cf. below, Appendix A.
93 Stubbs, p. 57.
94 Read, *Walsingham*, ii. 6, 19.
95 OA 178/24–5, 178/11–12.

'venereal pleasures'.[96] Were the aged absurdities of Basilius' pursuit of young Pyrocles any more repellent, in Sidney's mind, than the flirtation of Elizabeth – that 'old maid', as opponents of the Anjou match called her[97] – with a wooer half her age? That question, too, hangs in the air.

Basilius' flaws of temperament and policy put his survival at risk. The survival of Elizabeth, which her flaws of temperament and policy have already jeopardised, will become more gravely imperilled if she marries Anjou. Sidney explores the dangers created by Basilius, and thus those that have been created by Elizabeth or will soon be created by her if she marries Anjou. Those dangers await the two rulers both at home and abroad.

At home, there is the peril of rebellion. The misgovernment of Basilius provokes rebellion. Book Two, summoning the images of discord that were the dread of Sidney's class, describes the 'barbarous' rising of 'the many-headed multitude', that drunken outburst of 'enraged beasts' who are 'knit together only in madness', who emit 'savage howlings', and whose 'winy mirths' turn to 'bloody rages'.[98] Basilius' life is narrowly rescued from the rebels by Pyrocles. For his predicament the blame is his alone. The rising has occurred because he has spurned good counsel. Hideously as the rebels voice and exploit their grievances, they have sound points to make about his rule. Their complaints correspond to the counsel given by Sidney and others to Elizabeth against the Anjou match. Their hostility to the sway of 'foreign hands', and their resentment at 'the want of a prince', recall leading arguments in Sidney's 'Letter', which urges the queen not to submit England to foreign rule and advises her against 'the easing you of being a queen and sovereign'.[99] The rebels' question about Basilius, 'Who would call him duke if he had not a people?', echoes frequent expressions, by Sidney's friends and allies, of the same conviction about the responsibilities of monarchs to their subjects.[100]

Elizabeth risks provoking rebellion too. If she marries Anjou, advises Sidney's 'Letter', she will offer pretexts for disobedience to 'all discontented persons, such as want and disgrace keeps lower than they have set their hearts'. Basilius' dismissal of Philanax's advice gives scope to the same kind of social discontent: the grievances of the rebels are voiced by persons 'of wretched estates (and worse minds), whose fortunes change could not impair'.[101] With Stubbs, and with councillors who opposed the match, Sidney observed that the discontented English papists needed only a 'head' to set England on fire. In Anjou, he and they believed, they would find one. Once

---

96   Moffet, *Nobilis*, p. 79. Cf. the remark of Sidney's beloved Aristotle about the passions of old men which is cited by Duncan-Jones, *Sir Philip Sidney*, p. 84; though see too above, Chapter 2, n. 103.
97   Above, p. 101.
98   *OA* 129/16, 131/22, 124/2–6, 126/22, 128/7–8.
99   *OA* 127/32–3; *MP* 51/17–18.
100 *OA* 127/18; below, p. 224.
101 *MP* 48/24–5; *OA* 127/19–20.

installed as Elizabeth's husband, thought forward Protestants, Anjou would be ready to use in England the tactics which – like the Guises – he had adopted in France: to aggrandise his own power he would be as happy to work against as with the monarchy to which he was ostensibly allied. He could be expected, wrote Sidney, to 'draw together evil affected humours' against Elizabeth and to plunge the country into civil war: in the *New Arcadia*, where Basilius' misgovernment gives rise to civil war, the 'humours' of the disaffected are dextrously exploited by Amphialus, the prince who puts himself at the head of the revolt.[102] The social material of rebellion is the same in the uprising led by Amphialus as in that which besieges Basilius in Book Two of the *Old Arcadia*, and of the same kind as that in which Sidney sees a basis of revolt in England: Amphialus raises 'such whom any discontentment made hungry of change, or an over-spended want made want a civil war'. Later in the *New Arcadia* Clinias, turning against his master Amphialus, uses the same method, seeking to entice into mutiny those who are impelled by 'discontentment of some unsatisfied ambition' or who 'had not found such sudden success as they had promised themselves'.[103]

Amphialus, like the rebels of Book Two, puts good arguments to evil ends: he covers 'the foulness of his treason' with 'glosses of probability' and 'true commonplaces'.[104] In Protestant minds there were traitors in Elizabethan England who possessed the same arts of manipulation and dissimulation and who, given half a chance, would do as Amphialus does. Protestant England lived in fear and expectation of Catholic rebellion. In pressing upon the queen the gravity of that threat, Sidney recalled the Northern Rising of 1569. That revolt may seem to us a final spasm of protest by a dissolving feudal order. It seemed nothing so innocuous at the time. The memory of it haunted Protestant minds. So long as Mary Queen of Scots survived as a focus of discontent, revolt might easily come again. In 1581 Walsingham wrote to the Earl of Huntingdon, the President of the Council of the North, that though the north might be outwardly loyal, 'I . . . fear a great number of those which make now a good liking of the present state would be found very dangerous and doubtful in obedience to her majesty upon any such occasion to be offered them as the obstinate papists expect of foreign aid and of the return of such fugitives as were in the last rebellion.' The danger was all the greater now that England had lost control of Scotland and that northern English malcontents had 'Scotland so friend[ly]. And therefore I do wish in this case her majesty to fear the worst.'[105] Basilius, who should likewise fear the worst, is oblivious to the peril of it.

The threat of conspiracy and rebellion, which fed on the memory of 1569, grew with the mounting evidence of Catholic plotting in the early 1580s.

102   MP 49/5–6, 50/4 (cf. MP 49/19–20); GP 32/14–19; Stubbs, p. 80; Hatf. 148, fo. 48ᵛ; NRO, F(P)M 111, fos 2, 5, 15ᵛ; NA 325/2.
103   NA 324/35–6 (cf. NA 325/1–5), 386/24–7.
104   NA 325/13–15.
105   MP 49/1–5; Huntington Library, Hastings MS. HA 13065 (21 March 1581).

The subject grew in Sidney's fiction too, occupying a larger place in the *New Arcadia*, the product of the years 1582–4, than in the *Old*. In the *New Arcadia* Amphialus, knowing 'how violently rumours do blow the sails of popular judgements', 'caused rumours to be sowed and libels to be spread', just as Clinias, 'who was bold only in privy whisperings', had contrived, in plotting rebellion, to 'whisper rumours into the people's ears'.[106] Again, Sidney reproduces – whether or not by design – the language of contemporary politics and the anxieties it reported. In Elizabethan England, rumours, whispers and libels were taken to be the stock-in-trade of plotters of rebellion. In 1582 Sir Francis Hastings, Huntingdon's brother, told Walsingham of the 'secret seducers that run about to poison the land, and by privy whisperings to withdraw the simple sort into a detestation of the present government'.[107]

Amphialus, in launching his rebellion, distributes pamphlets which make 'most false applications' and are 'painted with rhetorical colours'. He takes other steps too 'to colour the better his action'.[108] The peril posed to Basilius' regime by that tactic would have been all too recognisable by Elizabethan readers. In 1569 Thomas Norton, writing against the northern rebels from a forward Protestant standpoint, had attacked the 'false' proclamation issued by the leaders of the rising, who had used plausible arguments so as to 'colour' their 'evil designs'; they had 'put on a vizor of great virtue'. Norton traced the support for the Northern Rising to the cause which likewise fills the ranks of Amphialus' rebel army and of the uprising of Book Two: 'each man is likeliest to desire a new estate, as he hath most cause to be weary of the old'.[109] The *New Arcadia* carries another parallel to 1569 too. The predicament of Cecropia, when she decides to incite (with Amphialus) the revolt of Book Three, corresponds to that which moved the northern earls to rise. They, like her, had been caught plotting against the regime. They, like her, knew that the government's 'examinations' were growing 'dangerous'. She does what they did in raising the north: she 'thought to play double or quit'.[110] Though Basilius has at last grasped the truth of her conduct, his awakening has come too late. Will Elizabeth awake in time, before Mary or Anjou overthrows her?

In Arcadia as in Elizabethan England, internal perils combine with external ones. Basilius, defective as a ruler at home, is defective in foreign policy too.

106 *NA* 325/9–10, 327/34–5, 337/36, 288/26.
107 Huntington Library, Hastings MS. HA 5086 (8 April 1582), fo. 2.
108 *NA* 325/11–15, 326/23, 352/13.
109 Norton, *To the Queenes Majesties Poore Deceyved Subjectes of the North Country* (London, 1569), sigs B4, A5, A6, A8ᵛ, C1ᵛ. Cf. Norton, *Warning*, sigs Eiii, Gi, Gii, Oi; Norton, *A Bull Granted by the Pope to Doctor Harding* (in *All Such Treatises . . . published by Thomas Norton*), sig. Cii.
110 *NA* 319/33–4; cf. Norton, *Bull*, sigs Biiiᵛ–Ci. The emphasis in Amphialus' propaganda on the low birth of the duke's 'hated' adviser Philanax (*NA* 325/38–9, 352/10) also corresponds to rebel propaganda of 1569 (McCoy, *Rites of Knighthood*, p. 35; cf. MacCaffrey, *Policy*, p. 135, and Sargent, *Dyer*, p. 17) – if also to much other sentiment of the time.

He has been remiss in his conduct towards his Grecian neighbours and in failing to perceive or resist the perils posed to all the states of Greece by their common enemies. His failings are those discerned by forward Protestants in Elizabeth's behaviour towards her co-religionists on the continent and in her unwillingness to recognise or confront the Catholic threat common to them and to England.

In addressing that theme in the *Arcadia*, Sidney does what Thomas Wilson, whose thoughts so often resemble his, does in history, the branch of instruction which Sidney's *Defence* ranks beneath poetry.[111] Wilson's pioneering translation and study of Demosthenes, a substantial scholarly achievement, was published in 1570 with the title *The Three Orations of Demosthenes*. It carried a bluntly topical preface and commentary. To William Cecil he described it as 'a book wherein he unfolded his thoughts of the present dangerous condition of England'.[112] 'I have reviewed the lessons of Greece,' explains Wilson's prefatory verse, 'and have prepared Greek remedies for my unfortunate country.'[113] The title-page describes the work as 'most needful to be read in these dangerous days, of all that love their country's liberty, and desire to take warning for their better avail, by example of others'. The message of the treatise anticipates Wilson's 'A discourse touching this kingdom's peril, with th[e] remedies', a memorandum apparently drawn up in the spring of 1578, that dark hour for forward Protestantism.[114] In his work of 1570, recalling how Demosthenes had inspired the Athenians to resist 'King Philip' of Macedon, Wilson urges Englishmen to emulate their example by withstanding a modern King Philip:

> Every good subject . . . should compare the time past with the time present, and ever when he heareth Athens, or the Athenians, should remember England and Englishmen . . . that we may learn by the doings of our elders how we may deal in our own affairs, and so . . . avoid all harm that else might unawares happen to us.[115]

Wilson was not the only forward Protestant to direct Elizabethan readers to parallels between the two Philips. The same strategy was adopted in an

---

111 Though Wilson belonged to an earlier generation than Sidney, the two men, both dependants of Leicester, would have found much to talk about – not least Wilson's *The Arte of Rhetorick*, which influenced the younger man. It has been observed that where Wilson believed that an English logic and an English rhetoric could serve the wider interests of England, Sidney saw the same function for English poetry: Sidney, *Apology for Poetry*, ed. Shepherd, pp. 13, 25; cf. Andrew Hadfield, *Literature, Politics and National Identity* (Cambridge, 1994), pp. 108–17, 132–69. But the only time we see Wilson and Sidney together is in their joint audience with Don John in Louvain in 1577.

112 BL, Lansdowne MS. 12, no. 9; cf. Medine, *Thomas Wilson*, ch. 6.

113 I adopt the translation by Medine, *Thomas Wilson*, p. 136.

114 PRO, SP 12/123/17.

115 Wilson, *Demosthenes*, sig. B1ᵛ. Two years after Wilson's publication an M.P. quoted Demosthenes on the threat of Philip of Macedon to Athens and warned that 'the like' was to be 'expected in England': Hartley, *Proceedings*, p. 373 (cf. p. 232).

anonymous, undated work entitled *Orations, of Arsanes against Philip the Trecherous Kyng of Macedon*. Its author was evidently the forward Protestant Thomas Norton. Norton, whose words often anticipate Sidney's, will be of interest to us in a later chapter as the co-author of *Gorboduc*, the play of 1562 which is commended by Sidney's *Defence of Poetry* and which we shall find echoed in the *Arcadia*.[116] In 1581 he was sent to the Tower for speaking out against the Anjou match.

I do not know the origin of the prevailing assumption that Norton's *Orations, of Arsanes* was published in 1560. Perhaps it was, but its language and preoccupations, and its unambiguous hostility to Spain, are characteristic of the forward Protestantism less of that time than of the years around 1570,[117] the year when Wilson's *Three Orations of Demosthenes* was published. In that same year Norton expressed anxieties, which conform to Wilson's, about the conduct of the Elizabethan government. Within the conventional codes of politeness he found ways to blame the 'timorous policy' of the regime, its needless 'fear', its 'lack of daring', its want of 'boldness and sharp execution upon enemies'.[118] Perhaps Norton's *Orations*, which refers to the efforts of 'the learned and eloquent' Demosthenes to arouse the Athenians against the threat of Philip of Macedon,[119] was written to complement Wilson's publication: perhaps Wilson's book was intended to complement Norton's. Certainly Norton makes the same points as Wilson about the events of their time. *Orations, of Arsanes*, explains Norton, offers a 'precedent of good admonition, and a mean of great efficacy, to awaken Christians, and a substantial teaching to trust in God and to fear shrinking from the defence of his cause and church'.[120] The parallel between the two Philips is heightened by Norton's account of Philip of Macedon as 'defender of the holy league'.[121]

Arsanes was the King of Persia's lieutenant in Lesser Asia when Philip, having subdued Greece, threatened Persia. For though Greece and Persia were ancient enemies, they now had a common enemy who threatened them both with extinction. Norton invents, or largely invents, an oration for Arsanes. Just as evangelical Protestants urged Elizabeth to waken to the peril on the continent and to intervene there before Philip II could invade England, so Norton, deploying an ingenious if strained geographical parallel, has Arsanes urge the Persians to 'cast [their] eye over the narrow seas into Europe' and observe the 'gathering of the clouds in the coasts of Europe'. For 'there is some great tempest a-brewing towards us'. Philip of Macedon,

---

116   Below, Chapter 11.
117   Cf. Michael Graves, *Thomas Norton. The Parliament Man* (Oxford, 1994), p. 41.
118   Norton, *Warning*, sig. Bi^v.
119   Norton, *Orations, of Arsanes*, sig. Eiii^v.
120   Ibid., sig. Ai^v. Wilson and Norton were both clients of Burghley, though Wilson was also close to Leicester and Walsingham, while Norton was close to Mildmay and Walsingham (Leimon, 'Walsingham', p. 75; Graves, *Thomas Norton*, p. 124). The eagerness of both Wilson and Norton for forward Protestant causes sometimes separated them from Burghley.
121   Norton, *Orations, of Arsanes*, sigs Aiii, Aiiii, Biii.

greedy for 'revenge', is 'creeping forward by little and little'.[122] Arsanes'
language is that which we have met in the state papers written by Elizabethan
forward Protestants. If we are to resist Philip's advances, says Arsanes, we must
'awake' from 'security';[123] we must show 'vigilant foresight'; we must seize
our 'opportunities' or 'occasions' before it is 'too late', for the preservation of
kingdoms consists 'chiefly in foreseeing and preventing of mischiefs . . . and in
accepting or following opportunities when they be proffered'.[124]

Thomas Wilson's edition of Demosthenes transposes the forward Protes-
tant case for the assistance of continental Protestantism to ancient Greece.
Norton transposes it to ancient Persia. Wilson explains that the 'ancient
Grecians', seeing that 'all Greeceland [was] in danger of King Philip',
'thought themselves bound in conscience to tender the preservation of all
Greeceland, not only of their own several state or country'.[125] Norton has
Arsanes remark that, Philip of Macedon having absorbed 'the most part of
the ancient Graecia', the Persians need to 'look upon our next neighbour'
and aid 'our trusty friends' against 'their and our common foe', who
'pursueth . . . our dear friends' 'with fire and sword'.[126] With Wilson, Norton
was in favour of taking the war to the enemy: by that means the threat of
invasion could be 'diverted' rather than 'drawn hither'.[127]

In the *Arcadia* as in Wilson's and Norton's books, Greece stands for
Protestant Europe. Arcadia, though it usually looks like an independent
kingdom, is a 'province' or part of a larger federation,[128] its fate indissolubly
connected to that of Greece, as England's is to that of international Protestantism. Where England and its Protestant neighbours must unite against the
threatened conjunction of Spain and France, Euarchus 'saw the Asiatics of the
one side, the Latins of the other, gaping for any occcasion to devour Greece,
which was no way to be prevented but by their united strength'. In seeking
to rally the Grecian states to unite, he presses a point that is especially
pertinent, by analogy, to England in the face of the international Catholic
peril: he 'by many reasons mak[es] them see that, though in respect of place
some of them might seem further removed from the first violence of the
storm, yet being embarked in the same ship the final wrack must needs be
common to them all'. Basilius is deaf to that plea, as Elizabeth is unresponsive
to its forward Protestant counterpart. In the retreat of Basilius, 'the mightiest
prince of Greece next to Euarchus', Euarchus discovers what forward Protestants saw in Elizabeth's passivity: 'he straight considered the universal case
of Greece deprived by this means of a principal pillar'.[129] (We have seen the

---

122 Ibid., sigs Bi^v–iii^v. Norton's book contains two other 'Orations' which illustrate parallels with
England's current problems.
123 Ibid., sigs Ui&^{v}, Ciii.
124 Ibid., sigs *iii^v–iiii, Bi, Di, Ciii^v, Diii^v–iiii.
125 Wilson, *Demosthenes*, sig. B4^v and pp. 67, 73.
126 Norton, *Orations, of Arsanes*, sigs Bii, Di^v, Ciii^v; cf. ibid., sigs Diiii^v–Ei.
127 Ibid., sig. Eii.
128 *OA* 4/3, 360/21, 388/19, 400/5; *NA* 158/37–159/2.
129 *OA* 358/35–359/1, 355n., 358/3–4, 358/28–9; cf. *OA* 414/16–17.

M.P. Thomas Digges describing the queen's 'safety' as 'the only pillar whereon God's church in Christendom at this day chiefly leaneth', and Thomas Norton using the same language.) It is now that Euarchus makes his melancholy assessment of Basilius' conduct: the duke 'did so suddenly without the advice or allowance of his subjects, without either good show of reasonable cause, or good provision for likely accidents, in the sight of the world put himself from the world, as a man that not only unarmed himself but would make his nakedness manifest'.[130] In marrying Anjou the queen would do the same. It was the mistake of advocates of the match, thought Sir Walter Mildmay, to suppose that it could provide 'good provision'– Euarchus' phrase too – against peril.[131]

There are other correspondences of language between the account of international politics in the *Arcadia* and forward Protestant assessments of the international politics of Elizabeth's time. On the death of Basilius the shepherds 'fear our hateful neighbours' might, / Who long have gaped to get Arcadians' treasure',[132] an anxiety given substance by Euarchus' observation that the Asiatics and Latins are 'gaping' to 'devour Greece'. In November 1578 the forward Protestant William Davison feared that the divisions among the Netherlanders were playing into the hands of their 'common enemy', 'who . . . hath long since gaped for this advantage'.[133] Councillors who opposed Elizabeth's prospective marriage to Anjou referred to 'the ambitious gaping for her death' by princes eager to annex her throne.[134]

At other points, too, the subject of foreign policy brings the vocabularies of fact and fiction together. Euarchus, seeing his enemies preparing for war against him even as they give 'many tokens of continuing still their former amity', is careful not to be deceived by 'such practices'.[135] The 'practices' of false 'amity' troubled forward Protestants too. England, as it struggled to navigate between the French and Spanish threats, received many intimations of friendship both from Spain, with which England's relations had been outwardly amicable for most of the 1570s, and from France, never more so than during the Anjou suit. Forward Protestants – among them Norton and Wilson in drawing their parallels with Greek history – intimated that Elizabeth was all too prone to yield to 'credulity . . . when cunning dealing is used under colour of love and friendship': too ready to be deceived or lulled by the professions of 'amity', by the false 'promises', of the great powers.[136] The word 'practices' was habitually used, particularly by forward Protestants, to describe the devious contrivances of Spain and France and their agents against

---

130   Above, pp. 152–3; *OA* 358/4–8.
131   BL, Harleian MS. 6265, fo. 104; *OA* 358/5–6.
132   *OA* 349/23–4.
133   K. de L., xi. 100.
134   *HMC Cecil*, ii. 268.
135   *OA* 355n.
136   K. de L., ix. 338, x. 711; *CSPF 1577–8*, p. 592; Norton, *Orations, of Arsanes*, sigs Bi[v], Cii; Wilson, *Demosthenes*, p. 53 (cf. pp. 3, 64, 65); Bodl., Rawlinson MS. A331, fo. 9[v] (cf. fo. 12[v]); Read, *Walsingham*, i. 217.

England and Protestantism.[137] The ambassadors of those powers, Sidney would remark in 1583, 'be noted for great practisers'.[138]

In foreign affairs, Sidney and his party knew attack to be the best form of defence. They knew about politics what the *New Arcadia* tells us in reporting the course of love: that 'who stands only upon defence stands upon no defence'; that 'as well the soldier dieth which standeth still as he that gives the bravest onset'; that 'lying still doth never go forward'.[139] Yet if the forward Protestants were a war party, they were not warmongers. Some of them did, in some moods and at some times, welcome the realisation that intervention in the Netherlands might bring fresh territorial influence to England. Yet there were, they believed, ethical rules which must govern and restrict the pursuit of conquest and dominion. We need to meet those rules in order to follow one theme of the *Arcadia*.

It is a theme that leaves Basilius behind, for the failings it addresses are not his. Equally they were not Elizabeth's. They characterised the kings who were her enemies and whose policies had wrought the slaughter and destruction of the wars of religion. Unfortunately they also characterised Anjou, the military adventurer whose martial activities had exacerbated those miseries, a man, in the eyes of opponents of the match, 'fed with an ambitious hope of his own greatness'.[140] If Elizabeth married him, would not England be led in his military wake? Prominent among Sidney's objections to the Anjou match, as Greville relates them, was the fear that the duke's 'ambition or necessities might entice or draw her' into his continental 'designs', to which her own 'moderate desires' would thus give place. Greville adds that Sidney, again with the Anjou match in mind, 'discovered the great difference between the wisdoms of quiet princes – in their moderate desires of subsistence – [and] the large and hazardous counsels of undertaking monarchs, whose ends are

---

137 See e.g. *GP* 30/34–31/2; K. de L., ix. 117, 338, x. 133, xi. 22, 65; BL, Harleian MS. 6265, fo. 106ᵛ; BL, Cottonian MS. Titus BII, fo. 493ᵛ; NRO, F(P)M, fo. 15, F(P)M 123, fos 1, 2, 3ᵛ; PRO, SP12/123/17 (fos 53ᵛ, 54); *HMC Cecil*, ii. 244; Wright, *Queen Elizabeth*, ii. 4; Read, *Walsingham*, i. 72, 163; Read, *Burghley*, p. 181; *Mémoires et correspondance de Duplessis-Mornay*, ii. 236–7.

138 Feuillerat, iii. 144. There is a further correspondence of language. An M.P. of 1572, quoting Demosthenes with Wilson's book perhaps in mind, warned against England's 'barbarous' enemy, Spain (Hartley, *Proceedings*, p. 373; cf. Wilson, *Demosthenes*, sig. B1ᵛ and p. 70). 'Barbarous', the term with which the Greeks had described their neighbours to the east, was the adjective that came to the minds of forward Protestants and their friends when they described the Spaniards (NRO, F(P)M, fo.1ᵛ; *CSPF 1575–7*, p. 488, *1577–8*, p. 592; *The Apologie or Defence, of the Most Noble Prince William* (Delft, 1581), sig. O2ᵛ). A motive of the princes in assisting a subject of the tyrant of Persia, Tiridates, is 'to save a Greek people from being ruined by such whom [the Arcadians] call and count barbarous' (*NA* 206/30–1). For they share 'the natural hate the Grecians bare the Persians'. (Thomas Norton has Arsanes remark on 'the natural hatred between the two realms of Persia and Greece', on 'the old grudge and well-near foresworn hatred between the realms of Persia and Greece': *Orations, of Arsanes*, sigs Biiᵛ, Ci, Eiᵛ.) In fighting the Persians Musidorus and Pyrocles use 'incomparable valour', a quality England would need against Spain (*OA* 68/17–19).

139 *NA* 197/7–8, 133/21–2, 128/37.

140 BL, Harleian MS. 288, fo. 148&ᵛ; cf. BL, Cottonian MS. Titus BII, fo. 493ᵛ.

only to make force the umpire of right'.[141] Sir Walter Mildmay, arguing against marriage to Anjou, declared that it was 'like[ly]' that it would 'draw her majesty into wars for the furtherance' of his ambition, 'as King Philip did Queen Mary'.[142]

Thus a queen whose fault had been timidity might swing to the opposite error. During the Anjou crisis it was not the opponents of the match but Leicester's enemies, Sussex and the Catholic nobleman Henry Howard, those warm advocates of it, who argued that her new alliance might enable Elizabeth to conquer the Low Countries and either annex them to the English crown or share them with her husband. Sussex and Howard were potential instruments, and would probably be principal beneficiaries, of the palace revolution at Elizabeth's court which forward Protestants dreaded in the late 1570s and of which the Anjou match seemed the harbinger. Alarmed by the domestic aims of those enemies, Sidney's party was repelled by their foreign ones too. The annexation of the Netherlands by Elizabeth and Anjou, Mildmay remonstrated, would be 'a thing void of justice'.[143] It was Howard's claim that the marriage would give England scope for 'increase and enlargement of dominion and empire'.[144] 'Wars grounded on ambition for increase of dominion', believed Walsingham, 'are always unjust.'[145] Greville, too, rebuked princes whose 'ambition' moved them to 'enlarge' their dominions and 'encroac[h]' upon others.[146] In speaking against the match, Mildmay referred disdainfully to those medieval wars which 'grew upon quarrels of . . . princes, either to recover or enlarge their dominions', and which were waged to gratify rulers, not for the benefit of their subjects.[147] We do not know how widely the expansionist sentiments expressed by Sussex and Howard were canvassed during the Anjou crisis. But according to John Stubbs the suit inspired among a number of Englishmen a reckless enthusiasm, encouraged by Anjou's agents, for a revival of their country's medieval glories.[148] Such a mood was alien to the principles and sober hearts of forward Protestants.

Territorial ambition, in their minds, does not justify war. But liberation from 'oppress[ion]' is, as Greville maintains, a different matter.[149] In September 1578 Sir Amias Paulet, believing (wrongly) that the queen had resolved to fight in the Low Countries after all, told her of his 'great joy' on learning that she would aid the Netherlanders 'not after the manner of ambitious

---

141 GP 28/16–19, 35/6–9.
142 BL, Harleian MS. 6265, fo. 109; NRO, F(P)M 111, fos 2, 5.
143 Above, Chapter 6; Lehmberg, Mildmay, p. 158.
144 Stubbs, p. 170; cf. Peck, Leicester's Commonwealth, p. 78.
145 Read, Walsingham, i. 153. Cf. K. de L., xi. 161; KAO, U1475: Z1/10, p. 653.
146 GP 14/16, 26/6, 30/3, 49/26–7, 68/11–12, 124/1–2, 127/23–5; Wilkes, pp. 150 (st. 461), 171 (sts 542, 544).
147 BL, Harleian MS. 6265, fo. 104ᵛ.
148 Stubbs, pp. 56–7; cf. Leimon, 'Walsingham', p. 123.
149 GP 124/1–5; Wilkes, p. 166 (sts 523–4); cf. Mornay, A Woorke concerning the Trewnesse of the Christian Religion, sig. ★3ᵛ, where it is explained that Sidney died while fighting 'in defence of persons oppressed'.

princes desiring to decide their neighbours' controversies with intent to enlarge their own territories, but in equity and charity to deliver the oppressed from thraldom and tyranny'.[150] It had been with the difficulties of the Netherlanders in mind that Walsingham had asked, in or around January 1576, 'What juster cause can a prince that maketh profession of the gospel have to enter into wars than when he seeth confederacies made for the rooting out of the gospel and religion he professeth?'[151] To Walsingham and his allies, the marriage of Elizabeth to the Catholic Anjou would be a repudiation of the cause of the oppressed. A war fought by England in the Netherlands as a result of the match would have no ethical warrant.

The view to which forward Protestants subscribed is that set out in the concluding section of Languet's and Duplessis-Mornay's *Vindiciae, Contra Tyrannos*, which addresses the question 'Whether neighbouring princes may by right, or ought, to render assistance to subjects of other princes who are being persecuted on account of pure religion, or oppressed by manifest tyranny?' The answer, of course, is yes. 'If a prince' – such as Philip II in the Low Countries – 'rides roughshod over the fixed limits of piety and justice, then a neighbour will be able to rush forth from his borders piously and justly, not in order to invade another's, but to command him to be content with his own.' There is no justification, on the other hand, for a prince who conceals 'ambition or pursuit of gain under the cloak of piety'.[152]

The 'ambition' to 'enlarge', then, is one source of wrongful war. Another is the pursuit of 'glory'. Languet's warnings to Sidney not to 'give the glorious name of courage' to military adventure and bloodshed[153] are paralleled in the *Arcadia*, which reveals what Pyrocles calls 'the vainness of these things which we account glorious'.[154] Sidney's fiction has much to say about the destructive character of war, about the slaughter and misery that kings inflict on innocent subjects in satisfying their own ambition and thirst for glory.[155] The *Arcadia* reproduces the language in which Sidney's party expressed its view of international morality. In that language, 'ambition' and 'glory' are enemies to the self-sufficiency with which a country should be content. Rulers should respect their 'neighbours' and behave towards them with 'justice' and 'moderation'.

That ideal was voiced in a pamphlet of 1583, translated into English in the same year, by a former ally of England's forward Protestants, the Humanist scholar, statesman and soldier Philip von Marnix. In 1576 Marnix had supplied Leicester with arguments showing that it would be legitimate for

---

150 *CSPF 1578–9*, p. 181. Cf. Bodl., Rawlinson MS. A331, fo. 88ᵛ; Norton, *Orations, of Arsanes*, sigs Ciiiᵛ, Di, Dii.

151 Read, *Walsingham*, i. 317; cf. K. de L., viii. 95.

152 Garnett, pp. 173–4, 183–4.

153 Pears, pp. 137, 147, 154.

154 *OA* 21/21–2.

155 *OA* 68/6–8, 154/9–10, 155/22–4; *NA* 178/17–24, 207/13–14; cf. Blenerhasset, *Revelation of the True Minerva*, sig. Bi.

England to aid Orange and liberate the Netherlands from Spanish oppression.[156] But for Marnix, too, liberation was one thing, expansion another. Nations must learn to live together and respect each other. Hitherto, explained his pamphlet of 1583, 'was there never province, town or valiant and virtuous citizen, but did account their safety, liberty and common quiet to depend upon the moderate and peaceable government of their mightiest borderers', valuing nothing more than that 'their neighbours' should:

> establish their estate in justice, or moderate affection, and in peaceable containing themselves within their own bounds and limits . . .. And assuredly as ambition is ever to be feared and suspected . . . so is it more dangerous in those, who being already of great power and strength, cannot nevertheless bridle their covetous affections, how large soever the extent of their bounds and limits be . . ..[157]

So the opening sentence of the *Arcadia* makes a contemporary political point:

> Arcadia among all the provinces of Greece was ever had in singular reputation . . . principally for the moderate and well tempered minds of the people who (finding . . . how the shining title of glory, so much affected by other nations, doth indeed help little to the happiness of life) were the only people which, as by their justice and providence gave neither cause nor hope to their neighbours to annoy them, so were they not stirred with false praise to trouble others' quiet, thinking it a small reward for the wasting of their own lives in ravening that their posterity should long after say they had done so.[158]

Englishmen must hold to the same rule. Later in the *Arcadia* Philisides dreams of his native Samothea, or England, which, says Sidney's source, retained that pristine name only until 'desire of rule endeavoured to take hold in the minds of men, and each prince began to enlarge his own dominions'.[159] That perversion is a parallel, in international relations, to the destruction of pristine constitutional and social harmony recorded in the song learned by Philisides on Ister Bank.

Just as the Arcadians are the 'only people' – 'only', in this context, meaning 'exemplary' – who are blessed with wisdom towards their neighbours, and are thus different from 'other nations', so Euarchus' attitude to

---

156 K. de L., viii. 113–18.
157 [Marnix], *A Pithie, and most Earnest Exhortation, concerning the Estate of Christendom . . . by a Germaine Gentleman, a Lover of his Countrey* (Antwerp, 1583), p. 3.
158 *OA* 4/3–14. *Gorboduc* (cf. above, p. 162) had observed what happens 'When kings on slender quarrels run to wars', the destruction they wreak being 'deck'd with glorious name / Of noble conquests': William Tydeman, ed., *Two Tudor Tragedies* (Harmondsworth, 1992), p. 80 (II. i. 608–17), and cf. p. 278.
159 Holinshed, *First and Second Volumes*, 'The Description of Britaine', p. 3.

foreign conquest is exceptional and exemplary too. For, just as that ideal king acts unlike 'most princes' as governor of his country, so in his foreign dealings is he unlike 'most princes', 'even those whom great acts have entitled with the holy name of virtue'. Those princes seek 'the enlarging of their dominions, wherein they falsely put the more or less felicity of an estate'.[160] Euarchus' philosophy links him to a Humanist tradition of distrust of the glory of war.[161] The tradition is expressed in More's *Utopia*, which complains that 'most princes' apply themselves to 'the arts of war' and 'are generally more set on acquiring new kingdoms by hook or crook than on governing well those they already have', so that the desire to 'enlarge . . . boundaries' has become 'the curse of all countries'.[162]

Euarchus, measuring 'his greatness by his goodness', has no 'lickerousness of dominion', only a concern for international 'justice'. He:

> never used war (which is maintained with the cost and blood of the subject) but when it was to defend their right whereon their well being depended. For this reckoning he made: how far soever he extended himself, neighbours he must have; and therefore . . . he did rather stand upon a just moderation of keeping his own in good and happy case than, multiplying desire upon desire, seeking one enemy after another, put both his honour and people's safety in the continual dice of fortune.

He thinks war 'never to be accepted until it be offered by the hand of necessity', a principle that aligns him with Walsingham, who believed that 'wars grounded on necessity', 'not for sovereignty but for safety, not to enlarge but to retain', were 'just'.[163] For Euarchus no more than for Walsingham are justice and restraint in international relations to be confused with weakness. Fully prepared, as Walsingham wanted his queen to be, to fight 'a just war', Euarchus wages it with 'no want of true courage', as 'the earth hath . . . borne enow bleeding witnesses'. 'To his eternal fame' he 'not only conquered' the 'enemies' who had unjustly sought to 'conquer' Macedon, 'but established good government in their countries'.[164] The young princes, who in liberating foreigners 'help the weaker', follow Euarchus' example when they deliver countries oppressed by tyranny: they give them 'good governors' and lay the foundations of good 'government'.[165] But between liberation and annexation there lies a firm line. Mercifully for Arcadia, Euarchus respects it. That is why, as Greville explains, he declines the 'opportunity', which any prince of 'ambition' would take, to seize

160   *OA* 358/9–13.
161   Robert Adams, *The Better Part of Valor. More, Erasmus, Colet, and Vives on Humanism, War, and Peace, 1496–1535* (Seattle, 1962).
162   More, *Utopia*, ed. George Logan and Robert Adams (Cambridge, 1989), pp. 14, 44.
163   *NA* 159/16–17; *OA* 361/14–15, 358/16–25, 355n.; Read, *Walsingham*, i. 153, 317.
164   *NA* 162/30, 159/10–11, 306/20–1; *OA* 10/9–15.
165   *OA* 68/17–18; *NA* 179/3–4, 175/9–15.

Arcadia and 'establish' the monarchy there 'successively to him and his forever'.[166]

Pastoral, explains Sidney's *Defence of Poetry*, can 'show that contentions for trifles can get but a trifling victory'.[167] Much warfare, he thought, is directed towards the trifling goal of establishing or recovering 'titles' of honour or possession. Languet agreed. The princely preoccupation with 'title[s]', he remarked to Sidney, is 'childish'.[168] Euarchus is as indifferent to them as to 'the shining title of glory'. As King of Macedon he inherits 'a kingdom which in elder time had such a sovereignty over all the provinces of Greece that even the particular kings' – those of Arcadia among them – 'therein did acknowledge . . . some kind of fealty thereunto'. Finding 'by his latter ancestors' either negligence or misfortune that in some ages many of those duties had been intermitted', he nonetheless:

> would never stir up old titles how apparent soever, whereby the public peace with the loss of many not guilty souls should be broken; but contenting himself to guide that ship wherein the heavens had placed him, showed no less magnanimity in dangerless despising, than others in dangerous affecting, the multiplying of kingdoms.[169]

The philosophy to which Euarchus subscribes is that which Greville attributes to Sidney. It is also attributed by Greville, as he ignores the gulf that separated Sidney from his queen, to Elizabeth. Elizabeth, after all, could scarcely be accused of having been a warmonger. But in Sidney's lifetime, when the queen's timidity had dismayed Sidney and Greville alike, Greville would not have thought to highlight the virtue which, after Sidney's and Elizabeth's deaths, he emphasised in her diplomacy. In retrospect he remembered that the queen, 'this mirror of justice', had 'restrain[ed] that unnatural ambition of getting other princes' rights within the natural bounds of well governing her own'. That had been Burghley's justification of Elizabeth's stance, not the view of it taken by Sidney's party.[170] The queen, Greville recalled, had been right not 'under any pretence of title' to 'question or conquer upon foreign princes' possessions'. Greville, who commends Euarchus for overlooking his ancient title to Arcadia, praises Elizabeth for having eschewed England's 'native, though discontinued rights' in France, which she could have invoked to sanction the 'reconquering any part of her ancient domains'. Instead, he recalled, her aim in aiding the Huguenots had been to keep them 'free from oppression'. England's medieval 'conquests', which the Anjou match seemed to its bolder advocates to offer the country a chance to emulate, had sprung, wrote Greville, from 'pride', and 'we strove

166   *GP* 9/27–10/5.
167   *MP* 95/5–6.
168   Pears, p. 99.
169   *NA* 158/36–159/9.
170   *GP* 127/22–5; Read, *Burghley*, p. 186.

to gripe more than was possible for us to hold'.[171] In the *Arcadia* the Latins are 'ready to lay an unjust gripe upon' Greece: Euarchus by contrast renounces the chance of 'laying an unjust gripe upon' Arcadia, 'which yet might have been beautified with the noble name of conquest'.[172]

Basilius, like Elizabeth, has no thirst for conquest. His errors of foreign policy, like hers, have derived not from ambition but from timidity and neglect. But those defects are quite as serious. They expose Arcadia and England to the prospect of conquest from without.

The two monarchs also expose their countries to the prospect of collapse from within. When Sidney wrote the *Arcadia*, England had lived for more than a decade with the peril of convulsion, both from without and from within. The most direct causes of that danger had been the presence of Mary Queen of Scots in England, and Elizabeth's failure to bring her to trial and execution. To Mary's place in Sidney's fiction we now turn. It is a place that alters between the *Old Arcadia* and the *New*, and so illuminates a difference of political perspective between the two versions.

---

171 *GP* 47/26–7, 56/29–35, 57/32–3 (though see *GP* 61/21–2); cf. Wilkes, p. 121 (st. 344). Mildmay maintained that Anjou's ignoble intervention in the Netherlands reflected France's ancient 'preten[ce of] title' to that land: BL, Harleian MS. 6265, fo. 109.
172 *OA* 355n., 358/26–8.

CHAPTER 10

Mary Queen of Scots

When Sidney wrote the *New Arcadia*, between 1582 and 1584, the Anjou crisis was past. There are many signs in the *New Arcadia* that he had not ceased to think about its lessons. By transporting Basilius' abdication, the parallel to the Anjou match in the *Old Arcadia*, into the plot of the *New*, he ensured that the parallel would persist there. Yet the duke's abdication, with which the *Old Arcadia* begins and which is the manifest source of the disasters that follow it, is less dominantly situated in the *New Arcadia*. The fresh political imagining of the revised version is mostly directed elsewhere.

Though the Anjou crisis heightened the dissatisfactions of forward Protestants with their queen, the dissatisfactions had been present long before it and would long outlast it. From 1568, when Mary Queen of Scots had fled to England, until her execution in 1587, discontent time and again centred on Elizabeth's failure to bring her to death. Over that period the arguments about Mary's fate, and the language which expressed them, changed little. The Anjou match, which brought the issue of the succession to the front of the nation's mind, did nothing to allay the anxieties which her presence in England aroused. Advocates of the match, it is true, were able to claim that it would remove the threat posed by Mary to England. But to its opponents, Anjou (son to Catherine de Medici) and Mary (once Catherine's daughter-in-law) seemed fellow demons of international Catholicism. Sidney's party held the deepest suspicions of the intentions which Anjou would bring to the marriage. They feared that, once the Catholic momentum in England and his own power-base there were strong enough, he would desert Elizabeth for Mary; or, even if not, that he would marry Mary after Elizabeth's death and join his new wife on the English throne.[1] If the Anjou match figures prominently in the *Old Arcadia*, so does the queen's failure to dispatch Mary. But where the issue of the marriage acquires little fresh life in the *New Arcadia*, the issue of Mary acquires much more.

---

1 Above, Chapter 6.

In the *Old Arcadia* the state is reduced to havoc by Basilius' apparent death. In the *New Arcadia* it is torn by civil war, fought in the duke's lifetime. There is a second shift too. In the *Old Arcadia* Basilius' death sharpens the danger, already present in his lifetime, of foreign invasion. In the *New Arcadia* the emphasis on foreign threats is much reduced.[2] The years which produced the *New Arcadia* were a time of diminishing conflict between forward Protestants and Elizabeth over foreign policy and of an ever more intense preoccupation among forward Protestants with the enemy within. The concern of Sidney's party with conspiracy peaked with the uncovering of the Throckmorton plot in 1583. As a friend and ally of Walsingham, who ran the queen's intelligence service, Sidney may have been privy to the government's knowledge of Catholic plotting. The possibility becomes stronger if, as has been forcefully argued, his and Fulke Greville's friend the philosopher Giordano Bruno was acting as an agent for Walsingham.[3]

The focus of Catholic conspiracy was Mary Stuart, whom John Stubbs's *Gaping Gulph* called that 'most hidden and pestilent adversary creature that lives to prince and state', 'the fairest daughter of the pope and sh[ee]t anchor of all papists'.[4] It was on the conduct and treatment of Mary, as the forward Protestant Sir Nicholas Bacon observed, that 'the only prosperity and adversity' of Elizabeth's reign depended.[5] Elizabeth, in the perception of Sidney's party, had time and again averted her gaze from the peril which her cousin posed to her. In the *New Arcadia* Basilius makes a parallel mistake. The centre of conspiracy against him is a character who does not appear in the *Old*, his sister-in-law Cecropia. Scheming, unscrupulous, diabolical, determined to topple the legitimate ruler from the thone, she conforms to the forward Protestant image of Mary Stuart. Even when Cecropia's plots do not correspond to Mary's own seditious conduct (or alleged conduct), they do correspond to plots that were formed on her behalf and probably with her knowledge.

Cecropia's ambitions, like Mary's, feed on the issue of the royal succession. Like Elizabeth's negotiations with Anjou, Basilius' decision to marry Gynecia was a striking departure from a resolve which time has appeared to confirm. Where Elizabeth liked it to be understood that 'of her own nature she did always forbear' to marry, Basilius in his younger days declared a 'bachelorly intention'.[6] He abandons his resolve only in his advancing years, as Elizabeth proposed to abandon hers well after the conventional age of marriage. Like the Anjou negotiations, Basilius' marriage upsets others with an eye on the throne. Cecropia is moved to conspire against him because her son Amphialus, who has been next in line, is now 'cut off' from 'all hope' and 'expectation' of the 'succession'. While it lasted, that 'expectation' was itself

2 Cf. Zeeveld, 'Uprising', p. 213.
3 Bossy, *Bruno*, passim.
4 Stubbs, p. 78; cf. Blenerhasset, *Revelation of the True Minerva*, p. viii.
5 NRO, F(P)M 99, fo. 4ᵛ.
6 Murdin, *Collection*, p. 328; *NA* 318/7–8.

7 Mary Queen of Scots in ?1578.

a danger to Basilius. Mary Stuart's 'expectation' of the English throne, declared Walsingham, spelled danger to Elizabeth.[7]

Before the action of the *New Arcadia* begins, Cecropia has already been thwarted in a 'plot' to assassinate the duke.[8] During that action the depth and wickedness of her contrivances emerge in three episodes.

The first is the pursuit of the princesses by the lion and bear at the end of Book One. In the *Old Arcadia* the beasts have strayed into the vicinity of Basilius' household 'by chance', but in the *New Arcadia* they belong to Cecropia. She claims, in self-defence, that they had appeared by 'mischance', their arrival 'being happened by the folly of the keeper'. However, Gynecia, the duchess, rightly 'took a further conceit of it, mistrusting greatly Cecropia because she had heard much of the devilish wickedness of her heart', and

7 *NA* 117/34–6, 318/33–4, 319/8; Read, *Walsingham*, ii. 14. The correspondence of Cecropia to Mary may yield a further analogy. The forward Protestants hoped that Mary's son James, their likely candidate to succeed Elizabeth, would prove to be what Cecropia's son Amphialus is, 'like a rose out of a briar, an excellent son of an evil mother' (*NA* 317/27–8).
8 *NA* 318/28–31.

'conjectur[ing] it proceeded rather of some mischievous practice than of misfortune'. The duke, 'good man', does not share his wife's suspicions, even though evidence of Cecropia's true character is already known to him.[9] Wrapped in the pleasures of his retreat, he is blind to the threat to himself and his country. His wife and daughters are left to 'marvel that Basilius looked no further into it, who . . . thought so much of his late-conceived commonwealth that all other matters were but digressions unto him'.[10]

Foiled by the princes, who save the princesses from the beasts, Cecropia tries other means. Her second attempt is the popular mutiny in Book Two. Here too there is a contrast between the two *Arcadias*. In the *Old Arcadia* the mutiny was a spontaneous uprising against 'foreign' influence.[11] In the *New Arcadia*, where the rebels no longer complain of interference from without,[12] it is set on foot from within, wholly or largely by Cecropia's agent Clinias. He was 'privy to all the mischievous devices wherewith she went about to ruin Basilius and his children'. He had been employed, 'ever since the strange retiring of Basilius, to whisper rumours into the people's ears'.[13] But Basilius has again been blind to the villainy practised against him. Being 'not the sharpest piercer into masked minds', and being 'tickled' by the flattery bestowed on him by Clinias 'in the hearing of his mistress', he swallows his professions of loyalty and his smooth account of the uprising, which naturally omits his and Cecropia's part in it.[14] The duke's gullibility mirrors that of Elizabeth, whom forward Protestants thought insufficiently alert to 'the cunning of the world' when listening to shows of friendship from her enemies.[15]

If Basilius shares Elizabeth's failing, Philanax does not. Nor does a man who has much in common with Philanax, the head of Elizabeth's intelligence service Sir Francis Walsingham. Like Walsingham, Philanax and his associates are thorough in their investigations. Their 'examinations' into the causes of 'this late sedition all touc[h] Cecropia with vehement suspicion of giving either flame or fuel unto it'. It is now that, finding his investigations 'grow dangerous', she resolves 'to play double or quit'.[16] The third episode, which has no counterpart in the *Old Arcadia*, duly follows. Where Mary Queen of Scots, in the judgement of forward Protestants, was guarded with insufficient security against her would-be deliverers, Basilius has confined his daughters 'in so unfit and ill-guarded a place' that they are in danger of being 'conveyed' to a 'foreign country', a fate that would be 'to the whole

---

9   *OA* 46/29; *NA* 92/2–8.
10 *NA* 117/23–118/6.
11 *OA* 127/32.
12 Zeeveld, 'Uprising', p. 213.
13 *NA* 288/21–8, 319/30–1.
14 *NA* 293/18–20, 290/19–20.
15 K. de L., ix. 338; above, p. 165.
16 *NA* 314/18–21, 319/33–4.

commonwealth pernicious'. The seizure of Mary from captivity had been the
continuous aim of English and foreign conspirators since her flight to England. It had been the goal of the northern rebels in 1569, of the Ridolfi
conspirators in 1571, of Don John of Austria in 1577–8. The fear that Anjou,
if spurned by Elizabeth, might seek to capture or 'deliver' Mary weighed on
the minds of the councillors who debated the Anjou match in 1579.[17]
Cecropia has Basilius' daughters kidnapped (though she is thwarted in her
plan to seize their parents).[18] She does not convey them abroad, but she does
plunge Arcadia into a civil war – as Mary's deliverance would plunge
England into one.

In the *Old Arcadia*, too, the succession issue convulses the land. Pamela, we
are repeatedly reminded, is the 'just' and 'undoubted heir' to Basilius'
throne.[19] But she is under-age. The age-restriction would lapse if she were
married, and she and Musidorus are ready to marry, but 'all the estates of her
country' are 'ill satisfied touching her father's death'. Some Arcadians want
Pamela to reign, others Philoclea; some want Gynecia to be regent; some
want to enthrone Philanax, some to prevent his rule at all costs; Timautus
wants to partition the country with Philanax.[20] Pamela's situation – though
not her age – resembles that of Elizabeth's legitimate heir Mary Stuart, first
when Pamela is under Dametas' guard, then when she is under Philanax's.
Sidney does not draw those correspondences together. They look less
pressing in his mind than other contemporary parallels in his fiction. They
nonetheless seem too many and too close to be accidental.

   Like Mary, Pamela is due to succeed by the laws of inheritance. But her
conduct, like Mary's, has raised question-marks against her claim, and
Arcadia's estates are an obstacle to her succession, as parliaments have been to
Mary's. Under Dametas' guard she thinks herself, as Mary thought herself, a
victim of 'unworthy bondage', of the 'unreasonable restraint of her liberty'.
There is an attempt, of the kind which Sidney and his party long believed
Mary and her allies and prospective husbands to be planning, to 'convey' her
from captivity and 'stea[l]' her away to the next seaport'.[21] When she is
captured and placed under Philanax's guard, her attitude again corresponds to
Mary's: she has 'spite to see herself, as she thought, rebelliously detained'.[22] If
Pamela succeeds in regaining the throne, she will be expected, as Mary is,[23]
to turn on those who have imprisoned her and have sought to prevent her
succession, and to 'revenge [the] wrong done her', a prospect for which she

17 Hatf. 148, fo. 29. Cf. K. de L., xi. 266; Wright, *Queen Elizabeth*, ii. 4; Read, *Walsingham*, i. 116–
    17; Feuillerat, iii. 144.
18 *NA* 325/40–326/4, 320/3–5.
19 *OA* 315/28–9, 319/16, 378/26.
20 *OA* 319/24–5, 321/3–23, 322/18–19.
21 *OA* 107/25–6, 172/30, 399/27, 401/33, 172/26.
22 *OA* 370/5–6; cf. *OA* 320/1–2, 402/8.
23 Below, p. 186.

indeed displays an appetite.[24] Yet in Arcadia the opponents of the due heiress are at sixes and sevens, torn between different candidates and different courses of action. The opponents of Mary's succession in England were likely to find themselves in comparable disarray.

The 'convey[ance]' of Pamela from captivity is as critical a moment in the *Old Arcadia* as in the *New*. In the earlier version it is Musidorus who conveys her, this time with her own connivance. He steals her from the captivity in which her father has placed her. The insecurity of her captivity, in the *Old Arcadia* as in the *New*, is the fault of her father. This time she is removed from the guard of Dametas, to whom Basilius has foolishly entrusted her confinement. Musidorus' intentions towards Pamela are akin to those of which Don John of Austria and the Duke of Anjou were suspected towards Mary:[25] he plans to 'brin[g] . . . an army hither', to impose his will on the native ruler, and – so Philanax charges – to 'tyranniz[e]' over Arcadia.[26] Pyrocles for his part is ready to 'take . . . away' Philoclea, 'though it were with the death of her parents'.[27] Later, when Philanax has placed Pamela under guard, others want to 'deliver' her, as Don John and Anjou were expected to seek to 'deliver' Mary.[28]

Yet the chief presence of Mary Queen of Scots in the *Old Arcadia* does not lie in the resemblances between her situation and conduct and those of Pamela. It lies in the trial and condemnation of the princes in Book Five. The young princes, like Mary, are princes of a foreign land who have committed treason in the country they have entered. From their trial we learn how, and on what grounds of legitimacy, Elizabeth should eliminate the threat from Mary. To follow Sidney's lesson, we must look first at the debates about Mary's fate which the *Old Arcadia* reproduces.

Elizabeth had long been under pressure to bring her cousin to trial. In the parliament of 1572, when the pressure was at its most intense, the M.P. Sir Thomas Scot spoke for most of his colleagues in claiming that if the queen were to 'tarr[y] . . . longer' she would find 'her realm conquered, and herself deposed'.[29] Walsingham, who campaigned for Mary's death from 1569, was sure that 'so long as that devilish woman lives, neither her majesty must make account to continue in quiet possession of the crown, nor her faithful subjects assure themselves of safety of their lives'.[30]

A besetting sin of Elizabeth's reign, in the opinion of Walsingham and Mildmay, was the 'lenity' of 'too merciful a princess' to its enemies, 'a thing

---

24 *OA* 315/28–30, 325/27–9, 370/6–7, 397/22–4.
25 Feuillerat, iii. 144; K. de L., xi. 266; Wright, *Queen Elizabeth*, ii. 4; Read, *Walsingham*, i. 116–17.
26 *OA* 173/25, 176/15–16, 399/27–30.
27 *OA* 216/30–1.
28 *OA* 323/35–6, 352/25.
29 Hartley, *Proceedings*, pp. 349–50.
30 Read, *Walsingham*, i. 184.

very commendable in a prince, if our corruption abused not the same'. As a result of it, there was too 'little awe . . . in the hearts of the subjects'.[31] Elizabeth, who amid the courtesies of Sidney's 'Letter' against the Anjou match looks to have the virtues of Euarchus,[32] is in plain truth opposite to that model king, lacking precisely the virtues he embodies. For the 'extreme severity' of his 'justice' has cured the 'corruption' of his realm; it has created an 'awful love' for him among his subjects; the Arcadians regard him with 'reverent awe'.[33] Thomas Wilson thought 'severity' to the opponents of the Elizabethan regime 'most necessary, lest both laws and the law maker through overmuch softness do grow into contempt'.[34] Thomas Norton, longing for 'justice' to be executed on Mary Stuart and her fellow Catholic conspirators, was dismayed by the royal 'lenity' and 'excess of clemency' that forestalled it.[35]

Euarchus embodies the principle of 'justice'. Elizabeth does not.[36] In 1579 Walsingham complained of the queen's 'irresolutions of doing justice' against Mary, of her failure to do what 'both reason and justice require'.[37] 'Justice' was the insistent cry of those who wanted Mary dead. The M.P.s of 1572 bemoaned Elizabeth's 'slackness of justice' against her.[38] It is 'dangerous for the state', they argued, 'to swerve from the ministration of justice and the due execution of law'; 'to spare offenders in the highest degree is an injury to the prince and state of the realm'.[39] Thomas Wilson told the Commons of the wonder expressed by 'foreign princes that, [Mary's] offences being so great and horrible, the queen's majesty suffereth' that 'traitor' 'to live', and declared that 'we ought importunately to conclude for justice, justice'.[40] 'Much pardoning offences', he believed, 'destroyeth a state.'[41]

Those who demanded the trial of Mary knew that she had two principal objections at the ready. She was to use both of them when she was at last brought to trial in 1586. First, as an 'absolute princess', she was exempt from the jurisdiction of any court. Secondly, as a 'stranger' in England she could not be tried by English laws. The court which tried her was prepared for those claims. As Walsingham reported, it ruled that Mary's 'prerogative of being an absolute queen could not in this case serve her for a privilege against the laws of this realm'. For 'all persons, of what calling soever, remaining in other princes' dominions, and committing an offence against

---

31   Ibid., 70, 73, 184; BL, Harleian MS. 6265, fo. 104; below, pp. 204–5; cf. Hatf. 148, fo. 58.
32   Above, p. 118.
33   NA 160/27, 160/36–7, 160/15; OA 382/31.
34   K. de L., ix. 303.
35   Norton, Warning, sigs Aiii[v], Bi[v], ii[v], iii[v], Mii[v]; Hartley, Proceedings, pp. 325, 408; Norton, Orations, of Arsanes, sig. Aiii.
36   Cf. below, pp. 203–4.
37   Read, Walsingham, i. 184.
38   Hartley, Proceedings, p. 277.
39   Ibid., p. 287.
40   Ibid., pp. 328–9, 365.
41   Wilson, Demosthenes, p. 103.

the said prince, were subject to the laws of the place where the offence was committed'.[42]

The question whether Mary could be legally tried, which was fundamental to the safety of England, also raised fundamental issues of political and legal thought, which imprinted themselves on the minds of Sidney's generation. They persisted there after her death, when Philip Sidney's brother Robert meditated, with Mary in mind, on the legal position of 'absolute princes who willingly or by fortune have come into other princes' dominions'.[43] Equally concerned was the reader of the composite *Arcadia* of 1593 whose notes survive in the Sidney family papers. Regretting that Elizabeth had been 'loath' to have Mary executed, he remarked that Mary had entered the realm 'unlawfully', and that in any case 'absolute princes are not exempt from all kind of punishment. For seeing they are men, and subject to commit the greatest faults, it cannot stand with divine justice. For they differ from other men but by the qualities of degree and function.'[44]

Similar views about Mary had been vigorously expressed by the M.P.s of 1572. It was Elizabeth's duty, they asserted, to punish Mary whether she 'be queen or subject, be stranger or citizen'. 'A king passing through another king's realm or there resident', they argued, 'is but a private person'; 'a confederate being in the country of his confederate is to be punished as though he were a subject'; 'every person offending is to be tried in the place where he committeth the crime without exception of privilege'.[45] The tiny minority in the Commons that wished to exempt Mary from trial appealed to the principle of *ius gentium*, the law of nations, which, in the case of an absolute queen who was also a stranger, must overrule England's own laws. To that argument there was a clear reply: 'What have we to do with *ius gentium*, having law of our own? Shall we say our law is not able to provide for this mischief?'[46]

There was another objection which M.P.s had to confront. Mary was Elizabeth's kinswoman, whose blood Elizabeth, on that ground as well as others, was loath to shed. Again M.P.s had their replies ready. Mary must be brought to justice 'be she kin or not kin', for 'God willeth his magistrates not to spare either brother or sister or daughter or wife or friend, be he never so high.'[47]

In the trial scene of the *Old Arcadia* the princes, who were earlier disguised as a shepherd and an Amazon, have second disguises. Musidorus appears as

---

42 Wright, *Queen Elizabeth*, ii. 319; Antonia Fraser, *Mary Queen of Scots* (London, 1989 edn), pp. 446, 594, 596.
43 KAO, U1475: Z1/1, pp. 119, 127, 403, 701; Z1/10, p. 299.
44 KAO, U1475: Z1/11, unfoliated passages. He did think that 'an absolute prince' should be exempt from punishment by 'his own people', but only by them.
45 Hartley, *Proceedings*, pp. 275, 286. Cf. ibid., p. 324; *Le Reveille-Matin*, dialogue ii, pp. 28–9; Kingdon, *Myths*, p. 135.
46 Hartley, *Proceedings*, pp. 324, 328.
47 Ibid., pp. 275, 276.

Prince Palladius, Pyrocles as Prince Timopyrus. Whether Musidorus is an 'absolute' ruler of Thessalia, and whether Pyrocles will become an 'absolute' ruler of Macedon, we do not know. But it suits their purposes to claim, in their disguises at their trial, to be 'absolute' princes. The claim suits Sidney's purposes too. The princes put forward, in their own defence, the arguments which were deployed by Mary and her defenders. Their pleas are answered by the objections which had been persistently raised by Sidney's party: objections which the court that tried her in 1586 would sustain. The answers to the princes are emphasised by repetition, being first provided by the prosecution or by a bench of judges – it is unclear which – and then sanctioned by the judgement of Euarchus. Brought before the court, the princes:

> demanded to know by what authority [it] could judge of them, since they were not only foreigners, and so not born under their laws, but absolute princes, and therefore not to be touched by laws. But answer was presently made them that Arcadia['s] laws were to have their force upon any [who] were found in Arcadia, since strangers have scope to know the customs of a country before they put themselves in it, and when they once are entered, they must know that what by many was made must not for one be broken, and so much less for a stranger, as he is to look for no privilege in that place to which in time of need his service is not to be expected.

Though Euarchus thinks that the princes are 'sufficiently answered' by that reply, he underlines and adds to it. Even if Musidorus and Pyrocles are truly 'princes absolute' in their own lands, he declares, that status cannot protect them in Arcadia. For 'betwixt prince and subject there is as necessary a relation as between father and son, and as there is no man a father but to his own child, so is not a prince a prince but to his own subjects'. So 'here they be no princes'.[48] In 1572 M.P.s had argued that Mary is 'here no queen'; that, in the words of Thomas Wilson, 'a king coming hither into England is no king here'; that, as Thomas Norton put it, even if 'she be queen at all' she 'is no queen of ours'.[49]

The appeal of the princes to *ius gentium* wins no more favour from the Arcadian court than Mary's appeal to it extracted from M.P.s. The princes claim that 'if they had offended . . . against the laws of nations, by the laws of nations they were to be chastised'. They are overruled. Just as Mary must be tried by England's 'laws of its own', so the princes are to be judged, decides Euarchus, according 'to the laws of Greece and municipal statutes of this dukedom'.[50] The 'laws of . . . nations', he decides, far from protecting the princes, demand that they be tried as 'private men': 'the Scottish queen',

48   *OA* 385/2–12, 403/25–33.
49   Hartley, *Proceedings*, pp. 391, 328, 335; cf. ibid., p. 353.
50   *OA* 385/18–20, 404/26–7.

declared Wilson in 1572, is 'but a private person with us'.[51] Philanax, deriding the disguises of Musidorus and Pyrocles and the want of retinue with which they have entered Arcadia, questions 'if they be princes'.[52] Mary's undignified entrance into England gave a similar opportunity to her parliamentary opponents: 'we have no record', observed Wilson sardonically, 'to prove her a queen'.[53] There is another similarity too. The forward Protestants' complaint that Mary had violated the rules of 'hospitality' in England, and their claim that she was thus not entitled to 'protection' there, are paralleled in the trial scene, where Philanax indicates that the princes, having 'broken all laws of hospitality', have forfeited the 'protection' which those laws afford.[54]

In (it seems) 1585, a civil lawyer drew up an answer to those who 'favour the impunity of Mary late Queen of Scots, notwithstanding her notorious and horrible treasons against the queen's most excellent majesty'. The document was compiled at Sidney's 'request'.[55] Its conclusions, fortified by an array of historical precedents and examples, are those which condemn Musidorus and Pyrocles. 'It cannot be denied that strangers are bound to such laws as they find in every country where they come', for 'a stranger is as well chargeable with treason as a subject'. It is of no consequence that Mary, who in England is 'a private person', 'either is or lately hath been sovereign prince of another country', for 'foreign princes are . . . within other territories . . . reputed for subjects'.[56]

Euarchus has no difficulty in perceiving or acting upon the truths that Sidney's lawyer spells out. It is when he has pronounced judgement on the princes that he confronts the gravest test of his character and of his commitment to justice. He discovers that the princes he has condemned are his son and nephew. If he holds to his sentence he will be, as Musidorus cries, 'a destroyer of his kindred' – just as Elizabeth, if she submits to the pressure to dispatch Mary, will end the life of her 'kin'. Euarchus' response resembles that with which Philanax meets a comparable dilemma in the *New Arcadia*, when Basilius, blackmailed by Cecropia's threat to his children's lives, proposes to put their survival before the interests of the commonwealth. Philanax, asked for his counsel, is left 'standing awhile in a maze, as inwardly perplexed', until 'at last' he advises his master to put 'public' before 'private' concerns: to act as 'father' of his 'people' first, as 'father' of his children only second. Only thus can he honour 'the heart of justice'.[57] Euarchus' response to the choice before him is related in similar terms. He 'stayed a good while upon himself . . . being vehemently stricken with the fatherly love of so

51 *OA* 404/1, 401/20–3; Hartley, *Proceedings*, p. 329; cf. *OA* 404/14–17.
52 *OA* 399/34–5.
53 Hartley, *Proceedings*, p. 329.
54 *Le Reveille-Matin*, dialogue ii, p. 34 (cf. p. 30); *OA* 390/19–20, 391/6–8; cf. *OA* 130/6–7.
55 BL, Additional MS. 48027, fo. 396ᵛ.
56 Ibid., fos 380–97ᵛ; Woudhuysen, 'Leicester's Literary Patronage', p. 72.
57 *NA* 416/25–6, 418/3–6.

excellent children, and studying with his best reason what his office required'. 'At length' he knows his own mind, just as 'at last' Philanax knows his.[58]

For Euarchus as for Philanax there can be only one answer. 'Private respects', Euarchus concludes, must be overridden. He reached his verdict against the princes, he declares, 'out of my assured persuasion what justice itself and [Arcadia's] just laws require'. He has thus condemned, unknowingly, 'such in whom I placed all my mortal joys. . . . But, alas, shall justice halt . . . ?' We must 'never, never, let' the 'sacred rightfulness' of 'justice' 'fall. It is immortal, and immortally ought to be preserved. If rightly have I judged, then rightly have I judged mine own children . . . .. No, no, Pyrocles and Musidorus, I prefer you much before my life, but I prefer justice as far before you.'[59]

Euarchus' decision struck 'such an admiration' into:

> all the beholders that most of them, examining the matter by their own passions, thought Euarchus (as often extraordinary excellencies, not being rightly conceived, do rather offend than please) an obstinate-hearted man, and such a one, who being pitiless, his dominion must needs be insupportable. But Euarchus, that felt his own misery more than they . . . loved goodness more than himself . . ..[60]

In holding to justice in Arcadia no less than in reforming Macedon, Euarchus has used 'extreme severity'. But as Philanax knows, it is 'an evil tongue' that 'can call severity cruelty'.[61] Elizabeth, shunning severity against Mary Stuart, shuns justice too.

Modern critical sentiment does not care for Euarchus' severity. It sympathises with Pyrocles, who suggests (in no impartial spirit) that Euarchus has been 'seeking too precise a course of justice'.[62] Yet Pyrocles and Musidorus between them – eloping with the heir to the throne, preparing to raise foreign armies, contemplating the murder of the ruler – commit in deed or thought the crimes which Mary Stuart and her allies commit in deed or thought.[63]

Sidney's decision to equate the conduct and situation of Pyrocles and Musidorus with those of Mary, and to reproduce, in the scene of their trial, the arguments for and against her execution, was a move, in both literary and political terms, of extraordinary courage and resourcefulness. The trial scene is a debate. Against Euarchus' claims of duty it sets those of love: against his claims for public rectitude it sets those of private experience. We can hardly doubt that there lay, behind the inventiveness of Sidney's parallel, the

---

58   *OA* 410/35–411/3.
59   *OA* 411/5–30.
60   *OA* 414/29–35.
61   *OA* 324/17–18.
62   *OA* 414/15–16. It is perhaps easier to mount a case against the sentence imposed by Euarchus than against his decision to adhere to it.
63   Their treasonous actions and intents are discussed further below, Chapter 17.

pressure of debate in his own mind. We shall come to that debate in Part Five. There is much about the princes' love to be forgiven, even sympathised with, even admired. Yet there is also much about it to be condemned. It is love that has driven the princes, whom we have come to think of as benign, to a wickedness equal to that of Mary Stuart. The parallel is a startling one, meant, it seems, to startle.

In this and the two preceding chapters we have watched Sidney's fiction disclosing the failures of Elizabeth's character, of her methods of rule, of her foreign policy, of her dealings with Mary Stuart. In 1579 she compounded her follies by proposing to marry Anjou. Just how serious Sidney believed the consequences of her misrule might prove becomes evident when we see the most serious consequences of misrule in Arcadia. They arise at the end of Book Four, when Basilius appears to be dead.

CHAPTER 11

The Death of Basilius

In the late summer and autumn of 1579, the critical period of the Anjou suit, the Spanish ambassador Mendoza reported attempts by the Earl of Leicester and his friends to exploit and intensify the public feeling against the match. The ambassador tried to exploit and intensify it too. The people, he wrote, 'hate' the marriage proposal and 'threaten revolution about it'. It was against that background, he explained in August, that members of Leicester's entourage had 'remarked that parliament shall have something to say as to whether the queen marries or not'.[1] In the autumn, parliament, which had last met in 1576, was prorogued again and again.[2] There was a widespread belief that it would meet soon and play a part in the Anjou crisis. 'It is said', Mendoza reported, that if the queen 'marries without consulting her people she may repent it'. In October, according to the same source, Leicester arranged for 'documents' to reach the queen which:

> gave her to understand that when she proposed to marry, parliament would urge her to declare an heir to the crown, as the people did not wish, in case of her death, to find themselves in the present position with their enemies within their own gates. She has been greatly alarmed by all this, as she has been given to understand that as soon as a successor is appointed they will upset her.[3]

That last sentence may owe at least something to Mendoza's imagination, but the rest of his statement is plausible enough. Leicester and his allies may well have intended, if they could not dissuade the queen from marrying Anjou, to use parliament, and the pressure of public feeling behind it, to exclude the heirs of the Catholic duke from the succession.[4] A hundred years

---

1 *CSPS 1568–79*, pp. 680, 692, 693, 705.
2 J. E. Neale, *Elizabeth I and her Parliaments*, 2 vols (London, 1953–7), i. 369.
3 *CSPS 1568–79*, pp. 692, 703.
4 Cf. above, p. 111; below, pp. 225–6.

later there would be an attempt to exclude, by pressure of parliament and of public feeling, a Catholic successor to the throne, James Duke of York. The Anjou suit of 1579–81 raised the spectre of popish rule that would again confront the nation during the exclusion crisis (as it can loosely be called) of 1679–81. During that later episode people would interpret, and inflame, the issues before them by remembering an earlier drama. They would recall the year 1641, that time of constitutional breakdown which in the common saying of the exclusion crisis was 'come again'.[5] In 1579–81 people interpreted, and inflamed, the issues before them by remembering the reign of Mary Tudor. The *Arcadia* remembers it. Sidney's story, which we have seen warning of the prospect of bloody rule by one Catholic Queen Mary, Mary Stuart, also recalls the bloody rule of another.

Mary Tudor had married the Catholic Philip II. Now Elizabeth proposed to marry the Catholic Duke of Anjou. Greville's account of Sidney's thinking during the Anjou suit dwells on parallels seen by Sidney between Mary's marriage and Elizabeth's prospective one. Thus 'the marriage of King Philip to Queen Mary . . . was yet so fresh in memory – with the many inconveniences of it – as, by comparing and paralleling these together, he found credible instances to conclude neither of these foreign alliances could prove safe for this kingdom'. For Mary's marriage, had it lasted longer, would have reduced England to popish slavery and compelled the English to 'wear the livery' of their new king 'and serve his ends'. The Anjou marriage would do the same.[6] Councillors who opposed the match agreed. Given time, they maintained, Philip would have 'usurped the state': given time, Anjou would usurp it too.[7] John Stubbs's *Gaping Gulph*, the partner of Sidney's 'Letter' to the queen in the campaign against the match, drew ominous parallels between Mary's marriage and Elizabeth's suit.[8]

To opponents of the suit, those parallels were indeed obvious and alarming. Would not the Reformation, under Elizabeth and Anjou as under Mary and Philip, be reversed, and Protestantism, now as then, be proscribed and persecuted?[9] Sidney, says Greville, thought that Anjou would follow 'a forerunning hand in the change of religion after King Edward's death'.[10] The dread that the persecution of the 1550s would return contributed to the political arsenal of forward Protestantism. In 1577 the Puritan Thomas Wood reminded Sidney's uncles, the Earls of Leicester and Warwick, whose opposition to Mary's accession in 1553 had placed their lives in danger, of that

5 Patrick Collinson describes the campaign to prevent Mary Queen of Scots from succeeding Elizabeth as a prolonged exclusion crisis, comparable to that of Charles II's reign: 'The Elizabethan Exclusion Crisis and the Elizabethan Polity', *Proceedings of the British Academy* 84 (1993), pp. 51–92.

6 *GP* 28/20–4, 29/22–3.

7 NRO, F(P)M 111, fo. 11.

8 Stubbs, pp. 48, 49.

9 Above, Chapter 6.

10 *GP* 29/15–16.

catastrophic episode. He remembered England's failure to heed the preachers who had condemned the nation's sinfulness 'in the last days of King Edward'. The earls, he urged, should consider whether 'our state is not far more dangerous' now than then. 'What followed then we know. And what is like to come to pass now, all godly men tremble to think of it.'[11] The Anjou suit gave a new edge to such memories. In the early spring of 1579, reported the Spanish ambassador acidly, a preacher before the queen, 'inspired from high quarters', 'said that marriages with foreigners would only result in ruin to the country, as was proved by what happened when the sainted King Edward died and was succeeded by Mary, who married a foreigner, and caused the martyrdom of so many persons, who were burnt all over the country'.[12]

Mary's reign had bequeathed Protestant memories not only of persecution but of exile: an exile in many cases voluntarily undertaken, but exile nonetheless. Walsingham was among the Protestants who had gone abroad. So was Thomas Wilson. So was Sidney's and Languet's friend Daniel Rogers, son of the Marian martyr John Rogers. So was the Earl of Bedford, who helped organise the resistance to the Anjou match. So was Bishop Richard Cox, who wrote privately to the queen urging her against the marriage.[13] Exile, forward Protestants knew, might come again. A Huguenot publication of 1574, which drew on an informed English source, pointed out that it needed only Elizabeth's death 'to change and reverse everything'. If Mary Stuart succeeded Elizabeth, remarked the tract, then those of Elizabeth's advisers who had been the Scottish queen's harshest enemies would be exposed to her hatred. Thus if Elizabeth fell ill it would make sense for them to 'pack their bags'. Their 'families' would be at risk too.[14]

No families would have been at greater risk than those to which Sidney belonged as a son and nephew. In the year in which the Huguenot tract appeared, Languet reminded him of his hazard. Bearing 'in mind how liable your country is to changes', he advised his protégé to plan an 'honourable and secure retreat' in Germany, in case 'some enemies' unjust power, or some other compulsion, should force you one day to go into exile'.[15] In 1579, by adopting the 'dangerous' course of writing against the marriage, Sidney took the risk of exile on his own account. His public quarrel with the Earl of Oxford was likewise perilous to him. Writing to Sidney from Antwerp in October, Languet remarked that 'you want another stage for your character, and I wish you had chosen it in this part of the world'. Sidney should be 'on your guard' in case Anjou returned to England 'with a crowd of French noblemen about him', for 'you know the fiery nature' of the French.[16]

11   Collinson, *Godly People*, p. 105.
12   *CSPS 1568–79*, pp. 658–9.
13   BL, Lansdowne MS. 28, fos 156&ᵛ.
14   *Le Reveille-Matin*, dialogue ii, pp. 11, 14, 44–5.
15   Osborn, *Young Philip Sidney*, p. 210.
16   Pears, p. 165. The rejection of the Anjou match, and 'that which was written against' Anjou in England, provoked some revengeful resentment in Paris: Peck, *Leicester's Commonwealth*, pp. 2, 4.

By January 1580 Languet's alarm had grown. Writing again from Antwerp, he advised Sidney to reflect that:

you may possibly be deserted by most of those who now think with you. For I do not doubt there will be many who will run to the safe side of the vessel, when they find you are unsuccessful in resisting the queen's will . . .. When you find that your opposition only draws on you dislike and aversion . . . I advise you to give way to necessity, and reserve yourself for better times . . ..

For Sidney should:

remember what Queen Mary, after King Edward's death, was enabled to effect, though at the first she had very few adherents . . .. The party and influence of Anjou is on the increase here, and if you should annoy him by your opposition in England, you will scarcely find a reception here, much less in France . . .. Your religion shuts you out of Spain and Italy, and so Germany would be your only refuge if you were compelled to leave your country.[17]

Protestants in exile under Mary Tudor had produced pamphlets vigorously demanding her overthrow. The most sensational of them has a bearing on the *Arcadia*. Christopher Goodman's *How Superior Powers Oght to be Obeyd of their Subjects* was published in Geneva in 1558. Its subtitle is more revealing: *and wherein they may lawfully by God's word be disobeyed and resisted*. Goodman had already been involved in a conspiracy to assassinate Mary.[18] Now his pamphlet urged the nation to overthrow her. That plea was made redundant by her death. But its revolutionary implications were no more welcome to the new queen than to her sister, particularly as Goodman, with his friend John Knox, had animadverted on the evils of female rule. In the early years of Elizabeth's reign Goodman was prevented from re-entering England. Though he was allowed to return in 1565, the government subsequently extracted a renunciation of what it saw as his seditious beliefs. Even thereafter the authorities remained nervous of him.[19]

Yet Goodman found powerful protectors. The chief of them were Leicester and Sidney's father Sir Henry.[20] In 1567, in support of Goodman's (unsuccessful) candidacy for the deanery of St Patrick's, Dublin, Sir Henry wrote a testimonial which would have been hard to cap: 'he hath been in my house almost a year; if ever man on earth, since the apostles' days, deserved to be held a saint, he is one'.[21] In 1570 Goodman was made Archdeacon of Richmond. Yet his radical instincts persisted. In 1578 Bishop Aylmer, no friend to forward Protestantism, urged the regime to keep a

17 Pears, p. 170; cf. *GP* 32/11–12.
18 C. H. Garrett, *The Marian Exiles 1553–1559* (Cambridge, 1938), p. 163.
19 J. E. Bailey, 'Christopher Goodman', *Journal of the Chester Archaeological and Historic Society* n.s. 1 (1887), pp. 138–57, at pp. 149–50; BL Additional MS. 29546, fos 28–32.
20 For Leicester: Phillips, 'Buchanan', p. 30; Collinson, *Godly People*, pp. 101, 207.
21 Myles Ronan, *The Reformation in Ireland under Elizabeth 1558–1580* (London, 1930), pp. 202–3.

watch on him.[22] In 1580, when Sidney was writing the *Arcadia*, Goodman, now aged around sixty and in bad health, sent greetings to Sidney's friend and correspondent George Buchanan. Buchanan's own justification of resistance to tyrants, his book *De Iure Regni apud Scotos*, had been published the previous year with the encouragement of Sidney's circle, which had long known the work in manuscript.[23] Goodman received one of the first copies of the book to come out of Scotland.[24] In 1583 he preached a contentious sermon on the failure of the Elizabethan church settlement to meet godly standards.[25]

We saw that the fear lest the 'stranger' Anjou should 'possess' the throne and strength of England was often expressed by opponents of the match in 1579 and is often echoed in the *Arcadia*.[26] Goodman's *How Superior Powers* gave voice to parallel fears in 1558. In 1579 Englishmen feared that England would become prey to France. Under Mary Tudor they had feared that, under the influence of her husband Philip II, it would become prey to Spain. In common with other pamphlets of the exile, Goodman's tract emphasised the biblical texts which prophesy 'that strangers shall devour the fruit of thy land. . . . The Lord shall bring them a people from afar off, whose tongue thou shalt not understand.' The Spaniards, wrote Goodman, were 'strangers', 'a people of afar and of a strange language', 'God's express adversaries', 'a cruel people, a proud nation . . . without all pity and mercy', who had 'put themselves in a readiness to enter the realm and make a general spoil and prey of all'.[27] Goodman reminded his readers that Wyatt's rebellion – the rebellion which, we have seen, Leicester was suspected of wanting to emulate in 1579[28] – had laudably aimed 'to keep out strangers, which were coming to rule over you, and to devour you'. Unless the English nobility awoke to the dangers before them, he warned, 'your fair houses and gorgeous buildings [will be] destroyed, your great possessions given to your enemies, your wives to be ravished, your maids deflowered, and children murdered without mercy'. 'Write this upon your doorposts,' urged the pamphlet, 'and in all your well-decked chambers.'

> For do you think that Philip will be crowned King of England, and retain in honour English councillors? . . . Shall his nobility be Spaniards, without your lands and possessions? And shall they possess your promotions and livings, and your heads upon your shoulders? Come they to make a spoil of the whole realm, and leave you and yours untouched?[29]

22   Nicolas, *Hatton*, p. 52.
23   Phillips, 'Buchanan', pp. 36–44. (Goodman's health recovered and he lived until 1603.)
24   Ibid., p. 30.
25   Huntington Library, Huntington MS. EL 34 C 2, no. 14.
26   Above, pp. 100–1.
27   Christopher Goodman, *How Superior Powers Oght to be Obeyd of their Subjects* (Geneva, 1558), pp. 178, 173–4, 35.
28   Above, p. 109.
29   Goodman, *How Superior Powers*, pp. 209, 94, 100.

The *Arcadia* asks similar questions. At the opening of the Fourth Eclogues the shepherds retreat to a hillside 'whose prospect extended it so far as they might well discern many of Arcadia's beauties'. For the purposes of subsequent commentary, I shall italicise some words of the passage which follows. The second paragraph of the passage is spoken by a figure who, like Goodman when the *Arcadia* is written, is an ageing man, a link with a former time.

And there, *looking upon the sun's as then declining race*, the poor men sat pensive of their *present miseries*, as if they found a wearisomeness of their woeful words; till at last good old Geron (who as he had longest tasted the benefits of Basilius's government so seemed to have a special feeling of the present loss), wiping his eyes and long white beard bedewed with great drops of tears, began in this sort to complain:

'Alas, poor sheep', said he, 'which hitherto have enjoyed your fruitful *pasture* in such *quietness* as your *wool*, among other things, *hath made this country famous*, your best days are now passed. Now must you become the victual of an army, and perchance an *army of foreign enemies*. You are now not only to fear home *wolves* but alien *lions*; now, I say, now that Basilius, our right Basilius is deceased. Alas, sweet *pastures*, *shall soldiers* that know not how to use you *possess* you? *Shall they* that *cannot speak Arcadian language* be *lords over your shepherds*? For, alas, with good cause may we look for any evil, since Basilius *our only strength* is taken from us.'[30]

Goodman, whose title-page refers to the 'present misery' of 'England', longs for the death of Mary Tudor and an end to tyranny. Geron, lamenting the 'present miseries' of Arcadia, weeps for the death of Basilius and expects the onset of tyranny. That tyranny, he fears, will take a Marian shape. Goodman predicts the rule of men speaking 'a strange language': Geron fears the rule of men 'that cannot speak Arcadian language'. Goodman warns, as Geron does, lest 'wolves . . . and lions' should destroy native 'pastures'.[31] Geron's rhetorical questions – 'shall soldiers . . . possess you? Shall they . . . ?' – recall Goodman's: 'Shall his nobility be Spaniards, without your lands and possessions? And shall they . . . ?'[32] Goodman foretells that foreign soldiers will make a 'spoil of the whole realm': the death of Basilius, which makes 'soldiers desirous of trouble as the nurse of spoil', exposes Arcadia to the threat of 'foreign force',[33] of (in Geron's phrase) 'an army of foreign enemies'.

Did Sidney, in writing of the death of Basilius and of its consequences,

---

30   *OA* 327/6–24; cf. *OA* 324/38.
31   Goodman, *How Superior Powers*, p. 178.
32   Cf. John Stubbs's rhetorical question about the 'possession' of Elizabeth by Anjou: Stubbs, p. 37. Stubbs's tract, whether or not by design, often brings Goodman's to mind. There is one respect, his emphasis on the theme of national sin and divine punishment, in which Stubbs is closer to Goodman than Sidney is.
33   *OA* 320/28, 360/24.

have Goodman's *How Superior Powers* beside him, or at least in his memory? We cannot be sure, though the chances will seem greater when, in a later chapter, we find reminders of *How Superior Powers* in the beast-fable sung by Philisides in the Third Eclogues.[34] What we can say is that the *Arcadia* drew on a fund of language and feeling which had persisted since the 1550s and which the Anjou crisis restored to the surface of political life.

For the perils foreseen by Goodman are foreseen by Sidney too. Sidney's *Defence of Poetry*, which has offered us precise guidance to his fiction, offers it again here. 'The poor pipe' of pastoral, the *Defence* explains, 'can show the misery of people under hard lords and ravening soldiers':[35] in Arcadia, a land made 'miserable' by Basilius' death,[36] it is amid the 'miseries' of the shepherds that Geron foretells the incursion of 'soldiers' and 'lords'. If the *Defence* once more illuminates the *Arcadia*, the *Arcadia* once more illuminates the thinking of Sidney and his allies in the Anjou crisis. Sidney's 'Letter' predicts that, if the marriage takes place, foreign 'soldiery' will seek, under Anjou's command, 'show of spoil'. John Stubbs observes the threat to England from the 'well-trained soldiery' of France, who 'for cruelty . . . are approved for anything'.[37] On the death of Basilius the Arcadians await 'the cruelty of the coming prince'.[38]

Whether or not Geron is directly indebted to Christopher Goodman, he speaks, no less than Goodman, with England in mind. Which 'country', after all, has been 'made famous' by its 'wool'? Speaking at a dinner-party on his German embassy of 1577, Sidney explained to his companions, Languet among them, why 'England hath no wolves', animals which do 'much harm to sheep, which England aboundeth with'. Thanks to the elimination of 'this ravenous and cruel beast', he observed, England now had 'great flocks whereof there be great revenues made every year, as appeareth by the good and great store of cloths that are made of their wool, and that are so much spoken of among all nations'.[39] In having Geron tell us that 'this country' has been made 'famous' by its wool, Sidney repeats a tactic he has used a little earlier in the *Arcadia*. There, to alert us to the correspondence of England to the land of its mythical past, Samothea, he has Philisides explain: 'The name of Samothea is so famous that, telling you I am of that, I shall not need to extend myself further in telling you what that country is.'[40]

Geron's speech points us not only to England but to its queen. The shepherds, surveying Arcadia's beauties from the hillside and meditating on

34   Below, Chapter 16; p. 349.
35   *MP* 94/35–95/1
36   *OA* 360/20–1.
37   *MP* 50/5–7; Stubbs, p. 79.
38   *OA* 320/11.
39   Osborn, *Young Philip Sidney*, pp. 464–5, 466 (I have modernised 'clothes' as 'cloths'); cf. *NA* 126/27.
40   *OA* 334/12–14; above, Chapter 4. Cf. the device of Philip Massinger, in alluding to England's wool in the *Maid of Honour*, a play set in a foreign land: Albert Tricomi, *Anticourt Drama in England 1603–1642* (Charlottesville, Va, 1989), p. 157.

their present miseries, 'loo[k] upon the sun's as then declining race'. Elizabeth's advisers, in their gloomier moods, spoke of her as the declining sun. So, in their more hopeful moods, did their enemies. The rising sun was Mary Queen of Scots. England's papists, observed Thomas Norton in 1570, looked to Mary as 'a sun rising to whose worship they would fain draw us from our sun declining', from Elizabeth 'our true sun'.[41] The simile came from Plutarch, where Pompey 'bad Sulla reflect that more worshipped the rising than the setting sun, intimating that his own power was on the increase, while that of Sulla was on the wane and falling away'.[42] During the Anjou crisis the queen's councillors, with that passage of Plutarch in mind, time and again alluded to Mary as 'the rising sun' or 'the sun rising', to which men 'begin to look' and which they were ready to worship.[43] Elizabeth herself described Mary as 'the rising sun', as Sidney's 'Letter' against the match (which reminds her of the Roman origin of the phrase) twice recalls.[44]

If, in Geron's speech, the 'declining' sun alludes to Elizabeth, 'Basilius our only strength', that indispensable preserver of Arcadia's tranquillity, alludes to her too. In 1572 Thomas Norton declared in parliament that the queen's survival was 'the . . . only stay', 'the singular stay', of England's quiet;[45] an entertainment given before the queen at Norwich in the summer of 1578 reminded her that her survival was 'our only stay';[46] England, it was observed during the council's debates on the Anjou match in 1579, had 'no further hope of any other stay, but only her majesty's life';[47] her death, observed Walsingham in the same year, would remove 'our only comfort and stay'.[48] Sidney, in opposing the match, made the same point. The queen, his 'Letter' reminds her, is 'the only head' of 'this body politic'; she is 'that jewel dear, the loss of which should bring us to we know not what'; by her 'loss, all blindness light upon him that sees not our fatal misery'.[49] As so often, Sidney's words had been anticipated by his fellow forward Protestant Thomas Norton, whose work Orations, of Arsanes looks forward to the Arcadia.[50] In the early 1570s Norton had explained 'how precious and how dear a jewel

41 Norton, Warning, sig. Ki; cf. OA 274/10–12, 335/14.
42 MP 184.
43 HMC Cecil, ii. 244, 268; NRO, F(P)M 111, fo. 15ᵛ; K. de L., xi. 409; Leimon, 'Walsingham', p. 177. Cf. OA 217/10–11; Le Reveille–Matin, dialogue ii, p. 42; Worden, 'Ben Jonson among the Historians', p. 83.
44 MP 53/24, 54/20–2.
45 Hartley, Proceedings, pp. 213, 203; cf. William Tydeman, ed., Two Tudor Tragedies, p. 119 (Gorboduc, l. 1629).
46 Nicholls, Progresses, p. 165; cf. Doran, 'Juno versus Diana', pp. 270–3.
47 Murdin, Collection, p. 323.
48 Read, Walsingham, ii. 15–16. Cf. NRO, F(P)M 96, fo. 7; p. 323; [William Allen], A True, Sincere, and Modest Defence of English Catholiques, ed. Robert Kingdon (London, Scolar Press facsimile, 1971), p. 185. Forward Protestant anxieties about the consequences of Elizabeth's demise were intensified by the thought that, having married Anjou, she might die in childbirth: NRO, F(P)M 111, fo. 6ᵛ; Hatf. 148, fo. 23ᵛ; above, p. 101.
49 MP 47/9, 54/19–20, 55/3–4.
50 Above, Chapter 9.

is the safety of the queen's most excellent majesty', by whose 'loss' there would follow 'unspeakable miseries', and 'what mischief may grow we do not know'.[51] In 1575, on returning from his grand tour, Sidney was perturbed to find Elizabeth 'somewhat advanced in years': 'it is God's will our safety should hang on so frail a thread . . .. She is to us a Meleager's brand; when it perishes, farewell to all our quietness.'[52] 'Quietness', which we saw to be a mixed blessing for England and for Arcadia,[53] is what Geron now sees departing from his native land.

In confronting the prospect of Elizabeth's death, Sidney's party looked back not only to the events of Mary's reign but to the coup that had launched it. In 1553 Leicester's and Sidney's fathers were at the centre of the Edwardian regime. On Edward's death Northumberland tried to preserve his ascendancy by enthroning Lady Jane Grey. So swift was Jane's fall, so feebly was it resisted, that we easily forget the daring and decisiveness that were needed to overthrow her. 'Mary's accession', as C. S. L. Davies remarks, 'was the only successful rebellion of Tudor England.'[54]

In 1579, as in 1553, it was obvious that on the monarch's death the realm would be there for the taking. Advocates of the Anjou match were as conscious of that peril as their opponents. Indeed it was a principal argument for the marriage that it might remove or at least diminish that spectre of fire and blood which the unresolved succession beckoned. The Catholic propagandist William Allen, deriding the 'uncertainty' of the succession, remarked that there was only one 'certainty': the queen's death would be followed by 'most bloody civil and foreign wars', which would bring with them 'confusion, persecution, blood, vengeance . . . spoils, ravishments'. So 'we shall be the most miserable nation in the world'.[55] Allen's point was the more effective because it had so often been made by Protestants.

They had made it, not least, in imaginative literature. Here too the *Arcadia* echoes writing produced in the period around Elizabeth's accession: this time, writing produced after rather than before that event. During her reign Elizabeth had been willing to watch a number of plays and masques which urged her to settle the succession.[56] Among them was *Gorboduc*, a play which Sidney's *Defence of Poetry* says that he has 'seen'[57] (though we do not know whether he saw it on the stage or on the page). It was given two performances – which may have been its only Elizabethan performances – in January 1562 (when Sidney was seven years old): the first at the Inner Temple, the

---

51 Norton, *Warning*, sig. Ai (cf. sig. Biii); Hartley, *Proceedings*, p. 203 (cf. p. 408).
52 Pears, p. 96; cf. Norton, *Orations, of Arsanes*, sig. Eii.
53 Above, pp. 130–1.
54 C. S. L. Davies, *Peace, Print and Protestantism* (London, 1976), p. 290.
55 Allen, *Defence of English Catholiques*, pp. 185, 186.
56 Marie Axton, *The Queen's Two Bodies. Drama and the Elizabethan Succession* (London, 1977); Doran, 'Juno versus Diana'.
57 *MP* 113/1–2.

second before the queen. Its authors were both experienced M.P.s: Thomas Norton; and Thomas Sackville, that leading contributor to the *Mirror for Magistrates*, who as Lord Buckhurst would be Burghley's successor as Lord Treasurer. *Gorboduc* is explicitly a 'mirror . . . to princes all', whom it warns to 'shun' the errors of government that it portrays.[58] The *Arcadia*, in describing the errors of Basilius and their consequences, is a mirror for magistrates too.

Gorboduc is one of the two works by living writers that are mentioned in Sidney's *Defence of Poetry*. The other, mentioned in its preceding paragraph, is Spenser's *Shepheardes Calender*. Sidney praises both works, but regrets that both of them depart from ancient literary rules. His objection to *Gorboduc* has attracted more attention than his praise of it. For our purpose the praise – like the praise of *The Shepheardes Calender* – is the more instructive. Sidney is 'grieve[d]' by the formal defects of the play because otherwise it might 'remain as an exact model of all tragedies'. He bestows on it the highest praise he knows: it is 'full of notable morality, which it doth most delightfully teach, and so obtain the very end of poesy'.[59] 'Delightful teaching', or 'virtue-breeding delightfulness', is for Sidney 'the right describing note to know the poet by'. In his fiction 'delight' is an essential component of instruction.[60]

His tribute to *Gorboduc*, which looks forward to the encouragement given to other exercises in austere Senecan drama by his sister after his death, can be read straightforwardly, as the expression of a literary conviction. But it has – designedly or not – a further function. It is another of the passages of the *Defence* which indicate to us how to read between the lines of the *Arcadia*.[61] For the delightful teaching of *Gorboduc*, and the delightful teaching of the *Arcadia*, are as close in content as they are distant in form.

Gorboduc is set in primitive or mythical Britain. Before the events which the play relates, that land was 'whilom in renown' – just as Philisides' Samothea, that mythical version of pristine Britain, 'whilom stood / An

---

58 Tydeman, *Two Tudor Tragedies*, p. 74 (*Gorboduc*, ll. 461–2). See too now Henry James and Greg Walker, 'The Politics of *Gorboduc*', *English Historical Review* 110 (1995), pp. 109–21. The first published text of *Gorboduc*, that of 1565 (which may have been pirated), attributed the first three acts to Norton, the last two to Sackville. But there is no discernible schism of style or argument between the earlier and later parts of the play.

59 *MP* 112/23–113/14.

60 *MP* 81/37–82/1, 92/8, 116/4–5; *OA* 8/7 (cf. *OA* 302/34–303/1); *NA* 163/31–3, 165/32–3, 254/1. Cf. Osborn, *Young Philip Sidney*, p. 537; above, Chapter 1. Sidney's understanding of delight and its purposes was Aristotelian: cf. Sidney, *Apology for Poetry*, ed. Shepherd, pp. 68–9. There is an oddity about the strictures passed by Sidney on *The Shepheardes Calender*. The rebuke to the 'old rustic language', which 'I dare not allow', of Spenser (with whom he was on familiar terms) is at odds with Sidney's deployment of such language in the 'Ister Bank' fable (below, Chapter 15; cf. p. 211, on 'durst not'). The contrast is the more striking in the light of the appeal in the same passage of the *Defence* to the practice of Sannazaro, Sidney's source for the *Arcadia*. The rebuke is also strangely schoolmasterly. He might be Musidorus reproaching the lovesick Pyrocles. Is the passage delivered tongue-in-cheek, in mock homage to the authority of opinion?

61 Above, p. 11.

honour to the world'.[62] The play relates the destruction of pristine Britain, as Philisides laments its degeneration. The two stories bear striking similarities. In both cases an ageing duke, after a long and peaceful reign, resolves to abandon his public responsibilities and to hand over the running of his country.[63] Both dukes, just before they undertake a 'change' of 'course',[64] overrule the pleas of a counsellor with a symbolic Greek name: in *Gorboduc* the adviser is Eubulus (giver of wise counsel); in the *Arcadia* he is Philanax (king-lover). In both cases the duke dies (or, in the case of Basilius, is seen to be dead) at the end of Act Four, after which we watch the calamitous consequences (or, in the case of the *Arcadia*, the all but calamitous consequences) of misrule, as both countries are plunged into crises over the succession to the throne. In the play, Duke Gorboduc divides his kingdom between his two sons, who quarrel for control of it. The younger slays the elder and is then slain by their mother, who in turn, with Gorboduc, is slain by their subjects. Naturally, no one in 1562 imagined that Elizabeth intended to abdicate or to divide her kingdom between two sons, any more than anyone imagined around 1580 that she had consulted an oracle or that she had two daughters next in line to the throne. Yet Gorboduc's misrule, like that of Basilius, has consequences akin to the prospects that appear to await Elizabeth's subjects on her death.

The *Old Arcadia* was written nearly twenty years after *Gorboduc*. Yet there is a frozen quality to Elizabethan politics. The issues and fears raised by the unresolved succession and by Europe's confessional strife persisted across the reign. In *Gorboduc*, Britain is subjected to foreign invasion and to 'the cruel flames' of 'civil fire' and 'hateful strife'. It is 'spoiled' and, for half a century, will 'wax desolate'.[65] The Arcadians, on the death of Basilius, confront 'neighbours' invasions, civil dissension',[66] and the disasters foretold by Geron. Both countries face the prospect summoned by Burghley during the Anjou match. The death of Elizabeth, he wrote, would 'accelerate the ruin of this kingly state, which no tongue can express how miserable it shall be . . . for destruction thereof by civil war'.[67]

Gorboduc is likely to have been sponsored by Sidney's uncle the Earl of Leicester, with the aim of persuading the queen to marry him.[68] On the

---

62 Tydeman, *Two Tudor Tragedies*, p. 123 (ll. 1746–7); *OA* 336/15–16.

63 In both cases the duke is sometimes referred to as the king. (John Dryden, in the preface to his *The Rival Ladies*, famously referred to 'Queen Gorboduc', a mistake repeated by his contemporary John Oldham. Alexander Pope, who greatly admired *Gorboduc*, would describe the errors of Dryden and Oldham as a 'scandal': E. G. Midgley, 'Pope's Knowledge of English Literature from Chaucer to Dryden' (Oxford Univ. B.Litt. thesis, 1950), pp. 35–6, 57. Yet Dryden's lapse may not be foolish: it may be related to the perception which revealed to him that the lion of Spenser's *Mother Hubberds Tale* is really a 'lioness', Queen Elizabeth: above, pp. 64–5).

64 Above, p. 134; Tydeman, *Two Tudor Tragedies*, p. 74 (l. 458). (In *Gorboduc* the 'change' is one of dynasty.)

65 Tydeman, *Two Tudor Tragedies*, pp. 94 (ll. 969–70), 108 (dumb-show), 111 (l. 1411), 123 (ll. 1745–9); cf. Norton, *Orations, of Arsanes*, sig. Eii&ᵛ.

66 *OA* 320/10–11.

67 *HMC Cecil*, ii. 250.

68 Doran, 'Juno versus Diana', pp. 260–1; Graves, *Thomas Norton*, pp. 92ff.

question of the succession it offers two warnings. First, it represents the 'tumults, rebellions, arms and civil wars' that are liable to follow from 'want of certain limitation, in the succession of the crown'.[69] The vocabulary in which it does so was echoed, a year after the play had been performed before the queen, in a parliamentary petition, read by Norton to her, 'for limitation of succession'.[70] Both the play and the petition urged that the 'limitation' be settled by parliamentary authority. In the Anjou crisis that proposal was revived by the opponents of the match on the council. Instead of marrying Anjou, they argued, the queen should 'ha[ve] authority by parliament to limit in time . . . the right of the crown to persons certain to be capable thereof', so that 'the realm might be provided of a successor'.[71]

The second warning, which was of still more immediate relevance to the Anjou crisis, was against the 'foreign thraldom', the 'unnatural thraldom of a stranger's reign', that might be brought either by marriage to a foreign prince or by a war fought over the unresolved succession. When Arcadia teeters on the brink of civil dissolution, Euarchus has the 'opportunity' to seize that land as 'prey': the disintegrating Britain of *Gorboduc* becomes, we are repeatedly told, 'an open prey'.[72] Where Euarchus, in the *Arcadia*, declines his opportunity, in the play the foreigner Albany seizes his: 'If ever time to gain a kingdom here / Were offered man, now it is offered me.'[73]

In 1570 *Gorboduc* was published together with Norton's collected tracts. Those tracts, and his parliamentary speeches, display recurrent preoccupations: the preservation of Elizabeth's safety; the bringing of her enemies – especially Mary Queen of Scots – to justice; the consequences – civil turmoil, foreign occupation – that would follow Elizabeth's death. His tracts dwell, as *Gorboduc* does, on the evils of 'foreign thraldom', of 'grievous bondage to a stranger's unjust power'. They emphasise, as *Gorboduc* does, the prospect that the realm will become a 'prey', subject to 'spoil' and 'conquest'.[74] Norton – like Thomas Wilson, whose translation of *The Three Orations of Demosthenes* we have viewed alongside Norton's *Orations, of Arsanes* – can transfer his preoccupations and language easily from one genre to another. Sidney, transferring the preoccupations and language of his 'Letter' against the Anjou match to the *Arcadia*, does the same. Norton and Wilson move between political writing or speaking and historical writing: Sidney, who elevated poetry above history, moves from political writing to poetry.

Sidney's starting point, in the 'Letter' and the *Arcadia* alike, is the

---

69 Tydeman, *Two Tudor Tragedies*, p. 108 (dumb-show).

70 Leonard Courtney, 'The Tragedy of "Ferrex and Porrex"', *Notes and Queries* 2nd ser. 10 (1860), pp. 261–2; Hartley, *Proceedings*, pp. 90–3.

71 Hatf. 148., fos 25, 34; cf. ibid., fo. 55. During the council debates of October 1579 it was also argued, probably by opponents of the match, that an act of parliament should be passed 'to disable all such persons from the claiming of the crown as shall by any means interrupt her majesty's quiet or endanger her person'. K. de L., xi. 407; cf. Collinson, *Elizabethan Essays*, pp. 48–55.

72 OA 358/11; Tydeman, *Two Tudor Tragedies*, pp. 119, 120, 122 (ll. 1630, 1657, 1708).

73 Tydeman, *Two Tudor Tragedies*, p. 113 (ll. 1479–80).

74 Norton, *Warning*, sigs Aiᵛ, Dii; Norton, *To the Queenes . . . Subjectes*, sig. Aiiii; Tydeman, *Two Tudor Tragedies*, p. 111 (ll. 1411–12); cf. Collinson, *Elizabethan Essays*, pp. 70ff.

overruling of good counsel, that insistent worry of forward Protestants under
Elizabeth.[75] *Gorboduc* has the same starting point. Where Philanax urges
Basilius to hold to the course that has given his country justice, obedience
and safety for thirty years, Eubulus pleads to Gorboduc:

> you that long have wisely ruled the reins
> Of royalty within your noble realm,
> So hold them, while the gods for our avails
> Shall stretch the thread of your prolonged days . . ..[76]

Philanax and Eubulus are alike 'faithful' counsellors who give 'bold' advice.[77]
Norton and his fellow author of *Gorboduc*, Thomas Sackville, were known
for the brave candour of their advice; indeed it was as a consequence of
Norton's 'overboldness' against the Anjou match, of his 'overmuch and
undiscreet speaking' on that subject, that he was sent to the Tower in 1581.[78]
He was no friend to 'the mannerliness of . . . courtesy' when the survival of
a kingdom was at stake. Rather – like Walsingham or Thomas Wilson, like
Philanax – he believed himself impelled by duty to speak out.[79]

In the *Arcadia* and *Gorboduc* alike, plain, bold counsel is contrasted with the
honeyed flattery of counsellors who tell princes what they want to hear.[80] In
both works, havoc has its source in the overruling of good counsel by royal
'will'. Basilius, having 'the authority of a prince whose power might easily
satisfy his will', acts 'without the advice or allowance of his subjects',
propelling his country towards disaster by 'making his will wisdom'. The
havoc wreaked in *Gorboduc* shows what happens 'when kings will not consent
/ To grave advice, but follow wilful will'. It is from Gorboduc's 'will alone'
that Britain's nightmare has 'sprung'; 'the course of governance' has been
'with wrong transpose[d]' because 'the present fancy of the prince' has been
indulged.[81]

Those like causes have like consequences. The Britain of *Gorboduc* is left 'as
ship without a stern', with 'empty place of princely governance': after Basilius
has 'left the stern of government' the Arcadians have 'a prince . . . keeping
and not exercising the place'.[82] On Basilius' death Arcadia loses, we are

75   Cf. above, Chapter 9.
76   Tydeman, *Two Tudor Tragedies*, p. 72 (ll. 395–8).
77   Above, p. 128; *OA* 285/25; Tydeman, *Two Tudor Tragedies*, p. 69 (cf. ibid., p. 75, dumb-show).
     Like Sidney (above, p. 150), Norton intimates that Elizabeth should treat her councillors with
     more respect: Norton, *Warning*, sig. niiii^v.
78   Hartley, *Proceedings*, p. 201; Charles Wilson, 'Thomas Sackville: an Elizabethan Poet as Citizen',
     in Jan van Dorsten, ed., *Ten Studies in Anglo–Dutch Relations* (Leiden, 1974), pp. 30–50, at pp.
     41–7; Graves, *Thomas Norton*, pp. 97, 391.
79   Graves, *Thomas Norton*, p. 336; Hartley, *Proceedings*, p. 352; above, Chapter 9.
80   For the theme of flattery in *Gorboduc*: Tydeman, *Two Tudor Tragedies*, pp. 65, 70, 72, 75, 86, 123
     (ll. 96–8, 360, 421; dumb-show; 779–80, 1753–4); in the *Arcadia*: below, Chapter 12.
81   Above, p. 151; Tydeman, *Two Tudor Tragedies*, pp. 123, 100, 60 (ll. 1750–2, 1136, 60–1).
82   Tydeman, *Two Tudor Tragedies*, pp. 118, 119 (ll. 1602, 1628); *NA* 23/5–6 (cf. *OA* 360/21–2);
     OA 358/32–4.

repeatedly told, its 'guide': the Britain of *Gorboduc*, the play stresses, becomes 'a guideless realm', 'left without a guide'.[83]

Both in the England of *Gorboduc* and in Arcadia, the errors of the governor create calamitous divisions among the governed. For Sidney's party, national unity – that recurrent preoccupation of Elizabethan politics and literature – is the necessary basis of England's self-reliance and independence. *Gorboduc* says the same:

> The strength that, knit by fast accord in one
> Against all foreign power of mighty foes,
> Could of itself defend itself alone,
> Disjoined once, the former force doth lose . . ..

For 'a state knit in unity doth continue strong, but being divided is easily destroyed'.[84] In 1578 Walsingham repeated the warning of *Gorboduc*. 'Our unity', he wrote, 'might be strength to ourselves and an aid unto our neighbours, but if we shall like to fall at division among ourselves, we must needs lie open to the common enemy, and by our own fault hasten or rather call upon ourselves our own ruin.'[85] Forward Protestants warned insistently that division leads a nation to 'ruin', that 'every kingdom divided in itself shall come to ruin'.[86] In 1579 opponents of the Anjou match emphasised the division, and hence the desolation, to which the marriage would lead.[87] 'Your estate', Sidney's 'Letter' told the queen, 'by inward weakness, principally caused by division' – division on which Anjou would know how to play – 'is fit to receive harm.'[88]

Division is a recurrent theme of the *Arcadia*. The First Eclogues alert us to the country's 'divided weakness' and to the 'discord' that 'flows' among its leaders.[89] On the death of Basilius 'was all the whole multitude fallen into confused and dangerous divisions'. The opening words of Book Five bring the theme to the fore: 'The dangerous division of men's minds, the ruinous renting of all estates, had now brought Arcadia to feel the pangs of uttermost peril.'[90] The nation is ready to 'run itself upon the rock of self-division'; the nobles divide into 'factions'; the people, 'divided in many motions', become 'tired with their own divisions'; only Euarchus can 'unite our disunions'.[91]

But for the arrival of Euarchus, the consequences of division would be

83 *OA* 320/6, 349/25, 360/21; Tydeman, *Two Tudor Tragedies*, pp. 119, 118 (ll. 1630, 1599, 1614).
84 Tydeman, *Two Tudor Tragedies*, pp. 73, 57 (ll. 445–8; dumb-show).
85 Wright, *Queen Elizabeth*, ii. 79; cf. *HMC Cecil*, ii. 268. Walsingham seems to have had in mind the divisions which weakened the godly cause in Scotland as well as in England.
86 BL, Harleian MS. 6992, no. 50; K. de L., x. 571, xi. 129; Leimon, 'Walsingham', p. 168.
87 *HMC Cecil*, ii. 270; Hatf. 148, fo. 48ᵛ.
88 *MP* 56/13–15, 50/19–22.
89 *OA* 76/19–24, 77/26.
90 *OA* 320/3–4, 351/2–4. For the 'ruinous' division of Arcadia see also *OA* 320/21–3; cf. *MP* 93/18–19.
91 *OA* 360/23, 320/25, 354/23, 323/3–4, 354/28–9, 354/1.

be as grave for Arcadia as they are for the Britain of *Gorboduc*. 'To our ruin',
declares Philanax on Basilius' death, has the duke 'left the frail bark of [his]
estate!'[92] The nation disintegrates. Its inhabitants are shown

> hearkening on every rumour, suspecting everything, condemning them whom
> before they had honoured, making strange and impossible tales of the duke's
> death . . . altogether like a falling steeple, the parts whereof (as windows, stones
> and pinnacles) were well, but the whole mass ruinous. And this was the
> general case of all, wherein notwithstanding was an extreme medley of diver-
> sified thoughts: the great men looking to make themselves strong by factions;
> the gentlemen, some bending to them, some standing upon themselves, some
> desirous to overthrow those few which they thought were over them; the
> soldiers desirous of trouble as the nurse of spoil; and not much unlike to them
> (though in another way) were all the needy sort; the rich, fearful; the wise,
> careful. This composition of conceits brought forth a dangerous tumult . . . .[93]

Sidney, then, reproduces, whether or not by design, the language and
preoccupations both of Christopher Goodman and of the authors of
Gorboduc.[94] There is another literary parallel to Basilius' demise. This one
places the *Arcadia* alongside writing, not of earlier decades, but of its own time.
For the lamentations with which Geron and the other shepherds respond to
the passing of the duke align Sidney once more with his fellow client of
Leicester, Edmund Spenser. *The Shepheardes Calender* was entered in the
Stationers' Company Register in December 1579 and printed by the printer
of John Stubbs's *Gaping Gulph*, Hugh Singleton, who had been sentenced to
the same penalty as Stubbs but been reprieved.[95] *The Shepheardes Calender* asks,
as the *Arcadia* does, what will happen when Elizabeth dies. The November
Eclogue 'bewaileth the death of some maiden of great blood'. 'The personage
is secret', but not hard to guess. In the *Arcadia* the shepherds resolve on 'endless
wailing' now that Basilius is 'absented': the shepherds of the November
Eclogue are repeatedly enjoined to 'waile' in response to the dead maiden's

---

92   *OA* 287/1–2
93   *OA* 320/10–31. Sidney's prose becomes jumpy or frenetic in and around that passage. Note the
     frequency of, and the number of sentences beginning with, the word 'but': *OA* 320–6.
94   *Gorboduc* itself often comes close to Goodman's tract. Though a number of the resemblances may
     be attributable to a common dependence of the two works on a common vocabulary, there is
     one moment when the languages of the two texts are perhaps more alike than that explanation
     would allow. We have heard Goodman's prophecy of foreign occupation: 'your wives shall be
     ravished, your maids deflowered, and children murdered without mercy': the concluding section
     of *Gorboduc*, which predicts the horrors awaiting Britain, foretells that 'the wives shall suffer rape,
     the maids deflowered, / And children fatherless shall weep and wail' (Tydeman, *Two Tudor
     Tragedies*, p. 122, ll. 1726–7). That resemblance was noted by Sarah Ruth Watson, ' "Gorboduc"
     and the Theory of Tyrannicide', *Modern Language Review* 34 (1939), pp. 355–66. Watson's
     detection of other debts of *Gorboduc* to Goodman's tract is generally less convincing.
95   Barnes, 'John Stubbe', pp. 423–4.

'absence'.[96] In Arcadia havoc ensues when the 'great shepherd', the 'shepherd high', 'is gone'. It ensues too in the eclogue, where Spenser summons the phrase 'great shepherd' in reporting the maiden's demise. Wolves 'chase the wandring sheepe' now that she 'is gone that safely did [t]hem keep'.[97]

That imagery spoke immediately to the concerns of 1579. We saw that the dread of convulsion on Elizabeth's death afflicted advocates as well as opponents of the Anjou match. One advocate of it, in a reply to Stubbs's *Gaping Gulph* that was sponsored perhaps by Burghley (whose views it echoes), certainly by someone at the centre of government, advised the queen to 'set before [her] eyes the plight of England' on her death, 'when the shepherd being taken hence the sheep will be dispersed and cast open to the wolf'. He envisaged a scenario close to that experienced by the Arcadians. If the succession were not settled, he warned, there would come a time:

> when there shall be no king in Israel but every man do what he list, when Lepidus will reach at all because the forces of the realm are in his hand, Octavius by title of the will, and Antony because he was the first that undertook to wreak the death of Caesar [*sic*]; when the noblemen shall put their houses, meaner men shall put their goods and lives, many their good name . . . in peril . . ..

There would follow 'violence', 'spoil', 'the flames of civil war', 'tyranny'; neighbouring states 'shall set upon us'; 'the widows and poor orphans shall exclaim without redress'; 'iniquity' would 'prevail without restraint and blood shall overflow . . . without measure'; 'every man will take upon him to command but none obey'; it would be in no man's power to 'save the state from wreck'.[98]

The panic that grips Arcadia on Basilius' death reveals the failings not only of a king but of a ruling class and of a nation. Public spirit, though it survives in a Philanax or a Kerxenus, has been generally overwhelmed by faction, greed, fear. On Basilius' death, at least, the shepherds give no sign of being

---

96 *OA* 282/15–16, 344/24; Stubbs, pp. li–lii.
97 Oram, pp. 189 (l. 48), 192 (ll. 136–7). I have generally been more hesitant in identifying allusions to current events in *The Shepheardes Calender*, where the problems of allegorical interpretation are complex, than in *Mother Hubberds Tale*, which, as S. K. Heninger argues (*Sidney and Spenser*, p. 359), differs from Spenser's other verse in its 'self-consciously simple' art. However, I am encouraged to see that Douglas Brooks-Davies, in his edition of *Edmund Spenser. The Shorter Poems* (London, 1995), detects an insistent preoccupation with the Anjou match in *The Shepheardes Calender*. I should add that the question of England's fate after Elizabeth's death, which is prominent in the *Old Arcadia*, persists into the *New Arcadia*. Even though the death of Basilius does not recur there, Sidney has Pyrocles remind the mutineers of Book Two what would happen should he die. What would they have done, he asks them, 'if you had lost Basilius? Under whose ensign would you go if your enemies should invade you?' (*NA* 286/28–9).
98 PRO, SP 15/26/★35, fo. 162&ᵛ. The same passage alludes to the succession crisis in Portugal, 'which in a dumb-show serveth to present our tragedies'. Were the dumb-shows which relate the tragedies of pristine Britain in *Gorboduc* somewhere in the author's mind?

factious or greedy. 'Finding no place for themselves in these garboils, to which their quiet hearts . . . had at all no aptness', they 'retired themselves from among the clamourous multitude'.[99] Their want of political appetite enables Sidney, here as elsewhere, to set pastoral innocence against political corruption. Whereas the 'great men' are convulsed, on Basilius' death, by the 'extreme ambition' of Timautus, the 'highest ambition' of the shepherds 'was in keeping themselves up in goodness'. To that extent they resemble Euarchus, who is immune to 'ambition' and of whom we are told that, 'if for anything he loved greatness, it was because therein he might exercise his goodness'.[100]

So the retreat of the shepherds to the hillside may seem to their credit. Yet there is another side to the picture. For the shepherds, serving as they do under their 'great shepherd' Basilius, are not separate from the ruling class or its responsibilities. They 'were not such base shepherds as we commonly make account of, but the very owners of the sheep themselves, which in that thrifty world the substantiallest men would employ their whole care upon'.[101] The conventions of pastoral analogy were flexible. Sidney's shepherds are sometimes commentators on the action, sometimes participants in it. As participants they are sometimes Arcadia's leaders: sometimes, as on the hillside, their association with the countryside distances them from the grandees and the court. Yet even in the countryside they have duties. They have not discharged them. Their impotence at the crisis of the Arcadian state that follows Basilius' death stems from their failings in his lifetime.

The shepherds are supposed to do, and have failed to do, 'justice'[s] work',[102] the work, among England's landowners, of J.P.s. In that respect they correspond to, and share the failings of, England's J.P. class (the class which is answerable to the monarchy for local government but does not form policy, or shape conflicts of power, at the centre). England's J.P.s, in the eyes of forward Protestants, have been as neglectful of their responsibilities as the queen has been of hers. They have largely failed to promote the true religion. They have been insufficiently watchful against the enemies of the realm, particularly Catholic ones, and insufficiently vigorous in acting against them. Their weaknesses are shared by too many clergy, the shepherds of the church, those 'lukewarm fellows' who, as the forward Protestant Sir Amias Paulet complained in 1577, failed 'to deal roundly, plainly and sincerely in their stations'. Paulet added the wish that the queen's 'sheriffs, justices and the like ministers were such as did worship God truly and serve her highness faithfully. Instead their winking or rather comforting in corners' was doing 'hurt'. Men of 'diligence and industry' were needed to serve the queen not only at the centre but 'in every other part of the realm'.[103]

---

99 OA 327/2–5.
100 OA 321/33–4, 327/3–4, 357/13; NA 159/17–18.
101 OA 56/11–14.
102 OA 77/28.
103 Bodl., Rawlinson MS. A331, fo. 82ᵛ.

Sidney told Elizabeth that 'the poison of division' had split England into 'two mighty factions'.[104] The poison has its equivalent not only among the 'factions' into which the noblemen and gentlemen of Arcadia divide, but among the shepherds. For if the shepherds shun the factions that flourish on Basilius' death, they are divided earlier. To describe their division, Sidney uses language which he has already applied to the public life of his own time. In 1574 he prophesied to Languet that the French, 'who are now cutting each other's throats, will be driven to join forces, and stand fast against the common foe: just as fighting dogs when they see the wolf at work among their sheep'.[105] In the First Eclogues there are fighting dogs who face the same threat, and who likewise need to stop fighting. Geron rebukes them:

> I set you o'er the flock I dearly love
> Them to defend, not with yourselves to fight.
> Do you not think this will the wolves remove
> From former fear they had of your good minds,
> When they shall such divided weakness prove?

Perhaps, in that passage and in his letter to Languet, Sidney took his cue from Thomas Wilson's translation and edition of Demosthenes, which foreshadows so much in the *Arcadia*. Demosthenes, recalls Wilson, told a fable of the animal kingdom, 'signifying by the wolf Alexander, by the dogs the magistrates and orators, by the sheep the people of Athens'. Wilsons text has a marginal note: 'Magistrates compared to mastiffs, that defend sheep against the wolf'.[106]

Whether Sidney was drawing on Wilson or not, the import of Geron's song is clear enough. It is partnered by the outburst of his fellow shepherd Mastix. Mastix bemoans the 'discord 'twixt greatest shepherds' and the 'faults' revealed by their 'justice'[s] work'.[107] He assails the cowardice and neglect of Arcadia's ruling class. England is lulled by 'security', by 'sleep'.[108] So, in Mastix's account, is Arcadia:

> we see our saddest shepherds out . . .
> Quickly secure, and easily in doubt,
> Either asleep be all if naught assail,
> Or all abroad if but a cub start out.
> We shepherds are like them that under sail
> Do speak high words when all the coast is clear,
> Yet to a passenger will bonnet vail.[109]

---

104 *MP* 50/19, 47/19–20.
105 Pears, p. 48.
106 Wilson, *Demosthenes*, p. 119.
107 *OA* 500, 76/20–4, 77/11, 77/26–8.
108 Above, pp. 61–5.
109 *OA* 77/12–19.

Mastix's lines recall words of the forward Protestant Sir Amias Paulet, to whom Englishmen's 'security' and 'sleep' were a constant worry. 'We are bold enough to fear nothing when the peril is most imminent,' Paulet wrote to Thomas Wilson in November 1577, but 'we are fearful and afraid of a very shadow where things are most easy. These be the fruits of security.'[110]

The Arcadians betray the same weakness on the death of Basilius: 'while they thought themselves in danger, wishing nothing but safety; as soon as persuasion of safety took them, desiring further benefits'. They are frightened by 'whatsoever in common sense carries a dreadful show'.[111] That is the failing of Basilius in response to the oracle and of Elizabeth in intending to hide from Spain behind Anjou. In Elizabeth, and in Basilius, fear induces the surrender of virtue to fortune.[112] So does it among the shepherds, who think of themselves as the victims of 'cruel' and 'filthy' fortune.[113]

Three times in the *Arcadia* the ruling dynasty, and thus the safety of the realm, are placed in mortal peril. There is the threat to the lives of the princesses, Basilius' heirs, when they are pursued by the lion and bear in Book One. There is the mutiny of Book Two. There is the death of Basilius in Book Four. On each occasion native resources are helpless before the crisis. On each occasion the state has to be rescued by a foreigner or foreigners: in Book One by Musidorus and Pyrocles, who rescue the princesses; in Book Two by Pyrocles, who withstands and pacifies the mutineers; and near the end by Euarchus.

The deficiencies of the shepherds are exposed by each of those challenges. The First Eclogues, where Mastix reproaches them, comment on the action that precedes them. Mastix's complaint points back to the account, near the end of Book One, of the response of the shepherds to the appearance of the lion and bear, when 'fear . . . possessed their inward parts'. They were 'like silly wretches that think all evil is ever next themselves'. When they saw the beasts they 'ran away as fast as they could; so that the one tumbled over the other, each one showing he would be glad his fellow should do valiantly, but his own heart served him not'.[114] Their failure of nerve, which exposes the heiress of Arcadia and her sister to mortal danger, may seem purely comical amid the high spirits of Book One. It assumes a graver aspect when we read the First Eclogues, and a still graver one when we watch the subsequent conduct of the shepherds. In the crises of Books One and Two their behaviour is placed in contrast with that of Pyrocles, whose 'courage was always ready without deliberation' and whose 'manner of fighting' is so dauntless. The 'excellent valour' of that 'stranger' saves the duke, and 'perchance the whole state', 'from utter ruin'.[115]

110 Bodl., Rawlinson MS. A331, fo. 89ᵛ.
111 *OA* 320/11–17.
112 Above, Chapter 8.
113 *OA* 284/10–285/20.
114 *OA* 45/27–32, 46/31–2.
115 *OA* 50/31–2, 48/6–7, 128/29, 129/26, 129/31, 300/30–1.

Even Basilius is troubled by 'the hasty and fearful running unto him of the most part of the shepherds' from the lion and bear. He is 'amazed to see such extreme shows of fear'. So 'he did, with a gentle manner, chastise the cowardice of the fugitive shepherds'.[116] A more fitting response than gentleness might have been the 'severity' which characterises the rule of Euarchus. Basilius' admonition seems to do little good. For although in the ensuing story there are brave and loyal shepherds,[117] there are evidently not enough of them. On the death of Basilius the defects of Arcadia's ruling class become evident once more. The shepherds are 'the first descriers' of the events surrounding that calamity. Yet they play no part in the drama that follows, being 'unused to be arbiters in princes' matters'. The 'quietness' of their 'hearts', and their innocence of ambition, no doubt reflect a becoming modesty;[118] but quietness can be the enemy to action and thus to virtue. Hitherto the shepherds have done a great deal of panic-stricken running away and running around.[119] Now, on the hillside, they 'sat pensive of their present miseries'. There, like Basilius in his lifetime, they are unactive. Their 'quiet' 'hearts', we learn when news of Basilius' death reaches them, are 'honest but over-tender'. Basilius himself is 'tender-minded', which is why he yields to blackmail during the civil war of the *New Arcadia*.[120] That surrender is a failure both of courage and of public spirit. So is the response of the shepherds to his death. They 'yielded themselves over to . . . forms of lamentation' and 'ran about his body tearing their beards and garments; some sending their cries to heaven; others inventing particular howling musics; many vowing to kill themselves at the day of his funerals'.[121] Their real concern is for themselves: they indulge in 'lamentation' in the manner of men who 'think the rebound of the evil falls to their own smart'.[122]

Among the roseate memories of the duke inspired by their grief is the conviction that his reign was characterised by justice. They bestow the 'sacred titl[e] of . . . just' upon him; they remember him as 'a prince under whom they had found . . . justice equally administered'; they complain that 'justice, justice is now, alas, oppressed'.[123] Their tributes, coming from men who have themselves failed in 'justice'[s] work', are not worth much. Nor are their other tributes. They bestow a no less 'sacred title' upon him, 'the father of the people',[124] a description flatly contradicted by his refusal, in the *New Arcadia*, of Philanax's plea that in the cause of 'justice' he act as 'a prince – and a father – of people'.[125] In death, cry the shepherds, the duke is

---

116   *OA* 45/24–5, 45/30–1, 56/34–57/1.
117   *OA* 126/5, 126/16–17, 274/3–4, 281/18–23.
118   *OA* 326/23–4, 282/21, 327/3.
119   *OA* 45/25–7, 46/32, 274/7, 283/28.
120   *OA* 283/13; *NA* 418/11.
121   *OA* 283/12, 283/28–31.
122   *OA* 283/14–15.
123   *OA* 283/27, 327/27–9, 348/13.
124   *OA* 283/27.
125   *NA* 418/3–5; cf. Tydeman, *Two Tudor Tragedies*, pp. 63–4 (ll. 148–50, 170–1).

'absented' from them: yet we have already witnessed the consequences of his 'absented manner of living'.[126]

Opponents of the Anjou match, in pressing the queen to gauge her strengths and take her stand on them, paid their own tributes to her. High among the qualities commended by them, as by the shepherds, was 'justice'. Where the shepherds praise Basilius' justice after his death, Sidney and his allies praise the queen's in her lifetime. They do so for a purpose. Like most bestowers of praise on Renaissance monarchs, they praise the quality they wish their monarch had, or at least had more of. In the same Renaissance manner they persuade one half of their minds to discern in reality the ideal qualities they describe. Perhaps Philanax's mind is similarly divided when, repeating Sidney's advice to the queen, he urges Basilius to build on the strength and obedience which royal 'justice' has created.[127] On that subject he is no more dependable a reporter of reality than the shepherds. The opponents of the Anjou match are unreliable reporters of it too. Even as they praise the justice of Elizabeth's reign, they urge her, in terms which point to its deficiency, 'to govern the people with justice indifferently'.[128] Sir Walter Mildmay, arguing against the Anjou match, struggles to have it both ways. Commending the 'justice' of the queen's rule, he also concedes that by reason of 'negligence', 'affection', 'partiality', 'corruption', 'lenity', on the part of 'those which should execute the laws under her majesty', 'justice [is] not delivered with that sincerity and expedition which it ought to be'.[129] Here Burghley was at one with the forward Protestants: there was needed 'more sincerity in the bishops and clergy and more dexterity in all temporal magistrates with distribution of justice equally to all persons'.[130]

For the 'justice' of Elizabeth's reign could be far to seek. Euarchus embodies justice in condemning his son and nephew: Elizabeth rejected the demand for justice against Mary Queen of Scots. Euarchus' 'severity' in reforming Macedon enables 'justice' to replace 'corruption': in forward Protestant eyes Elizabeth's 'lenity' and 'overmuch softness' left England's 'corruption' unremedied. The pleas of forward Protestants for an end to Elizabeth's 'immeasurable and dangerous clemency' in respect of papists, and to dispensations from 'penal laws . . . for private men's profits', went unanswered.[131] So did their calls for purges of the church and local government. England's J.P.s, no less than Arcadia's, failed to do 'justice'[s] work'. Passages of *Mother Hubberds Tale* that are likely to have been written around the time of the Anjou match describe the 'foul abuses both in realme and raine' that stain the rule of the 'sleeping lion', and complain of 'lawlesnes', 'infinite

126   *OA* 348/19–20, 127/1–2.
127   Above, pp. 128–9.
128   *HMC Cecil*, ii. 252.
129   BL, Harleian MS. 6265, fo. 104; cf. ibid., fo. 106ᵛ.
130   Hatf. 148, fo. 80.
131   *HMC Cecil*, ii. 268; Norton, *Warning*, sig. Niᵛ–ii; above, pp. 72, 177–8; cf. Feuillerat, iii. 144.

extortions', 'great oppressions'.[132] Spenser's fable inspects the corrupted condition of the commons, of the clergy, of the nobility.[133]

England's 'inward corruption', and the need for 'inward medicines' to cure a realm 'so corrupted at home', persistently worried Walsingham.[134] Arcadia is corrupted too, if corruption means the ascendancy of private interests, the loss or paralysis of public spirit, the erosion of a political community or of a common political will. The degeneracy of Arcadia becomes evident when Sidney describes the country's response to Basilius' death. It is not only the shepherds who, in the face of that crisis, fail in public spirit. The nation fails in it. In such a crisis, fears Sidney, the English nation would fail in it too.

In the event the Arcadian state survives because – as in Spenser's *Mother Hubberds Tale* - a *deus ex machina* saves a misgoverned realm. Instead of gobbling Arcadia, Euarchus rescues it from itself. Yet Sidney's heart, in those concluding paragraphs of the *Arcadia*, seems not to be in the rescue. Euarchus can restore peace, restore the 'quiet' which the Arcadians, like the English, have through good fortune enjoyed. Whether he has solved the underlying cause of the Arcadian crisis, a crisis, like England's, of misgovernment, is left doubtful.[135]

The *Arcadia*, we have seen, assimilates – whether or not by intention – material that had been written twenty years and more earlier, by Christopher Goodman and by Thomas Sackville and Thomas Norton. Thirty years after its own composition the *Arcadia* would itself be assimilated. This time, the presence of intention is unmistakable. Around 1611, a quarter of a century after Sidney's death (and at the time when Fulke Greville was writing his 'Dedication' to Sidney), the historian Sir John Hayward, that practised borrower of other men's words, wrote a history of the first four years of Elizabeth's reign. Its opening paragraph, which describes the dying sickness of Queen Mary and the nation's response to it, is silently lifted from, and mildly paraphrases, the account in the *Arcadia* of the crisis that follows the death of Basilius. Hayward uses the passage to show 'how in a royal state the surety of the common people depends much upon the life and safety of their prince'. Describing events of 1558 rather than those of 1553 or those predicted in 1579, he makes some tactical adjustments to Sidney's text. For example the Arcadian dread of the 'cruelty of the coming prince' yields to English nervousness about 'the doubtful disposition of the succeeding prince', Elizabeth. Hayward's alterations merely underline his understanding of the relevance of the *Arcadia* to the Tudor succession question and to the

---

132 Oram, pp. 372 (l. 1276), 377 (ll. 1310–12). In passages probably written later, it is said that there is 'no care of justice' and that 'justice' is 'solde': pp. 371 (l. 1131), 372 (l. 1147).

133 Heninger, *Sidney and Spenser*, p. 359.

134 Read, *Walsingham*, i. 239, 237, ii. 92; K. de L., viii. 358.

135 Greville does disclose that Sidney, had he completed the *New Arcadia*, would have shown us 'the return of Basilius from his dreams of humour to the honour of his former estate' (*GP* 10/ 13–15).

problems of government and society that the unresolved succession created and exposed.[136]

Those problems prompted in Sidney's mind, we shall now see, a meditation on the weaknesses not only of the present reign but of the monarchical system over which the queen presided.

---

136 The passage in Hayward, and the parallel passage of the *Arcadia*, are reproduced below in Appendix B.

Part Four: Political Thought

CHAPTER 12

Monarchal Dissipations

There was a notable example how great dissipations monarchal governments
are subject unto . . ..

(The Old Arcadia)

If we were to look for a programme of political theory in the *Arcadia* we
would be disappointed. It would serve us right. Sidney, as a poet will do,
supplies images of political degeneration, not analyses of it. He raises political
questions which he does not answer. Yet he was as interested as any
Elizabethan in the political thought of his time, which his friends did so
much to shape; he studied voraciously the subject which was agreed to be the
essential base of political thought, history; and he brought the language of
contemporary political argument to bear on the problems of government
experienced both by Renaissance Europe and by mythical Arcadia. To place
his fiction alongside the political thought of his time and of his allies is to
realise how far it belongs to it and is permeated by it.

In the Third Eclogues Philisides sings a beast-fable. Its last verse, which brings
its lesson together, has a warning for kings:

> But yet, O man, rage not beyond thy need;
> Deem it no gloire to swell in tyranny.
> Thou art of blood; joy not to make things bleed.[1]

The pertinence of those lines to the Europe which had witnessed the
Massacre of St Bartholomew and the other recent atrocities in France, and
the reign of terror conducted by the Duke of Alva in the Netherlands, would
have been obvious. Queen Elizabeth, by contrast, was (at least in Protestant
eyes) no bloodthirsty tyrant. No more is Basilius. Like Elizabeth he is no

1   *OA* 259/10–12.

Catherine de Medici, no Alva, no Philip II. No more than Elizabeth does he
practise the 'malice and cruelty' which Sidney and his fellow forward Protestants associated with popish rule.[2] No more than she does he oppress his
subjects or treat them with the brutality exercised by a series of tyrants in
Book Two of the *New Arcadia*. No more than she does he seek to extend the
powers of the crown.

Basilius is a 'doting fool' who commits 'absurd follies'.[3] Love deprives him
of all dignity. Euarchus, opposite to Basilius as usual, preserves a 'gravity' of
presence and countenance;[4] Basilius' wife Gynecia, coming more fully to her
senses than he, conducts herself with 'grave behaviour'; Philanax, after the
duke's death, acts 'with the grave behaviour of a wise father';[5] but Basilius
(that unwise father) lacks the gravity appropriate to his white hairs. We find
him, as a lover, falling on his aged knees or 'fetching a little skip'.[6] Yet his
failings seem human and forgivable. He looks a harmless, affable figure.
Though his love is a 'vice', it is the vice of 'the good old Basilius' (or 'the
poor old Basilius'), that 'good man', that 'prince not to be misliked'.[7] In the
New Arcadia Kalander, though gently indicating the duke's want of wisdom
and courage and 'princely virtues', commends his 'truth of word, meekness,
courtesy, mercifulness, and liberality'.[8]

Basilius, then, can look innocuous. He is not. He is 'a mighty duke',[9] with
mighty power for good or ill. In the *New Arcadia* we meet a king with flaws
similar to his: the King of Iberia, father to Plangus. Like Basilius he is 'of no
wicked nature, nor willingly doing evil'. But like Basilius he is gullible.
Basilius, being 'not the sharpest piercer into masked minds', fails to perceive
the designs of Cecropia, which bring chaos on his dukedom: the King of
Iberia tends to 'mistake the evil, seeing it disguised under some form of
goodness'.[10] Disaster awaits him too. If the misrule of Arcadia provides one
'notable example how great dissipations monarchal governments are subject
unto',[11] the misrule of Iberia supplies another.

Precisely because Basilius is not wicked or bloodthirsty, Sidney's fiction is
able to offer something more than an indictment of royal wickedness. It can
inspect not only the abuses of royal power but its inherent flaws. The name
of Euarchus, the antitype to Basilius, means 'good ruler'. Basilius' name
means 'kingly', not 'bad king'. The trouble is that kings tend to be bad.
Euarchus, so unlike 'most princes', is an exception: Basilius looks like a
norm. In the thinking of Sidney's revered Aristotle, the term 'good king' is

---

2 PRO, SP 78/2/27 (*CSPF 1577–8*, p. 592); above, p. 56.
3 *NA* 317/37; *OA* 45/21. Cf. *OA* 174/15; *NA* 223/24.
4 *OA* 359/29, 375/13–14, 386/12, 411/4.
5 *OA* 276/8, 353/1.
6 *OA* 96/19–20, 177/13, 95/30; cf. *OA* 218/26–7.
7 *OA* 45/20, 114/3, 124/12; *NA* 225/22; *OA* 45/7, 227/30–1, 280/34–281/1.
8 *NA* 16/26–33.
9 *OA* 4/20.
10 *NA* 215/13–15, 293/18.
11 *OA* 320/5–6.

in effect tautologous, for kingship is that which gives authority to goodness. Sidney leaves us to wonder whether, in Renaissance Europe, it is not the term 'bad king' that is tautologous.

Because Basilius – like Elizabeth – intends no harm, we do not think of him as a tyrant. In Pamela's opinion, it is true, he is a 'tyrant' over his daughters and has behaved 'cruelly' to them;[12] but his subjects would not use those words of him. Even the mutineers of Book Two complain only of sins of omission, not of commission. They resent 'the duke's living from among them', their 'want of a prince'.[13] Yet if we defer to the criteria of Aristotle, that root source of Renaissance political thinking, Basilius is unmistakably a tyrant. First, he pursues his private wishes rather than the public good.[14] In a realm where 'public matters had ever been privately governed' he declines 'to set down all private conceits in comparison of what, for the public, is profitable'.[15] Secondly, like Aristotle's tyrants he governs by will rather than law. He takes his decisions (we have seen) 'without the consent or allowance of his subjects', 'making his will wisdom', being 'fortified with the authority of a prince whose power might easily satisfy his will'.[16] The 'freedom of speech and behaviour' that is granted to the shepherds in the performance of their eclogues is conditional upon his 'wil[l]'.[17] His subjects are at his beck and call.[18]

Good-natured he may be, but he is not a man to trifle with. He is capable of 'choler', 'fury', 'anger', 'revenge'.[19] He threatens to put out the eyes of Miso, Dametas' wife, when she hesitates to connive at his adulterous plans.[20] The *New Arcadia* underlines the fear which Basilius commands. Thus the painter of Philoclea's portrait 'durst [not]', 'for fear of suspicion', ask the duke's permission to allude in his painting to her 'watched' condition; Kalander 'durst not' offer Basilius bold counsel; 'nobody durst' enter the area by the River Ladon reserved for royalty, it being 'so privileged a place, upon pain of death'; and it is in the *New Arcadia* that the shepherds utter, under the guise of pastoral, 'such matters as otherwise they durst not deal with'.[21]

For Greville, tyranny is characterised by 'will, which nothing but itself endures', and which overrides 'law'.[22] His golden retrospection contrasts the readiness of Queen Elizabeth to harmonise her 'own affections' with those of

---

12 *NA* 455/32, 155/5.
13 *OA* 127/15, 127/33.
14 Aristotle, *The Politics*, ed. Stephen Everson (Cambridge, 1988), pp. 61–2 (1279b), 130 (1311a).
15 *OA* 320/7–8; *NA* 418/5–6.
16 Above, p. 151.
17 *OA* 57/3–4 (though cf. *OA* 392/13–14).
18 *OA* 250/2, 251/33–4, 252/25–6.
19 *OA* 9/1, 313/25, 396/23; *NA* 353/21–2.
20 *NA* 228/21–2; cf. *NA* 278/1–2.
21 *NA* 15/26–31, 416/22–3, 188/38–189/1, 24/33–4. In the manner of Renaissance courts, 'misliking', which Basilius is spared, is visited instead on the counsellor he has wilfully raised, Dametas: *OA* 269/16–17.
22 Wilkes, pp. 51 (st. 66), 45 (st. 41), 60 (st. 100), 109 (st. 298), 200 (st. 659). Cf. ibid., pp. 49 (sts 57–8), 106 (st. 286).

'her subjects', and to govern by 'laws', with the ways of 'tyrants' who 'allow of no scope . . . but their own will'.[23] Yet in Sidney's lifetime Greville, and Sidney too, would have been more likely to concur with the view of Sir Francis Knollys that she preferred 'her own will and her own affections' to 'the sound advice of open counsel'.[24] 'Will', in Renaissance minds, is the enemy not only of law but of reason, which law embodies. Languet's and Mornay's *Vindiciae, Contra Tyrannos* cites Juvenal's condemnation of kings who resolve to rule by 'will' rather than by 'reason'.[25] The friends of will are passion and lust. Political disaster arises, thinks the forward Protestant Thomas Wilson, when men, instead of 'reason, follow will, and instead of law, use their own lust'.[26]

The same thinking is articulated in the *New Arcadia*. We find Erona, that prisoner of 'passions', 'arming her will with authority' when she becomes queen.[27] Then there is King Antiphilus. Antiphilus, like Basilius, has no taste for blood. He does not use his subjects 'cruelly'. But he is a 'weak fool', as Basilius is. His weakness and folly have cruel consequences. Having been 'suddenly borne into an unknown ocean of absolute power', he is 'like one carried up to so high a place that he loseth the discerning of the ground over which he is', and 'his mind' is 'lifted . . . far beyond the level of his own discourse'. 'Swayed' by 'every wind of passions', he turns his passion on the reason of his subjects. For 'imagining no so true property of sovereignty as to do what he listed, and to list whatsoever pleased his fancy', and 'remembering only that himself was in the high seat of a king', he 'could not perceive that he was a king of reasonable creatures'.[28] Basilius' head is not turned by power as Antiphilus' is. Yet he too is swayed by the 'wind' of passion,[29] with disastrous results for his subjects.

Basilius conforms in one more respect to Aristotle's account of tyranny. Aristotle describes 'our modern tyrants' who 'spend whole days in sensuality'.[30] That is what the lovesick Basilius does, or tries to do. At the same time his delight in the 'pleasant' eclogues sung by the shepherds confirms Aristotle's observation that 'those who show some dexterity' in 'pleasant amusements' are 'highly esteemed at the courts of tyrants'.[31] Sloth and sensuality are likewise criteria of tyranny in the *Vindiciae, Contra Tyrannos*,

23 *GP* 41/4–6, 41/24–5.
24 Above, p. 151; cf. Martin van Gelderen, *The Political Thought of the Dutch Revolt 1555–1590* (Cambridge, 1992), p. 132. Is there a glance at Elizabeth's wilfulness at *NA* 29/11–12?
25 Laski, *Defence*, p. 144; cf. Garnett, p. 96.
26 K. de L., xi. 130. Wilson was describing mob rule, but like many in his time he traced the excesses of tyranny and those of democracy to that common root.
27 *NA* 207/39, 206/5–6.
28 *NA* 299/3–17; cf. Goodman, *How Superior Powers*, pp. 148–9 ('as though they were not reasonable creatures'). Ironically it is Basilius, oblivious to his own failings, who relates those shortcomings of Antiphilus and the disastrous events of his reign: *NA* 298/15ff.
29 Above, p. 138.
30 Aristotle, *Politics*, p. 138 (1314b).
31 *OA* 6/25–6, 56/20; Aristotle, *The Ethics*, ed. Jonathan Barnes (Harmondsworth, repr. 1984), pp. 326–7; cf. Marlowe's *Edward II*, I. i. 49ff.

which explains that tyranny prevails when kings wrap themselves in 'a sleepy dream of voluptuous idleness' and retain only 'the bare name' of kings: Basilius, that sleepy dreamer of voluptuous idleness, is 'a prince . . . not doing like a prince, keeping and not exercising the place'.[32]

Basilius' is the tyranny exercised not by the strong but by the weak. The *Vindiciae* warns against the gift of unlimited power to a 'weak' master or 'weak mind'.[33] For Greville, tyrants are of two kinds: 'strong' ones and 'weak' or 'weak-minded' ones.[34] 'Which are worse', he asks, 'kings ill, or easily led'?[35] It seems a moot point. Greville, who calls Basilius an 'unactive' ruler,[36] explains elsewhere that a 'weak-minded' or 'unactive' tyrant, holding 'power absolute', is unequal to his responsibilities. 'Ease is made greatness'; 'power would shadow sloth' and 'make the crown a specious hive for drones'.[37] Greville's plays portray weak tyrants. In his *Mustapha* there is something of Basilius, that 'doting fool', in King Solyman,

> this dotard king
> (Who, swol'n with practice of long government,
> Doth stain the public with ill managing) . . ..[38]

More conspicuously close to Basilius is the 'old king' of Greville's play *Alaham*, who is 'weak both in good and ill'. Like Basilius, he has 'Sent to the gods to learn what should befall, / Having but peace; and wealth to doubt withal'. A 'frail king', a 'king effeminate', lacking 'active constantness', he has – again like Basilius, that 'mighty duke' – 'languished, and wantoned in a powerful throne'.[39]

Basilius' mind, we learn when we first meet him, has been 'corrupted with a prince's fortune'. Sidney went out of his way to reproduce those words in the *New Arcadia*.[40] They point to the inherent defects of kingship where kingly will prevails. In 1579 George Buchanan, a writer always alive to the frailties of princes, feared lest Mary's son James VI of Scotland might be 'corrupted' by 'false notions' implanted by 'flattery'.[41] John Stubbs declared in

32 Garnett, p. 143; *OA* 358/32–4.
33 Laski, *Defence*, p. 154; cf. Garnett, p. 129.
34 Wilkes, pp. 55, 71; cf. Macfarlane, *Buchanan*, p. 388.
35 Bullough, i. 93 (sonnet xxxvi, l. 13).
36 *GP* 8/21.
37 Wilkes, pp. 57–8 (sts 89–93).
38 Bullough, ii. 130 (V. iii. 78–80).
39 Ibid., 140 (Prologue, ll. 82, 86), 143 (I. i. 26–9), 145 (I. i. 103). In Thomas Norton's *Orations, of Arsanes*, the King of Persia, ignoring the external threat to his land as Basilius ignores the external threat to his, 'sat negligent with his wanton court at home, while Philip [of Macedon] by augmentation of victories armed his will with power'. Norton, *Orations, of Arsanes*, sig. Eiiii; cf. above, pp. 162–3.
40 *OA* 6/4; *NA* 23/3–4; R. W. Zandvoort, *Sidney's Arcadia. A Comparison between the Two Versions* (Amsterdam, 1929), p. 69.
41 Buchanan, *Powers*, ed. Arrowood, pp. 37–8; cf. Wilkes, p. 114 (st. 318).

the *Gaping Gulph*, with Elizabeth's conduct during the Anjou negotiations in mind, that 'the very place of a prince doth bring him some disadvantage through our old Adam, who when he is lift up will hardly yield to the poor good advice of them that speak truth in a bare simplicity'.[42] For Sidney and his allies the corruption of princes illustrated rules of 'nature'. It was the 'corruption of human nature' that led Languet and Mornay to conclude that kings must be restricted by contracts with their subjects;[43] William of Orange, urging resistance to Philip II, observed that it is 'in the nature of sovereign power not to brook any contradiction';[44] in 1579 a Dutch tract against Philip remarked on the failings that lie in 'the nature of kings', or at least in the 'nature' of 'most . . . kings';[45] Fulke Greville thought that it was 'in princes' natures' for passion to usurp reason;[46] in the *Arcadia* it is 'according to the nature of great persons' that Basilius, 'in love with that he had done himself', makes the preposterous appointment of Dametas as his 'principal herdman'.[47] Sidney often alerts us to the vices inherent in 'great persons', 'great personages', 'great men', 'great fellows', 'proud lords', on whose wills there is no check.[48]

In the *New Arcadia* the normally mild Kalander remarks of the appointment of Dametas, which the duke's sycophants have applauded, that 'princes whose doings have been often soothed with good success think nothing so absurd which they cannot make honourable'.[49] Sidney knows how power shapes opinion to its own advantage, and how opinion can yearn to be shaped by it. He sees how the 'great acts' committed by princes in the selfish pursuit of glory 'entitl[e]' them with 'the holy name of virtue'.[50] The shepherds of the *Arcadia* deceive themselves, on the death of Basilius, by thinking well of his reign: on the death of Cosimo I de Medici of Florence, Languet and Sidney jest about his people's lament for that tyrant, who no doubt 'will one day', says Languet, 'be spoken of as a sagacious and fortunate prince'.[51] In the *New Arcadia* the Queen of Laconia 'was a queen, and therefore beautiful'.[52]

The *New Arcadia* also reveals 'how soon rulers grow proud, and in their pride, foolish'.[53] The results of their pride and folly, in the late Renaissance, were plain to see. Greville noticed how 'rarely' kings were exemplary or public-spirited, how 'rarely' they listened to 'counsel uncorrupt'.[54] 'Learning

---

42 Stubbs, p. 30.
43 Charles Mercier, 'Les Théories politiques des Calvinistes dans les Pays-Bas à la fin du XVIᶜ et au début du XVIIᶜ siècle', *Revue d'histoire ecclésiastique* 29 (1933), pp. 25–73, at pp. 50–1; cf. Garnett, pp. 139, 140.
44 *CSPF 1575–7*, p. 430.
45 Martin van Gelderen, ed., *The Dutch Revolt* (Cambridge, 1993), p. 127.
46 Wilkes, p. 83 (st. 194).
47 *OA* 31/18–19.
48 *OA* 48/10–11, 244/34, 320/24–5; *NA* 142/19–21, 166/21, 178/27–8, 189/8, 363/21–2.
49 *NA* 18/35–6; *OA* 31/14–20.
50 *OA* 358/8–13.
51 Pears, pp. 55, 63–4.
52 *NA* 96/12.
53 *NA* 239/27–8.
54 Wilkes, pp. 156 (st. 482), 197 (st. 647), 66–7 (sts 126–7).

and judgement', remarked the forward Protestant Thomas Randolph to George Buchanan, were qualities 'in this age . . . amongst princes most rare'.[55] Friendship, a commodity valued highly in Sidney's fiction, is declared by the *New Arcadia* to be 'a rare thing in princes – more rare between princes'; to Languet Sidney wrote witheringly of 'the fruits of royal friendships'.[56] If virtues are exceptional in kings, vices are the norm. 'Most kings', according to the *Vindiciae*, 'are transported' with 'licentiousness and unbridled power'.[57] Euarchus, who in his foreign policy is unlike 'most princes',[58] is unlike them again in his government of his realm. For as Musidorus explains to Pamela in the *New Arcadia*:

> where most princes, seduced by flattery to build upon false grounds of government, make themselves as it were another thing from the people, and so count it gain what they get from them, and as if it were two counterbalances, that their estate goes highest when the people goes lowest, by a fallacy of argument thinking themselves most kings when the subject is most basely subjected; [Euarchus] contrariwise, virtuously and wisely acknowledging that he with his people made all but one politic body whereof himself was the head, even so cared for them as he would for his own limbs, never restraining their liberty without it stretched to licentiousness, nor pulling them from their goods (which they found were not employed to the purchase of a greater good), but in all his actions showing a delight in their welfare, brought that to pass, that while by force he took nothing, by their love he had all. In sum . . . I might as easily set down the whole art of government as to lay before your eyes the picture of his proceedings.[59]

It is, alas, an art little understood among the princes of Sidney's time.

Sidney's associates explained that, though opposed to tyrants, they were in favour of kings. When princes 'transgress the bounds and limits of the law', Walsingham warned James VI, 'they leave to be kings and become tyrants'.[60] Sidney himself, explains Greville, wanted to 'publis[h] the differences between monarchs and tyrants . . . clearly to the world'.[61] Greville for his

---

55 P. H. Brown, ed., *Vernacular Writings of George Buchanan* (Edinburgh, Scottish Text Society, 1892), p. 55.

56 *NA* 162/2–3; Pears, p. 41.

57 Laski, *Defence*, p. 137 (cf. Garnett, p. 89).

58 Above, p. 169.

59 *NA* 161/8–23; cf. *OA* 10/4–6.

60 Read, *Walsingham*, ii. 218.

61 *GP* 58/17–18; cf. Wilkes, p. 93 (st. 231). There is only one moment in Sidney's writing when he appears to repudiate not only tyranny but kingship. It occurs in the description, in the fable sung by Philisides in the Third Eclogues, of the displacement of the 'harmless empire' of senators (*OA* 256/19) by a king who rules them tyranically. (The fable is printed in Appendix C, below.) But (i) things go wrong for the beasts only when they allow kingship to slide into tyranny (*OA* 258/1ff.); (ii) Sidney leaves open the possibilities that initially the king not only ruled well but meant well, and that the descent from kingship into tyranny was not inevitable (*OA* 258/2–7); (iii) the compression inherent in the fable form may involve the elimination of distinctions or

own part declares that 'Tyrants through fear and malice feed on blood, / Good kings secure at home, seek all men's good.'[62] Buchanan agreed.[63] So did Languet and Mornay.[64] What their *Vindiciae, Contra Tyrannos* has to say against tyrants, it explains, 'is so far from detracting anything from kings, as on the contrary, the more tyrants are laid open in their proper colours, the more glorious does the true worth and dignity of kings appear'.[65]

That passage would be echoed by Milton in his *Defensio Secunda* of 1654.[66] For even among the republicans of the seventeenth century we sometimes glimpse a yearning for an Aristotelian good king. We glimpse it too in Sidney and his party. The majesty of Euarchus inspires 'reverent awe', for 'reverence' is the quality commanded by 'the very shining force of excellent virtue'.[67] Sir Walter Mildmay, in arguing against the Anjou match, noted that whereas 'tyranny' governs by the 'fear' which terrifies, 'monarchies' properly command 'reverend fear' and are thus 'ruled with fear and love together'.[68] Sidney, who gives the word 'sovereignty' favourable meanings, associates it with reverence and majesty (rather than with the recently formulated ideas of Jean Bodin about undivided constitutional supremacy). The *New Arcadia* regrets the abuse of 'sovereignty' by bad kings, its erosion by royal favourites or by oligarchy, the loss of reverence that leaves a monarch with 'nothing but the name of a king'.[69]

Yet if, as Sidney and his friends thought, kings are generally corrupt, how plausible can the distinction between kings and tyrants be in practice? Fiction can create a Euarchus, so unlike 'most princes', but where in the real world

---

subtleties within the historical process he describes, on which another form would dwell; (iv) the rule of 'harmless senators' imagined by Sidney, who is no friend to pure aristocracy (below, Chapter 13), may have had a monarchical element to it even before the elevation of 'man'. On that last point we may note that the *Vindiciae*, though it proposes simply that tyranny, which is evil, has replaced kingship, which is virtuous, nonetheless represents virtuous kingship as being controlled by a nobility (Garnett, p. 147). Perhaps Sidney's harmless senators exercised a similar control over a king. Perhaps their aristocratic rule was similar to (albeit an idealised version of) that unflatteringly portrayed on the title-page of Hobbes's translation of Thucydides, where, as Fritz Levy has pointed out to me, 'aristocracy' is rule by a group of men sitting at a table with a king at one end (Thucydides, *Eight Bookes of the Peloponnesian War* (London, 1629; cf. sig. a2); on the same theme see Richard Tuck, *Philosophy and Government 1572–1651* (Cambridge, 1993), p. 204). That possibility is strengthened by remarks of Greville, who describes the government of Poland, which had a king but a weak one, as a 'well-mixed and balanced aristocracy', and implies that Sidney regarded it in the same light (*GP* 49/28–50/4; though cf. below, p. 240). Greville thinks of the golden age, to which Sidney's rule of harmless senators effectively belongs, as ruled by kings (Wilkes, pp. 35, 43 (st. 35)).

62 Bullough, i. 141 (sonnet xcv, ll. 23–4).
63 Archibald Brown, ed., *The Sacred Dramas of George Buchanan* (Edinburgh, 1906), p. 110; Buchanan, *Powers*, ed. Arrowood, pp. 43, 92, 109, 111 (cf. p. 44); Macfarlane, *Buchanan*, pp. 380, 381, 387.
64 Patry, *Philippe Du Plessis-Mornay*, pp. 276–7.
65 Laski, *Defence*, p. 117 (cf. Garnett, p. 67).
66 F. A. Patterson, ed., *The Works of John Milton*, 18 vols (New York, 1931–8), viii. 24–5.
67 *OA* 382/31, 314/27–9; cf. *OA* 357n.
68 Lehmberg, *Mildmay*, p. 159.
69 *NA* 299/9–10, 160/1–2, 159/36–7, 182/8–10. Cf. *NA* 153/22–5, 156n.; Wilkes, p. 152 (st. 466); KAO, U1475: Z1/1, pp. 711–12.

are true kings to be found? Earlier in the century Baldesar Castiglione had made a tart observation on that subject: 'heaven is so reluctant to produce excellent princes that scarcely one has been seen over many centuries'.[70] The time since Castiglione wrote had evidently brought no improvement in the stock of kings. Greville admitted that, in passages of his own writing which criticised the abuses of regal power, he had failed to uphold the distinction between 'kings' and 'tyrants' because 'the image' of true kingship would not 'have proved credible to men'. Thanks to man's 'craft', which has destroyed pristine political harmony, 'many years are gone / Since any godhead ruled an earthly throne'.[71] Languet, reporting to Sidney the praises that were being bestowed on the King of Poland in 1578, was 'glad that we have in Christendom at least one king who possesses some goodness'.[72]

If there is one principal cause of the general corruption of kings, it is the 'servile flattery' which Sidney associates with courts in *The Lady of May*: the flattery by which, as Musidorus explains, 'most princes' are 'seduced'. For Sidney as for other writers of the Renaissance, flattery to princes is a poison, a 'poisonous sugar'.[73] Where Euarchus, the exception to the rule, is not 'anything tickled with . . . flatteries', Basilius, the norm, is 'tickled' by the flattery of Clinias, with dire results;[74] the *Vindiciae*, which has 'the minions and flatterers of princes' as a persistent target, explains that they 'tickl[e] their ears'.[75] In the *Arcadia*, Dametas, whom Basilius has whimsically raised to favour and into whose hands he has 'put his life', purveys 'the most servile flattery'.[76] His rise is hastened by the 'flattering courtier[s]' who applaud Basilius' misjudgement of his character.[77] In the *New Arcadia* the tyrants of Book Two are calamitously susceptible to flattery and sycophancy[78] and calamitously prone to advance 'favourites' and 'minions' and 'fit persons for faction'.[79]

Flattery was hardly a novel complaint. But in the minds of Sidney and his friends it was associated with a modern problem: with that narrowing of the range of opinion to which, in an age of declining representative institutions and emerging cabinet councils, the princes of the Renaissance were exposed. It was associated, too, with the slaughter and persecution of the wars of

70   Baldesar Castiglione, *The Book of the Courtier*, ed. George Bull (Harmondsworth, repr. 1981), pp. 315–16.
71   *GP* 92/10–14; Wilkes, p. 39 (st. 17).
72   Pears, pp. 141–2.
73   *MP* 28/17–18; *OA* 166/27; *NA* 238/5–14, 299/18; K. de L., ix. 337; Tydeman, *Two Tudor Tragedies*, pp. 75, 86 (*Gorboduc*, dumb-show; ll. 779–80); cf. Blair Worden, 'Shakespeare and Politics', *Shakespeare Survey* 44 (1991), pp. 1–15, at p. 15.
74   *OA* 364/25–6; *NA* 293/19–20.
75   Laski, *Defence*, p. 66.
76   *OA* 269/17, 31/22–3, 43/30, Sidney takes pains to reproduce the point at *NA* 109/19–20.
77   *OA* 31/14.
78   *NA* 169/34–5, 176/1–3, 218/13, 300/14.
79   *NA* 176/21–39, 182/8–10, 222/33, 249/33–4.

religion, which Sidney's circle blamed on evil counsel. All over Europe, it seemed, advice was being monopolised by enemies to truth and virtue. 'The minds of our princes', wrote Languet to Sidney in 1577 as he surveyed the destruction wrought by religious strife, 'are preoccupied by evil counsels, and as if they were gone mad refuse to take the advice of common sense'.[80] 'Always or most commonly', lamented Walsingham in 1578 with the counsels of Elizabeth in mind, 'the persons that wish best, and the causes that work best, are most misliked.'[81] Thomas Wilson offered the same diagnosis.[82] Greville regretted the sway, in the courts of 'modern princes', of 'favourites' at the expense of men of 'worth'.[83]

The *Arcadia* has its eye on modernity too. One sentence brings the modern age before us with unusual directness: 'Philanax was not one of the modern minds who make suitors magistrates, but did ever think the unwilling worthy man was fitter than the undeserving desirer.'[84] Sidney's own disfavour, which kept him 'from fit employments', heightened his alertness to the 'corrupt[ion]' of the 'age': Greville thought it characteristic of rulers in 'this crafty world's declining age' that 'worth they choose rather to suppress, than use'.[85] The 'noble virtues' of Sidney's father, thanks to a whispering campaign against him at court, 'were many times suppressed', just as, in Macedon before Euarchus has reformed it, 'men of virtue' are 'suppressed'.[86]

In Renaissance minds the evils of flattery and favouritism are inseparable from those of courts. 'In all courts', as Greville says with an eye to the Anjou crisis, the 'reigning faction' seeks to monopolise the advice that reaches the sovereign.[87] Sidney's criticism of courts is conventional in its themes and language, as Greville's is. Anti-courtly literature of the sixteenth century, as is often observed, is largely a courtly phenomenon. It can be seen as a safety-valve that allowed courtiers and would-be courtiers to discharge their resentments as they competed for power and place. A distaste for court life often existed, as it did in Sidney, alongside more positive feelings. Yet Sidney is uncomfortable at Elizabeth's court and uncomfortable in thinking about it. His anxieties are sufficiently sharp and troubled to suggest that he believes good courts to be as remote a possibility as good kings or the sway of good counsellors.

Because Basilius has broken up his court, Sidney has to work hard to inject the theme of courtly evils into the *Arcadia*. The scope that would have been open to him had he placed the work in a court is indicated by a play of 1606 by John Day, *The Isle of Gulls*, which uses Sidney's plot but sets it in a court

---

80 Pears, p. 111; cf. ibid., pp. 53, 83, 87.
81 K. de L., x. 832.
82 Wilson, *Demosthenes*, p. 128.
83 GP 95/21, 96/8, 105/12–13, 107/3–17; above, p. 69; cf. Bullough, ii. 170 (*Alaham* II. iv. 34).
84 OA 363/15–17.
85 Osborn, *Young Philip Sidney*, p. 537; Pears, p. 143; Wilkes, p. 162 (st. 507).
86 MP 4; NA 160/12.
87 GP 37/30–8/2.

intended to parallel that of King James I. The prologue remarks that Dametas, a central character of the play, 'expresses to the life the monstrous and deformed shape of vice'.[88] In the *Arcadia* it is easier to think of Dametas as a buffoon than as a villain, even if it is as evident from his conduct as from the duke's that folly can be as harmful as wickedness.

If Arcadia, in contrast to Day's play, has no court to satirise, it is spared other modern evils too. We are taken back to 'those worthy days' when 'virtuous courage' was properly esteemed[89] and 'the right honest hospitality' respected.[90] The modest 'throne of judgement seat in which Basilius was ever wont to sit', and which is carried 'into the midst of the green' for the trial of the princes, recalls Greville's invocation of an 'innocent' age of 'poor simplicity' when there was 'no throne, but open air'.[91] Yet the refuge from modernity proves illusory. Arcadia is no escape from present reality, though the lovers act as if it is. But equally it is not the setting for a sustained exploration of courtly corruption or of the consequences of flattery and favouritism.

When those subjects do appear in his narrative, Sidney underlines them. He labours the duke's irresponsibility in elevating Dametas, that 'moth of his prince's estate'.[92] In the *New Arcadia* Kalander steps out of character (or so at least it seems) to spell out his revulsion at Dametas' appointment.[93] In the *Old Arcadia*, where Sidney tends to tell us himself what in the *New Arcadia* he has his characters tell us, the introduction of Dametas prompts one of those infrequent moments when the narrator steps from the action to frame a moral: Dametas' advancement was 'a great error' in the duke, whose 'quality was not to make men, but to use them according as men were, no more than an ass will be taught to manage, a horse to hunt, or a hound to bear a saddle, but each to be used according to the force of his own nature'.[94] Another of those infrequent moments condemns the effects of flattery in private life,[95] for in Sidney's fiction flattery characterises both the courtship of courts and the courtships of love.[96]

In the *New Arcadia* Sidney finds fresh ways of working courts and their characteristics into his narrative. In Book Two, on the princes' travels, we catch glimpses of courts outside Arcadia. In Book One, even though Basilius has broken up his court and has forbidden access to his person, he is willing

---

88   John Day, *The Isle of Gulls*, ed. G. B. Harrison (London, 1936), sig. A2ᵛ; Tricomi, *Anticourt Drama*, pp. 35, 39–41.

89   *OA* 50/8–9; cf. above, p. 61.

90   *NA* 9/31–2, 12/17, 71/28–9, 73/20, 107/10–11, 285/29–30, 418/18–19.

91   *OA* 374/34–6; Bullough, ii. 190–1 (*Alaham*, Chorus Tertius, ll. 20–31). Cf. Wilkes, p. 149 (st. 454); Hackett, *Virgin Mother, Virgin Queen*, p. 106.

92   *OA* 288/20–1.

93   *NA* 17/34–6, 18/31–6.

94   *OA* 31/23–7.

95   *OA* 206/26–30.

96   Catherine Bates, *The Rhetoric of Courtship in Elizabethan Language and Literature* (Cambridge, 1992), pp. 27, 32.

to entertain the parade of courtly chivalry that Sidney describes so fully.
Thereafter the shadow of his court still falls on his subjects. Here there is a
change from the *Old Arcadia*. In the earlier version the shepherds, though
they sing eclogues at court and in doing so reveal facts about courtly power,
are all essentially countrymen. But in the *New Arcadia* there are certain
'specified' shepherds who enjoy courtly privileges.[97] Philisides, a shepherd in
the *Old Arcadia*, becomes a courtly knight in the *New*.[98] In the *Old Arcadia*
the court has to be observed from the outside, in the pastoral setting of the
eclogues, which provide a retreat from it but also a vehicle of commentary
upon those vexations and vanities and falsities of court life that so troubled
the Elizabethan political sensibility. Philisides recalls the retirement that freed
him from 'courtly pomps'; Musidorus delights in the 'sweet woods' that
separate him from the court and its abuses.[99]

Courts debase their occupants and entrap them. Among the features of
court life identified by Musidorus is 'envy's snaky eye'. In the *New Arcadia* it
is an 'envious counsellor' who turns the King of Phrygia into tyrannical
courses.[100] One poem of Sidney adapts Horace to emphasise the pressures of
court life, 'where envy needs must be';[101] in another, Lamon's song, the court
is 'the envy-hatching place'. To Lamon the court is also full of 'restless desires
in great men rife'.[102] For there can be no point of rest in courts, 'where', as
Greville says, 'no thought's peace is nourished'.[103] Courtiers are forever rising
and falling. 'The splendour of a court', Languet warns Sidney, rests on
'slippery ground'; Lamon is glad to escape from 'climb-fall court'; Astrophil
finds himself suspected of ambition, of 'still climbing slippery place'.[104] Those
sentiments recall the translation of Seneca's *Thyestes* made earlier in the
sixteenth century by Sir Thomas Wyatt, where the Chorus observes 'the
slipper top / Of court's estates'.[105] At the court of Henry VIII Wyatt had
been 'fettered with chains of gold'.[106] That language, too, persisted into
Sidney's generation. Greville wrote of the 'golden fetter' that adorns noblemen subjected to kings; Musidorus, in the 'sweet woods', escapes the 'golden
manacles' of the court; the courtier Astrophil finds his 'young brain captived
to a golden cage'.[107]

Sidney's young brain, too, was captived to a golden cage. Yearning for
action and fulfilment, he was obliged instead to take part in those stiff and

97   *NA* 23/19, 297/24–5, 315/21–3; cf. *NA* 198/22–3.
98   *NA* 255/18ff.
99   *OA* 335/27–8, 166/23–9. Cf. *OA* 250/5–253/5; Bodl., Rawlinson MS. A331, fo. 83.
100 *OA* 166/26; *NA* 176/22–39.
101 Ringler, p. 143 (sonnet 12, l. 6); Robert Stillman, *Sidney's Poetic Justice* (London and Toronto,
     1986), pp. 72–3; cf. Buxton, *Sir Philip Sidney*, p. 58.
102 Ringler, p. 243 (ll. 61–2).
103 Bullough, ii. 125 (*Mustapha* V. 1. i.).
104 Pears, p. 155; Ringler, pp. 243 (l. 61), 176 (sonnet 23, ll. 9–10).
105 Sir Thomas Wyatt, *The Complete Poems*, ed. Ronald Rebholz (Harmondsworth, 1978), p. 94
     (no. xlix).
106 Ibid., p. 102 (no. lxxi).
107 Bullough, i. 138 (sonnet xci, ll. 7–8); *OA* 166/33; Ringler, p. 176 (sonnet 23, l. 11).

elaborate formalities of the Elizabethan court which, as J. H. Elliott remarks, 'even foreigners accustomed to the style of Habsburg and Valois were amazed' to witness.[108] He had to adjust to the every mood and whim of a monarch who was turning her back on his party and his policies and, as he believed, leading her country to ruin. In January 1579 Daniel Rogers wrote a Latin poem to Sidney which described Sidney's life at court. The poem summons – inadvertently, unless there is irony in it that has not been suspected – the frustrations of the world which it commends and to which Rogers seems to yearn to belong. Since the queen's warm reception of Sidney on his return from his German embassy in 1577, Rogers reminds him, she has:

> commanded you to remain in her presence; and so, whether she walks with wandering steps through the green fields which one sees from the nearby court of Richmond, or whether she takes a walk through the sunny gardens, you are there, faithfully ready to wait upon her majesty. If it pleases the goddess to ride into the gay fields, you will mount your horse and presently keep your mistress company. . . . And whatever you are doing, you must be close to the queen, whether she is seriously occupied or pleases to be merry.[109]

In Sidney's portraits of courtly culture, revulsion is rarely far away. The *New Arcadia* records that in Asia 'great multitudes of many great persons, and even of princes', come to bestow 'right royal presents', 'the highest honours', indeed 'excessive honours', on Musidorus and Pyrocles, 'so as, in those parts of the world . . . in many hundreds of years, there was not seen so royal an assembly'. But Musidorus and Pyrocles are 'quickly aweary thereof'. They hasten away by ship, leaving their princely admirers to bid them farewell from the shore 'even upon their knees'.[110] Languet regretted that Sidney had not been present at the Polish coronation of 1573 – that 'sartorial sensation', as Elliott calls it – for the 'pomp and brilliance . . . were, it is said, unbelievable. And yet', he reflected, 'these spectacles might have proved boring to you.'[111] Indeed they might. There is plausibility enough in Sidney's announcement that his 'pen grows almost weary to set down' the 'honey words' with which the lovesick Basilius, at the expense of his country's needs, woos the disguised Pyrocles.[112]

How did Sidney contend with the subservience, the artificiality, the restlessness, the hollowness of the Elizabethan court? According to his early, laudatory biographer Thomas Moffet he spent a part of each day away from its 'clashing tumult', its 'foison of delights and desires', perhaps studying and

---

108 J. H. Elliott, *Europe Divided 1559–1598* (London, 1968), p. 70. Walsingham, a man of austere habits, may have been uneasy at Elizabeth's court: Leimon, 'Walsingham', pp. 12, 75.
109 Van Dorsten, *Poets*, pp. 65–6.
110 *NA* 271/15–33, 272/38–9.
111 Levy, 'Correspondence', letter of 18 March 1574; Elliott, *Europe Divided*, p. 235.
112 *OA* 178/11–12.

talking with scholars, 'all troubles banished from his mind'.[113] But when Languet witnessed Sidney's life at court in the winter of 1578–9 he found an altogether less pleasing picture. 'To speak plainly', he wrote to him afterwards,

> the habits of your court seemed to me somewhat less manly than I could have wished, and most of your noblemen appeared to me to seek for a reputation more by a kind of affected courtesy than by those virtues which are wholesome to the state, and which are most becoming to generous spirits and to men of high birth. I was sorry therefore, and so were other friends of yours, to see you wasting the flower of your life on such things, and I feared lest that noble nature of yours should be dulled, and lest from habit you should be brought to take pleasure in pursuits which only enervate the mind.[114]

Languet may privately 'speak plainly' to Sidney, but he knows that plain speaking can be imprudent at or around courts. Sidney knows it too. A beast-fable in the First Eclogues, a political allegory, shows:

> the swan of dignity deprived,
> And statute made he never should have voice,
> Since when, I think, he hath in silence lived.[115]

The swan's fate recalls that of the poet in *The Faerie Queene* whose tongue is 'nayld to a post'.[116] In the autumn of 1579 the punishment of John Stubbs, Leicester's client and Sidney's partner in the campaign against the Anjou match, provided a grim reminder of the dangers of literary bluntness. Perhaps there is an allusion to that episode in a jest made by Sidney in a letter to Leicester in August 1580, when the *Arcadia* was being written; if so, the jest is a dark one. Being 'so full of the cold as one cannot hear me speak', Sidney explains, he is kept from court, 'since my only service is speech and that is stopped'.[117] For on the scaffold, where his hand was struck off, Stubbs had remarked that 'my mouth is stopped', by royal order, from questioning his punishment; he repeated the point – 'the judgement . . . against me doth stop my mouth' – in asking the privy council for his release from prison.[118]

Courtiers could prosper only if they learned to speak indirectly and obliquely.[119] Languet, who besieged Sidney with injunctions to serve his country, warned him that the servants of princes must 'learn to dissemble', that without an acquaintance with 'Maranism', the art of saying one thing

---

113 Moffet, *Nobilis*, pp. 78, 83.
114 Pears, p. 167.
115 *OA* 78/35–79/1; cf. below, p. 245.
116 *The Faerie Queene* V. ix. 25.
117 Feuillerat, iii. 129.
118 NRO, F(P)M 204; Stubbs, p. xxxv.
119 Cf. Bates, *Rhetoric of Courtship*, p. 3.

and meaning another, he could not hope to 'attain any high station in England'.[120] In the Netherlands an ally of England's forward Protestants was horrified by the decision of Leicester's party to commission Stubbs's *Gaping Gulph*. 'The way to pacify kings', he urged, 'is not to oppose them, or announce by writings, signatures, or remarks that one does not approve their doings. It is necessary to be humble, or at least to hold one's tongue.'[121] That Sidney's patrons, who knew that general truth perfectly well, chose nonetheless to incite open opposition to the Anjou match, and to commission the writings of Sidney and Stubbs against it, indicates their desperation.

For the habits of courtly duplicity and concealment were second nature to them. This was the world in which the writings of Tacitus, the historian of dissimulation and concealment in the politics of imperial Rome, acquired so powerful an appeal to the late Renaissance.[122] Courts were Tacitean in another way too: they were places not only of guarded tongues but of watchful suspicion. The spying of courtiers on each other seems to have heightened in the late 1570s[123] – a time when, Philip Sidney believed, members of his father's entourage were passing information from Sir Henry's correspondence to Sir Henry's enemies.[124] Philip's fiction explains that princes operate through 'spies (the necessary evil servants to a king)', that the 'ears' of princes are 'manifold';[125] 'kings', says Greville, have 'many ears'.[126] By contrast Sidney's shepherds, in their pastoral innocence, are 'not limited to a whisp'ring note, the lament of a courtier'. 'Among the shepherds was all honest liberty; no fear of dangerous telltales (who hunt greater preys), nor indeed minds in them to give telltales any occasion.' The victim of spies and informers is truth, for, as the elderly shepherd Geron says, 'no man doth speak aright who speaks in fear'.[127]

Kings have elementary responsibilities of which, insulated by the servility of courts, they tend to be unaware. In 1580 the Dutch, seeking to educate the Duke of Anjou, their prospective sovereign, in the principles of sound government, explained to him that a king should be a 'father to his country'.[128] Sidney underlines the same point. Before Euarchus, the exception to the rule, reformed Macedon, 'the court of a prince' was 'rather

120 Levy, 'Correspondence', no. 54; Pears, p. 62.
121 *CSPF 1579–80*, p. 99.
122 Cf. below, Chapter 14.
123 Read, *Walsingham*, ii. 2. The place of spies in the Elizabethan political imagination is vividly illustrated by Lacey Baldwin Smith, *Treason in Tudor England. Politics and Paranoia* (London, 1986); see too John Michael Archer, *Sovereignty and Intelligence. Spying and Court Culture in the English Renaissance* (Stanford, Calif., 1993).
124 Feuillerat, iii. 123.
125 *NA* 216/11–13.
126 Quoted by Joan Rees, *Fulke Greville, Lord Brooke, 1554–1628* (Berkeley and Los Angeles, 1971), p. 170.
127 *OA* 86/14, 245/22–4, 262/23.
128 Gordon Griffiths, ed., *Representative Government in Western Europe in the Sixteenth Century* (Oxford, 1968), p. 491.

deemed as a privileged place of unbridled licentiousness than as a biding of him who, as a father, should give a fatherly example unto his people'.[129] 'Betwixt prince and subject', knows Euarchus, 'there is as necessary a relation as between father and son.' Basilius, opposite to Euarchus again, fails to act as a 'father' to his 'people'.[130] Instead of the path of public service, of 'well-doing', he pursues his private 'pleasure'. So a double irony lies in the description of him on his death, by the 'over-tender' shepherds, as 'the father of the people', who 'our father was in all affection, / In our well-doing placing all his pleasure'.[131]

In Book Two the rebels ask a fair question about Basilius: 'Who would call him duke if he had not a people?'[132] Their point echoes a series of sixteenth-century (and not only sixteenth-century) descriptions of the first principle of kingship: that kings exist for the benefit not of themselves but of their subjects; the descriptions often drew on the analogy between kings and fathers.[133] If the interests of subjects come before those of princes, should not a subject place the care of his country or commonwealth before that of the prince? That notion, voiced by the Marian exile John Ponet in 1556,[134] is present in the thinking of Walsingham, though he would not have spelled it out.[135] It is present too in the *New Arcadia*. Among the 'true commonplaces' that are explained there (even though Amphialus makes 'false applications' of them) are: 'the duty which is owed to the country goes beyond all other duties'; and 'the weal-public [i]s more to be regarded than any person or magistrate that thereunto [i]s ordained'.[136]

One way of restricting one's sense of obligation to a monarch was to put one's obligation to God before it. Sidney and Walsingham did so.[137] A more secular route was to think about commonwealths or states as separate from

129 *NA* 160/5–8.

130 *OA* 403/31–2; *NA* 283/35–7, 418/3–6; cf. *GP* 68/24–6.

131 *OA* 283/27–8, 349/17–18. Elizabeth, said the councillors who opposed the Anjou match, 'reigneth over her subjects as a most loving mother over her children' (K. de L., xi. 411; cf. Stubbs, p. 49). Was that tribute any more convincing?

132 *OA* 127/18.

133 See e.g. More, *Utopia*, ed. Logan and Adams, p. 33; Goulart, *Mémoires*, i. fo. 25; Felix Raab, *The English Face of Machiavelli* (London, 1964), p. 122; NRO, F(P)M 199; Stillman, 'Politics of Sidney's Pastoral', p. 798; van Gelderen, *Political Thought*, pp. 130, 154, 155; E. H. Kossmann and A. F. Mellinck, eds, *Texts concerning the Revolt of the Netherlands* (Cambridge, 1974), pp. 197, 210; Kingdon, *Myths*, p. 83; Julian Franklin, ed., *Constitutionalism and Resistance in the Sixteenth Century* (New York, 1969), p. 79; K. de L., viii. 54, 57; Samuel Daniel, *The Tragedy of Philotas*, ed. Laurence Michel (London, repr. 1970), p. 11.

134 John Ponet, *A Shorte Treatise of Politike Power* (Geneva, 1556), reproduced in facsimile in Winthrop Hudson, *John Ponet (?1516–1556). Advocate of Limited Monarchy* (Chicago, 1942), p. [61].

135 Hexter, *Reappraisals in History*, p. 70.

136 *NA* 325/14–25. Those views would have been endorsed by Walsingham, who during the negotiations for the Treaty of Blois in 1572 observed – admittedly with the purpose of securing a negotiating advantage – that terms which might be acceptable to Queen Elizabeth might not be so to all her councillors, and that 'leagues must be made not only to satisfy the prince but also the subjects'. Sir Dudley Digges, *The Compleat Ambassador* (London, 1655), p. 170.

137 Above, p. 46; Read, *Walsingham*, i. 133; K. de L., xi. 23; cf. MacCaffrey, *Policy*, pp. 265–6.

monarchs. An anonymous paper written around 1626 would relate that 'at the latter end of Queen Elizabeth, it was a phrase to speak, yea for to pray for the Queen and State. This word "State" was learned by our neighbourhood and commerce with the Low Countries, as if we were, or were governed by, States. This the queen saw and hated.'[138] Such talk of 'states' did not, in fact, necessarily carry republican implications. Equally, forward Protestants never said that subjects must choose between loyalty to the state and loyalty to the prince. Yet their words drew on a republican tradition and carried the possibility, however embryonic, of republican claims.[139] State and prince are sometimes linguistically separated in Arcadia. Philanax is instructed 'to take the government of the state', which Basilius has abandoned; loving both 'the duke' and the 'dukedom', he finds himself, in Arcadia's hour of need, 'equally distracted betwixt desire of his master's revenge and care of the state's establishment'; Pyrocles, in quelling the rebels, 'saved Basilius, perchance the whole state, from utter ruin'; on the duke's death there are those who want 'the state altered and governed no more by a prince'.[140]

The Elizabethan awareness of a distinction between the claims of a prince and those of a state or commonwealth was heightened by the succession problem. For Elizabeth's own interests would die with her, whereas her death would expose her subjects to dire peril. Her advisers, Sir Walter Mildmay among them, stretched and even exceeded the conventions of courtesy in indicating that the queen, in her apparent indifference to the need for an heir, was failing to show proper 'consideration of this realm committed to her charge'.[141] Sidney, more delicately, explained to her that on the subject of the succession the perspective of subjects who might outlive her was bound to differ from hers.[142] In 1584 Burghley advanced a plan for a regency to follow the queen's death, during which the succession would be placed in council and parliament. That proposal was born of necessity, not from any conversion on the part of Burghley or anyone else to the principle of parliamentary sovereignty or to a conviction that peoples have the right to choose their kings.[143] Leicester and his allies may have wanted to use

---

138 G. N. Clark, 'The Birth of the Dutch Republic', *Proceedings of the British Academy* 32 (1946), pp. 189–217, at pp. 194–5.

139 Quentin Skinner, 'The State', in Terence Ball et al., eds, *Political Innovation and Conceptual Change* (Cambridge, 1989), pp. 90–131, esp. pp. 104ff., 111–12, 133. Of course, the emergence of the language of 'state' did not always work against monarchs. On the contrary the ideal of service to the state, and the language of statecraft and of reason of state, would characterise the emergence of seventeenth-century absolutism. On the usage of 'state' see also Clark, 'Birth', pp. 213–17; Clark has suggestive thoughts about Sidney's deployment of the word 'state' in his letters to Languet.

140 *OA* 9/21, 5/31–2, 351/6–7, 300/30–1, 320/34. Cf. *OA* 312/12; *La Reveille-Matin*, dialogue ii, p. 38; Huntington Library, Hastings MS. HA 5359, the Earl of Huntingdon to Walsingham, 4 April 1581.

141 NRO, F(P)M 111, fo. 2ᵛ. Cf. PRO, SP 15/26/*35, fo. 162ᵛ; NRO, F(P)M 96, fo. 3; *NA* 325/40–326/1; above, pp. 106–7, 153.

142 *MP* 55/6–12.

143 Note however the commendation of Venetian, Roman and aristocratic political practices in one version of the plan to anticipate the expected succession crisis: NRO, F(P)M, fos 4–5.

parliament to put pressure on the queen to break with Anjou in 1579,[144] but no one in Elizabethan England seems to have supposed that parliaments should be more than occasional events, summoned to deal with special circumstances (such as the Anjou crisis). That is what the estates of Arcadia are. Yet Burghley's plan would have turned parliament, as the voice of the nation's collective will, into the ultimate source of authority.[145] That is what the estates of Arcadia are on Basilius' death.[146]

Arcadia is convulsed, as England can expect to be, by the basic weakness of its polity. The subjects of a monarch whose 'will' can be exercised without their 'consent or allowance', and under whom 'public matters had ever been privately governed', acquire no 'experience to rule'.[147] In the absence of a monarch the state dissolves. Good fortune may sustain the peaceful and superficially happy reign of a Basilius or Elizabeth, but a crisis will expose its lack of a political life. Sidney's standards of political life are evidently exacting. Historians have become alert to the social depth and the sophistication that characterised the participatory procedures of the local government and administration of Elizabethan England.[148] To Sidney 'experience to rule' evidently means something more than that: something that would be equal to the English crisis foreshadowed by the death of Basilius. He does not tell us what he means, and we cannot tell. But the phrase, and the 'monarchal dissipations' that prompt it, invite us to ask where he might have turned so as to reform the political condition of his time and country. In seeking the answer, we shall find how ambivalent is his thinking about the rule of kings.

---

144 Above, pp. 184–5.
145 Collinson, *Elizabethan Essays*, pp. 48–56; cf. Read, *Walsingham*, ii. 216. The Elizabethan succession problem enhanced parliament's potential importance in another way too: the argument was made that parliament, by ratifying treaties made by Elizabeth, would give her allies a guarantee that England's friendship would outlive her: K. de L., ix. 421; cf. *CSPF 1577–8*, p. 276.
146 For the role of the Arcadian estates see the passages cited below, Chapter 13, n. 106.
147 *OA* 320/7.
148 See particularly Collinson, *Elizabethan Essays*, ch. 2.

Forms of Government

Amid the 'confused and dangerous divisions' that beset Arcadia on the death of Basilius, the survival of the monarchy comes into question. 'For some there were that cried to have the state altered and governed no more by a prince; marry, in the alteration many would have the Lacedemonian government of few chosen senators; others the Athenian, where the people's voice held the chief authority.' Yet the republicans are swept aside. For 'these were rather the discoursing sort of men than the active, being a matter more in imagination than practice. But they that went nearest to the present case (as in a country that knew no government without a prince) were they that strave whom they should make' – that is, whom they should enthrone.[1]

We have seen the failings of the Arcadian system of monarchy. It provides 'no experience to rule'; under it 'public matters had ever been privately governed'; it is 'subject unto' 'great dissipations'. Yet at no other moment in the *Arcadia* are proposals for alternative forms of government voiced. Half a century before Sidney wrote, Thomas Starkey, the friend and adviser of Reginald Pole, had broken new ground in English political thought. From his studies of republican Greece and Rome, and from the knowledge he had acquired from his stay in Venice of its republican institutions, he inferred that to live 'in liberty' we must 'live the civil life' that characterises healthy republics.[2] The ideal of the civil life or of active citizenship, dear to the Italian republicanism of the Renaissance, can be found, around the time the *Arcadia* was written, in the writings of opponents of Spanish tyranny in the Netherlands, whose cause Sidney's party took to be their own.[3] Sidney had visited Venice and studied its history and institutions. He had read Machiavelli, the dominant figure of sixteenth-century republicanism; he had visited Florence, where Machiavelli had witnessed and expounded the

---

1   *OA* 320/4, 320/33–321/5.
2   Worden, 'Tolerant Repression'.
3   Van Gelderen, *Political Thought*, pp. 154, 192–9.

conflict between republican liberty and monarchical tyranny; he was keenly interested in the history of the Roman republic, that guiding light of Machiavelli's political thought. Might we not expect him to have looked to those models to supply the 'experience to rule' that the Arcadians lack?

For monarchy denies men the self-reliance, and the capacity to shape their destinies, which in Sidney's philosophical scheme are essential to the attainment of virtue. We saw what happens in politics when we 'depend' on others or on 'fortune', virtue's enemy.[4] Under monarchy, explains the *New Arcadia*, 'all favour and power depend' on the royal whim: under the monarchy of Turkey, explains Greville, men's 'lives and states depend' on the monarch.[5] Basilius may be no Turk, but his subjects are at the mercy of his 'will'. They are dependent too on the chances that will preserve or end his life. Thomas Norton noted that Englishmen 'depend[ed]' on Elizabeth's survival; his and Sackville's play *Gorboduc* showed how the 'life' of a nation 'doth hang' upon the determination of the royal succession;[6] when Sir John Hayward appropriated Sidney's description of the aftermath of Basilius' death for his own account of the death of Mary Tudor, it was in order to show 'how in a royal state the surety of the common people depends much upon the life and safety of their prince'.[7] Under hereditary monarchy, which can randomly allocate power to a weakling or a fool or a minor, the well-being of the subjects is a lottery, dependent on what the *New Arcadia* calls 'the true play that is used in the game of kingdoms'.[8] The hereditary principle, as Greville says, resigns 'true worth to chance', just as, in Greville's mind, Sidney's failure to win advancement in Elizabeth's service showed that under monarchies promotion is a matter of 'chance' rather than 'worth'.[9]

Yet if there is republicanism in Sidney's mind, it is, at the most, of a speculative and hypothetical kind. To Sidney, it transpires, a republic is no more the answer to England's problems than to Arcadia's.[10]

The Arcadians' rejection of the Athenian form may be less surprising than their decision not to imitate the Lacedemonian. For democracy Sidney had no time. Following events in the Netherlands as closely as he did, he must have known that there were thinkers there who, in arguing for the renunciation of Spanish rule, were willing to advocate democracy or 'popular

4 Above, Chapter 7.
5 *NA* 249/33–4; Bullough, i. 137 (sonnet xc).
6 Norton, *Warning*, sig. nii; Tydeman, *Two Tudor Tragedies*, p. 111 (ll. 1405–6).
7 Above, p. 205.
8 *NA* 302/29–30.
9 Wilkes, p. 43 (st. 35); above, p. 69. In the *New Arcadia* some men become 'dependents' on Amphialus' candidacy for the throne (*NA* 415/27–8). Yet, sharp as Sidney's intimations on the subject of inherited monarchy can be, he may have thought that the hereditary principle could give a proper 'reverence' to majesty: *OA* 378/6–9 (with which compare Bullough, ii. 100: *Mustapha* III. i. 39–41), 406/16–18; *NA* 158/9–10; *MP* 54/24–5.
10 The treatise *A Discourse of Civill Life* (London, 1606) by Sidney's friend Lodowick Bryskett shows how innocent of Italian republicanism English ideas of 'civil life' could be.

government', Machiavelli's goal, in its place.[11] They did not have our understanding of democracy. They did not envisage universal suffrage or anything like it. But they did want to entrust a large measure of power to men outside the elite: power which would be mixed with or balanced by that of a higher group or class but which might be decisive nonetheless. They tended to draw, at least implicitly, a distinction between the people and the rabble: between responsible citizens who could safely be entrusted with power and the multitude which could not. For Sidney, 'popular government', a principle which in the *New Arcadia* is derided by Pamela in her finest hour,[12] appears to mean simply popular licence. His eager study of Livy and his knowledge of Machiavelli seem to have inspired no sympathy in him for the 'popular estate' of republican Rome, where, he observed, 'men were to rise or fall according to the foolish breath of a many-headed confusion'.[13] The *Arcadia* reveals the 'weak trust of the many-headed multitude', just as, in the *Vindiciae, Contra Tyrannos*, the mob is a 'monster . . . with countless heads'.[14] Sidney's fiction shows how 'ill balanced be the extremities of popular minds', how 'inconstan[t]' is the multitude and how 'wavering' the people's 'affection', 'how violently rumours do blow the sails of popular judgements'.[15] The 'people's will', observes Euarchus, runs in 'circles of imagination' and builds on groundless 'conceits'.[16]

Popular government, in the minds of Sidney and his friends, was associated, as it always had been by its critics, with 'division', a political failing against which he persistently counselled.[17] 'Division' is the 'weakness' of the Phagonian rebels of the *New Arcadia*.[18] In republican Rome, Sidney recalls, 'the whole people . . . resolutely divided themselves from the senate, with apparent show of utter ruin'.[19] Greville in turn believed that the 'dissensions' of 'democracy' – which Machiavelli by contrast had generally regarded as an antidote to corruption – had 'corrupted' 'old Rome'.[20] According to Greville, Sidney noticed that the proneness of popular governments to division makes them prey to monarchies, which have the unitive virtue: that the democratic Swiss, being 'swollen with equality', were 'divided', a flaw which left them 'enemies, yet servants, to monarchies'; that the Dutch, having 'changed from their ancient dukedoms to popularity', had consequently 'been forced to seek protection among the monarchies then

11 Van Gelderen, *Political Thought*, pp. 189–90, 195.
12 *NA* 360/33–6.
13 *MP* 54/22–3.
14 *OA* 131/22; Garnett, p. 45.
15 *OA* 364/14–15, 131/22; *NA* 222/32, 288/1, 325/9–10. Cf. *OA* 355/6–8; Tydeman, *Two Tudor Tragedies*, p. 111 (*Gorboduc*, l. 1420).
16 *OA* 362/29–363/1, 363/10; cf. *MP* 102/31–3.
17 Above, Chapter 11; below, Chapter 19; cf. van Gelderen, *Political Thought*, p. 175.
18 *NA* 284/24, 284/36, 285/2, 289/29.
19 *MP* 93/17–19.
20 Wilkes, pp. 98 (st. 253), 191 (st. 621), 193 (st. 629).

reigning'.[21] Sidney and Languet agreed that unitive leadership was needed to save the Dutch revolt,[22] which they and their English and Dutch friends watched being torn by the 'monster of civil division'.[23]

Democracy, thought Sidney and his allies, tends innately not only to division but to tyranny. In establishing 'popular' government, thought his intimate friend Edward Dyer, the Netherlanders had become 'tyrannous over themselves making themselves miserable at home and despised abroad'.[24] Languet believed that the people naturally abuses its liberty and develops tyrannical instincts.[25] Thomas Wilson, quoting Livy, agreed: 'Populus aut humiliter servit aut superbe dominatur.'[26] Though the rebels of Arcadia affect 'the glorious name of liberty',[27] they represent not 'liberty' but 'licence', which is also the characteristic of tyrants,[28] and which in its 'popular' form 'is indeed the many-headed tyranny'.[29] Sidney's fiction attributes to rebels the same characteristics that it portrays in tyrants: 'rage', 'fury', 'hate', 'cruel[ty]', 'greediness', 'revenge', 'blindness'.[30] In mobs and tyrants alike, such passions are 'unbridled' and 'immoderate' and have an inherent tendency to 'multiply'.[31]

Even when the rule of the people is not tyrannical in itself, it can easily lead to tyranny, for the people, out of weakness, tends to set up tyrants and to ally with them against the nobility. The Spartan helots of Book Two of the New Arcadia, having fought for the people's rights against the nobility, idolise their leader Pyrocles, 'kissing the places where he stepped' and 'making temples unto him as to a demigod'. In the Old Arcadia the misguided 'multitude' of Philisides' beast-fable turns against the nobility, Sidney suggests, with the 'envy' that 'harb'reth most in feeble hearts': 'With neighing, bleaing, braying, and barking, / Roaring, and howling, for to have a king'.[32] Philippe Duplessis-Mornay anticipated a similar process in the wars of religion in his native France, where he saw 'a million beasts', empty of 'reason', ready to 'devour each other'. Drawing on historical examples, he warned that the wars could produce a 'popular licence', and that the people, in order to overthrow the nobility, would then set up 'the tyranny of someone' who 'will call himself protector of liberty' and subject them to harsher servitude.[33]

---

21   GP 50/23–4, 84/17–21; though cf. Read, Walsingham, i. 25n.
22   Pears, pp. 58, 132.
23   K. de L., x. 161.
24   Sargent, Dyer, p. 79.
25   Mercier, 'Théories politiques', pp. 39–40.
26   K. de L., ix. 352.
27   NA 292/12. Cf. OA 128/1–2; NA 174/7–14.
28   NA 160/5–6, 299/12.
29   OA 127/8; NA 174/15–16.
30   Rebels: OA 126/26, 128/3–24; NA 30/27, 33/10, 34/24, 34/34, 36/4, 41/28, 174/13. Tyrants: OA 259/10–11; NA 170/23, 175/28–9, 176/28, 206/10–11, 258/5, 265/25, 300/17. Cf. Tydeman, Two Tudor Tragedies, p. 115 (Gorboduc, ll. 1518–19).
31   Below, Chapter 18.
32   NA 42/10–11; OA 256/18–26.
33   Mémoires et correspondance de Duplessis-Mornay, ii. 74–7.

Forward Protestants feared lest popular rebels in the Netherlands, 'that inconstant mutinous brood', swayed by 'will' and 'appetite' and moved by 'hate' of the nobility and by 'rage' against it, should 'run headlong to their own ruin' by strengthening, albeit inadvertently, the hand of the Spanish tyrant. 'God keep England', reflected Thomas Wilson, 'from any such confused authority'.[34]

Wilson's fears for the Dutch revolt were intensified by the series of popular convulsions that broke out in the southern Netherlands in the winter of 1578–9. Critics normally and rightly connect Sidney's accounts of popular mutiny in Arcadia with the dread, ubiquitous in his class, of the 'many-headed multitude' in England. Yet the Dutch example may also have been in his mind. In the late 1570s William of Orange, seeing the Dutch nobility as the chief native obstacle to his cause, strove to break its influence in the towns by allying with non-noble groups there.[35] The movement which he thus launched escaped from his control, especially in Ghent, where a year earlier the ancient post of 'doyen' had been revived, 'an office', as William Davison explained to Walsingham, 'being of like quality and authority to the office of *Tribunus Plebis* sometime in the commonwealth of Rome'.[36] Popular discontent in Ghent now produced an orgy of destruction, which alienated Orange's following in the south and helped Parma to divide north from south in the early months of 1579, with consequences disastrous to the revolt of the Netherlands.

Languet was horrified by the conduct of the Ghantois, who, he told Sidney, were 'actuated by blind impulse' and who 'never show the least moderation in their proceedings'.[37] The Ghantois followed the pattern against which Mornay had warned and against which Philisides' fable warns. The year 1580 saw the revival of the proposal of 1578, which the Ghantois had vigorously opposed, to give the headship of the Netherlands to the Duke of Anjou. Languet, Mornay and other counsellors of Orange were determined that, if Anjou were made leader, his powers would be strictly limited. The Ghantois, swinging, as *demos* will, from one extreme to the other, had no such concern. 'What inconsistency is this in the men of Ghent!', wrote Languet to Sidney. 'A year ago they were cutting in pieces the name and character of Anjou . . ... They even formed designs upon his life; and yet now they are the first with their votes to give over the sovereignty of the country to him.'[38]

So the Arcadians are right, it seems, to reject the calls of those of the 'discoursing sort of men' who want the 'Athenian' form of government. But what of the alternative republican proposal that is put forward on Basilius'

34 K. de L., xi. 129–30, 144–5, 184; *CSPF 1575–7*, p. 419, *1578–9*, p. 263.
35 Van Gelderen, *Political Thought*, p. 49.
36 K. de L., x. 85.
37 Pears, p. 156.
38 Ibid., p. 174.

death, 'the Lacedemonian government of few chosen senators'? Philisides' beast-fable recalls the harmonious age before the erection of kingship, a time when the martial nobility, 'with courage clad', 'like senators a harmless empire had'.[39] Yet there is nothing else in Sidney's writings to suggest that he might have admired aristocratic government.[40] Book Two of the *New Arcadia* shows us the bad side of all three forms of government: monarchy, aristocracy, democracy. There is the gallery of tyrants; there is the perverted form of aristocracy, 'the worst kind of oligarchy', as it prevailed in Macedon before Euarchus put a stop to it;[41] there is *demos* at work in the popular mutiny in Arcadia. Book Two also gives us, in the rule of Euarchus, the good or pure form of monarchy;[42] but it does not show us a healthy form of either democracy or aristocracy.

The adjective 'aristocratic' has often been applied to Sidney and his writing. Used loosely, the adjective is warrantable enough, as it would be if applied with the same looseness to most people of his time and class. He was against the rise of base-born men above their station. He was opposed to popular government and mob rule and apparently failed to distinguish between them. He wrote within, and for, a culture which confined power to an elite. He thought it natural that the many should be led by the few and defer to them. His confidence in the authority of an individual's virtue, and in its capacity to effect political change, belonged to a world which only a small number of people could expect to have the power to alter: a world in which it made sense to suppose that a work available solely in manuscript, as Sidney's fiction was in his lifetime, might become an instrument of political reform. Though the *Arcadia* was written in English, for an English audience, the elite to which Sidney belonged extended across the national and religious boundaries of Europe, united by its common cultural inheritance.

Yet for Sidney's time the term aristocracy did not mean a class or summon the values of a class. It meant a form of government. That form was characteristically dominated, of course, by the class we would call the aristocracy. Yet Sidney is no spokesman for the political conduct of that class. In his fiction noblemen who seek power are factious or ambitious.[43] He is no friend to the 'oppressi[on]' which 'lords' and 'great men' inflict on those below them, on 'them that would defend their liberty against them'.[44] Even in Philisides' fable it seems that the apparently 'harmless' and 'hurtless' rule of the senators rested on their inferiors' 'fear' of them and that they enjoyed immunity from prosecution for 'murder'.[45]

---

39 *OA* 256/18–19.
40 The empire of the senatorial beasts may in any case not have been purely aristocratic: see above, Chapter 12, n. 61.
41 *NA* 159/34.
42 *NA* 160/24–161/26.
43 *OA* 320/24–5, 321/23–6; *NA* 160/8–10.
44 *NA* 35/26–7, 159/31–3, 160/8–9.
45 *OA* 256/17–19, 258/21–5. Thus, just as the flawless surface of Arcadian life that we glimpse on the opening page of Sidney's story is deceptive (above, p. 19), so in Philisides' tale there is a hidden flaw in the pristine harmony of the beasts.

The *New Arcadia* takes us inside Lacedemon (or Sparta, or Laconia), the state with the archetypal aristocratic government. Yet its inhabitants, who in Sidney's *Defence of Poetry* are called 'the incomparable Lacedemonians',[46] are less than incomparable in his fiction. The 'notable . . . hatred' of the Spartan rebels 'towards the very name of a king' is not reported sympathetically.[47] Sidney's account of Spartan politics would have disappointed the expectations held by readers with even a portion of his alertness to contemporary discussions of politics and government. He might even be thought to have gone out of his way to disappoint them. Spartan politics were celebrated for their stability, a quality conspicuously absent from his account, where the class war appears to be fought selfishly and destructively on both sides. The war deprives the country of the prosperity enjoyed by neighbouring, peaceful, monarchical Arcadia.[48] Again, the constitutional legacy of Theopompus in Sparta and the creation of the Spartan ephors were feats warmly admired among Sidney's allies.[49] They were invoked by those who imposed strict limitations on the powers of Anjou in the Netherlands.[50] Yet Sidney shows no interest in Sparta's constitutional arrangements. He forgets what the historian of Sparta's reputation down the centuries calls 'the most striking' feature of its constitution, that it had not one king but two.[51] Sidney's imagination silently absorbs Sparta (as it does other Greek republics) into the international courtly culture, essentially a Renaissance culture, which Musidorus and Pyrocles encounter everywhere on their travels. We learn of 'the Laced[e]monian king and nobility', of 'the prince and court of Laconia'.[52] A 'Laconian knight' chivalrously devotes himself to Andromana, the queen of Iberia. It is 'the queen of Laconia' who is 'a queen, and therefore beautiful'.[53]

In October 1577, when the leaders of the Dutch revolt were planning to depose Philip II and wondering how to replace his rule, Sidney wrote to Languet that 'you will there have a most excellent field for putting into practice, in the formation of this new commonwealth, those principles which you have so diligently studied during the whole course of your life'. The Frenchman Languet would be in the position enjoyed in Sidney's fiction by Euarchus and the young princes, who take their chances to establish good

---

46 *MP* 97/19.
47 *OA* 357n.
48 *NA* 11/19–29.
49 Wilkes, p. 85 (st. 199); Kingdon, *Myths*, pp. 83, 139; Franklin, *Constitutionalism and Resistance*, p. 80; Buchanan, *Powers*, p. 105; Quentin Skinner, *The Foundations of Modern Political Thought*, 2 vols (Cambridge, 1978), ii. 315–16. Cf. Hudson, *John Ponet*, p. [11]; Hartley, *Proceedings*, pp. 295–6; Elizabeth Rawson, *The Spartan Tradition in European Thought* (Oxford, 1969), p. 149.
50 Griffiths, *Representative Government*, p. 491; van Gelderen, *Political Thought*, p. 180.
51 *OA* 357n.; *NA* 30/20–1, 35/35, 36/2, 47/12–13, 47/24, 92/29; Rawson, *Spartan Tradition*, p. 2. (Machiavelli, it is fair to add, had made the same mistake: Rawson, *Spartan Tradition*, p. 140.) In the *New Arcadia* Sidney's character Lycurgus could scarcely have less in common with Sparta's lawgiver of that name.
52 *NA* 35/34–5, 91/20–1, 97/14–15.
53 *NA* 94/33–5, 96/9–12.

forms of government in foreign lands recently liberated from tyranny.[54] As far as we can tell, it does not occur to Euarchus or the princes to set up republics in the countries they have freed. As far as we can tell, it does not occur to Languet to seek to establish a republic in the Netherlands. Sidney seems to take it for granted that his friend's 'new commonwealth' will be built around a 'prince', William of Orange.[55] When Philip II was formally deposed in 1579, some Dutch thinkers did make proposals for republican rule.[56] Their schemes of government, like those of 'the discoursing sort of men' in Arcadia, were swept aside.

More influential was a Dutch pamphlet of 1580 which asked whether the Netherlands should be transformed into a 'republic' or adhere to a monarchical form. Its author assumed, as Sidney did, that the essential basis of political health is virtue. Unfortunately, he observed, the Dutch lacked it. Machiavelli had argued that a republic cannot be preserved among a corrupt people. The pamphleteer of 1580 concurred. He acknowledged that the Swiss, who had maintained 'the ancient military discipline' and 'do not care for riches', had sustained their virtue without corruption and so were able to sustain a democracy. But the Netherlanders were too 'effeminate and corrupt' to meet that challenge. They were also 'too corrupt' to sustain an aristocratic republic, being 'forlorn of the virtue which in former times had been the true source of the status of their ancestors'. Where the Arcadians rejected republicanism because they 'knew no government without a prince', the 'habits and conditions' of the Netherlanders have become so 'disposed to a principality' that the Low Countries 'are completely incapable of aristocracy'.[57] A premise of Machiavelli's republicanism is thus directed against the establishment of a republic. In 1583 another Dutch pamphlet repeated the stance of the mainstream Arcadians: a republic akin to the aristocracy of Venice or the democracy of Switzerland might be 'very good' in theory but would not work in practice.[58] A further Dutch pamphlet of 1583, deploying a similar argument, regretted that the Netherlanders lacked 'experience' of government; the Arcadians lack 'experience to rule, and had not whom to obey'; the Dutch, thought Thomas Wilson, are 'a people that can neither tell how to rule nor yet can yield to be ruled'.[59]

Orange himself despaired of the prospects for aristocratic rule in the Netherlands because of the feebleness and failings of the Dutch nobility, who had 'so much degenerat[ed] from the constancy and virtue of their ancestors'. In Arcadia 'public matters had ever been privately governed': the Netherlands, lamented Orange in 1581, were failing before the challenge of liberation because 'everyone has his private rather than the public interest at

54   Above, p. 169; below, p. 240.
55   Pears, p. 117.
56   Van Gelderen, *Political Thought*, ch. 5 and pp. 276ff.
57   Ibid., pp. 171–2.
58   Ibid., p. 175.
59   Ibid., p. 176; K. de L., xi. 182.

heart'.[60] Walsingham and Thomas Wilson observed the want of courage and resolution among the Dutch nobility, a defect on which Walsingham blamed the Netherlanders' failure to seize their chance of 'liberty' and which he took as a symptom of national degeneration.[61]

Machiavelli argued that, where the material of society is corrupt, a 'virtuous prince' is needed to reform it. Machiavelli's concept of virtue could be radically at odds with Sidney's.[62] Yet Sidney adapts Machiavelli's ethics to his own. It is the virtuous prince Euarchus, as tough and fearless a ruler as Machiavelli could have wished, who reforms Macedon. His 'virtu[e] and wis[dom]', his 'extreme severity', the 'awful fear engendered by [his] justice', cleanse a land where 'men of virtue [were] suppressed . . . and at length virtue almost forgotten, when it had no hopeful end whereunto to be directed; old men long nuzzled in corruption scorning them that would seek reformation'.[63] The Dutch pamphlet of 1580 which argued that the Netherlanders lacked the 'virtue' essential to a democracy or aristocracy turned to Machiavelli's distinctive language in holding out 'the virtuousness of a new prince' as the only solution. The ideal of the 'virtuous prince' was widespread in Dutch pamphleteering around that time.[64]

For the role of 'virtuous prince' in the Netherlands there was one obvious candidate: William of Orange. In England, Walsingham and others had come to regard William as the necessary unitive force of the revolt, as the only man who could rise above its contending factions. They saw him as a divinely appointed instrument of deliverance, on whose shoulders the fate of Europe and England rested.[65] Thomas Wilson, who regretted the political 'inexperience' of the Netherlanders, believed Orange to be their 'only man for authority, wisdom and experience . . . and the aptest to govern the people'.[66] (In Arcadia, whose citizens lack 'experience to rule', Euarchus draws on 'long experience' to resolve their crisis.)[67] Languet, as he repeatedly made plain to Sidney, was awed by the wisdom, the industry, the calmness in adversity, of Orange, whose leadership seemed to him too to be essential to Dutch hopes of success.[68] 'I beseech you,' he urged Sidney in a bleak moment for the revolt, 'mark well his virtues, and do not let yourself be deterred from cultivating his friendship by his fortunes'.[69] Sidney, 'burning' to get to know

60 Kossmann and Mellinck, *Texts concerning the Revolt of the Netherlands*, pp. 35, 235; *Apologie . . . of . . . William*, sig. M3ᵛ.
61 K. de L., viii. 358.
62 Above, p. 30.
63 *NA* 161/14, 160/12–37.
64 Van Gelderen, *Political Thought*, pp. 172, 179; cf. Pears, p. 91.
65 K. de L., ix. 426–7, x. 101, 590; Read, *Walsingham*, i. 215; Collinson, *Godly People*, p. 380; van Dorsten, *Poets*, p. 46; cf. BL, Cottonian MS. Titus BII, fo. 493ᵛ.
66 K. de L., ix. 141; cf. *CSPF 1575–7*, p. 419.
67 *OA* 362/14.
68 Pears, pp. 14–15, 68–9, 136–7, 139, 150, 159–60, 171, 173, 174.
69 Ibid., p. 160.

Orange better and to fight beside him, hardly needed that encouragement.[70] The numerous encomia of Orange by Sidney and his friends carry a recurrent hint: how different things would be, for England and for Europe, if England had an Orange at its helm![71]

How different, too, would things be for Arcadia and for Greece if Arcadia had a Euarchus at its helm. Arcadia, no less than England or the Netherlands, needs a virtuous prince. The descriptions of Orange by forward Protestants who met him bring Euarchus to mind. Moved by the 'particular virtues' of a man who dealt with them so 'plainly and uprightly' and 'frankly', they came to 'honour and love' him.[72] Euarchus, the exception to the norm of princely rule, is without 'ambition': in forward Protestant eyes, Orange, though opposed by 'princes' of whose 'ambition' there would be 'no end', was conspicuously devoid of 'ambition'. He resembles Euarchus too in pursuing the course of 'virtue' against 'vice' amid 'the greatest troubles and tempests', where the inducements of 'policy' or of 'worldly respects' would tempt the integrity of a lesser man.[73] Of course, Orange encountered bitter hostility, not least from those who did suspect him of personal ambition. But as Thomas Wilson observed, 'it is a great honour to be hated for virtue'.[74] Euarchus in turn has to bear with a misdirected charge of 'tyrann[y]'. 'Most' of his 'beholders' conclude that 'his dominion must needs be insupportable'. Euarchus, however, 'lov[ing] goodness more than himself', can bear that cross.[75] Orange can bear his cross too.

Orange resembles Euarchus not only in character but in action. In the military crisis of Macedon and Greece, Euarchus 'followed everywhere his commandment with his presence', 'arming' his subjects and 'fortifying' vulnerable places. After the shattering defeat at Gembloux in January 1578, reported William Davison, Orange remained at Gembloux and 'showed wonderful judgement and resolution in riding up and down to survey every corner and to provide where there was need: without whose stay, I doubt things would have grown to a marvellous confusion; but he hath now taken so good order . . . advancing the fortifications' and mobilising soldiers that 'now they are out of fear'.[76]

Both men are unaffected in demeanour. Greville, bowled over by Orange when he met him, retained a vivid memory of his 'posture of body and mind, familiarity and reservedness'. Though his 'natural worth' had carried the authority of a 'prince', his plain clothes and straightforward address had been those of a 'no-prince'; 'no exterior sign', only 'the outward passage of inward greatness', proclaimed his stature. Greville records that Orange con-

---

70 Ibid., p. 107.
71 Orange is commended as a 'pattern' to Elizabeth in NRO, F(P)M 96, fo. 7.
72 K. de L., x. 135; Wright, Queen Elizabeth, ii. 117.
73 CSPF 1577–8, p. 711; K. de L., ix. 230, 530, xi. 169.
74 K. de L., ix. 303.
75 OA 412/20, 414/29–35.
76 OA 356; K. de L., x. 271.

ducted himself 'fellow-like', the phrase that also describes the conduct of the king in Philisides' beast-fable while he rules well.[77] Euarchus, when we first meet him, is 'found taking his rest under a tree with no more affected pomps than as a man that knew, howsoever he was exalted, the beginning and end of his body was earth'.[78] He is unlike 'most princes': Greville contrasts Orange, to his advantage, with other 'princes'. Greville adds that Orange thought that those other princes had become inactive because they were 'so full of pleasures': Euarchus is immune to 'pleasure', the snare to which the 'unactive' Basilius, the princely antitype to Euarchus, succumbs.[79]

So the Netherlander cause, fighting, like the Greece of the *Arcadia*, for its survival, might well prefer, as the Arcadians do, the unitive principle of monarchy to republican alternatives. Even when it became clear that Orange would not be an acceptable sovereign to the Netherlanders at large, and even when, after Elizabeth had abandoned them, they could find no more attractive a candidate for leadership than Anjou, they persisted in their preference for a single ruler. What practical man, amid the exigencies of the Dutch revolt, would have sought to win over the Netherlands, that patchwork of ancient customs and local privileges, to a novel constitutional design? The revolt needed leadership, not a debate about political theory.

Would not the same priority assert itself in England on the death of Elizabeth, which that of Basilius foreshadows? Where Netherlanders judged their country to be too 'corrupt' to sustain a republic, Sidney's party were no less conscious of England's 'corruption'. Alongside that theoretical argument for monarchy there ran, in England as in the Low Countries, a practical one. On Elizabeth's death the different parties would contend, as those of 1553 had done, for the occupancy of the throne. On that occasion the Protestants had been defeated. On Elizabeth's death Mary Queen of Scots or Anjou would seek to defeat them. Protestants, living in a country which, like Arcadia, 'knew no government without a prince', were no more likely on Elizabeth's death than the Arcadians are on Basilius' to spend time on proposals 'to have the state altered and governed no more by a prince'. As in Arcadia, 'they that went nearest to the present case' would be those who 'strave whom they should make'. For that moment Sidney's party must be prepared.

In Arcadia the 'discoursing sort of men', whose republican proposals are 'a matter more in imagination than practice', are overruled by the 'active'. Sidney's phrasing illustrates a principle recurrent in his mind and language. For him, 'action' is virtue, 'practice' the test and fulfilment of 'philosophy precepts'.[80] It is in putting the ideas learned over a lifetime into 'practice', he writes, that his friend Languet will plan a 'new commonwealth' in the Netherlands, not on the basis of republican blueprints but around the man of

---

77 *GP* 13/19–14/12; *OA* 258/5.
78 *OA* 355/17–357/2.
79 *GP* 13/19–22, 14/31; above, p. 144.
80 Above, Chapter 2.

action who will meet the needs of the hour, William of Orange. Languet, we saw Greville saying, was 'wise by the conjunction of practice in the world with that well-grounded theory of books'.[81] Greville himself prefers 'practic use' to 'the mere contemplative'. He applies that priority, as the 'active' Arcadians do, to forms of government. The rule of 'many heads', he thinks, is antipathetic to 'active virtue'; it produces 'laws . . . and ordinances' which are 'fit for discourse, or books, not polity' and of which the 'practice' is unsatisfactory. 'Our books', he knows, are 'filled with praise' of aristocracy and democracy, but:

> let not man examine this by book,
> As states stand painted, or enamelled there;
> But rather upon life than pictures look,
> Where practice sees what every state can bear . . ..[82]

In Sidney's usage, 'discourse' is generally a disparaging word. The Italians, he tells his brother Robert, are 'given to . . . counterfeit learning', being 'all discoursers'.[83] In Arcadia, 'discourses' are 'idle', that besetting sin in Sidney's eyes.[84] Impotent on the death of Basilius, discourse is discarded at other moments of action and decision. Pyrocles, at the crisis of his own affairs, sees that 'to call back what might have been to a man of wisdom and courage carries but a vain shadow of discourse'; Euarchus knows 'the weak effect of fair discourses not waited upon with agreeable actions'; in deciding how to conduct the trial of the princes he sets 'philosophical discourses' aside.[85]

The predicament that disables the Arcadian discoursers on Basilius' death is one that has often confronted men troubled by the failings of kingship. Early in the sixteenth century it was acknowledged by Thomas More, who asked himself 'what is the best form of government'. In *Utopia* he opted for a utopian solution, framing a constitution which combined, on the principles of classical and republican antiquity, the strengths of monarchy, aristocracy and democracy. The monarchy is limited; it is elective not hereditary; the monarch may be deposed for tyranny. Yet in a poem written around the same time More explains the difference between utopia and reality. The rule of a senate, he suggests, is generally better than the rule of a king. Kings rarely rule moderately; their greed is never satiated; 'blind chance rules' instead of the 'firm counsel' characteristic of senatorial rule. And yet the whole matter, he declares, is hypothetical: 'Is there really anywhere a people

---

81 Above, p. 26.
82 Wilkes, pp. 156 (st. 484), 184 (sts 594, 595), 196 (st. 641), 181–2 (sts 584–5).
83 Feuillerat, iii. 127.
84 *NA* 25/24.
85 *OA* 291/1–2, 356, 404/24–33. Cf. PRO, SP 15/26/*35, fo. 114ᵛ ('praters and discoursers'); Daniel, *Tragedy of Philotas*, p. 20.

over whom you can place in authority a king or a senate by your own decision?'[86]

For More, like the Arcadians, lives 'in a country that knew no government without a prince'. So does Sidney. He does want to learn from alien forms of government. The 'good laws and customs' of China, he tells his brother Robert, 'are to be learned': in the *Arcadia* the polity of Egypt has 'good laws and customs, worthy to be learned'.[87] Philip urges his brother Robert to study, as he himself has done, the 'good laws and customs' of republican Venice. Yet, he warns him, 'we can hardly proportion [them] to ourselves, because they are quite of a contrary government'.[88] Walsingham, too, knew the gap between discourse and practice. In 1573 the French government proposed the establishment of a joint Anglo-French regime in Scotland, which would rule through 'a number of men' and would 'never make mention of king nor queen'. The result, thought Walsingham, would be an 'aristocratia' or 'headless government' which could never achieve unity. Anyway, he pointed out, the proposal was unreal. For – just as the Arcadians 'knew no government without a prince' – the Scots 'were never wont to be governed but under a king'.[89]

Republicanism, then, is utopian. Monarchy belongs to the here-and-now. Is there a cure for its 'dissipations'? Can the 'will' of a monarch be curbed and 'counsel' prevail? In that hope Sidney, and his friends at home and abroad, looked to the ideal of limited monarchy. They recalled the restricted Gothic monarchies which, they believed, had given way or were giving way to the unrestricted monarchies of modern times. In 1579, the year of the Anjou crisis and of the publication both of the *Vindiciae* and of Buchanan's *De Iure Regni*, arguments for limited monarchy were at the fronts of their minds. The English response to *De Iure Regni*, explained Sidney's friend Daniel Rogers, was divided between the advocates and opponents of limited monarchy. The first, who had the welfare of the kingdom at heart, warmed to the book, whereas 'those who study to conciliate by means of flattery the favour of princes, and who wish the reins of law to be relaxed according to their pleasure', rejected it.[90]

---

86 David Norbrook and H. R. Woudhuysen, eds, *The Penguin Book of Renaissance Verse* (Harmondsworth, 1992), pp. 80–2; More, *Utopia*, ed. Logan and Adams, pp. 48–9. The same point would be made in similar language by David Hume: Duncan Forbes, *Hume's Philosophical Politics* (Cambridge, 1975), p. 182.

87 Feuillerat, iii. 126: *OA* 155/31–2.

88 Feuillerat, iii. 127.

89 Digges, *Compleat Ambassador*, pp. 177–8, 178; cf. Walsingham's comment on the 'confused government' of the Dutch revolt, 'with many heads': K. de L., x. 730.

90 Irving, *Buchanan*, p. 250; cf. Phillips, 'Buchanan', p. 43 & n. Stubbs (p. 37) describes Elizabeth as the 'chief officer' of England, a term favoured by men wanting the limitation of royal power: for a seventeenth-century parallel see Blair Worden, 'Marchamont Nedham and the Beginnings of English Republicanism', in David Wootton, ed., *Republicanism, Liberty, and Commercial Society* (Stanford, Calif., 1994), pp. 45–81, at p. 55.

Advocates of limited monarchy knew that its terms must be secured at the outset. They returned to a principle which had been enunciated by Thomas Aquinas: 'a monarchy should be so constituted that there is no opportunity for the king, once he is reigning, to become a tyrant'.[91] That principle was adopted in the Low Countries, where it was agreed to impose firm restrictions on the ruler who replaced Philip II. Walsingham, swallowing his objections to the prospect of Anjou's leadership of the Dutch revolt, reasoned that the choice in the Netherlands was between the imposition of terms on Anjou that would make him a 'limited monarch' and the rule of the 'despot' Philip II.[92] In 1580 Orange, resigned as he was to the installation of Anjou as leader, pressed Philippe Duplessis-Mornay to join the negotiations with the duke. Mornay agreed, as his widow would recall, 'but only on the assurance that the new prince was to be bound by such conditions that, humanly speaking, no harm could follow'.[93] Beside that statement we can place the moment in the New Arcadia when Musidorus, having slain the tyrant of Phrygia, bestows the crown on a new ruler, 'but with such conditions, and cautions of the conditions, as might assure the people with as much assurance as worldly matters bear [compare Mornay's 'humanly speaking'], that not only that governor, of whom indeed they looked for all good, but the nature of the government, should be no way apt to decline to tyranny'.[94]

The contention between limited monarchy, which governs according to law, and unlimited monarchy, which governs by royal will, was being waged across the Europe of Sidney's time. There was Scotland, where Buchanan wanted 'laws' to set 'limits' on kings. Walsingham, voicing the anxiety of forward Protestants lest the young King James VI should turn not only to Catholicism but to tyranny, warned him that 'young princes were many times carried into great errors upon an opinion of the absoluteness of their royal authority' and were wont to 'transgress the bounds and limits of the law'.[95] There was Poland. In 1572 the Poles – 'that man-like nation', as Stubbs's Gaping Gulph calls them – had taken advantage of a succession crisis to impose strict limits on the royal prerogative, an episode of warm interest to Sidney and his friends.[96] But Greville tells us that, after Stephen Bathory had acquired the Polish throne in 1576, Sidney came to think that that 'dangerously aspiring king' was 'busy to encroach . . . and add more to his own limited sovereignty'.[97] There was the Holy Roman Empire, where

91   Thomas Aquinas, Selected Political Writings, ed. A. P. D'Entrèves (Oxford, 1948), p. 29.
92   Read, Walsingham, ii. 92.
93   Crump, Huguenot Family, pp. 179–80. The French reads: 'à quoi il s'employa avec assurance qu'il seroit obligé à certaines conditions qui feurent dressées, moyennant lesquelles il n'en pouvoit humainement arriver inconvénient': Mémoires et correspondance de Duplessis-Mornay, i. 131. Languet was also involved in the negotiations: Chevreul, Hubert Languet, pp. 156, 161–3.
94   NA 175/10–15.
95   Buchanan, Sacred Dramas, p. 154; Phillips, 'Buchanan', pp. 40–1; Read, Walsingham, ii. 218.
96   Stubbs, p. 66. Cf. Pears, pp. 5, 24, 41–2, 53; Levy, 'Correspondence', nos 57, 62, 63.
97   GP 49/28–50/2.

Sidney, Greville implies, believed that the House of Austria was undermining the 'native liberty' of the principalities.[98]

More pressingly there was the struggle between Spain and the Dutch for control of the Netherlands. Greville reports that Sidney believed it to be Philip II's aim to 'transform his Low Country dukedoms – fallen to him by descent – into the nature of a sovereign conquest'.[99] In Dutch eyes, a long and jealous tradition of self-governing independence and constitutional variety was being eroded by a centralised and unaccountable regime which overruled traditional laws and liberties.[100] Accused of extinguishing liberty in the Netherlands, Spanish tyranny was charged with having eliminated it in Italy, a land which Sidney, says Greville, longed to see liberated.[101] Languet remarked to Sidney that in Italy there flourished 'evil devices by which a great many princes have, in our memory and that of our fathers, turned moderate and well-ordered princedoms into tyrannies'. Languet attributed that development to 'Florentines'.[102] Doubtless he had one Florentine particularly in mind, Machiavelli: the Machiavelli not of the republican *Discourses* but of *The Prince*. The Huguenot writer Innocent Gentillet, describing a parallel process in France, had *The Prince* in mind too. Gentillet, who was close to Sidney and to England's forward Protestants, claimed that the 'pernicious' influence of Machiavelli had 'changed the good and ancient government of France into a kind of Florentine government', so that the 'diversity of ancient government' had surrendered to the uniform power of 'the modern and present government'.[103] Sidney, relates Greville, saw 'how that once well-formed monarchy [of France] had by little and little let fall her ancient and reverend pillars – I mean parliaments, laws and customs – into the narrowness of proclamations or imperial mandates'.[104]

What, then, under the influence of Anjou, would happen to England? Sidney, says Greville, believed that Anjou would seek to 'lift monarchy above her ancient legal circles . . . till the ideas of native freedom should be utterly forgotten', and to 'metamorphos[e] our moderate form of monarchy into a precipitate absoluteness'. Anjou would have proceeded towards that end 'by a public decrying of our ancient customs and statutes . . . from that ground giving proclamations a royal vigour in moulding of pleas, pulpits and parliaments – after the manner of [his] own and some other foreign nations'.[105]

It may be that Greville, by the time he wrote the 'Dedication', had

98 *GP* 16/10–12, 25/28–30.
99 *GP* 29/7–9.
100 Van Gelderen, *Political Thought*, pp. 29, 116–17, 123.
101 *GP* 61/7ff.
102 Levy, 'Correspondence', no. 29.
103 Gentillet, *A Discourse upon the Meanes of Wel Governing* (London, 1602), esp. ded., and preface, sig. Aiiii&ᵛ (and see the Roman parallel, pp. 237–8); below, Chapter 14. Gentillet's *Apology* for the Huguenots was published in English in 1579 by Leicester's client (and Thomas Norton's publisher) the bookseller John Day (Rosenberg, *Leicester*, p. 207).
104 *GP* 58/10–13.
105 *GP* 32/11–14, 32/20–1, 31/29–32.

acquired a stronger sense than Sidney had possessed of the European movement towards absolutism, and was readier than Sidney might have been to see the Anjou match as part of that trend. It may be too that Greville's emphasis on the threat to parliaments from the use of royal proclamations, an issue of large concern in Jacobean politics and of little if any around 1579, casts Sidney's anxiety in anachronistic terms. Sidney's thinking about political consent, as far as we can judge, was altogether less precise about the forms and functions of representative institutions than Greville's would be in James's reign. Though he sat in the parliament of 1581, he wrote next to nothing about parliaments.[106] However, while Greville may modernise Sidney in making him a spokesman for parliamentary liberty, his general point, that his friend saw the Anjou crisis as a conflict between limited and unlimited monarchy, between the rule of law and the rule of will, is true to Sidney's anxieties and to those of his allies.

Yet in Sidney's eyes the Anjou crisis, like the crisis on Basilius' death, did not so much create fresh dangers as expose and intensify existing ones. It is because of the corruption of the two lands that England and Arcadia are so vulnerable when the crises come. When and why has England become corrupt? What has become of Gothic monarchy, that curb to corruption, in England? The opponents of the Anjou match represented the suit as a threat to the liberty which sixteenth-century England had preserved while its continental neighbours had lost theirs. Yet when Greville explains that Sidney expected Anjou to create a 'tyranny' which would 'bring the English people to the poverty of the French peasants', the illustrative parallel to which he turns is not French but English: Anjou's 'instruments' would be 'Frenchified Empsons and Dudleys', that is, successors to the instruments of tyranny under Henry VII.[107] There are indications (we shall find) that Sidney thought of the reigns of Henry VII and his son as having brought a dangerous shift of power in the crown's favour.[108]

In comparison with early Tudor government, and (in Protestant eyes) with that of Mary Tudor, Elizabeth's rule was mild. In the *New Arcadia* Helen of Corinth, appearing as an idealised Elizabeth, rules gently a 'people' who were 'always before so used to hard governors as they knew not how to obey without the sword drawn'.[109] The real Elizabeth was no more 'hard' a

---

106   In his fiction there is a 'general assembly of the Arcadian nobility' (*OA* 397/1), and Arcadia has other representative '[e]states' too (*OA* 305/22, 319/24; *NA* 326/8–12); but his main interest is in the consent of 'the Lydian nobility' or of 'the principal Arcadians' rather than in the constitutional forms which their acquiescence might take (*OA* 69/14–15, 288/13–18). (During the Anjou negotiations it was proposed – on the basis of the earlier negotiations between Mary Tudor and Philip of Spain – that no children borne by Elizabeth should be permitted to leave England 'without consent of the nobility of the realm': Hatf. 148, fo. 28.) Greville's emphasis on the breaking of 'laws' and 'customs' in France may likewise bear a larger imprint of his own reflections than of Sidney's: see Bullough, i. 128 (sonnet lxxi, l. 21).

107   *GP* 32/3–10.

108   Below, Chapter 15.

109   *NA* 253/22–5.

'governor' than Sidney's idealised one. When Sir Francis Knollys complained that the queen followed 'will and affection' instead of 'counsel', he was lamenting the consequences of that proclivity for the formation of policy, not charting a rise of absolutism. Nonetheless, the political weaknesses that afflict Arcadia are England's too. Whether or not England's problems can be traced to the early Tudors, it is evident that in England as in Arcadia 'public matters' have been 'privately governed' and that its inhabitants, like the Arcadians, lack 'experience to rule'. If the queen marries Anjou, will not those failings prove as disastrous as they are in Arcadia?

Thus Sidney, dismayed by the monarchies of his time but unwilling to countenance republicanism, turns to the ideal of limited monarchy. Yet other sides to his mind think differently. Two aspects of his political thinking are in tension with his wish for limited monarchy. They are also in tension with each other. First, Sidney, the critic of courts, is a courtier; and the evolution of Renaissance courtesy belongs to the same process as the erosion of limited monarchy. Secondly, unlimited monarchy, which has so much capacity for evil, has an equal capacity for good.

Sidney knew his courts. During his youthful stay in Paris, King Charles IX had made him a 'gentilhomme ordinaire de nôtre chambre' and given him the title Baron de Sidenay. On his embassy of 1577 he was received at the court of the Emperor Rudolf II and at those of German princes. The court he knew best, of course, was Elizabeth's. His dislike of the artificiality, vanity and falsity of that arena is clear enough. Yet the same court was the necessary route to the 'service' for which he longed and to the political 'action' which he saw as the highest end of virtue. Only through management of the court could forward Protestant policies be implemented. Languet, dismayed as he had been by the effeminacy and affectation of the Elizabethan court, and fearful as he was lest his young friend's mind should be 'dulled' there, was still more troubled by Sidney's retreat from court: now Sidney, he feared, would be 'dulled by idleness'.[110] Musidorus may contrast 'the delight of solitariness' with the courtly evils from which it offers liberation, but solitariness is an evasion of our responsibilities to our fellow men.[111]

A writer who often seems present in Sidney's pages is Castiglione. The effeminacy and corruption and servility of court life are tolerable, Castiglione suggested, 'if the activities of the courtiers are directed to' a 'virtuous end'.[112] That is the end to which courtly activities are directed at the court of the King of Egypt in the *Old Arcadia* and at the court of Helen of Corinth, the 'Diana', or idealised Elizabeth, of the *New*. Helen educates her courtiers, as Sidney seeks to educate his readers, through 'delight': they become '(by sports) learned, her ladies (by love) chaste; . . . her sports were such as carried

110   Above, p. 65.
111   *OA* 166/23–167/2; above, p. 26.
112   Castiglione, *Book of the Courtier*, p. 284.

riches of knowledge upon the stream of delight . . . so as, it seemed that court
to have been the marriage place of love and virtue'.[113] That image reflects a
development, at once political and literary, which is largely new in England.
It is in Elizabeth's reign that negative criticism of the court, by itself a far
from novel occurrence, becomes balanced by the positive ideal of courtly
perfection.[114] Spenser's *Mother Hubberds Tale*, though merciless to 'common
courtiers', proposes an alternative image, indebted to Castiglione, of the good
courtier, free of the court's abuses.[115] The evils of the court are one side of
a coin: on the other, as Ben Jonson explains near the end of the reign, 'a
virtuous court a world to virtue draws'.[116]

Courts were expected to teach something more than virtue. It was their
role to impart 'manners' too. At the 'faery court' of *The Faerie Queene* the
ideals of virtue and manners merge:

> Of court it seemes, men courtesie doe call,
> For that it there most useth to abound;
> And well beseemeth that in princes hall
> That vertue should be plentifully found,
> Which of all goodly manners is the ground,
> And roote of civill conversation.[117]

'Courtesy', 'civil conversation', 'manners', are important to Sidney, as 'good
manners' are to Philisides.[118] They are the qualities summoned by Gabriel
Harvey's description of Sidney and Dyer as 'the two very diamonds of her
majesty's court'.[119] Dametas, though committing the courtly evil of flattery, is
chiefly contemptible not because he is a courtier but because, being a
courtier, he lacks courtly graces: because his coarseness and clumsiness – and
his 'base blood' – offend against 'courtesy'.[120]

Basilius, having recruited Dametas to his service, compounds that folly by
interpreting his 'bluntness' as 'integrity' and his 'rudeness' as 'plainness'.[121]
Plainness is a merit of Philanax in advising Basilius, and is the merit which
forward Protestants strove to promote among the queen's councillors.[122] But
plainness, thought Sidney and his friends, ought to be compatible with

---

113 *OA* 155/29–31; *NA* 253/32–254/5.
114 Javitch, *Poetry and Courtliness*, p. 119.
115 Oram, p. 358 (ll. 713ff.); cf. ibid., p. 329.
116 Jonson, *Cynthias Revells* V. xi. 173.
117 *The Faerie Queene* VI. 1. i; cf. Worden, 'Shakespeare and Politics', p. 10.
118 *OA* 254/14; cf. *NA* 343/38–344/1.
119 *Dictionary of National Biography*: Dyer, Sir Edward. It would be said that Dyer was 'one of those
     who would not fawn or cringe' at court (ibid.).
120 *OA* 30/10–11, 32/34, 34/6–8, 43/34–5; cf. *MP* 118/33–5. Dametas' base blood shows him to
     be no true 'courtier', a defect particularly evident in his absurd performances on horseback,
     which are placed in contrast to the noble Musidorus' exercise in *haute école*: *OA* 188/12–15,
     266/6; *NA* 153/22–33, 154/6–9, 383/34ff.; below, p. 324; cf. *NA* xxii–xxiii.
121 *OA* 31/10–17; *NA* 116/8–9.
122 Above, pp. 146–7.

courtesy and to be combined with it.[123] Philanax, plain-hearted as he is, has none of the 'obstinate austerity' of advisers who, in confronting rulers with reality, 'wholly neglect the prince's person'.[124] Sidney and his allies were embarrassed by the antics of his friend Dr Beuttrich, the inflammatory adviser to John Casimir, whose habit of using 'free and plain speech where he is discontented', 'unseemly to be used to any king or monarch', damaged the forward Protestant cause in the courts of England and France alike.[125]

Both civility and prudence require directness of speech to be rationed. Freedom of speech, in the minds of Sidney and his party, is essential to political liberty.[126] Yet it can be abused. The silencing of the swan in the First Eclogues of the *Arcadia*, like the nailing of the poet's tongue in *The Faerie Queene* ('for his trespasse vyle ... adiudged so by law'), is not a protest against the suppression of free speech but a warning against the abuse of it. The swan, as Geron reports, has abused his privilege of speech by 'defacing' the other animals, who unite to silence him. Geron explains the point to his fellow shepherd Mastix, whose name means 'scourge', and who has complained of the failings of Arcadia's – and England's – J.P. class with 'too much zeal': 'Let not thy tongue become a fiery match, / No sword so bites as that ill tool annoys.' Courtiers who make that mistake lose their scope for achievement:

> I pray thee what hath e'er the parrot got,
> And yet they say he talks in great men's bow'rs?
> A cage (gilded perchance) is all his lot.[127]

Courts, then, should have functions of virtue and civility. Yet can they fulfil them? And can virtue and civility truly meet in them? Before Euarchus reforms Macedon, the court, whose ruler ought to give a 'fatherly example', is a 'place of unbridled licentiousness'. But what sort of 'fatherly example' would a good court supply? Sidney never mentions Euarchus' court. Can we envisage Euarchus spending time on the chivalric pastimes practised at the court of Basilius in the first book of the *New Arcadia* and at that of Helen of Corinth in the second? We learn of his 'virtue' but not of his 'manners'. Would not the practice of courtly civility soften the resolve, or weaken the reforming energy, of that 'virtuous prince'? Can courts promote the 'action' which virtue serves to advance?[128]

---

123 Perhaps Thomas Norton, who was imprisoned for his outspoken attack on the Anjou match, failed to grasp that truth: above, p. 162.

124 *OA* 6/1–2; cf. Martin Bergsbuch, 'The "Subaltern Magistrate" in Sir Philip Sidney's *Arcadia*', *English Studies in Canada* 7 (1981), pp. 27–37.

125 *CSPF* 1575–7, pp. 539–40, 545, 1578–9, pp. 370–1, 424.

126 Above, p. 147; below, pp. 275, 279.

127 *OA* 78/11–79/4, 500; *The Faerie Queene* V. ix. 25.

128 Euarchus, it is true, is scrupulous in his 'courtesies' (*OA* 359/27) – as is William of Orange (Wright, *Queen Elizabeth*, ii. 117); but those courtesies, like Orange's, do not seem particularly courtly. (See also *OA* 283/25, 387/14–15.)

In the *New Arcadia* the tension between the demands of civility and those of action becomes evident in the character of Amphialus. Though a flawed personality, he is, like Euarchus, a man of bold and decisive action. Unlike Euarchus he is also shown to be a paragon of chivalry, that quintessential courtly virtue. Yet those two aspects of his character do not properly meet. Sidney works hard to identify the 'courtesy' of Amphialus and other characters with 'virtue' and with the valour which attends it.[129] Yet the figure who is 'commonly called "the courteous Amphialus"', the Amphialus in whose heart 'courtesy . . . seemed incorporate',[130] is at odds with the Amphialus who so ably organises and animates a military campaign. On the battlefield Amphialus' devotion to chivalric combat obscures the larger strategic picture from him and threatens to cost him the campaign.[131]

Not only do we never see Euarchus among courtiers. We never see him taking counsel. If there is a single cause of Arcadia's and England's problems, it is a failure of counsel. Yet in Macedon, counsel appears to be redundant. Euarchus does have men of 'greatest trust . . . about him',[132] but they appear to be mere executors of his will, as Philanax, after his advice has been spurned at the outset of the *Arcadia*, is the mere executor of Basilius'. There is no evidence, either, of representative institutions in Macedon or of any other curbs on the royal prerogative. Euarchus' methods of rule, it will transpire, are at odds with the ideal of limited monarchy.

So are Sidney's thoughts for the future of the Protestant cause. The English knew that on Elizabeth's death they would face the likelihood of a 'monstrous disordered interregnum', the outcome of which would be resolved by 'the sword'.[133] If, out of that chaos, Sidney's party succeeded in installing its own candidate on the throne, the new ruler would need all the resources and authority he could get. There would be rival claimants to be crushed, papists to be suppressed, godly wars to be fought and financed. Revolutions create their own pressures. A century later, in the Revolution of 1688–9, opponents of absolutism would rejoice in the accession to the throne of William III, the descendant of William the Silent. His regime, fighting off the deposed Catholic dynasty and its Catholic allies, would swell the resources of the state. Whig statesmen who in the exclusion crisis had been critics of the royal prerogative now became its advocates.

They were neither the first nor the last politicians to reveal that human trait. The trait was the subject of some mordant remarks by Pierre Bayle. He directed them at the authors of the work of political thought to which the *Arcadia* is closest: the *Vindiciae, Contra Tyrannos*, by Sidney's intimate friends

---

129   *NA* 61/36–62/4, 92/7–8, 198/14–15, 317/24, 369/35, 374/7–8.
130   *NA* 61/39, 196/33; cf. *NA* 27/26, 61/9, 92/24, 195/27, 196/25, 197/1, 235/26, 400/9, 407/36, 408/6.
131   *NA* 346/1–5. A little later the claims of 'courtesy' and 'violence' contend within him: *NA* 353/33–5.
132   *OA* 356.
133   NRO, F(P)M 96, fos 3&ᵛ, 7.

Languet and Mornay. 'Frequently the same persons who write for the rights of the people', Bayle observed, 'would write for arbitrary power if affairs should change; that is, if despotic power came to be exercised in their favour, and to the great prejudice of a party which they hate.'[134]

The tendency Bayle described might have found expression not only in England after Elizabeth's death but in the Netherlands, where Sidney ended his life. The queen believed that Sidney and William Davison had been the 'principal actors and persuaders' behind Leicester's assumption, which so angered her (and angered many in the United Provinces too), of 'full and absolute power' in the Low Countries, a position markedly in contrast with the merely token authority allowed to Anjou there six years earlier.[135] Justifying Leicester's decision to a Dutch audience, Sidney said of himself that:

> he had learnt from history that when the state of the republic of Rome had been in utter peril or danger, as the Netherlands nowadays are, which [the Dutch] fully acknowledge, it had been necessary to create a dictatorship, with absolute power and disposition over everything concerning the prosperity of the country, without any instruction, limitation or restriction . . ..[136]

Rome's dictatorships had been justified as temporary measures, to meet emergencies. But Sidney does not seem to have expected Leicester's powers to be temporary.

Those powers might one day be his own. At the banquet that followed Sidney's funeral, one of the Dutch mourners whom Walsingham had invited to attend made a speech. Sidney's death, he explained, 'is most sad for us, because we had hoped that through his help and advice our country would be rescued from this long and miserable war . . .. Through the outstanding and incomparable talents of his character he was, in the opinion of all, the desired and destined successor' to Leicester as Elizabeth's deputy and Governor-General.[137] According to Greville 'there was such a sympathy of affections' between Sidney, that 'adopted patriot of the States-General', and the Dutch leaders, and so much respect in the Netherlands for his 'exorbitant worth', that 'time and occasion had been like enough to metamorphose this new aristocracy of theirs into their ancient and much honoured form of dukedom'. Sidney, adds Greville, 'felt something in his own nature possible in time to become an elect commander' there.[138]

---

134 Pierre Desmaizeaux, ed., *Mr. Bayle's Historical and Critical Dictionary*, 5 vols (London, 1738), v. 740.

135 Bruce, *Leycester Correspondence*, p. 118; van Gelderen, *Political Thought*, pp. 199–200; Jonathan Israel, *The Dutch Republic* (Oxford, 1995), pp. 220–30. Van Gelderen suggests that there were those in the Netherlands who looked to Leicester as a 'virtuous prince'.

136 Poort, 'Desired and Destined Successor', p. 29; cf. van Gelderen, *Political Thought*, p. 201.

137 Poort, 'Desired and Destined Successor', p. 25.

138 GP 83/23–31.

The 'dukedom' of the Low Countries had been a limited monarchy. Would it, in Sidney's hands, have remained so? During his time in the Netherlands he was, as he knew, 'called very ambitious and proud at home'.[139] Greville acknowledged the presence of 'ambition' in him, though characteristically emphasising his hero's ability to 'balance' it with loyalty to queen and country.[140] As duke, Sidney would doubtless have seen himself as the heir in spirit of William of Orange. Over the next century the house of Orange sought, through a bitter and intense struggle with the Dutch republicans, to acquire monarchical powers. A seventeenth-century Dutch writer with republican sympathies thought that Sidney, 'had he lived', might have developed similar aspirations. 'Some', it was true, 'never doubted' that his 'wisdom and modesty (once time and experience had mollified his passions), would have persuaded his uncle'

> to discontinue his immature enterprises, which were a humiliation to the States. But others judged, that if [Sidney] should have used his industry, valour, and ability in undermining liberty (which his insistence, from the very first, that Leicester's governorship should embrace unlimited authority had given them reason to fear) . . . this would have disagreed with the country even more than the delusions of Leicester, the rash beginnings of whose enterprises caused him to halt half-way.[141]

Sidney, who justified the dictatorship of his uncle in the Netherlands, admired another dictator too: Julius Caesar, the destroyer of the Roman republic. We know of that enthusiasm from Gabriel Harvey, who studied Roman history at Sidney's side, and who reveals that Sidney admired 'the singular life and actions' of Caesar 'above all other'. Liking men of action as he did, he reputed Caesar, says Harvey, 'the greatest actor that ever the world did afford', knowing him to have been respected by his friends and enemies alike as:

> a most worthy man; modest in profession; pithy in discourse; discreet in judgement; sound in resolution; quiet in expedition; constant in industry; most vigorous in most danger; surmounting the wisest in policy, the bravest in valour, the terriblest in execution . . . . the only mirror of excellent valour . . ..[142]

Harvey might have been recording Sidney's judgement, not of Caesar, but of Euarchus.

---

139 Feuillerat, iii. 167.
140 *GP* 75/12–15.
141 Van Dorsten, *Poets*, p. 167.
142 Jardine and Grafton, 'Gabriel Harvey', p. 55; cf. Wilkes, p. 156 (st. 482).

One issue will highlight for us the opposing directions of Sidney's thinking about monarchical power: the sixteenth-century concern about the use of troops and of garrisons or citadels by monarchs to preserve order among their subjects. Machiavelli had distinguished between healthy commonwealths, whose citizens are trained to fight for themselves and their country, and corrupt or tyrannical states, whose rulers, fearful of their subjects, disarm and subjugate them and hire mercenaries to fight in their stead. Sidney registers such a distinction in advising his brother Robert to study, on his continental travels, 'the fortifications and garrisons' in the countries he visits and to discover 'how the people' are 'warlikely trained or kept under'.[143] Greville thinks on the same lines. Accepting Machiavelli's argument that only states which arm their citizens can hope to prosper in war, he condemns tyrants who, following 'a counsel out of hell', 'disarm' their subjects and who practise 'this art of tyrant citadel, / Not suffering free citizens but slaves'.[144] Through 'citadels' and 'forts', says Greville, rulers 'mow their people down'.[145] Languet and Mornay agreed. 'A tyrant', explains the *Vindiciae*, 'places foreigners in garrisons, and constructs fortresses against the citizens. He disarms the people, and . . . surrounds himself with barbarous and servile guards.'[146] Mary Queen of Scots's mother, Mary of Guise, had as regent of Scotland garrisoned fortresses with French soldiers:[147] French troops, warned Sidney and John Stubbs, would be instruments of Anjou's tyranny in England.[148]

In the *New Arcadia* the 'citizens' of Phrygia 'set upon the guard and soldiers as chief instruments of tyranny'. Plexirtus, the tyrant of Galatia (Paphlagonia), 'as he came to the crown by . . . unjust means, as unjustly . . . kept it by force of stranger soldiers in citadels, the nests of tyranny and murderers of liberty, disarming all his own countrymen'.[149] In the Netherlands, too, the citadels built by the occupying Spaniards were detested as 'nests of tyranny'.[150] Queen Elizabeth protested to Spain against its 'garrisons and soldiers of foreign countries' in the Low Countries and against Philip II's moves to 'plant a

---

143 Feuillerat, iii. 125. In the *New Arcadia* we watch the helots 'fighting' with all their might, in the spirit recommended by Machiavelli, 'for their livings, wives, and children' (*NA* 37/12); but Sidney does not idealise that disposition. Cf. Pears, p. 50.

144 Wilkes, p. 163 (st. 511).

145 Ibid., pp. 170 (st. 538), 163 (st. 511); Bullough, ii. 96 (*Mustapha*, Chorus Secundus, ll. 123–6, where Greville also makes use of Machiavelli's point that only regimes which arm their subjects can expand); cf. Wilson, *Demosthenes*, sigs B4, C1. It was a sign of England's virtue, claimed Sir Walter Mildmay during the council's debates over the Anjou marriage, that she might raise an army 'without trusting upon mercenary soldiers': BL, Harleian MS. 6265, fo. 106.

146 Garnett, p. 145.

147 Read, *Walsingham*, i. 41; cf. BL, Harleian MS. 6265, fo. 106ᵛ.

148 Above, p. 190.

149 *NA* 174/8–10, 182/16–19.

150 John Motley, *The Rise of the Dutch Republic* (London, 1876 edn), p. 700; cf. *CSPF* 1575–7, p. 414.

martial government there'.[151] Sidney, relates Greville, discerned Spain's intention 'to citadelise the long-oppressed Netherlanders into a tenure of uttermost bondage', and feared that, as a result of the European diplomatic
revolution that could be expected to follow Elizabeth's marriage to Anjou,
the Dutch would be made to 'submit their necks to the yoking citadels of
Spain'.[152] Where Sidney indicates to his brother Robert that 'people' are
'kept under' by garrisons, Hubert Languet observes that forts in the Dutch
towns are intended to 'keep' the 'people to their obedience'.[153] William of
Orange, as Sidney knew, regarded their demolition as an indispensable
condition of any negotiated peace.[154] Most of the 'calamities' of the Dutch
towns that had been made desolate by the war, declared Orange, had
proceeded from the building of their citadels.[155] There were Spanish citadels
or garrisons elsewhere too. Greville says that Sidney looked forward to the
liberation of Italy from Spanish and tyrannical rule by a Protestant army that
would 'chase away these . . . oppressing garrisons' with which the Italian
princes were 'busy' in 'keeping down' their 'people';[156] Sidney himself wrote
to Languet that Philip II aimed to 'keep down' his Italian subjects, of whom
he 'begins to be afraid';[157] Mornay complained of Spain's use of garrisons
against its subjects both in the Netherlands and in Italy, and lamented to
Walsingham the building of citadels to oppress French Protestants.[158]

And yet it seems that, in a virtuous cause, garrisons and citadels can have
their merits. For as Greville explains, the rules of strong government apply
'without distinction' both to kings and to tyrants. Kings will put their
strength to 'good uses', tyrants to bad; but the means to those opposite ends
are the same.[159] If Sidney and his friends protested against tyrants who 'keep
down' their virtuous subjects, they were also sure that virtuous monarchs
must 'keep down' their vicious ones. At the time of the Anjou match the
queen's councillors were agreed on the need to 'keep down' or 'keep under'
or 'keep . . . in awe' her papist and 'evil-contented subjects' in England.[160]
There was the same need in Ireland, at least in the judgement of Sidney's
father Sir Henry, the queen's deputy there. Sir Henry thought the queen's
Irish garrisons to be 'in effect the only monuments of obedience and nurseries
of civility' in that land.[161] His secretary William Molyneux explained how, by

151 BL, Harleian MS. 6992, no. 30.
152 GP 58/32–3, 33/23–4.
153 Pears, p. 175.
154 Osborn, Young Philip Sidney, p. 485; CSPF 1575–7, pp. 430, 502, 551 (cf. p. 414); cf. van
     Gelderen, Political Thought, p. 170.
155 CSPF 1575–7, p. 429; cf. Apologie . . . of . . . William, sig. K2.
156 GP 61/14–18, 50/30–1.
157 Pears, p. 66.
158 Mémoires et correspondance de Duplessis-Mornay, ii. 27 (cf. iii. 74); Patry, Philippe Du Plessis-Mornay,
     p. 73.
159 Wilkes, p. 115 (sts 320–1).
160 BL, Harleian MS. 6265, fos 104, 106ᵛ; Hatf. 148, fo. 37; above, p. 116.
161 Collins, Letters and Memorials, i. 20–1.

those and other military means, Sir Henry 'kept' the Irish 'in awe'. It was on that essential basis of security that he was able to establish 'justice' in Ireland and cleanse the land of 'corruption'.[162]

Molyneux's account of Sir Henry's achievements in Ireland has warrantably reminded critics of the methods by which, in the *Arcadia*, Euarchus reforms Macedon. At the time of the Anjou crisis, such methods were regarded as essential not only in Ireland but in England. That perception, as far as we can tell, was not divisive. Advocates of the match – Burghley perhaps in particular – were at least as convinced of the need for tough measures as were its opponents. But there was the usual difference. Opponents of the match were looking for ways by which England could survive without it: advocates were wondering how to rescue England if the match were broken off.

The measures recommended by Elizabeth's councillors are those taken by Euarchus in confronting the external peril to Greece. First, England, no less than Macedon, needs to be militarily prepared against its enemies. Euarchus' 'first care was to put his people in a readiness for war, and by his experienced soldiers to train the unskilful to martial exercises', a task to which he appoints men 'of greatest trust': the queen's councillors wanted her to keep soldiers 'in readiness' and to 'entrust . . . skilful persons' and 'good captains' with the 'furnish[ing]' of 'all her people able to serve . . . with armour and weapon'. Euarchus, in training and allocating his soldiers, 'ma[de] of his kingdom so many divisions as he thought convenient': councillors wanted to see the raising of 'horsemen' who would be 'divided into sundry quarters of her realm'. Euarchus 'giv[es] order for the repairing and increasing his navy': councillors wanted the queen's 'navy to be strongly furnished' and urged her to 'put . . . her realm in strength . . . by sea'. Euarchus provides for 'the fortifying of such places, especially on the sea coast, as . . . commodity of landing' might 'draw the enemy unto': the councillors, calling for 'the furniture of garrisons', particularly wanted troops to be sent 'towards places of landing by the sea'.[163]

If Euarchus' troops, and the troops for which Elizabeth's advisers call, will afford protection against invasion, that will not be their only role. Euarchus raises soldiers 'both for resisting the invading enemy, and punishing the disordered subject'. Councillors proposed that the English troops which would be raised to withstand foreign incursion 'might [also] at all times' be ready 'upon the sudden [to] stay all inward attempts of seditions'.[164] A few years after the Anjou match, one writer, seeking to forestall the national disintegration that seemed likely to occur on Elizabeth's death, proposed the immediate levy and training of 4000 troops to be 'maintained in readiness for

---

162 Holinshed, *First and Second Volumes*, iii. 1548ff.; cf. Hatf. 148, fo. 58. Sir Henry's administration in Ireland, as described by Philip, was admired by Languet: Osborn, *Young Philip Sidney*, p. 466.
163 *OA* 356; Hatf. 148, fos 51ᵛ, 80ᵛ; BL, Harleian MS. 6265, fo. 106ᵛ.
164 *OA* 356; Murdin, *Collection*, p. 327 (from Hatf. 148, fo. 51ᵛ).

service', 'as well against foreign forces as also for the suppressing of all seditious factions hereafter'.[165]

Euarchus 'ma[de] of the divers regions of his kingdom so many divisions as he thought convenient'. He gives the men who are to govern those divisions 'sufficient authority to levy forces within their several governments'.[166] He might be Oliver Cromwell dispatching his Major-Generals to the regions of England in 1655. Elizabeth's councillors, proposing that troops be maintained 'in readiness [and] divided into sundry quarters of her realm', anticipated Cromwell too. They wanted troops to disarm 'obstinate or suspected' people and to remove 'all suspected persons' from populous towns.[167] The same tasks would fall to Cromwell's Major-Generals.

The Major-Generals were entrusted not only with the preservation of order but with moral reform. The military leaders appointed by Euarchus assist 'the progress of wisdom and virtue' among his subjects.[168] Sidney's description of the conduct of Philanax likewise associates military rule with 'wisdom and virtue'. For Philanax, as the commander of troops that had been raised to protect Basilius, 'placed garrisons in all the towns and villages anything near the [royal] lodges, over whom he appointed captains of such wisdom and virtue as might not only with the force of their soldiers keep the inhabitants from outrage, but might impartially look to the discipline both of the men of war and people'.[169]

We have seen Musidorus creating, in Phrygia, constitutional conditions that would restrain any ruler, good or evil. Yet it seems that wisdom and virtue have their own prerogatives. 'Severity', the quality which characterises the rule of Euarchus and in which Sidney's party believed the rule of Elizabeth to be deficient,[170] is unlikely to be allied to constitutionalist scruples. Sidney, Greville tells us, believed that the 'humours' of his countrymen must be 'governed . . . by the active and yet steady hand of authority'.[171] It looks as if England, which on the one hand needs to avoid the tyranny of Anjou, needs no less strongly the smack of firm and virtuous government.

165 NRO, F(P)M 96, fo. 6&ᵛ.
166 *OA* 356.
167 Hatf. 148, fo. 80ᵛ.
168 *OA* 356.
169 *OA* 286/8–13. Troops raised in Macedon and Arcadia also have the purpose of guarding frontiers (*OA* 356, 6/28–9, 53/34–5, 285/31–286/1). Sidney welcomed the guarding of England's Scottish border as a source of English strength: Osborn, *Young Philip Sidney*, p. 466; cf. Wilkes, pp. 168–9 (sts 532–4).
170 Above, p. 204.
171 *GP* 47/13–14.

CHAPTER 14

History Lessons

Sidney's *Defence of Poetry* proclaims poetry to be the superior of history. In deciding to write the *Arcadia* he chooses poetry, not history, as his medium of 'delightful teaching'. Yet his fiction draws profoundly on history's resources. The *Defence of Poetry* has a case to prove. To do so it posits a false antithesis, for in Sidney's mind history is not the rival of poetry but its partner.

The *Defence* teases 'the historian', who is 'laden with mouse-eaten old records'. He cannot teach, being 'so tied, not to what should be but to what is, to the particular truth of things and not to the general reason of things, that his example draweth no necessary consequence'. Lacking philosophy, he can deliver only 'example', not 'precept': lacking imagination, he is capable only of 'reporting', not 'representing'.[1] What the *Defence* omits is Sidney's absorption in history and his commitment to the recovery of its lessons.[2] His historical perspectives add depth and breadth to the political content of the *Arcadia*.

'I need not speak to you of reading history,' wrote Languet to Sidney in 1574, 'by which more than anything else men's judgements are shaped, because your own inclination carries you to it, and you have made great progress in it.'[3] In 1580 Languet described Sidney as 'thoroughly well read in history'.[4] Surviving notes of conversations between Sidney and some of his English friends about the history of republican Rome confirm Languet's assessments, and convey something of the intensity and excitement that evidently animated those discussions.[5] In 1580, the year in which the *Arcadia*

1 *MP* 83/31, 85/8–21, 114/7–8.
2 Cf. F. J. Levy, 'Sir Philip Sidney and the Idea of History', *Bibliothèque d'Humanisme et Renaissance* 26 (1964), pp. 608–17; Elizabeth Story Donno, 'Old Mouse-Eaten Records: History in Sidney's *Apology*', in Kay, *Sir Philip Sidney*, pp. 146–67.
3 Pears, p. 26; cf. ibid., p. 11.
4 Ibid., p. 169.
5 Jardine and Grafton, 'Gabriel Harvey', esp. pp. 36–9, 55.

was principally composed, Sidney sent breathless but sophisticated and discriminating advice about the study of history to his friend Edward Denny and to his own brother Robert. Those letters reveal a formidable range of historical reading: classical, medieval, modern.[6]

History was a preoccupation of Philip Sidney's relations and friends: of Leicester, a leading patron of historical scholarship, interested in questions of historical philosophy and technique;[7] of Sir Henry Sidney, Philip's father, who shared his own enthusiasm with that sponsor of innovative historical scholarship Archbishop Matthew Parker;[8] of Robert Sidney, whose papers bear witness to the width and assiduity of his historical reading;[9] of Fulke Greville, whose writings draw on history at almost every turn. Sidney's friends and allies abroad were close students of history too. There was Languet; there was Philippe Duplessis-Mornay, who at Languet's instigation wrote a history (which seems not to have survived) of the French wars of religion;[10] there was Philip Marnix, the soldier–statesman and statesman–scholar; there was George Buchanan, the Humanist poet and scholar and the historian of Scotland.

History, in the minds of Philip Sidney and his circle, is for use. Because it repeats itself, it provides parallels with, and practical lessons for, the present. It supplies, or at least extends, the data on which political judgements can be based. Leicester, declared the epistle addressed to him in a work on historical method in 1574, 'delight[s] most in reading of histories . . . not as many do, to pass away the time, but to gather thereof such judgement and knowledge as you may thereby be the more able, as well to direct your private actions, as to give counsel like a most prudent counsellor in public causes, be it matters of war or peace'.[11] Walsingham believed 'knowledge of histories' to be 'a very profitable study for a gentleman': particularly Plutarch, Livy 'and all the Roman histories . . . as also all books of state both old and new'.

> And . . . in these the reading of histories, as you have principally to mark how matters have passed in government in those days, so have you to apply them to these our times and states and see how they may be made serviceable to our age, or why to be rejected, the reason whereof well considered shall cause you in process of time to frame better courses both of action and counsel, as well in your private life as in public government, if you shall be called.[12]

6 Osborn, *Young Philip Sidney*, p. 539; Feuillerat, iii. 130–2. In the same year the historical interests of Sidney's friend Gabriel Harvey, in whose company he studied Roman history, seem to have reached their peak: Jardine and Grafton, 'Gabriel Harvey', p. 49.

7 Woudhuysen, 'Leicester's Literary Patronage', pp. 74–81; Rosenberg, *Leicester*, ch. 3.

8 Rosenberg, *Leicester*, p. 11 (cf. pp. 85–6); Collins, *Sidney Papers*, i. 67; McKisack, *Medieval History in the Tudor Age*, pp. 19, 30–1, 40–1, 58–9, 133–4.

9 They are in the De L'Isle and Dudley Papers at Maidstone: KAO, U1475: Z1.

10 Crump, *Huguenot Family*, p. 171.

11 Rosenberg, *Leicester*, p. 62.

12 Read, *Walsingham*, i. 18.

Walsingham seems to have turned to Livy's history of Rome for guidance on the conduct of Elizabethan foreign policy.[13] The young James VI of Scotland was lectured by Walsingham on the lessons of Scottish and English history.[14] Walsingham's secretary, Sidney's friend Robert Beale, himself a man of wide historical knowledge, shared his master's outlook: 'by the reading of histories', he thought, one could learn to apply 'the examples of time past' to the present.[15] Thomas Wilson, whose parallels, in his learned edition of *The Three Orations of Demosthenes*, between the Athens of Demosthenes and the England of Elizabeth anticipate the warnings of the *Arcadia*, was no less alert to the present political relevance of Roman history and medieval English history.[16] The minds of Mornay and Marnix likewise roamed the past for parallels that would cast light on current events.[17] Languet thought in the same way.[18] The 'old true tales' with which he was wont to 'fill' the 'ears' of the young Sidney[19] find their contemporary application in Sidney's fiction. There too the historical component of the education arranged for the young princes by Euarchus prepares them for public action and government.[20]

The target of the *Defence* is ostensibly the historian but really, in the term we would use, the antiquarian. The historian is said to be 'better acquainted with a thousand years ago than with the present age',[21] the age which it is his duty to illuminate. The search for contemporary relevance in history can have banal results, and in the Renaissance it often did. Yet in the hands of Sidney and his friends it became something more searching. In England, Sidney is in at the birth of the 'politic' or 'civil' history which, in the late sixteenth and early seventeenth centuries, broke the antiquarian mould and invented, or reinvented, the science of politics.[22] In studying that science Sidney turned to

13 BL, Harleian MS. 288, fos 150–1; Leimon, 'Walsingham', p. 124.
14 Read, *Walsingham*, ii. 218 (though cf. 219n.).
15 Ibid., i. 443.
16 K. de L., ix. 292, 329, 337–8, 352; Hartley, *Proceedings*, pp. 232, 329, 365, 394; cf. Jardine and Grafton, 'Gabriel Harvey', pp. 55, 64.
17 Mornay: above, p. 250; Marnix: K. de L., viii. 113–18; *CSPF 1578–9*, pp. 227–8; cf. *Catalogue of the Library of Philips von Marnix* (Nieuwkoop, 1964). (Marnix, by looking to France rather than England for the liberation of the Netherlands, eventually fell out with England's forward Protestants.)
18 See e.g. Pears, pp. 102–3; Levy, 'Correspondence', letter of 10 April 1574; cf. Goulart, *Mémoires*, ii. fo. 26.
19 *OA* 255/26.
20 *NA* 35/6–7, 163/31–5. ('Stories', in the second passage I have cited, means, I think, 'histories' – as at *MP* 84/16.) At *NA* 163/31–2 Sidney seems to think of poetry as the partner (rather than the superior) of history. The same view is discernible even in the *Defence*. For his claim that poetry will teach 'you to serve your prince . . . better' than history, a lighthearted assertion, exceeds the drift of the passage to which it belongs, and of which the essential argument is that poetry can teach 'as much' or 'as well' about politics as history can (*MP* 89/9, 89/22–6).
21 *MP* 83/35–6.
22 A key figure in that enterprise was William Camden, Sidney's friend at Christ Church, Oxford, who would remain devoted to him despite Sidney's relationship to Leicester, whom Camden despised: above, Chapter 3, n. 43.

his beloved Aristotle.[23] But there were other ancient guides who took him further. Above all there was Livy and there was Tacitus.

Gabriel Harvey noted that Sidney 'esteems no . . . special Roman historian like Livy', and named Sidney as one of the three people who 'won my heart to Livy'. (One of the others was that pioneer of politic history Jean Bodin, whose seductively but misleadingly entitled *Method for the Easy Comprehension of History* Philip recommended to his brother Robert in 1580.)[24] 'Just before [Sidney's] embassy' to Germany, Harvey records, Sidney and he 'privately discussed . . . three books of Livy, scrutinizing them so far as we could from all points of view, applying a political analysis. . . .. Our consideration was chiefly directed at the forms of states, the conditions of persons, and the qualities of actions.'[25] In the recent decades of the century, studies of Livy, as of Tacitus,[26] had been largely chronological or philological in character. Harvey and Sidney 'paid little attention' to such commentaries.[27] It is in the same spirit that the education arranged by Euarchus for the young princes puts their preparation for public life before 'grammatical rules'.[28] That spirit likewise animated a work the English translation of which was dedicated to Sidney in 1585, *De Legationibus Tres* by Alberico Gentili, who recorded that he had had many discussions with Sidney and that the work was indebted to his influence.[29] The treatise observes that Livy's expositor Machiavelli, 'the shrewdest of men', 'in reading history . . . does not play the grammarian, but assumes the role of philosopher'.[30]

Yet if there was one Roman historian whose genius presided over the 'politic' history of Sidney's time, it was not Livy but Tacitus. The figure who did most to bring Tacitus alive for the late Renaissance was his Belgian editor Justus Lipsius. Though a much older man than Sidney, Lipsius was his friend; he was a friend too of Sidney's friends Daniel Rogers and Edward Dyer. In Sidney, to whom he dedicated his work on Latin pronunciation, Lipsius saw evidence that England's nobility 'is truly noble, educated as it is in the principles of *virtus* and *doctrina*'; Sidney, he declared, was 'the flower of England'; after spending time with him at Leiden he praised the younger man's 'remarkable prudence and wisdom'. Leicester, who visited Lipsius in

23   Pears, p. 28.
24   Feuillerat, iii. 130. Cf. the evidence of Edward Dyer's interest in Bodin recorded in Bodl., Rawlinson MS. A331, fo. 123ᵛ.
25   Jardine and Grafton, 'Gabriel Harvey', pp. 55, 36. The plot of the *Arcadia* may draw on Livy: Duncan-Jones, *Sir Philip Sidney*, p. 119. Livy's account of the Carthaginian war supplied a pressing parallel, in the minds of Sidney and his friends (and of many others of their time), with the struggle between Spain and its enemies: Pears, p. 48; *MP* 51/28–9 (cf. Ringler, p. 147: sonnet 17, l. 45); *GP* 27/12–14, 53/13–15; *Mémoires et correspondance de Duplessis-Mornay*, ii. 194; Read, *Walsingham*, ii. 85–6; Jardine and Grafton, 'Gabriel Harvey', p. 72 (cf. p. 38).
26   Kenneth Schellhase, *Tacitus in Renaissance Political Thought* (Chicago and London, 1976), ch. 5.
27   Jardine and Grafton, 'Gabriel Harvey', p. 36.
28   *NA* 163/35; above, Chapter 2.
29   Donald Stump et al., eds, *Sir Philip Sidney: An Annotated Bibliography* (New York, 1994), p. 240.
30   Quoted by Victoria Kahn, *Machiavellian Rhetoric from the Counter-Reformation to Milton* (Princeton, 1994), p. 128.

Leiden with Sidney, went to hear him lecturing there on Tacitus, and dined him afterwards; perhaps that was the occasion when Lipsius gave him a personally inscribed copy of one of his most celebrated works, *De Constantia*. Only a week or so before sustaining his fatal injury at Zutphen, Sidney wrote to Lipsius urging him to consider settling in England: 'The terms which I once obtained for you I shall get confirmed, so that even if I die they will not lapse.'[31] A number of students of Tacitus gathered around Sidney,[32] as around Leicester.[33] In 1585 an Italian translation of Tacitus' *Agricola* was dedicated to Philip's brother Robert,[34] whose annotated copy of Lipsius' edition of Tacitus, acquired on its publication in that same year, survives.[35] The annotations illustrate the readiness of Renaissance readers to apply their study of Tacitus to the political problems of their own time.[36]

In 1580 Philip had recommended the reading of Tacitus to Robert, praising the Roman historian's gift of 'witty word' and observing that he 'excelleth . . . in the pithy opening the venom of wickedness'. In the same letter he urged on his brother the friendship and historiographical guidance of his own friend and travelling-companion Henry Savile,[37] who in 1591, five years after Philip's death, would produce the standard English translation of Tacitus' *Histories*. We do not know whether Savile had begun the translation in Philip's lifetime. But it does seem that he had learned about Tacitus from Philip, or Philip from him, or the two men from each other.

The evidence lies in a footnote to Savile's translation. There Savile discusses Tacitus' celebrated phrase *arcanum imperii*, which he translates as 'secret of state'. He explains that, in the passage to which the footnote belongs, Tacitus used the phrase to mean 'the secret truths or appearances in affairs of estate; for [adds Savile] the mass of the people is guided and governed more by ceremonies and shows than matter in substance'.[38] The words point us to the passage in the *Arcadia* where Euarchus, making the arrangements for the trial of the princes, 'did wisely consider the people to be naturally taken with exterior shows far more than with inward consideration of the material

---

31 Van Dorsten, *Poets*, pp. 46–7, 79, 116–18, 148–51; Buxton, *Sir Philip Sidney*, pp. 73, 80; Duncan-Jones, *Sir Philip Sidney*, p. 294.

32 F. J. Levy, 'Sir Philip Sidney Reconsidered', in Kinney, *Sidney in Retrospect*, pp. 3–14, at p. 8.

33 Woudhuysen, 'Leicester's Literary Patronage', pp. 79–80.

34 Buxton, *Sir Philip Sidney*, pp. 69, 264.

35 BL, classmark C. 142 e. 13.

36 Blair Worden, 'Classical Republicanism and the Puritan Revolution', in Hugh Lloyd-Jones *et al.*, eds, *History and Imagination. Essays in Honour of H. R. Trevor-Roper* (London, 1981), pp. 182–200, at pp. 186–7. Languet shared Sidney's interest in Tacitus: Levy, 'Correspondence', letter of 10 April 1574. There is now a sizeable literature on the reading of Tacitus in the late Renaissance, much of it conveniently listed by J. H. M. Salmon, 'Seneca and Tacitus in Jacobean England', in Linda Levy Peck, ed., *The Mental World of the Jacobean Court* (Cambridge, 1991), pp. 169–88, at notes 2, 3. More recently the subject is approached by two essays in Sharpe and Lake, eds, *Culture and Politics*, viz.: Malcolm Smuts, 'Court-Centred Politics and the Uses of Roman Historians, c. 1590–1630' (pp. 21–43); Worden, 'Ben Jonson among the Historians' (pp. 67–89).

37 Feuillerat, iii. 131–3; cf. KAO, U1475: Z1/3, p. 191.

38 *The Ende of Nero and the Beginning of Galba. Foure Bookes of the Histories of Cornelius Tacitus. The Life of Agricola* (London, 1604 edn), 'The Histories', p. 8.

points'; for 'in these pompous ceremonies he well knew a secret of government much to consist'.[39] The reality perceived by Tacitus and by Euarchus
exercised Sidney. In the *New Arcadia* Amphialus 'knew . . . how few there be
that can discern between truth and truthlikeness, between shows and substance'; he was a connoisseur of 'secret[s] of government', which are enemies
to ethical 'truth'.[40] Watching the Dutch faltering in their struggle against
Spanish tyranny in 1585, Sidney noted sadly that 'this people . . . is carried
more by shows than substance'.[41] As so often, Sidney's words are echoed by
Greville, that devotee of Tacitus. It is because 'people' are 'caught with
shows', thought Greville, that they are wont to surrender their 'freedom'.[42]
The loss of freedom, Tacitus' theme, is a theme of the *Arcadia* too, as we shall
find.

There may be other moments in the *Arcadia* when Sidney alludes to
Tacitus. One of them is the occasion after Basilius' death when the 'discoursing sort of men' demand the abolition of the Arcadian monarchy and its
replacement by an aristocracy or democracy. 'But', says Sidney, their proposals were 'a matter more in imagination than practice'.[43] The section of
Tacitus' writing which spoke most powerfully to the late Renaissance, his
account of the tyranny of the Emperor Tiberius and his favourite Sejanus in
the *Annals*, contains the observation that a government mixing the three
forms of monarchy, aristocracy and democracy is 'rather a matter of fine
speculation than of practice'.[44] That statement accompanies Tacitus' famous
remark that whereas his predecessors, who had written the history of Rome's
republic, had been able to address grand themes, the subject-matter of the
historian of monarchy must be small, wretched and tortuous. Does the
shadow of Tiberian tyranny hang over the Arcadians' dismissal of republican
forms, as the shadow of French tyranny hangs over England at the end of the
1570s? Tacitus had described the extinction of senatorial independence, the
rise of imperial power at its expense, the emergence of a politics of mistrust
and espionage. The appeal of his writing to the late Renaissance drew on and

39   *OA* 375/1–6.
40   *NA* 325/9–11, 325/20–1.
41   Feuillerat, iii. 148.
42   Bullough, ii. 184 (*Alaham* III. iii. 89–90). Greville would be responsible, albeit unwittingly, for
     a political storm in 1627, when the man he had nominated to lecture on Tacitus in Cambridge,
     Isaac Dorislaus, glanced at the excessive powers of kings and vindicated the 'liberties' of the
     Netherlands 'against the violences of Spain'. Rebholz, *Greville*, pp. 271, 293–300; Levy, 'Fulke
     Greville', p. 445; Kevin Sharpe, *Politics and Ideas in Early Modern England* (London, 1989), ch. 8.
43   *OA* 320/33–321/3.
44   I use (for convenience) the translation of Robert Walpole's enemy Lord Bolingbroke:
     Bolingbroke, *The Works*, 4 vols (Philadelphia, 1841), ii. 120 ('A Dissertation upon Parties', letter
     xiii). (Savile did not translate the *Annals*.) The Latin reads: 'delecta ex iis et consociata rei
     ·publicae forma laudari facilius quam evenire' (*Annals*, iv. xxxiii). Sidney, of course, is not talking
     about mixed government, but the similarity between the two passages is more suggestive than
     the difference. Tacitus' point about mixed government may in any case not have been properly
     understood in Sidney's time (if indeed it is in ours). Richard Greeneway's translation of 1598 says
     nothing of mixture: 'a form of a commonwealth constituted of one of these' three forms 'may
     be better praised than found' (*The Annales of Cornelius Tacitus* (London, 1604 edn), p. 100).

reinforced the conviction that a parallel process was now at work: that limited monarchies, and with them the powers of noblemen and representative institutions, were giving way to the unlimited monarchies being forged in the secret and sinister consultations of Europe's courts.[45] A Huguenot pamphlet, published by a client of Leicester in an English version in 1579, cited Livy and Tacitus in outlining the moral decay of the Roman republic, and described the period of its collapse as 'a time in all points like to this sorrowful time of ours', to this time of 'extreme corruption'.[46] Languet had encouraged Sidney to study the 'causes' of the fall of the Roman republic.[47] The prospect of the queen's marriage to Anjou can only have added spice to that topic.[48]

The attraction of Tacitus to the late sixteenth century, an attraction largely political, was also literary. The literary attraction was related to the political one. Sidney's time produced a reaction against the Ciceronian prose which had been the dominant model for the early Renaissance.[49] Tacitus' pithy, aphoristic prose supplied an alternative to the rhetorical looseness that had come to be practised in Cicero's name.[50] While Sidney's prose is generally far from Tacitean, it has its Tacitean moments. He likes to tuck compressed and pregnant observations, half-proverbial, half-epigrammatic, into his long sentences, usually so as to convey truths which his characters have 'found' or 'experienced' or 'considered' or 'remembered': 'no vow is so strong as the avoiding of occasions'; 'deceit cannot otherwise be maintained but by deceit'; 'the more rage breeds the crueller punishment'; 'ambition, like love, can abide no lingering'; and so on.[51] The rise of Tacitus in the late Renaissance

---

45 Worden, 'Ben Jonson among the Historians', pp. 76–80; cf. PRO, SP 15/26/*35, fo. 137ᵛ.

46 Innocent Gentillet, *An Apology or Defence for the Christians of France* (London, 1579), ep. ded., sig. [Biiiᵛ].

47 Pears, p. 20. Cf. ibid., pp. 80–1, 154–5; *MP* 54/20–4, 55/21–2.

48 I suspect that Tacitus is again in Sidney's mind in the account of the 'corruption' of Basilius. Let me use italics to point to that possibility. The duke has been '*corrupted with a prince's fortune*' and by the '*flatter[y]*' that attends it. Spurning the sound advice of Philanax, he declines '*to set down all private conceits in comparison of what, for the public, is profitable*'. He gives preferment to Dametas '*according to the nature of great persons*', in the manner of 'princes whose doings have been often *soothed with good success*'. (*OA* 6/4, 31/14–18; *NA* 18/35–6, 23/3–4, 418/5–6; above, p. 214.) Tacitus reports that the Emperor Galba, in adopting Piso as his heir, warned him to beware of his consequent prosperity, for (in Henry Savile's translation) '*felicity corrupteth*'. However firm Piso's integrity, warns Galba, he will find that '*flattery* will break in, and pleasing speeches, and the most pestilent poison of all true meaning, *public respects for private advantages*'. (Tacitus, *The Ende of Nero*, 'The Histories', p. 13.) The annotator of the composite *Arcadia* of 1593 whose notes are among the Sidney family papers cited Tacitus for the observation that 'princes refuse that which is good', '*a rule true in the nature of all princes*'. KAO, U1475: Z1/11, fo. 52. (The annotator had just remarked on the 'corruption of the people by an ill prince'.)

49 Sidney, sharing that reaction, called 'great study in Ciceronianism the chief abuse of Oxford': Feuillerat, iii. 132.

50 The seminal works on that subject are George Williamson, *The Senecan Amble* (London, 1951) and the material by Morris Croll in J. Max Patrick, ed., *Style, Rhetoric and Rhythm* (Princeton, 1966). The findings of Croll and Williamson have been modified but not disproved.

51 *OA* 201/33–4, 206/35–6, 273/24–5; *NA* 218/36–7. The frequency of aphorisms in Sidney's fiction is noted by Hamilton, *Sir Philip Sidney*, p. 152.

accompanies the rise of the commonplace-book, where pithy maxims of prudence are recorded and learned. Thus Hamlet thinks it 'meet' to 'set ... down' in his 'tables' his perception that 'one may smile, and smile, and be a villain'.[52]

Hamlet lives in a court. The Tacitism of the Renaissance grew up in relation to courts, partly as a guide to existence within them, partly in ethical reaction against them. That tension is conspicuous in the career and reading of Sidney's brother Robert and in his notes on Tacitus.[53] The rhetorical and oratorical tradition to which Cicero belonged had thrived in the times of Athenian and Roman liberty. Tacitean prose, the close, epigrammatic prose of the empire, was better suited to the era of Renaissance monarchy, when power, now as in Rome, was passing from the floors of representative institutions to the hidden consultations of courts and cabinets.

Alongside the ancient historians admired by Sidney there were modern ones, all of them decisive contributors to the new 'politic' history of Sidney's time. There was Bodin. There were Gasparo Contarini and Donato Giannotti, who had described, in what Sidney called 'really choice books', the history and institutions of the republic of Venice.[54] There was Francesco Guicciardini.[55] Above all there was Guicciardini's fellow historian of Florence, Niccolò Machiavelli. Machiavelli's black reputation, and the vulgar identification of his name with the vilest principles of statecraft, gave rise to banter between Sidney and Languet on the subject of Sidney's admiration for the Florentine.[56] Behind the banter there may have been a certain unease, for the insights Sidney derived from Machiavelli were not always compatible with the philosophy of public virtue which he shared with Languet and with England's forward Protestants. There is a tension in Sidney between his ethical Humanism, which says how men ought to be, and his embrace of politic history, which says how they are. Ethical Humanism was inherited by his generation: political history was discovered by it. Though the first has the larger presence in his writing, the second has an important one. His debt to the approach to historical study which Machiavelli had helped to foster was extensive. From it, as from the legacy of Tacitus, he acquired an interest in recurrent historical laws and an ironic detachment in relating them. Machiavelli sought out patterns of behaviour and maxims of prudence that persist across variations of time and place. Particular events illustrate general rules. Sidney's advice to his brother Robert on the study of history illustrates his commitment to the exemplary approach.[57] Robert is urged to draw up

52 *Hamlet* I. v. 107–8.
53 Worden, 'Classical Republicanism', pp. 186–7.
54 Levy, 'Correspondence', no. 8 (cf. Pears, p. 10).
55 Osborn, *Young Philip Sidney*, p. 539; cf. BL, Harleian MS. 6265, fo. 106.
56 Pears, pp. 53, 60, 61–2, 78; Levy, 'Correspondence', nos 29, 50. Cf. Jardine and Grafton, 'Gabriel Harvey', p. 55; GP 79/8–12; NRO, F(P)M III, fo. 1ᵛ.
57 That commitment is not gainsaid by Sidney's mockery of an inadequate version of the same approach in the *Defence of Poetry*: MP 84/15–18; cf. MP 55/24–5.

'table[s]' of 'politic matters', in which 'the historical part, which is only the example', would be listed under general themes, such as 'good counsel'.[58] Robert's surviving historical notebooks follow that principle.

In one respect Philip Sidney's thinking is far removed from Machiavelli's. His confidence in the political authority of virtue (as distinct from Machiavelli's *virtù*, which in Sidney's terms is ethically neutral) measures the distance.[59] Chapter 17 of Machiavelli's *The Prince* asks 'whether it is better' for a ruler 'to be loved or feared', and concludes in favour of fear. The *New Arcadia* glances at that ethically bleak deduction through the eyes of that personification of Machiavellian wickedness Cecropia (whom Sidney has declare that 'a fair woman . . . need not dispute whether to govern by fear or by love').[60] Sidney maintains that 'love' between subjects and rulers is an essential basis of good government, and that the only healthy 'fear' in politics is the reverent fear that accompanies love.[61] The sway of loveless fear cannot be permanent. We are shown in the *New Arcadia* what happens to a tyrant when 'fear', 'having been the only knot that had fastened his people unto him', is 'untied': 'they all scattered from him like so many birds whose cage had been broken'.[62]

Yet there was much in Machiavelli's *The Prince* that Sidney could accommodate within his moral precepts. For although Machiavelli was often taken to have endorsed tyranny, others saw in him 'the supreme foe' of it, whose 'purpose' was not 'to instruct the tyrant' but 'by revealing his secret counsels to lay him bare'.[63] Mornay thought that Machiavelli had 'set down the true portrait of a tyrant'.[64] Tacitus, too, can be read, or at least used, as a straightforward enemy or exposer of tyranny. That is how, or largely how, Sidney read or used him, and how, or largely how, he read or used Machiavelli. In Book Two of the *New Arcadia* Sidney does through poetry what Machiavelli's *The Prince* does through history: he provides a gallery of tyrants whose particular vices exemplify general patterns of princely evil. The patterns, for Sidney as for Machiavelli, were aids to the understanding of the present time.[65]

Sidney not only learns from *The Prince*. He points his readers to it. At the outset of that work, Machiavelli explains that there are two kinds of prince: those who rule by hereditary right (as Basilius does and as Elizabeth does), and those who acquire power by their own exertions. Machiavelli's advice is directed principally to the second category, to the 'new prince', who must establish himself through the ruthless tactics for which *The Prince* became

---

58 Feuillerat, iii. 131–2.
59 Above, p. 30.
60 *NA* 356/24–33.
61 Above, p. 117–18.
62 *NA* 184/35–8.
63 Alberico Gentili, quoted by Levy, 'Sir Philip Sidney Reconsidered', p. 9; and see Kahn, *Machiavellian Rhetoric*, pp. 128–9.
64 Mornay, *Mysterie of Iniquitie*, p. 613.
65 Compare Sidney's comparison of the Duke of Tuscany with Dionysius of Syracuse: Pears, p. 55.

notorious. Pyrocles recalls those tactics in addressing the rebels in Book Two, just after he has exhorted them, with an ironic glance at the misgovernment both of Basilius and of Elizabeth, not to 'show yourselves so ungrateful as to forget the fruit of so many years' peaceable government'. The rebels should beware, he advises them, of exchanging Basilius' (hereditary) rule for 'the tyrannous yoke' of a usurper, 'the newness of [whose] estate' would 'bring forth . . . cruelty'.[66]

In Machiavelli's terms Basilius' plight is a terrible indictment of his reign. To Machiavelli the task of the hereditary ruler ought to be simple. If he 'be but a man of ordinary industry' he should 'be able to maintain himself in his state'; for 'the natural prince' has 'fewer occasions, and less [n]eed, to give offence, whereupon he must of necessity be more beloved'; to remain in power 'it suffices only not to transgress the course his ancestors took'.[67] In the *Arcadia* Pyrocles, and later the narrator, echo Machiavelli's words. Just before warning the rebels against enthroning a Machiavellian new prince, Pyrocles reminds them that Basilius is 'your natural duke', 'delivered unto you by so many royal ancestors'.[68] On Basilius' death, the narrator tells us, the 'over-tender' shepherds bemoan the duke's demise, some of them remembering 'his peaceable government', 'some of them remembering the nobility of his birth, continued by being like his ancestors'; 'others his liberality . . . a most amiable virtue'; and the shepherds 'generally giving a true testimony that men are loving creatures when injuries put them not from their natural course, and how easy a thing it is for a prince by succession [that is, by hereditary right] deeply to sink into the souls of his subjects'.[69]

Those passages of the *Arcadia* correspond not only to *The Prince* but to Sidney's doubtful tributes, in his 'Letter' against the Anjou match, to Elizabeth's hereditary and peaceful reign: she is a ruler 'to whom our fortunes are tied by long descent of your royal ancestors'; and she is among the princes who, 'the longer they reigned, the deeper still they sank into their subjects' hearts'.[70] It is the achievement of the 'Letter' to incorporate, beneath so courteous a surface, such sharp Machiavellian irony. The same irony and the same passage of Machiavelli have an interlinear presence on the opening page of the *Arcadia*, which to a superficial glance offers so carefree an image of the Arcadian land. The third sentence of Sidney's story introduces us to Basilius, 'a prince of sufficient skill to govern so quiet a country where the good minds of the former princes had set down good laws'.[71] In a manuscript variant,[72] 'sufficient skill' is 'sufficient virtue'. The latter phrase is surely an

---

66   *OA* 130/15–26.
67   *The Prince*, ch. 2. I have used the first translation of the work to be published in English: *Nicholas Machiavel's 'Prince'* (London, 1661 edn).
68   *OA* 130/18, 130/23.
69   *OA* 283/13–284/1; cf. below, Chapter 19, n. 34.
70   Above, p. 132; *MP* 54/4–6; cf. *OA* 406/17.
71   *OA* 4/20–2.
72   Cf. Woudhuysen, 'Leicester's Literary Patronage', pp. 276–7.

alternative attempt to translate Machiavelli's notoriously untranslatable term *virtù*. *The Prince* explains that 'a new prince', who has acquired his territory by conquest, has 'more or less difficulty' in maintaining it as his *virtù* 'is greater or lesser'.[73] By contrast, little if any *virtù* should be necessary in the hereditary prince. Irony is built into the political commentary of the *Arcadia* from the start.[74]

Sidney's historical judgements were formed in a wide field. He studied the history of Spain broadly enough to be able to detect recurrent patterns in its history.[75] At the age of nineteen, when Languet was in despair at the condition of his native France, Sidney told him that, but for his own 'youth and . . . deficiencies', he would venture to offer his mentor 'consolation, by citing from remote history examples of other kingdoms, which have . . . recovered from a far more desperate condition'.[76] Sidney's attitude to the future of the Netherlands, as related by Greville, was rooted in his alertness to historical parallels. 'He willed me', Greville records, to find 'in the examples of times past', from classical antiquity to the present era, the keys to present and future developments in the Low Countries.[77]

A subject of special interest to Sidney was the 'establishments or ruins of great estates' and the 'causes' of those developments.[78] Behind Philip's thinking there lay the cyclical theory present in Machiavelli and, behind Machiavelli, in Polybius.[79] 'Out of the credible almanac of history', says Greville, Sidney had 'registered the growth, health, disease and periods of governments (that is to say, when monarchies grow ready for change by over-relaxing or contracting, when the states of few or many continue, or forsake, to be the same)'. Sidney's interest in the 'disease and periods of governments', and in the historical cycles to which they belong, informs his fiction. There he aimed, Greville explains, 'lively to represent the growth,

---

73   *OA* 4n.; *The Prince*, ch. 6; cf. Quentin Skinner, *Machiavelli* (London, 1981), p. 35.
74   Sidney may also have Machiavelli in mind at *OA* 154/15–16: 'whosoever hath thoroughly offended a prince can never think himself in perfect safety under him'; and possibly too at *OA* 18/18–19, where Pyrocles associates with each other the words 'fortune', 'occasion' and 'industry', the English equivalents to Machiavelli's terms, which are closely related to each other in Machiavelli's mind, *fortuna*, *occasione* and *industria*. There is also a Machiavellian (or Tacitean) taste to *NA* 216/30–4. We might add that, whether or not they knew it, the attitude of Sidney and his party to (i) the growing Spanish threat, (ii) the divided and soporific response of Elizabeth and other princes to it, and (iii) the reasons for and the frailty of England's tranquillity, corresponds with striking proximity to a passage in Machiavelli's *Discourses*, II. i: Leslie J. Walker, ed., *The Discourses of Machiavelli*, 2 vols (London, 1950), i. 359. But it seems to be the Machiavelli of *The Prince*, rather than of the *Discourses*, who is the decisive influence on Sidney.
75   Pears, p. 76.
76   Ibid., p. 47.
77   *GP* 35/12ff.
78   Feuillerat, iii. 130–1.
79   Sidney evidently read Polybius (Osborn, *Young Philip Sidney*, p. 539), and his brother Robert read him extensively (KAO, U1475: Z1/10, pp. 109, 527–8, 581, 645–6, 653; cf. Z17, dedication, p. 4). But I know no sign that either brother had a first-hand knowledge of the sixth book of Polybius' *Histories*, where the cyclical theory is set out.

state and declination of princes, change of government and laws'.[80] Sidney places the crisis of the Arcadian state that follows Basilius' death – the crisis that demonstrates 'how great dissipations monarchal governments are subject unto' – within the perspective of the rise and fall of constitutional forms, 'such convulsions never coming but that the life of that government draws near his necessary period'.[81] For as Greville elsewhere asks,

> Who doth not by the course of nature know
> That periods in the growth of all states be
> Ordain'd?[82]

The *New Arcadia* confirms that the 'lastingest monarchies are subject to end'.[83]

Greville's verse has other words pertinent to the crisis that the misrule of Basilius has brought on Arcadia: 'But states grow old, when princes turn away / From honour, to take pleasure for their ends.'[84] Greville wrote a treatise entitled 'The Declination of Monarchy' (though he suppressed it).[85] For him 'this disease of monarch's state' was a recurrent preoccupation. He observed how 'hard' it is 'to prevent, or stay those declinations, / And desperate diseases of estate'.[86] Robert Sidney's historical notebooks recall his own interest, which Philip had pressed on him, in 'the signs of a commonwealth likely to continue, 2. to decay or 3. increase, [and in] reformations of commonwealths corrupted or declining'.[87] Walsingham argued that the want of 'courage' and 'judgement' in the Dutch nobility, who had let slip 'so apt a time to purchase their own liberty', made it 'most evident that that country is in his declination'.[88]

Did England, like Arcadia on the duke's death, face a crisis, not merely of the royal succession, but of the institution of monarchy? According to Francis Bacon the phrase 'declination of a monarchy' was applied to Elizabeth's reign by members of her court and gave her sharp offence.[89] The language of constitutional decay, though often loose, was in the air. During the Anjou crisis even Burghley, not a friend to conceptual speculation, was ready to argue that the premature death of the queen might 'accelerate the ruin of this kingly state'.[90] In the mind of a Philip Sidney or a Robert Sidney or a Fulke

---

80   GP 84/8–13, 10/26–8.
81   OA 351/4–5.
82   Wilkes, p. 192 (st. 627).
83   NA 434/32–3.
84   Bullough, i. 146 (sonnet ci, ll. 19–20).
85   GP 90/26–7; cf. Wilkes, p. 46.
86   Wilkes, pp. 194 (st. 636), 61 (st. 106).
87   KAO, U1475: Z1/10, p. 45 (cf. title-page – in the hand of Robert's son the second Earl of Leicester – and pp. 55, 437); Feuillerat, iii. 130–1.
88   K. de L., viii. 358.
89   James Spedding et al., eds, The Works of Francis Bacon, 14 vols (1857–74), vi. 30 ('Of Cunning').
90   HMC Cecil, ii. 250.

Greville, such language had a theoretical edge. Robert Sidney and Greville composed their reflections on politics largely or wholly after Philip's death, when the sources of his and their historical sophistication – Polybius and Tacitus and Livy, Machiavelli and Guicciardini, Contarini and Giannotti, Lipsius and Bodin – had entered the mainstream of English intellectual life. In Sidney's lifetime that process was only beginning. The *Arcadia* is a moment in the development not only of the writing of English poetry and fiction but of English historical thinking.

Deep as Sidney's debt to avant-garde authors and publications was, there seems to have been a still more fundamental influence on his historical thinking. Daniel Rogers reminded him that, during his grand tour, Hubert Languet 'guided you through the histories and origins of states'; he was 'the tutor who determined your judgement'.[91] We meet Languet in the Third Eclogues of the *Arcadia*, where Philisides acknowledges his own debt to 'old Languet', who 'with old true tales' was 'wont mine ears to fill'. Philisides' song relates the lessons about the origins and rise of tyranny which Languet 'taught' him or 'recounted' to him. Sidney sets that Aesopian 'tale . . . of beasts' 'on Ister bank', Ister being the Danube and its bank Vienna, where Sidney and Languet, 'the shepherd best swift Ister knew', had become close.[92]

Philisides' fable, faithful to the principles of the *Defence of Poetry*, transmutes history, 'old true tales', into poetry, which in Sidney's definition is fiction. In reading the fable we must remember to tell fiction from fact. The *Defence* reminds us to do so: a man who, reading Aesop, takes 'the tales of his beasts . . . for actually true were well worthy to have his name chronicled among the beasts he writeth of'.[93] Yet the origin of kingship, the subject of the song, was not one to supply 'actual truth'. It had left no evidence behind it. All political thinkers who addressed the topic knew that they were extrapolating, on the basis of imagination, from the evidence of human nature supplied by history and by the world around them. Sidney's fable does the same. The fable makes a virtue, it is true, of historical imprecision, even of historical evasiveness. It compresses historical developments where a historian might want to particularise them. It leaves alternative explanations open where a historian might want to decide between them.[94] It is nonetheless a history lesson, in its essence as true as the old true tales of Languet that it reproduces. We move next to its teaching.

91   Van Dorsten, *Poets*, p. 65.
92   *OA* 259/30–1, 255/15–256/4, 254/21.
93   *MP* 103/4–6.
94   *OA* 256/20–3, 258/2, 258/29.

CHAPTER 15

On Ister Bank

During the wedding festivities of the Third Eclogues, the lovesick Philisides agrees to sing 'one of his country songs', the beast-fable set on Ister Bank. (It is reproduced in Appendix C below.) Philisides' performance has a mixed reception.

> According to the nature of diverse ears, diverse judgements straight followed: some praising his voice; others the words, fit to frame a pastoral style; others the strangeness of the tale, and scanning what he should mean by it. But old Geron . . . said he never saw thing worse proportioned than to bring in a tale of he knew not what beasts at such a banquet when rather some song of love, or matter for joyful remedy, was to be brought forth.[1]

The fable is indeed a startling departure from the subject-matter that precedes it. Why is a song about tyranny sung at a wedding? The fable not only interrupts the nuptial celebrations. It introduces issues – the origins and rise of monarchy, the breaking of the nobility, the techniques of tyrannical rule – that are not raised elsewhere in the *Arcadia*. It is a departure not only of subject-matter but of style. In *A Defence of Poetry* Sidney, though praising Spenser's *The Shepheardes Calender*, adds that the 'framing of his style to an old rustic language I dare not allow'.[2] Yet the vocabulary of Philisides' 'country song' – 'couthe', 'gat', 'ycleped' and so on – is 'old'.[3] Such words cannot be satisfactorily modernised, as their Oxford editor recognised.[4] The archaisms are unique in Sidney's writing.

---

1 *OA* 254/13, 259/24–32. Geron's response resembles that against which Thomas North warned in introducing, and in pointing his readers to the political significance of, his translation of the collection of beast-fables, published in 1570: 'this treatise . . . at the first may seem to many a vain thing' (*Morall Philosophy of Doni*, sig. A3ᵛ).
2 *MP* 112/23–6.
3 *OA* 254/22, 254/24, 255/3; cf. Jan van Dorsten, *The Anglo-Dutch Renaissance* (London, 1987), pp. 72–3.
4 *OA* lxix.

The language is specifically English. Yet the setting, Vienna (Ister Bank), is specifically foreign. Philisides acknowledges his debt to a foreigner, Hubert Languet. Languet is the only person from the real world to be named in the *Arcadia*. Why does Sidney name him? An obvious answer is that he wants to alert the reader to a set of views with which, at the time when the *Arcadia* is written, Languet is identified: the views expressed in his and Philippe Duplessis-Mornay's *Vindiciae, Contra Tyrannos*, a work which was published in 1579 and to which the *Arcadia* has close correspondences. That explanation seems to me likely. But there is another possible explanation which, though it may complement the first, also may complicate it.

The passage about 'old Languet' is a personal tribute, a statement of affection and indebtedness.[5] Greville says that 'that reverend Languet' is 'mentioned for honour's sake in Sir Philip's *Arcadia*'.[6] When Languet lay dying in Antwerp, he asked that after his own death his intimate friend Duplessis-Mornay should record their friendship by mentioning him in print. Before his death Languet had begun a Latin translation of Mornay's *De la verité de la religion chrétienne* – a work of which Sidney, that intimate friend of both Languet and Mornay, began an English translation. In 1587 Mornay published a Latin translation of the book, perhaps the one that Languet had started. It is in the prefatory material that he pays homage to Languet and to their friendship.[7]

Languet died in September 1581. Is the tribute paid him by Sidney 'for honour's sake' likewise a posthumous one? That suggestion can be no more than a hypothesis, but is one worth exploring. If it is correct, and if the standard view that the *Arcadia* was completed by the spring of 1581 is also correct, it follows that Philisides' tribute to Languet must have been inserted after the *Arcadia* was written. That does not seem unlikely. The three stanzas which describe Sidney's relationship with Languet immediately precede the bcast-fable. May it not be that the remainder of the poem was written before the completion of the *Arcadia*, and that the three stanzas were inserted into the poem (or substituted for a stanza or stanzas in it) after Languet's death? The stanzas, admittedly, contain much that is pertinent to the fable which follows them and to the narrative which surrounds it. The allusion to the history lessons taught by Languet is thoroughly appropriate to the fable; and the account of Languet's religious teaching complements material elsewhere in the *Arcadia*. If Sidney did add the stanzas, he may have seen in them a means not only of honouring Languet but of adding edge and gravity to Philisides' song. Even so, the stanzas interrupt or divert the flow of the poem. The fable would follow more fluently from the stanza which precedes them.[8]

5   *OA* 255/15–256/5.
6   *GP* 5/32–6/1.
7   Mornay, *De Veritate Religionis Christianae* (Leiden, 1587), sig *1ᵛ; above, p. 54.
8   Henry Woudhuysen has gently pointed out to me that my hypothesis would fall if any of the surviving manuscript copies of the *Arcadia* – which all contain the three stanzas – could be shown to have been written before Languet's death. But I know of no evidence that they were. The

If we allow for that possibility, perhaps we should also entertain a larger though, I think, a weaker hypothesis: that the whole of Philisides' performance at the wedding is a tribute to Languet written after his death. The apparent separateness of the poem, in form and content, from the narrative that surrounds it could perhaps be explained in that light. Yet what appears to be separateness may be intentional contrast. The poem derives power from the suddenness with which it changes Sidney's subject and from the contrast it provides with what has gone before. Placed where it is, the fable also prepares us for the transition to the darker part of the *Arcadia*, Books Four and Five. The placing serves another function too: it helps (we shall find) to bring the public theme and the private theme of the *Arcadia* together.[9] Whenever the poem was written (or the three stanzas were written), the pertinence of Philisides' tale to the rest of the *Arcadia* will become clear.[10]

Philisides' fable draws both on classical and on biblical sources. The account of the harmony among the beasts before 'they all to changing did incline' remembers Ovid's account of the golden age and Isaiah's prophecy that 'the wolf also shall dwell with the lamb, and the leopard shall lie down with the kid'.[11] The story which follows, of the destruction of that harmony, re-enacts three ancient stories: the myth of Prometheus, who in creating man gives him the characteristics of each living creature; Aesop's fable of the frogs who ask Jupiter for a king;[12] and the episode, frequently cited in early modern debates about the origins and proper powers of kingship, which is related in I Samuel 8. There the Israelites demand and get a monarchy which, as God warns them, will become a bloodthirsty tyranny.

Like I Samuel 8 the poem can be read historically, as a meditation on the origins of kingship or tyranny. But, again like I Samuel 8, it can also be read typologically, as a meditation on men's recurrent proneness, and on their present proneness, to deprive themselves of their political liberty. Fulke Greville explained that I Samuel 8 told not only 'how inequality [was] raised' but how it 'still gathers'.[13] Sidney's fable does the same. Like Languet's 'old true tales' it tells not only 'how shepherds did of yore', but 'how now, they thrive'.[14] Sidney and his friends had watched with alarm and despair the loss

---

hypothesis, if correct, would perhaps lend support to Annabel Patterson's suggestion (*Censorship and Interpretation*, pp. 26, 35) that the beast-fable in the First Eclogues was written after, and alludes to, the act against seditious words passed by parliament in 1581, when the *Arcadia* had been written or mostly written. Some of the poems of the *Arcadia*, on the other hand, may have been written before rather than after the main body of the work: Ringler, p. 365; *OA* xvii–xviii.

9   Below, p. 347.
10 In the version of the *New Arcadia* published under Fulke Greville's direction in 1590, the poem is placed in the First Eclogues. It is possible that Greville had Sidney's sanction for that adjustment: Sukanta Chaudhuri, 'The Eclogues in Sidney's *New Arcadia*', *Review of English Studies* n.s. 35 (1984), pp. 185–202.
11 *OA* 256/22, 464; Isaiah 11: 6.
12 *OA* 465.
13 Below, p. 350.
14 *OA* 255/26–7.

of liberty on the continent, especially in the religious wars of France and the Netherlands. It had been a bloody process. 'For several years past,' declared the *Vindiciae*, 'many kings, being drunk in their Babylonian cups, have fought with the enemy of Christ against Christ,' and have 'boldly arrogate[d] to themselves immense power which is not derived from God'.[15] Well might Philisides' song warn kings to:

> rage not beyond thy need;
> Deem it no gloire to swell in tyranny.
> Thou art of blood; joy not to make things bleed.
> Thou fearest death; think they are loath to die.
> A plaint of guiltless hurt doth pierce the sky.[16]

If Elizabeth married Anjou, warned Sidney and his friends, England could expect to experience bloody tyranny too. It would be the tyranny, as they often declared, of a 'stranger' or 'foreign' prince. The Dutch faced the same prospect. Though generally hostile to foreign rule, they were contemplating offering the leadership of their cause to Anjou, a 'stranger' to the Netherlands as to England. Many forward Protestants expected the result of that plan to be the loss of Dutch liberty, with which they held the fate of English liberty to be inseparably bound.[17] Philisides' fable, and indeed the warnings insistently given by the *Arcadia* against rule by a 'stranger',[18] are as applicable to the Dutch predicament as to the English one. Yet the parallels established at the opening of the *Arcadia* between Philanax's advice to Basilius and Sidney's to Elizabeth suggest that, from the outset of Sidney's narrative, it is the English predicament that is foremost in his mind. So too do the linguistic archaisms of Philisides' song indicate that Sidney is there thinking more of the threat to English than to continental liberty. The stranger Anjou, if he brought continental tyranny to England – the tyranny in Languet's mind when he taught Sidney in Vienna – would destroy the Englishness which the poem embodies.

Between poetry and politics there is, inevitably, a gap. What Anjou's marriage to Elizabeth would terminate was not a golden age of the kind summoned by the poem, but a recent course of history. Sidney's poetic images, which encapsulate a long and complex historical process, thereby conceal its length and complexity. He and his friends have watched the erosion on the continent of a system of Gothic monarchy that was reined by a martial nobility. They fear that, insofar as that system has survived in England, it will succumb to Anjou. The pristine polity summoned by Sidney's fable is likewise controlled by a martial nobility. But there the resemblance ends. The poem, though it is at one level about historical

15   Garnett, pp. 26, 14.
16   *OA* 259/10–14.
17   See e.g. K. de L., viii. 55, xi. 130.
18   Above, pp. 100–1.

origins, is not about historical evolution. It does not tell us what happened in the middle ages.[19] Those are not, here, Sidney's purposes. His subject is the human proclivity which, in past and present alike, subjugates liberty and virtue to tyranny. The means by which tyranny triumphs in the poem are those by which it has prevailed in history and by which it prevails in Sidney's time.

Sidney's beasts are outwitted by the royalty they have needlessly and wantonly imposed on themselves. 'At the first' the king who is created by the beasts affects to rule for the common good, but once his power is 'rooted' he creates 'factions' among them. He divides and rules by succouring the 'weaker sort', who consequently become his allies against the 'nobler beasts'. The latter he provokes into committing crimes which he then punishes with death. He chooses his 'guarders' not from among the martial nobility, 'the beasts with courage clad', but from among the 'weaker' beasts, which are of 'not great, but gentle blood'. Those 'gentle' animals he tames 'by and by'. The 'commons', who initially rejoice in the overthrow of the nobles they have feared, soon find that they have lost their protectors. It is on the 'meanest herd' that 'worst fell'.[20]

The same charges are levelled against tyrants in the *Vindiciae, Contra Tyrannos*, the work of Languet and Mornay published in 1579 and evidently begun in 1574,[21] a year when Sidney had spent time with Languet in Vienna. The *Vindiciae* too traces the origin of tyranny and locates it in the free consent of the subjects. Some of the resemblances between the fable and the *Vindiciae* are in themselves inconclusive. There was a contemporary stock of anti-tyrannical imagery on which the two documents could have drawn independently of each other. It is the accumulation of similarities, which reflect the deployment not only of a common language but of common arguments, that underlines the significance in Sidney's thinking of his friendships with Languet and Mornay.

Like the fable, the *Vindiciae* looks back to a time of political innocence. Sidney's poem remembers an age when 'the harmless empire' of 'senators' gave protection to the 'weaker' beasts: the *Vindiciae* quotes Seneca to recall a 'golden age' when government 'was in the charge of wise men' who ruled with restraint and protected the weaker from the stronger.[22] In both texts, tyrants gain power through deceit. Sidney's 'man' – that is, king – is endowed with 'craft' and proceeds 'craftily' against his subjects, 'hiding' (Sidney suggests) his 'pride' behind an outward commitment to the public good. The *Vindiciae* explains that 'the adroit tyrant', knowing that men are

---

19   Cf. above, pp. 239–42.
20   *OA* 258/2–259/3.
21   Garnett, p. lxxv.
22   Ibid., p. 92. In the *Vindiciae* the pristine harmony is supervised by kings, not nobles; but see above, Chapter 12, n. 61.

deceivable by the shadow of virtue, 'wants to appear to be what the [virtuous] king actually is'. Much like Sidney's 'man' he 'affects devotion to the commonwealth', 'feigns praise for justice' and 'affects clemency'.[23]

In the fable, tyrants 'builden towers'. The tyrant figured by the *Vindiciae* oppresses his subjects through 'fortresses' and 'citadels', which are instruments of tyranny in Sidney's eyes.[24] Sidney's 'man' protects himself by 'guarders': the tyrant of the *Vindiciae* has 'bodyguards' and 'barbarous and servile guards'.[25] Both texts trace what Greville calls the 'declination of monarchy to violence'.[26] When Sidney's 'man' turns on the commons, he 'first' tears off their 'feathers'; then, 'when they were well used to be abused', he 'bruis[es]' 'their flesh' with his 'teeth'; and 'At length for glutton's taste he did them kill; / At last for sport their silly lives did spill.'[27] In the *Vindiciae* the instruments of tyrants 'ravage' their subjects,[28] who, as the seventeenth-century English translation has it, are 'fleeced and scorched to the very bones'.[29] Elsewhere the *Vindiciae* asks the tyrant: 'Just because someone has made you a shepherd for the sake of the flock, did he hand over that flock to be skinned . . . at your pleasure?'[30]

Like Sidney's 'man', the tyrant of the *Vindiciae* attacks the ancient nobility. 'A tyrant', we learn, 'crops the tallest ears in the cornfield; he oppresses the leading men of the commonwealth'. Sidney's 'man' punishes the nobles for the crimes he has lured them into committing. The tyrant of the *Vindiciae* is likewise ruthless in securing their arraignment and punishment, albeit by different means: he levels 'false accusations' against them and 'often fabricates conspiracies initiated against himself'. Like Sidney's 'man' he divides and rules. Sidney's 'man' 'gan factions in the beasts to breed': the tyrant of the *Vindiciae* 'nourishes factionalism' and 'sets his subjects at variance with each other'.[31] Sidney's 'man' ostensibly delivers the meaner beasts from noble oppression, but only so as to deprive them of their protection from his own tyranny, which he then brutally turns on them: the tyrant of the *Vindiciae* 'raises up against the nobles the low-born' and aids his meaner subjects 'in order that he might gut the people all the more easily afterwards'.[32]

Both in Sidney's England and in the native France of Languet and Mornay, the destruction of the ancient nobility was a theme of pressing relevance. It runs through the political literature of the French wars of religion, where it is used to explain the emergence of the corrupt absolutism of the

23   *OA* 257/15, 258/20, 258/2; Garnett, pp. 147–8.
24   *OA* 256/9; Garnett, p. 145; above, pp. 249–50.
25   *OA* 258/24; Garnett, pp. 129, 145.
26   Wilkes, p. 46.
27   *OA* 259/5–9.
28   Garnett, p. 139.
29   Laski, *Defence*, p. 136 (cf. Garnett, p. 89).
30   Garnett, p. 113. The *Vindiciae* speaks metaphorically.
31   Ibid., pp. 143–4; *OA* 258/15.
32   Garnett, pp. 144, 146.

Renaissance. In 1575 a tract probably written by the Huguenot scholar Henri Estienne, a friend of Sidney who may have influenced his views on poetry and who in 1576 would dedicate his text of the Greek New Testament to him,[33] ascribed to Anjou's mother Catherine de Medici a wish to 'root out the chief of the nobility: all such as by birth be mighty'.[34] In 1577 the Duke of Condé, the ally of the Huguenots and of Mornay's employer Henry of Navarre, protested against 'the most barbarous tyranny' of Anjou's brother Henry III, who was seeking to 'render the nobles tributary' and 'to ruin . . . the greatest and most illustrious families of France'.[35] John Stubbs's *Gaping Gulph* claimed that the intent of the French royal family was 'to raze all ancient French houses and to rear up new, bringing all, as near as they can, *à la Turkesque*'. If Anjou got his 'paws' on England, intimated Stubbs, he would 'first dispatch the ancient nobility, destroy the greatest kindreds, and scatter the mean sort into servile, unlearned, and unarmed trades'.[36] England's situation under French domination, Stubbs warned, would resemble that of Rome's provinces under imperial rule or of Spain's present-day colonies, whose governors and viceroys 'like boars in a fat new-broken ground . . . do root out the ancient home-growing nobility and turn under perpetual slavery, as clods, the country people'. Like Sidney's 'man', and like the tyrant of the *Vindiciae*, Anjou could be expected, wrote Stubbs, to divide and rule, 'sowing first some seeds of dissensions to breed partialities in the country'.[37]

The political process traced in Sidney's fable, in the *Vindiciae* and more briefly in Stubbs's *Gaping Gulph* is described too in another work related to the Anjou crisis: Spenser's beast-fable *Mother Hubberds Tale*.[38] Is Sidney's unwillingness, in *A Defence of Poetry*, to 'allow' the 'rustic language' of Spenser's *Shepheardes Calender*, a language which nonetheless recalls that of Philisides' beast-fable, one of those winks that point the reader of the *Defence* to the meanings conveyed by the *Arcadia* 'under hidden forms'?[39] Whether it is or not, the literary responses of Sidney and Spenser, those two clients of Leicester, to the Anjou crisis bear striking similarities.[40]

In *The Faerie Queene* Spenser would follow Sidney in recalling the biblical harmony of an 'antique age', a time of 'simple truth and blamelesse chastity', when:

33 *MP q.v.* 'Estienne'; Buxton, *Sir Philip Sidney, q.v.* 'Estienne'.
34 [Henri Estienne?], *A Mervaylous Discourse upon the Lyfe, Deedes, and Behaviours of Katherine de Medicis* (Heidelberg, 1575), p. 113; Kingdon, *Myths*, pp. 201–2.
35 *CSPF* 1575–7, p. 488; cf. *Mémoires et correspondance de Duplessis-Mornay*, ii. 75.
36 Stubbs, p. 89.
37 Ibid., pp. 52–3.
38 Cf. above, pp. 63–5, 204–5.
39 Cf. above, pp. 11, 193n.
40 Is it significant that both fables are set in August, the month, in 1579, of Anjou's visit to England to woo Elizabeth (Oram, p. 335n.; *OA* 255/7)? Sidney's choice of August, admittedly, may be explicable (or at least partly to be explained) by the fact that he had been in Vienna with Languet in August 1573 and August 1574.

> The lyon there did with the lambe consort,
> And eke the dove sate by the faulcons side,
> Ne ech of other feared fraud or tort,
> But did in safe securitie abide,
> Withouten perill of the stronger pride . . . .[41]

Where in Sidney's fable the rise of tyranny wounds 'guiltless earth', which 'good corn should send', and which instead is plundered for 'iron', *The Faerie Queene* remembers a time when 'all things freely grew out of the ground': 'No warre was knowne, no dreadfull trompets sound, / Peace universall rayn'd mongst men and beasts.'[42] In *Mother Hubberds Tale*, as in Sidney's fable, that peace is destroyed. The animal polity, which Sidney's fable subjects to 'man', is subjected in Spenser's to the ape and his adviser the fox. The ape contrives to:

> rule and tyrannize at will . . .
> And all wylde beasts made vassals of his pleasures,
> And with their spoyles enlarg'd his private treasures.
>
> (ll. 1127–31)

Like Sidney's 'man', Spenser's ape and fox take care to guard themselves. But there is a difference. Where the guards of 'man' are homegrown gentry, the ape and fox employ 'a warlike equipage / Of forreine beasts . . . / For tyrannie is with strange ayde supported' (ll. 1118–21). The parallels with those lines are to be found elsewhere in Sidney's fiction: in his account of the tyrant Plexirtus, who rules 'by force of stranger soldiers', and in Geron's expectation, on the death of Basilius, that Arcadia will become 'the victual of an army, and perchance an army of foreign enemies'.[43] There is a parallel too, or at least the threat of one, in the real world. Sidney's 'Letter' and Stubbs's *Gaping Gulph* both warn that Anjou's bid for tyranny in England would be backed by foreign troops. Those soldiers would be ready, says Stubbs, for 'cruelty' and 'blood': they would hunger, Sidney tells the queen, for 'spoil', and their 'appearance' would mark 'the manifest death of your estate'.[44]

In *Mother Hubberds Tale* as in Philisides' fable, tyranny is established by means of a social revolution. Like Sidney's 'man', Spenser's ape and fox break the martial nobility, who:

> for povertie
> Were forst their auncient houses to let lie,
> And their olde castles to the ground to fall,
> Which their forefathers famous over all

---

41 *The Faerie Queene* IV. viii. 30–1.
42 *OA* 258/10–12 (cf. *OA* 188/19, 266/2–3); *The Faerie Queene* V. proem 9.
43 *NA* 182/17; *OA* 327/18–19.
44 *MP* 50/5–7, 56/10–11.

Had founded for the kingdomes ornament,
And for their memories long moniment.
But [the fox] no count made of nobilitie,
Nor the wild beasts whom arms did glorifie. . . .

(ll. 1177–84)

Spenser's fox uses the tactic against the nobles which the tyrant of the *Vindiciae* deploys: he perverts the course of justice.

All these through fained crimes he thrust adowne,
Or made them swell in darknes of disgrace:
For none, but whom he list might come in place:
Of men of armes he had but small regard,
But kept them lowe, and streigned verie hard.

(ll. 1186–90)

Like Sidney's 'man', and like the tyrant of the *Vindiciae*, the ape and the fox appeal over the heads of the nobility and cultivate the classes beneath them. The lower beasts – the sheep and the ass – are initially frightened by the arrival of the ape and fox, but the fox:

disswaded them from needlesse feare,
For that the king did favour to them beare;
And therefore dreadles bad them come to corte:
For no wild beasts should do them any torte. . . .

(ll. 1075–8)

Where Sidney's beasts subject themselves to the king whom they create, Spenser's sheep and ass are 'perswaded . . . / Themselves to humble to the ape prostrate' (ll. 1082–3). The ape responds with initial courtesy – like Sidney's 'man', who behaves 'fellow-like' to his subjects until his power is entrenched.[45] The ape, 'gently to them bowing', 'receyv'd them with chearefull entertayne' (ll. 1084–5). Where Sidney's 'man' 'at the first' ruled amicably, the new regime described by Spenser 'promised of friendship store, / What time the ape the kingdome first did gaine' (ll. 1206–7). But the passage of time, which disabuses the humbler beasts of Sidney's fable, does the same to those of Spenser's. In *Mother Hubberds Tale* a sheep:

Came to the court, her case there to complaine,
How that the wolfe her mortall enemie
Had sithence slaine her lambe most cruellie;

45 *OA* 258/5.

> And therefore crav'd to come unto the king,
> To let him knowe the order of the thing.
>
> (ll. 1208–12)

The sheep's expectations are dashed. The fox, which has established a monopoly of 'accesse / Unto the prince' (ll. 1201–2), dismisses the sheep and reveals the extent of the regal oppression which he and the ape have built. 'So went the sheepe away with heavie hart, / So manie moe, so everie one was used' (ll. 1222–3).

Fulke Greville's verse likewise has a beast-fable to explain the rise of tyranny: a fable surely intended to recall Philisides' song. Just as the animals of that song each 'gave' their characteristics to tyranny,[46] so the tyranny against which Greville warns is made up of the 'gifts' of its contributory parts:

> For as when birds and beasts would have a king,
> To furnish this fair creature for a guide,
> Out of their own they gave him every thing,
> And by their gifts themselves more surely tied;
> Eyes, voices, wings, and of their natures' skill,
> To govern, raise, or ruin them at will ….[47]

Men yield to princes, observes Greville, 'some poor feathers out of their own wings'. He associates their loss of liberty with their surrender of 'freedom of speech'.[48] The elevation of 'man' in Sidney's fable has likewise ended that benefit: 'thenceforth … / No beast should freely speak, but only he'.[49] With Sidney, with Spenser, Greville looks back to a time of 'poor simplicity', in the 'infancy of time, when much was innocent', and when:

> power did thus really proceed,
> Not on advantage, humour, slight, or will ….
> Words grew in hearts, men's hearts were large and free,
> Bondage had then not brought in flattery.[50]

Alas, 'the art of powerful tyranny / Hath undermined man's native liberty'.[51] Where in Sidney's fable the 'craft' of 'man' destroys pristine virtue, Greville relates that 'man's craft' has 'altered' it.[52] Sidney's 'man' 'at the first' rules in the common interest: Greville writes that prospective tyrants 'at first'

---

46 *OA* 257/6, 257/10, 257/13, 257/21, 257/27, 257/31.
47 Wilkes, p. 65 (st. 122).
48 Ibid., p. 110 (sts 301, 299).
49 *OA* 257/34–5.
50 Bullough, ii. 190 (*Alaham* Chorus Tertius, ll. 20–6); Wilkes, p. 39 (st. 16).
51 Bullough, ii. 78 (*Mustapha* Chorus Primus, ll. 169–70).
52 Wilkes, p. 39 (st. 17); cf. *GP* 157/13–15.

restrained themselves, 'Till time, and selfness, which turn worth to arts, /
. . . Found out new circles to enthral men's hearts'. That enthralment,
explains Greville, has been the achievement of 'our modern tyrants', who
have aspired to 'make will law, man's wholesome laws but name'.[53]

Greville's 'Dedication' to Sidney recalls its hero's preoccupation with the
decline of the nobility and with the rise of monarchy at its expense. In
Greville's account, Sidney raised that subject, with supreme tact, in a discussion with the queen. Elizabeth had sought to end the quarrel that broke out
during the Anjou crisis between Sidney and the Earl of Oxford. In
reproaching Sidney for his obstinacy, records Greville, the queen

> lays before him the difference in degree between earls and gentlemen; the
> respects inferiors [owe] to their superiors; and the necessity in princes to
> maintain their own creations, as degrees descending between the people's
> licentiousness and the anointed sovereignty of crowns; how the gentleman's
> neglect of the nobility taught the peasant to insult upon both.[54]

Sidney would have known what she was talking about. His alertness to the
distinction between peers and gentry, and to the potential for conflict
between them, is reflected in the strategy of the 'man' of Sidney's fable, who
breaks the nobility and guards himself with men of 'not great, but gentle
blood'. It is reflected too in his account of the collapse of the Arcadian state:
'the great men looking to make themselves strong by factions; the gentlemen,
some bending to them, standing upon themselves, some desirous to overthrow those few which they thought were over them'.[55]

It is reflected again in Sidney's answer, as Greville records it, to the queen's
rebuke. He

> replied: first, that place was never intended for privilege to wrong. . . . Again,
> he besought her majesty to consider that although [Oxford] were a great lord
> by birth, alliance and grace, yet he was no lord over him, and therefore the
> difference of degrees between free men could not challenge any other homage
> than precedency. And by her father's act (to make a princely wisdom become
> the more familiar) he did instance the government of King Henry the Eighth,
> who gave the gentry free and safe appeal to his feet against the oppression of
> the grandees; and found it wisdom by the stronger corporation in number to
> keep down the greater in power, inferring else that if they should unite, the
> over-grown might be tempted, by still coveting more, to fall (as the angels did)
> by affecting equality with their maker.[56]

53 Bullough, i. 128–9 (sonnet lxxvii, ll. 3–9, 19–24).
54 *GP* 40/26–32.
55 *OA* 258/26, 320/24–7; cf. Sidney's comment on 'great personages' in Osborn, *Young Philip
    Sidney*, p. 206 (with which cf. p. 155).
56 *GP* 41/1–18.

A less tactful statement of the same case would have explained that Henry VIII, by giving 'the gentry free and safe appeal to his feet against the oppression of the grandees', had done what the 'man' of Sidney's fable does: he had ruled the nobility and gentry by setting them against each other.

Sidney's fable breaks new ground in historical understanding. It points ahead to the seventeenth-century interpretation, and to the twentieth-century interpretation, of early modern English history which the twentieth century has called 'the rise of the gentry'. For although there was nothing new in Sidney's perception that monarchs had curbed or were curbing noble power, the argument that another class or classes had been raised at the expense of the nobility, and that that change had had consequences for the powers of the crown, became familiar only around the end of the sixteenth century.[57] Early in the next century the thesis would be expounded in an influential form by Sir Walter Ralegh: 'the lords in former times were far stronger, more warlike, better followed, than now they are'. The king's writ, argued Ralegh, had come to run in territories previously controlled by magnates. As a result 'the power of the nobility' was 'now withered', with profound consequences for the power not only of the crown but of the commonalty.[58]

Ralegh's interpretation would be famously developed in 1656, in the *Oceana* of the republican thinker James Harrington. Harrington, too, follows where Sidney led. Sidney's fable records that, after the proscription of the 'great beasts', the 'meaner cattle', looking to 'man' to protect them, 'did . . . find, / The great beams gone, the house on shoulders light': Harrington wrote that the crown, having ruled through the nobility in the middle ages but broken it in the time of Henry VII and Henry VIII, found thereafter that the nobility 'had no shoulders' to support the throne.[59] Is that resemblance merely coincidental? Harrington makes a tantalising statement about the origins of his explanation of recent English history. His argument

---

57 R. H. Tawney, 'Harrington's Interpretation of his Age', *Proceedings of the British Academy* 27 (1941), pp. 199–223, at pp. 216–17. Of course, there were those before then who thought that 'upstart' men were taking over the role of ancient nobles in the king's counsels; but their complaints had not produced sociology.

58 *Remains of Sir Walter Ralegh* (London, 1681 edn), pp. 216–17.

59 *OA* 258/23, 258/30–1; J. G. A. Pocock, ed., *The Political Works of James Harrington* (Cambridge, 1977), p. 196. There is one significant difference of perspective. The view of Harrington (and Ralegh) is less fearful of tyranny than Sidney's. Sidney fears the tyranny of Anjou: Harrington, who has watched the overthrow of Charles I, regards the emancipation of the commons, as Ralegh does, as a source of princely impotence, not of princely power. Sidney portrays the freedom of the people as a mere interlude before the imposition of tyranny: Harrington (and Ralegh) see it as durable and as a guarantee of royal weakness. Yet within that difference there lies a similarity. For Sidney, tyranny is 'never secure' (*NA* 169/38, 183/1–2; cf. *NA* 184/35–8, and below, Chapter 18, n. 109); he knows 'upon how weak foundations gilded roofs are builded' (*MP* 96/26–7); with Languet he is impressed by lines of Seneca on the self-destructiveness of tyranny (Levy, 'Correspondence', no. 29; *MP* 60). He is as aware as Harrington that tyranny, no less than anarchy, can be a symptom of political weakness: an insecure or doomed ruler, sensing that he lacks a firm basis of authority over his subjects, may respond by lashing out at them. To Harrington, Oliver Cromwell was such a ruler: to Sidney, Anjou might prove to be one.

was anticipated, he tells us, in 'the reign of Queen Elizabeth' by 'the wisdom of her council. There is yet living testimony that the ruin of the English monarchy . . . was frequently attributed unto Henry VII by Sir Henry Wotton; which tradition is not unlike to have descended from the queen's council.' Has that statement any connection with the observations about monarchical 'declination' made by Sidney and his friends; or with Burghley's suggestion, made during the Anjou crisis, that the death of Elizabeth might 'accelerate the ruin of this kingly state'; or with Sidney's warning to the queen that the appearance of Anjou's troops in England would mark 'the manifest death of your estate'?[60] We cannot say. What we can say is that Sidney's fable, like much else in his fiction, is a moment of historiographical advance.

Harrington's evidence, and Greville's report of the queen's interview with Sidney after the quarrel with Oxford, both suggest the presence, in the thinking of Sidney's time about the historical developments of Tudor England, of a preoccupation with the early Tudor period. Greville's 'Dedication' associates Empson and Dudley, the servants of Henry VII sacrificed by Henry VIII, with 'the covetous, cruel or wanton excesses of encroaching tyranny'.[61] In a letter of 1574 Languet, explaining to Sidney that 'in monarchies virtue is more often the cause of ruin than vice for men of high rank', remarked that 'you do not have to look in ancient histories for examples of this; the life of Henry the Eighth alone can provide us with a good many'.[62] Robert Beale, the friend of Languet and Sidney, compared Henry VIII to the Old Testament tyrant Rheheboam.[63] George Buchanan described the reign of Henry VIII as a 'tyranny'.[64] He also regarded the 'ill' government of Edward IV and the 'cruelty' of Richard III, the predecessors of Henry VIII's father, as belonging to a wider European pattern of that time, when the rulers of Scotland, England, Burgundy, France and Portugal had 'laid the foundations of tyranny in their respective kingdoms'.[65] If there is one historical process to

---

60 Above, pp. 263–4. Sir Henry Wotton was half-brother to Sidney's close friend Edward Wotton. See too Malcolm Wallace, *The Life of Sir Philip Sidney* (Cambridge, 1915), p. 327.

61 GP 116/23–30.

62 Osborn, *Young Philip Sidney*, p. 155.

63 Read, *Walsingham*, i. 440 (cf. 437); cf. Louis Montrose, 'Of Gentlemen and Shepherds: the Politics of Elizabethan Pastoral Form', *English Literary History* 50 (1983), pp. 415–59, at p. 437 (quoting Puttenham, *Arte of English Poesie*, ed. Willcock and Walker, p. 269; cf. Puttenham, *Arte*, p. 294).

64 Macfarlane, *Buchanan*, p. 384.

65 *Buchanan's History of Scotland*, ed. William Bond, 2 vols (London, 1722), ii. 93; cf. Franklin, *Constitutionalism and Resistance*, pp. 85–7. (Where Sidney's 'man' rules well 'at the first' and later degenerates, Buchanan observes that James III of Scotland 'at first' showed 'a mind truly royal', but 'afterwards degenerated by degrees'.) A century after the writing of the *Arcadia*, Philip Sidney's great-nephew, the republican thinker Algernon Sidney, whose ideas stand in a strong line of descent from his great-uncle's and often repeat them (Worden, 'Classical Republicanism', pp. 185–7), would represent England's Wars of the Roses, and the subsequent purges of noble rivals to the first two Tudors, as England's equivalents to the wars and proscriptions that had ended republican liberty in ancient Rome. His account might have been intended to illustrate the process identified by Philisides' fable. Algernon writes that in those wars, which witnessed

which Sidney's fable alludes, it is likely to be the breaking of noble power in the later fifteenth and earlier sixteenth centuries, when England's kings, as the *New Arcadia* intimates, had been 'hard governors' ruling by 'the sword'.[66]

Whatever Sidney took the historical causes of England's danger in 1579 to be, the relevance of the fable to that danger is evident. Sidney, Greville tells us, believed that Anjou – assisted by his 'Frenchified Empsons and Dudleys' – would aim, as Elizabeth's husband, 'to lift monarchy above her ancient legal circles . . . till the ideas of native freedom should be utterly forgotten', and to 'metamorphos[e] our moderate form of monarchy into a precipitate absoluteness'. Elsewhere Greville writes – again with Philisides' fable in mind? – that the 'metamorphosing prospect' of tyranny under Elizabeth would have 'transform[ed]' the English 'into diverse shapes of beasts, wherein they must lose freedom, goods, fortune, language and kind all at once – an enchanted confusion imaged by the poets to warn princes' against 'forc[ing] a free people into a despairing state'.[67] By the loss of 'language' Greville presumably means the end either of free speech, which the 'man' of Sidney's fable usurps, or of native language, which, on Basilius' death, is expected to be submerged in Arcadia.[68] Sidney, for his part, appears to have seen the consequences of tyranny for language in metaphorical and biblical terms: tyranny, it seems, replaces the universal speech of Adam by a Babel of languages. Until the elevation of the tyrant in Sidney's fable, the 'language' of the beasts is 'a perfect speech': Sidney believed, says Greville, that the import of continental methods of government by Anjou would produce 'a confusion almost as fatal as the confusion of tongues'.[69]

According to Greville, Sidney believed that in Anjou's native land the elimination of liberty had been accomplished.[70] The same would surely happen in England if Elizabeth were to surrender her authority to the duke. Sidney's fable is not only an account of the historical developments of his time. It is an alert against them.

'a horrid series of the most destructive mischiefs', 'there were few, if any, great families in England, that were not either destroyed, or at least so far shaken, as to lose their chiefs, and many considerable branches of them'. In 1485 'all the Plantagenets, and the noble families allied to them, being extinguished, our ancestors were all sent to seek a king [cf. *OA* 256/27, 256/31] in one of the meanest in Wales', who was inclined 'to hate the nobility' and who 'exceedingly weakened' it. Algernon places Henry VII among the European kings of his time who, by 'king-craft' and 'tricks' and 'detestable arts', had achieved the 'subversion' of the nobility and had 'perverted' the healthy limited monarchy of the middle ages. After the 'covetousness and malicious subtlety of Henry VII' there came 'the lust, rage, and pride of Henry VIII', whose reign was 'turbulent and bloody'. Algernon Sidney, *Discourses concerning Government*, ed. Thomas West (Indianapolis, Liberty Classics, 1990), pp. 517, 239, 247–8, 575–6.

66   *NA* 253/23–5; above, pp. 239–42. (Are the proscriptions of the early Tudor period – and perhaps too the punishments of noble leaders of rebellions against the Tudors – represented by the punishment by Philisides' 'man' of the 'ill' deeds he has 'forced' them to commit?)

67   *GP* 32/6–21, 116/16–23.

68   *OA* 257/35, 327/22–3.

69   *OA* 256/27–8; *GP* 31/29–32/2; Genesis 11: 1; cf. Wilkes, p. 96 (st. 244).

70   *GP* 58/10–16.

Sidney's fiction, Greville tells us, offers guidance on two fronts: 'first on the monarch's part' and 'then again, in the subject's case'.[71] The concluding stanza of Philisides' fable follows that principle. Of its seven lines, the first five are those which address monarchs, urging them to 'rage not beyond thy need' and to 'deem it no gloire to swell in tyranny'. Those five lines endow the genre of the beast-fable with the function that Sidney's *Defence of Poetry* assigns to the genre of tragedy: tragedy, says the *Defence*, 'maketh kings fear to be tyrants'.[72] That standard aspiration of Renaissance dramatists was shared by Greville, who wanted to 'teac[h] kings and princes how to govern their people'. Following his own principle of warning princes against 'forc[ing] a free people into a despairing state', he gives them advice close to Sidney's, urging 'kings' to 'govern people, over-rack them not: / Fleece us; but do not clip us to the quick'.[73] George Buchanan's play *Baptistes*, that 'poetical draft', as it has been called, of his *De Iure Regni* of 1579, was dedicated to James VI in 1576 as a warning against the consequences of misgovernment.[74]

Thus the first five lines of Sidney's stanza, though making an urgent point, follow a conventional path. Their meaning is plain. The last two lines, which give advice 'in the subject's case', are unconventional. Their meaning is mysterious: 'And you, poor beasts, in patience bide your hell, / Or know your strengths, and then you shall do well.'[75] That charged and troubling couplet has attracted more critical attention than any other sentence in the *Arcadia*. In the course of the next chapter we shall ask what it means.

---

71   *GP* 10/26–30.
72   *MP* 96/21–4.
73   *GP* 91/18–19; Bullough, ii. 203 (Chorus Quartus, ll. 25–6); cf. Rebholz, *Greville*, pp. 200–1.
74   Phillips, 'Buchanan', pp. 40–1. Cf. Macfarlane, *Buchanan*, pp. 385–7; Mornay, *Woorke concerning the Trewnesse*, p. 201; Goodman, *How Superior Powers*, p. 149; W. A. Armstrong, 'The Eliza-bethan Conception of the Tyrant', *Review of English Studies* 22 (1946), pp. 161–81, at pp. 162, 175; W. A. Armstrong, '*Damon and Pithias* and Renaissance Theories of Tragedy', *English Studies* 39 (1958), pp. 200–7; Rebecca Bushnell, *Tragedies of Tyrants* (Ithaca and London, 1990), esp. pp. 1–2.
75   *OA* 259/15–16.

CHAPTER 16

Resistance

Sidney's generation was steeped in the habits and obligations of obedience. At a young age he was instructed by his father to be 'humble and obedient to your masters' and to 'feel in yourself what obedience is'.[1] Fulke Greville regarded 'obedience' as an 'inherent tribute of nature unto power', which 'refines man's reason' and 'rectifies his will'.[2] Greville was anxious to assure his Jacobean audience that Sidney had been a model of political obedience. When ordered by the queen not to sail with Drake to America, Greville records, Sidney was ready 'instantly' to 'sacrifice all these self-places to the duty of obedience'; indeed he might have given 'humble obedience, even to a petty tyrant of Sicily'.[3]

England's rulers and Protestants dreaded and vilified rebellion. In Arcadia, once the 'minds' of the Phagonian rebels were 'past the bounds of obedience more and more wickedness opened itself'.[4] Yet one man's rebellion is another man's lawful resistance. So long as Protestantism controlled the establishment, Sidney and his friends would never have contemplated taking up arms in England. They applied a different standard of rectitude, however, to events on the continent. They encouraged their friends there to rise against their Catholic oppressors and wanted to go to their aid. It was a common view among forward Protestants that Elizabeth's neighbour monarchs were 'tyrants' and, in particular, that Spanish rule in the Netherlands was tyrannical.[5] Not only were the Spaniards tyrannical in their methods: they were, in English as in Dutch eyes, usurpers rather than upholders of ancient and legal authority.[6] Even Burghley was willing to tell the Spanish

---

1 Osborn, *Young Philip Sidney*, p. 12.
2 *GP* 153/14–18.
3 *GP* 45/10–11, 25/1–2.
4 *OA* 128/25–6; cf. *NA* 286/22–4.
5 See e.g. K. de L., viii. 55, 57, x. 443, 525; Stubbs, p. 91; BL, Cottonian MS. Titus BII, fo. 493.
6 Van Gelderen, *Political Thought*, p. 96; Holt, *Anjou*, p. 132; Read, *Walsingham*, i. 339–40.

ambassador that the Dutch had been justified in rising against Spanish oppression.[7] Greville admires Sidney's desire to 'sti[r] up' Spain's new subjects in Portugal 'against the Castilian tyranny'; he is equally ready to commend Queen Elizabeth's willingness, early in her reign, to 'sti[r] up' the Huguenots against the French crown.[8] In the *New Arcadia* Musidorus and Pyrocles, on their Asian journeys, have no scruples about 'making forces' against tyrants in the lands they visit. In the *New Arcadia* too, the slayers of the King of Phrygia are subjected to 'unroyal reproaches' by the King of Pontus, 'as if they had done traitorously, and not heroically, in killing his tyrannical cousin'.[9]

The *Arcadia* was written at the moment of European history when the question of the legitimacy of resistance was most widely and urgently discussed. The slide of France and the Netherlands into Catholic tyranny and persecution had posed new dilemmas for Protestants brought up to obedience. What rights did kings and subjects have in relation to each other, and whence had those rights derived? The year 1579, in which Sidney apparently began to write the *Arcadia*, produced two of the classic works of Protestant literature that justify armed resistance to tyrants. One, in which Sidney's circle took a keen interest, was George Buchanan's *De Iure Regni apud Scotos*.[10] The second, perhaps the most influential treatment of the subject in the sixteenth century, was written by two men much closer to Sidney than Buchanan was: the *Vindiciae, Contra Tyrannos* by Hubert Languet and Philippe Duplessis-Mornay. Between them those works address the plight of persecuted Protestants in Scotland, in France, in the Netherlands. Protestants believed their religion to be under persecution by tyrants. If the tyrants were removed, persecution would or might be removed too. To secure their removal the claims of the political community had to be shown to be superior to those of its kings. In the theses of Buchanan and Languet and Mornay, as in Philisides' fable, the political community exists before the creation of kings, whose powers are those which the people has bestowed on them. Kings, the appointees of the community, are also, in the view of Buchanan and Languet and Mornay, its servants. That thinking was central to arguments for limited monarchy, a principle with which Sidney, or at least much of Sidney, concurred. Subjects, his fiction reminds us, 'have right' in their prince and have 'no less interest' in the happiness of the realm than he.[11] What right have they if their prince becomes a tyrant? To Languet and Mornay the answer was 'quite obvious': 'arms can be [legitimately] taken up' against him.[12]

---

7   Read, *Walsingham*, i. 318.

8   *GP* 54/17–18, 56/21; cf. *GP* 25/32–3, 47/3, 59/21, 65/24–66/2 (though also 32/18–19).

9   *NA* 184/33, 177/3–6. Cf. *OA* 68/17ff.; Norton, *Orations, of Arsanes*, sigs Ciiiᵛ-iiii. Elizabeth, of course, had a tyrannical cousin, Mary Stuart, whom Sidney wanted to see dead.

10 Phillips, 'Buchanan', pp. 36–44. Thomas Wilson, whose thought and language can so closely resemble Sidney's, was among those attracted to Buchanan's treatise: ibid., p. 43.

11 *OA* 413/4; *NA* 325/40–326/1. Cf. Bullough, ii. 276 (ll. 210–11); KAO, U1475: Z1/1, p. 383.

12 Garnett, p. 167; cf. ibid., p. 156. The essential guide to theories justifying resistance in the later sixteenth century is Skinner, *Foundations of Modern Political Thought*, vol. ii, *q.v.* 'resistance to lawful authority' and 'revolution, defence of'.

That claim of the *Vindiciae*, however, was hedged by three major qualifications. First, only the worst of tyrants, plunderers of their kingdoms and enemies to God and man, are to be resisted. It is folly to rise against a prince who is merely 'imprudent' or 'unwarlike' (the failings of both Basilius and Elizabeth).[13] Most if not all rulers have their imperfections, which may be subject to the imputation of tyranny, but it is normally better to bear with those failings than to risk a remedy which may prove worse than the disease; the 'wise man' will 'try all remedies before arms'.[14] Secondly, resistance is warrantable only 'while the tyranny is being formed; that is, so long as the tyrant is still struggling, scheming, and undermining'. Once a people, from choice or necessity, 'consents' to a tyrant's rule, it is obliged to observe the terms on which it has consented.[15] Thirdly, only those men to whom the people has committed its welfare – the nobles, or else the magistrates and office-holders – are entitled to sanction resistance. They are indeed obliged to do so, on the community's behalf. But without their authorisation, 'private persons' are forbidden to rise.[16] A quarter of a century earlier, Christopher Goodman and other advocates of armed resistance against Mary Tudor had argued that, when a nation's leaders fail to resist tyranny, private men have a right, even a duty, to take action themselves. Buchanan's *De Iure Regni* adopted the same principle. But Languet and Mornay, in the *Vindiciae*, turned their backs on it. Agitation and tumult distressed them. They saw legitimate resistance as representing the claims of order against the havoc which bloodthirsty tyranny brings. If a prince becomes a tyrant, the guardianship of order passes to the magistrates or noblemen below him. Independent initiatives by 'private persons' can only upset that order.

In the autumn of 1578 Sidney felt the force of Languet's dislike of rebellion by 'private persons'. Sidney wanted to fight alongside John Casimir against Spain in the Netherlands. From Languet he received, in the sharpest moment of their surviving correspondence, a stern rebuke. First, Sidney's motives were wrong: he wanted to fight 'out of mere love of fame and honour' and 'to have an opportunity of displaying [his] courage'. But even if his motives were right, he would not be justified in seeking, as a 'private person', a commission under Casimir, or to 'pas[s] a judgement' on the Dutch cause. He had no business to enlist under Casimir unless on the instructions of Elizabeth, his 'prince' and, as a lawful prince, his lawful 'magistrate'.[17]

---

13 On that point the language of the translation published in 1648 is the same as that used by Sidney in describing Basilius: we should not depose a prince merely because he is 'foolish' or because sometimes his 'passion overrule[s] his reason': Laski, *Defence*, pp. 196, 195.

14 Garnett, p. 155; cf. Buchanan, *Powers*, ed. Arrowood, p. 93. Though we rightly think of Languet and Mornay and Buchanan as theorists of resistance, they turned to resistance only against monarchs whom they were unable to influence through the conventional routes of court and council. Cf. Mercier, 'Théories politiques', p. 25; above, p. 280.

15 Garnett, pp. 151–2.

16 Ibid., pp. 59–63, 168, 170.

17 Pears, p. 154.

Pyrocles, in reproaching the rebels in Book Two of the *New Arcadia*, adopts Languet's stance: 'there could be no . . . obedience where every one upon his own private passion may interpret the doings of the rulers'.[18] The same spirit animates Walsingham's observation (though it was not addressed to the issue of resistance) that improvements to the Elizabethan settlement of religion must be achieved by 'public authority', the only bond that could hold Protestant England together, and that it would be 'very dangerous' to entrust reform to 'every private man's zeal'.[19] John Stubbs concurred. Though his *Gaping Gulph*, the partner of Sidney's 'Letter' in the campaign against the Anjou match, is an inflammatory document, much too inflammatory for the liking of Languet's continental friends, Stubbs is careful to say that 'private' men have no course open to them but subjection to the royal will.[20]

The *Vindiciae* was an inflammatory document too, however respectable its arguments might appear to its authors and however carefully restricted was the right of resistance which it sanctioned. Amid the religious wars on the continent, perhaps, it might not be difficult for resisters of tyranny to portray themselves as guardians of order and tradition. But amid the fragile peace and order of Elizabethan England, the claims of the *Vindiciae* might touch the rawest nerves of a society repetitively, even obsessively, insistent on the duty of obedience to kings. The Protestant establishment customarily associated disobedience either with the many-headed multitude, the monster that comes close to destroying the monarchy in Book Two of the *Arcadia*, or with Catholics, some of whom, as Protestants knew, were as willing to adopt theories justifying resistance as the beleaguered Protestants on the continent were. (One of them was the Earl of Oxford, the bitter enemy of Leicester with whom Sidney clashed on the tennis-court during the Anjou match.)[21] By the enemies to God and virtue the best of arguments might be put to the worst of uses. So are they by the mob of Book Two. So are they, in the *New Arcadia*, by Amphialus. Raising a wicked rebellion, he deploys – as Catholic leaders of revolt in England would surely do – what Sidney's narrative calls 'true commonplaces': he claims that the 'care of' the 'realm', in the crisis that confronts it, 'did kindly appertain to those who (being subaltern magistrates and officers of the crown) were to be employed, as from the prince, so for the people'. That principle is at the centre of the justification for armed resistance made by the *Vindiciae*. Yet Amphialus makes a 'false application' of it, much as the leaders of the Catholic rising of 1569 had, in Thomas Norton's words, used 'false' arguments to 'colour' their 'evil designs'.[22] In time Amphialus awakes to his own evil: he has, he acknowledges, 'lived to

---

18 *NA* 286/22–5.
19 *CSPF 1577–8*, p. 670.
20 Stubbs, p. 92.
21 Bossy, 'English Catholics', pp. 2–3.
22 Above, p. 160.

bear arms against [his] rightful prince' and 'to be accounted – and justly accounted – a traitor'.[23]

Yet if the pressures of obedience were mighty in Elizabethan England, so was the effect on forward Protestant minds of the advances of Catholic tyranny and persecution, which could not be checked without disobedience. Under those pressures, commitments to the principle of obedience could prove less firm than they looked. Greville, for all his endorsements of that principle, acknowledges that the 'obedience' which men give to kings can be 'credulous'.[24] He is ready to entertain (even if not necessarily to ratify) the notion that:

> Duties to kings they be conditional[.]
> When they from God, then we from them may fall.
> Not without cause goodness is weakness thought
> When our obedience nurseth tyranny . . ..[25]

Intentionally or not, Greville undermines his own assurances about Sidney's commitment to obedience. His friend, he says, believed 'tyrants' not to be 'anointed deputies of God, but rather, lively images of the Dark Prince'.[26] In Greville's England it was precisely as 'anointed deputies of God' that monarchs were held to be untouchable, even if their subjects believed them to be tyrants.

Elizabethan propaganda about the divinity of kingship, and about the place of kings in a divinely appointed hierarchy, left no mark on Sidney's writings. To him, kings were divine only if their minds or souls were divine and if their rule embodied the divine principle of justice.[27] In the *Arcadia* Philanax promises Pamela, the legitimate successor to Basilius, 'such obedience as by the laws was due unto her'.[28] Those laws were made on earth, not in heaven.

There was certainly nothing divine about the rule of the European tyrants for whose overthrow the *Vindiciae* looked. There would be no divinity in the rule of Anjou, or Mary Stuart, in England. For the first two decades of Elizabeth's reign her Protestant subjects had stood to gain from doctrines which enjoined obedience and subjection to kings. But if Anjou came to dominate England or Mary to reign over it, the arguments for resistance voiced by Protestants in the 1550s would become pertinent again.

In the late 1570s the world of Elizabeth's most powerful subject, the Earl of Leicester, Sidney's leader and patron, fell apart. The Anjou match signalled his defeat and humiliation. It signalled the defeat of forward Protestantism

---

23 *NA* 325/14–15, 325/29–32, 441/14–16. ('Commonplaces' means, not points conventionally accepted, but insights of the kind that can be appropriately recorded in a commonplace-book.)
24 Wilkes, p. 48 (st. 51).
25 Bullough, ii. 276 (ll. 202–5); cf. Rebholz, *Greville*, pp. 148–9.
26 *GP* 68/24–6.
27 Cf. Briggs, 'Political Ideas', p. 158.
28 *OA* 319/28–9.

too, reviving among them memories of persecution and exile of the 1550s. Those memories, we saw, surfaced in the *Arcadia*.[29] One aspect of the thinking of the 1550s, the authorisation of resistance by private subjects, had become an embarrassment a quarter of a century later, at least to Sidney's Huguenot friends. But what of resistance led from above? In 1579 opponents of the match mobilised opinion against it.[30] They succeeded: the queen, alarmed by their opposition, backed down. But what if she had persisted? During the 1570s and early 1580s, Leicester built up a formidable assembly of weapons at his castle at Kenilworth, which he heavily fortified.[31] As his enemies remarked, he had the makings of a powerful following in the regions, 'whatever chance may fall': the Earl of Huntingdon (his brother-in-law) was President of the Council of the North; Sir Henry Sidney was the queen's deputy in Wales; the Earl of Bedford was Lord Lieutenant of Dorset, Devon and Cornwall.[32] Leicester had, it was alleged, followers ready to be raised 'within an hour, / To daunt the queen, or true successor's power'.[33] During the Anjou negotiations Burghley encouraged the queen to think that Leicester was ready to rise in arms if the match went ahead.[34] Such imputations may, for all we know, have been unfair. Yet it seems unimaginable that the earl did not weigh his options, as, two decades later, the Earl of Essex would weigh his. In 1553 Leicester's father had tried, by a coup, to prevent the succession of Mary Tudor. Would there not have come a point at which the son, seeing either the imminence or the consequences of the Anjou match, attempted a coup of his own?

And what, in such circumstances, of Philip Sidney? Would not the claims of kinship have impelled him to follow Leicester? Would not the claims of conviction have done so, perhaps more strongly? We have seen how dark the political horizon seemed to him, how grave the threats to Protestantism and liberty at home and abroad, how disturbing he found the symptoms of 'monarchal dissipations', how grim and Tacitean was his sense of the nation's decay and corruption and of impending tyranny – and how ready he was to consider placing international loyalties above national ones. Now, in 1579, his country, and with it the cause of English and European Protestantism, reached a turning point.

To that turning point the arguments of the *Vindiciae, Contra Tyrannos* had a particular relevance. Philisides' fable describes a transition from kingship to tyranny, from benign to malign rule. The authors of the *Vindiciae* saw the same process at work in the Europe of their time. It was that transition, and its consequences for Protestantism, that brought the issue of resistance to the fronts of their and others' minds. A Dutch plea for resistance

29   Above, Chapter 11.
30   Above, Chapters 6, 11.
31   Lawrence Stone, *The Crisis of the Aristocracy* (Oxford, 1966), pp. 220–1.
32   Rogers, *Leicester's Ghost*, p. 17; Adams, 'Protestant Cause', pp. 25–6.
33   Rogers, *Leicester's Ghost*, p. 51.
34   Above, p. 109.

against Spain, which was translated into English (perhaps in 1580), declared that if a king, 'instead of a father, become a murderer . . . instead of a prince and protector a tyrant, then [the subjects] be no more bound to him, but take again to them their might and authority, which they had given unto him'.[35] Yet that 'might and authority', as the *Vindiciae* explains, is surrendered once a people has submitted to tyranny. In France and the Netherlands, believed Languet and Mornay, the crown was seeking to conquer its subjects and strip them of their liberties. Those subjects must act now, before the process had been completed and while armed resistance remained legitimate. The *Vindiciae* explains that Cicero and the younger Cato, and then Brutus and Cassius, had been right to take arms against Julius Caesar before he could establish a monarchy and obtain his people's consent to it. Once a people has 'subjected itself to another's right' and sworn obedience to him, the chance has passed.[36] It is now, in the seventeenth-century English translation of the *Vindiciae*, 'too late' for them to do what, in Philisides' fable, the owl sees that the beasts will likewise do too late: 'repent' of their choice.[37] The beasts, who 'at the first' discern only benign intentions in the king they have created, suffer from tyranny once his power is 'rooted': the *Vindiciae*, in the same translation, remarks that 'at the first' tyranny can be hard to recognise, and urges its victims to act before it is 'rooted'.[38] Sidney and his party believed that the queen's marriage to Anjou would be a moment of transition from monarchy to tyranny. If the authors of the *Vindiciae* were right, the transition could be legitimately resisted only before it was completed.

In the Second Eclogues of the *Arcadia* the shepherds Nico and Pas end a song by presenting 'riddles of the two monsters'. The perplexed audience debates 'what they should mean by' them.[39] The auditors of Philisides' fable are perplexed too, a number of them 'scanning what he should mean by it'.[40] Like the song of Nico and Pas, the fable becomes obscure at its end. The longer we look at its concluding couplet, the more it too looks like a riddle:

> And you, poor beasts, in patience bide your hell,
> Or know your strengths, and then you shall do well.

Even the syntax is uncertain. Are the two lines of the couplet placed in antithesis to each other? That is, will the beasts do well only if they know their strengths, and not if they bide their hell in patience? Or are the two courses which are open to the beasts, patience and knowing their strengths,

---

35 K. de L., viii. 55.
36 Garnett, pp. 152–3.
37 Laski, *Defence*, p. 193; *OA* 256/32.
38 *OA* 258/2, 258/8; Laski, *Defence*, p. 192.
39 *OA* 146/13–14. They seem to have meant something obscene: Stillman, *Sidney's Poetic Justice*, p. 124.
40 *OA* 259/26–7.

alternative means to doing well? On a first reading the ear is more likely to select the first interpretation, which in poetic terms is much the more striking, than the second. Yet a riddle may need to be read more than once. That ambiguity, which invests Sidney's meaning with mystery, also gives multiplicity to it.

The teasing words are those in the last line, 'know your strengths'. A number of critics, beginning with W. D. Briggs, have taken the words, together with the assurance that the beasts 'shall do well', to be an injunction to rise against tyranny, and thus an endorsement of the right of armed resistance proclaimed by the *Vindiciae, Contra Tyrannos*.[41] I believe that interpretation to be at once correct and, in the forms in which it has been generally presented, incomplete. It is incomplete in two main ways. First, in Sidney's mind the word 'strength' means something more than force. It summons the qualities which the beasts have squandered: virtues of which the use of force, if ethically motivated and prudently managed, can be a fitting expression, but of which it is not the essence. There are the strengths of reason and virtue within each of us, which flourish when they prevail over passion and fortune. In England there are those national strengths of unity and self-reliance upon which Sidney and his party urged the queen to 'stand alone' in 1579.[42] So, though the last two lines of the fable are about resistance, they are also about something more. Secondly, the commentaries which have interpreted the couplet as an injunction to resist have rarely given weight to the first of the two courses offered by the couplet, 'patience'. The balance of the couplet demands scrutiny of its first line as well as of its second. So do the writings of Sidney's friends and of Sidney elsewhere. 'Patience' under tyranny is a course which the *Vindiciae* takes to be obligatory in certain circumstances. For Fulke Greville, 'patience' is an 'armour against oppression'.[43] For Sidney, whose *Defence of Poetry* explains that pastoral 'can include the whole considerations of wrong-doing and patience', patience is a serious subject too. In his ethical scheme it can itself be a source of strength.[44]

Yet if the interpretation which equates 'know your strengths' with resistance is incomplete, it surely has a large measure of the truth. To name Languet in the song was inevitably to bring the *Vindiciae* before its readers' minds, or at least before the minds of readers sympathetic to Sidney's political and religious outlook. No Elizabethan courtier could have referred to the *Vindiciae* openly. But the 'hidden forms' of pastoral and of Aesopian beast-

---

41   Briggs, 'Political Ideas in Sidney's *Arcadia*', pp. 150–3. The other principal discussions of the couplet are: Irving Ribner, 'Sir Philip Sidney on Insurrection', *Journal of the History of Ideas* 13 (1952), pp. 257–65; Ernest Talbert, *The Problem of Order. Elizabethan Political Commonplaces* (Chapel Hill, N.C., 1962), ch. 4; Martin Bergsbuch, 'Rebellion in the *New Arcadia*', *Philological Quarterly* 53 (1974), pp. 29–41 (and see Bergsbuch, 'Subaltern Magistrate'); Martin Raitière, *Faire Bitts. Sir Philip Sidney and Renaissance Political Theory* (Pittsburg, Pa, 1984).
42   Cf. above, Chapters 2, 7, and below, Chapter 19.
43   *GP* 154/5–6; cf. *CSPF 1577–8*, p. 670.
44   *MP* 95/4–5 (cf. *MP* 90/8); Mervyn James, *Society, Politics and Culture. Studies in Early Modern England* (Cambridge, 1986), pp. 387–8.

fables at once gave their authors licence and alerted their readers to the exercise of it.[45] Under the hidden form of the Fourth Eclogues Sidney echoed that daring vindication of armed resistance published in 1558, Christopher Goodman's *How Superior Powers Oght to be Obeyd*.[46] Goodman's arguments about resistance, we have seen, were not identical to those of the *Vindiciae*. Yet to a reader searching beneath Sidney's hidden forms, the similarities would have seemed more significant than the differences. In the *New Arcadia* subterfuge is used to introduce the teaching of the *Vindiciae*. For by registering Amphialus' 'false application' of the teaching of the *Vindiciae* about subaltern magistrates, he contrives to indicate that the teaching itself is 'true'.[47]

To Sidney, 'knowing', or 'knowledge', is the key to 'well-doing' by 'active' men.[48] The beasts are told that if they 'know' their strengths they will 'do well'. Are they not, then, being encouraged to be active rather than to 'bide [their] hell' with 'patience', the quality of passive men? And if so, what kind of action other than resistance could Sidney have in mind for them? The likelihood that he has resistance in mind is fortified by the proverbial resonance of the words 'know your strengths'. At least from the early sixteenth century until the early eighteenth, a number of writers and speakers used the phrase 'know their strengths' – or, more commonly, 'know their strength' – in describing threats or alterations to the balance of political power. They turned to it to allude to the potential, sometimes of kings, sometimes of nations, sometimes of parliaments, sometimes of men of substance, sometimes of the commonalty or the poor, to challenge the might of rival institutions or nations or social groups.[49]

---

45 Above, Chapter 1.

46 Above, Chapter 11. The allusion on Goodman's title-page to England's 'present misery', which is echoed in the *Arcadia* (above, p. 189), is accompanied by the announcement that Goodman's tract will propose 'the only way to remedy the same': i.e., resistance.

47 The conclusion of John Stubbs's *Gaping Gulph*, warning his countrymen of the 'perpetual slavery' that will await them under Anjou, may adopt a similar ploy. By alluding to the kinds of resistance which the *Vindiciae* would not allow, Stubbs may intend to remind the reader of the kinds that it would (Stubbs, pp. 91, 92). If so, then the end of Stubbs's tract has a function parallel to that of the end of Philisides' fable. Unfortunately we do not know whether the *Vindiciae*, which appeared at some point in 1579, was in print by September, the month when the *Gaping Gulph* was published (though Sidney and his friends would surely have had advance knowledge of its contents).

48 Above, Chapter 2.

49 Thomas More, *The History of King Richard III*, ed. Richard Sylvester (New Haven and London, 1963: vol. ii of *The Yale Edition of the Complete Works of St. Thomas More*), p. ciii; Roger Lockyer, 'An English *Valido*? Buckingham and James I', in Richard Ollard and Pamela Tudor-Craig, eds, *For Veronica Wedgwood These: Studies in Seventeenth-Century History* (London, 1986), pp. 45–58, at p. 48 (quoting Sir Dudley Carleton); Huntington Library, Huntington MS. 55603 (journal of Sir William Drake), fo. 36ᵛ; Pocock, *Political Works of James Harrington*, p. 198; *Mercurius Politicus* 19 September 1650, p. 259, 6 March 1651, p. 623; [Marchamont Nedham], *The Excellencie of a Free State* (London, 1656: 1757 edn), p. xix; *Diary of Thomas Burton*, 4 vols (London, 1828), i. 272 (cf. *The Leveller* (London, 1659), p. 8); Algernon Sidney, *Discourses*, ed. West, p. 276; *The Works of John Sheffield . . . Duke of Buckingham*, 2 vols (London, 1753), ii. 74; H. Russell Smith, *Harrington and his Oceana* (Cambridge, 1914), p. 144 (quoting John Toland). Of course, the term 'know . . . strength' also has a proverbial tradition outside politics.

Yet the proverbial tradition is not a straightforward one. Sidney's deployment of the phrase is not straightforward either. It has been misunderstood. One reason for the misunderstanding is a speech made by Fulke Greville in a parliamentary debate on taxation in 1593. There Greville associated the phrase with popular mutiny: 'the poor are grieved by being overcharged . . . . If the feet knew their own strength as well as they know their oppression, they would not bear as they do'. Greville's words have been taken as evidence of a belief on Sidney's part that 'the common people may one day realise the power of their collective strength and justifiably overthrow their oppressive rulers'.[50] Yet Greville, like others who use the phrase 'know their strength' with the commonalty in mind, does not hope for the people's discovery of its strength. On the contrary he fears it. He warns his fellow M.P.s against it. The threat of it is realised in Greville's play *Mustapha*, where 'The mysteries of empire are dissolved. / Fury hath made the people know their forces.' We are invited to sense danger, not hope, when Achmat decides to encourage 'the people's rage' and urges them: 'Lend not your strengths to keep your own strengths under. / Proceed in fury.' Achmat soon thinks better of his decision to invite the 'fury' and 'rage' of a 'mutiny':[51] Book Two of the *Arcadia* shows the 'rage' and 'fury' of 'a mutinous multitude'. There is no more sympathy for popular rebellion in Greville or Sidney than in the *Vindiciae*.

The identification of Sidney with a populist position may rest on a misreading. Some critics have assumed that by 'poor beasts' he means the economically disadvantaged ones. Yet the adjective 'poor', which is frequent in his fiction, is for him normally a term to convey sympathy, rarely one to denote an economic or social category. He mostly uses it, in fact, to describe afflicted princes or princesses who are the chief characters of his fiction, or other characters whom we know not to be impecunious.[52] Philisides' fable describes the plight of the whole community of beasts. Why should we suppose that its concluding section addresses, and expresses sympathy for, only the impecunious section of that community?

Another reading is likelier: a reading which not only confirms the presence

---

50 William Drennan, '"Or Know your Strengths": Sidney's Attitude to Rebellion in "Ister Banke"', *Notes and Queries* 231 (September 1986), pp. 339–40. Drennan adds that Philisides' fable 'stands as . . . evidence of Sidney's conformity to Huguenot thought'. But Huguenot thought – with the *Vindiciae* at its head – was opposed to popular rebellion. Elizabethan attitudes to resistance are discussed by Gerald Bowler, '"An Axe or an Acte": the Parliament of 1572 and Resistance Theory in Early Elizabethan England', *Canadian Journal of History* 19 (1984), pp. 349–59, and J. E. A. Dawson, 'Revolutionary Conclusions: the Case of the Marian Exiles', *History of Political Thought* 11 (1990), pp. 257–72. (Bowler does not seem to me to establish his claim – pp. 351–3 – that the opponents of Mary Queen of Scots in the parliament of 1572 reproduced material from tracts by Marian exiles of the 1550s.)

51 Bullough, ii. 129, 131 (*Mustapha* V. iii. 7–8, 90–6); cf. ibid., 96 (l. 123), 248 (note to l. 92).

52 *OA* 12/3, 12/18–19, 45/7, 97/27, 109/1, 157/35, 230/7, 243/5, 274/3, 282/20, 287/22, 288/2, 327/9, 366/27–8, 417/19–20; *NA* 145/19–20, 216/19–20, 221/11, 233/33, 279/27–30, 400/8, 418/13–18 (though see also *OA* 250/7, 327/15–20). Sidney's adjective for the impecunious is 'needy': *OA* 320/29.

of the theme of resistance but helps to show what Philisides' injunction to 'patience' has to do with it. On this reading the couplet, though addressing all the beasts, divides them into the two categories distinguished by the *Vindiciae, Contra Tyrannos*: the leaders of the political community and the led. The lot of the second category is 'patience'. Private persons, enjoins the *Vindiciae*, should 'remain quiet' under oppression, 'should bear bad princes, and wish for better ones; and they should think that such a tyranny is to be suffered by them with resignation'.[53] Philisides' fable describes the plight of the 'weaker sort' or the 'meanest' beasts: Stubbs's *Gaping Gulph* enjoins the 'meaner sort' to 'know your place' to be 'in all subjection and peaceable patience'.[54]

If that interpretation is correct, perhaps the first line of the couplet – 'And you, poor beasts, in patience bide your hell' – will seem a counsel of despair. Yet it need not be. It is so only if, as in the fable, the leaders and the led have allowed themselves to be divided against each other. Such division plays into the hands of 'man' and removes their right and power to act against him, for the meaner beasts have no entitlement to rise without their leaders, while their leaders have no troops without their followers. By 'know your strengths', claimed the critic William Ringler, Philisides means 'be aware that the aristocrats are the protectors of the commons against tyranny'.[55] Though that is not, I think, the only meaning of the phrase, it is surely one of the meanings that the phrase contains. The *New Arcadia* gives support to Ringler's judgement when, in showing 'a popular licence' to be a hideous thing, it indicates that the people's discontent against tyranny should be guided by 'the wisest'.[56]

Immediately after the concluding couplet of the fable, Philisides turns his attention to animals which never lead and only follow: 'Thus did I sing and pipe eight sullen hours / To sheep whom love, not knowledge, made to hear.' 'Knowledge' is the essential source of virtue and the essential ally of the action which fulfils it. The sheep 'know' – they 'couthe' – Philisides' 'pipe', but that is a knowledge to equip them only to follow. What 'strength' can they 'know' on their own? They are 'now fancy's fits, now fortune's baleful stours': in other words they are swayed, like the wavering multitudes of Sidney's fiction, by inconstancy, passion, chance.[57] Philisides' relationship with his sheep is admirable. Their love for him and his care and affection for them[58] supply a unifying social relationship and thus a healthy contrast to the divisions wrought among the beasts by 'man'. What the relationship does not

---

53 Garnett, pp. 169, 170.

54 Stubbs, p. 92. Thomas North observed in 1570 that beast-fables could teach the 'inferior and common sort' how to behave: above, p. 12.

55 Ringler, p. 414. In *Mother Hubberds Tale* the nobility is 'the realms chief strength' – though also the 'girlond of the crown' (l. 1185); cf. Wilkes, p. 118 (st. 334).

56 *NA* 174/14–16; cf. *MP* 95/1–3.

57 *OA* 259/17–20, 254/22.

58 *OA* 254/21–3, 255/8–14, 259/20.

bring the sheep is 'knowledge'. 'Know[ing]' only their shepherd's 'pipe', they must trust and follow it. If they do so, his 'strengths' will be theirs too.

We have, then, an intelligible reading of the riddle which conforms to central tenets of the *Vindiciae*. The leaders may act against tyranny by resisting it. The rest of the community may follow them. If the leaders do not resist, however, the rest must bide their hell in patience.

That reading is persuasive as far as it goes. But alongside that answer the riddle has, I think, another. To it, too, the *Vindiciae* again provides the essential clue. In the *Vindiciae*, patience under tyranny is not demanded only of private persons. It is enjoined on the whole political community once that community has submitted to the tyrant. Resistance, we saw, must come in time, before tyranny is established and legitimised. A people – leaders and led – 'should struggle with every effort to retain its rights'; but once it has, by its 'consent', 'subjected itself to another's right', it must bear the new ruler 'with a patient heart'.[59] An influential Dutch pamphlet of 1580 confirmed the point. A people loses its right to resist when it 'willingly' subjects itself to a prince. Thereafter it can only 'wait patiently', for deliverance in God's time, not man's.[60]

The beasts of Philisides' fable subject themselves by consent. 'All' of them 'consen[t]' to 'g[i]ve' their powers and attributes to 'man'.[61] Heedlessly forgetful of their strengths of unity and self-reliance, they impose the 'hell' of voluntary servitude on themselves. The time to prevent tyranny – to 'know [their] strengths' and 'do well' – was earlier, before the rule of 'man' was 'rooted'.[62] They cannot now exercise their 'strengths', for they have surrendered both their powers and their rights to 'man'. So they must 'in patience bide [their] hell'. On that reading, biding our hell and knowing our strengths are thus activities separated in time. Knowing our strengths – and if necessary exercising them by force – will spare us the subsequent necessity of biding our hell.

The riddle, then, has answers. For Sidney they may soon be of urgent relevance. Philisides, having recounted his fable, concludes by describing the end of the fearsome night through which he sang it: 'The night grown old, her black head waxen grey, / Sure shepherd's sign that morn would soon

---

59 Garnett, p. 152.
60 Kossmann and Mellinck, *Texts concerning the Revolt of the Netherlands*, p. 210.
61 *OA* 257/31.
62 *OA* 258/8. There is here a difference of emphasis between Philisides' fable and the *Vindiciae*. Philisides stresses that the 'consent' given by the beasts to the rule of 'man' is both voluntary and needless: in the *Vindiciae* the 'consent' which empowers a tyrant may be given under duress. But (i) that duress is likely to be self-inflicted, the result of the failure of the nobles or magistrates to act to prevent it; and (ii) elsewhere the *Vindiciae* warns against needless servitude: below, p. 351. If I bypass some of the arguments for armed resistance made by the *Vindiciae*, and slide over some of the distinctions made in the course of them (above all that between tyrants without title and tyrants by practice), it is because Sidney's fable does the same. Once more poetry compresses what historical and political thought separates.

fetch day.'[63] Does the darkness of and around 1579 precede a dawn? Will England find, in its knowledge of its own strengths, the key to the survival of its liberty? To that end, peaceful means must of course be tried first. There is the route of counsel, through councillors and courtiers. If that fails, there is the route of public and parliamentary pressure. If that fails too, what course other than armed resistance will be left?

Let us speculate. Lalus, whose wedding the Third Eclogues celebrate, has remarked earlier that 'who frowns at others' feasts doth better bide away'. What should the melancholy Philisides do at the wedding-feast? He knows that 'good manners' require him to sing at it. He is a reluctant singer. In the First Eclogues he 'neither had danced nor sung' before Geron roused him to perform. In pointing to Philisides' reticence in the Second and Fourth Eclogues, Sidney connects it not only with Philisides' melancholy but with the shepherd's relationship to his monarch. Thus in the Second Eclogues Philisides is 'very unwilling' to sing, but when Basilius 'will[s]' him he yields to 'the duke's commandment': in the Fourth Eclogues, during the 'doleful time' that follows Basilius' death, Philisides, 'who by no entreaty of the duke would be brought unto it', sings of his own surrender to Mira.[64]

If the Anjou match went ahead, Sidney too could expect, with his fellow courtier–poets, to be called on to produce poetry for a wedding: the wedding which, he believed, would be a prelude to the destruction of England's religion and liberty. He too could expect to be 'willed' by his monarch to perform against his own will. Sidney wrote very little poetry in praise of Elizabeth.[65] Never would he have written for her with less enthusiasm than in the period around the Anjou negotiations. Within the 'gilded' 'cage' of the court he could not openly oppose the match. But how could he bring himself to offer the 'song of love' or the 'matter for joyful melody' that Geron deems appropriate to a wedding? Philisides' solution is to find 'a mean way betwixt both'.[66] Sidney – we are speculating – finds a mean way too, by taking up his pen. He writes, with 'good manners', a letter of advice against the match; and he writes Philisides' fable and the fiction to which it belongs. But in the final couplet of the fable he goes beyond that 'mean way'. He threatens to take up not only his pen but his sword.

That couplet is sometimes analysed more or less on its own, in isolation from the fable which it concludes.[67] Yet it is properly intelligible only in the light of what has gone before, of the choices and divisions by which the beasts

63 OA 259/22–3. Some suggestive remarks about the fable as a 'dawn poem' are made by van Dorsten, *Anglo-Dutch Renaissance*, pp. 78–9.
64 OA 59/3, 71/32, 159/24–8, 334/9–10.
65 Ringler, p. li; Stephen May, *The Elizabethan Courtier Poets* (Columbia, Mo., 1992), pp. 97–8.
66 OA 78/19, 259/31–2, 254/18–19.
67 Ringler's interpretation avoids that pitfall. See also Bergsbuch, 'Rebellion in the *New Arcadia*', p. 40; van Dorsten, *Anglo-Dutch Renaissance*, p. 78.

have destroyed their 'strengths'. Arguments justifying resistance answer the question whether we are entitled to get ourselves out of the hole we are in. The thrust of Sidney's fable addresses what is for him a larger question: how we got into the hole in the first place.[68] The poem describes not the removal of tyranny but its creation.

The theme of the surrender of liberty permeates not only Philisides' fable but the whole of the *Arcadia*. At the end of this book we shall see how the fable, even as it departs in form and in content from the rest of Sidney's fiction, encapsulates one of its central meanings, perhaps its central meaning. But before we can do that, we need to bring the public theme of the *Arcadia* together with its private theme. In love as in politics, it transpires, we need to know our strengths.

68   The authors of the *Vindiciae* have the same concern (pp. 350–1, below).

PART FIVE: LOVE AND POLITICS

CHAPTER 17

Falling in Love

Before they enter Arcadia the young princes travel thousands of miles around the Mediterranean and in Near Asia. Their journeys, related in brief in the *Old Arcadia* and at length in the *New*, are a saga of exploits and adventures. They are also the completion of their education. In the princes' time as in Sidney's, education is a preparation for public life. Like many young men schooled for statesmanship in the Renaissance, the princes undertake a grand tour. Sidney undertook one, on a scale surpassed only by that of his princes. 'Even to contemplate Sidney's European travels', observes his recent biographer, 'is exhausting.'[1] He travelled, not least, to understand his own country better. 'Hard sure it is to know England', he advised his younger brother Robert, 'without you know it by comparing it with others': Philisides, the surrogate Philip of the *Arcadia*, who by resembling both its author and its young princes links him to them and England to Arcadia, travels so as to 'compar[e]' other countries with his own, for 'who doth know none but his own, doth not know his own'.[2]

On his travels Sidney sought, in the Renaissance manner, information about foreign lands that would be useful to him, and to his patrons, in royal counsels.[3] The princes do the same. Sidney had, as Languet told him, a quality 'almost necessary to those who aspire to be statesmen': 'you feel the strongest desire to learn the state of things in those nations with which we have any relations, and the changes that may occur among them'.[4] When Musidorus comes to Arcadia he informs himself 'fully of the strength and riches of the country; of the nature of the people, and of the manner of their laws'; Pyrocles is wont to make similar inquiries.[5] Sidney's brother Robert,

---

1 Duncan-Jones, *Sir Philip Sidney*, p. 63.
2 Feuillerat, iii. 125; *OA* 334/30–4.
3 See e.g. Pears, pp. 89–91; Feuillerat, iii. 111.
4 Pears, pp. 95–6.
5 *OA* 13/1–3, 13/29–34.

preparing for his own grand tour, is urged by Philip to study the laws and
politics of the countries he visits, 'the topographical description of each
country', its 'fortifications and garrisons'.[6] Philip, too, sought information
about 'fortifications and garrisons' abroad; his friend Philippe Duplessis-
Mornay, on his own youthful travels, made a 'very careful study' of the Low
Countries, especially its 'castles and garrisoned places'; Musidorus and
Pyrocles, inquiring into the 'strength' of the countries they visit, consult
'excellent men in . . . soldiery'.[7] Military expertise was a principal goal of
noble education in the Renaissance. Sidney in his youth wanted to study
geometry and astronomy because of their usefulness to 'the art of war';[8] a
knowledge of history, thought Languet, would enable Sidney to understand
'the military system of our day'; Musidorus flourishes in battle, being
'acquainted with stratagems', 'especially by reading histories'.[9]

The education of the princes, as of Philisides and Sidney, has a practical
cast. But in Arcadia as in the Renaissance, the practical goals of education are
understood to be the servants of ethical ones. There is one purpose of the
princes' travels to which all others are subordinate: the 'trial' and 'exercise' of
their virtue. The princes, we saw, are 'desirous more and more to exercise
their virtues'; they have 'a youthful longing to have some trial of their
virtue', 'to employ those gifts esteemed rare in them for the good of
mankind'. For the princes as for Sidney, 'virtue' exists for public 'service' and
public 'use'.[10]

In Arcadia the princes meet the most searching 'trial of their virtue'. It
comes from the least expected quarter. On their travels, when they 'seemed
to love anything better than love',[11] they carried the world before them. Yet
their chivalric triumphs, being improbably difficult, are the deeds of super-
men and thus improbably easy. In the *Old Arcadia* Sidney relates them with
occasional winks of irony. He lacks the 'higher style' needed to tell 'how
many ladies they defended from wrongs, and disinherited persons restored to
their rights'. The princes, after assisting the princess Erona, are 'called away
by one of the notablest adventures in the world'. The 'many notable accidents' that befall them between Palestine and Egypt are 'worthy to have
whole books written of them'; but they are not the books Sidney writes.[12]
When, in Book Two of the *New Arcadia*, he does relate the princes' chivalric
feats, he produces, by common consent, the least compelling portion of his
fiction.

6 Feuillerat, iii. 125; cf. ibid., 131–2.
7 Pears, pp. 112–13; Crump, *Huguenot Family*, p. 102; *OA* 13/1–2, 13/31–2; cf. Read, *Walsingham*,
   i. 19.
8 Pears, pp. 25, 28.
9 Ibid., pp. 169–70: *NA* 35/6–7; cf. Feuillerat, iii. 131–2.
10 Above, pp. 26–7.
11 *OA* 155/15–16.
12 *OA* 11/4–6, 69/16–17, 155/33–5.

The princes, whose travels are the last stage of their education, enter Arcadia on the last stage of their journey to Macedon. They are now 'so near' Pyrocles' 'home', and the 'main career' on which he has embarked is now 'almost performed'.[13] Pyrocles' father Euarchus awaits them with 'tedious expectation', 'fear of their miscarrying', 'melancholy'.[14] Soon, it seems, his ears will be delighted with 'all the excellent things' which his son has done and 'which have filled the world with [Pyrocles'] fame'. To fail now, Musidorus tells his cousin, would be to 'drown your ship in the long-desired haven', or to resemble 'an ill player' who 'should mar the last act of his tragedy'.[15]

Yet fail the princes do. They confront a test which confounds their chivalric values and confounds the expectation of chivalric adventure which our introduction to the princes has created in us. Their education, which has been so carefully planned and executed, has not equipped them for the trial of love. They prove unequal to that trial. Pyrocles, having succumbed to love, relates to Musidorus the vain resistance offered to it by the lessons of his upbringing: 'I take to witness the eternal spring of virtue that I had never read, heard, nor seen anything; I had never any taste of philosophy, nor inward feeling in myself which, for a while, I did not call for my succour.'[16] Soon Musidorus succumbs too, and the two princes are plunged into idleness and self-absorption. Virtue consists in action. Yet the call of action, which hitherto the princes have always answered without a backward glance, can no longer summon them. Musidorus declines the chance to 'exercise his valour in soldiery': all his thoughts are now 'bent' instead to his pursuit of Pamela. Philisides' love of Mira has the same effect: 'from all other exercises of my mind', he admits, he has 'bent [him]self only' to winning her.[17]

Philisides, like the princes, fails the hopes that are held of him. Those hopes are high. Pyrocles, 'the greatest hope of the world',[18] has proved himself, by the time he nears home, worthy of the 'rare . . . expectation' that has attended his upbringing: Philisides, 'being home returned', is 'thought of good hope (for the world rarely bestows a better title upon youth)'.[19] No one can have known better the burden of 'expectation' and 'hope' than Sidney, the object of Languet's high 'expectation'.[20] The conduct of his embassy to Germany in 1577, remarked Walsingham on his return, gave 'arguments of great hope'.[21] He was held to be 'a gentleman of great hope, and exceeding

---

13 OA 19/8, 13/24–5.
14 OA 359/9–12.
15 OA 19/10–13.
16 NA 79/15–18.
17 OA 53/33–54/2, 173/15–16, 341/1–3.
18 NA 171/7.
19 OA 19/6–7, 334/34–335/1.
20 Pears, pp. 183–4.
21 Osborn, *Young Philip Sidney*, p. 494.

expectation', the 'very hope of our age'. Yet instead of fulfilling that hope through virtuous action, he found himself yielding to 'indolent ease'.[22]

Philisides, too, permits himself a 'state' of 'ease'. He thus succumbs to the 'deadly disease' of love.[23] The disease sweeps through the 'princely crew' of Arcadia.[24] It turns Basilius' kingdom into 'a notable dumb show of Cupid's kingdom'.[25] The blame lies with idleness, which is the opposite of action and thus the enemy of virtue.[26] Its partner is lust. Love is 'engendered betwixt lust and idleness': an 'active mind' is the antidote to its 'passion'.[27] The 'unactive' Basilius, oblivious again to the gap between his preaching and his practice, reproaches 'young companions' who talk themselves into love 'for want of other business'.[28]

In the political thinking of Sidney's party, we saw, 'idleness' is the partner of 'sleep'. Sleep is a recurrent metaphor of the romantic plot of the *Arcadia*. In the experience of Prince Pyrocles, in particular, it has a persistent significance. His exploits on his travels show him to have 'an excellent strength, and courage to make that strength awake'. Yet, falling in love, he abandons the search for virtue which he has pursued through 'knowledge' and instead 'let[s his] mind fall asleep'.[29] That is the danger against which Sidney, during the composition of the *Arcadia* in 1580, warned his friend Edward Denny, whom he urged to 'keep yourself awake with the delight of knowledge'.[30] In the *Arcadia*, Sidney draws repeated attention to Pyrocles' sword, which he teaches us to recognise as the symbol of a 'virtuous courage' that, until his fall, 'was ever awake'.[31] Before making love to Philoclea he 'had never separated himself' from his sword 'in any occasion'. But when he falls asleep on her bed, after 'the too high degrees of their joys had overthrown the wakeful use of their senses', he is 'deprived of his sword' by, of all people, the coward Dametas, who 'from his childhood had ever feared the blade of a sword'. Pyrocles thus loses his capacity to fight (as England, in Sidney's judgement, is losing hers). As Dametas slips away with the sword, Sidney describes Pyrocles with a phrase that takes us back to the poem of Spenser which, we saw, comments upon Queen Elizabeth's state of mind during the Anjou crisis, *Mother Hubberds Tale*: he is a 'sleeping lion'.[32]

In the *New Arcadia* the travels of Pyrocles and Musidorus disclose the same lesson. The princes allowed themselves, 'while [they] slept', to be 'deprived . . . of [their] arms'. Advised that they should 'stand upon [their]

22 Holinshed, *First and Second Volumes*, iii. 1151; above, p. 65.
23 *OA* 160/17–18.
24 *OA* 222/32.
25 *NA* 88/3.
26 Above, Chapter 4.
27 *OA* 19/37–20/1, 75/33.
28 *NA* 91/28–30.
29 *OA* 153/31–2, 13/28–35.
30 Osborn, *Young Philip Sidney*, p. 537.
31 *OA* 27/14–17, 32/33–6, 47/12, 50/31–2, 124/10–11, 129/6, 228/5–6.
32 *OA* 289/17–18, 273/4–5, 32/35–6, 273/18–19.

guard', they decide that henceforth they will 'no more disarm [them]selves, nor the one sleep, without his friend's eyes waked for him'. But in the *New Arcadia* as in the *Old*, love dulls Pyrocles' vigilance. This time his disarmament is occasioned by idleness rather than sleep. While he and the princesses 'sat devising how to give more feathers to the wings of time', the kidnappers sent by Cecropia were able to seize him 'before [he] could draw [his] sword'. It may be an accident, but it is fitting, that the final, uncompleted sentence of the *New Arcadia* describes an exploit accomplished by Pyrocles, now back on ethical form, with his 'right-hand sword'.[33]

When we want to understand a writer's thinking in the Renaissance we usually need to go back to Aristotle. So it is with Sidney. He revered Aristotle, thought Greek worth learning in order to reach a 'perfect understanding' of him, and apparently made a translation of the first two books of his *Rhetoric* (though we do not know from which language).[34] In 1574 he regarded Aristotle's *Politics* as the work of his 'the most worth reading'.[35] By the time he wrote the *Arcadia* his preference was for the teaching of the *Ethics*, that 'good end [to] which every man doth and ought to bend his greatest actions', that surpassing guide to the attainment of the classical virtues of justice, valour, temperance, friendship.[36]

Aristotle, like Plato before him, had a low opinion of erotic love. Plato saw it as an enemy to reason.[37] To Aristotle it was a false allurement or a 'pleasure', which for Sidney, too, is a pejorative word.[38] Aristotle held that the soul has rational and irrational parts. They correspond to reason and appetite (or desire or passion). In Sidney's understanding of Aristotle's scheme, virtue represents the sovereignty of reason; the appetites contest that sovereignty; the task of virtue is to master them. In that task it has one essential ally: knowledge (and its servant, learning). Early in the sixteenth century Baldesar Castiglione, in that handbook of Renaissance conduct *The Book of the Courtier*, presented Aristotle's thinking in terms which Sidney would have endorsed: 'reason is always overcome by desire because of ignorance, and true knowledge can never be defeated by the emotions, which originate in the body rather than the soul. And if the emotions are properly governed and controlled by reason, then they become virtuous, and if otherwise, then vicious.'[39]

33 *NA* 250/29–30, 273/29–34, 314/26–7, 316/28–9, 465/32.
34 *MP* 88/9; Pears, p. 28 (cf. p. 121); the evidence for the translation is given in Wallace, *Life of Sir Philip Sidney*, p. 327.
35 Pears, p. 28.
36 Feuillerat, iii. 124; Osborn, *Young Philip Sidney*, p. 538; cf. Donno, 'History in Sidney's *Apology*', p. 153.
37 Arthur Kinney detects the presence of Plato's teaching on that subject in the *Arcadia*: Kinney, 'Sidney's Journey to Flushing and Zutphen', in van Dorsten, *Sir Philip Sidney*, pp. 125–48, at p. 135.
38 Aristotle, *Ethics*, ed. Barnes, p. 263 (1156b).
39 Castiglione, *Book of the Courtier*, p. 293.

The 'knowledge' in which Musidorus and Pyrocles have been schooled seems to embody pure Aristotelian principles. Pyrocles, Musidorus tells him, should

> remember (for I know you know it) that, if we will be men, the reasonable part of our soul is to have absolute commandment, against which if any sensual weakness arise, we are to yield all our sound forces to the overthrowing of so unnatural a rebellion. . . . Nay, we are to resolve that if reason direct it, we must do it; and if we must do it, we will do it; for to say I cannot is childish, and I will not womanish.

Love, he continues, is 'the basest and fruitlessest of all passions'.[40] Time and again in the *Arcadia* love is represented as a mutiny of the passions against reason. In Basilius and Gynecia 'passion . . . reign[s]' until Gynecia understands 'how much fancy doth . . . darken reason'. Then, her 'reason' at last answering 'the filthy rebellion of sinful sense', she tells her husband that she and he must 'let reason enjoy his due sovereignty'.[41]

Aristotle, who as Sidney says teaches us to be 'rightly temperate',[42] associates reason with temperance: with the mean or moderation or 'mediocrity'. He regards excess as the territory of the passions. 'All well-doing', Philanax reminds the Arcadians, 'stands . . . in the middle betwixt his two contrary evils.' The *New Arcadia* repeatedly recalls the merits of the mean or moderate way. There is Kalander's house, which has reminded readers of the Sidneys' home at Penshurst, and in which 'each place' is 'handsome without curiosity and homely without loathsomeness, not so dainty as not to be tro[d] on, nor yet slubbered up with good fellowship'; the Arcadians offer hospitality 'though not with curious costliness, yet with cleanly sufficiency'; Argalus is 'friendly without factiousness'; Parthenia, his lady, holds 'her silence without sullenness, her modesty without affectation'.[43]

'Love', acknowledges Philisides in the *Old Arcadia*, is supposed to 'learn temp'rance'. But 'whence', he inquires, 'should love be so learned?'[44] Well might he ask, for the love of Arcadia's 'princely crew', of the 'great personages', of 'all this noble company', is as intemperate as could be.[45] Instead of holding to the mean, the lovers are in 'extremity'.[46] They 'burn' in 'fire' or 'flames' or a 'furnace'.[47] Love 'rages' within them, or they themselves are gripped by its 'rage' or 'fury'.[48] 'Vehement love' causes 'vehement

40 *OA* 19/13–21, 19/32.
41 *OA* 49/22–3, 276/5–6, 279/15–16, 277/22–3.
42 Osborn, *Young Philip Sidney*, p. 538.
43 *NA* 12/23–5, 107/11–12, 27/17, 28/12–13; cf. Justus Lipsius, *Six Bookes of Politickes or Civil Doctrine* (London, 1594), p. 105.
44 *OA* 343/23–4.
45 *OA* 48/10–11, 91/4.
46 *OA* 17/24, 48/23, 105/18–19, 111/23, 203/24.
47 *OA* 35/31–2, 63/2–3, 86/24, 93/7–10, 94/22, 107/17, 109/5, 123/10–16, 184/23–4.
48 *OA* 20/5, 49/17, 122/12, 122/32, 140/29, 171/26, 184/28, 202/1, 287/24–5, 306/21, 343/23–7; cf. *OA* 415/21.

pain'.[49] The lovers 'shak[e] all over [their] bod[ies]'.[50] They are plunged into 'a lake of wretchedness' or 'sea of miseries'; they suffer 'torments', 'deathful torments', 'torment . . . beyond all succour', 'torment' of the 'soul' as upon a 'rack';[51] they endure 'a hell of dolours', 'hellish longing', 'hellish agonies', 'raging agonies', 'infernal agonies'.[52] Love is variously a 'wound', an 'infection', a 'disease', a 'fever', a 'plague-sore', a 'poison', an 'inward evil', a 'lasting hell'.[53] The lovers expect or half expect to die of it.[54]

If daytime is bad for them, night is worse. They sleep irregularly and badly. Their 'agonies' subject them to 'long tossing' and allow them, at most, 'unquiet sleeps' or 'a little sleep' or 'broken sleep'.[55] They lie in bed until 'near noon' so as to feed on their solitary thoughts.[56] When at last sleep comes it is taken with 'greediness'.[57] Yet when Gynecia, 'to whom rest was no ease', does get to sleep she is 'torment[ed]' by 'fearful' and 'wretched' dreams.[58]

Love is not always wretched. Yet its happiness is intemperate too. Pyrocles, having approached Philoclea's chamber in a state of 'extremity', of 'excessive forefeeling', experiences 'too excessive joy' there.[59] Musidorus, who, being 'never acquainted with mediocrity', and having a 'heart . . . framed never to be without a passion', enters, as his cousin does, 'uninhabitable climes of cold despairs and hot rages'. When Pamela at last smiles on Musidorus he is 'like one frozen with extremity of cold over-hastily brought to a great fire'.[60] In that respect he resembles the Duke of Anjou, who courts Queen Elizabeth, says Sidney, with an 'ague-like manner of proceeding, sometimes hot and sometimes cold in the time of pursuit'.[61]

Musidorus shares another proclivity with Anjou. Like Anjou's religion, the love of Sidney's princely lovers is idolatrous. The lovers practise a popery of the heart. They worship their loved ones as 'saints' or 'images' or 'goddesses';

49 OA 117/30, 41/12.
50 OA 115/16, 16/3-4.
51 OA 176/11, 104/31, 86/7, 92/5, 94/22-3, 105/10, 215/1; NA 320/1.
52 OA 220/11, 183/21-2, 105/24, 96/16, 80/6.
53 OA 12/4, 12/12, 15/10, 17/8, 28/15, 28/18, 41/3-7, 41/10, 47/32, 66/10, 91/3-6, 91/18, 94/24, 105/23, 111/13, 160/15-18, 181/16, 229/17, 333/26-7; NA 143/14-15; cf. John Carey, 'Structure and Rhetoric in Sidney's Arcadia', in Kay, Sir Philip Sidney, pp. 245-64, at pp. 260-1.
54 OA 93/16, 105/10, 160/13-14, 181/6, 184/10, 219/8-9, 235/15; cf. OA 146/21-3. Admittedly Pyrocles, who wonders 'whether loving, I shall live or die', later restores a sense of proportion by mocking Basilius' claim to be threatened with death by unrequited love; but in the New Arcadia lovesickness may literally put Musidorus' life in danger. OA 17/31-2, 219/20-1; NA 308/9-10, 309/20-1.
55 NA 224/19-23; OA 115/31, 213/7-8, 214/4-5, 367/17, 367/27-8. Cf. OA 167/21-2; NA 119/7, 225/4-5. There are exceptions to prove the rule: OA 237/11-16, 306/11.
56 OA 167/23-4.
57 OA 314/12-14.
58 OA 91/9-10, 115/31-2, 280/18-20, 367/17-18; NA 277/21-31.
59 OA 229/4, 228/22, 242/35, 237/5-6.
60 NA 308/24; OA 53/9-10; NA 127/11-12, 308/20-1.
61 MP 50/29-30; cf. NA 133/16-17, 401/36-8. 'I freeze, and yet am burned', declares (in conventionally Petrarchan language) the voice of a poem said to have been written by Queen Elizabeth in grieving for the departure of Anjou from England: Leicester Bradner, ed., The Poems of Queen Elizabeth I (Providence, R.I., 1964), p. 5.

they make 'pilgrimage[s]' on their behalf; they offer 'oblation' or 'sacrifice' at
their 'shrines' or 'altars', or keep 'temples' to them in their 'hearts'; they
'superstitiously ador[e]' 'pictures' of their loved ones as 'idols'.[62] Regarding
criticism of those loved ones as 'blasphemy' against them,[63] they are driven by
their own extremities of passion to 'blaspheme' against God.[64] Musidorus and
Pyrocles, in defending their conduct as lovers, blasphemously invoke the
divine power to sanction the hollow casuistry of their pleas.[65]

Love, an offence to God, is also an enemy to public order. Sidney shows
the 'force' love 'hath' to 'change the most settled estates'.[66] The loves of the
princes, who once in love cease 'to be like princes',[67] drive Arcadia towards
breakdown. They also break the rule of public commitment that has been
the guiding theme of their education. The survival of Greece in the face of
the Latin and Asiatic threats rests upon the stability and preparedness of the
kingdom of Macedon, to which Pyrocles is heir. His father and country need
him. Instead he 'divert[s his] thoughts from the way of goodness' and
jeopardises the 'honour' of his 'royal parentage'. He is 'made' by his love for
Philoclea to 'neglect his country, forget his father, and lastly forsake himself'.
He and Musidorus embark, in their disguises (Pyrocles as the Amazon
Cleophila, Musidorus as the shepherd Dorus), on a course of 'evil' and
'secretest cunning'. Musidorus sees what has happened to them: 'To what a
pass are our minds brought, that from the right line of virtue are wried to
these crooked shifts!'[68]

At their trial, Philanax calls Musidorus and Pyrocles 'disguisers, falsifiers,
adulterers, ravishers, murderers, and traitors'.[69] Each of his six accusations is
understandable on the evidence at his disposal. The first two (disguise and
falsification) are accurate. Pyrocles whets the appetite of Basilius and Gynecia
for the third offence (adultery); Musidorus is foiled in attempting to commit
the fourth (ravishment), a charge which his cousin in effect levels at himself;
Pyrocles, ready to slay the duke and duchess, would in doing so commit the
fifth (murder).[70]

The sixth charge (treason), at least as grave as any of them, is accurate. It
summons a dreadful truth: so dreadful as to warrant Sidney's parallels between
the princes' conduct, both before and during their trial, and that of the arch-

---

62 *OA* 15/29–31, 20/31, 67/16–18, 88/10–11, 114/24–5, 137/13, 149/26, 170/31–2, 177/4–33,
    208/32–4, 212/12; *NA* 58/35–6, 268/32–4, 309/38, 387/35–7, 399/21, 441/38. Cf. *OA* 83/9;
    NA 93/8–9; below, Chapter 18, n. 77; Margaret Aston, *England's Iconoclasts*, vol. i: *Laws Against
    Images* (Oxford, 1988), pp. 466–7.
63 *OA* 162/19, 209/26.
64 *OA* 148/26–30, 165/29–166/3, 177/4–10.
65 *OA* 311/7–13, 380/5–7. Pyrocles would also have committed the sin of suicide had not
    Philoclea stopped him.
66 *OA* 119/36–120/2, 46/25–6; cf. Bates, *Rhetoric of Courtship*, p. 127.
67 *OA* 404/13–14.
68 *OA* 19/7–9, 176/20, 120/14–15, 265/7–8; *NA* 109/28–30.
69 *OA* 400/21–2.
70 *OA* 216/30–1.

traitor of Elizabethan England, Mary Queen of Scots.[71] George Buchanan traced the calamities visited on Scotland by Mary's amatory adventures, 'love', he explained, being a passion 'usually . . . carried with a rash violent motion of a muddy and troubled mind'.[72] The 'violence' and 'rashness' in the 'troubled mind[s]' of the lovesick Musidorus and Pyrocles[73] have the potential to produce much the same effects.

So long as the interests of Arcadia coincide with their own amatory ambitions, it is true, the princes display a proper allegiance to the realm they have entered. Their valour rescues the princesses from the beasts in Book One and thus preserves the royal line. In Book Two Pyrocles rescues Philoclea, whose life again depends on his intervention,[74] from the mutineers, and in the process again saves the realm. But thereafter the interests of love and duty part. Before he came to Arcadia, Pyrocles had promoted good government in Greece and Asia. Had he not now fallen in love he would doubtless have applauded Basilius' announcement, after the mutiny, of his intention to resume the reins of government. Instead he is troubled to learn of that 'great bar to [his] hopes' of winning Philoclea.[75]

The descent of the princes into treasonous intent and conduct is rapid. They plan to raise armies that will 'make Basilius (willing or unwilling)' grant them his daughters.[76] Musidorus, as Philanax and Euarchus maintain at his trial, cannot 'deny the stealing away' of 'the undoubted inheritrix of this country', of 'as it were the whole state and well being' of the Arcadians, 'which is no less than treason'.[77] 'No man can deny', adds Euarchus, that the princes 'have been accidental, if not principal, causes of the duke's death'.[78] Of course, the duke proves not to be dead. Yet if Euarchus had been able to watch the action of the first four books of the *Arcadia*, if he had seen his son and nephew shattering the rules of virtue in which he had had them educated, would his judgement of their conduct have been any less censorious?

The love of the princes, then, breeds both private and public disorder. But there is love and love. We are invited − or so it seems − to learn the difference between 'true love' and the love which passion rules. True love, in its premarital form, is shown in two guises, the one Platonic, the other pastoral. Platonic love, the love which is commended by Musidorus to Pyrocles before his own descent into passion and which is later contrasted by Euarchus with the 'ill-governed passion' of his son and nephew, is a union of

71 Above, pp. 179–83.
72 George Buchanan, *A Detection of the Actions of Mary Queen of Scots* (London, 1651), p. 47.
73 *OA* 41/3–4, 103/4–5, 237/17, 58/20 (cf. *OA* 13/35–6, 23/4).
74 Cf. *OA* 126/20–1.
75 *OA* 185/10–11.
76 *OA* 173/25–7, 176/15–16, 216/31–2.
77 *OA* 388/7–8, 400/4–14, 406/16–17.
78 *OA* 405/11–13.

minds and souls, with 'no other knot than virtue'.[79] Platonic lovers love the essence of their loved ones, of which bodily beauty is merely the formal and outward expression. In the *New Arcadia* the 'true love' of Argalus for Parthenia survives the apparent destruction of her physical beauty.[80] Our subsequent glimpse of the married household of that 'happy couple' shows them at a point of rest, 'sitting at a parlour' while he reads improving stories to her.[81] Their poise supplies a contrast to the 'restless desire',[82] the frenzied amatory declamations, and the sometimes ruthless methods, of the central characters.

The pastoral or shepherdly love of the *Old Arcadia* provides a contrast to them too.[83] In Book Three Pyrocles has his way with Philoclea, and Musidorus, who has undertaken to respect Pamela's virtue, seeks to destroy it. In the ensuing eclogues we are wryly invited 'to remember a little our shepherds while the other greater persons are either sleeping or otherwise occupied'. Those eclogues celebrate the wedding of the shepherd Lalus, 'honest Lalus', to the shepherdess Kala, 'the honestest wench in all those quarters'.[84] The methods by which Lalus has won his bride are very different from the amatory tactics of the 'greater persons'. Musidorus and Pyrocles are experts in the artificialities of courtship, its flatteries and deceptions. Pyrocles perfects the art of flattery in implying to Philoclea, of whom he had evidently never heard before his arrival in Arcadia, that his and his cousin's principal motive in visiting the country has been to witness 'the beauty of you and your sister', which has won Arcadia international renown.[85] For, Sidney emphasises, flattery is the easy route to others' hearts, as, in public life, it is the easy route to rulers' favour.[86]

Musidorus' courtship of Pamela exposes another flaw of his character: the 'promise-breaking' that 'deceive[s]' her 'trust' in him.[87] The opening words of the Third Eclogues rebuke that failing: Lalus has won Kala's consent 'not with . . . false-hearted promises'. In the same passage the word 'not' establishes other contrasts with the princes' conduct: Lalus has wooed Kala 'not with many painted words'; he has 'not forc[ed] himself beyond his reach'; his 'love songs were not dainty'.[88] Musidorus aims to force Basilius to 'consent' to the marriages of his daughters: Lalus and Kala are married with the (evidently unforced) 'consent of both parents (without which neither Lalus would ask nor Kala grant)'.[89] The song of well-wishing to Lalus and

---

79 *OA* 20/13–16, 407/1–5; cf. *NA* 91/30–1.
80 *NA* 30/37, 373/19. Cf. *NA* 28/15–20, 31/28–9, 215/32–4, 356/5–6; *OA* 219/19–20; Ringler, p. 190 (sonnet 52, ll. 7–8).
81 *NA* 371/35–40.
82 *OA* 173/13.
83 Cf. Bates, *Rhetoric of Courtship*, pp. 112–13.
84 *OA* 244/22–245/1.
85 *NA* 272/4–13.
86 *OA* 206/26–30; above, pp. 217–18.
87 *OA* 202/6, 306/22, 306/15.
88 *OA* 244/1–14.
89 *OA* 393/1–2, 173/26, 244/29–31; cf. *NA* 30/11–13, 357/31–3, 456/15–16, 459/16.

8   Courtly love,
portrayed in the *Allegory
of Divine Love, c.*
1560–70.

Kala sung by the shepherd Dicus sets the integrity of 'justest love', of 'simple
love, which chasteness doth impart', 'not needing charming skill', against the
'hurtful art' of 'foul Cupid, sire to lawless lust'. It is Cupid's 'empoisoned
dart' that pierces the princely lovers, who are forever 'tittle-tattling of
Cupid'.[90]

   In the manner of Cupid's triumphs, the descent of the princes into love has
been 'sudden'.[91] In Sidney's fiction good things happen gradually, bad things
suddenly. There is no indication that Lalus or Kala has been suddenly
smitten. Lalus woos Kala patiently, choosing presents for her – spring flowers,
a lamb, strawberries – in time with the rhythms of nature. We need not
over-edify the courtship of Lalus and Kala, which is related with the hint of
a satirical smile. Yet the contrasts between their conduct and that of the
'greater persons' have a bearing on the larger narrative. Sidney's tale, if told
only a little differently, might seem throughout what it occasionally seems
even as he tells it: a sorry, even sordid, tale of the lies that lovers tell
themselves and each other.

90   *OA* 245/31, 247/17–22; *NA* 210/33.
91   Above, p. 143.

Yet it can also seem something much more pleasing. When it does so the distinction between pure and impure love becomes less clear. Sidney's Astrophil finds that 'desire' 'oft so clings to my pure love, that I / One from the other scarcely can descry'.[92] Readers of the *Arcadia* can have difficulty in descrying one from the other too. If the Third Eclogues contrast Lalus' love with that of Musidorus and Pyrocles, the difference is less marked in the singing contest between Lalus and Musidorus in the First Eclogues.[93] In the Aristotelian scheme invoked by Musidorus before his fall into love, the supremacy of passion is the victory of the beast in us over manhood. Yet how solid is that scheme? Sidney's *Defence of Poetry*, and Musidorus (now fallen) in adapting it, point out that the ability to discern and love beauty is what distinguishes men, even men whose love is 'lustful', from beasts.[94] The lovesick Pyrocles, likewise with the authority of the *Defence* behind him, justifies his passion by recalling that 'notable men have attributed unto' love 'the highest power of the mind'.[95] The narrator lends support to Pyrocles' claim that his 'desire' for Philoclea is 'noble'.[96] Besides, passion, however faulty, may be no more so than the lack of it. The *Defence* rebukes the 'col[d]' love poetry of writers who do not 'feel' the 'passions' they describe.[97] In the *New Arcadia* lovers who do not feel their passions are repeatedly reproached.[98]

Sidney's princely quartet – Musidorus and Pamela, Pyrocles and Philoclea – are without that failing. They are themselves sometimes credited with 'true love', or at least with a commitment to the ideal of it.[99] Their love, which in Musidorus' scheme is the enemy of virtue, is portrayed elsewhere as its ally. To Musidorus' lecture against passionate love, which derides the frailty of women, who are love's object, Pyrocles replies that women 'are capable of virtue. And virtue, you yourself say, is to be loved.'[100] In Book Three of the *New Arcadia* the gap between love and virtue in the conduct of the princely quartet closes. Pamela, with 'chaste plainness', now accepts Musidorus' love for her as a mark of his 'virtue'.[101] The love between Pyrocles and Philoclea is now said to express their 'virtue' too.[102] If passionate love can aspire to virtue, virtuous love has its passions. 'Even that heavenly love you speak of', Pyrocles reminds Musidorus, 'is accompanied in some hearts with hopes,

---

92 Ringler, p. 202 (sonnet 72, ll. 1–3).
93 *OA* 58/23ff.
94 *MP* 103/29–104/4; *NA* 106/7–9; cf. *NA* 356/5–16.
95 *OA* 22/6–7; *MP* 104/4–7.
96 *OA* 11/35–6, 23/5.
97 *MP* 117/2–7.
98 *NA* 91/28–33, 104/8–9, 454/39–455/2; cf. *NA* 215/29–31.
99 *OA* 58/34 (cf. 58/27), 101/30, 223/11, 232/14, 294/6, 372/13; *NA* 145/25, 146/35–6, 252/32, 324/12; cf. *OA* 96/4, 177/1.
100 *OA* 22/1–3, 21/31–2.
101 *NA* 308/15–19.
102 *NA* 430/10–19.

griefs, longings, and despairs.' In the Platonic love of Argalus and Parthenia, 'reason' is mixed with the passions of 'hope' and 'despair'.[103]

The victory of virtue in Argalus and Parthenia is a testament to 'virtuous constancy'.[104] Yet the love of the principal young characters is 'constant' too.[105] The fidelity of the princesses during their incarceration by Cecropia in the *New Arcadia* is a feat of Stoic heroism. They and their wooers are distinguished from those 'inconstant' lovers who wear love 'like a fashion'.[106] Constancy in love is allied to unselfishness. Musidorus and Pyrocles put the 'care' and 'safety' and 'life' of their loved ones before their own.[107] In that respect their love replicates 'the true laws of friendship', that other 'coupling of . . . souls', at which the young princes, both of them loving the other 'more than himself' and willing to risk 'life' on the other's behalf, are faultlessly good.[108]

The *New Arcadia* in general elevates the lovers. The *Old Arcadia* is readier to tease them but also to indulge them, at least during the first three books, where the public consequences of their loves are yet to be made fully apparent.[109] There Sidney builds a mood of mock-complicity with the 'fair ladies that vouchsafe to read this', whom he invites to share his 'compassion' for the lovers.[110] They know what the lovesick princes and princesses are suffering; Sidney knows it; we know it. Time and again he winks at readers who 'know' or who, 'untold, can guess what love means' and who will 'easily fall to compassion of them who taste of like misery'.[111] However many 'philosophy precepts' are levelled against it, love belongs to 'the common course of humanity'.[112] Sidney's accounts of the discoveries and uncertainties and pangs and desolations of love, especially of first love or of love in its early stages, endorse that humanity and appeal to our recognition of it. The first mention of love in the *Arcadia* is such an appeal: Pyrocles' 'heart . . . received straight a cruel impression of that wonderful passion which to be defined is impossible, by reason no words reach near to the strange nature of it. . . . It is called love.'[113] What is human may be avoidable only at a cost to humanity. If love is an 'evil', it transpires, 'he must fly from himself that will shun his evil'.[114] At the least there is a case for charitable constructions of love. The lovers defend love both as a 'venial' fault and as 'a passion far more easily reprehended than refrained'.[115]

103   *OA* 22/24–6; *NA* 28/17–22.
104   *NA* 30/38–9; cf. *NA* 29/34, 43/35–7.
105   *OA* 233/20; *NA* 430/27.
106   *NA* 91/32–3, 104/8–9.
107   *OA* 370/26–8, 378/3.
108   *OA* 12/31, 168/16–17, 18/27, 28/21–2, 312/33–4, 373/18–19. Cf. *OA* 174/1–2, 174/20–30; *NA* 269/10–11.
109   Cf. below, Appendix A.
110   *OA* 27/21, 39/17–18, 40/21, 45/33–4, 55/1, 55/14, 227/11, 242/30, 243/9.
111   *OA* 43/1–3, 57/19, 88/17, 211/31–4, 230/7.
112   *OA* 43/3–4.
113   *OA* 11/37–12/3.
114   *OA* 49/20–1.
115   *OA* 402/20–4, 392/27–8; cf. *OA* 342/26, 343/28, 394/28–9.

Musidorus, before he succumbs, is 'high in the pulpit against love'. He warns Pyrocles against it like 'a schoolmaster'. 'A mind well trained and long exercised in virtue, my sweet and worthy cousin,' he begins, 'doth not easily change any course it once undertakes.'[116] Has he been talking like that all through Greece and Near Asia? Soon he will be wiser. He will learn that 'those pains must be felt before they be understood'; that 'all is but lip-wisdom which wants experience'; that, as Pyrocles has it, 'none can speak of a wound [of love] with skill, if he have not a wound felt'.[117] Alongside Sidney's creed of virtue, which tells mankind what qualities it ought to have, there lies his knowledge of mankind as it is and is bound to be. It is the 'nature of man', Sidney repeatedly indicates, to act 'according to' the 'nature' of his passions or humours or characters: to the 'nature' of 'sorrow', 'pain', 'anger', 'ambition'.[118] The demands of virtue, which are supposed to bring out the best in our nature, can be at odds with our nature. Virtue enjoins altruism: yet Sidney understands our natural 'selfness of affection'.[119] He knows that our compassion for others can derive from the reflections which we instinctively find, in their misfortunes, of our own.[120] He understands that in grieving for death we grieve, no less 'naturally', for ourselves.[121]

The 'nature of love', as of the other passions, has its own claims to assert.[122] They may be unanswerable. The language of virtue spoken by the princely lovers is deflated by a series of comic metaphors and similes which establish the lovers' subjection to nature's biological imperative. Philoclea's 'excellent fair hair' is 'a net indeed to have caught the wildest disposition'; as Pyrocles' 'prey' she is 'like a young fawn . . . coming in the wind of the hunters'; Pamela's warning to her against love's snares comes 'too late to clip the bird's wings'.[123] When Musidorus, pursuing Pamela, seeks by a love-song to 'bring her to a dull yielding-over her forces', she tries to divert his attentions 'lest in parley the castle might be given up'.[124] Metaphor gets us to the point. Pyrocles, having explained his lovelorn abstractedness to Musidorus in eva-sively edifying terms, then 'brok[e] the ice' and 'made the breach' so as to put his real preoccupations across.[125] In reporting the biological imperative within his characters, Sidney colludes with the same imperative within his readers. We are invited to savour the moment when Philoclea and Pyrocles, pressed next to each other in 'imparadised neighbourhood' in a coach, make the blushing tactile discoveries of adolescence.[126] The imagination not only of

116 *OA* 42/16, 168/28, 13/9–11.
117 *OA* 105/29; *NA* 106/4–5; *OA* 85/3; cf. *OA* 72/19–20.
118 *OA* 129/16–17, 314/13–15, 368/16; *NA* 178/10–11, 160/9; cf. *NA* 178/33–6.
119 *OA* 133/34.
120 *OA* 43/2–5, 152/21–2.
121 *OA* 283/12–15, 327/26–328/2.
122 *OA* 303/15–16. Cf. *OA* 11/37–8; *NA* 152/3–4.
123 *OA* 37/24–6, 47/17; *NA* 144/8–9, 152/6–7.
124 *OA* 107/1–2, 107/28–9; cf. *OA* 121/19–20.
125 *OA* 17/23, 18/5.
126 *NA* 141/25–142/2.

Pyrocles, but of 'any man', is tempted to venture beneath Philoclea's filmy garment.[127]

At such moments love could not look more innocuous. Arcadia for long seems to be a holiday world, and we seem to be on holiday too. Yet love, the delight of that world, shatters it. But for Euarchus, the *deus ex machina*, it would shatter Arcadia. The 'delight' which is Sidney's declared instrument of instruction depends upon our readiness, which he encourages, to identify with the lovers. Yet that identification lures us into connivance with their deceit and with the destruction it causes. The fair ladies, instruments of our complicity, slip away when destruction looms.[128]

Geron's fellow shepherd Dicus, 'whether for certain mischances of his own, or out of a better judgement, which saw the bottom of things, did . . . detest and hate love'.[129] Sidney leaves us to choose, if we can, between those two explanations. There are conflicting signposts at almost every turn of his narrative.

Pyrocles and Philoclea, and Musidorus and Pamela, agree to marry. Pamela argues that her and her lover's 'consciences' would be 'stained' if they made love before marriage, or at least (for the passage is ambiguous) before their engagement had been rightfully recognised.[130] Philoclea and Pyrocles act on different principles. By doing so they bring Sidney's debate about love into its sharpest focus.

Philoclea gives her 'consent' to her lovemaking with Pyrocles. She thinks of it as 'our virtuous action', as the 'innocencies' and 'solemnities' of 'our virtuous marriage'.[131] Pyrocles attests, and the narrator confirms, that her 'soul' remains 'innocent' and her 'virtue' 'unstained'.[132] Sidney leaves Pyrocles and Philoclea sleeping at the end of Book Three, 'lest my pen might seem to grudge at the due bliss of those poor lovers'. Who indeed could grudge that 'mutual sleep' into which, as Sidney's benign irony discloses, they have fallen, 'yet not forgetting with viny embracements to give any eye a perfect model of affection'?[133]

The answer, of course, is that the law grudges it and that Pyrocles' father grudges it. When Pyrocles awakes he belatedly 'remember[s]' what he must have learned before he set eyes on Philoclea, in the days when, his mind still fixed on his preparation for public service, he noted the laws and customs of

---

127 *OA* 33/28–9, 37/26–9, 47/29–32.
128 They are addressed frequently in Book One and, though absent in Book Two, return in Book Three. We do not hear of them in Books Four and Five (or in the *New Arcadia*, where in any case the narrator who has conversed with them rarely announces himself).
129 *OA* 64/11–13.
130 *OA* 197/7–8.
131 *OA* 299/14, 299/19, 304/2–3.
132 *OA* 290/14, 290/25–6, 379/34, 380/12. Pyrocles, admittedly, pretends for Philoclea's sake that he 'offered force to her' (*OA* 394/27–8). Yet neither he nor she sees anything to repent in their communion.
133 *OA* 243/4–5, 273/9–11.

the countries he visited. He recalls 'the cruelty of the Arcadian laws which, without exception, did condemn all to death who were found in act of marriage without solemnity of marriage'. In Sidney's writing, 'cruelty' is a word normally conveying strong and unqualified disapproval. Is it so here? Pyrocles 'saw' that 'the weak judgement of man would condemn' his and his partner's lovemaking 'as a death-deserving vice'. His prediction is apparently borne out, for Euarchus, who condemns him to death, has on his own admission conducted the trial as 'a creature whose reason is often darkened with error'.[134]

Yet Euarchus' errors are mistakes of fact, not, as far as Sidney allows us to conclude, of principle. He has two main arguments. First, the law is the law and must be upheld if it is to be respected. Secondly, what the princes call their love is not 'a right love', which is faithful to the virtue from which it springs, but an 'unbridled desire'. Philanax, who has claimed that there was no 'bridle' to Pyrocles' 'lust', thus seems to be vindicated. Admittedly Euarchus and Philanax are both deceived by the version of events with which Pyrocles protects Philoclea; it was to deceive them that Pyrocles himself called his conduct 'unbridled'. Yet the death penalty does not cover only the rape or attempted rape of which Pyrocles falsely charges himself. It extends, Euarchus explains, to 'the wickedness of lust . . . though both consent'.[135]

Euarchus condemns Pyrocles to be 'thrown down from a high tower to the earth – a death', he declares, 'which doth no way exceed the proportion of the trespass'.[136] Philoclea, being judged by Euarchus' 'wisdom' to be 'not altogether faultless', is sentenced 'all her life long [to] be kept prisoner' in a convent, there to expiate the 'honour of her house'.[137] Such is to be the price of those viny embracements. Sidney has jolted us into observing the opposition between the principles he portrays: between Pyrocles' and Philoclea's belief in their own innocence and Euarchus' unbending commitment both to the spirit and to the letter of the law. The opposition is not resolved. The awakening of Basilius clears all the accused characters of murder or complicity in murder. It does nothing to remove or excuse the sexual offences which Euarchus has condemned in his son and nephew, and about which the amnesty that ends the story keeps a loud silence.

How are we to respond to the tension in the *Arcadia* between the criticisms and claims of erotic love? Is Euarchus right, or are his death-sentences a denial of life in a larger sense too? Pyrocles and Philoclea appeal to the language of instinct and experience, Euarchus to 'philosophy precepts'. Is Sidney's humanity at war with his philosophy?

---

134   OA 290/7–9, 290/24–5, 365/14–15.
135   OA 407/1–5, 406/30–1, 390/20, 301/36, 406/4–5.
136   OA 405/28–30.
137   OA 380/32–381/2.

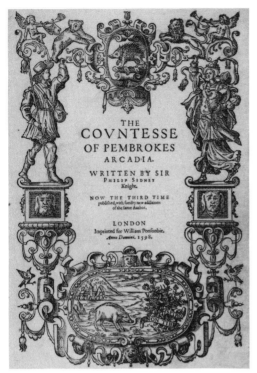

9 From the title-page of *The Countess of Pembroke's Arcadia*. The porcupine (top-centre) is the Sidney family crest.

He certainly seems to have been at war with himself. Sidney is older than his princely heroes but, if Philisides is a measure of him, no better at commanding his emotions or at resisting distractions from public duty. The title-page of the composite *Arcadia* of 1593 associates Musidorus with the Dudley arms and Pyrocles with the Sidney arms.[138] 'The two brave knights, Musidorus and Pyrocles', observed Sidney's friend Gabriel Harvey, are 'combined in one excellent knight, Sir Philip Sidney'.[139] Early in the *Old Arcadia* Musidorus, distressed by the effects of love on Pyrocles without yet knowing their cause, discerns, as he tells him, 'I will not say an alteration, but a relenting, truly, and slacking of [your] main career'. The 'main career' of Sidney has relented and slacked too; it may even be altering. Pyrocles, thinks his cousin, has abandoned 'action' for 'contemplation', that 'glorious title to idleness': Sidney, for whom virtue consists in action, retreated from it in his 'idlest times' and composed 'this idle work of mine'.[140] Sidney's friends, he was told by Languet, feared lest 'the sweetness of your lengthened retirements may somewhat relax the vigorous energy with which you used to rise to noble undertakings, and a love of ease, which you once despised, creep by degrees over your spirit'.[141]

138 *OA* xlviii–xlix.
139 Quoted by Hamilton, *Sir Philip Sidney*, p. 125.
140 *OA* 13/23–4, 16/14–15; above, p. 65.
141 Pears, p. 183.

On his youthful travels, Languet reminded him, Sidney 'used sometimes to say' that he was 'by nature entirely averse to the excitement and fascinations of a court, and that when you returned home, nothing would delight you more than to pass your life with your friends in dignified ease'. In 1578 Languet was 'especially sorry' to learn from Sidney of the younger man's 'desire to fly from the light of your court and betake yourself to the privacy of secluded places to escape the tempest of affairs by which statesmen are generally harassed'. Pyrocles, postponing his journey to Macedon, 'neglect[s] his country': in 1580, after Sidney had spent several months in Wiltshire writing the *Arcadia*, Languet enjoined him to 'consider well . . . how far it is honourable to lurk where you are,' 'in that hiding place of yours', 'whilst your country is imploring the aid and support of her sons'.[142] Musidorus lurks too. He − or a figure with whom he identifies himself − exchanges 'the pomps of a palace' for woods and open sky; the lovesick Philisides, another lurker, has shunned 'courtly pomps'; Pyrocles, lurking too, turns his back on the 'pomp' of power.[143] Musidorus' admonition to Pyrocles − 'A mind well trained and long exercised in virtue . . . doth not easily change any course it once undertakes' − has its unmistakable counterpart in Sidney's experience. Languet, that anxious monitor of his development, had long pressed him to 'adhere steadfastly' to the 'excellent intentions' which had already enabled his 'virtue' to bear 'such sweet fruit'.[144] In 1578−80 Languet's injunctions rained upon him: let him not leave court but 'stand firm on your principle and strength of mind'; let him not 'stray from the good path which hitherto you have trodden so steadfastly'; let him persist, with 'constancy', in 'your good intentions'; let him not tire of 'that toilsome path which leads to virtue, which you formerly pursued with so much earnestness'.[145]

The *Arcadia* removed Sidney from the life of action. It was written in a language Languet did not know, and belonged to a territory of the imagination which the scholar−statesman had not entered.[146] 'Lurking' in the country in 1580, Sidney was free of what has been called Languet's 'oppressive paternalism'.[147] He was free of something more: of that austere, manly philosophy to which not only Languet but England's forward Protestants subscribed. Sidney is far from rejecting that philosophy. No one can expound it more beautifully or feelingly. Yet so much of what he expounds has been taught him by old or older men. Like theirs, his political thinking is rooted in that of the 1550s, the time when he was born. How old a head was expected to sit on such young shoulders! Is it an accident that the *Arcadia*

---

142   Ibid., pp. 184, 155, 185.
143   *OA* 86/7−15, 335/27−8, 228/28−9.
144   Osborn, *Young Philip Sidney*, p. 149.
145   Pears, pp. 155, 166, 183. (Languet's implication that he does not share the anxieties about Sidney mentioned in that last letter is unconvincing.)
146   Duncan-Jones, *Sir Philip Sidney*, pp. 76, 143; Pears, p. 89.
147   Buxton, *Sir Philip Sidney*, p. 62.

gives the princes the scope for adolescence that Sidney himself has been denied? Once Musidorus has stopped talking like Languet, the argument about the legitimacy of love becomes a conflict of generations. The shepherd Geron, whose 'age' has 'taken from him both the thoughts and fruits' of love, derides it as a 'toy' and warns Philisides sharply against it. 'O gods,' protests Philisides, 'how long this old fool hath annoyed / My wearied ears!'[148]

Philisides and Pyrocles know that they have failed the expectation held of them, as Sidney must have known the failure of the expectation held of him. 'Behold here before your eyes', Pyrocles exclaims to Philoclea as he remembers his obligations to his father and country, 'Pyrocles prince of Macedon, whom you only have brought to this fall of fortune and unused metamorphosis.'[149] Yet when his 'imagination' looks forward to the 'blissfulness' that awaits him in Philoclea's chamber, he sees the world in a new way: 'All the great estate of his father seemed unto him but a trifling pomp, whose good stands in other men's conceit, in comparison of the true comfort he found in the depth of his mind.'[150] Must there not have been some moment in Sidney's life to which that insight corresponds? Is the awakening of his powers as a writer separable from his discovery of a world of feeling and self-realisation which the prescriptions of public life do not permit and cannot accommodate? The private world needs and allows the qualities of leisure and softness, which public virtue prohibits. Can Sidney, so highly strung, grow only by allowing his mind to do what, in March 1578, that bleak month for the forward Protestant cause, he admits to Languet that it is doing, and what it can only do outside public life: to 'relax without any reluctance'? 'In your letters', he had written to Languet in 1574, 'I fancy I see a picture of the age in which we live: an age that resembles a bow too long bent; it must be unstrung or it will break.'[151] What was true of the age might be true of Sidney too. It is true of Pyrocles, whose reply to his cousin's charge that he is straying from the path of virtue is that 'the mind itself must, like other things, sometimes be unbent, or else it will be either weakened or broken'.[152]

Sidney's ethical system is Ciceronian, sometimes sternly so. But Cicero himself is not always stern. Richard McCoy writes of the 'yearning for some respite from the stringencies of submission and self-control' that became 'a concern' for Sidney and 'other young aristocrats of the period'. He aptly quotes the response of Henry Wriothesley, the young Earl of Southampton, when assigned in 1586 a Latin theme on 'the arduous studies of youth'. The response contains a plea:

---

148   *OA* 64/8–10, 74/1–2. The eternal conflict between old and young is evenly handled at *NA* 160/14–16.

149   *OA* 120/12–15.

150   *OA* 228/26–229/1.

151   Pears, pp. 143, 36.

152   *OA* 14/27–8; cf. Rudenstine, *Sidney's Poetic Development*, ch. 2.

young men may, with justice, relax their minds and give themselves up to enjoyment . . . .. Cicero . . . says (in his speech in defence of M. Caelius) 'Let some allowance be made for a person's years, let youth be allowed greater freedom, let not everything be denied to the passions. Let not that severe and unbending reason always prevail, let desire and pleasure sometimes triumph over reason.'[153]

On the path to virtue, urge its custodians, not a moment must be wasted. That is why Sidney, as Languet warns him, must guard against the 'many temptations to waste time' at court, courts being 'by no means a frugal economy of time'.[154] Sidney in turn counselled his friend Edward Denny not to 'lose your time' and thus 'lose so much of your life', for 'the consideration and marking of [life] stands only in time'.[155] The shepherds of the *Arcadia*, who should be attending to their pastoral (and thus public) duties, 'spend their days' and 'pass [their] time' in trifles, 'feel[ing]' too 'small account of time';[156] Basilius, having abandoned his kingdom, did 'pass great time in writing of verses';[157] Musidorus, again sounding like Languet, fears lest the 'delays' which preceded his own travels 'devoured too much of his good time', and lest Pyrocles, in his abstractedness, will 'lose, nay . . . abuse, your time'.[158]

Love gives Pyrocles a different perspective. The delights of his emotional awakening are, to him, 'sufficient reward for any time lost'.[159] So Musidorus should not forbid 'my mind sometimes to enjoy itself, nor blame . . . the taking of such times as serve most fit for it!' Are not the discoveries of youth dependent on, inseparable from, the wasting of time? Sidney's elders would not have enjoyed that thought. Sir Henry Sidney, exhorting Philip at a tender age towards 'virtuous life and good action', warned him that 'otherwise, through vice and sloth, you may be counted *labes generis* [the stain or ruin of his family], one of the greatest curses that can happen to man'.[160] It is a dire warning. Yet Philip's acknowledgements of his own capacity for 'slothfulness', of his inclination to 'relax without reluctance', sound less like self-reproach than stirrings of self-knowledge.

Musidorus, Pyrocles, Philisides, all withdraw from action and virtue into love. Sidney, withdrawing from them too, does so in order, not to love, but to write. Yet Sidney loves too. We do not know when love struck him, but we have ample evidence of its effects. Of course, Philisides, and then

---

153   McCoy, *Rebellion in Arcadia*, p. 57; from G. P. V. Akrigg, *Shakespeare and the Earl of Southampton* (London, 1968), pp. 29–30.
154   Pears, pp. 97, 95.
155   Osborn, *Young Philip Sidney*, pp. 537–8; cf. Duncan-Jones, 'Philip Sidney's Toys', p. 169.
156   *OA* 77/32–5.
157   *OA* 97/4–5; cf. *OA* 56/3.
158   *NA* 164/37; *OA* 19/9.
159   *OA* 15/13, 15/3–5.
160   Osborn, *Young Philip Sidney*, p. 13.

Astrophil, are literary creations. That Sidney injects his amatory experiences into theirs is nonetheless obvious enough. 'Those pains', after all, 'must be felt before they be understood.'[161]

Philisides, obsessed by Mira, has, like the princes, abandoned his public preoccupations and succumbed to solitary and melancholy self-absorption. When we first meet him he is reposing beneath a tree. Euarchus, when we first meet him, is doing the same. But where Euarchus is 'taking his rest' from strenuous public exertion, Philisides is brooding idly on himself.[162] The first crisis of the Arcadian state, the mutiny in Book Two, finds Philisides singing dolefully and, it seems, putting the afflictions of his heart before the protection of his sheep. The second crisis, the death of Basilius, finds him no less melancholy or self-absorbed. He has to be asked to 'leave particular passions, and join in bewailing' Arcadia's 'general loss'.[163]

If the experience of Philisides in love resembles that of Musidorus and Pyrocles, so does that of Astrophil. He, like those princes and like Sidney, has borne 'great expectation'.[164] Like Sidney's, his career has faltered:

> For since mad March great promise made of me,
> If now the May of my years much decline,
> What can be hoped by harvest time will be?

The lovelorn Astrophil, like the lovelorn Pyrocles, is reproached by a 'friend' who opposes the claims of virtue and learning to those of love. But like Pyrocles, who answers his friend Musidorus by linking the beauties of Philoclea to the 'heavenly dwelling' of the landscape and posing rhetorical questions about it, Astrophil finds a rhetorical reply: 'Hath this world ought so fair as Stella is?'[165]

In common with the princely lovers of the *Arcadia*, Astrophil 'burn[s]' and 'quake[s]' and 'rage[s]' with love.[166] Like them he is 'poisoned' by it; like them he suffers 'torments' and 'hellish' feeling; like them he 'adore[s]' his beloved as a 'saint' or 'image' in the 'temple' of his 'heart'.[167] Like the distracted lovers of the *Arcadia* he cannot cope with company or take in what is said to him or answer it to the purpose.[168] Like them he cannot concentrate on public duty. In 1574 Sidney (at the age of nineteen) had declared to Languet that the bleak condition of the Protestant cause in Europe 'seems to demand, of all who care for the true religion, to dismiss every other thought,

---

161 Cf. Helgerson, *Elizabethan Prodigals*, pp. 135ff.
162 *OA* 71/32–4, 355/17.
163 *OA* 125/14–32, 344/20–1.
164 Ringler, p. 175 (sonnet 21, l. 8).
165 *OA* 15/12–32; Ringler, p. 175 (sonnet 21).
166 Ringler, pp. 173 (sonnet 16, l. 5), 177 (sonnet 25, l. 14), 191 (sonnet 53, l. 10), 195 (sonnet 62, l. 2), 213 (l. [15]).
167 Ibid., pp. 173 (sonnet 16, ll. 5, 14), 214 (l. 59), 205 (sonnet 78, l. 4), 167 (sonnet 5, ll. 6–7), 234 (l. [24]).
168 *OA* 20/31–2, 46/20–1, 173/31–3; Ringler, p. 178 (sonnet 27, ll. 1–4).

and concentrate on it alone the full powers of their mind'.[169] In the years of
and around the Anjou crisis, the years that produced both the *Arcadia* and
Astrophil and Stella, the fate of 'the true religion' hung in the balance. Yet
when 'busy wits' ask Astrophil questions about international politics, he can
think only of Stella. The questions are on subjects of overwhelming concern
to the Sidney whom we meet in his letters to Languet: the conduct of the
King of Poland, the French wars of religion, the fate of the Dutch revolt
'now so good towns be lost', the effectiveness of Sir Henry Sidney's policies
in Ireland, the court politics of Scotland.[170] Elsewhere Sidney set a love-poem
to the marching-song of William of Orange, on whose austere public
commitment the survival of the Protestant cause rested.[171]

Astrophil's love, like those of the princes, sets experience against precept.
His response to that conflict is an iconoclastic review of Sidney's public
values. The philosopher Sidney most admired was Aristotle, the statesman he
most admired Julius Caesar. Yet, says Astrophil, 'I do not envy Aristotle's wit,
/ Nor do aspire to Caesar's bleeding fame.'[172] Astrophil, by applying it to
love, pokes fun at the principle of contractual monarchy on which Sidney's
friends based the right of armed resistance to Catholic tyranny.[173] Kingship is
the object of a further moment of Astrophil's defiance: he hails Edward IV,
who in the terms of Sidney's public philosophy was the most irresponsible of
kings, as the most praiseworthy of them.[174]

Astrophil casts doubt on other convictions of Sidney too. France, the
source of the tyranny that Anjou threatens to bring to England, becomes 'that
sweet enemy'.[175] Astrophil embraces 'love', which has fled from its birthplace
Greece to England, 'pleased with our soft peace':[176] the peace which, in
Sidney's judgement, has made England 'idle' and 'corrupt'.[177] When, in the
Arcadia, Euarchus discovers that he has condemned his son and nephew to
death, he conducts himself 'with such a sad assurance as Cato killed himself
withal': Astrophil tells 'virtue' to 'use' its 'sceptre . . . in some old Cato's
breast'. Cato's principle of virtuous patience is a large presence in the *Arcadia*.
Astrophil derides it: 'Fie, school of patience.'[178] Here he is on the same side
as Pyrocles, who objects that Musidorus is 'high in the pulpit against love',
that his advice about virtue is 'fitter for quiet schools than my troubled brains'.
'Churches or schools', Astrophil tells 'virtue', 'are for thy seat more fit.'[179]

169   Pears, p. 58.
170   Ringler, p. 180, sonnet 30. Cf. Hamilton, *Sir Philip Sidney*, pp. 93–4; H. R. Woudhuysen,
      '*Astrophel and Stella* 75: A "New" Text', *Review of English Studies* n.s. 37 (1986), pp. 388–92.
171   Ringler, pp. 151–2.
172   Ibid., p. 198 (sonnet 64, ll. 9–10).
173   Ibid., p. 200 (sonnet 69, ll. 12–14).
174   Ibid., p. 204 (sonnet 75, ll. 1–2); cf. Stubbs, p. 176.
175   Ringler, p. 185 (sonnet 41, l. 4).
176   Ibid., p. 168 (sonnet 8, ll. 1–4).
177   Above, p. 61.
178   *OA* 414/35–6; Ringler, pp. 166 (sonnet 4, ll. 1–5), 192 (sonnet 56, l. 1).
179   *OA* 42/16, 23/3–4; Ringler, p. 166 (sonnet 4, ll. 1–6).

Yet if Astrophil's experience of passion, like that of the young princes, answers back to the precepts of reason and virtue, the precepts are ready with their own replies. The Sidney of 'Certain Sonnets' hears them:

> For virtue hath this better lesson taught,
> Within my self to seek my only hire:
> Desiring nought but how to kill desire.[180]

Astrophil hears them too. He sees what is happening to him, as the princes and Philisides know what is happening to them. Love, he perceives, has made his 'wits . . . in virtue lame'.[181] Idleness, which diverts the lovers of Arcadia, and Sidney, from the 'course' of life for which they have been prepared, diverts Astrophil from his 'course' too:

> I in my self am shent,
> When into reason's audit I do go:
> And by just counts my self a bankrupt know
> Of all those goods, which heav'n to me hath lent:
> Unable quite to pay even nature's rent,
> Which unto it by birthright I do owe:
> And which is worse, no good excuse can show,
> But that my wealth I have most idly spent.
> My youth doth waste, my knowledge brings forth toys,
> My wit doth strive those passions to defend,
> Which for reward spoil it with vain annoys.
> I see my course to lose my self doth bend . . ..[182]

In Astrophil, as in Philisides and the young princes, 'a strife is grown between virtue and love'. 'Virtue awake', he demands of himself, for 'beauty but beauty is'. Yet he begs 'sleep', that persistent enemy to virtue in Arcadia, to release him: 'O make in me those civil wars to cease.'[183]

There are the same civil wars in Arcadia. Is there a cure for them? Or is the 'heart', as is hinted by the exchange with which Musidorus and Pyrocles conclude their debate about love, doomed to eternal conflict with 'the head'?[184] So it might seem. Yet 'philosophy precepts', which Sidney commends because they teach us how to live, prove to be more resourceful aids in the tests of life and of love than we might expect or than his characters always grasp.

---

180 Ringler, p. 161 ('Certain Sonnets' no. 31, ll. 12–14).
181 Ibid., p. 175 (sonnet 21, l. 4).
182 Ibid., pp. 173–4 (sonnet 18).
183 Ibid., pp. 190 (sonnet 52, l. 1), 188 (sonnet 47, l. 9), 184 (sonnet 39, ll. 1–7).
184 OA 23/26–8.

CHAPTER 18

Public and Private Respects

at length he found that, both in public and private respects, who stands only
upon defence stands upon on no defence . . ..

(The *New Arcadia*)

The Second Eclogues open with 'the skirmish betwixt Reason and Passion'.
It brings Sidney's public and private themes together. It is 'occasion[ed]' by,
and points back to, 'the rude tumult of the Phagonians'[1] near the end of
Book Two, where the passions of the mutineers escape the government of
reason. It is followed by, and points forward to, an anatomy of the conflict
between reason and passion in the heart. Passion is the source of disorder in
the heart and in the state. For Sidney, as for most writers of the Renaissance,
the public world and the private world are to be interpreted within a
common vocabulary: the Aristotelian vocabulary of reason and passion, of
moderation and excess. Reason and passion contend for sovereignty both
over the individual – over the heart or soul – and over the public realm. The
Vindiciae, Contra Tyrannos of Languet and Mornay, deploying that principle,
offers a straightforward explanation of the prevalence of misgovernment:
'Always those are the greater [in number] who are led by passion, than those
who are ruled by reason, and therefore tyranny has more servants than the
commonwealth.'[2] For Greville, too, the defeat of 'reason' by 'passion'
extends from the soul to the state, 'Vice getting forces far above her own, /
When it spreads from a person to a throne'.[3]

Sidney's language of politics is full of the language of private life. His
language of private life is no less full of the language of politics. It is full,
above all, of the language of rebellion and tyranny, those opposite yet allied
forces in passion's struggle against reason. To Musidorus, remembering his

---

1   *OA* 135/2–4.
2   Laski, *Defence*, p. 194 (cf. Garnett, p. 153).
3   Wilkes, p. 83 (sts 193–4).

Aristotle, love is an 'unnatural . . . rebellion' of 'sensual weakness' against 'the reasonable part of our soul'. In the soul of Pyrocles 'passion rebel[s]' against 'reason's strength', 'shake[s]' it and deposes it:

> the stormy rage of passions dark . . .
> With rebel force hath closed this dungeon dark
> My mind ere now led forth by reason's light . . ..

Geron urges Philisides to 'suppress' the 'rebel thoughts' of love, which are properly reason's 'slaves'.[4]

Rebellious 'love' or 'lust' becomes, in its victories over Sidney's lovers, a tyrant. That is what happens to Astrophil, the 'foul rebellion' of whose passion secures 'unjustest tyranny' for it; to Musidorus, who succumbs to 'the tyrannical power of lust'; to Amphialus, over whose 'reason' 'love' or 'lust' becomes a 'tyrant'.[5] Sidney's characters, as they acknowledge, become 'slaves' to love,[6] its 'prisoners',[7] 'captived'[8] or 'enchained'[9] or 'thralled'[10] or 'possessed'[11] by it.

So Musidorus, however inexpert in human sympathy, is right to point Pyrocles towards Aristotle. Unfortunately he has got his Aristotle wrong, or half wrong. His own descent into love illustrates not merely the helplessness of his precepts before experience but the flaws of the precepts themselves.

Aristotle tells us that the intellect, or reason, rules the appetites, or passions, not with a 'despotical' but with a 'constitutional and royal rule': that is, as a king not a tyrant.[12] Musidorus' error is to claim for reason an 'absolute commandment' over passion.[13] For Aristotle, despots or tyrants rule by will and force, true kings by law and consent. Because passion is irrational, because it tends to the extreme, it will always seek to rule despotically. But reason, if it is true to itself, inclines to moderation. So it should rule passion moderately, not tyrannically. In the skirmish that begins the Second Eclogues, 'Reason', making the same mistake as Musidorus, calls 'Passion' a 'rebel vile'. Musidorus would have us 'summon all our sound forces' to its 'overthrow'. 'Reason', which shares his aspiration to 'absolute commandment', likewise thinks in military terms: it rebukes 'Passion' for daring to 'fight' against 'our strength'. Like tyrants or unlimited kings, 'Reason' seeks

---

4   *OA* 19/14–16, 218/7–8, 179/33–180/2, 73/14–15; cf. *OA* 279/15–17.
5   Ringler, p. 214 (ll. 56–63); *OA* 306/23; *NA* 323/28–9, 401/34–5.
6   *OA* 24/3, 24/30, 29n., 48/23, 61/28, 94/25–6, 138/6, 173/14, 408/31.
7   *OA* 12/19, 24/29, 288/34–289/1; *NA* 146/10–11; cf. *OA* 333/25–6.
8   *OA* 18/17, 29n., 43/13, 105/32.
9   *OA* 230/8; *NA* 321/23.
10 *OA* 103/11, 151/24, 197/22.
11 *OA* 23/5, 23/26, 39/30, 61/27–8, 103/10, 175/33, 182/2, 306/8–9.
12 Aristotle, *Politics*, ed. Everson, p. 6 (1254b); cf. p. 180 (1334b).
13 *OA* 19/14–15.

to impose its 'will' on 'Passion', forbidding it to be 'free'. It is consequently 'counted' a 'tyrant' by it.[14]

In aiming at tyranny, 'Reason' plays 'Passion' at its own game, which 'Reason' cannot win. Musidorus wants 'the reasonable part of [Pyrocles'] soul' to 'overthrow' love, but what Pyrocles experiences is the 'overthrow' of 'poor reason' and its subjection to passion's 'will'.[15] In Sidney's political thought, 'passion' is represented in politics by the exercise of royal 'will': the political representative of 'reason' is good 'counsel', that basic preoccupation of the forward Protestants around the time of the writing of the *Arcadia*. The sway of will characterises unlimited monarchies: the rule of counsel characterises limited ones. Will and counsel stand for passion and reason in private life too. When Pyrocles' 'reason', conquered by passion, urged it to delight 'more moderately' in its conquest, passion, which 'of a rebel was become a prince, disdained almost to allow [reason] the place of a councillor'.[16] Musidorus, 'overmastered' with 'the fury of delight' as he watches the sleeping Pamela, allows his 'will' to draw him to assail her chastity; 'and each thought that rase against those desires was received but as a stranger to his counsel'; for his 'lust' was 'past the calling back of reason's counsel'.[17] The episode confirms what the elderly shepherd Geron, with the pitfalls of love in mind, tells Philisides: 'The wits abused with will no counsel take.'[18] When Pamela at last smiles on Musidorus, and rescues him from his misery, he is carried to the opposite extreme: he 'could not set bounds upon his happiness, nor be content to give desire a kingdom but that it must be an unlimited monarchy'.[19]

By subordinating reason to passion, asserts Musidorus, love 'utterly subverts the course of nature'. He is wrong again. Passion and love are not contrary to our nature. They belong to it. If we come to terms with them we may find the accuracy of what the opening sentence of the *Arcadia* tells us: 'how true a contentation is gotten by following the course of nature'. Reason and passion gain nothing by fighting, by thinking of each other as enemies. In the skirmish it is 'Passion' which gets it right, in observing that it and 'Reason' are 'fellowlike together born'.[20] It is true that, as Sidney's *Defence of Poetry* insists, virtue can prevail only if it 'master[s]' passion. Yet there is more than one kind of mastery. There is mastery over servants and mastery over slaves. Geron may think of the 'rebel thoughts' of love as 'slaves

14 *OA* 135/13, 136/7, 135/15–21.
15 *OA* 29/1–6.
16 *NA* 87/1–4.
17 *OA* 201/30–202/1; *OA* 306/23–4.
18 . *OA* 72/25.
19 *NA* 308/24–6; cf. Ringler, p. 214 (l. 60). For political or constitutional imagery in the romantic plot see also *OA* 277/22–3; *NA* 96/29–30, 144/35–145/3, 377/14–15; cf. *The Faerie Queene* II. i. 57–8.
20 *OA* 20/11–12, 4/6–7, 135/25; cf. *OA* 258/5.

by kind', but Amphialus learns better, finding that 'true love . . . is a servant'; Pyrocles too sees that passions should be 'servants' to 'reason'.[21]

In lecturing Pyrocles, Musidorus is willing to recognise that passions other than love can be serviceable: 'Fear breedeth wit; anger is the cradle of courage; joy openeth and enableth the heart; sorrow, as it closeth it, so yet draweth it inward to look to the correcting of itself. And so all of them generally have power towards some good, by the direction of reason.'[22] His point is amply confirmed in the *New Arcadia*. There fear, anger, courage and sorrow are shown to be 'servants' of reason and virtue. Only when free from the benevolent discipline of those masters do they manifest themselves as cowardice, fury, brutality, despair.[23] Musidorus' error is to deny to the passion of love what he allows to the rest. For him 'this bastard love', this 'hateful . . . humour', 'is nothing but a certain base weakness'.[24]

Passions, in conventional thinking, were feminine, holding greater sway in women than in men. Sidney's women are in general not more passionate than his men; often they are less so. At the outset of the *Arcadia* he stands up for 'that sex', 'how much soever the rugged disposition of some men, sharp-witted only in evil speaking, hath sought to disgrace them'. That judgement prepares the ground for, and gives weight to, Pyrocles' complaint against the 'cruelty' and 'tyrannous ambition' of men towards women, whom nature has made as well equipped 'for the exercise of virtue as we are'. Geron confirms the point, observing that the virtue of women flourishes when they are 'by wisdom's rules directed', not 'forced' into 'thraldom' or treated like 'cattle'.[25]

Instead, it seems, Sidney thinks they should be treated like horses. That distinction might not be enough to appease every late twentieth-century sensibility, though Sidney has the highest esteem for horses, higher than for many men, and recognises the measure of independence belonging to the horse, that 'only serviceable courtier without flattery'.[26] He indicates that men may 'withhold' women with 'bridle', and that a husband, though owed 'obedience' by his wife, should govern her with 'never hard hand, nor ever reins too light'.[27] 'Bridling' is a movement of authority; but the good rider, in bridling, works with the horse, not against it. His concern is harmony and order, not subjugation. His rule is an image of moderation. The political

---

21 *MP* 83/21–5; *OA* 73/15; *NA* 401/35 (echoed in Massinger's *The Bondman*: Philip Edwards and Colin Gibson, eds, *The Plays and Poems of Philip Massinger*, 5 vols (Oxford, 1976), i. 352); *OA* 29/5, 297/10–14.

22 *OA* 19/23–6.

23 *NA* 34/28–35, 61/36–7, 140/29, 167/30–2, 308/9–10, 342/27–30, 345/29–32, 388/5, 391/3–4, 394/11, 395/4–5, 432/6, 461/28–9. Cf. *NA* 153/37–9; *OA* 51/31–2, 368/9–10; *GP* 72/10–11; Spenser, *The Faerie Queene* VI. vi. 5. When Sidney indicates to his brother Robert that 'passions' can be 'virtuous' he is presumably thinking of them as servants to reason: Feuillerat, iii. 126.

24 *OA* 19/36–20/2.

25 *OA* 4/32–5/1, 21/13–18, 263/6–9, 262/21–2.

26 *MP* 73/19–20.

27 *OA* 73/27; *NA* 373/19–20 (cf. *NA* 87/5–6); *OA* 253/28.

language of the time conveys the same understanding of the function of the bridle – as when Walsingham, warning James VI of Scotland against a 'course of violence', recommends the 'bridl[ing]' of his 'passions' by 'temperance and wisdom'.[28] 'Bridle' is a key word in Sidney's understanding of the proper relationship between reason and passion, 'violence' a key word in his understanding of the improper one. His characters, slaves to love, are devastated by its 'violence'.[29] By contrast his picture of Musidorus on horseback offers a model of government appropriate to the relations of men and women, indeed to the entire geography of the emotions, both private and public. Musidorus':

> spurs and wand . . . seemed rather marks of sovereignty than instruments of punishment; his hand and leg with most pleasing grace commanding without threatening, and rather remembering than chastising . . . he ever going so just with the horse, either forthright or turning, that it seemed, as he borrowed the horse's body, so he lent the horse his mind (in the turning, one might perceive the bridle-hand something gently stir, but indeed so gently as it did rather distil virtue than use violence) . . ..[30]

The bridling of violence, emotional and political, is what Sidney calls good 'government' (or sometimes 'direction' or 'discretion'). His characters explain their amatory travails in terms of their own or each other's 'ill govern[ment]'.[31] Basilius, in pursuing his own 'unbridled' amorous 'enterprise' with 'unbridled hope', is 'governed by the force of his passions'; he comes to his senses only when enjoined by his wife 'to govern yourself'.[32] Euarchus, opposite to Basilius as usual, condemns as 'ill-governed' the 'unbridled' passion of his son and nephew.[33] He is right at least in Musidorus' case, for it was Musidorus' failure to 'govern [his] love towards' Pamela[34] that subjected him to 'the tyrannical power of lust'.

Good government of the heart or soul sets 'limits' and 'bounds' to passion. Basilius, promising to reform, intends marital love to be henceforth the 'limit of his affection'; extremity of amorous joy, to which Musidorus cannot set 'bounds', extends Pyrocles' heart beyond its 'wonted limits'.[35] Against the 'tyrannical' claims of desire, reason stands for 'proportion' and for what the

---

28 Read, *Walsingham*, ii. 216; cf. J. H. Hexter, *The Vision of Politics on the Eve of the Reformation* (New York, 1973), p. 224.
29 *OA* 41/3–4, 96/7, 103/4–5, 111/23–4, 113/23, 165/5, 173/7–8.
30 *NA* 153/22–32; cf. above, Chapter 13, n. 120. In the *Defence*, 'poesy must not be drawn by the ears; it must be gently led': *MP* 111/28–9.
31 *OA* 121/17–18, 223/8–9. Cf. *NA* 232/25–6, 368/4–5, 465/26; Osborn, *Young Philip Sidney*, p. 296.
32 *OA* 119/11, 275/30, 218/26, 277/10.
33 *OA* 407/1, 406/30. Cf. *NA* 401/7–9; Feuillerat, iii. 110 ('her wise and noble governing of herself').
34 *OA* 197/4.
35 *OA* 278/12–13, 229/4–5. Cf. *OA* 50/4; *NA* 185/5–6.

New Arcadia calls 'bounds of mediocrity',[36] the Aristotelian mean which guides us towards divinity and away from bestiality.[37] Basilius and Gynecia are 'immoderat[e]' in emotion and conduct; Musidorus, that 'child of passion', was 'never acquainted with mediocrity'. The immoderation of the lovers is set against the 'moderate and well tempered minds' of the Arcadians at large.[38]

When loosed from mediocrity, passion is greedy. It demands to be 'fed'. Basilius 'feed[s] his mind' with amorous thoughts; he and Gynecia 'immoderately fee[d] their eyes' on the disguised Pyrocles. Pyrocles himself, charged by Musidorus with deserting virtue, claims to be 'feed[ing]' his 'mind' with 'higher thoughts', but in reality his imagination persistently 'feed[s]' on the 'conceits' and 'fancies' of love.[39] Musidorus in turn 'greedily draw[s] into his mind all conceits which might more and more torment him'. For the passions always want 'more'. The 'more' they consume the more 'unsatisfied' they become; they are like a 'fire' which 'the more fuel is put to it, the more hungry still it is to devour more'.[40] Just as the love or practice of virtue makes us 'more' virtuous, so wrong-doing generates 'more' wickedness.[41] Nature and weakness and time provide 'new matter to increase' or 'ad[d] . . . to' the lovers' 'passions'.[42]

Beyond the bounds of mediocrity the extreme of tyranny meets the extreme of servility.[43] The tyranny of love thrives on the servility of the lovers, who long to surrender their reason to their loved ones, to 'obey' or 'yield wholly' to their 'pleasure' or their 'liking' or 'commandment' or 'will'.[44] The most servile of the lovers is Basilius, who begs to know and satisfy the every whim of Cleophila (the disguised Pyrocles). His subjection is rich in political irony. The absolute monarch becomes an absolute slave. It is because 'passion' has gained 'the absolute masterhood' of him that he pursues Cleophila, 'fortified with the authority of a prince whose power might easily satisfy his will'. The duke rules his subjects according to his 'pleasure' and abandons them without their 'advice or allowance': yet as a lover he resolves 'perfectly to yield a willing obedience to all [Cleophila's] desires', and shows, by his 'consenting countenance', that his beloved's 'pleasure' is a 'law unto' him, her words being 'to him more than a divine ordinance'.[45] Because he has abandoned his duties, the young princes are

36   *OA* 150/24–7; *NA* 337/34.
37   Davis, 'Map of Arcadia', p. 71.
38   *OA* 112/11, 112/16; *NA* 308/24; *OA* 4/5–6.
39   *OA* 97/4, 112/16, 14/30–1, 17/4–5, 39/29–30, 179/15, 228/28; cf. *OA* 187/34–5.
40   *NA* 309/31–2, 406/38–407/2; cf. *NA* 328/31–2.
41   *NA* 423/8–11, 363/21–2.
42   *OA* 72/5, 113/22–3, 168/2–4, 208/11–12; *NA* 328/31–2; cf. Lipsius, *Six Bookes of Politickes*, p. 104.
43   *OA* 321/36–322/5; *NA* 164/2–5.
44   *OA* 39/11–13, 43/20–1, 56/30–1, 96/30, 136/32, 146/20–1; *NA* 61/16, 223/17–18; cf. *OA* 173/18–20.
45   *OA* 45/12–15, 358/4–5, 146/21, 215/24–6; *NA* 290/11–12.

denied 'access' to him: yet he seeks 'a more free access unto Cleophila'.[46] In his political capacity he spurns the 'counsel' of Philanax: yet as a lover he is persuaded by the 'power' of Cleophila's 'beauty' to ask her 'counsel', so far has he 'become a slave to' her. 'In my bondage', he proclaims, 'consists my glory.'[47]

How then are the passions to be 'governed' and the bounds of mediocrity secured? Musidorus, and 'Reason' in the skirmish, propose to meet violence with violence, will with will. Instead we should accept and respect the passions within us. Rather than suppressing them we should learn to direct their course. The opening sentence of the *Arcadia*, in commending the benefits of 'following the course of nature', points ahead to a series of images that amplifies the point. We can usefully think of passion, it emerges, as a river with its own 'currents'. If we are to master the currents we must begin by 'following' them. The currents, it is true, need to be restrained. As horses are to be guided by reins and bridles, so the 'river' of love must be channelled by 'rampires' if it is not to 'overflo[w]'.[48] But guidance is one thing, opposition another. To 'resist' or 'strive against' passion is merely to intensify it. The amatory obstacles confronting Philoclea 'made [her] love increase', for 'to a mind once fixed in a pleasing determination, who hopes by annoyance to overthrow it doth but teach it to knit together all his best grounds, and so perchance of a changeable purpose make an unchangeable resolution'. Gynecia 'found in herself a daily increase of her violent desires which, as a river, his current being stopped, doth the more swell, so did her heart, the more impediments she met, the more vehemently strive to overpass them'.[49] In Sidney's fiction the imprisonments, physical and emotional, that are intended to prevent the course of love become causes of it or intensifiers of it.[50]

  Prudent observers of others' passions learn how to steer them. At the outset of the *New Arcadia* the shepherds Claius and Strephon 'gave way unto' the 'melancholy' of the shipwrecked Musidorus, 'knowing that the violence of sorrow is not at the first to be striven withal', that it is 'sooner tamed with following than overthrown by withstanding'.[51] In the *Old Arcadia* Musidorus himself grasps the same principle in respect of Pyrocles (though not of himself). Finding his cousin's love of Philoclea to be 'so deeply grounded that striving against it did rather anger than heal the wound . . . he was content to yield to the force of the present stream, with hope afterwards, as occasion fell out, to prevail better with him'. Pyrocles himself adopts that tactic when confronted with the passion of Gynecia and Basilius for him. He

46 *OA* 392/30–1, *OA* 116/26.
47 96/22–4, 114/29–30.
48 *NA* 146/8–9; cf. *OA* 165/18.
49 *OA* 208/11–12, 113/22–5.
50 *OA* 8/8–12, 11/33–6, 172/28–30; *NA* 308/3–11.
51 *NA* 10/16–20.

saw that 'there was no way but to yield to the violence of their desires, since striving did the more chafe them; and that following their own current, at length of itself it would bring [Pyrocles] to the other side of [Gynecia's] burning desires'.[52]

If we risk strengthening the passion of others by resisting it, our own passions may likewise be strengthened by our resistance to them. Sidney suggests that Musidorus' 'very resisting' of his love of Pamela 'made the wound the crueller'. The 'more' he and Pyrocles 'argu[ed]' with themselves against their love, the 'more' it 'increased' and the 'deeper' it 'sank into' their hearts. The experience brings home to Musidorus – though not, alas, for long – a lesson characteristically cast by the narrator in political terms: 'love to a yielding heart is a king, but to a resisting is a tyrant'.[53]

Love declares its tyranny not only in political but in military language. The characters succumb to the 'force' of love.[54] Force, in Sidney's fiction, is an enemy to reason and to virtue. As Euarchus observes, 'it were very barbarous and preposterous that force should be made judge over reason'.[55] It is with 'force' that Musidorus makes his attempt on Pamela's chastity.[56] Within the lovers' hearts, too, force usurps the throne of reason. Love conquers[57] and invades[58] and assails[59] the lovers; it turns their hearts into battlefields[60] littered with arms and ammunition[61] or into besieged castles;[62] it seeks 'revenge' on those who have resisted it.[63] From so much violence it is a relief to turn to the wedding of Lalus and Kala, where 'war of thoughts is swallowed up in peace'.[64]

Sidney longed to go to war. He had (what is not necessarily the same thing) a violent and irascible streak. He threatened to 'thrust my dagger' into his father's secretary William Molyneux. His tennis-court quarrel with the Earl of Oxford was potentially disastrous to his career and to his fellow opponents of the Anjou match. Yet 'by nature and inclination', Languet told

52 *OA* 28/17–21, 185/16–19. (I hope, but am not sure, that I have correctly interpreted the perplexing personal pronouns of that last passage.) Cf. Bullough, i. 140 (sonnet xcv, ll. 1–4).
53 *OA* 41/6–7, 12/6–8; *NA* 108/5–8.
54 *OA* 38/5–6, 49/19–20, 117/25–30, 120/1, 123/21–2, 137/22, 148/20, 150/28, 179/5–6, 218/5, 218/26, 229/5, 229/19, 230/7, 235/19, 306/17, 394/28, 402/19; *NA* 234/6.
55 *OA* 398/31–2.
56 *OA* 306/17.
57 *OA* 28/31, 111/15, 151/25, 165/30, 199/26; *NA* 95/30, 155/4, 357/7–9; cf. *NA* 401/7–8.
58 *OA* 111/14, 138/15.
59 *OA* 199/25–6; *NA* 155/3–4.
60 *OA* 29/2, 107/1, 177/2–3, 220/10; *NA* 95/19–20.
61 *OA* 60/14, 165/10ff.; *NA* 152/4, 356/34–5.
62 *OA* 107/28–9, 121/19–20, 199/25–6, 210/17–18. Cf. *NA* 121/21–5; Ringler, p. 171 (sonnet 12, ll. 9–14), 202 (second song, l. 15). The prevalence of military imagery is discussed by L. A. Knoop, 'Sir Philip Sidney: Politics and Metaphor' (Univ. of London Ph.D. thesis, 1993), pp. 230–2.
63 *OA* 41/5, 66/28.
64 *OA* 245/32.

him in 1580, Sidney was 'formed for gentleness'.[65] A dislike of violence, physical and emotional, runs through the *Arcadia*. Violence and gentleness are poles of his personality and of his writing. So are hardness and softness; and so are what his time understood as the masculine and the feminine. Musidorus warns Pyrocles that to 'soften' his heart towards love would be 'the very first down step to all wickedness'. Yet in captivity, when Sidney shows us the princes at their best, 'like men indeed (fortifying courage with the true rampire of patience)', a thin crack appears in that hard surface. Their cares centre on their ladies and each other, 'wherein (if at all) their hearts did seem to receive some softness'.[66]

'Like men indeed' . . .. According to Musidorus it is 'if we will be men' that our reason will suppress our passion. Pyrocles, even in his Amazonian disguise, is resolved 'to prove myself a man'.[67] But 'if we will be men', must we be only men? 'Those two brave knights, Musidorus and Pyrocles', who are 'combined in one excellent knight, Sir Philip Sidney', face each other on the title-page of the composite *Arcadia* of 1593 as they support the Sidney crest,[68] the one in male, the other in female costume. In the opening dialogue between the princes, Musidorus' arguments for masculinity are matched and balanced by what he calls the 'womanish' arguments of Pyrocles. Soon Pyrocles acquires his female attire; 'and thus did Pyrocles become Cleophila – which name for a time hereafter', explains the narrator, 'I will use, for I myself feel such compassion of his passion'.[69] 'Do not permit yourself', Languet had warned Sidney in urging him to stick to the path to virtue, 'to be transformed into another person.' Pyrocles' 'mind' is 'wholly turned and transformed' into Cleophila. He is 'transformed in show', 'transformed in mind', 'transformed . . . in sex', 'transformed' into passion's slave.[70] Perhaps a part of Sidney is transformed with him.

Musidorus' counsel to Pyrocles against love is delivered in the terms of a masculine philosophy. Philanax counsels Basilius against abdication from public duty in the same terms. Musidorus then breaches that philosophy: Philanax adheres to it. In the thinking of Sidney's party Philanax is a model counsellor. He personifies the public virtue which the forward Protestants demanded. Yet in prosecuting the princes for the consequences of their loves he becomes a monster. He is 'overgone with rage', 'more greedy than any hunter of his prey', 'short-breathed' with 'extreme vehemency', driven by 'malice' and 'spit[e]' and 'revenge'. He 'utterly suppress[es]' evidence – the letters from the princesses – that might assist the prisoners.[71] Musidorus

65   Pears, p. 177. Perhaps that quality explains Sidney's dislike of bloodsports: Duncan-Jones, *Sir Philip Sidney*, pp. 57–8, 95–6.
66   *OA* 19/26–7, 370/24–9.
67   *OA* 19/13–14, 22/35.
68   Above, p. 313.
69   *OA* 19/20–1, 27/17–19.
70   Pears, p. 6; *OA* 18/22–3, 26/9, 28/30, 29/6, 43/13–14; cf. *OA* 111/32, 234/30.
71   *OA* 399/3, 408/10, 386/7–8, 391/22, 398/25, 410/30, 398/20–5; cf. Bergsbuch, 'Subaltern Magistrate'.

senses, in Philanax's conduct, evidence of a loveless life. 'Thy narrow heart', he answers him, 'hath never had noble room enough in it to receive' 'love'.[72] Has Philanax ever been in love? Has Euarchus? If he had been, might not the education he provided for the princes have prepared them for emotional experience outside the public realm? For all Sidney knew, had Languet or Walsingham been in love? Had Philip's father Sir Henry?[73] Could Sidney have shared the kind of wit that illuminates the *Arcadia* with any of those men?

And yet, even as Philanax prosecutes the princes, his hard surface cracks too. The imperative of revenge, he has told himself, allows him no room for 'womanish' conduct.[74] Yet at the point at which it becomes evident that Euarchus has unwittingly been judging his own son and nephew, 'even Philanax's own revengeful heart' is 'mollified' when he s[ees] how from diverse parts of the world so near kinsmen should meet in such a necessity'; his 'face' is 'unclothed . . . of all show of malice'. During the trial he decides not to read the princess's letters even to himself, 'doubting [lest] his own heart', 'so bent upon revenge', 'might be mollified'. Since learning of Basilius' death he has wanted to demonise Pyrocles, to visit 'hateful passion' on him as the duke's murderer. Yet when he first sees him he is 'stricken with admiration at the goodly shape of Pyrocles', feeling 'a kind of relenting mind towards him'.[75]

Forward Protestants themselves had a relenting experience – or feared to do so – when they came face to face with the figure whom the princes parallel at their trial: Mary Queen of Scots. A correspondent of William Cecil in 1569 warned him that 'very few should have access to or conference with that lady', for she had 'an alluring grace, a pretty Scottish accent, and a searching wit'. The austere forward Protestant Sir Francis Knollys, when he met her, had to admit that she was 'a notable woman', a person of 'policy, ready wit and constant courage'.[76] Philanax's arguments against the princes, and thus against Mary, are endorsed by Euarchus, that personification of justice. In the terms of Sidney's scheme of virtue and of his political anxieties they have everything to be said for them. Yet the spirit in which they are advanced is also that in which Philanax and Euarchus proscribe the humanity of the princes' loves. Could every part of Sidney join the hunt?[77]

72 *OA* 402/19–20.
73 He may have been. Lorna Hutson has kindly shown me her transcription of poems written in partnership by Sir Henry and his wife in 1551, when they were newlyweds: the verses are inscribed in Richard Grafton, *The Union of the Two Noble and Illustrious Families of Lancastre and Yorke* (London, 1548): Folger Shakespeare Library, copy 2.
74 *OA* 287/7–20.
75 *OA* 410/30–4, 398/23–4, 287/11–20, 300/27–301/3.
76 Patrick Collinson, *The English Captivity of Mary Queen of Scots* (Sheffield, 1987), p. 10.
77 A forthcoming essay by Katherine Duncan-Jones, to appear in a commemorative volume on Edmund Campion published by Oxford University Press, emphasises the evidence that Sidney may at one stage have been attracted to Roman Catholicism. Though that evidence is far from conclusive, it provides a further reason for asking whether the politics and religion of Sidney's party can have accommodated every aspect of his personality. It may also cast suggestive light on

If forward Protestants preferred to harden their hearts against Mary, they liked to entertain black thoughts too of Elizabeth's prospective husband, the Duke of Anjou. Walsingham, who had met Anjou, knew that he was no demon.[78] Sidney must also have known it. Yet, where Philanax suppresses evidence that may favour the princes, Sidney stretches evidence that may harm Anjou. His 'Letter' against the marriage, as Languet says, 'exaggerat[ed] some circumstances'.[79] Sidney brings Anjou close to monstrosity, as the speeches of Philanax project monstrosity on to the princes. The opponents of the Anjou match were participants in the polarisation and intense antagonisms which characterised English politics in the late 1570s. Polarisation and antagonism are not friends to openness of mind. Burghley and the advocates of marriage caught their opponents off their guard, exposing weaknesses in their arguments and turning those arguments against them. The forward Protestants responded defiantly, with a philosophy which renounced human weakness and permitted England and the English no compromise with it.[80] They could not afford the humanity of self-doubt. But could they wholly escape it?

The narrator of Sidney's fiction, though so critical of emotional violence, himself directs it at two targets. First there is the 'many-headed multitude', whose drunken dissonance, whose folly and fury, whose 'very unbridled use of words', are assaulted with an immoderation of Sidney's own. The mob's statements of grievance are attacked too. 'It were tedious', Sidney declares, to relate the 'far-fetched constructions' of the rebels' arguments against 'the duke's living from among them'.[81] Yet those arguments repeat the case made in Sidney's 'Letter', and elsewhere in the *Arcadia*, against the Anjou match. Why is Sidney so fierce to them? The second target is Cecropia, the counterpart to Mary Stuart. In the *New Arcadia* she and Pamela debate the existence of God. The dice are loaded mercilessly against Cecropia, that 'wicked woman', the 'filthiness' of whose 'impiety' is set off against the shining 'majesty' of Pamela's 'unconquered virtue'. Yet Cecropia too has, in the terms of Sidney's political thought, a plausible case. Her argument that 'fear was the mother of superstition' corresponds both to Sidney's account of the sway of fear and superstition in Basilius and to the complaints of Sidney and his party against those Catholic princes of Europe whom fear and superstition were preventing from standing up to Spain and the pope.[82] Of course Cecropia, like the rebels in the *Old Arcadia*, is at fault. The rebels, though it suits them to use public-spirited arguments, are without public spirit: Cecropia cannot see the difference between superstition and faith. Yet

his representation of love as idolatrous, a representation which does not invariably seem unsympathetic.
78   Above, Chapter 5.
79   Pears, p. 187.
80   Above, Chapter 7.
81   *OA* 127/11–17; cf. *OA* 306/28–307/1, 309/10ff., 317/4–17.
82   *NA* 359/17–20, 363/12–15, 359/38.

in the belligerence and righteousness of the narrator's rebukes we glimpse the impulse that pursues Anjou, Mary Stuart and, in Book Five, Musidorus and Pyrocles. On what terms does the side of Sidney that is 'made by nature and inclination for gentleness' live with that impulse?

Sidney's favourite character, he indicates, is 'sweet Philoclea' (as she is so often called). To her 'memory principally all this long matter is intended'.[83] Philoclea does not subscribe to the stern unbending doctrine of virtue learned by Musidorus and Pyrocles and enforced by Euarchus. She, if ever anyone, is 'formed for gentleness'. Where her sister's 'beauty used violence' against men's hearts, 'and such violence as no heart could resist', 'Philoclea's beauty only persuaded'. She is said to have a less 'constant temper' than Pamela's and to be 'apter to yield to . . . misfortune' than she.[84] Confronted, with Pyrocles, by the prospect of death, she faces it in a vein less strenuous than his.[85] She does not crave ethical exertion. Virtue is for her solely, or at least mainly, the avoidance of evil.[86] She is content to live by 'nature': the 'eyes' and 'senses' of 'the amiable Philoclea . . . received nothing but according as the natural course of each thing required'; in her we watch 'that most natural effect of conforming herself to that which she did like'.[87] On Arcadia's emotional battlefield between reason and passion, between virtue and nature, Philoclea's passivity, like the love of Lalus and Kala, offers an image of peace.

What then of the public world? In the opening pages of the *Arcadia* Pyrocles answers Musidorus' case for masculinity with the case for femininity. In those same pages Basilius has, and can have, no parallel answer to Philanax. There is no room for femininity in politics. Yet if there is that essential difference between the public and the private world, there are also essential similarities. To observe them is to perceive the argument that gives the *Arcadia* its unity.

In the public world, no less than in the private, passion causes havoc 'when it is not governed with reason',[88] when extremity prevails. 'Passion' gains 'the absolute masterhood' of Basilius the lover: Basilius the king surrenders to 'passions' which proceed from his 'weakness'.[89] In politics as in love, passions – or 'desires' – are violent when they escape reason's control. What the *New Arcadia* calls the 'evil consort of love and force'[90] has its political counterpart. Euarchus, the antithesis to 'most princes', rules by 'love', not 'force'; Sir Walter Mildmay, in arguing against the Anjou match, contrasts the 'hearty

83   OA 108/20–1. Cf. OA 306/6–10; Victor Skretkowicz, 'Philisides in "Arcadia"', in Allen, *Sir Philip Sidney's Achievements*, pp. 194–200, at p. 197.
84   NA 17/7–10, 17/17–18; OA 369/32.
85   OA 294/2–8.
86   OA 108/23–5, 121/1–2, 294/1–4 (cf. MP 84/31–5). Cf. Pears, p. 87, and the reference to Sidney in Bryskett, *Discourse of Civill Life*, preface.
87   OA 108/31–3; NA 144/30–1.
88   OA 33/26–7.
89   OA 45/12–13, 5/24–5.
90   NA 458/39–459/1.

love and affection' of subjects for kings with the 'constrained or enforced' fear, void of 'true love', that marks the subjects of tyrants.[91] Healthy political life, like healthy love, is created not by force but by 'consent'. In love, Lalus wins Kala's 'consent'.[92] In politics, it is the 'consent' of a nation or a people that sanctions the authority responsibly exercised by Euarchus in Arcadia and Musidorus in Phrygia; by contrast Basilius and Antiphilus, those irresponsible kings, act without consent or in opposition to it.[93]

In politics as in love, 'resistance' to passion only strengthens it. The conduct of the rebels of Book Two shows 'the nature of m[e]n' to be 'such that . . . they leave no rageful violence unattempted while their choler is nourished with resistance'. Pyrocles, in dealing with the rebels, grasps the point. In private life, where he has to deal with Gynecia's passion, we saw him 'yielding' to the 'violence' of her 'desires', 'following' rather than 'striving against' the current: in public life he quietens the rebels by channelling, with 'sweet magnanimity and stately mildness', their 'fury' and 'rage' towards 'reverence'.[94]

In public as in private life, passions are healthy when 'serviceable', destructive when not. The 'anger' of two brothers in the *New Arcadia*, which 'in the time that they obeyed a [royal] master' was 'a serviceable power of the mind to do public good', becomes 'unbridled' once they break free of him. Their lives are now unhinged, 'almost to the ruin of the country', by 'wickedness', 'excess', 'rage', hunger for 'revenge', delight in 'slaughter'.[95] In the public as in the private world passions need limits and bounds. The 'desires' of the rebels who follow Amphialus are 'unlimited'; England's foreign enemies, in Greville's account of Sidney's thinking, seek 'a deluge of boundless power'.[96] In private life the unwise lover 'forc[es] himself beyond his reach': in politics the 'liberty of the subject', if not duly governed, will 'stretc[h] to licentiousness'.[97]

In public as in private life the instruments of 'moderation' or the 'mean', the quality that draws and guides the service of the passions, are 'government', 'discretion', 'discipline', the 'bridle'. Philanax, as a commander in battle, 'mak[es] force and fury wait upon discretion and government', and then 'striv[es]', with reverence of authority, to bridle the flight of astonishment, and to teach fear discretion'.[98] The 'unbridled' rebels of Arcadia are 'governed', to their cost, by 'rage' and 'fury': the 'beastly fury' of their counterparts in Laconia has to be 'brought down', by 'discipline', 'to . . . a

91   *NA* 458/39–459/1, 161/21; Lehmberg, *Mildmay*, p. 160; above, pp. 117–18.
92   *OA* 244/3; cf. *OA* 107/27, 185/34.
93   *OA* 364/35; *NA* 174/38–9 (cf. *NA* 177/16–17); *OA* 358/4–5; *NA* 209/31–2. Alas, there can be unwise 'consent', in love and politics alike: *OA* 215/25, 257/31.
94   *OA* 129/16–18, 128/19–20, 131/6–9.
95   *NA* 178/6–23.
96   *NA* 324/34; *GP* 59/30; cf. Wilkes, p. 45 (st. 41).
97   *OA* 244/4; *NA* 161/16–17.
98   *NA* 342/27–8, 394/9–11.

mean of good government'.[99] The conduct of Sidney's rebels answers to Thomas Wilson's description of the 'unbridled' rebels and iconoclasts of Ghent in 1578.[100] It answers too to the judgement of Hubert Languet, who thought 'the people' ('populus') of the Low Countries wont to 'abuse' their liberty 'in the manner of an unbridled horse' ('instar effraen[i]s equi').[101]

Excess of passion strikes the lovers of Arcadia 'blind'.[102] Rulers and politicians are struck 'blind' by it too.[103] King Antiphilus is 'incredibly blinded' when 'suddenly borne' into 'royalty' and 'absolute power'. 'Licentiously abusing' his subjects, and being so 'swayed' by 'passions' that he 'could not perceive that he was a king of reasonable creatures', he brings to mind George Buchanan's account of the 'unbridled licentiousness' of Mary Queen of Scots, 'a woman raging without measure or modesty, and abusing, to all her subjects' destruction, the force of her power that she had received for their safety'.[104] Antiphilus' career shows that, in politics as in love, ungoverned or unbounded passion always demands 'more'. Where the lovers 'feed' on their 'imaginations', his 'imagination had crowned him king of Armenia, and had made that but the foundation of more and more monarchies'. For 'great persons are wont to make the wrong they have done to be a cause to do the more wrong'.[105] In the tumult of Book Two 'more and more wickedness opened itself' once the rebels were 'past the bounds' of obedience.[106]

In politics as in love, ungoverned passion will always 'increase' or 'add to' itself, for 'an evil mind in authority does not only follow the sway of the desires already within it, but frames to itself new desires not before thought of'.[107] The rebels of Book Two are seen 'adding fury to fury and increasing rage with running', 'mischief' being 'of such nature that it cannot stand but with strengthening one evil by another, and so multiply in itself till it come to the highest'.[108] The passions of rulers 'multiply' too. Whereas Euarchus, whose foreign policy adheres to a 'just moderation', 'despis[es] . . . the multiplying of kingdoms', 'most princes' seek to 'enlarg[e] their dominions', 'multiplying desire upon desire'.[109]

---

99   *OA* 127/11–12, 128/10–20; *NA* 34/28–34; cf. *OA* 351/29–30.
100   K. de L., xi. 130.
101   *Huberti Langueti Viri Clarissimi Epistolae* (Frankfurt, 1633), pp. 251–2.
102   *OA* 73/4, 176/13–14; *NA* 295/6–7.
103   *NA* 178/21–2.
104   *NA* 300/17–18, 299/7–17 (cf. *NA* 423/35); Buchanan, *Detection*, pp. 75–6. Cf. NRO, F(P)M 96, fo. 3ᵛ; Goodman, *How Superior Powers*, pp. 148–9.
105   *NA* 300/3–5, 363/21–2. An opponent of the Anjou match remarked that, as King of England, Anjou would never allow himself to be 'bridled by laws', for he was 'fed' by an ambition for greatness: above, p. 165.
106   *OA* 128/25–6.
107   *NA* 249/14–16.
108   *OA* 128/19–24.
109   *NA* 159/8–9; *OA* 358/9–12, 358/22–3. 'Men', Greville explains, 'delight to multiply desire' and, if they fail to 'fix . . . on good desire', are susceptible to 'ambitious dreams or fears of overthwart' (Bullough, i. 140: sonnet xciv, ll. 1, 13–14). But Greville knows too that it is 'vain'

Excess, then, is to be curtailed, in love and politics alike. Moderation curtails it. Yet moderation is not to be confused with weakness. On the contrary, by controlling the passions it promotes the ethical resolution and the independence that are the goals, in love and politics alike, of Sidney's philosophy.

In the eyes of Sidney and his fellow opponents of the Anjou match, we saw, it was essential that Elizabeth 'stand' upon God, upon her virtue, upon the strength and loyalty of her country. She must 'build' on those 'foundations' or 'grounds' and shun 'dependence' both on foreigners and on the whims of 'fortune'.[110] The same vocabulary runs through the romantic plot of the *Arcadia*. The lovers tie themselves to insecure dependencies and stand or build on insecure grounds and foundations. Basilius allows 'all the powers of his spirits' to 'depend' on Cleophila; Philisides, in sacrificing virtue to love, chooses a false 'foundation of his honour'; Pamela is alarmed to realise 'upon what ground she built' her determination to elope with Musidorus; Musidorus himself, having reproached the lovesick Pyrocles for his 'want of a true-grounded virtue', allows Pamela to become 'the very foundation whereon my life is built'.[111]

If love can create unhealthy dependencies, so can friendship. Friendship is, or is analogous to, a passion. Provided it is subordinate to 'virtue' it is as pure and delightful a quality as any in Sidney's fiction; but the subordination is essential.[112] In the *New Arcadia*, where the difference of age between Musidorus and his younger cousin is widened from (apparently) about one year to about three,[113] 'most of' Pyrocles' well-being 'stands in' his friendship with Musidorus. He notices in himself 'such a kind of depending upon him as without him I found a weakness and a mistrustfulness of myself, as one strayed from his best strength'.[114] So for a while the two cousins go separate and solitary ways. Sidney has much to say against solitariness, which in his fiction is a failing both of unwise and of evil characters. Yet his most reliable and public-spirited characters – Euarchus, Kalander, Philanax – are also solitary agents, leading, it seems, solitary lives, their solitariness marking their self-sufficiency. Euarchus and (apparently) Kalander are widowers. If they have friends we do not hear of them. We hear of no wife or children to Philanax. The only friend of his we learn of is Basilius, from whom his virtue sets him apart.

---

for 'infinite ambition to extend / The bounds of power' (Wilkes, p. 85, st. 200). Sidney perceives the same truth: mischief eventually 'fall[s] with its own weight', 'excess' leading to 'a headlong overthrow' (*OA* 128/19–25; *NA* 178/7–8). In Sidney's fiction, where 'tyranny' is 'never secure' (above, Chapter 15, n. 59), the 'pleasure' of love is likewise doomed to transience, despite Pyrocles' fond belief that in Arcadia 'no beauty . . . should ever fade' (*OA* 20/6–7, 15/22).

110 Above, Chapter 7.
111 *OA* 116/4–5, 162/30–163/1, 196/20, 24/1, 173/6–7 (cf. *OA* 13/11).
112 *NA* 184/13–14.
113 *OA* 377/25–6; *NA* 7/37, 14/5–6, 164/12–13.
114 *NA* 8/19, 235/39–236/5.

Solitariness casts us on our own resources and tests them. If those resources are infirm, sociability will not make up their deficiency. Nor will it help our companions. For though an essential feature of virtue is that it directs itself to the good of 'others', not merely of our 'selves', it is equally true that 'no man [is] good to other that is not good in himself'.[115] The only true foundation both of virtue and of freedom lies in what Sidney calls the 'inward self'.[116] Near the end of his life, in dire straits in the Netherlands, he told Walsingham of his resolution to be true to 'himself' and not to be 'drawn from [him]self'.[117] Philanax's declaration to Basilius that we are to follow the guides 'within ourselves' has its counterparts, in the romantic plot, in the warnings and confessions which reveal that the lovers have 'turned from themselves' or 'forsake[n] [them]sel[ves]' or lost authority 'in' or 'within' or 'upon' themselves or are 'divided in [them]sel[ves]'.[118] Cast into 'inward bondage' or 'inward darkness', they can 'no more sustain [them]sel[ves]'.[119] They thus cannot 'stand'. After Pyrocles abandons his inner resources his 'help stands without himself',[120] and proves no help at all. In the *Old Arcadia* only Pamela, who seeks 'a reasonable ground' to 'build her love upon', can claim to have a 'heart . . . standing upon itself', and she only in the later stages. In the *New Arcadia*, where her virtue is perfected, her 'determination' to adhere to it is 'built upon so brave a rock' that no suffering or temptation can threaten it.[121]

In Duke Basilius and Queen Elizabeth, self-reliance is eroded by 'fear', a passion, maintains Sidney, serviceable when taught 'discretion' and when properly 'used', but disastrous when it becomes the 'ground' of our conduct.[122] A function of heroic poetry, he argues, is to make 'magnanimity and justice shine through all misty fearfulness'.[123] It is a function of the *Arcadia* too. 'Who for each fickle fear from virtue shrinks', advises Geron, 'Shall in this life embrace no worthy thing.'[124] By 'fear' in love, which witnesses to a 'guilty heart',[125] Sidney alludes, I think, to the palpitations of the suppliant lover, the starts of undeclared passion, the dread of rejection, submission to the beloved's moods and whims. Amorous fear produces consequences to parallel those of political fear. Rebukes to fear, even when delivered at moments in the *Arcadia* when politics are not in sight, are administered in

---

115 *NA* 264/31–2; above, pp. 25–6.
116 *MP* 98/24–5.
117 Feuillerat, iii. 166–7.
118 *OA* 43/13, 73/20, 93/33, 120/15, 140/19, 147/15, 173/13, 183/7 (cf. *OA* 318/18–19); cf. Ringler, pp. 161 (sonnet 31, ll. 12–14), 174 (sonnet 18, l. 12).
119 *OA* 61/30, 182/28, 116/5–6.
120 *OA* 180/19–20; cf. *OA* 73/20.
121 *OA* 106/32–3, 311/32–3; *NA* 419/5–7.
122 Above, pp. 121, 135, 138; *OA* 294/30.
123 *MP* 98/4–5.
124 *OA* 261/31–2.
125 *OA* 137/27–8.

terms hard to distinguish from those in which Sidney reproaches Elizabeth
and Philanax Basilius. Those rulers hide from imaginary fears (from what
Philanax calls 'imagined' evil),[126] the queen by courting Anjou, the duke by
consulting the oracle. The fearful Elizabeth proposes to jeopardise England's
native political and military independence; the fearful Basilius has to be told
to 'arm [him]self'; Musidorus, before he falls in love, declares that:

> Fear is more pain than is the pain it fears,
> Disarming human minds of native might;
> While each conceit an ugly figure bears,
> Which were not ill, when viewed in reason's light.

The shepherd Dicus explains about love what Sidney's party told Elizabeth
and what Philanax tells Basilius: that 'safety' sought in cowardice will prove
no refuge. He makes points about 'defence' and 'weakness', and about 'fear'
and 'folly', that are as applicable to Elizabethan diplomacy as to love:

> A man to fear a moody woman's eye,
> Or reason lie a slave to servile sense,
> There seek defence where weakness is the force,
> Is late remorse in folly dearly bought.[127]

In love and politics alike, the princes, following virtuous principles at least
in this, do what Sidney thought Elizabeth should do in her foreign policy.
Seeing the vulnerability of a posture of 'defence', they contrive to 'offend',
to 'go forward' rather than 'l[ie] still', and 'with extraordinary boldness to
overcome boldness, and with danger to avoid danger'.[128] Boldness, we learn,
enables us to 'stand'. Amphialus, when assailed by the jealous lover Zelmane
(the disguised Pyrocles), was content to 'stand upon' defence and avoid
'offence' until 'at length he found that, both in public and private respects,
who stands only upon defence stands upon no defence'.[129] The passage signals
the correspondence between Sidney's public and private themes, for the
presence of the subordinate phrase, 'both in public and private respects',
derives no warrant from the context.[130]

Fear, in love and politics alike, has an opposite and complementary
passion, which, when beyond the control of virtue, is equally inimical to self-
reliance: the passion of hope. 'Great inclining' to either 'fear' or 'hope',
explains Pyrocles, 'shows but a feeble reason, which must be guided by his

126 *OA* 8/32.
127 *OA* 373/23–32, 139/22–7.
128 *NA* 464/16–17; above, p. 165; *OA* 128/36–129/2.
129 *NA* 196/33–5, 197/6–8.
130 Cf. *OA* 383/4. Mornay noted that the epigrams of that 'excellent poet' Sannazaro (Sidney's
     source) provide 'an abridgement of all wickedness both public and private': Mornay, *Mysterie
     of Iniquitie*, p. 615.

servants'.[131] 'Reason' asserts itself in Pamela's 'heart' when 'hope' and 'fear'
are quietened there, but is powerless in the 'heart' of 'the weak fool'
Antiphilus, who is thralled to 'hop[e]' and 'fear'.[132] In Sidney's fiction hope
provides no firm 'grounds' for our conduct. If we 'build upon' it we rob the
mind of 'resolution'.[133]

Hope and fear are the baits of fortune. To be swayed by them, or by worldly
prosperity or adversity, is to subject our inward selves and inward strengths
to the vagaries of accident or appearance or reputation. That was the failing
addressed by Stoicism, the doctrine which was articulated for the late Renaissance by Sidney's friend Justus Lipsius, and which is an essential component of Sidney's philosophy of self-reliance. We saw that Basilius relies, as a
ruler, on fortune rather than inner strength, and that in Sidney's judgement
Queen Elizabeth does so too.[134] The same temptation confronts the lovers of
the *Arcadia*.

Stoicism, and Sidney's fiction, insist that the gains and losses of fortune
must be servants, not masters, of virtue. Otherwise we become, in the words
of Plangus in the *Arcadia*, 'thralls to fortune's reign'.[135] Fortune is the ally of
passion. The passion of love is a matter of fortune, at least to those lovers
who, not 'feel[ing] indeed that divine power which makes the heart find a
reason in passion', 'inconstantly lean . . . upon the next chance that beauty
casts before them'.[136] Eventually, in the face of adversity, the lovers of the
Arcadia rise above fortune, or at least largely do so. Musidorus and Pyrocles,
awaiting trial, know not to be daunted by 'accidents': Pamela sees that
'chance is only to trouble them that stand upon chance'.[137] Pyrocles, foreseeing the consequences of his night with his beloved Philoclea, explains to her
that 'true fortitude' and its 'persisting resolution' are not swayed by external
pleasures or displeasures. Philoclea in turn identifies external 'honours' and
'shames' as distractions from the attainment of inner virtue, which 'stand'
only 'in other men's true or false judgements'.[138]

The young lovers are not always so wise. The principle explained by
Philoclea to Pyrocles is precisely that which he, while approaching her
chamber in 'extremity of joy', has applied in an opposite spirit. It was then
that 'all the great estate of his father seemed unto him but a trifling pomp',
the 'good' of which 'stands in other men's conceit'. Instead he found 'true
comfort . . . in the depth of his mind' in the prospect awaiting him in
Philoclea's arms.[139] Stoic comfort is indeed to be found in the mind, not in

131   *OA* 297/11–14.
132   *OA* 196/16–18; *NA* 303/13–14.
133   *OA* 92/17–18, 174/8–9; *NA* 295/5, 456/6–8.
134   Above, pp. 120, 138–9.
135   *OA* 147/14. Cf. *OA* 386/1–2; *NA* 342/30–1, 455/31–2.
136   *NA* 91/30–3.
137   *OA* 318/18–20, 413/10–11, 311/28–9.
138   *OA* 296/19–21, 298/17–18.
139   *OA* 229/4, 228/28–229/1.

the greatness of estates. Yet can the 'comfort' in the depths of Pyrocles' mind have been truly 'true'? The judgement he passes on his father does no justice to that man of 'well grounded' inclinations. Euarchus' 'great estate' may seem to his son a 'trifling pomp', empty of true 'good'; but the truth is that he shuns 'affected pomps' and surmounts 'the greatness of his fortune with the greatness of his mind', welcoming 'greatness', and the 'goods of fortune', solely as means to 'goodness'.[140] Nowhere else in the *Arcadia* is the self-discovery of love pitted more defiantly against 'philosophy precepts' than by Pyrocles' moment of insight. Sidney's narrative contains other challenges to its own philosophy of virtue, but none so startling. Yet is not the insight falsely based? The father follows Stoic principles which the son, blinded by joy and desire, has forgotten.

Stoicism, the pursuit of internal virtue, offers 'a quiet mind', 'an assured tranquillity'.[141] 'Quietness', a vice in Elizabethan foreign policy, is a virtue in the mind.[142] 'Kee[p] still your mind in one state of virtuous quietness,' Sidney urged his father amid the family's political afflictions of 1578.[143] Sidney's romantic plot tells us, in words that again contrive to link the private to the public world without warrant from the context, of the benefits that derive from the 'contentment of the mind, which once obtained, no state is miserable; and without that, no prince's seat restful'.[144] Essential to that contentment is the Stoic quality of 'patience'.[145] Alas, the Stoic 'resolution' of Musidorus, that 'child of passion', yields to 'impatience'. Earlier the 'contentment of the mind' which love has seemed to bring him proves – like the 'comfort' in Pyrocles' 'mind' – to be a mirage. For he has yielded 'the balance of [his] contentation' from '[him]self' to Pamela, who thus 'holds' it.[146] He acknowledges, in a flood of tears, the dreadful truth. Having surrendered his 'virtue' to 'fortune', 'I go blindfold whither the cause of my ill-hap' – his ill fortune – 'carries me'. It is in the desperation induced by that perception that he plots treason against Basilius.[147]

The relationship of virtue to fortune is a continuous preoccupation of Sidney. He knew what Languet told him, that men should be valued for their 'virtues', not their 'fortunes'.[148] Poetry, explains Sidney's *Defence*, can show us the 'goodness' of 'a virtuous man in all fortunes'.[149] One such man is Euarchus, who knows the goods of 'fortune' to be 'servants' to 'virtue' and 'well-doing'. Once more Basilius is Euarchus' opposite: cowering from the

140　*OA* 357/1–10; *NA* 159/16–18.
141　*OA* 140/19, 296/22–3.
142　*OA* 20/4, 52/4, 54/34–5, 109/24, 115/31, 141/3–8, 183/26, 228/2, 237/13–14; *NA* 421/37, 455/24.
143　Feuillerat, iii. 122; cf. *OA* 237/13–14.
144　*OA* 44/36–45/3.
145　Above, p. 33.
146　*OA* 413/10–11, 45/1, 141/7.
147　*OA* 176/10–16.
148　Above, p. 235.
149　*MP* 86/13–14; cf. *MP* 90/4–6.

rebels of Book Two, he owes the good 'fortun[e]' of his survival to the 'virtue' not of himself but of his rescuer Pyrocles.[150] To Pyrocles and Musidorus, as to Euarchus, 'fortune' is properly the 'serv[ant]' of 'virtue', even though Musidorus discovers that it can be a 'rebellious handmaid against' it.[151] On their travels, 'following the course which virtue and fortune led them', they are determined to be independent of fortune. They 'seek exercises of their virtue, thinking it not . . . worthy to be brought to heroical effects by fortune'; Pyrocles, while not 'foolishly . . . ungrateful to good fortune', wants 'not [to] be beholding to fortune' in military 'victory', which properly owes itself to 'virtue'.[152] Likewise Amphialus, fighting Musidorus, 'would not have fortune come to claim any part of the victory'.[153]

Yet fortune devastates Amphialus. It devastates Pyrocles and Musidorus. Musidorus, the victim, in his own eyes, of 'filthy fortune', claims that it has 'crossed' his 'best framed intent'.[154] Pamela puts him right: 'methinks you blame your fortune very wrongfully, since the fault is not in fortune but in you that cannot frame yourself to your fortune'. 'A man', she explains, need not think upon the accidents of worldly prosperity: he 'is bound no further to himself than to do wisely'.[155] That statement recalls Geron's belief that 'for th'event we never ought be sad', and recalls too Philanax's advice that if Basilius follows 'wisdom and virtue' he will be 'never in evil case', 'either standing or falling with virtue'.[156]

In seeking its sway over us, fortune has an ally: 'necessity'. The patience and endurance displayed by the princes in awaiting their trial make them 'rather appear governors of necessity than servants to fortune'. On their travels in the New Arcadia they want their heroic deeds to be the products of their 'own choice and working', not of 'fortune or necessity'.[157] For Sidney as for Milton after him – and for Aristotle before them – choice, freedom and virtue are an ethical triangle. Freedom, defined by choice, is the victory of virtue.[158] It is the victory of reason too. Where 'reason hath . . . overmastered passion', declares Sidney's Defence, 'the mind hath a free desire to do well'. Musidorus' reason, alas, is instead 'overmastered' by the passion of love. Having become a 'slave' to 'restless desire', he has 'no more freedom in mine own determinations'. The passion of 'fear', as Pyrocles indicates, is likewise an enemy to freedom – to 'well-choosing'. Friendship, the New Arcadia discloses, can be virtuous only when it is the fruit of 'choice'.[159]

The princes lose their power of choice, and with it their freedom. On

150 OA 357/7–10, 286/4–5.
151 OA 175/4–5, 176/10–11, 101/8.
152 NA 206/20–1, 179/9–11, 462/8, 242/7–8; above, pp. 30–1.
153 NA 408/5–6; cf. NA 140/16, 248/36–249/1, 397/23, 407/7–8, 452/14–15, 458/29–30.
154 OA 103/15–18, 311/13–14; cf. OA 178/18–19.
155 OA 100/30–2 (cf. OA 100/1–3), 311/25–8.
156 Above, pp. 33–4.
157 OA 370/25–6; NA 179/10–12.
158 Cf. Wilson, Demosthenes, p. 89; Lindheim, 'Sidney's "Arcadia", Book II', p. 185.
159 MP 91/26–7; OA 173/13–15, 296/30; NA 184/13–16.

their travels, before love smote them, 'their courages disdained to be compelled to anything'; and yet Musidorus is 'compelled' by his passion to
attempt the rape of Pamela.[160] Pyrocles recognises in his love of Philoclea 'the
fatal overthrow of all my liberty'; she in turn laments, as a lover, her 'given
away liberty'; Amphialus, in loving her, 'lost [his] liberty'.[161]

   The subjects of monarchy, as Philisides' beast-fable discloses, have lost their
liberty too. Their well-being rests upon the whims and fortunes of their
monarchs. Rulers who seek glory in war, explains the *Arcadia*, 'put [their]
people's safety in the continual dice of fortune'.[162] Queen Elizabeth, though
not a warmonger, has another failing which likewise emphasises the sway of
chance in monarchies: her refusal to listen to her counsellors, complained
Walsingham, was a source of 'grief' to those who 'depend' on 'her fortune'.[163] That dependence was exacerbated by the hereditary system. Sidney
knew that the 'fortunes' of Queen Elizabeth's people were 'tied' to her
survival, that they 'hung' on 'so frail a thread'.[164] A people's 'whole state and
well-being', observes Euarchus, is 'tied' to the royal succession.[165]

Lovers and subjects, then, are subjected to a dependency incompatible with
true liberty, the liberty within. The *Arcadia*, our concluding chapter will
show, asks whether, and if so how, that plight can be avoided.

---

160 *OA* 155/19–20, 201/26; cf. *OA* 119/31.
161 *OA* 17/27, 209/14; *NA* 409/13.
162 *OA* 358/23–5; cf. *OA* 358/18–19.
163 K. de L., x. 819.
164 *MP* 53/15–16; above, pp. 191–2. Cf. Allen, *Defence*, p. 185; Strype, *Sir Thomas Smith*, p. 198;
     Worden, 'Ben Jonson among the Historians', p. 101.
165 *OA* 406/16–17. Speaking as a friend to monarchy, Euarchus nonetheless discloses one of the
     'dissipations monarchal governments are subject unto', for 'in all monarchal governments', he
     explains, the 'prince's person' is 'the very knot of the people's welfare', to which they are 'in
     necessity bound to be loyal' (*OA* 383/12–15). Again, 'necessity' is a signal of dependence and
     the opposite of freedom.

CHAPTER 19

Causeless Yieldings

this bastard love . . . his adjoined companions be unquietness, longings, fond comforts, faint discomforts, hopes, jealousies, ungrounded rages, causeless yieldings . . ..

(The *Old Arcadia*)

During the Second Eclogues the shepherd Dicus asks the lovesick Musidorus 'if love took thee by force, or caught thee guilefully'. Parallel questions are repeatedly raised in Sidney's fiction. Philoclea, Pyrocles, Pamela, ask themselves 'if' they could have avoided Cupid's darts: 'if' they have submitted 'willingly', or 'if' they should have 'ma[d]e resistance', or 'if' they have been conquered by 'a small or unworthy assault'.[1] The question is raised 'if' any 'indifferent soul . . . could resist from subjecting itself' to the beauty of Helen of Corinth. 'Have I', asks the love-smitten Astrophil, 'betrayed my liberty', 'or am I born a slave, / Whose neck becomes such yoke of tyranny?'[2]

Musidorus' reply to Dicus' inquiry – whether love has taken him by force or guile – is an open one:

> how [love] doth by might or by persuasion
> To conquer, and his conquest how to ratify,
> Experience doubts, and schools hold disputation.

Sidney's writing 'holds disputation' too. Because 'reason direct[s] it', rules Musidorus in admonishing his cousin, we 'must' and 'will' suppress the passion of love, 'for to say I cannot is childish, and I will not womanish'. Yet he finds that 'no reason of mine own can' dissuade him from pursuing his

---

1 *OA* 137/31, 111/20–4, 165/4–5; *NA* 155/3–4. (The syntax of Pyrocles' speculation is problematical.)

2 *NA* 96/29–30; Ringler, p. 188 (sonnet 47, ll. 1–4); cf. Leland Ryken, 'The Drama of Choice in Sidney's *Astrophel and Stella*', *Journal of English and Germanic Philology* 68 (1969), pp. 648–54.

own passion, and that he who 'will resist' love 'must either have no wit, or put out his eyes'. He has yielded to Pamela, he concludes, 'by force, not choice'.[3] Astrophil, like Musidorus, yields to that against which he has set his face. 'I must, I can, I will . . . / Leave following' love. Then: 'Soft, but here she comes.'[4] Time and again the lovers of the *Arcadia* decide that they 'can' not or 'could' not resist their loves, that love is or was 'unresistible' by them.[5]

Yet there is an opposite view too: the view which represents the lover of the seventeenth of Sidney's 'Certain Sonnets' as a man 'whom free choice slave doth make'.[6] The lovers of Arcadia are repeatedly described as 'yielding' to love.[7] At those moments, or at least at many of them, their surrender seems no more warrantable than that of the 'over-tender' shepherds who 'yielded themselves' to tears on the death of Basilius.[8] Musidorus, before he himself yields to love, takes it to be characterised by 'causeless yieldings'; Geron thinks it a 'cause of causeless woe' and condemns men who have their 'freedom sold' to it.[9]

In Sidney's philosophy, we saw, our strength and virtue lie 'within ourselves'.[10] It is there that the lovers fail their test. 'The given-over Pyrocles' is, in his own judgement, guilty of 'inward treason', 'false in myself', 'forsaken [by my]self', 'weakened by myself'.[11] Musidorus, by yielding to love, is 'impaire[d]' by 'myself'.[12] Philoclea, having failed to 'exercis[e] any way her mind' against the advance of passion, decides that she has 'betrayed [her]self', that she has 'given away [her]self' by 'too much yielding'. Before love came to her she was pledged to chastity, which in Pyrocles' words is 'the most noble commandment that mankind can have over themselves'.[13] Basilius, having 'abandon[ed] himself', 'utterly gave himself over' to his desire. With the 'willing blindness of affection' he resolves 'perfectly to yield a willing obedience' to the disguised Pyrocles.[14]

Is it all right to fall in love? In the *Arcadia* the virtues and vices of love, its choices and necessities, are in incessant collision and debate. We are left to judge love's claims as best we can, or to decide that Sidney intends, or is driven, to juxtapose contrary claims. Yet amid that multiplicity of stances there is one theme which all the others serve. Again and again his narrative

3   *OA* 138/25–7, 19/19–21, 173/20; *NA* 106/6–7, 139/37–140/2.
4   Ringler, p. 188 (sonnet 47, ll. 10–12).
5   *OA* 24/22, 48/27, 49/19–20, 92/2–3, 109/9, 204/33–4, 220/12–13, 226/13, 296/14; cf. *NA* 17/ 7–10, 215/29–31.
6   Ringler, p. 146 (l. 9).
7   *OA* 28/35, 39/11, 72/5, 98/2, 209/14; cf. *OA* 109/9, 121/21, 215/24.
8   *OA* 283/12–13.
9   *OA* 20/5, 75/15, 73/25.
10   Above, p. 335.
11   *OA* 230/22, 28/33, 29/2, 120/15, 165/20.
12   *OA* 141/3.
13   *OA* 98/3, 121/21, 209/18–20, 211/23, 209/14, 220/17–18.
14   *OA* 7/35, 45/17–18; *NA* 295/6–7; *OA* 215/24–5.

directs us to the issue of individual choice and responsibility. It underlines those moments when the lovers do what Sidney and his party urged Elizabeth and her country to do at the time of the Anjou suit: they examine and discover the extent of their ethical resources. They look within themselves.

The lovers come to crossroads, to decisive moments of inward stocktaking and of self-definition. 'Whenever . . . any feeling new to yourself shall agitate your mind,' Languet advised Sidney in 1577, 'do not hastily indulge it'; 'before you give it entrance, reflect carefully what it is that tempts you'.[15] Sidney's lovers, their minds agitated by novel feelings and temptations, pause at critical moments of their lives for what his narrative calls 'judgement' upon the 'self', 'judgement' being for him a word usually synonymous with or related to the exercise of reason.[16] Their judgements are mostly overruled. Gynecia's 'judgement', as her passion for Pyrocles deepens, observes the 'evils she was like to run into', the infamy and terrors of conscience awaiting her, the loss of 'her long-exercised virtue'; 'and . . . no small part of her evils was that she was wise to see her evils'. Her foresight will not, or cannot, stop her.[17] Musidorus reflects that love has diverted him and his cousin 'from the right line of virtue.' 'But' he overcomes that scruple.[18] Pyrocles, plotting daring designs on Philoclea, 'had leisure to sit in judgement on himself, and to hear his reason accuse his rashness'. 'But' he goes ahead. In what is probably an earlier version of the same passage, Pyrocles 'stayed a great while', 'oppressed with a dead amazement'. 'But', 'within a while', he overcame 'all inward objections'.[19] The passions of 'desire' and 'fear' deny to Pamela 'free scope of judgement' to examine her decision to elope, until 'reason began to . . . make her see herself in herself'. 'But', even then, love has its way.[20]

Later, however, Pamela's judgement prevails. Learning of the death of her father and its attendant calamities, she 'look[ed] a great while on the ground'. 'But', 'in the end remembering how necessary it was for her not to lose herself', 'she strengthened her well created heart'.[21] In the public domain, virtuous characters pause 'awhile' to judge themselves or their situations or to make decisions. Philanax 'paus[ed] a while with himself' before deciding how to meet one crisis of the Arcadian state, and 'st[ood] a while in a maze, as inwardly perplexed', before resolving how to answer another. When confronted with the conflict between the black image he has formed of Pyrocles and the goodly reality, he 'rested awhile upon himself'.[22] On Euarchus' arrival in Arcadia, Philanax 'stood a while' before him, like 'a man

15 Pears, p. 126.
16 *OA* 237/16–17, 296/4–5, 296/30, 317/33–6.
17 *OA* 91/13–20.
18 *NA* 109/29–30.
19 *OA* 237/16–20, 174/11–20.
20 *OA* 196/12–21.
21 *OA* 319/9–15.
22 *OA* 351/21; *NA* 416/25; *OA* 300/27–8.

gone a far journey from himself, calling as it were with his mind an account of his losses'. Euarchus for his part, on discovering that he has condemned his son and nephew to death, 'stayed a good while upon himself', 'studying with his best reason' before deciding 'what his office required'.[23]

If the decisions or commitments of love, as of politics, inspect our inner resources, there are two kinds of lovers whose inner resources are understandably limited and to whose predicament Sidney consequently extends sympathy. First there are women. Their subordination to men, and their economic dependence on them, can make it harder for them than for men to 'stand' on their own 'virtue' and to defy 'fortune', particularly if they are tied to men who themselves have deserted virtue. 'Hard I must needs say', declares Gynecia to her feckless husband, 'is the destiny of womankind, the trial of whose virtue' has to 'stand' upon the love of men undeserving of love. She 'care[s]' for his 'well-doing' because, her maintenance depending on his estate, she cannot 'separate [her]self' from his 'fortune'.[24] Pamela tells Musidorus that she is 'content' to 'build' her 'pleasure' on his 'comfort'. She reminds him that the 'judgement' of the world 'stands upon . . . fortune', and that women are 'bound to have regardful eye to men's judgements'. She speaks teasingly, it is true, with an amorous intent, but the plight of women becomes apparent when, in eloping, she 'bequeathe[s] the care of herself upon him to whom she had given herself' and reposes in Musidorus 'my estate, my life, my honour'.[25]

A second group, which naturally overlaps the first, is at a disadvantage among the contests of Venus: the very young. Sidney is more indulgent to the younger pair of princely lovers than to their seniors: to Pyrocles, that 'poor youth' who 'did not . . . at first know his disease', and to Philoclea, that 'poor soul' and 'tender youth' who is 'ignorant of her own disease'.[26] The Arcadians are unequal to the crisis on Basilius' death because 'they had not experience to rule': the 'reason' of Philoclea, when she becomes enthralled to Pyrocles, fails her because it is 'not yet experienced in the issues of such matters', she being 'but yet a prentice in the painful mystery of passions'.[27] She shares a problem with the young Parthenia: both girls, having been properly 'obedient' to parental authority, have consequently lacked opportunities to develop the 'judgement' on which to base the 'choice' or 'forechoosing' of their affections.[28]

Adults have less excuse, the elderly least of all. Basilius' age, and 'the long

---

23   *OA* 359/33–4, 410/35–411/3.
24   *OA* 276/26–9, 277/35–278/3.
25   *OA* 174/30–175/1, 102/29–31, 196/15–16, 196/33–4. She would have reposed them there even if she had not eloped, for the marriages of her and her sister to the princes were to have been arranged anyway, even if Basilius had not closeted his daughters and driven them into subterfuge and their lovers into treason (*OA* 359/7–9). Philoclea would then have been no less dependent on Pyrocles, for whom her 'true loving . . . made her think no life without him' (*OA* 294/6–7).
26   *OA* 12/3–4, 109/1, 108/33, 109/10.
27   *NA* 144/37–145/1; *OA* 208/29; cf. *OA* 97/36–98/1, 109/1–2; *NA* 144/8–11.
28   *OA* 108/33–109/1; *NA* 28/31–3, 29/3–4. Cf. *NA* 95/27–9, 155/5–6. On the place of choice in the experience of love, see also *OA* 195/18–22, 197/12, 197/27, 212/14, 224/16–17.

experience he had had of the world', make the 'follies' of his love 'the more absurd'.[29] The imprudent love of Plangus, that 'poor young prince', is 'excused by the greenness of his youth', whereas his father has amorous 'desires, which were in his son far more excusable'.[30] Another helpless victim of Cupid is the fourteen-year-old Erona; another still is Helen of Corinth, whose court 'swarmed full of suitors' before her 'age was ripe for it'.[31]

What the lovers lose by loving is shown by their songs, which chart and lament love's conquest of them. Philoclea's song of the 'woes' wrought by the love that has possessed her is sadly opposite in spirit to the hymn to chastity which she wrote 'while she was mistress of herself', while she held to the 'constant course' of virtue.[32] Musidorus, who sings of the surrender of his freedom to Pamela, later remembers and sings a song of Stoic wisdom which 'he had made before love turned his muse to another subject'.[33] Philisides sings of his enslavement to Mira: yet in the Third Eclogues he sings the beast-fable which he learned on Ister Bank before he had 'given over himself' to the 'passion' of love, 'before he had ever subjected his thoughts to acknowledge no master but a mistress'.[34]

Through the long and fearful night, through the 'eight sullen hours' in which, as a 'watching shepherd', he sings that song, Philisides keeps awake.[35] 'Sleep', we remember, and the 'security' that caused and accompanied it, had enfeebled Queen Elizabeth's response to the threat of international Catholicism,[36] a deficiency that in turn had induced her to contemplate the surrender of her own and her country's strength and independence to the Duke of Anjou. Sleep is perilous in private life too. When Pamela and Musidorus pause on their journey of elopement, Pamela, 'having been long kept from [sleep] with the perplexity of her dangerous' escapade, 'grow[s] extreme sleepy'. Musidorus spots his chance. Earlier, with a love-song, he tried to 'bring her to a dull yielding-over her forces'. Now, 'invited by him to sleep with . . . softly uttered verses', she 'was brought into a sweet sleep', where she was exposed to 'two dangers', the rape attempted by Musidorus and the incursion of the Phagonian rebels which thwarts him.[37]

In public life, we saw, sleep can protect our illusions. So can it in private life. One of the moments of irony that derive from Basilius' inversion of

---

29 *OA* 45/9–10, 45/18–21.
30 *NA* 216/19–20, 215/27–9, 216/29–30. Plangus is prone to the 'youthful' failing of 'credulity': *NA* 221/12, 272/24.
31 *OA* 67/15–25; *NA* 60/9–10.
32 *OA* 109/22–3, 110/10 (cf. *OA* 110/24, 110/34, 111/6).
33 *OA* 139/19–21, 141/7, 373/23–4.
34 *OA* 254/18–20. The songs of Basilius disclose his ethical plight too. He sings, without understanding it, a 'yearly-used' hymn to virtue and Apollo. He soon afterwards sings, understanding it all too well, a blasphemous love-song to Cleophila, 'not left me by my ancestors, but begun in myself'. *OA* 134/5–6, 177/32–3.
35 *OA* 259/17–23, 254/27, 255/9–14.
36 Above, pp. 61–5.
37 *OA* 200/20–201/9, 107/1–2, 202/13.

ethical rules has him looking forward to 'sinless sleep' with the disguised
Pyrocles and telling himself that 'the rest of thy time hath been but a dream
unto thee'. Book Three of the *Old Arcadia* is preceded by a 'night full of
passions' among the self-absorbed princely lovers: it ends with 'the greater
persons . . . sleeping or otherwise occupied'. Thereafter, as Walter Davis
observes, 'all the characters involved arise from sleep to find out what they
have really done, and what they should have done'.[38]

While Pyrocles sleeps with Philoclea, Dametas, that 'right pattern
of . . . fear',[39] removes the prince's sword, that symbol of 'a virtuous courage
that was ever awake'.[40] Philisides suffers an analogous fate: while 'asleep' he
is 'unarmed' by 'coward Cupid'. 'Deadly sleep', 'traitor sleep', 'took' him
from the path of virtue, nullifying the earlier exertions of his 'wakeful
mind'.[41] The shepherds, earlier as faultily 'asleep' and 'secure' as the English
ruling class to which they correspond, opt out of the crisis that follows
Basilius' death, 'hoping by a sleep, forgetting themselves, to ease their present
dolours'.[42] The shepherds of *Mother Hubberds Tale*, we saw, sleep too: it is
'careles sleep' that exposes their flock to destruction.[43] Geron, who warns
Philisides against excessive 'sleep', urges him instead to 'let special care upon
thy flock be stayed'. He pleads in vain, for Philisides in his lovesickness seems
indifferent to the protection of his sheep. Instead he writes a poem, a lover's
lament.[44] The shepherd Histor likewise writes poetry when he should be
attending to his pastoral – that is, his public – duties.[45] Perhaps the author of
the *Arcadia* does the same.

Philisides behaved differently 'before he had given over himself' to love.
Then it was that he guarded his flock and sang the beast-fable, a poem not
about love but about the peril of tyranny in the state. He sings it sitting on
the ground. When we first met him he was reclining on the ground,
absorbed in himself.[46] Now he is dedicated to his public duties. Vigilance,
which elicits the fable from him, is also a subject of it.

The construction of monarchy in the beast-fable, a process to which each of
the animals contributes its gift, has its parallels in the romantic plot. In the
Second Eclogues it is love, rather than monarchy, that is built or imposed by
its separate components. Pyrocles describes the allurements of Philoclea
which have 'undermine[d]' him and led him to 'yield' to 'conquest': 'her
loose hair be the shot, the breasts the pikes be', while her hands, lips, legs,

---

38 *OA* 275/6, 275/12, 168/1, 244/34–245/1; Walter Davis, 'A Map of Arcadia', in Davis and
     Lanham, *Sidney's Arcadia*, p. 159.
39 *OA* 266/29–30.
40 Above, p. 300.
41 *OA* 335/10, 336/3–9, 340/25–8.
42 *OA* 350/12–14; above, p. 201.
43 Oram, p. 346 (ll. 333–6); above, pp. 64–5.
44 *OA* 75/25, 75/32, 125/15–29.
45 *OA* 152/14–15.
46 *OA* 255/13, 71/32–3.

eyes, have each played their military part. But there is one difference from Philisides' fable. Philoclea's attributes, though their task is eased by Pyrocles' inner weakness, conquer him from without.[47] The beasts of the fable are conquered from within, building tyranny with their own attributes. The Second Eclogues provide a closer parallel to their predicament in the afflictions of Musidorus, who sees what his own 'mischiefs have contributed' to love's conquest of him. His 'sight', 'thought', 'wonder', 'attention', 'delight', each plays its part in his downfall. Other characteristics of Musidorus give his love 'eyes', 'wings', 'hands': in the fable the beasts bestow the same bodily parts on 'man'.[48]

Musidorus' self-surrender invites upon him the fate that visits the beasts. Again the private and public worlds come together. Turning to love, as the beasts turn to 'man', for 'protection', Musidorus risks instead, as Dicus warns him, the 'destruction' of his 'safety'.[49] Just so, in Sidney's warning to her, does Elizabeth, 'the continuance of [whose] safety' his 'Letter' seeks, risk destroying that safety by surrendering her and her country's liberty to Anjou.[50] The owl of Philisides' fable advises the other animals 'not to seech / So hastily that which they would repent': the price of Musidorus' love, Dicus warns him, will be 'late remorse in folly dearly bought'.[51] The beast-fable, describing the surrender of public liberty, is flanked by material describing the surrender of private liberty. Before the fable Sidney places a song that shows a husband needlessly throwing away his marital happiness through the passion of jealousy.[52] After it he places Geron's warning to the lover 'late to repent' of the effects of his 'fear' and 'fond thraldom'.[53]

'Fear' and 'fond thraldom', the sources of our subjection in private life, cause our public subjection too. There too they impel 'causeless yieldings'. There too we are left to count the cost of our surrender.

The beasts have 'consented' to their slavery.[54] Indeed they have devoted art and industry to its construction. Here is a persistent and under-explored

---

47 *OA* 165/10–166/1; cf. *OA* 332/14–17.
48 *OA* 139/16, 138/16–24, 257/18–31.
49 *OA* 139/22.
50 *MP* 46/16–17.
51 *OA* 256/31–2, 139/27; cf. *OA* 276/33, 351/31. Philippe Duplessis-Mornay, writing of the conflicts of classes (akin to those which destroy pristine unity in Philisides' fable) that are wreaking destruction in the French wars of religion, fears that 'too late we shall repent of having been so badly advised not to have lived together . . . in peace and union': *Mémoires et correspondance de Duplessis-Mornay*, ii. 75. Forward Protestants had long argued that the queen would 'repent', 'too late', the inaction of her foreign policy (above, p. 78). Greville records Sidney's view that she would have realised 'too late' the consequences of her marriage to Anjou: *GP* 32/31. The exiles of the 1550s had often expressed the fear that their countrymen would awake 'too late'.
52 *OA* 249–53.
53 *OA* 262/35, 261/31, 262/23, 263/9. For the correspondence between destruction in the soul and destruction in the state, compare too *OA* 147/8–10 with *OA* 258/3, 258/10–12 (and see *OA* 188/17–19, 266/2–3).
54 *OA* 257/31.

theme of the political literature of the early modern period. It is the theme
encapsulated in a book written by a friend of Montaigne and published on
the eve of the French wars of religion or perhaps a little earlier: Etienne de
la Boétie's *Discours de la servitude volontaire*, 'of voluntary servitude'. In de la
Boétie's eyes the tyranny imposed on us by others is bad enough, but the
tyranny we have built by our choices, and which we are powerless to
remove, has a peculiar agony. De la Boétie's treatise was recycled in leading
Huguenot tracts of the 1570s.[55] 'We are all naturally free,' he observes,
asking, like Rousseau after him, how and why we come to lose our freedom.[56] 'It is the people', he decides, 'who enslave themselves, who cut their
own throats: who, having the choice of being vassals or freemen, reject their
liberty and submit to the yoke, who consent to their own evil, or rather
procure it.' 'The tyrant enslaves his subjects' – as 'man', that creation of the
beasts' 'consen[t]', enslaves them – 'by the means of one another'.[57]

Voluntary servitude is as profound a preoccupation of Sidney as of de la
Boétie. According to Greville, Sidney wished to 'publis[h] the differences
between monarchs and tyrants so clearly to the world as hereafter all states
that would take upon their necks the yoke of tyranny must justly be reputed
voluntary slaves in the choice of that passive bondage'.[58] That is how
Languet, whose 'old true tales' lie behind the beast-fable, 'reputed' them.
Time and again Languet interpreted the disasters of contemporary Europe in
terms of self-surrender, of the success of 'baits' which 'tempt' men 'to betray
their country', of the political 'folly' that leads to self-inflicted 'ruin' and
'suicidal destruction'.[59] That was a failing, he believed, of those princes who,
confronted by the popish threat, were 'wilfully and knowingly . . . giving
themselves over to ruin', or who were allowing the religious wars, which
they had brought on themselves, to 'wear out' their 'strength' and so expose
them to external conquest.[60]

Self-surrender, a fault of princes, can be a fault also of the subjects who
submit to them. In a letter to his brother Robert, Sidney remarked on the
submission of Italian peoples to foreign or princely domination: 'there is little
there but tyrannous oppression and servile yielding to them that have little or
no rule over them'.[61] Languet, writing to Sidney in 1574, contrasted nations
that are healthily governed with 'the custom of the people who, through

---

55   Kingdon, *Myths*, pp. 73, 87, 168–72.
56   Etienne ['Stephen'] de la Boétie, *A Discourse of Voluntary Servitude* (London, 1735), p. 63. (That
     translation carries the French text on facing pages.) The *Vindiciae*, invoking Aesop in a discussion
     of the origins of monarchy, notes that 'men are free by nature': Garnett, p. 92. I am grateful to
     David Wootton for introducing me to de la Boétie.
57   Ibid., pp. 53, 111.
58   *GP* 58/17–20.
59   Pears, pp. 98, 111, 135; Levy, 'Correspondence', nos 25, 57, 62.
60   Pears, pp. 63, 44. Languet's hero William of Orange warned the Dutch not to allow posterity
     to accuse their generation of having 'lost' their ancestral rights to a foreign tyrant
     'by . . . cowardice': *CSPF 1577–8*, p. 56.
61   Feuillerat, iii. 127.

choice or fear, have so enslaved themselves that they actually think it sinful even to suspect a prince of acting wrongly'.[62] In the Netherlands Languet noticed the yearning of the Ghantois to 'give over' their liberty to Anjou.[63] Though strict conditions were imposed on Anjou's sovereignty there, 'carelessness', as Philippe Duplessis-Mornay's widow remembered, squandered them; 'these conditions . . . were immediately relaxed solely because people were too ready to be deceived'.[64] What then of the 'credulous' English, as Stubbs's *Gaping Gulph* called them when they hearkened to French blandishments at the height of the Anjou crisis? Must not they, like the lovers in *Arcadia* who succumb to fear, expect 'late remorse in folly dearly bought'? And what remorse might await their queen, who in 1579 seems, like Basilius, 'a prince unconquered [ready] to become a slave to a stranger'?[65]

Voluntary servitude was not a new preoccupation of English public life. The subject had exercised the Marian exiles of the 1550s, a decade with so large a presence in the thinking of Sidney and his party. The exiles had watched their countrymen yielding their liberty to Mary Tudor. In Philisides' fable the tyrant 'at the first' behaves well, or affects to behave well, to his subjects: the famous treatise of 1556 by the exile John Ponet, *A Shorte Treatise of Politick Power*, recalls, with an eye on the present, that William the Conqueror 'at the first' made 'very fair promises of peace, quietness and justice', with which 'the foolish fond people were soon beguiled'.[66] The theme is stated more fully in the pamphlet of 1558 which we have heard echoed more than once in the *Arcadia*, Christopher Goodman's *How Superior Powers Oght to be Obeyd*. Goodman turns, as Philisides' fable does, to I Samuel 8 to explain the rise of modern tyranny. 'The people', he declares, 'ought not to suffer themselves to be made slaves' or to allow:

all power and liberty to be taken from them and thereby to become brute beasts, without judgement and reason . . . as though they were not reasonable creatures, but brute beasts: as if there were no difference betwixt bond slaves and free subjects . . . . The people, if they suffer this right to be taken from them, then are . . . an occasion that their kings and rulers are turned to tyrants and cruel oppressors, according as Samuel promised the people of Israel should come upon them . . . .[67]

---

62   Osborn, *Young Philip Sidney*, p. 209.
63   Pears, p. 174.
64   Crump, *Huguenot Family*, pp. 179–80.
65   *OA* 96/23–4.
66   Hudson, *John Ponet*, p. [168]. The fable contains further memories of Ponet's tract. Sidney's 'man' reveals his true character once he is 'rooted' in power: Ponet relates that William, 'once settled . . . beginneth to play Rex'. William, like Sidney's 'man', 'spoiled the nobility of their goods and possessions' and 'made them slaves'. In Ponet's account, the subjects of Mary Tudor await a fate akin to that of Sidney's beasts: 'your wings must be dubbed, your feathers must be pulled . . . your substance shall be gotten by little and little out of your hands'. Ibid., pp. [168], [166]. The opponents of the Anjou match recalled the tyranny of William the Conqueror: Murdin, *Collection*, p. 329.
67   Goodman, *How Superior Powers*, pp. 148–50.

The anxieties of the 1550s resurface in Sidney's generation and among his friends. Fulke Greville warns against voluntary subjection to tyranny. His mind, following Sidney's, turns to Aesop and to analogies with beasts.[68] Men become the 'beast[ly]' subjects of tyrants, he thinks, because they allow themselves to be 'hoodwinked' or 'deceiv[ed]' into subordination.[69] The flatterers and favourites who 'corrupt' kings exploit our credulity:

> And as the bird in hand, with freedom lost,
> Serves for a stale, his fellows to betray:
> So do these darlings raised at princes' cost
> Tempt man to throw his liberty away . . ..
> Whereby, like Aesop's dog, men lose their meat . . ..[70]

In lines likewise reminiscent of Philisides' fable, Greville explains that tyranny is built of the components of self-surrender:

> mankind is both the form,
> And matter, wherewith tyrannies transform:
> For power can neither see, work, or devise,
> Without the people's hands, hearts, wit, and eyes:
> So that were man not by himself oppressed,
> Kings would not, tyrants could not make him beast.[71]

Like Sidney, like Goodman, Greville turns to I Samuel 8 to illustrate the origin of servitude in men's choice:

> Man then repine not at these boundless kings,
> Since you endure the fate of your forefathers,
> To whom God did foretell, on human wings,
> How inequality, once raised, still gathers;
> Their choice offended him . . ..[72]

'People', regrets Greville, 'are superstitious, caught with shows: / To power why do they else their freedom give . . .?'[73]

The threat of voluntary servitude troubled Duplessis-Mornay too. He addressed it in a memorandum which roams history for parallels and which warns against the process that we have watched in Philisides' fable: amid the

---

68 GP 68/19–20; Wilkes, pp. 43 (st. 35), 163 (sts 510, 513). In the *Vindiciae* tyrants are beasts: Garnett, p. 98.

69 GP 38/17, 175/13–14; cf. Bullough, i. 148 (sonnet cii, ll. 63–4).

70 Bullough, i. 129–30 (sonnet lxxviii, ll. 4, 19–25).

71 Ibid., ii. 98 (*Mustapha*, Chorus Secundus, ll. 205–10).

72 Wilkes, p. 41 (st. 25). It is then that Greville, in a warning akin to that in which Sidney urges 'man' not to glory in tyranny, tells princes to 'over-rack not your creation' (st. 26).

73 Bullough, ii. 184 (*Alaham* III. iii. 89–92).

destruction of the French wars of religion, Mornay feared, the people would overthrow the nobility which ruled them and subject themselves to the harsher servitude of a single tyrant.[74] The *Vindiciae* of Mornay and Languet turns to I Samuel 8, where, it explains, the Israelites 'voluntarily brought on themselves' their 'servitude'. In that chapter 'God wanted to reveal to the people its own fickleness' and to show them 'how prone' are royal powers to 'lapse into violence', 'how precipitate [is] . . . the change from kingdom to tyranny'.[75]

Voluntary servitude is a principal theme, perhaps the principal theme, of Philisides' fable. It is a principal theme, perhaps the principal theme, of the *Arcadia*.

Philisides' song ends with a riddling couplet: 'And you, poor beasts, in patience bide your hell, / Or know your strengths, and then you shall do well.' 'Know your strengths', we saw, alludes to arguments, particularly those present in the *Vindiciae, Contra Tyrannos*, justifying armed resistance to tyranny. But we saw too that the words point back to the story that precedes them, to the gratuitous surrender of the beasts' 'strengths' to tyranny. Those 'strengths' are something more than armed force. They are the qualities and virtues of which arms, when well used, are the expression.

One of the strengths yielded by the beasts is unity. Unity is harmony: 'the lion by the lamb did lie'.[76] That and other images of harmony – between Philisides and his sheep, between Musidorus and his horse – show the polity of the emotions to be in good order. Unity is a virtue promoted by reason, disunity a vice born of passion. Reason is constant, passion mutable. Those princes of the present time, says Languet, who turn moderate governments into tyrannies exploit the mutability of the people, and thus deprive them of the 'strength' to 'recapture their liberty'.[77] In Sidney's thinking, what is true of reason and passion is true of practical politics. Unity was essential to the forward Protestant cause, to its 'strength'. 'Our unity', declared Walsingham, 'might be strength to ourselves and an aid unto our neighbours' against the Catholic menace: Euarchus urges the states of Greece to 'unit[e] their strength' against foreign peril. 'Division', Sidney tells the queen, has caused the 'inward weakness' of her government.[78] It was through 'division among ourselves', knew forward Protestants, that England and Protestantism faced the prospect of 'ruin' and 'destruction' 'by our own fault', 'through [our own] folly'. Opponents of the Anjou match, who wanted Elizabeth to 'stand alone' against her enemies, knew that division would destroy that prospect and might destroy the realm. 'Regnum in se divisum desolabitur', they

74 Above, p. 230.
75 Garnett, p. 128; cf. van Gelderen, *Dutch Revolt*, pp. 104–5.
76 *OA* 256/15.
77 Levy, 'Correspondence', no. 28.
78 Above, p. 197; *OA* 355n.

warned. If a divided kingdom cannot 'stand', neither can a divided soul. 'I am divided in myself', laments the lovesick Gynecia; 'how can I stand?'[79]

The beasts lose their unity. 'Man', who at first rules them 'fellow-like',[80] then puts an end to their harmony with him and with each other. He subjugates them by dividing them against themselves. They learn what Greville, who so often amplifies the lessons of Philisides' fable, tells about our divisions (or 'distractions'), which:

> keep our strengths unknown;
> One holding that, which others give away,
> The base whereon all tyranny doth stay . . ..
> Hence came those false monarchal counsels in . . ..

Greville believes that virtuous or 'true monarchy . . . works a perfect unity' which serves 'mutual ends';[81] that the people of a harmonious common-wealth will be 'strengths' to 'their king', just as, 'knew kings their strength, our freedom were to serve'.[82] But when men 'yield' their liberty to 'thrones' which have 'gr[own] idols',

> these strengths which did before concur
> To build, invent, examine, and conclude,
> Now turn disease, bring question, and demur . . ..[83]

A principal source of division is fear. As Greville says, fear makes us selfish, indifferent to 'neighbours' overthrow'.[84] Fear is the passion about which Sidney's analyses of politics have most to say. It is healthy when we employ it in the service of reason and virtue, as Philisides does in his 'dread', in 'fear[ing] sore', as he guards his flock on Ister Bank.[85] But the *Arcadia* more often shows fear free of those restraints. Then it becomes a source not of strength but of weakness, 'disarming human minds of native might'.[86]

It was to 'fear', we saw, that Sidney attributed both Basilius' abandonment of his duties and Elizabeth's readiness to yield her country's liberty and religion to Anjou.[87] Instead, both monarchs should take virtue, which masters fear, for their foundation. Virtue is the ally of, even synonymous with, true religion, the religion which inspires us to virtuous action, religion purged of the superstition and idolatry that intimidate or anaesthetise us.[88] Of the

---

79 Above, pp. 141, 197; HMC *Cecil*, ii. 270; *OA* 183/7; cf. *OA* 63/14–15.
80 *OA* 258/5.
81 Wilkes, pp. 48 (sts 52–3), 163 (st. 513).
82 Ibid., p. 141 (st. 424); Bullough, ii. 203 (*Alaham*, Chorus Quartus, l. 10).
83 Wilkes, p. 52 (st. 69).
84 Ibid., p. 51 (sts 63, 65).
85 *OA* 255/8–12.
86 Above, p. 336.
87 Above, pp. 121, 135, 138.
88 Above, Chapters 2, 4.

'strengths' which we are to 'know', and which will help us to withstand fear and disunity, virtue and religion are the essence. In 'standing alone', Sidney explained to Elizabeth, she would 'make that religion upon which you stand to carry the only strength', for England's Protestants were 'your chief, if not your sole, strength'.[89]

By 'strength' Sidney there meant political strength. But political strength, in his judgement, has its centre in ethical strength, in 'strength of mind'. It was 'strength' which, he admitted to Languet in 1578, his 'mind' was 'beginning, by reason of my indolent ease, imperceptibly to lose'. It was on 'strength of mind', on 'steadfastness of . . . mind', that Languet in return urged him to 'stand firm'.[90] Pyrocles follows Languet's principle in parting company with Musidorus, his 'depend[ence]' on whom has made him 'as one strayed from his best strength'.[91] 'Strength of virtue', Pyrocles recognises, is properly men's 'assured foundation'.

That foundation, he explains, lies 'in themselves'.[92] For it is 'within ourselves', as we have found, that the ethical battles of Arcadia, both in love and in politics, are fought out. As Philanax tries to make Basilius understand at the outset, 'the heavens', the source of 'wisdom and virtue' and thus of 'inward comfort', 'have left us in ourselves sufficient guides'.[93] If we desert their guidance the fault is in ourselves. Both in love and in politics the true tyranny is internal. Sidney's fiction shows the lovers to be 'captiv[ed] . . . within [them]selves':[94] men 'inwardly defective' in wit and courage, believes Greville, 'though they be born free in the laws of nations, are yet slaves in the narrow moulds of their own affections'. Again Greville projects Sidney's voice beyond the grave. It is, he maintains, upon our frailties – sloth, ignorance, baseness, the sway of passion – that 'power' builds and that 'the inferior sort of men' are 'made captive'.[95] Tyrants too are captive, no less than the subjects who empower them. The reign of Mary Tudor, Greville thinks, shows that 'princes captived in nature can seldom keep anything free in their governments'.[96] But it is our own passions and deficiencies that make possible the rule of a Mary Tudor over us. Drawing again on Aesop and beast-fables,[97] Greville maintains that 'absolute governments' 'stroke us with our own hands' and 'threaten us with our own strengths' so as to swell their powers. They will retain their supremacy 'till the beasts begin to know their strengths'.[98]

89 *MP* 56/22–6, 47/31–2.
90 Pears, pp. 143, 155, 183.
91 Above, p. 334.
92 *OA* 35/29–30.
93 *OA* 7/3–14.
94 *OA* 43/13.
95 *GP* 38/17–18, 147/17–25.
96 *GP* 130/27–9.
97 *GP* 157/9–11, 157/31–2.
98 *GP* 157/14–19, 158/10–11.

What form will that knowledge take? Greville, in reproducing Philisides' injunction to the beasts (the injunction to 'know your strengths'), is not alluding to the justifications of armed resistance with which critics are readiest to associate it. His concern is the threat posed to virtue and liberty by two passions which are twin servants to fortune, 'the one bewitching, the other amazing us'. The first is 'fear'. Where the *Arcadia* shows 'fear . . . disarming human minds of native might', Greville argues that 'fear' erodes our 'native freedom', 'enticing, or forcing us to give away our rights'. The second is 'hope', which, in the process of subjugating us to power, 'master[s] the strength of number with a multitude of scattered desires'. 'Fear and hope' are 'temptations' against which we must 'stand firm'. They are the 'crafty spies' of 'tyranny', 'giving intelligence what may be forced within us'.[99]

Sidney, too, knows what may be forced within us. He too knows that subservience to hope and fear, and to their mistress fortune, is the enemy within. Yet if our weaknesses lie within us, so do our strengths. 'Outward accidents', as Sidney's 'Letter' tells Elizabeth, 'do [not] much prevail against a true inward strength.'[100]

Behind that conviction there lie the 'philosophy precepts' to which we have watched his fiction giving 'pregnant images of life'. They can be simply summarised. Where passion rules, tyranny will prevail in the heart and in the state. Where reason rules, 'moderate' and 'limited' government will prevail in the heart and in the state. The sway of reason, in heart and state alike, is the victory of virtue over fortune; of learning over ignorance; of unity over discord; of gentleness over violence; of consent over will; of service over servitude. It teaches us to know our strengths.

In guarding the sway of reason we must, like Philisides through the night on Ister Bank, be ever awake. Otherwise 'causeless yieldings', whether in the private or in the public world, will lose us our liberty. Sidney, so conscious of the peril to liberty, does not underestimate the challenge of preserving it. He acknowledges the loneliness of the responsibility on which it will call. But the courage to 'stand alone', if we can find it, will bring us to safety, whether as lovers or rulers or peoples. The shepherd Geron may be old, testy, sometimes wrong, but he is right at least in his advice to the lovelorn Philisides: 'upon thyself to stand'.[101] It is the advice given too by Philanax to Basilius in Arcadia's hour of impending crisis and by Sidney to Elizabeth in England's. By that rule of virtue, and by it alone, the survival of Sidney's country and religion can be won.

---

99   *GP* 157/25–158/6, 164/1–2.
100   *MP* 47/14–15.
101   *OA* 73/20.

Greville, Sidney and the Two Arcadias

Fulke Greville's 'A Dedication to Sir Philip Sidney' (or, as it has more usually been called, his 'Life' of Sidney) is an essential source both for Sidney's career and for his writing. It is also a problematical one, invaluable if used with caution but potentially deceptive if not. It was evidently written largely in or around the years 1610–12, though it may have been begun in some form as early as 1604 and may not have been completed until 1614.[1] It is really three books in one: a biography of Sidney; a tribute to Queen Elizabeth; and an account of Greville's own writings. But the first two subjects inevitably overlap. One problem in assessing Greville's treatment of them is obvious: the failures and tricks of memory that led him into identifiable errors of fact and may have led him into unidentifiable ones. But there are more subtle difficulties too. With respect to Sidney's career, they arise from Greville's Jacobean political perspective. With respect to Sidney's writing they have two causes. First there are the changes in Greville's values which occurred between the composition of Sidney's fiction and the writing of the 'Dedication'. The second is that, in writing about that fiction, Greville thinks mainly of the *New Arcadia*. Though much of what he says is as pertinent to the *Old Arcadia* as to the *New*, some of it can be a misleading guide to the earlier version. Yet that difficulty can also be a help to us. To notice where Greville's observations fit the *New Arcadia* and not the *Old* is to be alerted to differences between the two versions.

Once it was plain that James I would succeed her smoothly, the death of Queen Elizabeth in 1603 was received with general relief. Her last years had been troubled by political unrest, by a pervasive sense of political corruption,

---

1 *GP* xxii–xxiv. John Gouws's introduction to that edition is indispensable to the study of the 'Dedication', though I occasionally part company with his conclusions. Some of my own conclusions about the 'Dedication' are set out, more fully than here, in Worden, 'Friend to Sir Philip Sidney'.

by the prospect of civil war, by fears of tyranny.[2] James's accession brought hopes of fresh political health. The hopes did not last. By the time Greville wrote the 'Dedication' (or the greater part of it), opinions of Elizabeth were being radically revised in her favour.[3] Critics of James, who could not attack him openly, found an alternative method of condemnation in the praise of his predecessor, with whom James was silently contrasted. Greville's 'Dedication' is a pioneering and leading essay in that strategy. He wrote it with a view not merely to lamenting present failings but to correcting them – perhaps through the agency of James's heir, Henry Prince of Wales, around whom critics of the regime gathered in the two years before Henry's early death in 1612. Greville's account of Sidney's views on foreign policy is in effect a state paper, in which Sidney, 'our unbelieved Cassandra', foretells the failings of Jacobean diplomacy and hopes that his own militantly anti-Spanish programme will be 'revived'.[4] It was among advocates of that programme that the cult of nostalgia for Elizabeth was strongest. It was also among them that the cult of nostalgia for Sidney was strongest. The problem was that Elizabeth and Sidney had profoundly disagreed. For Greville the problem was acute.

Elizabeth, in the 'Dedication', is 'this miracle of princes', 'this she-David of ours', 'this mirror of justice', 'this unmatchable queen and woman'.[5] How many disasters, we are invited to reflect, would have been avoided 'if God had either lengthened the days of that worthy lady' or if 'time' had 'not neglected her wisdom so suddenly'?[6] Unlike one monarch who cannot be named, she did not turn her court into a 'farm' or 'suffe[r] public places to be made particular farms of private men'. Her 'council-board', 'that glorious type of civil government', was not 'compelled to descend, and become broker for money, executioner of extremity'. She forbade 'the latitudes which some modern princes allow to their favourites'.[7] She respected and sustained the nobility and yeomanry. She resisted the general movement of European monarchies towards the suppression of representative institutions and non-parliamentary taxation. Instead she 'chose that narrower but safer medium of state assemblies, concluding that these two honourable houses [of parliament] were the only judicious, faithful and industrious favourites of unencroaching monarchs'. She honoured the 'native birthrights' and 'native liberties' of her subjects and spared them 'tyrannies'.[8]

Greville had been less enthusiastic about Elizabeth's rule when Sidney was alive. So had Sidney. On occasion Greville does allow the memory of the

---

2 Worden, 'Ben Jonson among the Historians'.
3 C. V. Wedgwood, *Oliver Cromwell and the Elizabethan Inheritance* (London, 1970); Anne Barton, *Ben Jonson, Dramatist* (Cambridge, 1984), ch. 14.
4 *GP* 68/11, 70/30–1.
5 *GP* 103/14, 98/31, 127/22–3, 129/29; cf. *GP* 128/27–8.
6 *GP* 126/33–127/2.
7 *GP* 117/3, 110/5–6, 117/5–7, 105/12–13.
8 *GP* 114/22–5, 106/4–8, 114/11.

conflicts between Sidney and the queen to rise, albeit unobtrusively, to the surface. Thus Sidney, he intimates, was unable to persuade 'this excellent lady' of the merits of an 'offensive war' with Spain. She had settled for a 'defensive war – which commonly falls out rather to be an impoverishing of enemies than any means to enrich or discipline their states that undertake it'. Yet when Greville's focus shifts to the failings of James I, his tune changes. Elizabeth's 'defensive wars', it now appears, were an 'active, victorious, enriching and balancing course', which 'time' has 'exchang[ed] . . . for an idle, I fear deceiving, shadow of peace'.[9] Greville contrasts 'this effeminate age' with the 'active times' of that 'active prince'.[10] It was, in fact, precisely for the 'inactivity' of her diplomacy, and for its 'idleness' and 'effeminacy', that Sidney and his friends had repeatedly blamed her. Repeatedly too they had complained of the want of 'foresight' and 'courage' in her foreign dealings, her failure to build up military and naval strength, her want of sympathy with the 'oppressed' Protestants of France and the Netherlands, her reluctance to form confessional alliances.[11] Yet when Greville contrasts her with her successor he tells us that she 'wanted . . . neither foresight, courage nor might . . . to support her neighbours unjustly oppressed'. He calls it 'worthy of reverence in this queen that she was never afraid or ashamed to avow the quarrel of religion for a ground of her friends or enemies'.[12] If Sidney has ever turned in the grave, it must have been upon hearing those words of his intimate friend. Greville's retrospective portrait of Elizabeth's reign is not merely different from what he and Sidney would have said to themselves and each other at the time: sometimes it is opposite to it.

Greville's hindsight raises many problems for the student of Sidney's political beliefs (though it would raise more of them if it were less transparent). The general grounds on which Sidney had opposed Elizabeth's policies were those on which Greville opposed James's. A diplomacy of militant or forward Protestantism was the ideal of the two friends and was overruled by both rulers. It was the continuity of that ideal that made Sidney's memory, late in Elizabeth's reign, dear to the followers and then to the mourners of the Earl of Essex. The same continuity made that memory, around the time Greville wrote the 'Dedication', dear to the followers and then the mourners of Prince Henry.[13]

Yet even the most continuous of policies has to adapt to changes of circumstance. Greville is rarely interested in such changes. He mainly ignores the alterations to the diplomatic map of Europe that occurred between the composition of the *Arcadia* and the writing of the 'Dedication'. To that rule

---

9   *GP* 47/27–48/3, 127/1–4.
10 *GP* 7/11–12, 76n.
11 Above, Chapter 5.
12 *GP* 124/2–5, 102/3–5.
13 Dennis Kay, *Melodious Tears. The English Funeral Elegy from Spenser to Milton* (Oxford, 1990), ch. 5; Roy Strong, *Henry Prince of Wales* (London, 1986), pp. 159, 220–4; Worden, 'Friend to Sir Philip Sidney'.

there are two exceptions that prove it. He makes them not in order to acknowledge that the problems of diplomacy have changed since Sidney's time, but rather to demonstrate his friend's powers of diplomatic prophecy. Thus, first, Sidney 'prophes[ied]' the union of the crowns of England and Scotland of 1603 and 'foresaw' its consequences for both nations; and, secondly, he 'fores[aw]', as a 'prophet', the long-term strains that would arise in the alliance formed in 1585 between England and the Dutch.[14]

It is likely that Sidney said things that could retrospectively be interpreted in those lights. Greville, so concerned to be true to his friend's memory, would not have cheated on it. The most his recollections can plausibly be charged with are confusions and distortions. If we are alive to his retrospective purpose, and if we measure his evidence, when we can, against the documentary legacy of Sidney's lifetime, he can be a penetrating guide to his friend's political career and beliefs. But he is never an easy one.

He is no easier a guide to Sidney's fiction. His description of what he says that he 'know[s]' to have been his friend's purpose is reproduced above on page 15. It is characteristically abstract. Has any reader been entirely sure what Greville means by it? Perhaps its lack of condensation explains why little attention has been paid to the question which version or versions of Sidney's story Greville has in mind.

In 1590 he published the uncompleted *New Arcadia*, a version which (we shall see) he had reasons to prefer to the *Old*. The 'Dedication' is more reliable as a guide to the *New Arcadia* than to the *Old*. The *Old Arcadia* does have a place in its thoughts. The 'Dedication' remembers the whole process of the composition of Sidney's fiction, not merely the writing of the *New Arcadia*. Thus the 'intent and scope' of Sidney which Greville discerns and describes was, he 'know[s]', 'the first project' of his friend's fiction.[15] Again, Greville emphasises the rescue of Arcadia by King Euarchus, a subject which belongs to the *Old Arcadia*, not to the *New*.[16] Other remarks of Greville may allude to passages of the *Old Arcadia* which either do not appear in the *New Arcadia* or, if they do, are less conspicuous there.[17] Even so, it is the *New Arcadia* that is closer to the front of his thoughts.

---

14   *GP* 66/12–20, 84/7–25.

15   *GP* 11/9.

16   *GP* 9/14–10/5. It was of course added to the *New* in the composite edition of 1593. But Greville, who describes Sidney's story as uncompleted, does not mention the 1593 version, which repudiated his own version and which gave the impression of completeness.

17   (i) Would Greville have made so much of the failings of Basilius if he had remembered only the revised version, where that theme is less prominently situated? After all, those failings, the theme noticed by Edwin Greenlaw very soon after the rediscovery of the *Old Arcadia* early in this century, had gone unremarked during the three centuries since Greville wrote. (ii) Greville's remark that Sidney's fiction shows the danger of innovation 'even in a quiet and equally tempered people' (*GP* 9/22–3) may point to the opening sentence (which we saw on p. 168 to be politically charged) of the *Old Arcadia*, where we learn of 'the moderate and well tempered minds of the people' (*OA* 4/5–6); the corresponding passage of the *New Arcadia* (where the words 'moderate and' are omitted) is less prominently positioned (*NA* 16/5–6).

There are two principal indications of that priority. The first is Greville's list of Sidney's topics 'in the subject's case', which fits the revised version better than its less capacious predecessor.[18] The second is his statement that Sidney's 'purpose was to limn out . . . exact pictures of every posture in the mind'.[19] The *Old Arcadia*, it is true, does contain what Sidney calls 'pictures' or 'examples' which have the illustrative purpose to which Greville's words point. One of the favoured devices of the earlier version is to capture, as a mischievous photographer might do, a group of characters each pursuing his or her variation on the theme of human folly.[20] Yet that technique, though fertile, is used only occasionally. In the *New Arcadia*, a more emblematic work, the pictorial and exemplary method becomes at once more stately and more prominent. It takes its place in Sidney's architecture, which deploys, for much of the time, symmetrically arranged moral tableaux.[21] In the text of 1590, which Greville prepared for the press, that characteristic is highlighted by the insertion into Sidney's narrative of chapter headings containing such descriptions as 'inconstancy and envy portrayed'.[22]

Greville's concentration on the *New Arcadia* has a bearing on his political commentary too. The *New Arcadia*, where the presence of contemporary events is usually less immediate than in the *Old*, is gentler about the failings of Queen Elizabeth and her regime than the earlier version (though far from silent on them).[23] Without a knowledge of the *Old Arcadia* we might miss

(iii) Greville's reference to men who undergo 'traverses' of (among other things) 'private fortunes or misfortunes', and who are 'forced in the strains of this life to pass through any straits or latitudes of good or ill fortune' (GP 11/2–6), recalls three pieces of information which are given early in the *Old Arcadia* and which do not reappear in the *New*: the first, that the young princes have received 'great traverses, both of good and evil fortune' (*OA* 10/37–8); the second, that it is Pyrocles' 'either good or evil fortune' to fall in love (*OA* 11/21); the third, that the princes vow 'to continue partakers of all either good or evil fortune' (*OA* 43/16–17). On the other hand the theme of Stoicism, which Greville's comment on good and ill fortune summons, is (we shall see) more fully developed in the *New Arcadia* than in the *Old*.

18 GP 10/30–11/8. Admittedly even readers of the *New Arcadia* might be pressed to identify the moments when Sidney addresses some of the subjects listed; but Greville may mean not that the whole list is covered by the *New Arcadia* but that it would have been covered if the *New Arcadia* had been completed (GP 10/8ff.). In regretting Sidney's failure to complete his story, Greville provides another indication that his own mind is on the *New Arcadia*, for he refers to characters who appear only in the revised version (GP 10/17).

19 GP 11/3–4.

20 *OA* 46/34–47/1, 48/9–17, 49/15–20, 132/11–18, 152/19–20, 167/21–4, 174/12–18, 222/32, 230/22, 266/29–30, 270/31–2, 281/9–12, 293/36–294/2.

21 *NA* (e.g.) 171/3–4, 171/9–10, 179/18–19, 230/36, 245/14–15, 254/9–11, 294/6–8, 377/18–19, 415/3, 415/18–19, 452/3–4, 463/28; Davis, 'Map of Arcadia', p. 5; Jon Lawry, *Sidney's Two 'Arcadias'. Pattern and Proceeding* (Ithaca, N.Y., 1972), pp. 156ff.

22 *NA* lviii, 175n.

23 That change of emphasis is assisted, I think, by the introduction into the later version of the themes of courtesy and chivalry. The words 'courteous' and 'courtesy' appear only occasionally in the *Old Arcadia*. We do momentarily glimpse a chivalric world at 'the King of Egypt's court', which is 'full of valiant knights' (*OA* 155/30–1), but they are the only fictional people called knights in the *Old Arcadia* (though cf. *OA* 376/27). The *New Arcadia* is full of knights and full of courtesy. The politeness of the chivalric mode smooths and limits the political criticism in Sidney's narrative. Greville's account of Sidney's purpose omits the chivalry, a subject which by the time of James's reign had lost something of its appeal, and which in any case Greville may

such sharpness as survives in the political commentary of the *New*. Greville passes over that sharpness. Even as he emphasises Sidney's political intention he omits both its radicalism and its contemporary application. Since those features presented criticisms of the queen who was now Greville's heroine, the omission is not surprising. In any case it would not have been in his interest, even if it had been his wish, to cast doubt on the loyalty of Sidney, whose character and views the 'Dedication' held up – perhaps to the heir to James I's throne – for present emulation. Greville's writings take loyalty to be an indispensable condition of virtue.

His evasiveness about the contemporary targets of Sidney's writing becomes the more conspicuous when we notice his evasiveness about the contemporary targets of his own works. In his verse treatises, Greville claims, he kept to a 'general scope', thinking that a 'perspective into vice, and the unprosperities of it, would prove more acceptable to every good reader's ends than any bare murmur of discontented spirits against the present government'.[24] He does hope, he says, that his readers will find, in his history plays, 'some affinity of resemblance' between past and present, 'the vices of former ages being so like those of this age'. But such parallels, he assures us, would be 'beyond the author's intention or application'.[25]

Perhaps so. Yet Greville, no less than Sidney, wrote with his eye on the present.[26] The reason he burned his play 'Antony and Cleopatra', he tells us, was that it contained passages of 'childish wantonness' that were 'apt enough to be construed or strained to a personating of vices in the present governors and government'.[27] It does not sound as if they would have had to be strained hard. Whatever the truth about the play, Greville's account of Sidney's fiction in the 'Dedication', the work where he denies the contemporary application of his own writing, is itself not innocent of it. His remarks about Basilius are too close for coincidence to contemporary judgements about James I. The 'contempt' to which, says Greville, Basilius 'unactively' exposes his crown at home and abroad; the sway of 'ambitious' favourites at his court; the 'change' which reduces 'the commanding manners of princely birth into the degrading images of servile baseness'; the tendency to 'innovation' pro-

---

have come to regard, as he had come to regard so much else, as frivolous. Yet the emollient influence of that theme helps to bring the *New Arcadia* closer to Greville's account of Sidney's purpose than the *Old*. There are, it is true, other ways of thinking about the political import of the chivalric theme. Richard McCoy argues eloquently that Sidney's representation of chivalry contains the aggression and resentment characteristic of a martial nobility half-tamed by the Tudor court (McCoy, *Rites of Knighthood*, ch. 3; and see McCoy's essay 'Sir Philip Sidney and Elizabethan Chivalry', in Allen, *Sir Philip Sidney's Achievements*, pp. 32–41). A comparable and comparably stimulating case is made by David Norbrook (*Poetry and Politics in the English Renaissance*, London, 1984, pp. 106–7). If McCoy and Norbrook are even half right, the politeness of the *New Arcadia* cannot go very deep. Its presence is nonetheless, I suggest, a restraining influence.

24   GP 90/8–13.
25   GP 135/7–9.
26   Cf. Rebholz, *Greville*, pp. 102–3, 199–206.
27   GP 93/9–12.

moted by the duke's 'effeminate' regime – the contemporary application of those reproaches would have been obvious.[28] What Greville thought about James was not exactly what Sidney had thought about Elizabeth, but it was close to it: close enough for Greville to be able to turn Sidney's fiction, which criticised Elizabeth, against her successor.

The length of the list of topics which Greville locates in Sidney's fiction makes his most obvious omission the more striking. He refers to Sidney's 'Arcadian romances'[29] but says nothing of the romantic plot. He makes no mention, either, of his friend's love poetry.

Men change over thirty years. Greville changed more than most. His own love poetry, as far as we can tell, belongs wholly or mostly to his youth and to Sidney's lifetime.[30] Thereafter he scorned such indulgence. Instead he wrote stern Senecan plays, austere verse treatises on monarchy and religion, dark laments upon the world's iniquity and his own. Those works often echo Sidney's fiction, and in this book we have heard a number of the echoes. Yet Greville, for all his addiction to Sidney's memory, came to mistrust 'witty fictions, in which the affections or imaginations may perchance find exercise and entertainment, but the memory and judgement no enriching at all'.[31] He pondered the defects of 'corrupting reason', that 'twilight of deliberation'. He saw the world as a place of vain 'shadows', of 'shops of deceit'. For Sidney the aim of poetry was 'virtue-breeding delightfulness': for the older Greville the enticements of art are more likely to ensnare than improve.[32]

The 'Dedication' relates that Sidney, on his deathbed, reached the same conclusion. Speaking of his fiction while 'his piercing inward powers were lifted up to a purer horizon', he 'discovered not only the imperfection, but vanity, of these shadows, however daintily soever limned: as seeing that even beauty itself, in all earthly complexions, was more apt to allure men to evil than to fashion any goodness in them'.[33] It is likely that Sidney, as he contemplated the afterlife, said some such thing. Perhaps, contemplating posterity, he also had doubts about the literary quality of his work. He had, after all, been sufficiently dissatisfied with the *Old Arcadia* (though also sufficiently pleased with it) to want to rewrite it, and had then left the rewritten version unfinished.[34]

---

28 *GP* 8/21–6, 9/4–22; cf. *GP* 116/34–5.
29 *GP* 8/10.
30 That conventional view is however challenged by May, *Elizabethan Courtier Poets*, pp. 88–9.
31 *GP* 134/2–5.
32 Rebholz, *Greville*, pp. xxiv, 67, 107, 135–6, 139–40, 151–2, 213, and ch. 18; Worden, 'Friend to Sir Philip Sidney'.
33 *GP* 11/12–17.
34 Greville adds that Sidney, 'in that memorable testament of his', 'bequeathed no other legacy but the fire' to his fiction (*GP* 11/18–20). The word 'testament' has an ambiguity characteristic of the 'Dedication'. The obvious meaning – Sidney's testamentary will – is unlikely, for the will, as Greville must have known, does not mention his literary works. If on the other hand the term refers to Sidney's deathbed pronouncements, then Greville's words do not necessarily mean, as

Greville takes Sidney's fiction, that 'unpolished embryo', to be a failure. Though it 'live[s] after him admired even by our sour-eyed critics', 'they that knew him well will truly confess this *Arcadia* of his to be, both in form and matter, as much inferior to that unbounded spirit of his as the industry and images of other men's works are many times raised above the writers' capacities'. Sidney's 'Arcadian romances' were 'scribbled rather as pamphlets for entertainment of time and friends than any account of himself in the world: because, if his purpose had been to leave his memory in books, I am confident in the right use of logic, philosophy, history and poesy – nay, even in the most ingenious of mechanical arts – he would have showed' exemplary 'traits of a searching and judicious spirit'.[35] In other words, Sidney ought to have written books comparable in theme and character to Greville's own later verse – except, Greville would have been the first to add, that Sidney's books would have been much better.

For all his reservations about the *Arcadia*, Greville did publish it. He did see an improving role for the 'pregnant images' of this 'excellent image-maker'. 'Sounder judgements' could be trusted to 'exercise their spirits in' the 'moralities' which 'offer themselves throughout that various and dainty work'.[36]

> And though my noble friend had that dexterity – even with the dashes of his pen – to make the Arcadian antiques beautify the margents of his works, yet the honour which (I bear him record) he never affected I freely leave unto him with this addition, that his end in them was not vanishing pleasure alone, but moral images and examples, as directing threads, to guide every man through the confused labyrinth of his own desires and life; so that . . . I liked them too well – even in that unperfected shape they were – to condescend that such delicate, though inferior, pictures of himself should be suppressed . . . .[37]

So Greville published the *New Arcadia* – and made no mention of the *Old*.

There was another respect in which the *New Arcadia* came nearer to Greville's taste than the *Old*. At least by the time he wrote the 'Dedication', he looked to literature for unadorned contrasts between good and bad. In the *Old Arcadia* the princely lovers are sometimes good, sometimes bad. At some times they invite our approval, at others our disapproval or at least our doubt. They appear to sacrifice their virtue yet also to retain it. Goodness and badness, though they never quite blend, jostle with each other and impart

critics have generally supposed them to, that Sidney asked for the work to be burned; they may simply mean that he took no steps to ensure its survival. For the growth of the idea that Sidney burned his fiction see *MP* 224 (note to 171/10–11); *GP* 186 (note to 11/18–20); *The Countess of Pembroke's Arcadia* (London, 1655), sig. b3ᵛ.

35   *GP* 8/10–11, 11/22–12/2.
36   *GP* 10/6–12, 10/25.
37   *GP* 134/8–18.

humanity to each other, most memorably perhaps in the characterisation of Gynecia but in that of the princes too. In the *New Arcadia* goodness and badness are more often to be found in opposition to each other, dividing the characters down the middle. Amphialus, the principal new creation of the *New Arcadia*, is a fissured being.

In the revised version the battle between good and bad is fought not only within characters but between them. There are now simply good characters and simply bad ones. Some characters are now straightforwardly described, in phrases which have no counterparts in the *Old Arcadia*, as virtuous ('the virtuous nobleman, Timotheus', 'the virtuous Leonatus'). Others are straight-forwardly described as wicked ('thc wicked Demagoras', 'the wicked Cecropia').[38] That too does not happen in the *Old Arcadia*, a relatively gentle tale which has more to say about folly than wickedness and which (outside Philisides' beast-fable and the brief account of the princes' adventures on their travels) has only rare moments of cruelty. White is whiter in the revised version, black blacker. Virtuous conduct is pitted more sternly against its opposite, against failings which are now liable, or more liable, to be called 'sin',[39] 'evil',[40] 'guilt',[41] 'dust-creeping' iniquity.[42] In the *New Arcadia* the lovers imprisoned by 'the wicked Cecropia' surpass their counterparts of the earlier version by leaving evil behind them, Pamela triumphantly. So 'if ever the beams of perfection shined through the clouds of affliction, if ever virtue took a body to show his else-unconceivable beauty, it was in Pamela'.[43]

In the *New Arcadia*, as critics notice, Sidney aspires to write a heroic poem. The word 'heroical', not to be found (I think) in the *Old Arcadia*, is awarded in the *New* to Musidorus and Pyrocles, as well as to two other young princes who were not present in the *Old Arcadia*, Argalus and Amphialus.[44] The 'heroical virtue' which is now displayed by Musidorus and Pyrocles raises them above the Musidorus and Pyrocles we have got to know in the *Old Arcadia*; they are now less like us. Allusions to classical mythology, which in the *Old Arcadia* more often than not tease or deflate the characters, in the *New Arcadia* more often than not elevate them. The triumph of virtue in the *New Arcadia* is won at the cost of irony, which by Book Three is in far retreat. The gap between the lovers' conduct and their own assessment of it closes. Greville would probably have welcomed the retreat of irony, for his 'Dedication' to Sidney rebukes 'ironia' as a 'hypocritical figure . . . wherein men . . . seem to make toys of the uttermost they can do'.[45] From the *Old Arcadia* to the 'Dedication' there runs an uphill moral path. The *Old Arcadia*

38 *NA* 60/17, 272/28, 30/12, 317/7.
39 *OA* 111/26: *NA* 149/10–11.
40 *OA* 92/5: *NA* 120/13.
41 *OA* 91/15–16: *NA* 119/16.
42 *OA* 91/25–6: *NA* 119/25; cf. *NA* 109/28–30.
43 *NA* 421/33–5.
44 *NA* 27/18, 61/11, 152/22, 163/8, 179/11, 460/2; cf. *NA* 177/4, 248/35–6.
45 *GP* 92/1–3; cf. Montrose, 'Of Gentlemen and Shepherds', p. 437.

yields to the purer *New*; Sidney on his deathbed regrets that the *New* is not pure enough; Greville's subsequent standards of purity are (it is likely) more exacting still.

In revising the *Old Arcadia* Sidney launders much (though by no means all) of the love story. Musidorus and Pyrocles, who plot against the chastity of the princesses in the *Old Arcadia*, in the *New* pledge themselves to inflict no 'spot' on the 'virtue' of their loved ones.[46] Playful metaphors in the *Old Arcadia* which savour threats to the princesses' virginity[47] are eliminated in the *New*. A glance at the contrasting treatments of one episode by the two versions will convey the improving purpose of Sidney's revisions. In Book Two of both versions, Philoclea, after her amatory awakening, takes a walk in a wood at night. The romantic properties of the episode are reduced in the *New Arcadia*. The moon, no longer said to be 'full', no longer lightens 'her most perfect beauty'; the self-reproach induced by her emotional self-discovery becomes keener; her eyes, seekers of sensation in the first version, become recipients of it in the second.[48] She becomes not only more pure in heart but more dutiful. Whereas in the *Old Arcadia* she 'secretly stale from her parents' to visit the wood, she now leaves the lodge 'by her mother's commandment'.[49] Her submissiveness towards her parents receives new emphasis elsewhere, as does that of her sister.[50] The two daughters have more to be submissive about, for Sidney's revisions add weight to the cruelty of Basilius' decision to seclude them and to deny them opportunities for marriage.[51]

In writing the *New Arcadia* Sidney does not change his spots. The edge and impishness of the earlier version, and its alertness to moral complexity, are not lost in the later one. But amid the graver and higher ambitions of the revised version, the ambitions preferred by Greville, they are sometimes reduced. Though, in exploring the higher-spirited *Old Arcadia*, we often need to remember Greville's account of Sidney's fiction, we sometimes need to forget it.

One theme on which Greville's account of Sidney's purpose places particular emphasis is Stoicism, a philosophy with a prominent place in Greville's own thinking. Sidney, he explains, prepares his readers for 'private fortunes and misfortunes': he teaches them how 'to pass through any straits or latitudes of good or ill fortune' and 'how to set a good countenance upon all the discountenances of adversity, and a stay upon the exorbitant smilings of chance'.[52] We have seen the place of Stoicism in the *Old Arcadia*. Yet on this

---

46   *NA* 187/22, 276/28.
47   *OA* 37/24–6, 107/1, 107/28–9.
48   *OA* 109/13–14: *NA* 146/34; *OA* 111/26–7: *NA* 149/10–11; *OA* 109/18: *NA* 146/33.
49   *OA* 109/14–15: *NA* 146/29–30.
50   *OA* 115/30: *NA* 227/16; *NA* 357/31–3, 358/12–14.
51   *NA* 15/26–31, 21/32–7, 23/13–15, 80/6–7, 147/7–8 (with which cf. *OA* 109/28), 155/5, 358/ 9–11, 455/32–3.
52   *GP* 11/2–8.

subject as on others, Greville's account is a better guide to the *New Arcadia*, where Stoic philosophy is the more fully developed, than to the *Old*.

It is in one respect a misleading guide to both of them. In the late Renaissance there is Stoicism and Stoicism. If we mean by Stoicism a philosophy which elevates permanence above mutability, virtue above fortune, inner integrity above the outward appearances of reputation or prosperity, then Stoicism permeates both the *Old* and the *New Arcadia*. But the term carries a narrower conception which derives from the larger one but which can go its own way. It sets man on the defensive, viewing him not as an initiator of events but as a recipient or object of them, even as a victim of them. That is the perspective emphasised by Greville.[53]

The narrower version of Stoicism is present in both the *Old* and the *New Arcadia*. But in both of them it is unevenly distributed. In both cases it becomes prominent only towards the end. There Stoicism, which has hitherto reinforced Sidney's creed of activity, becomes a doctrine of passivity. It becomes, what amid the religious wars of the late Renaissance it often was, a philosophy of endurance under affliction and suffering. In the first three of the five books of the *Old Arcadia*, and in the first two of the three books of the *New*, Musidorus and Pyrocles aspire to 'exercise' or 'make trial of their virtue' not by suffering but by action.[54] In those earlier books of the *New Arcadia* there are, it is true, indications of an alternative perspective, as there are not in the earlier books of the *Old*: in Book One of the revised version the 'virtue' of Argalus is 'tried' by the affliction of his beloved Parthenia and by his (apparent) loss of her; Book Two tells us that the upbringing of the young princes has prepared them not only for action – for 'doing' – but for 'suffering'. But it is only in Book Three of the *New Arcadia*, where Sidney's narrative breaks wholly free of the earlier version, that the theme of suffering grows. Under the torments inflicted by Cecropia, it is Pamela's suffering that 'exercises' and 'tries' her virtue.[55]

In the *New Arcadia* the theme of Stoicism under affliction arises from the imprisonment and torture of Pyrocles and the princesses in Book Three. In the *Old* it arises from the imprisonment of the princes in Books Four and Five. That thematic link between the later parts of the two versions may explain why the composite text of 1593, where Books Four and Five of the *Old Arcadia* are added (together with much of Book Three) to the first three books of the uncompleted *New*, achieves such tonal continuity as it does.[56] Even so, the theme of suffering is less prominent and less searching in the *Old Arcadia* than in the *New*. That is partly because the first two books of the *New Arcadia* have done more to prepare the ground for it than the first three books of the *Old*. First, they have elevated the virtuous characters. Secondly,

53   *GP* 11/2–8, 134/13–15.
54   *OA* 11/10–11, 13/9, 18/33–4; *NA* 186/30–1.
55   *NA* 29/23, 97/18–23, 163/35–6, 336/11–12, 422/14.
56   Mervyn James, approaching Sidney's fiction through the composite *Arcadia* of 1593, finds a consistent thread of Stoic teaching in it: James, *Society, Politics and Culture*, pp. 388–90.

they have subjected them to larger afflictions: the young lovers, now of heroic stature, endure ordeals more taxing than in the corresponding portions of the earlier version. In the *Old Arcadia* the princes come to Basilius' kingdom near the completion of their travels, 'taking Arcadia in their way'. Once they have seen and done most of the things that high-born travellers are expected to see and do, Musidorus is ready to move on, 'seeing the duke's court could not be visited'.[57] In the later version, by contrast, the princes' arrival is preceded by a series of grave ordeals, which reach their climax in the shipwreck that opens the narrative. Musidorus' attitude is now, understandably, altogether less casual. He 'greatly desired a speedy return to his country after the many mazes of fortune he had trod[d]en'.[58] When the princes complain in the *Old Arcadia*, as they frequently do, of their harsh treatment at fortune's hands, their protests can seem self-indulgent. In the *New Arcadia* the princes have a more convincing case. The princesses too are now 'trodden underfoot by the wheel of senseless fortune'.[59]

When the crises come, the Stoic fortitude of the lovers is more impressive in the *New Arcadia* than in the *Old*. Pyrocles' reasons for wanting to kill himself, which in the *Old Arcadia* seem a pretext on Sidney's part for the staging of a cerebral debate – or which, at least, deserve graver afflictions to sustain them – are more persuasive in the *New*.[60] When, near the end of the *Old Arcadia*, Musidorus is momentarily unequal to the claims of 'patience' and of 'well-suffering', his lapse illuminates the recurrent weakness of an over-passionate character: when, in Book Three of the *New Arcadia*, Pyrocles momentarily fails the test of patience, the lapse signals less a flaw in his character than the extremity of his ordeal.[61]

In the *Old Arcadia* the theme of Stoicism is bound with the theme of divine providence.[62] Like Stoicism, providence provides a striking but problematical and perhaps flawed dimension of Sidney's fiction. There is no mistaking its presence. Providence is the 'justice',[63] or else the 'wisdom',[64] that governs the world. It operates, in pagan Arcadia as in Christian Europe, in God's 'time', not man's, at the command of a deity who pierces the 'depth' and 'darkest . . . secrets' of our 'hearts' and 'souls'.[65] 'Using ourselves to be the

57   *OA* 11/16, 13/1–6 (cf. *OA* 36/27).
58   *NA* 48/31–2.
59   *NA* 421/17–18. And compare *OA* 24/32 ('need') with *NA* 76/23 ('extremity').
60   *OA* 291/11ff.; *NA* 431/20ff.
61   *OA* 413/10–11; *NA* 431/20–4. It is true that the virtue of the princesses – in this as in much else superior to that of the princes – does not weaken under Cecropia's tyranny as Pyrocles' does; and it is likely that had Musidorus, who remains over-passionate in the *New Arcadia*, been among Cecropia's prisoners his patience would have weakened sooner than his cousin's.
62   Above, pp. 33–4.
63   *OA* 148/34, 265/2, 286/31–2, 292/17, 307/10, 317/14–15, 366/33, 385/30; *NA* 178/29, 362/ 33, 431/22–4, 435/20. Cf. *GP* 69/12; Rice, *Renaissance Idea of Wisdom*, p. 87.
64   *OA* 265n., 311/8–9; *NA* 360/37, 361/22, 362/18–22, 378/22–3, 458/30–1.
65   *OA* 297/28–9, 311/8–9, 335/2–3; *NA* 362/37–363/2.

punishers of our faults, and making our own actions the beginning of our chastisement', providence employs 'second causes' and human 'instrument[s]' so as to 'guide' us towards self-understanding.[66] It so orders events that 'human reason may be the more humbled' and that 'our shame may be the more manifest, and our repentance follow the sooner'.[67]

Perhaps the word 'repentance' raises expectations which are not met. At least it may do so in the minds of readers who have met the stricken souls of early modern Protestantism and who expect repentance to plumb larger depths than 'shame'. The submission of Musidorus and Pyrocles to affliction does not appear to be the product of repentance, even though the 'chastise[ment]' of Musidorus by 'the everlasting justice' has produced, at least for a time, 'a repentant shame' in him.[68] Basilius and Gynecia suffer 'shame' for their amorous follies, but their repentance is really a matter of their coming to their senses. Though the duke does pause to thank 'the destinies . . . that had made his own striving to go amiss to be the best mean ever after to hold him in the right path', no spiritual odyssey seems in store for him.[69] Sidney's treatment of the duke's self-examination is a critical moment in the moral economy of the *Arcadia*. Had Basilius' repentance been made deeper or more convincing, the restoration of harmony on the last page of the story, after his awakening, would have been deeper and more convincing too.

There is more than one possible explanation of the thinness of that treatment. Sidney may not want a rounded ending. Or he may judge it unfitting, or find it impossible, to give a capacity for depth of virtue to Basilius, on whose failings the public theme of the *Arcadia* has turned. But the answer may also, or instead, lie elsewhere: in a gap between paganism and Protestantism which the issue of repentance exposes and which Sidney's narrative, not for the first time, neither acknowledges nor crosses.[70] The gap is revealed too by the providentialist vocabulary of the *Old Arcadia*, the vocabulary which reports the 'secret working' of providence and its mastery of the 'darkest . . . secrets' of our 'souls'. There Protestantism, albeit a theologically undefined and perhaps indefinable Protestantism, hovers diffidently on the edge of a pagan world. Sidney may have been diffident too. He seems to have been uncertain, when announcing the theme of providence, in which direction to pursue it. Should he emphasise the pattern of divine chastisement and human shame and repentance? Or should he underline the weakness of human reason and calculation before God's sovereignty over events?[71]

---

66 *OA* 265/2–7 (cf. *OA* 317/14–15, 388/19–21); *NA* 63/28–30, 378/22–3; cf. *OA* 272/20–1, 307/10.

67 *OA* 265n., 265/4–5.

68 *OA* 278/6–16, 277/9ff., 287/28–9, 416/19–20 (though cf. *OA* 367/30).

69 *OA* 306/22, 307/10. Pyrocles, for his part, is determined not to 'repent' of making love to Philoclea: *OA* 291/22.

70 Cf. above, p. 35.

71 *OA* 265/1–9, 265n.

The theme of providence, like that of Stoic suffering, is unevenly distributed in the *Old Arcadia*. When we first meet the princes we learn that the
origin of their adventures in Asia and Africa was a storm at sea that diverted
them from their journey to Byzantium, where they were to join Pyrocles'
victorious father, Euarchus. For 'God . . . reserved them to greater traverses,
both of good and evil fortune'. Yet there is no further indication during the
first three books that God is governing events.[72] Those books – or, more
often, the eclogues that follow them – do measure our spiritual frailty and
mutability and short-sightedness against the wisdom and permanence of the
all-seeing deity. But they have little to say about divine intervention in the
affairs of this world. It is at the opening of Book Four that the 'strange and
secret working' of providence is introduced as a principal subject of the
work. The result is unsatisfying. The information at the end of the story that
'all had fallen out by the highest providence' seems an incomplete key to the
story we have read.[73]

There are other signs of gingerliness in Sidney's handling of the theme of
providence. Well there might be. As the story-teller it is Sidney, not God,
who writes the providential script. That is a presumptuous exercise, for God
withholds his secrets from the fallen understandings of men. Of course,
Sidney puts providence in charge not of life but of art. Yet the difference
between art and life complicates and perhaps undermines the theme of
providence. Fiction, as Sidney's *Defence of Poetry* explains, departs from fact in
arranging the triumph of the virtuous and the defeat of the wicked: it 'ever
sets virtue so out in her best colours, making Fortune her well-waiting
handmaid, that one must needs be enamoured of her'.[74] Here there is another
possible reason why the happiness of the ending of the *Arcadia* is so tentative.
Providence, unlike poetry, is not in the business of happy endings on this
earth.[75]

---

72   It might be argued that, in the *Old Arcadia*, the consequences of Basilius' submission to the oracle
      provide a continuous providential thread. Yet the duke's error, as the first spoken words of the
      Arcadia emphasise (*OA* 6/36ff.), is to think too much (or at least to think misguidedly) about
      providence (or its pagan equivalent). His dependence on the oracle is a mark of superstition, not
      of religion.
73   *OA* 10/37–8, 385/30, 416/18; cf. *OA* 325/33.
74   *MP* 90/4–6; cf. *MP* 89/5–6.
75   It may be that in one respect, in contemplating the relationship of providence to chance, Sidney
      the providentialist is at odds with Sidney the politician; if so we perhaps have another reason
      why the theme of providence in the *Arcadia* can lack conviction. Whereas Basilius concludes, at
      the end of the story, that 'all had fallen out by the highest providence', Greville describes the
      rescue of Arcadia not as providential but as 'chanceable' (*GP* 9/14). His point, which underlines
      Sidney's warnings in the *Arcadia* against the consequences of misgovernment, is that the events
      which save the country – the arrival of Euarchus, his selfless response to the situation before him,
      the resurrection of Basilius – would find no parallels in the real world. The warning, which
      Sidney would have wanted to be as effective as possible, is more effective in Greville's
      interpretation of events than in Basilius', for an Arcadia exposed to the winds of chance is more
      vulnerable than one sheltered by providence. (Admittedly Greville, like Sidney, took fortune to
      be under the government of providence: cf. *GP* 48/22–3. His choice of the adjective
      'chanceable' is nonetheless revealing.)

In Books Four and Five the theme of providential intervention, like that of Stoicism under affliction, is imposed on a narrative that in the previous three books has mostly managed without it. Did Sidney, in those first three books, keep those themes up his sleeve, to be produced later in response to the sufferings of his characters or in illustration of their – and perhaps our – blindness to the higher causes and lessons of events? Or does the presence of the themes in Books Four and Five reflect a shift in the balance of his interests, which the argumentative structure of the *Arcadia* accommodates but imperfectly?

The uncertainty in which the reader is left on that point may reflect uncertainty in Sidney. It may be too that Sidney came to regret the emphasis placed by the last two books of the *Old Arcadia* on the theme of providence. For whereas the theme of Stoic suffering, having been introduced in the later portion of the *Old Arcadia*, is developed in the *New*, providence supplies only the thinnest of threads in the later version.[76] Once more Greville's account is truer to the *New Arcadia* than to the *Old*. For his description of Sidney's fiction, which places so much emphasis on the theme of Stoicism, is silent on that of providence. In any case the Greville of the 'Dedication', who wrote so long after Sidney's death and whose aesthetic proscriptions had in the interim become so severe, might have resisted the notion that a work of pagan fiction could illustrate the workings of providence.

---

76 There is, it is true, the celebrated exchange about providence, in Book Three of the *New Arcadia*, between Pamela and Cecropia. Yet that conflict is not made integral to the surrounding narrative.

Sir John Hayward and the Old Arcadia

I explained at the end of Chapter 11 that Sir John Hayward, in describing the condition of England on the approach of Mary Tudor's death in 1558, borrows from Sidney's description of the condition of Arcadia on the death of Basilius. The two passages are reproduced below, where I have italicised some phrases to aid the reader's navigation. I reproduce Sidney's text from *OA* 320/4–31, which differs only diminutively from the corresponding passage of the composite *Arcadia* of 1593, the text used by Hayward. Hayward's own text is reproduced from his *Annals of the First Four Years of the Reign of Queen Elizabeth*, ed. John Bruce (London, Camden Society, 1840), pp. 1–2.

SIDNEY

There was a *notable example how* great dissipations monarchal governments are subject unto; for now their prince and guide had left them, they had not experience to rule, and had not whom to obey. Public matters had ever been privately governed, so that they had no lively taste what was good for themselves, but *everything was either vehemently desireful or extremely terrible. Neighbours' invasions, civil dissension, cruelty of the coming prince*, and whatsoever in common sense carries a dreadful show, was in all men's heads, but in few how to prevent: hearkening on every rumour, *suspecting everything*, condemning them whom before they had honoured, making strange and *impossible* tales of the duke's death; while *they thought themselves in danger, wishing nothing but safety*; as soon as persuasion of safety took them, desiring further

HAYWARD

a *notable example* might have been seen *how* in a royal state the surety of the common people depends much upon the life and safety of their prince. For every man's mind was then travailed with a strange *confusion of conceits, all things being immoderately either dreaded or desired*. Every report was greedily both inquired and received, *all truths suspected*, diverse tales believed, many *improbable* conjectures hatched and nourished. *Invasion of strangers, civil dissension, the doubtful disposition of the succeeding prince*, were cast in every man's conceit as present perils; but no man did busy his wits in contriving remedies. *They who held themselves in danger seemed to desire nothing but safety*: they who apprehended any opinion of safety did rise into unreasonable desire of liberty; wherein they were as various as in any thing beside, as well for benefits as amendment of forepassed faults (which faults notwithstanding none could tell either the grounds or effects of); all agreeing in the universal names of liking or misliking, but of what in especial points infinitely disagreeing; altogether like a falling steeple, the parts whereof (as windows, stones, and pinnacles) were well, but the whole mass ruinous. And this was the general case of all, wherein notwithstanding was an extreme *medley of diversified thoughts*: the *great* men looking to make themselves strong by factions; the gentlemen, some bending to them, some *standing upon* themselves, some desirous to overthrow those few which they thought were over them; the soldiers desirous to make *trouble as the nurse of spoil*; and not much unlike to them (though in another way) were all the needy sort; *the rich, fearful; the wise, careful.* This *composition of conceits* brought forth a dangerous tumult . . ..

the particulars, as for the limits of that which they desired. In this *medley of thoughts*, some thought to serve themselves by adherents, some by adjoining to those who had more to lose than themselves; some *stood upon* their proper strength, either for their own preservation, or for abating of such as they esteemed too *great.* Generally, *the rich were fearful, the wise careful,* the honestly disposed doubtful, the discontented and the desperate, and all such whose desires were both immoderate and evil, joyful, as wishing *trouble, the gate of spoil.*

Philisides' Fable

The song sung by Philisides in the Third Eclogues is reproduced below. The line and page numbers (the latter in square brackets) are those of the Oxford University Press edition of the *Old Arcadia*, from which it is reproduced.

[254]   As I my little flock on Ister bank
         (A little flock, but well my pipe they couthe)
         Did piping lead, the sun already sank
         Beyond our world, and ere I gat my booth
25   Each thing with mantle black the night did soothe,
            Saving the glow-worm, which would courteous be
            Of that small light oft watching shepherds see.

[255]   The welkin had full niggardly enclosed
         In coffer of dim clouds his silver groats,
         Ycleped stars; each thing to rest disposed:
         The caves were full, the mountains void of goats;
5   The birds' eyes closed, closed their chirping notes.
            As for the nightingale, wood-music's king,
            It August was, he deigned not then to sing.

         Amid my sheep, though I saw naught to fear,
         Yet (for I nothing saw) I feared sore;
10   Then found I which thing is a charge to bear,
         For for my sheep I dreaded mickle more
         Than ever for myself since I was bore.
            I sat me down, for see to go ne could,
            And sang unto my sheep lest stray they should.

15   The song I sang old Languet had me taught,
         Languet, the shepherd best swift Ister knew,

For clerkly rede, and hating what is naught,
For faithful heart, clean hands, and mouth as true.
With his sweet skill my skill-less youth he drew
   To have a feeling taste of him that sits   20
   Beyond the heav'n, far more beyond our wits.

He said the music best thilke powers pleased
Was jump concord between our wit and will,
Where highest notes to godliness are raised,
And lowest sink not down to jot of ill.   25
With old true tales he wont mine ears to fill:
   How shepherds did of yore, how now, they thrive,
   Spoiling their flock, or while twixt them they strive.

He liked me, but pitied lustful youth.
His good strong staff my slipp'ry years upbore.   30
He still hoped well, because I loved truth;   [256]
Till forced to part, with heart and eyes e'en sore,
To worthy Coredens he gave me o'er.
   But thus in oak's true shade recounted he
   Which now in night's deep shade sheep heard of me.   5

Such manner time there was (what time I not)
When all this earth, this dam or mould of ours,
Was only woned with such as beasts begot;
Unknown as then were they that builden towers.
The cattle, wild or tame, in nature's bowers   10
   Might freely roam or rest, as seemed them;
   Man was not man their dwellings in to hem.

The beasts had sure some beastly policy;
For nothing can endure where order nis.
For once the lion by the lamb did lie;   15
The fearful hind the leopard did kiss;
Hurtless was tiger's paw and serpent's hiss.
   This think I well: the beasts with courage clad
   Like senators a harmless empire had.

At which, whether the others did repine   20
(For envy harb'reth most in feeblest hearts),
Or that they all to changing did incline
(As e'en in beasts their dams leave changing parts),
The multitude to Jove a suit imparts,
   With neighing, bleaing, braying, and barking,   25
   Roaring, and howling, for to have a king.

A king in language theirs they said they would
(For then their language was a perfect speech).
The birds likewise with chirps and pewing could,
30   Cackling and chatt'ring, that of Jove beseech.
Only the owl still warned them not to seech
    So hastily that which they would repent;
    But saw they would, and he to deserts went.

[257]   Jove wisely said (for wisdom wisely says):
'O beasts, take heed what you of me desire.
Rulers will think all things made them to please,
And soon forget the swink due to their hire.
5   But since you will, part of my heav'nly fire
    I will you lend; the rest yourselves must give,
    That it both seen and felt may with you live.'

Full glad they were, and took the naked sprite,
Which straight the earth yclothed in his clay.
10   The lion, heart; the ounce gave active might;
The horse, good shape; the sparrow, lust to play;
Nightingale, voice, enticing songs to say.
    Elephant gave a perfect memory;
    And parrot, ready tongue, that to apply.

15   The fox gave craft; the dog gave flattery;
Ass, patience; the mole, a working thought;
Eagle, high look; wolf, secret cruelty;
Monkey, sweet breath; the cow, her fair eyes brought;
The ermine, whitest skin spotted with naught;
20   The sheep, mild-seeming face; climbing, the bear;
    The stag did give the harm-eschewing fear.

The hare her sleights; the cat his melancholy;
Ant, industry; and cony, skill to build;
Cranes, order; storks, to be appearing holy;
25   Chameleon, ease to change; duck, ease to yield;
Crocodile, tears which might be falsely spilled.
    Ape great thing gave, though he did mowing stand:
    The instrument of instruments, the hand.

Each other beast likewise his present brings;
30   And (but they drad their prince they oft should want)
They all consented were to give him wings.
And ay more awe towards him for to plant,
To their own work this privilege they grant:

That from thenceforth to all eternity
No beast should freely speak, but only he.

Thus man was made; thus man their lord became;   [258]
Who at the first, wanting or hiding pride,
He did to beasts' best use his cunning frame,
With water drink, herbs meat, and naked hide,
And fellow-like let his dominion slide,   5
   Not in his sayings saying 'I', but 'we';
   As if he meant his lordship common be.

But when his seat so rooted he had found
That they now skilled not how from him to wend,
Then gan in guiltless earth full many a wound,   10
Iron to seek, which gainst itself should bend
To tear the bowels that good corn should send.
   But yet the common dam none did bemoan,
   Because (though hurt) they never heard her groan.

Then gan he factions in the beasts to breed;   15
Where helping weaker sort, the nobler beasts
(As tigers, leopards, bears, and lions' seed)
Disdained with this, in deserts sought their rests;
Where famine ravin taught their hungry chests,
   That craftily he forced them to do ill;   20
   Which being done, he afterwards would kill

For murder done, which never erst was seen,
By those great beasts. As for the weakers' good,
He chose themselves his guarders for to been
Gainst those of might of whom in fear they stood,   25
As horse and dog; not great, but gentle blood.
   Blithe were the commons, cattle of the field,
   Tho when they saw their foen of greatness killed.

But they, or spent or made of slender might,
Then quickly did the meaner cattle find,   30
The great beams gone, the house on shoulders light;
For by and by the horse fair bits did bind;
The dog was in a collar taught his kind.
   As for the gentle birds, like case might rue   [259]
   When falcon they, and goshawk, saw in mew.

Worst fell to smallest birds, and meanest herd,
Who now his own, full like his own he used.

5   Yet first but wool, or feathers, off he teared;
       And when they were well used to be abused,
       For hungry throat their flesh with teeth he bruised;
           At length for glutton taste he did them kill;
           At last for sport their silly lives did spill.

10   But yet, O man, rage not beyond thy need;
       Deem it no gloire to swell in tyranny.
       Thou art of blood; joy not to make things bleed.
       Thou fearest death; think they are loath to die.
       A plaint of guiltless hurt doth pierce the sky.
15   And you, poor beasts, in patience bide your hell,
           Or know your strengths, and then you shall do well.

       Thus did I sing and pipe eight sullen hours
       To sheep whom love, not knowledge, made to hear;
       Now fancy's fits, now fortune's baleful stours.
20   But then I homeward called my lambkins dear;
       For to my dimmed eyes began t'appear
           The night grown old, her black head waxen grey,
           Sure shepherd's sign that morn would soon fetch day.

Bibliography

The principal purpose of the lists of primary and secondary printed works which appear below is to give the full titles of publications to which my footnotes have referred more than once and which I have normally cited in shortened form after the first citation. I also include a few publications which I have cited only once.

MANUSCRIPTS

Bodleian Library
Rawlinson A331 (letter-book of Sir Amias Paulet)

British Library
Additional 29546, 48027
Cottonian: Vitellius CXI, CXVI, Titus BII
Egerton 1693
Harleian 288, 6265, 6992
Lansdowne 12, 28

Hatfield House
Cecil Papers 140, 148 (available on microfilm in the British Library, M485)

Huntington Library
Hastings MSS
Huntington MSS

Kent Archives Office (Maidstone)
U1475: De L'Isle and Dudley Papers

Northamptonshire Record Office (Northampton)
F(P)M (Fitzwilliam of Milton Papers)

Public Record Office
PRO 31/3/27 (French transcripts)
SP: 12 (Domestic), 15 (Domestic), 63 (Ireland), 78 (France), 81 (German States), 83 (Holland and Flanders), 104 (Foreign Entry Books)

PRIMARY PRINTED SOURCES

Acts of the Privy Council

[Allen, William,] *A True, Sincere, and Modest Defence of English Catholiques*, ed. Robert Kingdon (London, Scolar Press facsimile, 1971)

The Apologie or Defence, of the Most Noble Prince William (Delft, 1581)

Aristotle, *The Ethics*, ed. Jonathan Barnes (Harmondsworth, repr. 1984)

Aristotle, *The Politics*, ed. Stephen Everson (Cambridge, 1988)

Blenerhasset, Thomas, *A Revelation of the True Minerva*, ed. Josephine Waters Bennett (New York, 1941)

Boétie, Etienne ('Stephen') de la, *A Discourse of Voluntary Servitude* (London, 1735)

Bradner, Leicester, ed., *The Poems of Queen Elizabeth I* (Providence, R.I., 1964)

Bruce, John, ed., *Correspondence of Robert Dudley, Earl of Leycester* (London, Camden Society, 1844)

Bryskett, Lodowick, *A Discourse of Civill Life* (London, 1606)

Buchanan, George, *Buchanan's History of Scotland*, ed. William Bond, 2 vols (London, 1722)

Buchanan, George, *A Detection of the Actions of Mary Queen of Scots* (London, 1651)

Buchanan, George, *The Powers of the Crown of Scotland*, ed. Charles Arrowood (Austin, Tex., 1949)

Buchanan, George, *The Sacred Dramas of George Buchanan*, ed. Archibald Brown (Edinburgh, 1906)

Buchanan, George, *Vernacular Writings of George Buchanan*, ed. P. H. Brown (Edinburgh, Scottish Text Society, 1892)

Calendar of State Papers Domestic

Calendar of State Papers Foreign

Calendar of State Papers Spanish

Calendar of State Papers Venetian

Camden, William, *The History of . . . Princess Elizabeth . . . Selected Chapters*, ed. Wallace MacCaffrey (Chicago and London, 1970)

Castiglione, Baldesar, *The Book of the Courtier*, ed. George Bull (Harmondsworth, repr. 1981)

Collins, Arthur, ed., *Letters and Memorials of State*, 2 vols (London, 1746)

Crump, Lucy, ed., *A Huguenot Family in the XVI Century* (London and New York, n.d., ?1926)

Daniel, Samuel, *The Tragedy of Philotas*, ed. Laurence Michel (London, repr. 1970)

Day, John, *The Isle of Gulls*, ed. G. B. Harrison (London, 1936)

Digges, Sir Dudley, *The Compleat Ambassador* (London, 1655)

Duplessis-Mornay, Philippe, *De Veritate Religionis Christianae* (Leiden, 1587)

Duplessis-Mornay, Philippe, *Mémoires et correspondance de Duplessis-Mornay*, 12 vols (Paris, 1824)

Duplessis-Mornay, Philippe, *The Mysterie of Iniquitie* (London, 1612)

Duplessis-Mornay, Philippe, *A Woorke concerning the Trewnesse of the Christian Religion* (London, 1587)

[?Estienne, Henri,] *A Mervaylous Discourse upon the Lyfe, Deedes, and Behaviours of Katherine de Medicis* (Heidelberg, 1575)

Franklin, Julian, ed., *Constitutionalism and Resistance in the Sixteenth Century* (New York, 1969)

Garnett, George, ed., *Vindiciae, Contra Tyrannos* (Cambridge, 1994)

Gelderen, Martin van, ed., *The Dutch Revolt* (Cambridge, 1993)

Gentillet, Innocent, *An Apology or Defence for the Christians of France* (London, 1579)

Gentillet, Innocent, *A Discourse upon the Meanes of Wel Governing* (London, 1602)

Goodman, Christopher, *How Superior Powers Oght to be Obeyd of their Subjects* (Geneva, 1558)

[Goulart, Simon, ed.,] *Mémoires de l'estat de France*, 3 vols (Geneva, 1578 edn)

Grafton, Richard, *The Union of the Two Noble and Illustrious Families of Lancastre and Yorke* (London, 1548)

Greville, Fulke, *Poems and Dramas of Fulke Greville*, ed. Geoffrey Bullough, 2 vols (Edinburgh and London, 1939)

Greville, Fulke, *The Prose Works of Fulke Greville, Lord Brooke*, ed. John Gouws (Oxford, 1986)

Greville, Fulke, *The Remains*, ed. G. A. Wilkes (Oxford 1965)

Griffiths, Gordon, ed., *Representative Government in Western Europe in the Sixteenth Century* (Oxford, 1968)

Harrington, James, *The Political Works of James Harrington*, ed. J. G. A. Pocock (Cambridge, 1977)

Hartley, T. E., ed., *Proceedings in the Parliaments of Elizabeth I 1558–1581* (Leicester, 1981)

Hayward, Sir John, *Annals of the First Four Years of Queen Elizabeth*, ed. John Bruce (London, Camden Society, 1840)

Historical Manuscripts Commission Report: Cecil II

Holinshed, Ralph, *The First and Second Volumes of Chronicles* (London, 1587)

Kervyn de Lettenhove, Baron J., ed., *Relations politiques des Pays-Bas et de l'Angleterre*, 11 vols (Brussels, 1882–1900)

Kossmann, E. H., and Mellinck, A. F., eds, *Texts concerning the Revolt of the Netherlands* (Cambridge, 1974)

Languet, Hubert, *Huberti Langueti Viri Clarissimi Epistolae* (Frankfurt, 1633)

Laski, Harold, ed., *A Defence of Liberty against Tyrants* (London, 1924)

Lettenhove, *see* Kervyn de Lettenhove

Levy, Charles Samuel, ed., 'The Correspondence of Sir Philip Sidney and Hubert Languet' (Cornell Univ. Ph.D. thesis, 1962)

Lipsius, Justus, *Six Bookes of Politickes or Civil Doctrine* (London, 1594)

Liques, David de, *Histoire de la vie de Messire Philippe de Mornay* (Leiden, 1647)

Lodge, Edmund, *Illustrations of British History*, 3 vols (London, 1838)

Machiavelli, Niccolò, *The Discourses of Machiavelli*, ed. Leslie Walker, 2 vols (London, 1950)

Machiavelli, Niccolò, *Nicholas Machiavel's 'Prince'* (London, 1661 edn)

[Marnix, Philip,] *A Pithie, and Most Earnest Exhortation, concerning the Estate of Christendom . . . by a Germaine Gentleman, a Lover of his Countrey* (Antwerp, 1583)

Moffet, Thomas, *Nobilis or the Life and Death of a Sidney*, ed. Virgil Heltzel and Hoyt Hudson (San Marino, Calif., 1940)

The Morall Philosophy of Doni, trans. Thomas North (London, 1570)

Morfill, W. R., ed., *Ballads Relating Chiefly to the Reign of Queen Elizabeth* (Ballad Society, Hertford, 1873)

Mornay, *see Duplessis-Mornay*

Murdin, William, ed., *A Collection of State Papers relating to Affairs in the Reign of Queen Elizabeth from 1571 to 1596* (London, 1759)

Nicholls, John, ed., *The Progresses and Public Processions of Queen Elizabeth*, 3 vols (London, 1823)

Nicolas, Sir Harry, *Memoirs of the Life and Times of Sir Christopher Hatton* (London, 1847)

Norbrook, David, and Woudhuysen, H. R., eds, *The Penguin Book of Renaissance Verse* (Harmondsworth, 1992)

Norton, Thomas, *All Such Treatises as have been lately published by Thomas Norton* (London, 1570): *A Warning agaynst the Dangerous Practices of Papistes; A Bull Granted by the Pope to Doctor Harding*

Norton, Thomas, *Orations, of Arsanes against Philip the Trecherous King of Macedon* (London, n.d.)

Norton, Thomas, *To the Queenes Majesties Poore Deceyved Subjectes of the North Country* (London, 1569)

Pears, Steuart, ed., *The Correspondence of Sir Philip Sidney and Hubert Languet* (London, 1845)

Peck, D. C., ed., *Leicester's Commonwealth* (Athens, Ohio, 1985)

Ponet, John, *A Shorte Treatise of Politike Power* (1556), facsimile reproduction in Hudson, *John Ponet*

Puttenham, George, *The Arte of English Poesie*, ed. Gladys Willcock and Alice Walker (Cambridge, 1936)

Le Reveille-Matin ('Edinburgh', 1574)

Rogers, Thomas, *Leicester's Ghost*, ed. Franklin Williams (Chicago, 1972)

Sidney, Algernon, *Discourses concerning Government*, ed. Thomas West (Indianapolis, Liberty Classics, 1990)

Sidney, Philip, *An Apology for Poetry*, ed. Geoffrey Shepherd (Manchester, 1973)

Sidney, Philip, *The Countess of Pembroke's Arcadia* (London, 1655)

Sidney, Philip, *The Countess of Pembroke's Arcadia*, ed. Carl Dennis (Kent State University Press, Ohio, 1970)

Sidney, Philip, *The Countess of Pembroke's Arcadia*, ed. Maurice Evans (Harmondsworth, 1977)

Sidney, Philip, *The Countess of Pembroke's Arcadia (The New Arcadia)*, ed. Victor Skretkowicz (Oxford, 1987)

Sidney, Philip, *The Countess of Pembroke's Arcadia (The Old Arcadia)*, ed. Jean Robertson (Oxford, 1973)

Sidney, Philip, *Miscellaneous Prose of Sir Philip Sidney*, ed. Katherine Duncan-Jones and Jan van Dorsten (Oxford, 1973)

Sidney, Philip, *The Old Arcadia*, ed. Katherine Duncan-Jones (Oxford, 1985)

Sidney, Philip, *The Poems of Sir Philip Sidney*, ed. William Ringler (Oxford, 1962)

Sidney, Philip, *The Prose Works of Sir Philip Sidney*, 4 vols, ed. A. Feuillerat (Cambridge, 1912–26)

Spenser, Edmund, *The Faerie Queene*, ed. A. C. Hamilton (London, repr. 1984)

Spenser, Edmund, *The Works of Edmund Spenser. A Variorum Edition: The Minor Poems*, ed. Edwin Greenlaw *et al.*, 2 vols (Baltimore, 1943–7)

Spenser, Edmund, *The Yale Edition of the Shorter Poems of Edmund Spenser*, ed. William Oram *et al.* (New Haven, 1989)

Strype, John, *The Life of the Learned Sir Thomas Smith* (Oxford, 1820 edn)

Stubbs, John, *John Stubbs's Gaping Gulph*, ed. Lloyd Berry (Charlottesville, Va, 1968)

Tacitus, Cornelius, *The Ende of Nero and the Beginning of Galba. Foure Bookes of the Histories of Cornelius Tacitus. The Life of Agricola*, trans. Henry Savile (London, 1604 edn)

Teulet, Alexandre, *Relations politiques de la France et de l'Espagne avec l'Ecosse au XVIe siècle*, 5 vols (Paris, 1862)

Tydeman, William, ed., *Two Tudor Tragedies* (Harmondsworth, 1992)

Whetstone, George, *Sir Phillip Sidney* (London, 1587)

Whitney, Geoffrey, *A Choice of Emblems* (London, 1586)

Wilson, Thomas, *The Three Orations of Demosthenes* (London, 1570)

Wright, Thomas, ed., *Queen Elizabeth and her Times,* 2 vols (London, 1838)

Wyatt, Sir Thomas, *The Complete Poems*, ed. Ronald Rebholz (Harmondsworth, 1978)

SECONDARY WORKS

Adams, Simon, 'The Dudley Clientele, 1553–1563', in G. W. Bernard, ed., *The Tudor Nobility* (Manchester, 1992), pp. 241–65

Adams, Simon, 'The Dudley Clientele and the House of Commons, 1559–1586', *Parliamentary History* 8 (1989), pp. 215–39

Adams, Simon, 'Eliza Enthroned? The Court and its Politics', in Christopher Haigh, ed., *The Reign of Elizabeth I* (London, 1984), pp. 55–77

Adams, Simon, 'Favourites and Factions at the Elizabethan Court', in Ronald Asch and Adolf Birke, eds, *Princes, Patronage and the Nobility* (Oxford, 1991), pp. 265–87

Adams, Simon, 'The Patronage of the Crown in Elizabethan Politics', in John Guy, ed., *The Reign of Elizabeth I. Court and Culture in the Last Decade* (Cambridge, 1995), pp. 20–45

Adams, Simon, 'The Protestant Cause: Religious Allegiance with the West European Calvinist Communities as a Political Issue in England, 1585–1630' (Oxford Univ. D.Phil. thesis, 1972)

Allen, M. J. B. *et al.,* eds, *Sir Philip Sidney's Achievements* (New York, 1990)

Altman, Joel, *The Tudor Play of Mind* (Berkeley and Los Angeles, 1978)

Archer, John Michael, *Sovereignty and Intelligence. Spying and Court Culture in the English Renaissance* (Stanford, Calif., 1993)

Armstrong, W. A., '*Damon and Pithias* and Renaissance Theories of Tragedy', *English Studies* 39 (1958), pp. 200–7

Armstrong, W. A., 'The Elizabethan Conception of the Tyrant', *Review of English Studies* 22 (1946), pp. 161–81

Axton, Marie, *The Queen's Two Bodies. Drama and the Elizabethan Succession* (London, 1977)

Bailey, J. E., 'Christopher Goodman', *Journal of the Chester Archaeological and Historic Society* n.s. 1 (1887), pp. 138–57

Barnes, Kenneth, 'John Stubbe, 1579: the French Ambassador's Account', *Historical Research* 64 (1991), pp. 421–6

Bates, Catherine, *The Rhetoric of Courtship in Elizabethan Language and Literature* (Cambridge, 1992)

Bergsbuch, Martin, 'Rebellion in the *New Arcadia*', *Philological Quarterly* 53 (1974), pp. 29–41

Bergsbuch, Martin, 'The "Subaltern Magistrate" in Sir Philip Sidney's *Arcadia*', *English Studies in Canada* 7 (1981), pp. 27–37

Bossy, John, 'English Catholics and the French Marriage, 1577–81', *Recusant History* 5 (1960), pp. 2–18

Bossy, John, *Giordano Bruno and the Embassy Affair* (London and New Haven, 1991)

Bowler, Gerald, '"An Axe or an Acte": the Parliament of 1572 and Resistance Theory in Early Elizabethan England', *Canadian Journal of History* 19 (1984), pp. 349–59

Brady, Ciaran, *The Chief Governors. The Rise and Fall of Reform Government in Tudor Ireland, 1536–1588* (Cambridge, 1994)

Briggs, W. D., 'Political Ideas in Sidney's *Arcadia*', *Studies in Philology* 28 (1931), pp. 137–61

Briggs, W. D., 'Sidney's Political Ideas', *Studies in Philology* 29 (1932), pp. 534–42

Buxton, John, *Sir Philip Sidney and the English Renaissance* (London, 1966)

Carey, John, 'Structure and Rhetoric in Sidney's *Arcadia*', in Kay, *Sir Philip Sidney*, pp. 245–64

Catalogue of the Library of Philips von Marnix (Nieuwkoop, 1964)

Chaudhuri, Sukanta, 'The Eclogues in Sidney's *New Arcadia*', *Review of English Studies* n.s. 35 (1984), pp. 185–202

Chevreul, Henri, *Hubert Languet* (Paris, 1852)

Clark, G. N., 'The Birth of the Dutch Republic', *Proceedings of the British Academy* 32 (1946), pp. 189–217

Collinson, Patrick, 'The Downfall of Archbishop Grindal and its Place in Elizabethan Political and Ecclesiastical History', in Peter Clark *et al.*, eds, *The English Commonwealth 1547–1580* (Leicester, 1979), pp. 39–59

Collinson, Patrick, *Edmund Grindal 1519–1583* (London, 1979)

Collinson, Patrick, *Elizabethan Essays* (London, 1994)

Collinson, Patrick, 'The Elizabethan Exclusion Crisis and the Elizabethan Polity', *Proceedings of the British Academy* 84 (1993), pp. 51–92

Collinson, Patrick, *The Elizabethan Puritan Movement* (London, 1967)

Collinson, Patrick, *The English Captivity of Mary Queen of Scots* (Sheffield, 1987)

Collinson, Patrick, *Godly People* (London, 1983)

Connell, Dorothy, *Sir Philip Sidney. The Maker's Mind* (Oxford, 1977)

Courtney, Leonard, 'The Tragedy of "Ferrex and Porrex"', *Notes and Queries* 2nd ser. 10 (1860), pp. 261–2

Davies, C. S. L., *Peace, Print and Protestantism* (London, 1976)

Davis, Walter, 'A Map of Arcadia', in Walter Davis and Richard Lanham, *Sidney's Arcadia* (London and New Haven, 1965)

Dawson, J. E. A., 'Revolutionary Conclusions: the Case of the Marian Exiles', *History of Political Thought* 11 (1990), pp. 257–72

Donno, Elizabeth Story, 'Old Mouse-Eaten Records: History in Sidney's *Apology*', in Kay, *Sir Philip Sidney*, pp. 146–67

Doran, Susan, 'Juno versus Diana: the Treatment of Elizabeth I's Marriage in Plays and Entertainments, 1561–1581', *Historical Journal* 38 (1995), pp. 257–74

Doran, Susan, *Monarchy and Matrimony. The Courtships of Elizabeth I* (London and New York, 1996)

Dorsten, Jan van, *The Anglo-Dutch Renaissance* (London, 1987)

Dorsten, Jan van, *Poets, Patrons and Professors* (Leiden and London, 1962)

Dorsten, Jan van, 'Sidney and Languet', *Huntington Library Quarterly* 29 (1965), pp. 215–22

Dorsten, Jan van, *et al.*, eds, *Sir Philip Sidney. 1586 and the Creation of a Legend* (Leiden, 1986)

Drennan, William, '"Or Know your Strengths": Sidney's Attitude to Rebellion in "Ister Banke"', *Notes and Queries* 231 (September 1986), pp. 339–40

Duncan-Jones, Katherine, 'Philip Sidney's Toys', *Proceedings of the British Academy* 66 (1980), pp. 161–78

Duncan-Jones, Katherine, 'Sidney and Samothea: a Forgotten National Myth', *Review of English Studies* n.s. 25 (1974), pp. 174–7

Duncan-Jones, Katherine, *Sir Philip Sidney. Courtier Poet* (London, 1991)

Elliott, J. H., *Europe Divided 1559–1598* (London, 1968)

Elton, W. R., *King Lear and the Gods* (San Marino, Calif., 1966)

Evans, R. J. W., *Rudolph II and his World* (Oxford, 1973)

Evans, R. J. W., *The Wechel Presses: Humanism and Calvinism in Central Europe 1572–1627* (Past and Present supplement 2, 1975)

Ferguson, Arthur, *The Articulate Citizen in the English Renaissance* (Durham, N.C., 1965)

Fraser, Antonia, *Mary Queen of Scots* (London, 1989 edn)

Garrett, C. H., *The Marian Exiles 1553–1559* (Cambridge, 1938)

Gelderen, Martin van, *The Political Thought of the Dutch Revolt 1555–1590* (Cambridge, 1992)

Gouws, John, 'The Nineteenth-Century Development of the Sidney Legend', in Allen, *Sir Philip Sidney's Achievements*, pp. 251–60

Graves, Michael, *Thomas Norton. The Parliament Man* (Oxford, 1994)

Greenblatt, Stephen, 'Sidney's *Arcadia* and the Mixed Mode', *Studies in Philology* 70 (1973), pp. 269–78

Greenlaw, Edwin, 'The Captivity Episode in Sidney's *Arcadia*', *The Manly Anniversary Studies in Language and Literature* (Chicago, 1923), pp. 54–63

Greenlaw, Edwin, 'Sidney's *Arcadia* as an Example of Elizabethan Allegory', *Anniversary Papers by Colleagues and Pupils of George Lyman Kittredge* (Boston and London, 1913), pp. 327–37

Hackett, Helen, *Virgin Mother, Virgin Queen. Elizabeth I and the Cult of the Virgin Mary* (London, 1995)

Hadfield, Andrew, *Literature, Politics and National Identity* (Cambridge, 1994)

Hamilton, A. C., 'Sidney's Humanism', in Allen, *Sir Philip Sidney's Achievements*, pp. 109–16

Hamilton, A. C., *Sir Philip Sidney* (Cambridge, 1977)

Hannay, Margaret, '"This Moses and This Miriam": the Countess of Pembroke in the Legend of Sir Philip Sidney', in Allen, *Sir Philip Sidney's Achievements*, pp. 217–26

Helgerson, Richard, *The Elizabethan Prodigals* (Berkeley and Los Angeles, 1976)

Heninger, S. K., *Sidney and Spenser* (Pa, 1989)

Hexter, J. H., *Reappraisals in History* (Evanston, Ill., 1962)

Holt, Mack, *The Duke of Anjou and the Politique Struggle during the Wars of Religion* (Cambridge, 1986)

Hudson, Winthrop, *John Ponet (?1516–1556). Advocate of Limited Monarchy* (Chicago, 1942)

Irving, David, *Memoirs of the Life and Writing of George Buchanan* (Edinburgh, 1817)

James, Mervyn, *Society, Politics and Culture. Studies in Early Modern England* (Cambridge, 1986)

Jardine, Lisa, and Grafton, Anthony, ' "Studied for Action": How Gabriel Harvey Read his Livy', *Past and Present* 129 (1990), pp. 30–78

Javitch, Daniel, *Poetry and Courtliness in Renaissance England* (Princeton, 1978)

Kahn, Victoria, *Machiavellian Rhetoric from the Counter-Reformation to Milton* (Princeton, 1994)

Kay, Dennis, *Melodious Tears. The English Funeral Elegy from Spenser to Milton* (Oxford, 1990)

Kay, Dennis, ed., *Sir Philip Sidney. An Anthology of Modern Criticism* (Oxford, 1987)

Kingdon, Robert, *Myths about the St. Bartholomew's Day Massacres 1572–1576* (Cambridge, Mass., 1988)

Kinney, Arthur, 'Sidney's Journey to Flushing and Zutphen', in van Dorsten, *Sir Philip Sidney*, pp. 125–48

Kinney, Arthur, *et al.*, eds, *Sidney in Retrospect* (Amherst, Mass., 1988)

Knoop, L. A., 'Sir Philip Sidney: Politics and Metaphor' (Univ. of London Ph.D. thesis, 1993)

Lanham, Richard, 'The Old *Arcadia*', in Walter Davis and Richard Lanham, *Sidney's Arcadia* (London and New Haven, 1965)

Lawry, Jon, *Sidney's Two 'Arcadias'. Pattern and Proceeding* (Ithaca, N.Y., 1972)

Lehmberg, S. E., *Sir Walter Mildmay and Tudor Government* (Austin, Tex.; 1964)

Leimon, M. M., 'Sir Francis Walsingham and the Anjou Marriage Plans 1574–1581' (Cambridge Univ. Ph.D. thesis, 1989)

Levy, Charles Samuel, 'The Sidney–Hanau Correspondence', in Kinney, *Sidney in Retrospect*, pp. 15–24

Levy, F. J., 'Fulke Greville: the Courtier as Philosophic Poet', *Modern Language Quarterly* 33 (1972), pp. 433–48

Levy, F. J., 'Sir Philip Sidney and the Idea of History', *Bibliothèque d'Humanisme et Renaissance* 26 (1964), pp. 608–17

Levy, F. J., 'Sir Philip Sidney Reconsidered', in Kinney, *Sidney in Retrospect*, pp. 3–14

Lindheim, Nancy, 'Sidney's "Arcadia", Book II: Retrospective Narrative', *Studies in Philology* 64 (1967), pp. 159–86

MacCaffrey, Wallace, *Elizabeth I* (London, 1993)

MacCaffrey, Wallace, *Queen Elizabeth and the Making of Policy, 1572–1588* (Princeton, 1981)

McCoy, Richard, *The Rites of Knighthood. The Literature and Politics of Elizabethan Chivalry* (Berkeley and Los Angeles, 1989)

McCoy, Richard, 'Sir Philip Sidney and Elizabethan Chivalry', in Allen, *Sir Philip Sidney's Achievements*, pp. 32–41

McCoy, Richard, *Sir Philip Sidney. Rebellion in Arcadia* (New Brunswick, N.J., 1979)

Macfarlane, I. D., *Buchanan* (London, 1981)

McKisack, May, *Medieval History in the Tudor Age* (Oxford, 1971)

May, Stephen, *The Elizabethan Courtier Poets* (Columbia, Mo., 1992)

Medine, Peter, *Thomas Wilson* (Boston, Mass., 1986)

Mercier, Charles, 'Les Théories politiques des Calvinistes dans les Pays-Bas à la fin du XVIᵉ et au début du XVIIᵉ siècle', *Revue d'histoire ecclésiastique* 29 (1933), pp. 25–73

Montrose, Louis, 'Of Gentlemen and Shepherds: the Politics of Elizabethan Pastoral Form', *English Literary History* 50 (1983), pp. 415–59

Myrick, Kenneth, *Sir Philip Sidney as a Literary Craftsman* (Loncoln, Nebr., repr. 1965)

Neale, J. E., *Elizabeth I and her Parliaments*, 2 vols (London, 1953–7)

Norbrook, David, *Poetry and Politics in the English Renaissance* (London, 1984)

Osborn, James, *Young Philip Sidney 1572–1577* (New Haven and London, 1972)

Parker, Geoffrey, *The Dutch Revolt* (Ithaca, N.Y., 1977)

Patrick, J. Max, ed., *Style, Rhetoric and Rhythm* (Princeton, 1966)

Patrides, C. A., *Milton and the Christian Tradition* (Oxford, 1966)

Patry, Raoul, *Philippe Du Plessis-Mornay* (Paris, 1933)

Patterson, Annabel, *Censorship and Interpretation. The Conditions of Writing and Reading in Early Modern England* (Madison, Wis., 1984)

Phillips, James, 'George Buchanan and the Sidney Circle', *Huntington Library Quarterly* 12 (1948–9), pp. 23–55

Poort, Marjon, '"The Desired and Destined Successor": a Chronology of Sir Philip Sidney's Activities 1585–1586', in van Dorsten, *Sir Philip Sidney*, pp. 25–37

Raab, Felix, *The English Face of Machiavelli* (London, 1964)

Raitière, Martin, *Faire Bitts. Sir Philip Sidney and Renaissance Political Theory* (Pittsburg, Pa, 1984)

Rawson, Elizabeth, *The Spartan Tradition in European Thought* (Oxford, 1969)

Read, Conyers, *Lord Burghley and Queen Elizabeth* (London, 1960)

Read, Conyers, *Mr. Secretary Cecil and Queen Elizabeth* (London, 1955)

Read, Conyers, *Sir Francis Walsingham*, 3 vols (Oxford, 1925)

Rebholz, Ronald, *The Life of Fulke Greville, First Lord Brooke* (Oxford, 1971)

Rees, Joan, *Fulke Greville, Lord Brooke, 1554–1628* (Berkeley and Los Angeles, 1971)

Ribner, Irving, 'Sir Philip Sidney on Insurrection', *Journal of the History of Ideas* 13 (1952), pp. 257–65

Rice, Eugene, *The Renaissance Idea of Wisdom* (Cambridge, Mass., 1958)

Ronan, Myles, *The Reformation in Ireland under Elizabeth 1558–1580* (London, 1930)

Rose, Mark, 'Sidney's Womanish Man', *Review of English Studies* 25 (1964), pp. 353–63

Rosenberg, Eleanor, *Leicester Patron of Letters* (New York, 1955)

Rudenstine, Neil, *Sidney's Poetic Development* (Cambridge, Mass., 1967)

Ryken, Leland, 'The Drama of Choice in Sidney's *Astrophel and Stella*', *Journal of English and Germanic Philology* 68 (1969), pp. 648–54

Salmon, J. H. M., 'Seneca and Tacitus in Jacobean England', in Linda Levy Peck, ed., *The Mental World of the Jacobean Court* (Cambridge, 1991), pp. 169–88

Sargent, Ralph, *The Life and Lyrics of Sir Edward Dyer* (Oxford, 1968)

Schellhase, Kenneth, *Tacitus in Renaissance Political Thought* (Chicago and London, 1976)

Sharpe, Kevin, *Politics and Ideas in Early Modern England* (London, 1989)

Sharpe, Kevin, and Lake, Peter, eds, *Culture and Politics in Early Stuart England* (London, 1994)

Skinner, Quentin, *The Foundations of Modern Political Thought*, 2 vols (Cambridge, 1978)

Skinner, Quentin, 'The State', in Terence Ball *et al.*, eds, *Political Innovation and Conceptual Change* (Cambridge, 1989), pp. 90–131

Skretkowicz, Victor, 'Philisides in "Arcadia"', in Allen, *Sir Philip Sidney's Achievements*, pp. 194–200

Smith, Lacey Baldwin, *Treason in Tudor England. Politics and Paranoia* (London, 1986)

Smuts, Malcolm, 'Court-Centred Politics and the Uses of Roman Historians, c. 1590–1630', in Sharpe and Lake, *Culture and Politics*, pp. 21–43

Stillman, Robert, 'The Politics of Sidney's Pastoral: Mystification and Mythology in the *Old Arcadia*', *English Literary History* 52 (1985), pp. 795–814

Stillman, Robert, *Sidney's Poetic Justice* (London and Toronto, 1986)

Stump, Donald, *et al.*, eds, *Sir Philip Sidney: An Annotated Bibliography* (New York, 1994)

Tennenhouse, Leonard, 'Arcadian Rhetoric: Sidney and the Politics of Courtship', in Allen, *Sir Philip Sidney's Achievements*, pp. 201–13

Trevor-Roper, Hugh, *Renaissance Essays* (London, 1985)

Tricomi, Albert, *Anticourt Drama in England 1603–1642* (Charlottesville, Va, 1989)

Wallace, Malcolm, *The Life of Sir Philip Sidney* (Cambridge, 1915)

Watson, Sarah Ruth, '"Gorboduc" and the Theory of Tyrannicide', *Modern Language Review* 34 (1939), pp. 355–66

Weiner, Andrew, *Sir Philip Sidney and the Poetics of Protestantism* (Minneapolis, Minn., 1978)

Williams, Penry, *The Tudor Regime* (Oxford, 1979)

Williamson, George, *The Senecan Amble* (London, 1951)

Wilson, Charles, *Queen Elizabeth I and the Revolt of the Netherlands* (London, 1970)

Wilson, Charles, 'Thomas Sackville: an Elizabethan Poet as Citizen', in Jan van Dorsten, ed., *Ten Studies in Anglo-Dutch Relations* (Leiden, 1974), pp. 30–50

Worden, Blair, 'Ben Jonson among the Historians', in Sharpe and Lake, *Culture and Politics*, pp. 67–89

Worden, Blair, 'Classical Republicanism and the Puritan Revolution', in Hugh Lloyd-Jones *et al.*, eds, *History and Imagination. Essays in Honour of H. R. Trevor-Roper* (London, 1981), pp. 182–200

Worden, Blair, 'Friend to Sir Philip Sidney', *London Review of Books* 3 July 1986, pp. 19–22, and 24 July 1986, p. 4

Worden, Blair, 'Shakespeare and Politics', *Shakespeare Survey* 44 (1991), pp. 1–15

Woudhuysen, H. R., '*Astrophel and Stella* 75: A "New" Text', *Review of English Studies* n.s. 37 (1986), pp. 388–92

Woudhuysen, H. R., 'Leicester's Literary Patronage: a Study of the English Court, 1578–1582' (Oxford Univ. D.Phil. thesis, 1982)

Woudhuysen, H. R., 'A "Lost" Sidney Document', *Bodleian Library Record* 13 (1990), pp. 353–9

Zandvoort, R. W., *Sidney's Arcadia. A Comparison between the Two Versions* (Amsterdam, 1929)

Zeeveld, Gordon, 'The Uprising of the Commons in Sidney's *Arcadia*', *Modern Language Notes* 48 (1933), pp. 209–17

Index